Fertility Rates: United States, 1930-1993

68.2
(1993 est.)

Note: Beginning with 1959, trend line is based on registered live births; trend line for 1930-1959 is based on live births adjusted for underregistration. Source: U.S. Bureau of Census

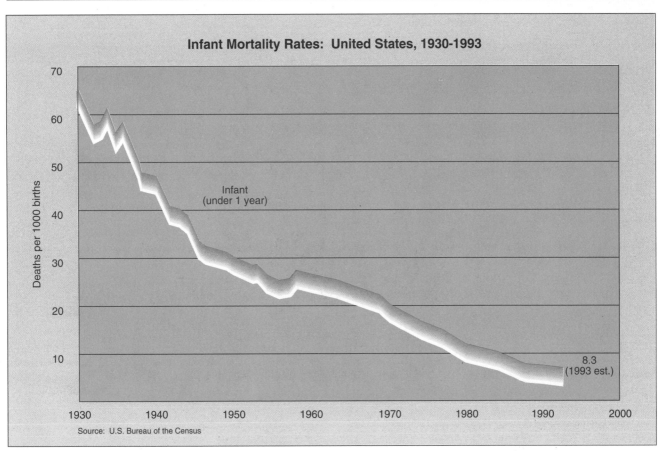

Infant Mortality Rates: United States, 1930-1993

Deaths per 1000 births

Infant
(under 1 year)

8.3
(1993 est.)

Source: U.S. Bureau of the Census

HUMAN INTIMACY
MARRIAGE, THE FAMILY AND ITS MEANING

SIXTH EDITION

HUMAN INTIMACY
MARRIAGE, THE FAMILY AND ITS MEANING

SIXTH EDITION

FRANK D. COX
SANTA BARBARA CITY COLLEGE

WEST PUBLISHING COMPANY
MINNEAPOLIS/ST. PAUL • NEW YORK • LOS ANGELES • SAN FRANCISCO

Copyeditor: Patricia Lewis
Composition: Parkwood Composition
Cover Image: © Bryan Peterson/The Stock Market
Illustrations: Barbara Barnett; Brenda Booth; John Foster; Sue Sellers; Precision Graphics

Additional credits follow index.

WEST'S COMMITMENT TO THE ENVIRONMENT

In 1906, West Publishing Company began recycling materials left over from the production of books. This began a tradition of efficient and responsible use of resources. Today, up to 95 percent of our legal books and 70 percent of our college and school texts are printed on recycled, acid-free stock. West also recycles nearly 22 million pounds of scrap paper annually—the equivalent of 181,717 trees. Since the 1960s, West has devised ways to capture and recycle waste inks, solvents, oils, and vapors created in the printing process. We also recycle plastics of all kinds, wood, glass, corrugated cardboard, and batteries, and have eliminated the use of styrofoam book packaging. We at West are proud of the longevity and the scope of our commitment to the environment.

Production, Prepress, Printing and Binding by West Publishing Company.

Library of Congress Cataloging-in-Publication Data

Cox, Frank D.
    Human intimacy: marriage, the family, and its meaning / Frank D. Cox.—6th ed.
        p.   cm.
    Includes bibliographical references and index.
    ISBN 0-314-01067-X (hard)
    1. Family—United States. 2. Marriage—United States. 3. Sex customs—United States. I. Title.
    HQ536.C759 1993
    306.8'0973—dc20
                                                        92-35570
 CIP

CONTENTS IN BRIEF

TABLE OF CONTENTS

CHAPTER 4
DATING, SEXUAL MORES, AND MATE SELECTION 91

CHAPTER 7
ROLE EQUITY:
THE CONVERGING OF THE SEXES 211

CHAPTER 8
THE FAMILY AS AN ECONOMIC SYSTEM 253

CHAPTER 9
THE DUAL-WORKER FAMILY:
THE REAL AMERICAN FAMILY REVOLUTION 303

CHAPTER 10
HUMAN SEXUALITY 341

CHAPTER 11
FAMILY PLANNING 387

CHAPTER 12
PREGNANCY AND BIRTH 435

CHAPTER 13
THE CHALLENGE OF PARENTHOOD 471

CHAPTER 14
FAMILY LIFE STAGES:
MIDDLE-AGE TO SURVIVING SPOUSE 517

CHAPTER 15
FAMILY CRISIS 551

CHAPTER 16
THE DISSOLUTION OF MARRIAGE 593

CHAPTER 17
REMARRIAGE:
A GROWING WAY OF AMERICAN LIFE 627

CHAPTER 18
ACTIVELY SEEKING
MARITAL GROWTH AND FULFILLMENT 657

PREFACE

"Family values" has become one of the catch phrases of the 1990s, but its meaning is far from clear. Politicians argue about it. All Americans say they believe in family values but are quick to criticize those who do not share their own particular brand. Certainly, the family is an institution that touches all kinds of values and morally defined relationships. Some pessimists see the family as declining, unable to survive in an immoral society. Others are more optimistic and maintain that the family is adapting to change just as it always has in the past in all societies.

Graham B. Spanier, the thoughtful past president of the National Council on Family Relations, raises serious family issues when he suggests, "The ultimate question, which I lack the vision to answer, is whether the American family, with its contemporary variations and character, can and will persist, given the demographic and social changes that continue to evolve." He goes on to say:

> When you knock on the front door of a house or apartment today, what do you find? Thirty percent of households are married couples with no children. Even fewer will include married couples with children; many of these couples are remarried and many of the children are stepchildren. Nearly one-fourth of the households contain a single man or woman. The others consist of cohabiting couples, unmarried women and their children, and a small proportion of other arrangements. The number of households maintained by a man or woman with no spouse present has increased substantially over the past 20 years. One in four of the nation's children live with only one of their parents. Viewed from another vantage point, whereas 85% of children under 18 lived with two parents [20 years ago], only 76% are now in that status.

After citing many other statistics that raise questions about the continuing viability of the American family, Spanier concludes by saying: "The health of the family of the future, I believe, hinges on our ability to marshall the forces of resiliency in the face of the forces of discontinuity. *Stated differently, my thesis is that we must adapt to today's structurally weakened state by building on individual and interpersonal strengths*" (Spanier 1989, 3–14).

As readers of past editions of *Human Intimacy: Marriage, the Family, and Its Meaning* know, your author takes an optimistic view of the American family and focuses on family well-being rather than on ideological or political agendas. Even now when the family is clearly afloat in stormy seas and seems at times as if it might flounder, marriage and the family remain a prominent part of the American scene. Most of us grow up in families, and over 90 percent of us will be a marriage partner at some time in our lives. Although this percentage is dropping, Americans are still among the most marrying people in the world. Consequently, it is important to stress those characteristics of intimate relationships (families) that help to reinforce the strength and resilience of the marital relationship and of the family. Accordingly, this sixth edition of *Human Intimacy* continues to incorporate research on family strengths throughout this book. Spanier is correct to end his discussion of family deterioration by calling on Americans to build their families on "individual and interpersonal strengths," and this edition is dedicated to that task.

Human Intimacy starts on a very positive note, by looking at the characteristics that lead to successful, enduring, and satisfying relationships. Even more than previous editions, this edition emphasizes how the characteristics of strong, successful families can be nurtured in all intimate relationships so that the family's full potential is realized. The book not only examines the entire range of family life in a positive and constructive manner but also incorporates lessons learned from studying strong, successful families.

Families tend to get into trouble because people believe that they cannot do much to change their relationships and/or because they are unwilling to take the time to nourish and enrich those relationships. In contrast this book stresses that every person has the ability to improve his or her intimate relationships.

One advantage of American society is the wide spectrum of choice it offers individuals in most aspects of life. Although family patterns were somewhat limited in the past, a wider variety of intimate relationships is becoming acceptable. For example, with the loosening of traditional sex roles, individuals have greater freedom to adapt relationships to their own liking. Marriage now involves personal satisfaction, not just the proper fulfillment of duties and roles. At the same time, greater freedom of choice also means greater freedom to err. Hence knowledge about relationships and the family is even more important today.

It is my hope that *Human Intimacy* will contribute to your ability to make intelligent decisions about intimate relationships. Individuals who make satisfying choices have the best chance of being fulfilled. And persons who are fulfilled are likely to enjoy exciting intimate and family relationships that contribute to the growth of all concerned. Furthermore, these persons are likely to contribute to the society at large, thus making the community a better place to live.

This sixth edition tries to present a realistic picture of marriage and the family as they are today. More important, it offers hope for tomorrow by emphasizing what the family can become. The beauty of the institution we call the family is that it is adaptable and flexible. Families can change for the better; intimate relationships can become more satisfying. Individuals with knowledge of themselves, the family, and their culture can establish enduring and successful family relationships. It is to further these goals that *Human Intimacy* has been written.

The edition contains several features designed to aid your reading:

1. Each chapter is preceded by a comprehensive outline that provides an overview of the material.
2. "Insets" supply interesting detail, allow hypothesizing, present controversial topics, and add variety. Insets entitled "What Research Tells Us about . . ." are a reminder of the quantity of scientific research underpinning our knowledge about intimate relationships and the family.
3. "Scenes from Marriage" appear at the end of each chapter. These condensed excerpts from other sources add new dimensions and/or conflicting viewpoints.

4. Case studies are scattered throughout the book. They highlight the principles being discussed and illustrate how they might be applied in everyday life. Most of the cases are composites, based on real-life experiences shared by my students over the years.

5. The "Debate the Issues" features present both sides of a controversial topic such as the single-parent family or abortion. Taking definite stands on both sides of the topic helps make the discussions both lively and thought-provoking.

6. A new chapter on crises in the family has been added. It discusses such topics as death, violence, drug and alcohol abuse, accidents, poverty, and unemployment.

7. To make the book more readable, most statistics have been set off from the text. This enables the reader to peruse the supportive data as needed.

It goes without saying that the whole book has been updated, and much new material has been added throughout, especially on ethnic families, i.e., African-American, Hispanic and Asian-American families.

As with all such undertakings, many people besides myself have contributed to *Human Intimacy*. The most important are the family members with whom I have interacted all my life, parents, grandparents, aunts, uncles, cousins, siblings, and, of course, my immediate family—Pamela, my wife, Randy and Linda, and Michelle and Steve. In addition, many fine researchers and writers have influenced and contributed to my thoughts. Also important are the contributions of the direct reviewers of the previous edition. Without them, *Human Intimacy* could not exist, and I wish to extend a special thanks to them:

Douglas A. Abbott, University of Nebraska, Omaha
Henry Bagish, Santa Barbara City College
Richard D. Berrett, California State University, Fresno
John Bowman, Santa Barbara City College
Denny Braun, Mankato State University
Raymond V. Burke, University of Nebraska, Omaha
Preston M. Dyer and Genie H. Dyer, Baylor University
Richard A. Hanson, North Dakota State University
Sherry L. Kirksey, Shelton State Community College
Ollie Pocs, Illinois State University
Joseph H. Stauss, University of Arizona
Ken Stewart, North Dakota State University
Isaac W. Williams, Central Florida Community College
James Friedman, Law offices of Davis, Friedman, Zavett, Kane and MacRae, Chicago
Mary Ann Shall, Santa Barbara, California

I would like to give special recognition to those who have contributed to the revision of the ancillaries—Barbara Brockhoeft of Lamar University for her outstanding work on the instructor's manual and Isaac Williams of Central Florida Community College for his extensive revision of the study guide.

Last, but extremely important, are all the wonderful students who have passed through my classes. They have contributed to the classes and to my writing, made me think, and in many ways let me know that the American family is alive and well.

Although *Human Intimacy* has my name on it, the actual production of the book rests with Clyde Perlee of West Educational Publishing, Beth Kennedy, the designer, the wonderful editorial staff at West Publishing, and above all those oft-forgotten production people at West who turn the final copy into a beautiful book and place it in the hands of many teachers and students who use it. I am always grateful for your fine work and consider *Human Intimacy* to be *our* book, not my book.

Frank D. Cox
Santa Barbara City College

THE ELOQUENT STORY OF LIFE IN ANCIENT SYMBOLS

Man

Friendship between men

Woman

Men quarrel and fight

Man and woman united

Man dies

Woman becomes pregnant

The widow and her children

And bears a child

The mother dies

The family: Man, woman, and children

Surviving children bearing within themselves the seeds of new families

CHAPTER

1

STUDYING SUCCESSFUL RELATIONSHIPS

CONTENTS

PROLOGUE: STRENGTHS OF SUCCESSFUL RELATIONSHIPS

Intimate relationships: What an exciting and important field of study! By **intimate,** we mean experiencing intense intellectual and emotional communion with another human being. Communicating and caring. Boyfriend/girlfriend. Husband/wife. Parent/child. Grandparent/grandchild. Family and friends. These are the relationships that give meaning to life, the relationships that give us a sense of identity, of well-being, of security, of being needed. These are the relationships that ward off loneliness and insecurity, the relationships that allow us to love and be loved. Without intimacy where would the human be? Perhaps the human part of "human being" would disappear and we'd all simply "be"—we'd become automatons similar to our home computers, capable of solving problems and delivering information but lacking in those markedly human qualities of loving, caring, and compassion. In a phrase, we'd lack the characteristics that allow human beings to become intimate.

The study of intimate relationships is both essential and exciting because we live in a society where intimate relationships are important to social, psychological, and emotional survival. What better way to begin this journey than by examining the strengths exhibited by successful intimate relationships, by families in particular. What would intimate relationships be like if we could make them the best possible? Even if we succeed in solving the major problems that will surely arise in an intimate relationship, can we build enduring relationships that are better than just satisfactory? Can people create intimate relationships that are secure and comfortable, yet growing and exciting at the same time? Will today's young families be able to rear children who care about themselves and the community of which they are a part, children who will grow into adults who are capable of being intimate, caring, and loving human beings?

Why discuss an ideal? Won't we all fall short of the ideal? Yes, of course, we will. But ideals can be goals, and goals give us something at which to aim. They give us direction in life. They motivate us. They can be the rudder that keeps us on course as our ship sails through life.

Having a vision of what we want ourselves—and our relationships, our families, our children, our society, and our world—to be is of the utmost importance to human beings. It is the ability to visualize the ideal that enables human beings to change. Without a vision of what could be, there would be little if any change. If all of our behaviors were inborn, biologically determined, and preordained, then nothing could change and no vision of the ideal would be necessary to survive.

We will begin our study of intimate relationships by examining the ideal qualities of strong families because it is within families that all of us learn about intimate relationships. After all, our **family of origin,** the family in which we were born and grew up, is the first seat of all of our learning, and human relationships are the essence of the family. Throughout this book we will often return to the theme, "How can we build into our intimate relationships those characteristics that lead to strong and successful friendships, marriages, and families?"

Intimate
Experiencing intense intellectual and emotional communion with another person.

Family of origin
Family into which you are born and/or grow up.

QUALITIES OF STRONG AND RESILIENT FAMILIES: AN OVERVIEW

Researchers who study strong, healthy marriages and successful families point out that volumes have been written about what is wrong with the family but little has been written about what is right in the successful family (Mace 1983). "We don't learn how to do anything by looking only at how it shouldn't be done. We learn most effectively by examining how to do something correctly and by studying a positive model" (Stinnett 1979, 24). "Some families appear to endure even in the face of great adversity. We need to discover why this is true" (McCubbin and McCubbin 1988, 247). By discovering what the strengths of enduring intimate relationships are, perhaps we all will be better able to cope with the adversities that are inevitable in every person's life.

The basic thrust of this book is to create and develop a vision of what the strong family is and to weave this image throughout the book. Of course, we will spend time discussing family problems. But by holding out an ideal vision of what a family can be, we take the first, and perhaps most important, step toward resolving problems that will arise throughout our lives. This ideal will help us understand how our relationships can be improved and made better.

Vera and David Mace (1983, 1985) coined the phrase "family wellness" to describe the strong family that is functioning successfully. The Maces maintain that the quality of life in our communities is determined, in part, by the quality of relationships in the families that make up the communities. Healthy families help to maintain healthy community environments (Stokols 1992). The quality of life in families in turn is strongly affected by the quality of relationships between the couples who founded those families.

> We take the view that family wellness, in its full and true meaning, grows out of marriage wellness. A family begins when a marriage begins. We do not mean that a one-parent family cannot be a well family. It can. But since four out of five one-parent families are really in transition between marriages, and most of them are one-parent families because the first marriage broke down, it is the marriage relationship that is still the foundation stone [to family success]. So the key to nearly everything else is to enable marriages to be what they are capable of being and what the people involved want them to be. (Mace and Mace 1985, 9)

What are the relationship qualities that lead to family strength and wellness? Numerous researchers have sought answers to this question, and there has been considerable agreement among their findings (Morgan 1987).

The research suggests six major qualities shared by all strong, healthy families:

1. *Commitment:* The major quality of strong families is a high degree of commitment. The family members are deeply committed to promoting each other's happiness and welfare. They are also very committed to the family group and invest much of their time and energy in the family. "The individual family member is integrated into a web of mutual affection and respect. By belonging and being committed to something greater than oneself, there is less

chance that individualism will sour into alienation or egocentrism" (Gardner 1981, 94).

An important point about strong families is that they take the initiative to structure their lifestyle to enhance the quality of their family relationships. They are on the "offensive." They do not just react; they make things happen. Families can do a great deal to make life more enjoyable, and strong families exercise that ability.

Each Monday Don and Linda spend part of the dinner hour discussing plans for the week with their two children. Each individual explains what his or her activities for the week are likely to be. In this way all of the family members try to work out scheduling conflicts ahead of time, thus avoiding last-minute decisions that can often be upsetting.

2. *Appreciation:* This quality seems to permeate the strong family. The family members appreciate one another and make each other feel good about themselves. All of us like to be with people who make us feel good. Yet many families fall into interactional patterns in which they make each other feel bad. In strong families, members are able to find good qualities in one another and to express appreciation for them.

3. *Good communication patterns:* Members of strong families spend time talking to each other. Sometimes families are so fragmented and busy and spend so little time together that they communicate with each other only through rumor. By this we mean that families may communicate indirectly through hearsay, assumption, guesswork, and innuendo rather than directly through good communication techniques.

Strong families also listen well. By being good listeners, the family members say to one another, "You respect me enough to listen to what I have to say. I'm interested enough to listen too."

Families that communicate well also fight fairly. They get angry at each other, but they get conflict out into the open and are able to discuss the problem. They share their feelings about alternative ways of dealing with problems and are able to select solutions that are best for everybody.

4. *Desire to spend time together:* Strong families do a lot of things together. This is not a "false" or "smothering" togetherness; they genuinely enjoy being together. Another important point is that these families actively structure their lifestyles so that they can spend time together. This togetherness extends to all areas of their lives—meals, recreation, and work—and they spend much of their time together in active interaction rather than in passive activities such as watching television.

5. *A strong value system:* Members of a strong family share a strong value system. Stinnett and DeFrain (1985) found this quality most often expressed as a high degree of religious orientation. This finding agrees with research from the past forty years, which shows a positive correlation among religion, marriage happiness, and successful family relationships. The old saying, "A family that prays together stays together," appears to be based on more than wishful thinking. Families that share a strong value system experience "spiritual wellness." This is a unifying force, a caring center within each person that promotes sharing, love, and compassion for others. It is a force that helps a person transcend self and become part of something larger (Stinnett and DeFrain 1985). Spirituality gives one a sense of community and support. Organized religion may be advantageous to family life by (1) enhancing the family's support network, (2) sponsoring family activities and recreation, (3) indoctrinating supportive family teachings and values, (4) providing family social and welfare services, and (5) encouraging families to seek divine assistance with personal and family problems (Abbott et al. 1990, 443). These researchers also point out, however, that rigid religious doctrines that promote only traditional sex roles or negative approaches to family planning, for example, might be detrimental to family life.

Of course, religion has no monopoly on spirituality. Strong values can be demonstrated in many ways such as community involvement, education, and work. The underlying factor that adds strength to a family is a strongly held and mutually shared value system.

6. *Ability to deal with crises and stress in a positive manner:* Strong families have the ability to deal with crises and problems in a positive way. Such families are resilient and are able to bounce back from adversity. They may not enjoy crises, but they are able to handle them constructively. Even in the darkest situations, they manage to find some positive element, no matter how small and focus on it. In a particular crisis, they may rely to a greater extent on each other and the trust they have developed in one another. Confronted by a crisis, they unite to deal with it instead of being fragmented by it. They cope with the problem and support each other.

Families with a high degree of these six characteristics are pleasant to live in because members treat one another in beneficial ways. (These six characteristics are discussed in more detail throughout the remainder of the book.) Members of strong families can count on one another for support and love. They feel good about themselves both as individuals and as members of a family unit or team. They have a sense of "we," yet this sense of belonging does not overpower their individuality. The family supports and respects individuality. Perhaps strong families can best be defined as those that create homes we enter for comfort, development, and regeneration and from which we go forth renewed and charged with power for positive living (Stinnett and DeFrain 1985, 8). Within a healthy family, individuals learn how to be intimate with family members. This sets the stage for successful future intimate relationships.

It is not unreasonable for family members to exhibit the characteristics we have listed. We usually start our family feeling mutual appreciation, wanting to spend time together, feeling committed, and trying to communicate well. Yet many families seem to lose these characteristics as time passes. How can a family keep these characteristics? How can families get them back once they start to lose them? The first step is to improve our understanding of intimate relationships in general and the family in particular.

In a national survey of over a thousand families, family scientists (Olson et al. 1983; McCubbin et al. 1988) identified the family strengths that appear to facilitate a family's efforts to manage stress and strain in their lives over the various life cycle stages. The following five stages of the family life cycle were used: (1) single, (2) couples, (3) preschool and school-age children, (4) adolescence and launching of children, and (5) empty nest (children gone) and retirement.

Note that the researchers found that specific family strengths vary in importance with different life stages. "Celebrations," for example, are important in every life stage, but "support networks" appear most important to family health during the childbearing–school-age and teenage–young adult stages.

The researchers identified the following as characteristics of successful families and indicated the period in the life cycle when each characteristic appears to be most important:

■ *Accord:* The family relationships allow members to resolve conflicts and reduce strain. Family members have developed ways of reaching agreements satisfactory to each other. This characteristic seems most important early in the life cycle from the time when the couple first gets together through the period of school-age children. Working out methods to achieve accord starts the family out in a positive manner.

■ *Celebrations:*Acknowledging birthdays, religious occasions, and other special events across the life cycle improves family solidarity.
■ *Communication:* Exchanging information, sharing beliefs and feelings, and demonstrating love and affection are all essential skills needed to create and maintain intimate relationships.
■ *Financial management:* Sound decision-making skills for money management lead to economic satisfaction, which contributes to family well-being. This characteristic appears most important through children's teen years. With economic planning early in the relationship, later years seem to take care of themselves barring catastrophe.
■ *Hardiness:* This characteristic is more difficult to understand, but it is vitally important across the entire life cycle. Hardiness encompasses family members' sense of control over their lives, their commitment to the family, their confidence that the family will survive no matter what, and their ability to grow, learn, and challenge each other.
■ *Health:* The physical and psychological well-being of family members reduces stress and helps create a healthy home atmosphere. This characteristic appears especially important at the beginning and end of the life cycle.
■ *Leisure activities:* This characteristic focuses on similarities and differences in family members' preferences for ways to spend free time. This is probably most important in early stages of the relationship. If

the couple agrees on and shares leisure activities, they will be drawn more closely together. Agreement by the couple also increases chances that the family will agree on leisure activities if and when children arrive.
■ *Personality:* This involves acceptance of a partner's or child's traits, behaviors, and general character.
■ *Support network:* Although often overlooked by courting couples, relations with in-laws, relatives, and friends contribute to marital and family success. This seems especially important through the middle of the life cycle.
■ *Time and routine:* Family meals, chores, togetherness, and other routines play important roles in creating continuity and stability in relationships throughout the life cycle.
■ *Traditions:* This characteristic overlaps "celebrations" but refers more to honoring important family experiences carried through generations. Gathering of the extended family at the grandparents' house every Thanksgiving would be an example. This seems important throughout the life cycle.

WHAT DO YOU THINK?

1. How many of these characteristics are in your family of origin?
2. Which characteristics are most important to you? Why?
3. Do you have family traditions that you'd like to carry on in your own family? What are they? Why are they important to you?
4. How would you establish characteristics that are important to you in your family or future family?

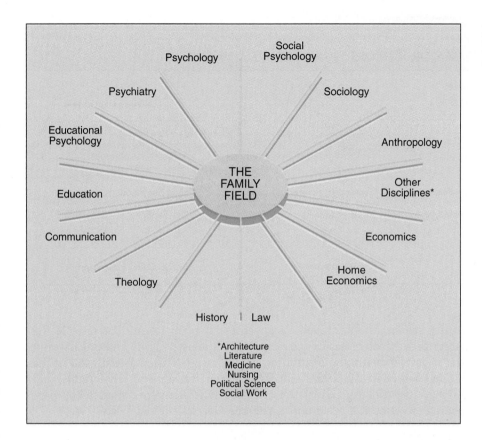

FIGURE 1-1
Family science involves many disciplines.

Psychology
Social Psychology
Psychiatry
Sociology
Educational Psychology
Anthropology
Education
THE FAMILY FIELD
Other Disciplines*
Communication
Economics
Theology
Home Economics
History | Law

*Architecture
Literature
Medicine
Nursing
Political Science
Social Work

THEORETICAL APPROACHES TO FAMILY STUDY

As Figure 1-1 demonstrates, many disciplines inform us about the family. Some marriage and family textbooks are written from a sociological perspective, which focuses on the family as an organization that functions independently as well as interacting with its individual members. Others are written from a psychological perspective, which focuses on the individual within the family; this emphasis occurs in part because psychologists believe that the individual creates the institution rather than the institution creating the individual. **Macrosociology** focuses on social structures (family, school, and so forth) and organizations and the relationships between them. **Microsociology** focuses on interactions between individuals.

It is not our purpose to turn the reader into a theoretician. Yet it is important to understand that research is always based on some theoretical foundation. There are so many perspectives in sociology today that we cannot do justice to all of them. Nevertheless, an examination of three different theoretical perspectives will help the reader understand the often differing approaches that researchers take in studying marriage and the family.

1. The *structural-functional approach* identifies the relevant social structures and examines how they function. This approach concentrates on institutions such

Macrosociology
Study of social structures and organizations.

Microsociology
Study of interaction between individuals.

TABLE 1-1
THREE MAJOR THEORETICAL PERSPECTIVES

	STRUCTURAL FUNCTIONALISM	CONFLICT THEORY	SYMBOLIC INTERACTIONISM
Nature of society	Interrelated social structures that fit together to form an integrated whole	Competing interest groups, with each group seeking to secure its own ends	Interacting individuals, social networks, and groups
Basis of interaction	Consensus and shared values	Constraint, power, and conflict	Shared symbolic meanings
Focus of inquiry	Social order and maintenance of society	Social change and conflict	Development of self and adaptation of individual to society
Level of analysis	Social structure	Social structure	Interpersonal interaction

Source: Brinkerhoff and White 1988, 14.

as the family, school, church, or government. Such institutions provide the patterns by which a society operates and maintains stability and order within the society. When these institutions break down—as they partially did in the United States in the 1960s and 1970s when the antiwar, civil rights, and women's movements were at their height—unrest usually occurs in the population. We saw this again during the Los Angeles riots in 1992.

> Structural-functional analysis often takes the approach of looking at the consequences of social structures. Positive outcomes are called *functions* and negative consequences are called *dysfunctions*. In addition, sociologists draw a distinction between those consequences that are manifest and those that are latent. *Manifest functions* are consequences that are intended and recognized by participants in the system; *latent functions* are consequences that are neither intended *nor* recognized. (Brinkerhoff and White 1988, 10)

For example, making birth control more available to the population was thought to be a way to make unwanted pregnancies a thing of the past (a manifest function). However, unwanted pregnancies appear to have increased (a latent dysfunction). Although we recognize the problem of unwanted pregnancies, we do not clearly understand the reasons for such pregnancies in light of the increased availability of contraceptive methods.

2. *Conflict theory* tends to see the world in terms of conflict and change. This approach tends to produce a critical picture of society with an emphasis on social activism and criticism. For example, the ongoing debate over abortion is best viewed from this perspective. Social activists who desire to make abortion a personal decision lobbied the courts and finally won a Supreme Court decision (*Roe v. Wade*, January 22, 1973) making abortion a woman's personal decision. Right-to-life activists are trying hard to overturn this decision and return control of abortion to the states.

Conflict theory also tends to emphasize economic determinism and sources of power and control. In looking at the family, conflict theorists might ask, who has the power, the man or the woman? Is inequality built into family roles? This perspective would be concerned with the women's rights and civil rights movements.

3. *Symbolic-interaction theory* is the third perspective. It tends to focus on how individuals interact by using symbolic actions such as language. This viewpoint examines the subjective personal meanings of human acts. How do individuals interpret and negotiate their way through society? A man opens a door for a woman. Is this simply a symbolic behavior indicating politeness and respect or is it a symbolic statement indicating that men are strong and women are weak? Symbolic-interaction theory attempts to answer such questions.

No perspective by itself can offer a complete picture of the family; all theoretical perspectives need to be explored.

> Together [the three theoretical perspectives] emphasize the key elements of social life, from the consequences produced by social systems to the mechanics of social interaction. Although [researchers] often prefer one perspective over the others, it is possible—even desirable—to use them as a single integrated perspective in order to have an awareness of the different aspects of social life that they emphasize. (Johnson 1989, 25)

Knowledge of theoretical perspectives is indispensable to researchers. Without a theoretical foundation, research cannot be done efficiently, if at all. For people interested in improving their own relationships, however, the findings of research are more important than its theoretical foundations. But some knowledge of the researchers' theoretical position can help people judge the validity of the research findings.

CAN WE STUDY INTIMACY?

Can we study "intimacy"? (See p. 3 for a detailed definition.) We can, if we study relationships that can be and often are intimate. We most often find intimacy within marriage and the family. Although intimacy can exist between any two people, it is within the family that most of us learn to be intimate, caring, loving people. Thus, to study the family is also to study intimacy.

The study of the family deals with many topics, as the table of contents of this book reveals. It is clear that such a study cuts across many disciplines: psychology, sociology, anthropology, economics, and so on (see Figure 1-1). To identify the study of marriage and family more clearly, we will use the term *family science* (NCFR Report 1985, 14).

Because each of us is born into a family (the family of origin or orientation) and approximately 90 percent of us marry and establish a family at some time in our lives (U.S. Bureau of the Census May 1991, 2), we usually have strong feelings about marriage, families, love, and intimacy.

> The vast majority of adults (71 percent) believe that marriage is a lifelong commitment that should not be ended except under extreme circumstances (Bumpass and Sweet 1988). Even more Americans (85 percent) say they would remarry their spouses if they had to do it all over again (Weiss 1988, 20). Yet only 39 percent of Americans polled expect marriage to last forever (CBS News/New York Times Poll 1989).

Such mixed feelings are natural, and we must examine them to understand how our own personalities have been influenced by our upbringing. Thus, to study family science is also to study one's own feelings about the institutions of marriage and family. The statement that the birthrate in the United States in 1991 was 16.3 births per 1000 population (U.S. Department of Health and Human Services March 12, 1992) may appear simple and clear, but such a statistic has little to do with one's personal decision about having children. One's personal experience may or may not be represented by a scientific statistic describing the general condition of American families. That is why there seems to be so little agreement about how marriages and families are changing and what the changes mean.

OPTIMISM VERSUS PESSIMISM

Some Americans feel that today's families are in deep trouble because they are different from their own family of origin. The pessimists see the high divorce rate, increasing numbers of children born out of wedlock, and the devaluation of children because mothers are entering the workplace as signs of family decline.

The optimists feel the wide variety of acceptable relationships now available to Americans allows people to create a family that is best for themselves. This, in turn, will improve the quality of family life. Pessimists see the high divorce rate (4.7 divorces per 1000 population in 1991) as sounding the death knell of marriage. Optimists see it as normal behavior in a society that emphasizes personal happiness. Given the present freedom to seek happiness through divorce, one no longer need endure an unhappy marriage. Regardless of what you may feel about the changes taking place in American marriages and families, it is clear that all individuals interpret the data in a personal manner based in part on their own family experiences.

This does not mean that there are *only* personal opinions about family institutions; a rich foundation of scientific information is available about this

most personal and intimate of relationships. People who know the scientific facts as well as their personal feelings about marriage and family are in a better position to understand themselves and build successful and satisfying intimate relationships that will create strong, resilient families. As we have said, to study family is also to study intimacy.

SOME WORDS ABOUT MARRIAGE AND FAMILY DATA

Hard and fast data in such an intimate field of study as the family are difficult to produce. Most data come from surveys and from clinicians who work in the field. Some data come from direct observation of families.

Survey data are often problematic for three reasons.

1. *The sample may not be representative of the population in which you are interested.* For example, if you are interested in the cohabiting behavior of college students, which college students do you survey? Certainly, the answers of state university students will differ from those of students at a small denominational college where dormitory residence is required. You must always ask whether the sample surveyed accurately represents the population about which you want to draw conclusions.

2. *Survey data only reflect the opinions of those who actually respond.* In most cases the researcher sets up a representative sample, but responding to surveys is voluntary, not mandatory. Although 100 percent of the sample may indeed be representative of the population about which you want to generalize, you will be fortunate if 50 to 80 percent of those in the sample cooperate. You need to know if those who cooperated are the same as those who did not. For example, in creating their monumental studies *Sexual Behavior of the Human Male* (1948) and *Sexual Behavior of the Human Female* (1953), Alfred Kinsey and his associates worked hard to draw a representative sample of Americans to interview about sexual behavior. They took people from all geographic areas and from various social classes. But can we be sure that the people who volunteered to discuss their most private sexual behavior were the same as those who did not volunteer? Of course, we can't, so there will always be a question about how representative of Americans the two Kinsey studies really were. The studies would be more accurately titled *Sexual Behavior of the Humans Who Volunteered Information.*

3. *It is difficult to validate respondents' answers.* Are they telling the truth? The more intimate the questions, such as those about marriage and sex habits, the more likely the respondents are to hedge on their answers or not to answer at all. Although researchers try to overcome this problem by making surveys anonymous, we can never really be sure the answers are true. While respondents may not actually lie, sometimes memories are inadequate, or what we think we'd do in a hypothetical situation is not what we would actually do in real life. We must always be careful about accepting survey data uncritically.

Clinicians, such as marriage counselors, clergy, psychologists, psychiatrists, and others who work with families, also supply data to the research field. These data are usually anecdotal (storytelling), and the clinicians' conclusions may be overgeneralized. Because they work with those seeking help, they may see only troubled families. Working eight hours a day over months with people who have problems, clinicians may acquire overly pessimistic views of the family. Writings from clinicians often turn up on best-seller lists. Some examples are, *How to Marry the Man of Your Choice, Men Who Can't Love, Women Who Love Too Much,* and *A Return to Love, How to Satisfy a Woman Every Time.*

Data for individual cases are valid for those cases, but can such data be generalized to the entire population? In most cases, probably not. Also, group data do not accurately predict what an individual will do. For example, data from large group studies indicate that an individual's chances of divorce go up if her or his parents are divorced. Yet we all know persons who are long married and indeed have worked harder to make their marriage succeed because their parents were divorced. Does this mean that group data are incorrect? Not at all. The statistics are correct for the group but do not necessarily predict the behavior of any one individual within the group. As Sherlock Holmes (in *The Sign of the Four*) said to his friend Dr. Watson: "While the individual man is an insoluble puzzle, in the aggregate he becomes a mathematical certainty. You can never foretell what any one man will be do, but you can say with precision what an average number will be up to. Individuals vary but percentages remain constant."

Direct observation of families is difficult to arrange. What family wants to have a stranger observing their intimate daily interactions? Even if direct observation can be arranged, the presence of the observer usually modifies the family's behavior to some degree.

In general, then, remember to be cautious about immediately accepting all supposed research facts in the field of marriage and family.

FAMILY AND NATION: GOVERNMENT FAMILY POLICY

In recent years people have started to study the effect that government policies and laws have on the family. The family after all exists within a society and that society is governed by laws. The family is affected by those laws.

Houlgate (1988, 7–8) suggests six legal functions that affect or concern families.

1. *Penal.* These are laws that impose fines or use imprisonment to ensure compliance. An example is a criminal statute forbidding the sexual abuse of children. Most family laws are not criminal in nature, however.

2. *Remedial.* This group of laws defines particular grievances and specific remedies. Statutes that make parents liable for at least a limited amount of damage to others' property caused by their child's vandalism are an example.

3. *Regulatory.* Many family laws use regulatory techniques designed to protect specific persons, usually children, from harm. Penalties may be involved, but criminal sanctions are not imposed. Examples of such regulatory family laws include those that set standards for child neglect and the conditions under which children may be removed from their parents.

4. *Conferral of private power.* A common function of law is to confer on private persons legal powers to make private arrangements and to indicate the legal duties, rights, status, and remedies that result from those arrangements. Laws of marriage, some laws on divorce or dissolution of marriage, and adoption law are all examples of family laws that confer power on individuals.

5. *Conferral of public power.* Some family laws establish public persons—the courts, for example—as a mechanism for settling disputes between private parties. Child custody laws are an example of this type of law applied to families.

6. *Benefit/burden distribution.* Cash assistance, housing, and employment programs designed for families are examples of this type of family law. Laws in this category are commonly referred to as *family policies.*

In his book *Family and Nation* (1986), Senator Patrick Moynihan discussed the need for the nation to consider the effects of government policy on the family. As one example of the harm that government action can have on the family, Moynihan cited the diminishing income tax exemptions allowed for family members.

> The exemption per person, which was $600 in 1948, had risen to $1000 by 1984. If the exemption had been indexed for inflation, however, it would have been $2589 per person in 1984. All told, combining Social Security taxes and federal income taxes, an American family of median income in 1948 paid about 4.4 percent of its income to the federal government. By 1982, the federal government was claiming 18 percent of the median family's income (Moynihan 1986, 161).

The Tax Reform Act of 1986 increased personal exemptions, indexed them to the inflation rate, and also reduced some tax rates. With personal exemptions indexed for inflation, families falling below the poverty line are now exempt from taxes. Consequently, indexing should help reduce various welfare payments to families because exemption from taxes will leave them with more spendable income.

Moynihan also pointed out that government policy has recognized the problems of the elderly for some time and has wrought a miraculous transformation: the virtual disappearance of poverty among the elderly. Thirty years ago the elderly were, in the words of the Economic Report to the President (Council of Economic Advisors 1985), "a relatively disadvantaged group." Their income levels have increased so dramatically since then that "poverty rates for the elderly were approximately the same as for the rest of the population."

> In 1990, 11 percent of persons over sixty-five years were poor compared to 13.5 percent of the total population. (U.S. Bureau of the Census August 1991, 15.)

If government policy can help the elderly, it seems obvious that government policies ought to be able to help the American family. Although such a conclusion seems reasonable, it is not always easy to understand the effects a change in policy will have on the family or on society in general. Recently, the government has tried various income maintenance (guaranteeing all families a minimum income) experiments that ensure support to all members of a family even if the marriage is terminated. One rationale for these experiments was that a family that survives economically is less apt to break up than one that does not. Actual research data on this idea are inconsistent. For some families, the economic help leads to the "independence effect" for the wife. If a wife is guaranteed an income for herself and her dependent children, divorce is sometimes the outcome because the guaranteed income allows the wife to be economically independent of her husband.

Yet Danziger and Gottschalk (1986) reviewed the various studies on the effects of welfare on family stability and concluded that welfare policies have no real dramatic effect on family structure. Zimmerman (1991) compared state divorce rates with state welfare support and failed to uncover any family destabilization caused by state welfare programs. Family policy research is aimed at uncovering these kinds of practical relationships between governmental actions and the family.

Sweden is often cited as the best example of a country where government policies help families. Poverty has almost been eliminated, equal employment opportunities are available for all, literacy is universal, parental leaves with job protection are available, and decent child care is provided. Nevertheless, as supportive of people as the Swedish government's policies have been, the country still has a high percentage of family dissolution and single-parent, female-headed families. Marriage itself has fallen out of favor to some degree with Sweden having the lowest marriage rate and the oldest average age at first marriage of any developed nation. Sweden also has the largest percentage of people living alone. Although the Swedish government has long tried to help its people and families through supportive family policies, it is clear that government policies do not always encourage family stability.

The Family Support Act of 1988 is an example of government policy specifically concerned with American families. This welfare reform bill included the following provisions:

1. Single parents on Aid for Dependent Children (AFDC) are required to get jobs or enroll in job-training courses at state and federal expense.
2. Persons under age twenty without a high school diploma are encouraged to finish high school.
3. Child-care, transportation, and Medicaid benefits are supplied for persons in various programs aimed at upgrading their skills.

Recipients incur an obligation for receiving these services; states are allowed to charge on a sliding scale for them. Among many other things, the act called for improved monitoring of child support payments and automatic withholding of wages for child support payments (Aldous & Dumon 1990).

Americans have mixed feelings about the government formally declaring an interest in their families. Many fear such policies will lead to more governmental interference in their lives. A national survey to determine the extent to which state governments were actively involved in addressing family issues found all states were involved to some degree. Five states—California, Connecticut, Illinois, Massachusetts, and New York—were particularly active in proposing family-oriented legislation (Wisensale 1990). Like it or not, the

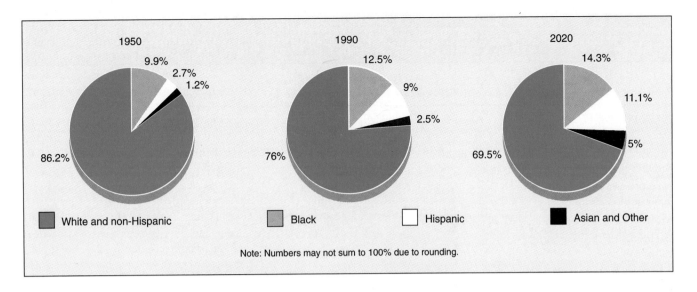

FIGURE 1-2
U.S. racial and ethnic composition,
1950–2020

government influences every family. Consequently, it is important that all proposed government policies and laws be examined for their effects, if any, on the family. Those laws that harm the family in any way should be discarded.

AFRICAN-AMERICAN, HISPANIC AND ASIAN-AMERICAN FAMILIES

The United States is made up of a great variety of peoples. The 1990 census found that over 16 million Americans were foreign born. All races and nationalities are represented in the American population.

Blacks make up 12.5 percent of the population (thirty-one million), and that proportion is projected to rise to 14.3 percent by the year 2020. Hispanics represent 9.0 percent of the population (approximately twenty million), a proportion that is projected to rise to 11.1 percent by 2020. Asian-Americans represent 2.5 percent of the population (approximately five million) with 5.0 percent projected by 2020.

Although the American dream of social "melting pot" is often espoused, the **principle of homogamy** is dominant in most relationships. This principle states that people are attracted to others who share similar objective characteristics such as race, religion, ethnic group, education, and social class. In other words "like tends to marry like."

Principle of homogamy
People are attracted to others who share similar characteristics.

Thus, rather than a melting pot, the United States resembles a "tossed salad," with numerous familial subgroups—the Chinese-American family, the black family, the Hispanic family, and so forth. The families in each of these subgroups share certain characteristics with all American families but also have specific characteristics that are unique to that subgroup.

Although this book tends to focus on aspects of family life common to all families regardless of race or nationality, it is important to note that *each* family

African-American, Hispanic and Asian-American Families

TABLE 1-2
SOME DEMOGRAPHIC VARIABLES FOR FOUR FAMILY GROUPS

VARIABLE	ASIAN-AMERICAN[1]	AFRICAN-AMERICAN	HISPANIC	CAUCASIAN
Percent population*[2]	3% (7.5 million)	12.1% (30 million)	9% (22 million)	75.6% (188 million)
Percent married couple families[3]	62%	50%	70%	83%
Birthrates per 1000 women, 15–44 years[4]	58	78	93	65
Percent women childless 18–44 years	40%	34%	29%	43%
Out-of-wedlock births[4]	9%	57%	23%	17%
Percent one-parent families[5]	15%[5]	56%[4]	30%[5]	20%[4]
Children under 18 living with:[6]				
2 parents	85%	38%	67%	79%
1 parent	15%	55%	30%	20%
Mother only	10%	51%	27%	16%
Father only	2%	4%	3%	3%
Divorced persons per 1000 married persons with spouse present[6]	low	208 (men) 358 (women)	103 (men) 155 (women)	112 (men) 153 (women)
Mean years of schooling completed by males 25 years and over[7]	13 +	11.3	10	12.8
Median family income[7]	high	$21,423	$23,431	$36,915
Median income married couples[7]	high	$33,784	$27,996	$40,321
Percent persons below poverty level[8]	12.2%	31.9%	28.1%	10.7%
Percent children below poverty level[9]	low	44%	38%	15%

*The population of the United States was approximately 254 million January 1, 1992.

1. Some figures for the Asian-American population are estimates.
2. U.S. Bureau of the Census. June, 1991. "Race and Hispanic Origin." *1990 Census Profile.*
3. _____. December, 1991. "Household and Family Characteristics: March 1990 and 1989." *Current Population Reports.* Series P-20 No. 447 Table 1.
4. _____. October, 1991. Fertility of American Women." *Current Population Reports.* Series P-20 No. 454 p. 2, 17, 18.
5. _____. October, 1991. "Studies in American Fertility." *Current Population Reports.* Series P-23 No. 176.
6. _____. May, 1991. "Marital and Living Arrangements: March 1990: *Current Population Reports.* Series P-20 No. 450 pp. 3, 5.
7. _____. August, 1991. "Money Income of Households, Families and Persons in the United States: 1990." *Current Population Reports.* Series P-60 No. 174. pp. 3, 156.
8. _____. August, 1991. "Poverty in the United States: 1990." *Current Population Reports.* Series P-60 No. 175. p. 4.
9. Bianchi, Suzanne M. June, 1990. *"America's Children: Mixed Prospects." Population Bulletin.* 45 No. 1 p. 14.

is not *all* families. Table 1-2 compares a few demographic characteristics for four different family groups, Asian-Americans, African-Americans, Hispanics, and Caucasians. This overview is followed by a brief discussion of each family (other than the Caucasian). These discussions are not meant to be exhaustive. They are aimed at alerting the reader to the fact that the United States is made up of diverse family groups representing many subcultures. Further detailed discussion of these various subgroup families will be found throughout the remainder of the book. Note also that the table gives statistics about an entire group of people and overlooks differences within the groups. For example, the table shows that African-American income is lower than in some other groups, but does not reveal that the African-American middle class has been growing faster as a percentage of all blacks than the middle classes in the other groups. Remember also the table only presents averages that may or may not describe individual families.

African-Americans make up the largest minority in the United States. Just as there is no one family type in the United States, there is no single type of black family. For example, much past literature has focused on African-American families near or below the official poverty level.

Poor African-American families account for 32 percent of black families down from 56 percent during the 1950s. Over one-third of black families have an annual income at or above the national median (Willie, 1988, 221). In 1989, nearly one in seven African-American families had an income of $50,000 or more (in constant dollars) compared to one in seventeen in 1967 (O'Hare et al 1991, 29).

Yet the more important economic story of the last 40 years for African-Americans has been the emergence of the middle class, whose income gains have been real and substantial (Smith and Welch 1986, ix). It is important to realize that the term "African-American or Black family" encompasses many kinds of families, both economically and in other ways.

In 1991, Hispanic families comprised approximately 9.0 percent of the American population. This subpopulation has been growing rapidly, especially in the border states such as California, Texas, and Florida. It is comprised mainly of persons from Mexico (62 percent), Puerto Rico (13 percent), Cuba (5 percent), and Central and South America (12 percent). Hispanics may constitute a higher percentage of the population than the census figure indicates because many Hispanic people, especially those from Mexico, enter the country illegally and do not participate in the census.

It should be noted that there is conflict over what Hispanic families should be called. The Census Bureau uses "Families of Spanish Origin," but "Latinos" and "Hispanics" have also been used. In addition, some groups prefer names that identify their country of origin such as "Mexican-American" or "Cuban-American." For clarity we will use "Hispanic families" throughout the book.

Here again Table 1.2 masks the differences found between the many different Hispanic families. For example, 60 percent of Hispanic males graduate high school but only 54 percent of Mexican-Americans graduate while 74 percent of Puerto Rican males graduate from high school (Knouse, et al 1992, 20).

In 1965 all discriminatory immigration quotas against Asians were lifted. Such quotas originated in 1882 when Congress passed the infamous Chinese Exclusion Act. This act remained in force until 1943 when China and the United States became allies during World War II. Since 1965 a large number of Asians, mainly those dislocated by the wars in Vietnam and Cambodia, have entered the United States. From 1981 to 1985, immigrants from Asia accounted for 48 percent of all legal immigration to the United States (Bouvier and Gardner 1986, 17).

The major Asian-American groups in order of size are Chinese, Filipinos, Japanese, Vietnamese, and Koreans. The most recent Asian immigrants have largely kept to themselves, setting up their own subcommunities and maintaining many of their family traditions. As with any group of immigrants, however, Asians who came early to this country (mainly Chinese, Japanese, and Koreans) have slowly become acculturated. Thus, their families have become increasingly similar to American families in general.

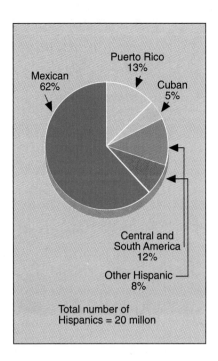

FIGURE 1-3
Hispanic population groups (Source: U.S. Bureau of the Census 1989)

African-American, Hispanic and Asian-American Families

Despite being discriminated against in earlier years, Asian-Americans are now often perceived as a "model minority" because as a whole they are better educated, occupy higher occupational positions, and earn more than the general U.S. population (Gardner et al. 1985, 4). Asian families generally tend to exhibit some of the characteristics of strong, successful families that we have described.

Again Table 1.2 does not discriminate between different Asian-American subgroups. For example, the overall birthrate for Asian women is 58 per 1000 women aged 15 to 44. However the current fertility rates range from 47 births per thousand women born in Vietnam to 158 births per thousand women born in India (U.S. Bureau of the Census October 1991, 52).

SUMMARY

1. Research indicates that strong, successful families share a number of characteristics, including the following:

- Commitment to the family
- Appreciation of family members
- Good communication skills
- The desire to spend time together
- A strong value system
- The ability to deal with crises and stress in a positive manner

2. Research on relationships, marriage, and the family is guided by a variety of theoretical perspectives. These perspectives include structural functionalism, conflict theory, and symbolic interactionism. Many disciplines such as psychology, sociology, and economics also study the family. Our approach tends to emphasize the psychological aspects of relationships. An individual who is functioning in a healthy manner is more likely to have successful relationships, which in turn will lead to a healthy family life.

3. Research on relationships, marriage, and the family is more prone to subjective bias than is research in such fields as physics and chemistry because everyone, including researchers, is personally involved with the subject matter. Therefore one must be careful in evaluating research findings in this field. Being aware of the kinds of problems that family researchers face will help the reader better evaluate research data.

4. Social institutions, especially governmental bodies, greatly influence the family as well as individual Americans. It is important that we study the effects that proposed changes in the law may have on family functioning.

5. American society is made up of a great diversity of peoples. People come from different ethnic backgrounds and are of different races. Therefore when we speak of the American family, we are actually speaking of many kinds of families. There is no one universal family form in the United States.

There is widespread fear among policy makers and the American public today that the family is disintegrating. Much of the anxiety stems from a basic misunderstanding of the nature of the family in the past and a lack of appreciation for its resiliency in response to broad social and economic changes. Change has always been characteristic of the family.

In the last twenty years, historians have been reexamining the nature of the family and have concluded that we must revise our notions of the family as an institution, as well as our assumptions about how children were perceived and treated in past centuries. A survey of diverse studies of the family in the West, particularly in seventeenth-, eighteenth-, and nineteenth-century England and America shows something of the changing role of the family (defined as kin living under one roof) in society and the evolution of our ideas of parenting and child development.

We have tended to believe that in the past children grew up in "extended households" including grandparents, parents, and children. Recent research has cast considerable doubt on the idea that as countries became more urban and industrial, the Western family evolved from extended to nuclear. Historians have found evidence that households in preindustrial Western Europe were already nuclear and could not have been greatly transformed by economic changes. Rather than finding sharp declines in household size, we find surprisingly small variations, which turn out to be due to the presence or absence of servants,

boarders, and lodgers rather than relatives. Most households in the past were quite small (mean household size was about 4.75 compared to 3.19 now). It seems unlikely that in the past few centuries many families had grandparents living directly with them.

The medieval family was nevertheless quite different from its modern counterpart because the boundary between the household and the larger society was less rigidly drawn, and the roles of parents, servants, or neighbors in the socialization of children were more blurred. Relationships within nuclear families were not much closer, it seems, than those with neighbors, relatives, or other friends.

Another difference was that in property-owning classes, in sixteenth-century England, for example, marriage was a collective decision, involving not only the immediate family but also other kin. Protection of the long-term interests of the lineage and consideration for the needs of the larger kinship group were more important than individual desires for happiness or romantic love. In addition, because the strong sense of individual or family privacy had not yet developed, access to the household by local neighbors was relatively easy. But in the late sixteenth century, this type of family gave way to a "restricted patriarchial nuclear family," which predominated from 1580 to 1640, when concern for lineage and loyalty to the local community declined, and allegiances to the state and church and kin within the household increased. The authority of the father, as head of the household, was enhanced and bolstered by the state and church. The drive toward parental dominance over children was especially characteristic of the Puritans; upper-class parents in particular sought to extend control to their children's choices of both career and spouse.

By the mid-seventeenth century, the family was increasingly organized around the principle of personal autonomy and was bound together by strong ties of love and affection. The separation, both physical and emotional, between members of a nuclear family and their servants and boarders widened, as did the distance between the household and the rest of society. Physical privacy became more important, and it became more acceptable for individual family members to pursue their own happiness.

Throughout most of the preindustrial period, the household was the central productive unit of the society. Children either were trained for their future occupations in their own homes or were employed in someone else's household. As the economic functions of the household moved to the shop or factory in the late eighteenth and nineteenth centuries, the household, no longer an economic focal point or an undifferentiated part of neighborhood activities, increasingly became an escape from the outside world. Children growing up in fifteenth-century England were expected and encouraged to interact closely with many adults besides their parents, but by the eighteenth and nineteenth centuries, they had come to rely more and more upon each other and their parents for their emotional needs.

The families that migrated to the New World, especially the Puritans, brought with them the ideal of a close and loving family, and although the economic functions of the American household were altered in the

nineteenth century, the overall change was less dramatic than it had been in Western Europe. This quick history of the European-American family makes it clear that the family does change across time, yet such changes do not destroy the family; instead the family adjusts to the changing times and beliefs (adapted from Maris Vinovekis, "Historical Perspectives on the Development of the Family and Parent-Child Interactions," in Lancaster et al. 1987.)

WHAT DO YOU THINK?

1. What do you see as the major change of this century in the American family?

2. How will the family you start differ from the family in which you were raised?

3. If you decide to have children, what effect will these changes have on them? How might they differ from you?

4. As the American population ages, what kinds of problems will this create for the young family?

HUMAN INTIMACY, THE FAMILY AND ITS MEANING

CONTENTS

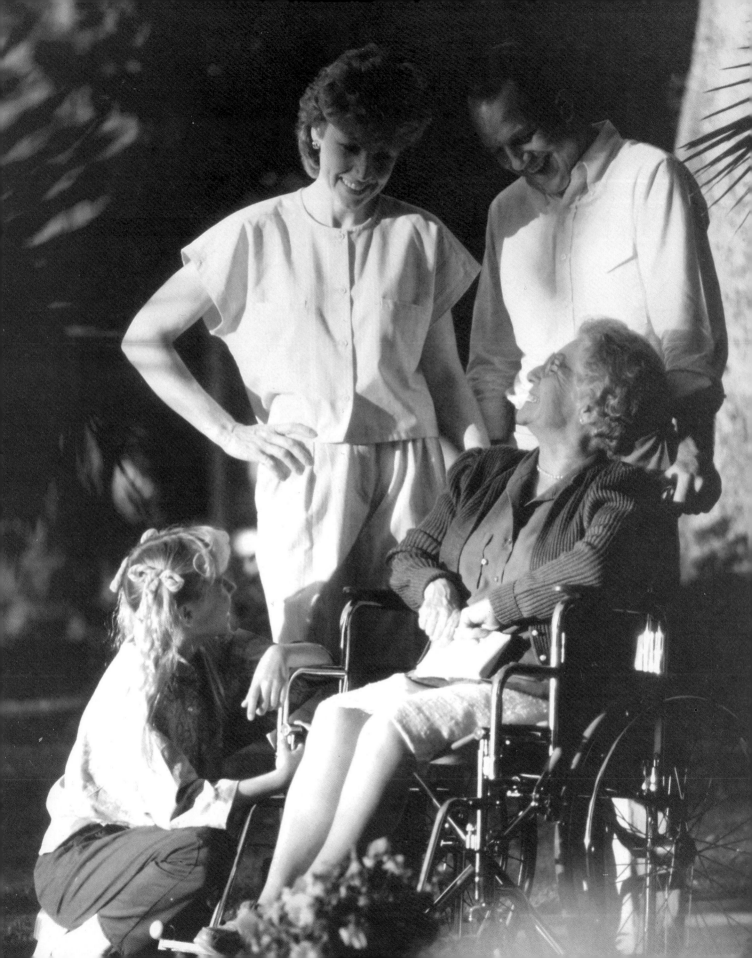

THE BASIC ASSUMPTIONS

All people hold beliefs about marriage and the family. Because these beliefs color an author's writing, it is important to recognize and make clear the major assumptions on which this book is based. While discussing the various assumptions, the chapter introduces information about today's American family. The discussion of each assumption is necessarily cursory, but appropriate cross-references are given to the chapter or chapters within the text where additional information can be found.

Each assumption is supported by some facts that also introduce many of the basic statistics about American families. Remember, an **assumption** is a belief that may or may not be well supported by the facts. Although the author believes that the various assumptions are supported, acceptance is left to the reader's discretion.

Assumption
The supposition that something is true

In general, the most important change that has occurred in the modern American family seems to be the shift from child centeredness to adult centeredness. There are two schools of thought about this change. The optimists emphasize the positive results of the change, particularly for women. The new individual freedoms that adults enjoy form the core of the optimists' case. Pessimists, on the other hand, believe the family as a social institution is in decline. They emphasize the negative consequences of the change for children. Devaluation of children is the core of the pessimists' case (Blankenhorn 1990, 8). It will be interesting for you, the reader, to evaluate your own attitude about the changes taking place in the American family.

FAMILY: THE BASIC UNIT OF HUMAN ORGANIZATION

Assumption 1 *The family is the basic unit of human organization. If defined functionally, the family is essentially universal. However, its structural form and strength vary greatly across cultures and time.*

The term *family* is used here in the broadest possible sense: It is defined as whatever system a society uses to support and control reproduction and human sexual interaction. This broad definition avoids many apparent conflicts over the meaning of the changes currently taking place in family functions and structure. For example, according to this assumption, Israeli kibbutzim are families, even though persons other than parents assume major childrearing responsibilities. On the other hand, a definition of family will be meaningless if it is so broad that each and every relationship qualifies for family status.

Following are several narrower but more meaningful definitions:

■ Lucille Duberman (1977, 10) says the family is "an institution found in several variant forms, that provides children with a legitimate position in society and with the nurturance that will enable them to function as fully developed members of society."

■ The New York Court of Appeals in 1990 says the family can be defined by examining several factors, including "exclusivity and longevity" and the "level of emotional and financial commitment" of a relationship. "It is the totality of the relationship as evidenced by the dedication, caring and self sacrifice of the partners." (Jacoby 1990)

■ Webster's Ninth New Collegiate Dictionary (1991) defines the family as "the basic unit in society having as its nucleus two or more adults living together and cooperating in the care and rearing of their own or adopted children."

■ The U.S. Census Bureau (May 1988, 130) defines *family* as a group of two or more persons related by birth, marriage, or adoption and residing together.

Ivan Beutler et al. (1989, 806–7) suggests that any definition of the family must include ties across generations that are established by the birth process. The main difference between family and other relationships, such as those between friends or work colleagues, is the permanence of the lineage ties. Nonfamily relationships are usually entered into voluntarily and fostered as a means to achieve specific ends. They can be broken at any time. But family ties exist as an end in themselves. A divorce may end a marriage, but it can't end generational ties between children and their parents, grandparents, and other relatives.

Part of the reason for the debate over the state of the American family is confusion between the functions of the family institution and the structure by which these functions are fulfilled. Many structures can fulfill the responsibilities of the family. In modern America the duties and thus the functions of the family have been reduced, and new structures, or alternative family forms, are being tried to fulfill some functions. Let us take a closer look at these functions.

FAMILY FUNCTIONS

The family serves both the society and the individual. Sometimes, of course, social and individual needs come into conflict; recent laws mandating one child per family in China are an example. Although having more children may benefit a particular family, the Chinese government believes that too many children will harm the larger society. For the family to remain a viable social institution, it must meet the needs of society as well as individual family members. Thus, the family must keep conflict between the individual and the society to a minimum.

The family has handled a broad range of functions in different historical periods and societies. In some primitive societies, the family is synonymous with the society itself, bearing all the powers and responsibilities for societal survival. As societies become more complex and elaborate, social institutions take over many responsibilities that formerly belonged to the family.

The following functions are necessary for the maintenance of society:

1. Replacements for dying members of the society must be produced.
2. Goods and services must be produced and distributed.
3. Provision must be made for solving conflicts and maintaining order within the family as well as within the larger society.
4. Children must be socialized to become participating members of the society.
5. Individual goals must be harmonized with the values of the society, and procedures must be established for dealing with emotional crises and maintaining a sense of purpose.

As the society grows more complex, social institutions are formed that assume the primary responsibility for some past family functions. For example, most families are no longer production units per se. Individuals within the family may produce goods and services, but they usually do this outside the family setting in a more formalized job setting. The family is still an economic unit, however, because it demands goods and services. It is the major consumption unit in the United States (Assumption 8). In addition, although the courts and police maintain external order, the family is still primarily responsible for maintaining order within its own boundaries. Formal education now trains children to become participating members of society, but the family begins and maintains and remains primarily responsible for the socialization process.

Thus we find that the contemporary American family has full responsibility for only two of the primary functions:

1. *Providing emotional gratification and intimacy to members and helping them deal with emotional crises so they grow in the most fulfilling manner possible.* Expecting emotional gratification from intimate family relationships seems to cause Americans more trouble than any of the other family functions. When couples report problems in their relationship, they often cite unhappiness and emotional misery as their major complaint.

2. *Providing continuing replacements for individuals so that society continues to exist.* Despite sperm banks and surrogate mothers, reproduction is still being carried out in the age-old, time-honored fashion. Birth follows pregnancy, which has followed sexual intercourse. The family is also the most efficient way of nurturing the human newborn, who is physically dependent during the first years of life. Without some kind of stable adult unit to provide child care during this long period of dependence, the human species would have disappeared long ago.

SEXUAL REGULATION

Each family structure, then, has reproduction as its primary function. An extension of this function is regulation of sexual behavior. Unlike other animals, human sexual behavior may be sought and enjoyed at any time, regardless of the stage of the female reproductive cycle. Humans are free to use sex not only for reproduction but also for pleasure. As in so many other aspects of human life, freedom of choice is a mixed blessing. Humans must balance their relatively continual sexual receptivity and desire with the needs of other individuals and with the needs of society as a whole. They must find a system that provides physical and mental satisfaction in a socially acceptable context of time, place, and partner. In most societies, the family is the basic institution controlling sexual expression.

No matter how sexuality is handled, humans seem to be comfortable only when they can convince themselves that the system is proper, just, and virtuous. When each culture has established a satisfactory "correct" system of sexual control, it bolsters this system with a complex set of rules and punishments for transgressions.

Western literature on marriage and the family is filled with arguments about proper sexual expression. Were men and women originally **promiscuous, polygamous,** or **monogamous?** We have even applied Darwin's theory of evolution to the male/female relationship in an effort to demonstrate that the monogamy of Western cultures is the highest and therefore the only proper form of relationship. Yet close and objective study of the various methods devised by humans to work out their sexual and family life tends to destroy most of the historical arguments for any straight-line evolutionary theory of family development. In their book *The Family in Various Cultures* (1985), Stuart Queen and Robert Habenstein conclude that because there is such variance among family patterns and in the way sexuality is controlled, no single family form need be regarded as inevitable or more "natural" than any other. They state: "We assume that all forms of the domestic institution are in process, having grown out of something different and tending to become something still different. But there is no acceptable evidence of a single, uniform series of stages through which the developing family must pass."

NEW FAMILY FUNCTIONS

Although consensus has it that the modern family has lost some functions, it may also have gained new ones. For example, the middle-class American family has assumed three new roles:

1. *The recreational role:* Family members spend their leisure time, especially vacation time, together.
2. *The therapeutic role:* Each family member assists the others in solving individual problems that may either originate in the family or be external to it. As we become more isolated from the larger ongoing society, such support becomes more crucial.
3. *Changed sexual roles:* Traditionally, the woman's role was to meet her husband's sexual needs. Now the feminist movement has emphasized that the husband's responsibility to meet his wife's sexual needs is equally important, thereby imposing a new responsibility on the man as well as changing the female role.

We have seen the family's functions changing over time. And we can certainly assume that its functions will continue to change. Do changing functions mean that the family as we know it will disappear? Not necessarily. The family's secret of survival over the past centuries has been its flexibility and adapt-

Promiscuous
Having many sexual partners

Polygamy
Having multiple spouses

Monogamy
Having one spouse in a sexually exclusive relationship

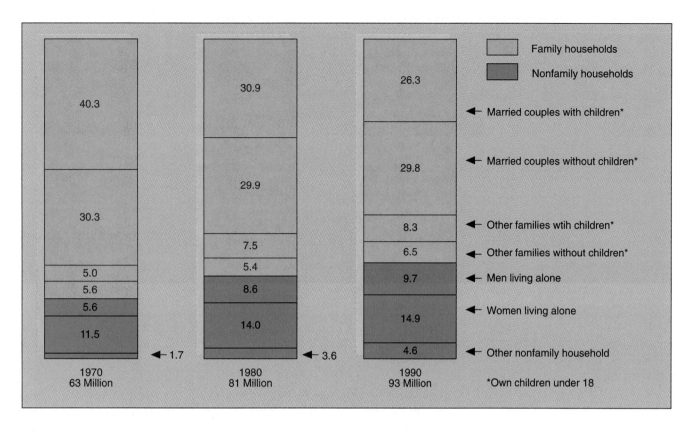

Legend:
- Family households
- Nonfamily households
- ← Married couples with children*
- ← Married couples without children*
- ← Other families wtih children*
- ← Other families without children*
- ← Men living alone
- ← Women living alone
- ← Other nonfamily household

1970 — 63 Million
1980 — 81 Million
1990 — 93 Million

*Own children under 18

ability. The family is a system in process rather than a rigid unchanging system. As John F. Crosby has pointed out:

> No one can yet foresee what the structure of the future family will look like because no one can know with certainty what the functions and needs of the future family will be. It is likely, however, that the needs for primary affection bonds, intimacy, economic subsistence, socialization of the young, and reproduction will not yield to obsolescence. To the extent that human needs do not change drastically, the family structure will not change drastically. (1980, 40)

THE AMERICAN FAMILY: MANY STRUCTURES AND MUCH CHANGE

Assumption 2 *A free and creative society offers many structural forms by which family functions, such as childrearing, can be fulfilled (Chapters 5, 8, and 16).*

Mom and Dad, Sissy and Junior, a dog, and maybe a cat represent the stereotypical American **nuclear family.** Yet to talk of the American family perpetuates the myth that one family structure represents all American families. If we examine the structure of the family, we find that there are, in fact, many kinds of American families. (By *structure* we mean the parts of which a family is composed and their relationships to one another. The nuclear family has a mother, a father, and their children. On the other hand, a single-mother-headed family has just a mother and her children.)

The single-parent family has been one of the fastest-growing family structures during the past decade (see Figures 2-1 and 2-2). Single-parent families

FIGURE 2-1
Household composition: 1970 to 1990 (percent)

Nuclear family
A married couple and their children living by themselves

The Basic Assumptions

29

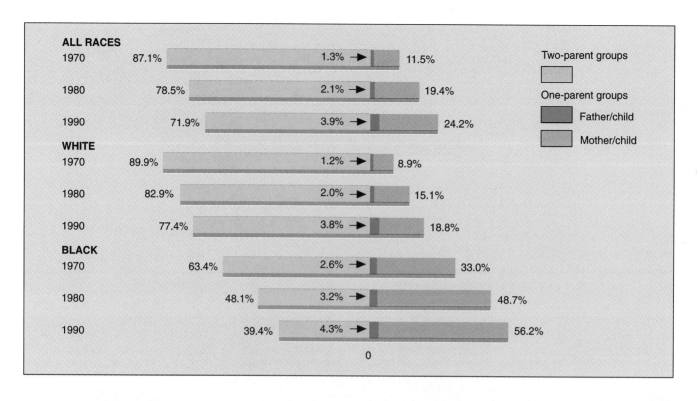

ALL RACES
1970	87.1%	1.3% → 11.5%
1980	78.5%	2.1% → 19.4%
1990	71.9%	3.9% → 24.2%

WHITE
1970	89.9%	1.2% → 8.9%
1980	82.9%	2.0% → 15.1%
1990	77.4%	3.8% → 18.8%

BLACK
1970	63.4%	2.6% → 33.0%
1980	48.1%	3.2% → 48.7%
1990	39.4%	4.3% → 56.2%

Two-parent groups

One-parent groups
Father/child
Mother/child

0

FIGURE 2-2
Composition of Family Groups with Children, by Race: 1970 to 1990 (Percent)

Reconstituted/Blended family
A husband and wife, at least one of whom has been married before, and one or more children from previous marriage(s)

account for 28 percent of the 34.7 million families with children, up sharply from 1970 when they accounted for only 13 percent. During this period, the proportion of children under eighteen years of age living with one parent doubled, from 12 percent to 25 percent (U.S. Bureau of the Census December 1990, 1).

Single-parent families tend to be temporary, but this family structure accounts for a significant number of American families at any one time. The large increase can be accounted for by the greatly increased divorce rate in America. To a lesser extent the greater social acceptance of the unwed mother who keeps her child has also contributed to the growing number of single-parent families.

Divorce is a good example of changing family structure within an individual family. The family begins as a nuclear family, becomes a single-parent family, and, in many cases, becomes a **reconstituted** or **blended family** when the single parent remarries. These kinds of changes signal the end of the initial relationship, at least as an intimate love relationship.

Even in a stable relationship, structure can change over time. Such a relationship usually begins as a couple relationship and then broadens to include children, sons- and daughters-in-law, and finally grandchildren. When the children leave home, the couple returns to a two-person household. Table 2-1 indicates some of the many structural forms families can take in various cultures.

During the 1970s, Americans experimented widely with different family structures. In fact, a popular cliché was that marriage as we had known it was dead. Communal living, multiple sex partners, cohabitation, childlessness, and other family experiments blossomed and were quickly reported and dramatized in the mass media. Experiments, such as cohabitation, have become a relatively

TABLE 2-1
DIFFERENT FAMILY STRUCTURES

KIND	COMPOSITION	FUNCTIONS
Types of Marriage		
Monogamy	One spouse and children.	Procreative, affectional, economic consumption.
Serial monogamy	One spouse at a time but several different spouses over time. Married, divorced, remarried.	Same.
Common-law	One spouse. Live together as husband and wife for long enough period that state recognizes couple as married without formal or legal marriage ceremony. Recognized by only a few states.	Same.
Polygamy	Multiple spouses.	Same.
Polygyny	One husband, multiple wives.	Any,* power vested in male.
Polyandry	One wife, multiple husbands.	Any, power vested in female.
Group	Two or more men collectively married to two or more women at the same time.	Any, very rare.
Types of Families		
Nuclear family	Husband, wife, children.	Procreative, affectional, economic consumption.
Extended family	One or more nuclear families plus other family positions such as grandparents, uncles, etc.	Historically might serve all social, educational, economic, reproductive, affectional, and religious functions.
Composite family	Two or more nuclear families sharing a common spouse.	Normally those of the nuclear family.
Tribal family	Many families living in close proximity as a larger clan or tribe.	Usually those of the extended family.
Consensual family (cohabitation)	Man, woman, and children living together in legally unrecognized relationship.	Any.
Commune	Group of people living together sharing a common purpose with assigned roles and responsibilities normally associated with the nuclear family.	Can provide all functions with leadership vested in an individual, council, or some other organized form to which all families are beholden.
Single-parent family	Usually a mother and child. Father/child combination less common.	Same as monogamy without a legally recognized reproductive function.
Concubine	Extra female sexual partner recognized as a member of the household but without full status.	Usually limited to sex and reproduction.
Reconstituted (blended)	Husband and wife, at least one of whom has been previously married, plus one or more children from previous marriage or marriages.	Any.
Authority Patterns		
Paternalistic	Any,* power vested in male.	Any.
Maternalistic	Any, power vested in female.	Any.
Egalitarian	Any, powers divided in some fair manner between spouses.	Any.

*"Any" means that the family may assume any or all compositions or functions that have been taken or fulfilled by families in the past.

permanent family structure for some Americans. Other experiments, such as **swinging** (acceptance of additional sexual partners outside of the spouse), have lost much of their appeal.

Many Americans thought criticism of the family was new. Yet throughout time, criticisms of marriage and the family have been voiced. In every era,

Swinging
Acceptance of additional sex partners outside of one's spouse

critics of the status quo have offered suggestions for "new" family forms. For example, in 1936, Bertrand Russell believed marriage would collapse as a social institution unless drastic changes were made:

> In the meantime, if marriage and paternity are to survive as social institutions, some compromise is necessary between complete promiscuity and lifelong monogamy. Although it is difficult to decide the best compromise at a given time, certain points seem clear:
>
> Young unmarried people should have considerable freedom as long as children are avoided so that they may better distinguish between mere physical attraction and the sort of congeniality that is necessary to make marriage a success.
>
> Divorce should be possible without blame to either party and should not be regarded as in any way disgraceful.
>
> Everything possible should be done to free sexual relations from economic taint. At present, wives, just as much as prostitutes, live by the sale of their sexual charms: and even in temporary free relations the man is usually expected to bear all the joint expenses. The result is that there is a sordid entanglement of money with sex, and that a woman's motives not infrequently have a mercenary element. A woman, like a man, should have to work for a living, and an idle wife is no more intrinsically worthy of respect than a gigolo. (1957 reprint, 171–72)

Perhaps the major contribution the turmoil of the 1960s and 1970s made to the family was the increase in the available alternatives for intimacy. Families have become more differentiated. Family patterns and sex roles are less stereotyped and rigid. It is no longer considered disgraceful not to marry. Most Americans marry but they don't feel that they have to. Having children can be a more conscious decision. One is no longer obligated to have children. It is far more acceptable to leave a marriage one doesn't like. Intimate cohabitation does not make a person unmarriageable. Acceptance of homosexual relationships has increased although it is still far from universal.

Modern America is remarkably tolerant of multiple forms of intimate relationships. Other cultures have had different marital systems, but they have usually disallowed deviance from their current system. A free and creative society, however, offers many structural forms of the family to fulfill such functions as childrearing and meeting sexual needs. The reasons for America's tolerance are partly philosophic but mainly economic. Marriage forms historically have been limited because women have been economically tied to the men who support them and the family. The women's movement, changes in the law exemplified by affirmative action and civil rights legislation, increased education for women, and ever-larger numbers of women in the work force have all helped women become more independent.

Industrialization and affluence have made it more possible to consider alternate lifestyles and marital forms. For example, affluence allows people to further their education, which exposes them to new ideas and knowledge. Affluence also brings mobility, and mobility brings contact with new people and new lifestyles. If a person discovers greater personal satisfaction in some alternate lifestyle, affluence makes it possible to seek out others who have the same interests. Affluence often enables people to postpone assuming adult responsibility (earning one's own living) and thus encourages experimentation by lessening the consequences of failure. Affluence has also given rise to the mass media, which have spread news about various lifestyles and experimental

YES

In 1989 San Francisco became the first municipality to pass a law (Domestic Partners Bill) permitting unmarried couples to register their domestic partnerships in much the same way as other couples file marriage licenses. The ordinance sets up a new nonmarried, nonsingle category of relations called "domestic partners." The legislation also grants hospital visitation rights and bereavement leave for city employees in such cohabitation relationships. Under the law, it might be possible to extend health benefits to the live-in lovers of city employees.

The ordinance defines domestic partners as "any two persons who have chosen to share one another's lives in an intimate and committed relationship of mutual caring, who live together."

Gay rights activists have for many years sought the right to "marry" their lovers or at a minimum have their relationships legally recognized. They have gained some support from long-term cohabiting hetereosexual couples.

The rationale behind the ordinance is that couples who live together in a close, intimate, committed relationship regardless of sex deserve the same rights as couples who legally marry. "We love and care about one another. We share households both physically and monetarily. Our relationship is long-lasting. To all intents and purposes we are married except for the legalities. So why can't we enjoy some of the advantages that married couples have?"

The law is humane in that it grants intimate couples some rights to care for one another. For example, one partner in a lesbian relationship recently was hospitalized for severe trauma, but her parents refused to allow her long-term partner hospital visitation rights because they objected strongly to the homosexual relationship. The law would allow the partner to visit.

NO

It is impossible for a person to be a "little bit pregnant," yet this law is trying to allow people to be a "little bit married." If, as the advocates protest, they are married in every way but legally, why not just go ahead and marry? This would not be possible for gay couples since the state bans marriage between two persons of the same sex, but it would apply to cohabiting couples of the opposite sex. Why be a little bit married when you can have all of the rights and protections that married couples have enjoyed for years under the law?

Such a law could be used by anyone in a cohabiting relationship to get from the partner those things allowed by the law. Many cohabiting couples cohabit rather than marry for the very reason that they wish to exclude their relationship from the laws. Such a law might be the beginning of numerous laws spelling out cohabitor's rights and obligations—the very thing that many cohabitors are trying to avoid.

Such a law could be costly if such things as medical coverage were to be extended to live-in lovers. Medical insurance is the most costly of the fringe benefits offered to workers. If any duly registered partner could receive such care, the cost could be enormous. In addition, a simple registration procedure without some penalties for misrepresentation would be highly susceptible to fraudulent claims.

Perhaps most important, such laws would undermine the whole concept and legal basis for marriage. Marriage demands commitment and legally protects partners to some extent if the relationship breaks up. Even with these legal sanctions and protections, American marriages are none too stable. Sanctioning simple cohabitation would undermine the stability of all relationships and hence the family itself. We might just as well do away with legal marriage.

WHAT DO YOU THINK?

1. Should society allow persons of the same sex to marry?

2. If you were cohabiting, would you register your relationship so that at least some laws would apply to it?

3. Do you think such laws would destroy legal marriage?

4. What are the advantages to living together without legal sanction? The disadvantages?

5. What are the advantages to legal marriage? The disadvantages?

INSET 2-1
THE FAMILY RIDDLE

Marriage, children, forever together, mom, dad, apple pie, love, Sunday softball in the park, grandmother's for Sunday dinner—The American Family.

Cohabitation, childlessness, divorce and remarriage, stepdad, stepmom, junk food, child abuse and wife beating, spectator sports in front of the TV, Pizza Hut for Sunday dinner—The American Family.

STUDENT: But these two descriptions can't both be of the American family.

FRIEND: Oh, but they are, and infinite other descriptions would also fit. American families, each and every one, are unique and represen-

tative of the individuals and their interactions within the family.

STUDENT: But how then can we study the American family if each is unique?

FRIEND: Because they all have certain things in common. They are all alike in some ways.

STUDENT: But they can't be. You just said they were all unique.

FRIEND: They are, and they are also always changing.

STUDENT: But how can you study something that is unique and also always changing?

FRIEND: Because change occurs in the midst of continuity and conti-

nuity can remain despite change.

STUDENT: You are saying then that each family is unique but has things in common with all other families and, besides, families are always changing but have continuity.

FRIEND: Yes.

STUDENT: It sounds like a riddle.

FRIEND: It is a riddle because in order to understand the family one must be able to understand two abstract principles:

1. Change can occur within continuity.
2. Uniqueness can exist within commonality.

relationships and helped create new lifestyles by portraying them as desirable, exciting, or "in."

In part then because of America's affluence, the young have a broader choice of acceptable relationships (family structures) than their grandparents did. Perhaps by choosing wisely the roles that best fit them as individuals, couples will be able to create growing intimate relationships that are more fulfilling than those of the past. On the other hand, wider choice involves greater risks, and freedom of choice does not seem to have made intimate relationships any more stable.

In the past, we knew more clearly what our roles would be. Sons often followed in their father's footsteps. Women became wives and mothers and ran the home. But today the pattern has changed. Individuals now must make their own choices about their lifestyles, vocations, marriages, and families. If one does not make conscious choices, the choices are made by default. The idea that love will automatically make the decisions for us is the source of much disappointment. One goal of this book is to help the reader make conscious, knowledgeable decisions about intimate relationships.

The major risk in opening up choice is that errors may be made. When more choices are available, one must carefully consider priorities. The older restricted system exacted a price; it often placed people in molds that did not enable them to choose a lifestyle that would allow maximum self-growth and social contribution. In a more open system, people run the risk of acting impulsively. Thus, the price of a more open system is the greater need for a rational examination of the alternatives.

In the old system, many people were trapped in a rut; in the new one, many people seem to run constantly from one lifestyle to another, unable to choose wisely or find permanence. On the other hand, the new system may also encourage experimentation that leads to better decisions. Free inquiry leading to reasoned decisions with opportunities to test those decisions is the way of science. There is no reason why this method should not improve the intimate life of people just as it has improved their material life. Moreover, free choice of a lifestyle can counteract the feelings of entrapment that long-married couples often express.

Certainly, then, one characteristic of today's society is that people have more structural alternatives with which to build their intimate relationships and families. Knowledge and understanding of the alternatives and being able to choose well have become increasingly important to living a successful life and building a strong family. As a society, we need more than ever to teach people how to make good, reasoned decisions about the growing number of relational alternatives that are becoming available.

■ CHANGE WITHIN CONTINUITY AND ■ UNIQUENESS WITHIN COMMONALITY

Assumption 3 *Family life involves continuity as well as changes.*

Assumption 4 *Each family is unique but also has characteristics in common with all other families in a given culture.*

As you try to understand the family and what is happening to it, remember that the American family covers a vast territory and is far from uniform in design. Everyone is aware that family life has changed. Yet the central core of family life continues much the same as it has for many generations. Grasping these two ideas—*change within continuity* and *uniqueness within commonality*—will help you cope with the seeming riddles of the American family (see Inset 2-1).

Some statistical examples that can be interpreted in different ways will help clarify these two principles. For example, the divorce rate has risen steadily throughout this century. In 1900 about one divorce occurred for every twelve marriages. Today about one divorce occurs for every two marriages in a given year.

Some people use this dramatic statistic to support the contention that the American family is in real trouble and will soon be dead and buried. Yet many others see a high but steady divorce rate as positive. The divorce rate per 1000 population has hovered between 4.8 and 5.3 since 1975. Americans will have better marriages and more fulfilling family lives because they no longer need put up with the dissatisfactions of empty marriages that previous generations accepted. Indeed, statistics indicate that divorced persons have high remarriage rates. Most divorced persons leave a particular mate but not the institution of marriage. It should also be remembered that approximately the same proportion of marriages broke up in 1900 as today. The difference was that the majority of marriages in 1900 ended with the death of one of the spouses rather than with divorce. Thus, despite the high divorce rate, family permanence has continued at about the same level for the past century.

A second example also illustrates the conflict evoked by statistics about changing family characteristics. The birthrate in the United States has generally been falling for the past two hundred years with the major exception of the baby boom between about 1947 and 1965, which was related to dislocations and prosperity brought on by World War II. Since 1965, however, the birthrate has fallen dramatically, reaching a low of about 14.5 births per 1000 population in 1975. That figure rose to 16.6 per 1000 population in 1990, although it dropped a bit to 16.2 in 1991 (National Center for Health Statistics April 15, 1992).

Some suggest that the decline in the birthrate was caused by young women deciding not to have children. During the 1970s, many young women were saying, "Having children is no longer an important part of marriage for me." "Careers are more important and children are only troublesome to the pursuit of one's own goals." The proportion of women who stated they expected to remain childless did go up between 1967 and 1974, but there is a difference between a statement made when one is eighteen years of age and what one actually does later in life. As these women approach the end of their childbearing years, they may decide to have a child despite their youthful decision to forgo childbearing and rearing. The birthrate is decreasing not because more women are remaining childless, but because mothers are having fewer children.

> The average woman born between 1846 and 1855 had 5.7 children. Women born between 1931 and 1935 had an average of 3.4 children. Women born between 1940 and 1945 average fewer than three children. Although it is too early to be sure, it appears that women born between 1950 and 1955 will average even fewer.

Thus, the decreasing birthrate may not mean that families are abandoning having children at all. Rather, it seems to mean that families are having fewer children, which is probably positive for the children. Evidence suggests that children do better in smaller families where they receive more adult time and attention. In 1990, 26 percent of married couples had children under eighteen years of age. This is down from 31 percent in 1980 but hardly represents the total demise of childbearing among American couples.

These two examples help point out just how confusing and controversial interpretation of marriage and family data can be. Furthermore, they demonstrate both principles presented in Inset 2-1, "The Family Riddle." Both examples show change within continuity. The divorce rate did increase dramatically in the early 1970s, which is indicative of change. Yet remarriage by divorcing people is common, which indicates the continuity of the marriage institution. Families are having fewer children, a change from the past. But they are indeed having and rearing children as families have always done, again an indication of continuity.

Both examples also demonstrate uniqueness within commonality. All married couples share the commonality of being married. But for some couples, the marriage is the first for each partner. For others, the marriage is the second for one or both partners. Thus, all couples share the characteristic of being married, but are unique in terms of their previous marriage experience. Some couples opt for no children, others for one or two or three. So all couples share the opportunity to have children (except those with fertility problems, although they may adopt), but are individual in the way they use the opportunity.

Many changes are occurring in the American family. As we discuss these changes, keep in mind the continuity. There were 2,371,000 marriages in 1991, but because the population grew, the marriage rate per 1000 population

INSET 2-2
TRICKY STATISTICS: COHABITATION AND REJECTION OF MARRIAGE

The news media usually interpret cohabitation statistics to mean that more and more young couples are living together in a sexually and emotionally intimate relationship without being married. However, the U.S. Bureau of the Census clearly states in all of its publications covering cohabitation data that the census takers do not ask questions about the nature of the couple's personal relationship.

In fact, the Census Bureau goes further and states that many cohabiting households undoubtedly contain couples with no emotional or sexual involvement. For example, a young male college student who rents a room in the home of an elderly widow causes that household to show up under cohabitation data. Whenever times are hard economically such as during recessions, many people double up in their living arrangements. Thus, a man and a woman who live together only for economic reasons would also show up in the cohabitation data.

In 1990, the Census Bureau reported 2,900,000 unmarried-couple households. Yet we really do not know what percentage of the un-married couples are involved in sexually intimate relationships.

Despite the Census Bureau's clear statement that it says nothing about the couple's personal relationship, the media tend to present cohabitation data as a rejection of marriage by American young people. Yet just what percentage of cohabiting couples see their relationship as a permanent rejection of marriage is impossible to determine. Studies of cohabitation indicate that most intimately cohabiting couples either break up or marry with time (see Chapter 4).

dropped from 9.8 in 1990 to 9.4 in 1991 (National Center for Health Statistics April 15, 1992). So we see that marriage remains popular even though the rate of marriage has declined.

The marriage and family statistics found throughout this book point out some of the changes in the American family. For example, we noted earlier the rapid rise of single-parent families. Yet America has always had single-parent families. In fact, the proportion of such families remained at about one in ten between 1870 and 1970. Early single-parent families resulted largely because of death rather than because of divorce as is true today.

As you peruse such statistics, keep in mind that when the statistics of family life are plotted for the entire twentieth century and longer, a surprising fact emerges: today's young people appear to be behaving in ways consistent with long-term historical trends (Skolnick and Skolnick 1986, 6). The recent changes in family life appear deviant only when compared to what people were doing in the 1940s and 1950s. The now middle-class adults who married young, moved to the suburbs, and had numerous children were the generation that deviated from twentieth-century trends. Had the 1940s and 1950s not happened, today's young adults would appear to be behaving normally. If we focus only on recent history of the family, we may remain blind to the broader picture of social change and continuity in family life (Kain 1990, 3–4).

An examination of other statistics demonstrates clearly the principle of change within continuity. How great are the changes? Unmarried-couple co-habitation increased 500 percent from 1970 (523,000) to 1990 (3 million), yet these couples account for only 3 percent of the total number of American households. Compared to married-couple households, they represent only 5 percent (U.S. Bureau of the Census May 1991). Change (an increase in

The Basic Assumptions

unmarried cohabitation) and continuity (most couples living together are married) are clearly demonstrated in these statistics. And how new is cohabitation to American society? Not so new. During the 1920s, common-law cohabitation involved about one in five couples (Ramey 1981).

Perhaps the biggest change of all is the increasing acceptance of various forms of intimate relationships. We are, after all, a pluralistic society, a society made up of diverse groups. Thus, it seems natural that different family structures should become increasingly acceptable.

FAMILY: A BUFFER AGAINST MENTAL AND PHYSICAL ILLNESS

Assumption 5   *The family becomes increasingly important to its members as social stability decreases and people feel more isolated and alienated. Indeed, the healthy family can act as a buffer against mental and physical illness.*

We've noted that one of the remaining functions of the family is providing emotional gratification and intimacy to family members and a new function was each family member assisting other family members in solving these individual problems. In general, as the pace of life quickens and people become increasingly alienated from their larger society, the family may become more important as a refuge and source of emotional gratification for its members. The family has been called the "shock absorber" of society—the place where bruised and battered individuals can return after doing battle with the world, the one stable point in an ever-changing environment. If you do not belong to a family, where do you turn for warmth and affection? Who cares for you when you are sick? What other group tolerates your failures the way a devoted wife, husband, mother, or father does? The family can serve as "portable roots," anchoring one against the storm of change. Furthermore, the family can provide the security and acceptance that lead to the inner strength to behave individually rather than always in conformity with one's peers. The family can be a source of security, a protective shield against environmental pressures.

Of course, to be all of this, the family must be healthy and strong. As we all have learned from the recent media emphasis on family violence, all of the problems faced outside the family can also penetrate into the family. An unhealthy family may not supply nurturing and love. It can be a place from which individual members may wish to escape rather than a place to which they return for warmth and security. Nevertheless, even an unhealthy family system may still have stability and even provide safety for its members.

However, to the degree that environmental stress on individual family members can be reduced, the healthy family can act as a buffer against mental and physical illness of its members. It is important that we emphasize the word "can." Again, the family can act as a buffer only if it is healthy, well integrated, fully functioning, and successful. This status is an ideal that not all families will achieve.

As families have become smaller and more isolated from societal supports, intimate relations within the family have become more intense, more emotional, and more fragile. For example, if a child has no other significant adults to interact intimately with besides his or her parents, then this emotional interaction becomes crucial to the child's development. If this interaction is positive and healthy, the child develops in a healthy manner; if it is not, then the child is apt to develop in an unhealthy manner. The family, in a sense, is a hothouse of intimacy and emotionality because of the close interaction and intensity of relationships. It has the potential to do either great good or great harm to its members. Because of the potential for harm, it becomes even more important to understand how to create a strong and healthy family that can help individual members grow and expand in healthy directions.

We all will spend a good part of our lives in a family unit. Within this setting most of us will achieve our closest intimacy with other persons—the shared human intimacy that promotes feelings of security and self-esteem. Such feelings lead to improved communication, and good communication tends to be therapeutic. According to Carl Rogers (1951, 1), "the emotionally maladjusted person is in difficulty first, because communication within himself or herself has broken down, and second, because, as a result of this, communication with others has become damaged." To the degree that our family can help us become good communicators, it can help us toward better life adjustment.

When health statistics on married, single, divorced, separated, and widowed people are compared, married people seem to be the healthiest (Anson 1989). Lois Verbrugge (1979, 1983, 1985, 1986) surveyed a great deal of data on six general health indicators: (1) incidence of acute health conditions; (2) percentage of people limited in activity by a chronic condition; (3) percentage of people with a work disability; (4) rates of restricted activity, bed disability, and work loss; (5) average number of physician (or dental) visits per year; and (6) percentage of people with a hospital stay in the past year, average length of stay, and hospital discharge rates. She adjusted rates for age and found that significant differences existed between the various groups. Divorced and separated people appeared to be the least healthy, while married people appeared to be the most healthy. Robert Coombs (1991) reviewed more than 130 empirical studies on a number of well-being indices and found that married men and women are generally happier and less stressed than the unmarried.

Interpretation of such data is complex and controversial. The differences between various marital groups, however, are substantial enough to suggest that they are real rather than simply chance. The fact that married persons generally appear most healthy and divorced and separated persons least healthy suggests that the family may have a strong influence on health. The successful family operates to improve its members' health, while the unsuccessful family may do the opposite. If this is true, it becomes a matter of health to work toward improved family functioning and increased levels of intimacy.

THE NEED FOR INTIMACY

Seeking physical, intellectual, or emotional closeness with others is a basic need of most people (Fromm 1956; Maslow 1971; Morris 1971; Murstein 1974). To feel close to another, to love and feel loved, to experience comradeship, to care and be cared about are all feelings that most of us want to experience. Such feelings can be found in many human relationships. It is within the family, though, that such feelings ideally are most easily found and shared. Families that do not supply intimacy are usually families in trouble, and often these families disintegrate because members are frustrated in their needs for meaningful, intimate relationships. Some successful families are not "close," but studies of strong families generally find that such families do supply intimate relationships to family members and through this intimacy contribute to their health.

The Basic Assumptions

Intimacy
Being emotionally, intellectually and perhaps physically close to another person

WHAT DO YOU THINK?

1. Is intimacy a goal for you?
2. If it is, why is it difficult for you to be intimate?
3. In what action realm (intellectual, physical, emotional) do you share intimacy most easily? Why?
4. Which realm is most difficult? Why?
5. In what ways is your relationship with your parents intimate? Why?
6. In what ways can you not be intimate with your parents? Why?

WHAT DO YOU THINK?

1. With which people in your life do you find it easiest to be intimate?
2. Why is it easier with each of these persons than with others?
3. Is it easier for you to be intimate with men or women? If there is a difference, what do you think that difference is?
4. Is your family of orientation generally close and intimate?
5. Do your friends generally consider you to be a person with whom they can be intimate?

The term **intimacy** generally covers all of the feelings mentioned previously as well as being a common euphemism for sexual intercourse. Because of the many meanings, providing a clear and concise definition is difficult. For our purposes we will use Carolynne Kieffer's definition: "Intimacy is the experiencing of the essence of one's self in intense intellectual, physical and/or emotional communion with another human being" (1977, 267).

The primary components of intimacy are choice, mutuality, reciprocity, trust, and delight (Calderone, 1972). Two people like one another and make overtures toward establishing a closer relationship. They have made a choice. Their act, of course, must be mutual for an intimate relationship to develop. As confidence in the other grows, each reveals more and more thoughts and feelings. *Reciprocity* means that each partner gives to the relationship and to the other: sharing confidences and feelings back and forth. This sharing nurtures acceptance and trust, which in turn increase the sharing, which eventually leads to the delight in one another that true intimates always share.

B. J. Biddle (1976) suggests that intimacy must be considered on each of three dimensions—breadth, openness, and depth. *Breadth* describes the range of activities shared by two people. Do they spend a great deal of time together? Do they share occupational activities, home activities, leisure time, and so on? *Openness* implies sharing meaningful self-disclosures with one another. They feel secure enough and close enough to share intellectually, physically, and emotionally. They trust each other enough to be honest most of the time, and this encourages further trust in one another. *Depth* means that partners share really true, central, and meaningful aspects of themselves. Self-disclosure leads to deeper levels of interaction. In the ultimate sense, both individuals are able to transcend their own egos and fuse in a spiritual way with their partner. Such an experience is difficult to attain, yet many believe that it is in the deepest intimate experiences that love and potential for individual growth are found. Abraham Maslow (1968), for example, holds that each individual must find deep intimacy to become a self-actualizing and fulfilled person.

Kieffer (1977) adds to Biddle's three dimensions the age-old idea of intellectual, physical, and emotional realms of action. A totally intimate relationship would have breadth, openness, and depth in each activity realm. Table 2-2 describes a highly intimate relationship. Kieffer cautions that such a description is simplistic and does not include the numerous psychological processes that characterize the interaction of the partners or that brought them to their level of involvement. In addition, she reminds us that intimacy is a process, not a state of being. Thus, this description only indicates where this particular couple is at one particular time.

In the past intimacy was maintained throughout one's life by the geographical and physical proximity of the family. As economic patterns in this country changed and increasing geographical mobility separated people from their families, social emphasis shifted from family closeness to individual fulfillment. Many have found intimacy more difficult to achieve because of this shift.

But life today offers many different opportunities for fulfilling intimacy needs. Marriage is no longer seen as the only avenue to intimacy. If we examine our lives, we will probably find we have a "patchwork intimacy." By this Kieffer means that most people are involved in many intimate (not sexual) relationships of varying intensity.

If intimacy is as rewarding as we have suggested and if American society is allowing each person to seek it in ways other than marriage, we need to develop an ethic for intimates. For example, how do we keep the quest for

TABLE 2-2
INTENSITY MATRIX FOR THE ANALYSIS OF AN INTIMATE RELATIONSHIP

	INTELLECTUAL	PHYSICAL	EMOTIONAL
Breadth (range of shared activities)	Telling of the meaningful events in one's day Participating in a political rally Years of interaction resulting in the sharing of meanings (phrases, gestures, etc.) understood only by partners Decision making regarding management of household	Dancing Caressing Swimming Doing laundry Tennis Shopping Gardening Sexual intercourse Other sensual/sexual activities	Phone calls providing emotional support when separated Experiencing grief in a family tragedy Witnessing with pride a child's graduation from college Resolving conflict in occasional arguments
Openness (disclosure of self)	Disclosing one's values and goals Discussing controversial aspects of politics, ethics, etc. Using familiar language Not feeling a need to lie to the partner Sharing of secrets with the partner and using discretion regarding the secrets of the partner	Feeling free to wear old clothes Grooming in presence of the other Bathroom behavior (elimination, etc.) in presence of the other Nudity Few limitations placed on exploration of one's body by the partner Sharing of physical space (area, possessions, etc.) with few signs of territoriality	Describing one's dreams and daydreams Feeling free to call for "time out" or for togetherness Maintaining openness (disclosure regarding one's emotional involvement with other intimates) Telling of daily joys and frustrations Emotional honesty in resolving conflict Expressing anger, resentment, and other positive and negative emotions
Depth (sharing of core aspects of self)	"Knowing" of the partner Having faith in the partner's reliability and love Occasional experiencing of the essence of one's self in transcendental union Working collectively to change certain core characteristics of the self and of the partner	Physical relaxation, sense of contentment and well-being in the presence of the other	Committing oneself without guarantee, in the hope that one's love will be returned Caring as much about the partner as about oneself Nonjealous supportiveness toward the other intimate relationships of the partner

Source: From *Marriage and Alternatives: Exploring Intimate Relationships* by Roger W. Libby and Robert N. Whitehurst. Copyright © 1977 by Scott, Foresman and Company. Reprinted by permission.

individual intimacy and fulfillment within boundaries acceptable to our spouse? How do we keep the quest from lapsing into the selfish pursuit of always "doing one's own thing"? Questions such as these must be considered by all couples seeking intimacy.

▨ THE FAMILY AS INTERPRETER OF SOCIETY ▨

Assumption 6 *The attitudes and reactions of family members toward environmental influences are more important to the socialization of family members than are the environmental influences themselves (Chapters 5 and 6).*

The Basic Assumptions

To seek and find intimacy with another is highly rewarding. Yet people often avoid intimacy for many reasons. To open ourselves to another invites intimacy but also risks hurt. What if we open ourselves to others and trust them to reciprocate, but they do not? Each of us has probably had such an experience. Who hasn't liked someone and been rejected by that person? We may now be able to laugh at some of our early failures with intimacy (label them "puppy love," and so forth), yet each time we fail at intimacy, we become more guarded and apprehensive.

Fear of rejection is one of the strongest barriers to intimacy. Each time we are hurt by another, it becomes more difficult to be open, trusting, and caring in a new relationship. To be the first to share our innermost feelings, to say "I like you" or "I love you" leaves one open to rejection. The first steps toward an intimate relationship are especially hard for the insecure person who lacks self-confidence. To build an intimate relationship, one must first be intimate, accepting, and comfortable with oneself. To the degree that we are not these things with ourselves, we will probably be fearful to enter an intimate relationship.

Intimacy demands active involvement with another. Often passive spectator roles seem more comfortable—let the other person supply the intimacy. Our society teaches us to be spectators via television. Society often conditions us to play roles, always to please others, to deny our feelings. We shall see how intimacy is avoided when we play our stereotypical masculine and feminine roles (macho males don't cry or show caring emotions, for example).

Anger can be another barrier to intimacy if it is not dealt with openly. When we suppress, deny, and disguise anger, we do not rid ourselves of it. Rather the anger lingers as growing hostility. Of course, we all become angry on occasion with our most intimate loved ones. Anger does not destroy intimacy. Suppressed anger, though, leads to hostility and will, over time, tend to destroy intimacy. Remember that intimacy implies openness between intimates. Suppressed anger is unexpressed and thus keeps us closed rather than open. Suppressing anger also implies lack of trust in the partner. Without trust there cannot be intimacy.

Fear of rejection, nonacceptance of ourselves, spectator roles, and unexpressed anger are four of the strongest barriers to intimacy.

A family with small children is watching the evening news describe a protest at a nuclear power plant. The parents either support or criticize the actions of the protesters. The parental reaction to this social event is more influential on the children than is the event itself.

We have seen that the family supplies the society's population by reproducing children. But the family also physically and psychologically nurtures the offspring into adulthood. Because humans have such a long period of dependence before becoming independent adults, the family is the main avenue for **socialization** of young children to their culture. Formal education takes over part of the job of socializing the young when they reach school age, but the family retains the greatest overall influence on preschool children. Indeed the family's continuing formal and informal socialization of its children may supply the most deeply lasting lessons. However, with increasing numbers of mothers joining the work force when their children are young, formal preschool child-care programs and television are assuming ever more influence over American children. Without socialization by adults, children cannot internalize society's rules, mores, taboos, and so forth. Society cannot exist unless its members

Socialization
Acquiring skills necessary to survive as an individual and as a member of society

internalize at least a minimum socialization level. In fact, people who fail to be socialized to their society are known as a **sociopaths** or *psychopaths*. Such people are characterized by inadequate conscience development, irresponsible and impulsive behavior, inability to maintain good interpersonal relationships, rejection of authority, and inability to profit from experience (see Scenes from Marriage, Chapter 13).

Social learning theory has long pointed out the importance of modeling in learning, especially for young children (Bandura 1969). **Modeling** is learning by observing other people's behavior. Parents and other family members are the most significant models for young children. How they react to their society is often more important than what they formally teach their children about it. If, for instance, a father teaches his children the importance of obeying rules and then asks them to watch for police officers when he exceeds the speed limit, he is teaching them that not getting caught breaking the rules is more important than obeying them.

Although society often tends to blame families for the problems of their individual members, it must be remembered that social problems—economic depression, inflation, unemployment, civil unrest, and so on—also greatly influence families. General social upheavals such as the United States went through during the Vietnam War in the 1960s and the 1992 riots in Los Angeles and the continuing furor over minority rights, abortion, surrogate parenting, availability of illegal drugs, pornography, and so on affect the family drastically. Each family will have an opinion about such behaviors based on its own value orientation. These opinions may lead the family to take certain actions when the social controversies touch the family or its members. For example, if a child is to be bused twenty miles into a new neighborhood and school to promote racial equality, there will certainly be consequences within the family. The parents will lose some control over the child. The distance to school may mean that they cannot participate in school activities such as PTA and class parties. They will not know the families of the child's playmates. The child will be exposed to different social mores and expectations that the parents may or may not find acceptable.

More important than the political fact of busing will be the family's reaction to it. Will the family accept and support it? Will the family decide that the overall social benefits of busing outweigh inconveniences to the family? Will it picket, riot, and protest? Will it transfer children from public to private school? Each family's reaction to busing teaches its children values about minority groups, racial prejudice or tolerance, law, and authority.

An additional function of the family, then, is to help family members interpret social influences. This function also brings the possibility that an individual family may teach an interpretation unacceptable to others in the society as a whole. However, if the family and society are working together, the family will help its children grow into responsible community members. Thus, by strengthening families, the community strengthens itself.

Sociopath
Person with inadequate conscience development

Modeling
Learning vicariously by observing others' behavior

UNIQUE CHARACTERISTICS OF THE AMERICAN FAMILY

Assumption 7 *The American family, especially the middle-class family, has certain characteristics that make it unique. Among these, the following stand out (Chapters 4, 8, and 9):*

Through socialization, the family teaches social values. We hear a lot about "family values," especially from people who feel that such values are being lost. But just what are "family values"? Table 2-3 lists the top fifteen "family values" as found in research conducted by Mark Mellman and others (1990). Table 2-4 asks, "How important is each of the following values to you?" The table lists the values by rank ordered by mean, with five (5) points awarded for "very important" and one (1) point for "not important at all." A comparison of the two tables shows that items defined as family values also tend to be the most important values in people's personal lives.

TABLE 2-3
FAMILY VALUES

How well does the term "family value" describe each particular value? (Rank ordered by mean)

Being able to provide emotional support to your family	3.67
Respecting one's parents	3.66
Respecting other people for who they are	3.65
Being responsible for your actions	3.64
Being able to communicate your feelings to your family	3.61
Having a happy marriage	3.59
Respecting one's children	3.59
Respecting authority	3.52
Living up to my full potential	3.46
Having faith in God	3.45
Leaving the world to the next generation in better shape than we found it	3.40
Being married to the same person for life	3.39
Following a strict moral code	3.37
Having good relationships with your extended family, including aunts, uncles, and cousins	3.31
Being physically fit	3.30
Being married	3.28

A score of four (4) means that "family value" describes this term "very well." A score of one (1) means that "family value" is not descriptive of the term.

■ *Relative freedom in mate and vocational selection*. Historically, most cultures believed that mate and vocational selection were too important to be left to inexperienced people. Decisions that would influence an individual's entire life were often made long before she or he reached puberty. To this day, in many countries children enter the labor market early. Whether tending the family's goats in Morocco or tying the thousands of knots in an Iranian carpet, children contribute to their family's economic well-being and learn their lifetime vocation early.

Western society, especially the United States, has rejected child labor. Childhood (an historically recent concept) has increasingly became a protected period of freedom from adult responsibility. Today children are encouraged to seek out their own vocations. Families may make suggestions about possible vocations, but the final decision is usually left to the child.

This freedom is even more evident in mate selection. As we shall see in Chapter 4, unstructured dating as a method of mate selection is a relatively new American contribution to the mate selection process. When Americans are asked why they marry, invariably they list "love" as their most important reason. Marrying for romantic love is another American contribution to the mate selection process. Although romantic love has always been recognized historically, it has almost never served as a basis for marriage. Marriages were contracted by parents for their children. The contracts were made for economic, political, power, and prestige reasons, not for love. If love were to appear in the contracted relationship, generally it would have to grow as time passed. The lyrics to the song "Do You Love Me?" from *Fiddler on the Roof* exemplify a contracted marriage.

TEVYE TO HIS WIFE GOLDE

Do you love me?

Do I what?

Do you love me?

Do I love you? With our daughters getting married and this trouble in town, you're upset, you're worn out. Go inside, go lie down. Maybe it's indigestion.

Golde, I'm asking you a question: Do you love me?

You're a fool!

I know, but do you love me?

Do I love you? Well, for twenty-five years I've washed your clothes, cooked your meals, cleaned your house, given you children, milked the cow. After twenty-five years why talk about love right now?

Golde, the first time I met you was on our wedding day. I was scared, I was shy, I was nervous.

So was I.

But my father and mother said we'd learn to love each other, and now I am asking, Golde, do you love me?

I'm your wife.

I know, but do you love me?

Do I love him? For twenty-five years I've lived with him, fought with him, starved with him. Twenty-five years my bed is his; if that's not love, what is?

Then you love me.

I suppose I do.

And I suppose I love you too.

It doesn't change a thing, but even so, after twenty-five years it's nice to know.

■ *Relative freedom within the family,* fostered by a relatively high standard of living compared to other countries, physical mobility, lack of broader familial responsibilities, and the pluralistic nature of American society. Freedom of vocational choice and mate selection stem from the general freedom that exists for the young within the American family and society. We have already examined the role that societal affluence plays in allowing broader choice of family structure.

■ *High economic standards and abundant personal possessions.* As we saw, affluence, increased education, and the proliferation of mass media all widen the experience of American youth. Such experiences increase youth's freedom both within the family and in the life choices that all youth must make. Of course, such freedom increases the need for decision making, because along with freedom comes responsibility for one's actions. Without responsibility freedom becomes anarchy.

Freedom also means freedom to make mistakes. Thus, the freedom that American youth enjoys tends to increase anxiety and insecurity. This increased anxiety and insecurity may partially explain the interest of some young Americans in cults, most of which ask their members to live by strict rules.

■ *An extremely private character.* The private character of the American family is another result of the general affluence of our society. Throughout most of the world, housing is in short supply. Many families are fortunate if they have more than one room. Living quarters often house not only the nuclear family but also more distant relatives.

The average size of American families living together has decreased over the years.

TABLE 2-4 VALUES IN GENERAL	
How important is each of the following values to you? (Rank ordered by mean)	
Being responsible for your actions	4.35
Being able to provide emotional support to your family	4.32
Respecting one's parents	4.32
Respecting other people for who they are	4.30
Having a happy marriage	4.30
Respecting one's children	4.27
Being able to communicate your feelings to your family	4.23
Having faith in God	4.15
Respecting authority	4.13
Leaving the world to the next generation in better shape than we found it	4.12
Living up to my full potential	4.11
Being physically fit	4.02
Being married to the same person for life	4.00
Following a strict moral code	3.99
Being independent	3.97
Having a rewarding job	3.95

The Basic Assumptions

> In 1790 the average American household living together was 5.6 persons. By 1970 the size had dropped to 3.14 persons and by 1990 had further dropped to just 2.63 persons (U.S. Bureau of the Census December 1990).

This decrease is due mainly to the loss of the additional relatives and roomers that used to live with families.

The number of single persons living alone has also increased lately although there are still fewer than a hundred years ago.

> More than one in every nine adults age fifteen and over lived alone in 1990 (23 million). The majority were women (61 percent). Since 1970, the number of women living alone has increased 91 percent, while the number of men rose by 156 percent (U.S. Bureau of the Census May 1991, 13).

Shrinking household sizes and growing numbers of persons living alone are possible only in a society affluent enough to supply abundant housing. An American family living in a 1400-square-foot, three-bedroom, bath-and-a-half house uses enough space to house approximately twenty persons in a country such as Afghanistan. This ability of the American nuclear family to live separately from relatives and neighbors has allowed it to become private. Such privacy is a luxury of economic affluence. Our society's privacy brings both advantages and disadvantages. Living with fewer people increases individual freedom but also increases the duties and responsibilities of the adults. Living alone certainly increases privacy, but it also increases the chances of loneliness.

■ FAMILY: THE CONSUMING UNIT OF THE AMERICAN ECONOMY ■

Assumption 8 *The family is the basic economic unit in modern American society (Chapters 8 and 9).*

The members of early American farm families were also production workers. The industrial revolution removed much of the economic production from the American family. Family members remained production workers, but the production was moved from the home into factories and did not necessarily include all family members. The money earned by outside work supported the family. Thus, the family's economic well-being came to be subject more to the whim of the anonymous marketplace than to the industry of individual family members. Rather than each family producing what it needed to survive, the family had to go to the marketplace and buy what it needed. Thus, the family became the consuming unit of society's agricultural and industrial output.

Of course, the family still provides services to its members, such as meal preparation and home maintenance, which require productive work from family members. However, such production is largely unpaid and unrecognized by the larger society. Some feminists suggest that those who provide the services—mainly women—should be paid. Payment for such family services would probably have a significant impact on husband/wife relationships, as family power, in part, relates to who earns the money. Estimates based on current wage scales of cooks, baby sitters, and so forth place the value of services provided by the full-time mother/housewife at $25,000 to $45,000 per year. Feminists suggest that such productive work should be recognized not only by the woman's husband but also by the government by granting Social Security benefits in

Read any newspaper, watch the television news reports and specials, and you will conclude that the American family is in trouble. Rather than dwell on the problems facing families—they are covered throughout the book—let us examine some possible agendas for change.

What should be done to counteract or remedy the negative effects of family decline? This question is the most controversial of all, and the most difficult to answer according to David Popenoe. Among the agendas for change that have been put forth, two extremes stand out as particularly prominent in the national debate. The first is a return to the structure of the traditional nuclear family characteristic of the 1950s; the second is the development of extensive government policies.

Aside from the fact that it probably is impossible to return to the structure of an earlier time, the first alternative has major drawbacks. It would require many women to leave the work force and, to some extent, become "de-liberated," an unlikely occurrence indeed. Economic conditions necessitate that even more women take jobs, and cultural conditions stress ever-greater equality between the sexes.

In addition, the traditional nuclear family may not work in today's world. One must realize that the young people who led the transformation of the family during the 1960s and 1970s were raised in 1950s households. If these households were so wonderful, why didn't their children seek to copy them?

Be that as it may, the traditional nuclear family is still the choice of millions of Americans. They are comfortable with it, and for them it seems to work. It seems reasonable, therefore, at least not to place roadblocks in the way of couples with children who wish to conduct their lives according to the dictates of the traditional family. Women who freely desire to remain outside the labor force and to spend much of their lives as mothers and housewives should not be penalized economically or psychologically by public policy for making that choice.

The second major proposal for change that has been the focus of national debate is the development of extensive government programs offering monetary support and social services for families, especially "nonnuclear" families. In some cases, these programs would assist with functions the families are unable to perform adequately; in others, the government would take over the functions, transforming them from family to public responsibilities.

The European welfare states have followed this path, but it has won less acceptance in the United States than in any other industrialized country. The European welfare states have been far more successful than the United States in minimizing the negative economic impact of family decline, especially on children. In addition, many European nations have established policies making it much easier for women (and increasingly men) to combine work with childrearing. With these successes in mind, it seems inevitable that the United States will slowly move in this direction.

Moving too far down this road entails clear drawbacks, however. If

49

children are to be served best, we should seek to make the family stronger, not replace it. At the same time welfare states are minimizing some of the consequences of decline, they also may be causing the breakup of the family unit. This phenomenon can be seen today in Sweden, where the institution of the family probably has been weakened more than anywhere else in the world. If the United States moves in this direction, it will be important to keep in mind that the ultimate goal is to strengthen families.

Though each of the preceding alternatives has some merit, there is also a third alternative, premised on the fact that we cannot return to the 1950s family, nor can we depend on the welfare state for a solution. Instead, we should strike at the heart of the cultural shift that has occurred, point up its negative aspects, and seek to reinvigorate the cultural ideals of family, parents, and children within the changed circumstances of our time. We should stress that the individualistic ethos has gone too far, that children are being woefully shortchanged, and that in the long run, strong families represent the best path toward self-fulfillment and personal happiness. We should return to the cultural forefront the old idea of parents living together and sharing responsibility for their children and for each other.

What is needed is a new social movement whose purpose is the promotion of families and their values within the new constraints of modern life. It should point out the supreme importance to society of strong families, while at the same time suggesting ways they can adapt better to the modern conditions of individualism, equality, and the labor force participation of both women and men. Such a movement could build on the fact that the overwhelming majority of young people today still say their major life goal is a lasting, monogamous, heterosexual relationship that includes procreation of children. It is reasonable to suppose that this goal is so pervasive because it is based on a deep-seated human need. The time is ripe to reassert that strong families concerned with the needs of children are not only possible, but necessary.

Source: This material is adapted from "Breakup of the Family: Can We Reverse the Trend?" by David Popenoe 1991.

CHAPTER

3

AMERICAN WAYS OF LOVE

CONTENTS

When God would invent a thing apart from eating or drink or game or sport, and yet a world—restful while in which our minds can melt and smile. He made of Adam's rib an Eve creating thus the game of love. Piet Hein

It is proper to begin our study of intimacy by discussing "love," for to most Americans, love and marriage are like hand and glove, apple pie and ice cream, bacon and eggs—they belong together. Of course, we all know of marriages without love, and romantic literature is full of examples of love without marriage. But the traditional ideal, the ultimate in human relationships for most Americans, is the steady, time-honored, and sought-after combination of love and marriage.

When Americans are asked, "Why do you want to marry?" they often reply, "Because I love . . . ." So we Americans marry for love. But, doesn't everyone? What other reasons could there be? Indeed, love as a basis for marriage may be a unique American contribution to the world. As Ralph Linton pointed out many years ago, "All societies recognize that there are occasional violent emotional attachments between persons of the opposite sex, but our present American culture is the only one which has attempted to capitalize on these and make them the basis for marriage" (Linton 1936, 175).

In most societies love has historically been an amusing pastime, a distraction, or, in some cases, a godsent affliction or even an addiction. Paul Chance likens the lover to the heroin addict:

> At first, lovers are satisfied to be with their partners for short periods, but their tolerance soon builds and they must increase the dosage. "I can't get enough of you." When dope addicts are unable to get a fix, they begin to sweat, feel nauseous, get the chills, etc. That's withdrawal. Lovers experience much the same thing when the joy of their life is torn from their arms. Longer separations create more intense agony, which the suffering lover feels obliged to describe in microscopic detail to anyone within earshot. (1988, 22)

Courtly love or love as an amusing distraction began as a diversion among the feudal aristocracy. It exalted both chastity and adultery. Courtly love glorified love from afar and made a fetish of suffering over love affairs. It made love into a great game where men proved their manliness on the jousting field in the name of love and a woman's honor. Adultery was an integral part of courtly love. The intrigue and excitement of adultery added to the sport and made the love even more sweet. Marriage was not considered the proper place for courtly love. Married love was too mundane and unexciting.

The story of the knight Ulrich von Lichtenstein highlights courtly love which seldom found consummation in marriage. At an early age Ulrich pledged his love and admiration to an unnamed lady. He accepted every challenge in an effort to prove himself worthy of serving his love. He was filled with melancholy and painful longings for his lady, a condition which he claimed gave him joy. The heartless lady, however, rejected his admiration even after his ten years of silent devotion and his many feats of valor. Undaunted, perhaps even inspired by her rebuffs, he undertook a stupendous journey in 1227 from Venice north to Bohemia during which he claimed to have broken the incredible total of three hundred and seven lances fighting his way to Vienna and his lady love. It comes as something of a shock when by his own statement he stopped off for three days to visit his wife and children. For the fact is that this lovesick Galahad, this kissless wonder, this dauntless knight-errant had long had a wife to lie with when he had the urge, and a family to live with when he felt lonely. He even speaks of his affection for his wife, but, of course, not his love; to love her would have been improper and unthinkable to the ethic of courtly love. (Hunt 1959, 132–39).

On the other hand, ancient Japan regarded love as a grave offense if it was not properly sanctioned, for it interfered with proper marriage arrangements. Etsu Sugimoto describes this in *A Daughter of the Samurai* (1935, 115–16):

When she was employed in our house, she was very young, and because she was the sister of father's faithful Jiya, she was allowed much freedom. A youthful servant, also of our house, fell in love with her. For young people to become lovers without the sanction of the proper formalities was a grave offense in any class, but in a samurai household it was a black disgrace to the house. The penalty was exile through the water gate—a gate of brush built over a stream and never used except by one of the Eta, or outcast class. The departure was public and the culprits were ever after shunned by everyone. The penalty was unspeakably cruel, but in the old days severe measures were used as a preventative of law-breaking.

Surprising as it may be, such attitudes are still widespread. Marriage in many cultures has been and still is based on considerations other than love. In India, the Hindu place responsibility for finding a suitable mate on the parents or older relatives. The potential mate is judged by his or her economic status, caste, family, and physical appearance. These criteria are not by any means simple snobbery; they reflect the couple's prospects for rapport, financial stability, and social acceptance, all valid concerns in marriage. Even in the United States, such considerations are often hidden in the ephemeral concept of love. Although an American may find it difficult to believe, most young

Love is such a tissue of paradoxes, and exists in such an endless variety of forms and shades that you may say almost anything about it that you please, and it is likely to be correct.

Henry Fink

Romantic Love and Personal Beauty

Love is patient and kind; love is not jealous or boastful; it is not arrogant or rude. Love does not insist on its own way; it is not irritable and resentful; it does not rejoice at wrong, but rejoices in the right. Love bears all things, believes all things, hopes all things, endures all things.

I Corinthians 13:4–7

How do I love thee? Let me count the ways.
I love thee to the depth and breadth and height
My soul can reach, when feeling out of sight
For the ends of Being and ideal Grace.
I love thee to the level of everyday's
Most quiet need, by sun and candlelight.
I love thee freely, as men strive for Right;

I love thee purely, as they turn from Praise.
I love thee with the passion put to use
In my old griefs, and with my childhood's faith.
I love thee with a love I seemed to lose
With my lost saints—I love thee with the breath,
Smiles, tears, of all my life!—and, if God choose,
I shall but love thee better after death.

Elizabeth Barrett Browning

Let me not to the marriage of true minds
Admit impediments. Love is not love
Which alters when it alteration finds,
Or bends with the remover to remove.
O, no! It is an ever-fixed mark,
That looks on tempests and is never shaken;
It is the star to every wandering bark,
Whose worth's unknown, although his height be taken.
Love's not Time's fool, though rosy lips and cheeks
Within his bending sickle's compass come;
Love alters not with his brief hours and weeks,

But bears it out even to the edge of doom.
If this be error and upon me proved,
I never writ, nor no man ever loved.

William Shakespeare
Sonnet 116

Love birds burn in the sky,
The Flame of Passion carries them high.
Beaks touching as one,
Wings beginning to melt, as they ride the crest of the flames.
With nothing to hold them in their flight
They fall
Into the inferno
Of their own passion.

Cynthia Moorman

Love is the triumph of imagination over intelligence.

H. L. Mencken

Love is a game of exaggerating the difference between one person and everybody else.

George Bernard Shaw

adults in India feel strongly that it is best for them if their marital partner is selected by their parents or a marriage broker. Students at Women's Teacher's College in Kashmir, northern India, felt that older adults would make a much better selection of their mate than they were capable of at their age. The women also felt that the American system of mate selection was degrading because it forced young people to compete with their friends for potential mates. For young Americans, parental interference in the mate selection process would undoubtedly cause a rift in the family.

THE AMERICAN MYTH THAT ROMANTIC LOVE SHOULD ALWAYS LEAD TO MARRIAGE

John Crosby (1985, 295) has suggested that the American idea that romantic love should lead to marriage is a myth. The myth implies that love alone is the one indispensable ingredient that should determine whom and when one marries. A corollary to the myth states that love will always overcome, never mind the obstacles.

Crosby goes on to say that the reader may protest, "Oh, but nobody really goes to that extreme! People don't really marry just because they fall in love, and if they do, they know there are other important factors in the selection of a mate." Yes, it appears that people are more thoughtful than the myth suggests, yet when it comes to behavior, our emotions tend to cancel out and override our reasonableness. Who in the midst of falling in love is always reasonable? Indeed, the myth suggests that if you are always reasonable about being in love, you probably aren't really "in love."

Because Americans tend to believe the romantic myth that love must lead to marriage, numerous marriages have little other than "love" going for them. So little, that within a short time the union dissolves because the couple has no basis on which to build a lasting relationship. Crosby goes further:

> In the name of "falling in love" with another man or woman, many a triangle is born; and many a marriage, destroyed. In the name of "falling in love," many a career has been abandoned, and many an education disrupted, postponed, or aborted. In the name of "falling in love," many a fetus has been conceived and then followed with the nuptial ritual giving legal status to an unplanned pregnancy. In the name of "falling in love," many a family has been torn with strife because an adolescent insists on marriage with the person they love when it is clear to all others except the person blinded by love that a mistake is being made. (1985, 296)

For Crosby, the belief that the love attraction should lead to wedlock is folly. To believe that wedlock could be sustained only by the love attraction is more than folly. It is the first step toward destroying the relationship.

Lest the reader feel that such strong criticism means that love should play no role in marriage, it must be pointed out that love does indeed play a role in all intimate lasting relationships. Even in the arranged marriages of India, couples who marry without intense love often build a loving relationship over time. Much of the confusion about the love-as-a-basis-for-marriage myth has to do with the many definitions of love. Love does not take just one form; it assumes many forms. I love my wife. I love my child. I love Mozart. I love a T-bone steak. Obviously, love is many things. It is "romantic" love as a basis for marriage that Crosby criticizes.

DEFINING LOVE

Trying to define love has kept poets, philosophers, and sages busy since the beginning of history. What is this phenomenon that causes two people to react to one another so strongly? Is it physical? Spiritual? A mixture of the two? Why does it only occur with some people and not others? Is it the same as infatuation? The questions are endless, yet we speak of love, seek it, and recognize it when it happens even if we can't define it.

Twenty-five centuries ago the Greek poet Sappho described the physical state of love:

For should I but see thee a little moment,
Straight is my voice hushed;
Yea, my tongue is broken, and through and through me
'Neath the flesh impalpable fire runs tingling;
Nothing see mine eyes, and a noise of roaring
Waves in my ear sounds;
Sweat runs in rivers, a tremor seizes
All my limbs, and paler than grass in Autumn,
Caught by pains of menacing death, I falter
Lost in the love-trance.

The Greeks divided love into a number of elements, the three most important being eros (carnal or physical love), agape (spiritual love), and philos (brotherly or friendly love). **Eros** is the physical, sexual side of love. It is needing, desiring, and wanting the other person physically. Sappho's poem describes the effect of eros. The Romans called eros Cupid, and, as we know, Cupid shoots the arrow of love into our hearts. Eros is that aspect of love that makes our knees shake, upsets our routine, and causes us to be obsessed with thoughts of our lover.

Agape is the altruistic, giving, nondemanding side of love. It is an active concern for the life and growth of those whom we love. It is most clearly demonstrated by a parent's love for a child. Agape is an unconditional affirmation of another person. It is the desire to care for, help, and give to the loved one. It is unselfish love.

Theologian Paul Tillich (1957, 114–15) sees the highest form of love as a merging of eros and agape:

No love is real without a unity of eros and agape. Agape without eros is obedience to moral law, without warmth, without longing, without reunion. Eros

Eros
The physical, sexual side of love; called "Cupid" by the Romans

Agape
Greek term for spiritual love

Defining Love

without agape is a chaotic desire, denying the validity of the claim of the other one to be acknowledged as an independent self, able to love and to be loved.

Philos
Greek term for the love found in deep, enduring friendships; a general love of humanity

Philos is the love found in deep and enduring friendships. It is also the kind of love described in the biblical injunction "Love thy neighbor as thyself." It can be deep friendship for specific people, or it can be a love that generalizes to all people. Philos is often nonexclusive, whereas eros and agape are often exclusive.

The philos element of love is most important to a society's humanity. A loving person creates loving relationships, and enough loving relationships make a loving society. A society that has a high level of philos among its members fosters the other elements of love. Lack of this kind of love creates a society of alienated, isolated individuals. When people are alienated and isolated from one another, the chance of dehumanized conflict between them escalates. Crime statistics in the United States make it clear that the Christian command to "Love thy neighbor" (philos) is often ignored in our society. This kind of love turns strangers into friends, and it is more difficult to perpetrate a crime against a friend than against a stranger.

THEORIES OF LOVE

There are probably as many theories of love as there are persons in love, but it should be noted that such theories do not enjoy much empirical support. Nevertheless, it is worthwhile to examine a few of them, even if only superficially. Learning how other thoughtful people have theorized about love will help us understand our own feelings about love. The better we know our own attitudes and definitions of love, the better we will become in making long-lasting intimate relationships.

In his classic book *The Art of Loving*, Erich Fromm defines love as an active power that breaks through the walls that separate people from each other. In love we find the paradox of two beings becoming one, yet remaining two (Fromm 1956). Like the Greeks, Fromm discusses several kinds of love, including brotherly and maternal love. *Brotherly love* is characterized by friendship and companionship with affection. *Maternal love* is characterized by an unselfish interest in your partner in which you place yourself second to your partner's needs. To Fromm, mature love includes attachment plus sexual response. More importantly, it includes the four basic elements necessary to any intimate relationship: *care, responsibility, respect,* and *knowledge.* People who share all of the elements of mature love are pair-bonded. The relationship is reciprocal. Fromm goes on to suggest that a person's need to love and be loved in this full sense arises from feelings of separateness and aloneness. Love helps us escape these feelings and gain a feeling of unitedness and completeness.

Taking off from this idea, Lawrence Casler (1969) considers that love develops in part because of our human needs for acceptance and confirmation. These needs are heightened in a society as competitive and individualized as ours. Thus, we are relieved when we meet someone whose choices coincide with our own, who doesn't try to undermine us in some way. We tend to attach ourselves to such a person because he or she offers us validation, and such validation is an important basis for love (see Rubin 1973, Chapter 7).

Casler points out that love feelings in dating partners may be more a by-product of American dating than the result of some innate attraction. For example, a person pretends to like her date more than she really does for any number of reasons including simple politeness. The date, also seeking validation, responds favorably. This favorable response makes the first person feel good, and she feels fondness for the individual who has made her feel good. As one person's feelings increase, the other's are likely to also. Obviously, it is easier to love someone who loves you than someone who is indifferent.

Of course, falling in love is more complex than in this example because we have many needs besides validation. Sex is another of these needs:

> Society emphasizes the necessity for love to precede sex. Although many disregard this restriction, others remain frightened or disturbed by the idea of a purely sexual relationship. The only way for many sexually aroused individuals to avoid frustration or anxiety is to fall in love—as quickly as possible. More declarations of love have probably been uttered in parked cars than in any other location; some of these are surely nothing more than seduction ploys, but it is likely that self-seduction is involved in most cases. (Casler 1969, 33)

Ira Reiss (1988, 100–106) suggests the wheel as a model of love:

■ Stage 1: In the *rapport* stage, the partners are struck by the feeling that they have known each other before, that they are comfortable with one another, and that they both want to deepen the relationship. Social and cultural background, education, style of upbringing, and other broad background factors operate to enhance or inhibit feelings of rapport.

■ Stage 2: During the *self-revelation* stage, the partners share more and more intimate thoughts and feelings. This sharing deepens the relationship because such sharing is only done with special people. Self-disclosure is associated with increased commitment, mutual trust, and feelings of love. Zick Rubin (Rubin et al. 1980) found that women are more likely than their partners to reveal their thoughts and feelings. He also found that self-revelation is higher among couples with relatively equalitarian attitudes toward gender roles.

■ Stage 3: As the sharing becomes more and more intimate, a feeling of *mutual dependence* develops. With it comes a feeling of loss when the partner is not present. The partner is needed in order to feel complete.

■ Stage 4: The partners experience more and more *personal need fulfillment* as they deepen their relationship. Reiss suggests that perhaps the initial rapport itself was caused by the hope of having these deeper needs met. The common characteristic of deeper needs is that they concern intimacy.

> They are needs which, as they are fulfilled, express the closeness and privacy of the relationship. For example, the needs for emotional support and sympathy are expressions of the underlying need for intimacy. We have other needs, but they are not related to intimacy and are thus less relevant for explaining love relationships. (Reiss 1988, 102)

These four processes are in a sense really one process for when one feels rapport, he/she reveals him/herself and becomes dependent, thereby fulfilling his/her personality needs. The circularity is most clearly seen in that the needs being fulfilled were the original reason for feeling rapport. (Reiss 1960, 143)

WHAT DO YOU THINK?

1. What do you personally mean when you say, "I love you"?
2. What do your parents mean when they say, "I love you" to each other? To you?
3. Does saying "I love you" carry a commitment to marriage? To sexual intercourse?
4. How do you recognize if a person is sincere in saying that he or she loves you?
5. How does love make you feel physically?

FIGURE 3-1
The wheel as a model of love
(Source: Reiss 1988, 103)

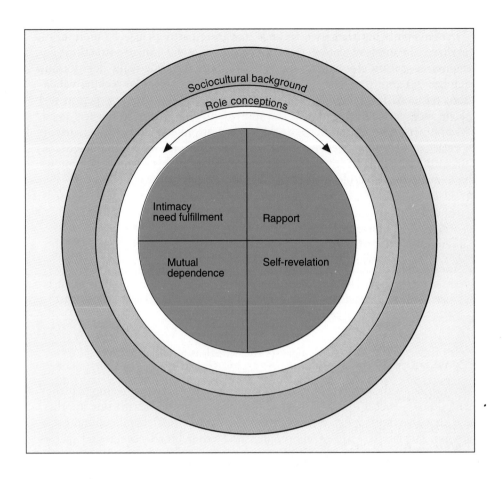

Note that the outermost ring of the graphic presentation of the Wheel Theory of Love (Figure 3.1) is labeled "sociocultural background." One's general background factors (education, religion, and so forth) account for the second ring, "role conceptions." What do I perceive "love" to be? What is my role in expressing love? What role do I expect my partner to play in an intimate relationship? What will my role be as a lover, husband or wife, father or mother? These two rings influence how quickly the wheel of love is formed if it is formed at all.

Goldstine (1977) suggests that love occurs in three stages:

■ Stage 1, *falling in love*, is characterized by excitement, emotional highs, good feelings both about oneself and one's partner, and the belief that this new love will transform one's life (romantic love). Both partners strive to put their best foot forward, and each perceives the other through "rose-colored" glasses; that is, they see the good points and are blind to negative aspects. Stage 1 is fleeting at best. Over time, satiation dilutes the intense pleasure the partners originally found in each other. As real-life obligations encroach on the relationship and evidence of shortcomings accumulates, Stage 1 gives way to disappointment. Delightful in and of itself, Stage 1 doesn't necessarily ensure that a relationship can endure and flourish. All it really says is that two people are strongly attracted to one another.

■ Stage 2, *disappointment*, begins when the rose-colored glasses come off. Conflicts and failure pile up, and the partners begin to realize that perhaps their lives are not being transformed. The question now becomes one of how the partners work out their differences, how they learn to accept one another's shortcomings, and how they handle the resentments that arise as each finds the other is a real live human being rather than the idealized image with whom they fell in love. The troubles people experience in Stage 2 do not necessarily mean that they have chosen the wrong partner, that they are no longer in love, or that their relationship must end. Ups and downs will always occur in a relationship, and with persistence and goodwill, the couple can move on to the third stage.

■ Stage 3, *acceptance*, finds the couple bringing their relationship into some kind of balance. Frustrations and anxieties do not stop, but they no longer trigger doubts in the couple about the goodness of their mate or their relationship. They have confidence in each other, they know they can work out differences; they trust one another and can share a deep intimacy, not of illusion, but of earned knowledge.

ROMANTIC LOVE

Many Americans' thoughts about attraction and intimacy are profoundly influenced by the idea of *romantic love*. This concept of love encompasses such ideas as "love at first sight," "the one and only love," "lifelong commitment," "I can't live without him/her," and "the perfect mate."

In essence the concept of romantic love supplies a set of idealized images by which we can judge the object of our love as well as the quality of the relationship. Unfortunately, such romanticized images usually bear little relationship to the real world. Often we project our beliefs onto another person, exaggerating the characteristics that match the qualities we are looking for and masking those that do not. We transform the other person into an unreal hero or heroine to fit our personal concept of a romantic marital partner. *Thus, we often fall in love with our own romantic ideas rather than with a real human being. We fall in love with love.*

Romantic love is only a set of attitudes about love. The confusion between "romance" and "love" causes great trouble in forming long-lasting intimate relationships. For example, the traditional romantic ideals dictate a strong, confident, protective role for a man and a charming, loving, dependent role for a woman. A woman holding this stereotype will tend to overlook and deny dependent needs of her mate. She will tend to repress independent qualities she discovers in herself. The man who has traditional romantic ideals will ignore both his own dependence needs and the woman's need for independence.

Those who "fall in love with love" in this way will suffer disappointment when their partner's "real person" begins to emerge. Rather than meeting this emerging person with joy and enthusiasm, partners who hold romanticized ideals may reject reality in favor of their stereotypical images. John Robert Clark provides a pithy description of this process:

> In learning how to love a plain human being today, as during the romantic movement, what we usually want unconsciously is a fancy human being with no flaws. When the mental picture we have of someone we love is colored by wishes of childhood, we may love the picture rather than the real person behind it.

Defining Love

Naturally, we are disappointed in the person we love if he does not conform to our picture. Since this kind of disappointment has no doubt happened to us before, one might suppose we would tear up the picture and start all over. On the contrary we keep the picture and tear up the person. Small wonder that divorce courts are full of couples who never gave themselves a chance to know the real person behind the pictures in their lives. (1961, 18)

Dating and broad premarital experience with the opposite sex can help correct much of this romantic idealism.

Sometimes people cling to their romantic expectations and try to change their partner into their romantic ideal. Changing one's partner is difficult, however. The person being asked to change may resent the demand or may not wish to change.

Because romantic love constantly seeks passion (emotional arousal), such love becomes increasingly difficult to maintain within long-term relationships (for example, marriage). Fixing dinner every night, writing the checks to pay the bills, changing diapers, going to work each morning, and doing the household chores are not romantic activities. Yet in the long run, these are the activities that make a relationship succeed. One must be able to find love within the sharing of such daily tasks as well as within the excitement of romance. But when one confuses romance and love or believes the two to be synonymous, true love can never emerge. The moment the fires of romantic love begin to die down, those trapped by their belief in romantic love turn away from their partner in a never-ending search for the "ideal" mate with whom they can share a lifetime of romantic love. The fact that no such ideal mate exists means that they will be doomed to continue the search forever.

Generally, romantic love's rose-colored glasses tend to distort the real world, especially the mate, thereby creating a barrier to happiness. This is not to deny that romantic love can add to an intimate relationship. Romance will bring excitement, emotional highs, and color to the relationship. From there one can move toward a more mature love relationship. As emotional, intellectual, social, and physical intimacy develops, romance becomes one of several aspects of the relationship, not the only one.

■ INFATUATION ■

Romantic love and infatuation are often confused. Some (Hatfield and Walster 1978) say that they are actually the same thing. Lovers use the term "romantic love" to describe an ongoing love relationship. The couple's feelings, bodily reactions, and interactions when they are romantically in love are the same as occur in infatuation. The difference may be only semantic. The term *infatuation* is used to negate past feelings of love that have now changed. Love is supposed to last forever, so falling out of love means that the feeling for the other person was not really love; it must have been something less—namely, infatuation (Udry 1974). "You were infatuated with him (not in love) before you met me." According to this line of thinking, perhaps infatuation can only be distinguished from romantic love in retrospect.

Others suggest that infatuation may be the first step toward love. The feelings of physical attraction, the chemical arousal, the intense preoccupation with your partner, all characteristics of infatuation and romantic love, are also

In his analysis of "The Romance of Tristan and Isolde," Robert Johnson (1983, 113) suggests that romantic love can never produce a long-lasting human friendship.

Romance by its very nature will deteriorate into egotism. Romantic lovers are in love with their own ideal image of what their spouse should be. The romantic lover looks to the ideal lover to be completed, to have weaknesses made strong, to overcome odds and avoid failure. This figment of the romantic lover's imagination is supposed to make the individual happy, to fulfill all his or her needs. Every marriage counselor has a steady stream of clients asking, "Will I never find someone to heal me of my unhappiness? My spouse is failing me." Because romantic lovers expect the impossible of their mate, only disappointment can occur.

There is no friendship in romantic love. Sometimes people say, "I don't want to be friends with my husband (wife); it would take all the romance out of marriage." This is true: Friendship does take the artificial drama and intensity out of a relationship, but it also takes away egocentricity and impossibility and replaces the drama with something human and real.

If a man and woman are friends, then they are "neighbors" as well as lovers; their relationship is suddenly subject to Christ's dictum "Love thy neighbor as thyself." One of the glaring contradictions in romantic love is that so many couples treat their friends with so much more kindness, consideration, generosity, and forgiveness than they ever give one another! When people are with their friends, they are charming, helpful, and courteous. But when

they come home, they often vent their anger, resentments, moods, and frustrations on each other.

They do this because the cult of romance teaches that they have a right to expect their spouse to be perfect, to make them complete. When they fail to feel complete, it is the fault of the spouse. No one asks friends to carry such a large burden. In reality romantic lovers ask the object of their love to do a job that can only be done inside each person. No one can complete the work of growing up into a mature, secure, happy, fulfilled adult for anyone else. This task must be undertaken by each individual. Romantic lovers try to impose this task on the object of their love. It is no wonder then that romantic lovers are so often dissatisfied and unhappy with their partner, so often unfriendly (197).

the precursors to "real" love. From the many ways the terms are used, it is apparent that we probably cannot agree completely on the difference between love and infatuation. Ann Landers periodically reprints a suggested list of differences between the two terms:

Love or Infatuation?

Infatuation is instant desire. It is one set of glands calling to another.

Love is friendship that has caught fire. It takes root and grows—one day at a time.

Infatuation is marked by a feeling of insecurity. You are excited and eager, but not genuinely happy. There are nagging doubts, unanswered questions, little bits and pieces about your beloved that you would just as soon not examine too closely. It might spoil the dream.

Love is the quiet understanding and mature acceptance of imperfection. It is real. It gives you strength and grows beyond you—to bolster your beloved. You are warmed by their presence, even when they are far away.

Infatuation says "We must get married right away. I can't risk losing you."

Love says, "Be patient. Don't panic. Plan your future with confidence."

Infatuation has an element of sexual excitement. If you are honest, you will admit it is difficult to be in one another's company unless you are sure it will end in intimacy.

Love is the maturation of friendship. You must be friends before you can be lovers.

Infatuation lacks confidence. When they are away you wonder if they are being true.

Love means trust. You are calm, secure, and unthreatened. Your partner feels that trust and it makes him/her even more trustworthy.

Infatuation might lead you to do things you'll regret later, but love never will.

Love lifts you up. It makes you look up. It makes you think up. It makes you a better person than you were before.

Such a list makes love sound grown-up and infatuation childish. Yet playfulness and childishness are also acceptable and are important parts of any intimate relationship.

How can we avoid the pitfalls of romantic love and infatuation? How can we be sure that we love someone just as they are and are not being dazzled by our own romantic image of them? Perhaps we can't. Love is learned, and learning to move toward a mature, realistic love may be trial and error.

Furthermore, the most important prerequisite for true love may be knowing and accepting ourselves, complete with faults and virtues. If we cannot deal with our own imperfections, how can we be tolerant of someone else's? As Erich Fromm puts it:

> Love of others and love of ourselves are not alternatives. On the contrary, an attitude of love toward themselves will be found in all those who are capable of loving others. Love, in principle, is indivisible as far as the connection between "objects" and one's own self is concerned. Genuine love is an expression of productiveness and implies care, respect, responsibility and knowledge. (1956, 59)

■ LOVING AND LIKING ■

In the play *Who's Afraid of Virginia Woolf?* Edward Albee depicts a couple who are in love but who also dislike and at times hate one another. Can you really be in love with someone whom you dislike? The answer is that you can be

passionately in love with someone you don't like, but your love probably will not evolve into a mature, enduring love. Instead, it will diminish as the dislike grows and ultimately leads to the breakdown of the relationship. In Albee's play the dislike leads to hate and horrendous fighting.

Elaine Hatfield and William Walster suggest that

> liking and companionate love have much in common. Liking is simply the affection we feel for a casual acquaintance. Companionate love is the affection we feel for those with whom our lives are deeply intertwined. The only real difference between liking and loving is the depth of our feelings and the degree of our involvement with the other person. (1978, 9)

It is probably more important to like someone than it is to love them if you are to live together over an extended period of time. Roommate situations clearly demonstrate this. Living closely together on a day-to-day basis is difficult. Sharing cooking, eating, cleaning, and the many mundane chores that make daily living successful is next to impossible if you dislike your roommate. On the other hand, you don't have to love your roommate to live successfully together.

It is difficult to distinguish in concrete terms between liking and loving. It is possible that the emotional aspects of these two states differ. On the other hand, perhaps the emotional aspects are the same and all that differs is your interpretation of the situation. (Hendrick and Hendrick 1992, 88)

Positive reinforcement and positive associations are important to the maintenance of a liking relationship. It is obvious that someone you feel good being with is easier to like than someone with whom you feel rotten. It is also important that the liked person be associated with positive experiences.

> You must associate your mate with pleasure if you're going to keep on loving [and liking]. Romantic dinners, trips to the theater, evenings at home together, and vacations never stop being important. It's critical that you don't come to associate your partner with wet towels thoughtlessly dropped on the floor, barked out orders, crying and nagging, or guilt ("You never say you love me"). If your relationship is to survive, it's important that you both continue to associate your partner with good things. And this requires some thought and effort. (Hatfield and Walster 1978, 12)

Defining Love

We have discussed many kinds of love and love in many contexts in this chapter. Keith E. Davis (1985) published the results of some fascinating research he did in an effort to describe how love and friendship, two essential ingredients to a fulfilling and happy life, differ.

Davis suggests friendship includes the following essential characteristics:

■ *Enjoyment:* Friends enjoy one another's company most of the time even though there may be temporary anger or disappointment.

■ *Acceptance:* Friends accept one another as they are, without trying to change one another.

■ *Trust:* Friends share basic trust, and each assumes that the other will act in light of the friend's best interest.

■ *Respect:* Friends respect each other in the sense of assuming that each exercises good judgment in making life choices.

■ *Mutual assistance:* Friends are inclined to assist and support one another. They can count on each other in a time of need.

■ *Confiding:* Friends share experiences and feelings with one another.

■ *Understanding:* Friends have a sense of what is important to the other and tend to understand each other's actions.

■ *Spontaneity:* Friends feel free to be themselves in the relationship.

Davis felt that romantic relationships would share all of the characteristics of friendship but would also have additional characteristics, over and beyond friendship. He identified two broad categories unique to love relationships. The first he termed the passion cluster set of characteristics.

PASSION CLUSTER

■ *Fascination:* Lovers tend to be preoccupied with one another, obsessed with one another, and desirous of spending all their time together.

■ *Exclusiveness:* Lovers are so intensely occupied with one another that their relationship precludes having a similar relationship with another. Romantic love is given

priority over all other relationships in one's life.

■ *Sexual desire:* Lovers desire physical intimacy with their partners.

Davis termed the second cluster of characteristics related to romantic relations the caring cluster.

CARING CLUSTER

■ *Giving the utmost:* Lovers care enough to give the utmost, even to the point of self-sacrifice, when their partner is in need.

■ *Being a champion/advocate:* Lovers actively champion one another's interests and make positive attempts to ensure that the partner succeeds.

The accompanying figure shows the way in which friendship and love were theoretically related for the research. In general, the reports of Davis's subjects supported this love-friendship model. However, there were some interesting results that differed from the model.

The caring cluster did not show as strong a difference between lovers and friends as had been expected. In fact, the "being an advocate/champion

■ LOVE IS WHAT YOU MAKE IT ■

The more one investigates the idea of love, the harder it becomes to pin down. Everyone is quick to describe it, most have experienced it, and all know the mythology of the romantic ideal even though many disclaim their belief in it. Although there does seem to be some agreement on at least a few of the aspects of love, much of what love is appears to be unique to each person. We each define love for ourselves. This may lead to problems for a couple if the partners define love somewhat differently. Therefore it is important to understand your own concept of love so that you can recognize differences between what you

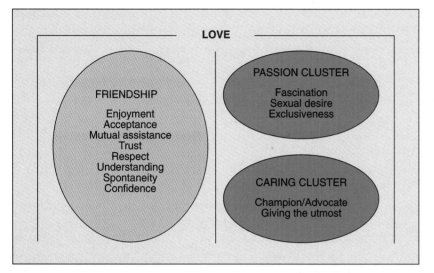

The initial model: Love is friendship plus the "passion cluster" and the "caring cluster"

One clear implication of these differences is that love relationships tend to have a greater impact on both the satisfaction and frustration of the person's basic needs.

WHAT DO YOU THINK?

1. Why might lovers be more critical of one another than friends?
2. How important is it that one's lover also be a friend?
3. Can men and women be friends and lovers at the same time?
4. Are there other aspects of friendship that are important but not listed by the researcher?
5. For a long-lasting relationship, do you feel that the friendship factors or the extra lover factors are more important?
6. Why do love relationships have a greater potential for distress and conflict?

scale" did not show a difference at all. Friends championed each other as much as lovers did.

Another unanticipated finding was that best friendships were seen as more stable than spouse/lover relationships. Perhaps this is related to the finding that the level of acceptance was significantly lower among spouses and lovers than among friends. In other words, lovers tend to be more critical and less tolerant of each other than friends.

Davis concluded that typical love relationships will differ from even very good friendships in having higher levels of fascination, exclusiveness, and sexual desire (the passion cluster), a greater depth of caring about the other person, a greater potential for enjoyment, and other positive emotions. Love relationships will also have a greater potential for distress, ambivalence, conflict, and mutual criticism, however.

and your partner may mean by love. For example, A. Lynn Scoresby suggests that

since love is the word symbol we are accustomed to use in explaining great varieties of marital events, if actual feelings of love are not determinant of happy marriages, then mutual agreement about what love means is. Love is, after all, the most often given reason for getting married, and loss of love is the most often given reason for dissolving a marriage. (1977, 168)

So, if a couple can agree on what love is, and on what loving acts are, and can act on this agreement most of the time, their chances are greater of

Defining Love

maintaining love in their relationship. When people were asked to describe and rate the central features of love, they listed the following in order of importance (Fehr 1988):

- Trust
- Caring
- Honesty
- Friendship
- Respect
- Concern for the other's well-being
- Loyalty
- Commitment
- Acceptance of the other the way he or she is
- Supportiveness
- Wanting to be with the other
- Interest in the other

Most people also agree that there is a *strong physical attraction* between lovers at least during the early stages of their relationship. This attraction is often accompanied by a variety of physiological reactions such as more rapid breathing, increased pulse rate, and muscular tension. In other words, the person "in love" experiences general emotional arousal when thinking of the loved one or when in his or her presence.

Of course, such a reaction could be just sexual attraction and infatuation rather than love. But if the physical attraction is accompanied by a strong and growing *emotional attachment*, and if there is a marked tendency to idealize and be preoccupied with the person, then the reactions are more indicative of love.

Generally, there is a *feeling of openness* between lovers. Both feel they can confide in the other. Both believe the other likes them as they really are, so they can be more open, honest, and communicative—in a word, more intimate—than in nonlove relationships. One way of viewing love may be as "intimate self-disclosure."

Open sharing of your true feelings can be risky. A person in love is easily hurt, as lovers will attest. However, the greater the risk, often the greater the return. Thus, to love is an adventure because danger is involved.

Indifference is the opposite of love. Lovers care, they reveal more of themselves, and therefore they are vulnerable to being hurt. When hurt occurs, a lover may react to the pain with hostility and anger and, at times, with hate. Someone who doesn't care, who isn't hurt, and who isn't in love will be indifferent. The indifferent person, the person who cares least in a relationship, exercises more control over the relationship. This is called the *principle of least interest*. The most loving person in the relationship is more vulnerable and therefore often goes to great lengths to placate and please his or her mate.

Another way of thinking of love is to ask whether the love experience is leading to *personal growth*. Most people in love experience an expansion of self. Being loved by another leads to feelings of confidence and security. Many people are encouraged to venture into new and perhaps unknown areas of themselves. "I feel more emotions than I've ever felt before." "I used to feel awkward meeting new people, but when I'm with Mary, I have no trouble at all." "Bill makes me feel like I can do anything I want."

Most Americans agree on the characteristics of love discussed thus far: physical attraction, emotional attachment, self-disclosure and openness, and feelings of personal growth. Yet individuals express these characteristics in a variety of ways, and such variance can lead to communication breakdowns. To say and mean "I love you" is one thing. We all recognize the word, but it has been used so indiscriminately through time that we can no longer identify love with certainty or tell what it represents (Lasswell and Lobsenz 1980, xii).

Two people very much "in love" may have quite different ideas about what this means and how to express it. For example, it is not uncommon for one partner to feel loving toward the other at the same time that the other feels unloved. It is as if they are on different emotional wavelengths. "But you never tell me that you love me," one may say. "I shouldn't have to tell you. I do loving things for you," the other replies. Those "loving things" may include such actions as bringing home a paycheck, fixing broken appliances, avoiding arguments. In her eyes these are merely things any good husband does routinely. She defines evidence of love as words of endearment, gifts, touching, tenderness—the kinds of behavior that may make him uncomfortable. He knows he loves her, but she is not getting the message. In other words love is more than emotion. Love is also an intellectual concept. It is what you think it is. It is how you define it, which will probably differ to some extent from how your partner defines it (Lasswell and Lobsenz 1980).

Because we usually assume that our meaning of love is the same as our partner's, we may often feel unloved when, in fact, we are simply failing to recognize our partner's expression of love. The emotional script in this case is:

> I, like every man and woman, want to be loved. But I have my own idea, grounded in my personality and attitudes and experience, of what loving and being loved means. Moreover, locked in the prison of my own ways of thinking and feeling, I assume that my definition of love is the only correct one. As a result, I want and expect to be loved in the same way that I love others, with the same responses that I interpret as the evidence of lovingness.
>
> But I am not loved in that way. Instead (and quite logically, if one could be logical about love), I am loved the way my partner thinks and feels about love, the way he or she understands and expresses it. In my own distress, I do not recognize that my partner is experiencing the same incongruity in reverse. Puzzled, hurt, unable to communicate our confusion to each other, we both unreasonably feel unloved. (Lasswell and Lobsenz 1980, 15)

In a truly loving relationship, each partner's concept of love grows to include the other's concept. As our personal definitions of love move closer together, our chances of feeling loved increase.

Jill and Bob are much in love. When Bob is alone with Jill and feels particularly loving, he often grabs her and wrestles her down to the floor or couch. She hates this behavior and tells him, "If you really loved me, you wouldn't act like this. People who love one another don't wrestle." His feelings are hurt by her rejection of his wrestling. Jill feels most loved when Bob approaches her slowly and gently; she feels unloved when he is rough with her. He feels that she doesn't love him because she never enthusiastically wrestles with him.

In Jill and Bob's case, it is clear that they are demonstrating love of the other in different ways. Bob's physically wrestling with Jill is perhaps the way he feels most comfortable touching her. Certainly, it is the way American men are taught to display affection toward other men, as one can easily observe during a football game. On the other hand, Jill has been taught that the more you love someone or something, the gentler you are. Both Jill and Bob are expressing their love, yet their different forms of expression are causing them both to think that they are loved less than they really are. Love, it seems, is what you make it through your attitudes and behaviors.

LOVE IN STRONG FAMILIES: APPRECIATION AND RESPECT

As we saw in the inset about love and friendship, it is astounding to realize that people often treat those they claim to love worse than they might treat a stranger. Most of us would excuse ourselves if we bumped into a stranger in a crowded department store. Yet, when we bump into our brother at home, we may say, "Why don't you look where you are going? You are so clumsy." In strong families where there is a mature, loving relationship, the expression of appreciation permeates the relationship (Stinnett and DeFrain 1985, 44). Mature love will always include appreciation of the loved ones, whether it be spouse, children, parents, grandparents, or simply good friends. Stinnett (1986) defines appreciation with the help of a story he calls "Dirt and Diamonds":

> Diamond miners spend their working lives sifting through thousands of tons of dirt looking for a few tiny diamonds. Too often, we do just the opposite in our intimate relationships. We sift through the diamonds searching for dirt. Our strong families are diamond experts.

Many young people report that they can be "good" and obey all the family rules for weeks on end, yet when their conduct finally lapses, that seems to be all their parents remember.

When I was a teenager and started to date, my parents set 11 P.M. as the time I had to be home from a date. For the first six months I dated, I was always home on time. Finally, I got home one Friday evening at midnight and they blew a fuse. It was all I heard about for the next three months. It was as if my six months of getting home on time counted for nothing. One slip had cost me the entire previous six months. It made me wonder why I had even bothered to get home on time during the prior months.

Many spouses and/or families take each other for granted until something happens to upset their routine. The routines of daily living often dull appreciation. For example, parents often forget to let their children know how much their good behavior is appreciated. Too often children fail to let their parents know how nice it is to come home to a good meal, a clean house, a regular allowance. Each forgets to find the diamonds. It is amazing how far a little appreciation goes in a family where there is little of it. Parents in strong families emphasize positive behaviors and attitudes exhibited by their children. They avoid overemphasizing minor negative transgressions. When discussing appreciation, I sometimes suggest to my classes that a simple phone call home to say that you had a good day in school and really appreciate your parents' support can work wonders.

The ability to appreciate others starts with appreciating oneself. When we don't feel good about ourselves, it is difficult to feel good about and love another. And, of course, we learn to feel good about ourselves by having others appreciate and love us. Thus, strong families seem to start a circular process: "I appreciate and respect you, you learn to appreciate and respect yourself, which leads you to appreciate and respect me." Strong families start this pattern early in their children's lives. Unfortunately, some families start what we call a vicious circle pattern of behavior instead: "I don't appreciate you, you don't learn enough self-respect to appreciate others." A **vicious circle** is a pattern of behavior in which a negative behavior provokes a negative reaction, which in turn prompts more negative behavior.

Respect is another important quality of strong families. We can't appreciate what we don't respect. Curran (1983, 90–111) suggests that respect is shown in many ways in strong families. First, the family respects individual differences. Parents, for example, don't expect all their children to be just the same or to be carbon copies of themselves. They respect each other's privacy. The family accords respect to all groups, even those with whom they may not agree. McCubbin (1988) describes a support network around strong families that emphasizes the positive aspects of relationships. Family members also respect those outside the family, the property of others, and society's institutions. For example, parents who ridicule the school system as inadequate can hardly expect their children to go happily to school. *Constructive* criticisms can and should be made not only of society's institutions but also of the family and its members as long as appreciation is also shown.

Appreciation includes respect for privacy. Family team work does not necessarily mean that everything about every member of the family is shared. A parent may have a particular problem that is shared only with the spouse. A child may do something wrong that does not affect others in the family, so the parent may keep it just between the child and him or herself. Even in large families each member needs some place and times for privacy. Fathers and mothers employed outside the home rarely have any time to themselves at home. When they are home, someone else is always there. In strong families parents may take turns allowing each other some private time around the house by taking the rest of the family elsewhere.

We have spoken mainly about giving appreciation but members of strong families realize that the ability to receive appreciation gracefully is also important. When we offer a sincere compliment to another person only to have it rejected, we feel stupid. For example, you may tell your brother, "My, you look handsome today." If he answers, "Well, I feel ugly today," what do you say? Inability to give or accept compliments stifles the flow of appreciation.

STYLES OF LOVING

A number of theorists have described various styles of loving (Lee 1989; Lasswell and Lobsenz 1980; Shaver 1988; Hendrick and Hendrick 1992). Marcia Lasswell and Norman Lobsenz agree with our thesis that each person defines love in a unique manner based on life experiences. They believe that one's definition of and attitude toward love, although individual, can be classified into six general styles: best friends, game playing, logical, possessive, romantic, and unselfish. Most people will include a mixture of styles in their definition, with one or two predominating. Understanding various styles of loving is valuable because they are basic to all of us and will characterize our intimate loving relationships.

■ Best Friends' Love ■

> When Jennifer and Gary told their families they were going to be married, the news was a pleasant surprise to everyone. "We knew they were close," said Jennifer's mother. "After all, our families have lived on the same block for years, and the children went through school together. But we never dreamed they would fall in love." Neither did Jennifer and Gary. "Actually, it's not that we fell in love at all. It's more that we're comfortable with each other. We have a really warm and easy relationship, so why bother to search for anyone else?"

In this case a comfortable intimacy has developed out of close association over a substantial period of time. For persons in whom this style predominates, love grows through companionship, rapport, mutual sharing and dependency, and gradual self-revelation. There is seldom any assumption at the outset of the relationship that it will flower into love or marriage. Friendly lovers find it hard to conceive of becoming emotionally involved with someone they do not know well. They rarely fantasize about other potential lovers. Even if this thought should occur to them, they would probably want to share it with their partners. After all, isn't that what a best friend is for? Such persons tend to speak of their love as "mature" compared with other styles of love, which they are likely to see as infatuation.

A person with the best-friend love style is typically the product of an emotionally secure and close-knit family. He or she has usually been able to count on parents and siblings for companionship, warmth, and support. In many respects this style of love resembles a good sibling relationship. The divorce rate is low for best-friend couples, but if such a relationship does break up, the partners will most likely want to remain close. After all, two people who have once loved one another cannot become enemies simply because they cease to be lovers.

■ Game-Playing Love ■

To the game-playing lover, an emotional relationship is a challenge to be enjoyed, a contest to be won. The more experienced one grows at the game, the more skilled one's moves can be, and often a wide range of strategies is developed to keep the game interesting. Commitment is anathema to this style of lover. The object of the game is to play amiably at love, to encourage intimacy, yet to hold it at arm's length. The other person is usually kept emotionally off balance, and the game player's affections are never to be taken for granted.

Game-playing lovers have many artifices. For example, they avoid making long-range plans with partners. Dates are usually arranged on a spur-of-the-moment basis. Game players are careful not to go out with the same person

Styles of Loving

too often; this might lead him or her to believe in some prospect of stability. Much of this kind of love style is found before marriage when a one-to-one commitment is not required or expected. Obviously, men and women who play at love have both charming and infuriating qualities. They are usually self-sufficient, make few demands on the other person, and prefer not to have demands made on them. They tend to be amusing, quick-witted, and self-confident; they also tend to be self-centered. The charge is often made that game-playing love is not truly love at all, that it is hedonism at best and promiscuity at worst. But the true game player believes in playing fair and tries not to hurt the other person.

■ LOGICAL LOVE ■

Logical love concentrates on the practical values that may be found in a relationship. This style has been called "love with a shopping list." "I could never love anyone who didn't meet my requirements for a husband and father (or wife and mother)." Moreover, logical lovers are quite realistic. They usually know exactly what kind of partner they want and are willing to wait for the person who comes closest to meeting their specifications.

It is not uncommon for a lover of this pragmatic bent to avoid any relationship that he or she does not think has a good chance of becoming permanent. "Why should I waste my time?" In one sense logical love is an updated version of the traditional "arranged" matchmaking of earlier times. The modern logical lover may think that romance does have some place in love, but he or she believes more strongly that love should be an outgrowth of a couple's practical compatibility.

Pragmatic lovers consider themselves in love as long as the relationship is perceived as a fair exchange. If matters turn out not to be what they seemed, logical love calls for a two-step response. First, an effort is made to help the partner fulfill his or her original potential. If such efforts fail, the relationship is ended. Not surprisingly, logical love requires patience: to find the proper partner; to work out problems; and if the relationship should break up, to wait to end it until a reasonable and logical time.

▓ POSSESSIVE LOVE ▓

Possessive love is perhaps the most unfulfilling and disturbing love style. Alternating between peaks of excitement and depths of despair, capable of shifting instantly from intense devotion to intense jealousy, this style of lover is consumed by the need to possess the beloved totally and to be possessed by the lover. The fear of loss or rejection is omnipresent. Despite this bleak picture, the pattern is considered one of the most common definitions of being in love.

At the root of possessive love are two seemingly contradictory emotional factors. On the one hand, such lovers are enormously dependent. At the outset of the love affair, they may be too excited to sleep, eat, or think clearly. Unable to control their intense reactions, they often feel at the mercy of the beloved. At the same time, such lovers are demanding, often placing great emotional burdens on the other person. Supersensitive, the possessive lover is constantly on the alert for the slightest sign that the partner's affection may be slackening.

If such a sign is detected, or even imagined, the anxiety-ridden lover demands immediate reassurance.

When possessive love affairs break up, the ending is usually bitter and angry. The possessive lover finds it almost impossible to see the former partner again or to retain any concern or affection for him or her. It is easy to scorn possessive love and concentrate on its unpleasant characteristics, but many perfectly adequate and emotionally healthy people evidence this style of love to some degree. They prefer intense togetherness. They see jealousy as a natural part of being in love.

ROMANTIC LOVE

Cupid's arrow piercing the heart and instantaneously awaking passionate devotion is the definitive image of romantic love. The romantic lover is often as much in love with love itself as with the beloved. Love at first sight is not only possible but almost a necessity. The typical romantic lover seeks a total emotional relationship with the partner. Moreover, he or she expects the relationship to provide a constant series of emotional peaks. The fires of this love style are fueled in large part by a powerful sense of physical attraction.

Once they have found each other, the romantic lovers are likely to be in each other's arms quickly. There is a great urgency to merge physically as well as emotionally. Obviously, the intensity of this initial attraction and passion cannot be maintained indefinitely at the same high level. When it begins to taper off, the romantic lover must either substitute fantasies for realities or learn to cope with growing evidence that the other person is not perfect.

One must be willing and able to reveal oneself completely, commit oneself totally, risk emotional lows as well as highs, and survive without despair if one's love is rejected. A romantic does not demand love but is confidently ready to grasp it when it appears.

UNSELFISH LOVE

Unselfish love (agape) is unconditionally caring and nurturing, giving and forgiving, and, at its highest level, self-sacrificing. A characteristic of this love style is that one has no sense of martyrdom, no feeling of being put upon. The style rests on the genuine belief that love is better expressed in giving than in receiving. In a sense men and women with this style of love never actually "fall in love." Instead, they seem to have a reservoir of loving kindness that is always available. They are ruled less by their own needs than by the needs of others. Unselfish love occurs less often in real life than is imagined. Not many people have the emotional fortitude to be so giving. And even if they have, their altruism is not necessarily complete. An unselfish lover experiences in return feelings of satisfaction, recognition, even gratitude.

LEARNING TO LOVE

If the styles of loving set forth by Lasswell and Lobsenz really exist, where do they come from and how do we learn them? Essentially, we learn the meaning of love and how to demonstrate it from those around us—our parents, siblings, peers—and from the culture in which we are raised. For example, family size may influence our definition of love. An only child is accustomed to a great deal of adult attention. Later, as an adult, such a child may feel unloved if his or her spouse (who is the third of four children and received relatively little adult attention) does not attend to him or her all of the time.

Conversely, the person whose attention needs were well met as a child may demand less as an adult. Someone who grew up receiving little attention may demand a great deal from an adult intimate relationship.

Our experiences mold our attitudes and behaviors. Thus, the way we express love and what we define as love are the results of our past experiences.

▪ ACTIONS AND ATTITUDES ▪

The attitudes a person brings to love, to dating, and later to marriage have developed over many years. Because no two people experience the same upbringing, it is not surprising to find great attitudinal differences between people, even when they are "in love." Many of the difficulties we experience in our interpersonal relationships stem from conflicting attitudes and unrealistic expectations rather than from specific behavior. For example, a few socks on the floor are not as upsetting to a new wife as is her husband's general attitude toward neatness. Does he expect her to wait on him? Often it is necessary to change underlying attitudes if behavior is to change, but this is difficult to do. We take our attitudes for granted without being aware of them. For example, a young man roundly criticized the double standard. But a day later, when discussing spouses' freedom to be apart occasionally, he stated that he certainly deserved time out with "the boys," but women probably shouldn't go out with their girlfriends after marriage. He suggested this might be misunderstood as an attempt to meet other men.

Attitudes generally consist of three components: affective, cognitive, and behavioral. The *affective* aspect is one's emotional response resulting from an attitude, such as "I like blondes." The *cognitive* component consists of a person's beliefs and/or factual knowledge supporting the particular attitude, such as "blondes have more fun." The *behavioral* component involves the person's overt behavior resulting from the attitude, "I date blondes."

Unfortunately, these components are not necessarily consistent. For example, my attitudes may not be founded on fact. I may not act on my attitudes. Or I may voice attitudes that I really don't believe. The young man above is an example of someone who voices one attitude—against the double standard—but favors another—for the double standard. Where do attitudes come from? We are not born with them. We learn our most basic attitudes as we grow up. A society passes its values on beginning at birth. This process is termed **socialization.** This is why we must trace our attitudes toward sex, love, and marriage from early childhood in order to understand adult behavior.

▪ DEVELOPMENTAL STAGES IN LEARNING TO LOVE ▪

Children pass through various stages of development as they grow to adulthood. These stages are actually arbitrary classifications set up by theorists, but

Socialization
Society teaching cultural mores and values to new members, i.e. children

they are useful in efforts to understand development. Sigmund Freud delineated four psychosexual stages leading to adult sexual and love expression. Eric Erikson expanded on these to suggest eight general stages of development across a person's life span (see pages 496–497). The following overview of Freud's four psychosexual stages will help us understand how we learn to love.

SELF-LOVE STAGE: INFANCY AND EARLY CHILDHOOD

During their early years young children are so busy learning about their environment that almost all of their energy is focused on themselves and exploring the environment. Many believe that this early period of self-involvement sets the foundation for subsequent attitudes toward the self. It is important during these early years for the child to receive stimulation, including physical fondling. As Ashley Montagu writes, "By being stroked, and caressed, and carried, and cuddled, by being loved, the child learns to stroke, and caress, and cuddle and love others" (1972, 194). Montagu concludes that involvement, concern, tenderness, and awareness of others' needs are communicated to the infant through physical contact in the early months of life. It is here that the child begins to learn the meaning of love and to develop attitudes about intimacy, although the infant cannot intellectually understand these concepts. The child who is deprived of early physical contact may later be unable to make relationships based on love and caring because he or she has not experienced loving relationships. Whether breast- or bottle-fed, the infant needs to be held, cuddled, and fondled. Feeding becomes a time of psychological as well as physical nourishment for the child (see Chapter 12).

If children are given love and security and are generally successful in learning to master the environment during this first stage, the chances are that they will have an accepting and positive attitude toward themselves. They will have positive self-esteem. These positive self-attitudes are necessary for us to relate lovingly to others: "The affirmation of one's own life, happiness, growth, and freedom is rooted in one's capacity to love, i.e., in care, respect, responsibility, and knowledge. If an individual is able to love productively, he loves himself too; if he can only love others, he cannot love at all" (Fromm 1956, 59–60).

By loving oneself, Fromm means coming to terms with oneself, realistically accepting both one's shortcomings and assets, and feeling at ease with oneself. People who hate or despise themselves have great difficulty loving others. Persons who lack love early in their lives often try to compensate for their lack of self-love by selfishness and heightened interest in personal gain.

In order to love, we must be loved. Thus, even as small children, we learn about love from the way in which we are loved.

PARENTAL IDENTIFICATION STAGE: EARLY AND MIDDLE CHILDHOOD

During this stage children learn the masculine or feminine role that goes with their biological gender. In many respects children act in a neuter way until they are about five or six years old, even though they start learning their gender roles much earlier. Many parents start guiding their children toward the appropriate gender role at birth. However, children are usually five or six before they make a commitment to the gender role by identifying with the like-sexed parent.

Although the parental identification stage is quite short, usually lasting a few months to a year, it is a crucial period since the child makes the basic identification with the proper sex role at this time. In a culture where the sex

"I DON'T PLAY WITH GIRLS, MARGARET...."

"... WHERE PEOPLE CAN *SEE* ME!"

roles are moving closer together as in the United States, it is more difficult for the child to pass through this stage since the gender roles are more overlapping and not as clear-cut.

During this stage it is important for children to have close contact with an adult of their own sex. Under normal circumstances this is the father or mother. However, with the increasing number of single-parent families, this person may be a grandfather or grandmother or a male or female companion of the parent. One can usually recognize when children have made this transition because they become more certain of their gender. Boys will probably not want to do things that they regard as being for girls and vice versa. Girls and boys will want to take the proper gender roles when playing house. Children usually talk a lot during this time about what is proper for a girl and for a boy. The importance of this stage to development suggests that the child's transition will be smoother if the parents can maintain a comfortable relationship even if apart and can work together to help the child make the proper identification. If identification does not occur during this stage, it may occur later, but it will be more difficult for the child to achieve.

Bernard Murstein (1986) reminds us of the common saying "women give sex for love, men give love for sex." Peplau and Gordon (1985) in a survey of college students found that men tended to say that sex was more important to them than love, and women said that love was more important, thus lending some empirical support to the saying. Murstein goes on to report on various research results (117–19) that describe further romantic differences between men and women:

■ Men more than women enter a relationship with the desire to fall in love and report being initially more attracted to their eventual fiancées.

■ Men tend to fall in love earlier than women.

■ Men are less willing to marry without being in love.

■ In general, men appear initially much more geared to romance than women. (However, "romantic" for men may well be a code word for sex.)

■ Once serious courtship is under way, the woman's love may be a better predictor of the course of the relationship. Even if she is more involved with him, she may break up the relationship if she thinks it is going nowhere. The man who is involved is more likely to enjoy the fruits of involvement and not be so concerned about where the relationship is going.

■ Once a woman commits herself to a man, she becomes more expressive than he is.

■ Men tend to enjoy love *now* and reflect on it later whereas women tend to reflect more *now*, hoping to enjoy love later.

■ Women tend to take more time to love and commit themselves to a relationship than do men.

■ Women generally seek emotional relationships while men tend initially to seek physical relationships.

The sex role that we learn is an important determinant of our definition of love and an even more important influence on how we display love. If a boy learns that it is not masculine to show tenderness, for example, tenderness may not be part of his style of love.

GANG STAGE: LATE CHILDHOOD AND PREADOLESCENCE

This stage coincides fairly well with the usual elementary school years in our society. It is called the gang stage because each gender tends to avoid the other, preferring to spend time with groups of same-sex friends. Freud called this the "latency" period because it appeared to be a relatively calm time sexually. Recent research has indicated that there is more sexual experimentation during this period than was first thought.

The main tasks of this stage are consolidation of the socially appropriate gender role and adjustment to cooperative endeavor and formal learning. The gang, or peer group, helps the child learn cooperative behavior and the give and take of social organization. In addition, masculine and feminine roles are strengthened by the gang members' approval and disapproval as well as by adult models the gang admires.

During this period the average boy or girl is often openly hostile toward the opposite sex. But the onset of puberty usually signals the end of this stage. The age at which puberty begins varies so widely in our culture that each child will probably enter it at a slightly different time. Thus, the primary importance

Learning to Love

of the gang diminishes only gradually as the members one by one begin to turn their attention toward the opposite sex. The girls' groups dissolve first because on the average they reach puberty two years ahead of boys. Girls have been ahead biologically all along, but the distance is greatest at the onset of puberty.

HETEROSEXUAL ADULT STAGE

Most young persons entering this stage turn their attention toward the opposite sex and soon begin dating. Each preceding stage of development becomes the foundation for the next stage. And we must assimilate the lessons of all stages to become mature, loving individuals. People who have passed successfully through the first three stages of development reach the heterosexual stage with a positive attitude toward themselves, a fairly clear idea of their roles as men or women, and a heightened interest in the opposite sex. They have learned several different kinds of love in their relationships with their parents and their peers. Their definitions of and attitudes about love are fairly well set and so is their own personal style of loving.

LOVE OVER TIME: FROM PASSIONATE TO COMPANIONATE LOVE

Many of the characteristics of love described thus far can be labeled passionate or romantic love and are most apparent early in a love relationship. Being in love at age twenty with your new mate will probably be quite different from the love experienced with your mate after twenty years of marriage. In an enduring relationship, romantic love tends to become companionate love. Murstein (1986, 110) defines *companionate love* as a strong bond including tender attachment, enjoyment of the other's company, and friendship. It is not characterized by wild passion and constant excitement, although these feelings will be experienced from time to time. The main difference between romantic and companionate love is that the former thrives on deprivation, frustration, a high arousal level, and absence. The latter thrives on contact and requires time to develop and mature. With time the emotional excitement of passionate love tends to fade into a lower-key emotional state of friendly affection and deep attachment.

David Orlinsky (1972) postulates various kinds of love relationships over the life cycle, starting in infancy and moving through eight stages into parenthood. Let us briefly examine his ideas about love and then consider what further changes in love might occur in the later years of a love relationship.

Each stage of the life cycle is marked by the emergence of a new form of love experience that is not only exciting but also necessary to the full development of the person. Each love relationship is a medium or vehicle of personal growth.

> One grows as a person through loving, though not only in this way. As one becomes a new and different self through this experience, one also becomes ready to engage in a new and different mode of relatedness to others. Love relationships are not merely pleasant or edifying but essential experiences in life, "growthful"

in the same generous sense in which travel is "broadening." They are in fact necessary links in the process of personal growth. (144)

What Orlinsky is saying, as Freud and many others have also noted, is that children become loving adults through interacting in loving relationships as they grow up. This preparation is necessary to experience mature love relationships. We looked at these early stages and their contributions to mature love in the last section. At this point we will quickly review the early stages to help us understand how love might change over time. Orlinsky's first four stages are *infancy* and *early, middle,* and *late childhood.* Each stage involves dependency on others. For example, infants must be nursed and children taught. If they are nursed and taught in a loving environment, the chances are good that they will have a positive self-image, a prerequisite for mature adult love. By the fifth stage, *preadolescence,* relations with peers are becoming more important, and the love experience changes to one between equals rather than unequals. In the sixth stage, *youth,* the exciting, passionate, romantic love we have discussed becomes dominant. If a partnership is formed during the seventh stage, *adulthood,* the couple will grow together and find the emotional attachment becoming stronger, and some of the passion may give way to a more enduring, caring, and comfortable relationship. During the last stage, *parenthood,* a couple's love broadens to include children. There will then be a greater proportion of agape or selfless love.

Where might love go from here? Hopefully, it will become more and more a mixture of romantic, selfless, and companionate love. Rollo May (1970) calls this mixture "authentic love." Erich Fromm (1956) uses the phrase "mature love" to describe healthy adult love. Mature love preserves the integrity and individuality of both persons. It is an action, not just a passive emotion. Giving takes precedence over taking. Yet this giving is not felt as deprivation but as a positive experience.

One must be able to accept as well as give love if a relationship is to remain loving. Loving is a reciprocal relationship. By accepting your partner's love, you affirm that person as an accepted and valued companion (Scoresby 1977).

The expression of love has social, physical, intellectual, and emotional aspects. At different periods in one's life, one or another of these aspects may be dominant, and thus the way in which love is shown will vary from time to time. Such changes do not necessarily mean an end of love but may only signal a changing interplay of all of its factors.

Thus, the route love might take in a relationship that lasts a lifetime is basically the pattern of dependency, mutuality, passion, caring, and respect, and then perhaps dependency again in old age. Of course, there are other courses that love can take when couples find their love has diminished or died.

American culture presents some obstacles to an enduring love relationship. Our culture, especially through mass media, exalts passionate or romantic love, which is usually linked closely to sexual expression. For those who equate true love only with passionate love, intimate relationships are doomed to end in disappointment. It is impossible to maintain a constant state of highly passionate love with its concomitant elation and pain, anxiety and relief, altruism and jealousy, and constant sexual preoccupation. Certainly, no one newly in love wants to hear that the flame will burn lower in time. Who, newly in love, preoccupied from morning till night with thoughts of their love, can think, much less believe, that the feelings they are experiencing so strongly will ever

Love over Time: From Passionate to Companionate Love

fade? On the other hand, who could tolerate being in this highly charged emotional state forever? The fact that love changes over time makes it no less important, no less intimate, no less meaningful when some of the passion is replaced by a warm, deeply abiding and caring, quieter companionate love.

Mass media's exaltation of passionate love and sex has led many Americans to equate sex with love. Unfortunately, this concentration on the sexual element in love may cause other important personal and interpersonal potentials to be neglected and may diminish the overall quality of love in a relationship. Luther Baker (1983, 299) points out "that sex is not the 'pièce de résistance' of the good life, and our present concentration upon it often prevents people from developing other aspects of personal functioning which will produce a good life." The best sex, he says, flows

> spontaneously out of a life and a relationship filled with love, joy, struggle, growth and intimacy. Good sex is a by-product and, like happiness, is most likely to occur when one is not worried about having it. We may find that when we come to know one another better in non-sexual ways, the expression of sexual intimacy will take on a new and more fulfilling dimension.

Following Baker's suggestion to deemphasize the "sex is love" philosophy would make it easier for two people passionately in love to accept the changes that slowly transform their love feelings into a subtler, more relaxed companionate love style.

Another obstacle to an enduring love relationship is our culture's emphasis on the individual, which leads to a preoccupation with oneself, self-improvement, self-actualization, and so forth. As Amitai Etzioni (1983) suggests, in this age of the individual ego, marriage (love) is often less an emotional bonding than a breakable alliance between two self-seeking individuals. Love must involve a strong feeling of community—the caring and loving of mate, children, and other intimates within one's environment. Passionate love tends to preclude all but oneself and the object of one's love. Indeed, if all Americans remained passionately in love, there would never be a sense of community. Passionate love ultimately is selfish love. As it is transformed into companionate love, the selfish element is reduced, and there is once again time for other aspects of the loving relationship besides the passionate and sexual. As the preoccupation with the loved one subsides, one can again attend to the broader community.

It should be remembered that companionate love does not preclude passionate love. Ideally, there will always be times of high passion in a loving relationship, no matter how long the relationship has lasted. These times are to be savored and enjoyed. Because such times will become less frequent with the passage of time in even a successful loving relationship, one must not value the "loving" less.

From our discussions it is clear that it takes little effort to fall passionately in love even if we don't exactly understand what such love is or just why we fall into it. It is equally clear that thought and work are required to remain in love. Love neglected will not survive in most cases. Falling passionately in love is not the end. It must be a beginning that when nurtured and cared for will endure, albeit in a changed form to some degree. To love lastingly and well—to like and care for another over a period of time—is a unique gift that humans can give one another. The idea that enduring love will simply occur because one is passionately "in love" is a false belief that may destroy a relationship.

INSET 3-5
LOVE AND THE LOSS OF ONE'S SELF-IDENTITY

As time passes, couples often report escalating conflict between sharing love together and the feeling of loss of identity. Robert Bellah et al. in *Habits of the Heart* (1985) discuss conflict between individualism and commitment in American life. One woman reported that during the first years of her marriage she acted out the role of good wife, trying continually to please her husband. "The only way I knew to be was how my mother was a wife. You love your husband and this was the belief I had, you do all things for him. This is the way you show him that you love him—to be a good wife." Trying so hard to be a good wife, she failed to put her "self" into the relationship. She put aside her willingness to express her own opinions and act on her own judgment. As time passed, she felt the loss of herself more and more strongly. "All I thought about was what he wanted. The very things I was doing to get his approval were causing him to view me less favorably."

Losing a sense of who one is and what one wants can make one less attractive and less interesting. To be a person worth loving, one must assert one's individuality. Having an independent self is a necessary precondition to joining fully in a relationship.

Love creates a dilemma for Americans. In some ways, love is the quintessential expression of individuality and freedom. At the same time, it offers intimacy, mutuality, and sharing. In the ideal relationship, these two aspects of love are perfectly joined—love is both absolutely free and completely shared. Such moments of harmony among free individuals are rare, however. The sharing and commitment in a love relationship can seem, for some, to swallow up individuality. Paradoxically, since love is supposed to be a spontaneous choice by free individuals, someone who has "lost" him/herself cannot really love. Losing a sense of one's self may also lead to being exploited, or even abandoned, by the person one loves.

If enduring love is to evolve from passionate love, it must be worked at and tended so that it will not wilt and die with the passage of time.

LOVE'S OFT-FOUND COMPANION: JEALOUSY

Jealousy, the green-eyed monster, is an unwelcome acquaintance of nearly everyone who has ever been in love. Because it is a personal acquaintance, it is described in many different ways, almost as many as the descriptions of love. **Jealousy** may be defined as the state of being resentfully suspicious of a loved one's behavior toward a suspected rival. "Jealousy is an aversive emotional reaction evoked by a relationship involving one's current or former partner and a third person" (Buunk and Bringle 1987). Jealousy refers to the belief that what has been promoted—that is, a relationship—is in danger of being lost.

Jealousy is sometimes used to mean "envy." *Envy*, however, represents a discontent with oneself and/or a desire for the possessions or attributes of another. Jealousy is characterized by a sense of feeling lonely, betrayed, afraid, uncertain, and suspicious. Envy elicits more shame, longing, guilt, denial, and a sense of inferiority (Parrott and Smith 1987).

Jealousy
The state of being resentfully suspicious of a loved one's behavior toward a suspected rival

Jealousy relates as much, if not more, to one's own feelings of confidence and security than it does to the actions of a loved one. As Margaret Mead (1968) has said: "Jealousy is not a barometer by which the depth of love can be read. It merely records the degree of the lover's insecurity. . . . It is a negative miserable state of feeling having its origin in the sense of insecurity and inferiority." Jealousy usually involves feelings of lost pride and threatened self-esteem, feelings that one's property rights have been violated. Whether the threat or violation is real, potential, or entirely imaginary, the jealous feelings aroused are real and strong.

Jealousy is also related to what one's culture teaches about love and possession inasmuch as the culture prescribes the cues that trigger jealousy (Hatfield and Walster 1978).

On her return trip from the local watering well, a married woman is asked for a cup of water by a male resident of the village. Her husband, resting on the porch of their dwelling, observes his wife giving the man a cup of water. Subsequently they approach the husband and the three of them enjoy a lively and friendly conversation into the late evening hours. Eventually the husband puts out the lamp, and the guest has sexual intercourse with the wife. The next morning the husband leaves the house early in order to catch fishes for breakfast. Upon his return he finds his wife having sex again with the guest. The husband becomes violently enraged and mortally stabs the guest. (Hupka 1977, 8)

This story seems unintelligible to an American. How can the husband condone his wife having sexual intercourse with another man on one occasion and be enraged by it a short time later? The answer lies in the cultural ways of the Ammassalik Eskimo. In this culture the husband would be considered inconsiderate if he did not share his wife sexually with his overnight guest. "Putting out the lamp" is a culturally sanctioned game that acts as an invitation for the guest to have sex with the host's wife. Yet it is not unusual for an Ammassalik Eskimo husband to become so enraged as to try to kill a man who has sex with his wife outside the prescribed game rules.

Such behavior illustrates that jealousy is to some extent rooted in social structure. Hupka (1981, 1985) identified several characteristics that differentiate jealous from nonjealous cultures. Cultures low in jealousy discourage individual property rights and view sexual gratification and companionship as easily available. Such cultures place little value on personal descendants or the need to know whether the children in the family are one's own progeny. Marriage is not required for economic survival, companionship, or recognition of the individual as a competent member of society (Salovey and Rodin 1989, 241). Such cultures are obviously quite the opposite of American culture.

In American society we are also taught the rules of love. In the past love meant exclusivity, monogamy, and lifelong devotion and faithfulness. Lovers were possessions of one another. Historically, adultery was grounds for divorce in every state. Thus, jealousy was usually nearby when a young American fell in love.

For most who experience it, what an unpleasant condition jealousy is. Its characteristics include suspicious feelings that seem to manufacture their own evidence to support the jealousy at every turn; compulsive preoccupation with the perceived infidelity; anger, sorrow, self-pity, and depression all wrapped into one continual emotional upheaval; eating and sleeping problems; and an assortment of physical ills evolving out of the continual emotional turmoil.

Researchers have shed some light on the manifestation of jealousy among Americans. The following characteristics have emerged from various studies (Adams 1980):

■ Jealousy goes with feelings of insecurity and an unflattering self-image.
■ People who feel jealous because of a mate's real or imagined infidelity are often themselves faithless (Salovey and Rodin 1985).
■ People who report the greatest overall dissatisfaction with their lives also feel jealous most often.
■ Happy or not, jealous people feel strongly bound to their mates. Desire for exclusivity is the strongest predictor of jealousy (Salovey and Rodin 1989, 233).
■ Younger people report jealousy more often than older people.
■ It is difficult to conceal jealousy from others.
■ Jealousy seems to cause women greater suffering than men.
■ Women tend more often to try to repair the damaged relationship, whereas men try to repair their damaged egos (self-esteem).
■ Men are more apt to give up a relationship in which jealousy is triggered by the woman's infidelity than are women in the reverse situation.
■ Women are more apt to induce jealousy in their partner to test the relationship, bolster their own self-esteem, gain increased attention, get revenge, and/or punish the mate for some perceived offense (White 1980).

Jim asks his steady to go out Friday night. She says she's sorry, but she has to go out of town to visit her grandparents. (She is actually going to do this.) Jim becomes jealous and angry and accuses her of having a date with someone else. No matter how she reassures him that she is indeed visiting her grandparents, he remains unconvinced. When she returns from her visit, he is even more angry and upset because in his view she has refused to tell him the "truth" as he perceives it.

We can see that Jim's behavior is being dictated by his own subjective view of the world, not reality. Yet even though both we and his girlfriend know that his view is incorrect, the difficulty is just as real as if he were correct.

Love's Oft-Found Companion: Jealousy

Because he is angry, they may fight and not speak to each other for a week. If Jim finds out from others that she was indeed visiting her grandparents, he will be apologetic and sorry that he has acted this way. Remember, we act on our perceptions, and they are not necessarily the same as objective reality.

One last point: To the degree that one's culture teaches the cues that trigger jealousy, changes in the culture may change the characteristics and incidence of jealousy. As American sexual mores have loosened, as increased divorce has eroded long-term monogamy, as cohabitation and premarital sexual intimacy have become more acceptable, the need for jealousy has also changed. Although the evidence is unclear at this time, greater sexual freedom may be leading to decreased sexual jealousy for some people. Gary Hansen (1982) found that nontraditional sex role subjects were less jealous than traditional sex role subjects in their reactions to hypothetical jealousy-producing events.

Is there anything that one can do to manage and control irrational jealous feelings? This question is difficult to answer, especially for a person in the midst of a jealous emotional reaction. Naturally, any steps we can take toward becoming confident, secure individuals will help us cope with our own jealousy. We can try to learn what is making us jealous. What exactly are we feeling and why are we feeling that way? We can try to keep our jealous feelings in perspective. Remember that jealousy is also a sign that one's relationship is meaningful and important. We can also negotiate with our partners to change certain behaviors that seem to trigger our jealousy. Negotiation assumes that we too are working to reduce unwarranted jealousy. Choosing partners who are reassuring and loving will also help reduce our irrational jealousies. Unfortunately, following such advice is difficult because jealousy is so often irrational and unreasonable and, for the jealous partner at the moment of jealousy, all too often uncontrollable. It remains one of the puzzling components of love relationships.

SUMMARY

1. *American youths are given relative freedom to choose a mate.* Unlike other societies where mate choice is directed by rigid prescriptions and parental and social guidance, ours permits young people to seek their own mates with a minimum of social interference or parental participation. American mate choice is usually based on the nebulous concept of romantic love: "I will marry the person I fall in love with."

2. *"Love" is a difficult word to define.* One helpful approach is the view of the ancient Greeks who classified love into three possible types: *eros*, sexual love; *agape*, spiritual love; and *philos*, brotherly and friendly love. Mature love includes all three aspects.

3. *Our attitudes about and personal definition of love guide mate selection and lead each of us to form a set of idealized expectations about the kind of mate we desire.* These expectations, if highly unrealistic, often cause disappointment because the partner cannot live up to them. Overromanticized expectations of what a mate and a marriage should be almost ensure disappointment in, and subsequent failure of, a relationship.

4. *Attitudes about love and marriage develop through a number of stages as one grows from infancy to adulthood.* Each stage presents problems that the developing person must successfully overcome if mature love relationships are to be sustained during adulthood. The first stage is the *self-love* stage. During this early period, children begin to come to terms with themselves, establishing security, trust, and self-respect. In the *parental identification* stage, children identify with their like-sexed parent and begin to incorporate the masculine or feminine roles of their culture. In the *gang* stage, further consolidation of appropriate roles is accomplished in addition to learning interpersonal relations and communication skills. Finally, the *heterosexual adult* stage is reached, which is the stage of adult sexuality and eventual marital fulfillment.

5. *Such stages, of course, are only theoretical and will vary with cultures and individuals.* Yet the idea that we develop our attitudes toward love and marriage as we grow up is important. Childrearing practices, the immediate family, and the general subcultures in which one is reared will all influence one's attitudes toward intimacy. Conflicting experiences during childhood may lead to confusion as an individual strives for intimacy. And differing childhood experiences may later lead to conflicts between lovers as they try to relate to one another. Awareness of these differences and concern for the other individual will make the transition to mature love more likely. And, finally, knowing and accepting ourselves is a necessary first step on the path to a successful love relationship.

6. *It is important that we like as well as love our mate if our relationship is to endure.* Passionate love can withstand dislike of the loved one for a short time, but unless the dislike can be changed into liking, passionate love can never evolve into a more permanent companionate love.

7. *Jealousy is an oft-found, yet unwanted companion of love.* The reasons for jealousy are many; it is closely related to one's own security and self-confidence. Although we are starting to understand some of its characteristics, thus far we have had little success in helping people control and manage jealousy. There is some evidence that sexual jealousy may be declining as sexual freedom has increased in the United States.

SCENES FROM MARRIAGE
ARE YOU A ROMANTIC OR A REALIST?

This Love Attitudes Scale is intended to assess the degree to which you are a romantic or a realist in terms of love and does not relate to being a happy or mature person.

Instructions: Circle the response you believe is most appropriate: 1 = strongly agree (SA); 2 = mildly agree (MA); 3 = undecided (U); 4 = mildly disagree (MD); and 5 = strongly disagree (SD).

1. Love doesn't make sense. It just is.	1	2	3	4	5
2. When you fall head-over-heels-in-love, it's sure to be the real thing.	1	2	3	4	5
3. To be in love with someone you would like to marry but can't is a tragedy.	1	2	3	4	5
4. When love hits, you know it.	1	2	3	4	5
5. Common interests are really unimportant; as long as each of you is truly in love, you will adjust.	1	2	3	4	5
6. It doesn't matter if you marry after you have known your partner for only a short time as long as you know you are in love.	1	2	3	4	5
7. If you are going to love a person, you will "know" after a short time.	1	2	3	4	5
8. As long as two people love each other, the educational differences they have really do not matter.	1	2	3	4	5
9. You can love someone even though you do not like any of that person's friends.	1	2	3	4	5
10. When you are in love, you are usually in a daze.	1	2	3	4	5
11. Love at first sight is often the deepest and most enduring type of love.	1	2	3	4	5
12. When you are in love, it really does not matter what your partner does since you will love him or her anyway.	1	2	3	4	5
13. As long as you really love a person, you will be able to solve the problems you have with that person.	1	2	3	4	5
14. Usually there are only one or two people in the world whom you could really love and be happy with.	1	2	3	4	5
15. Regardless of other factors, if you truly love another person, that is enough to marry that person.	1	2	3	4	5
16. It is necessary to be in love with the one you marry to be happy.	1	2	3	4	5
17. Love is more of a feeling than a relationship.	1	2	3	4	5
18. People should not get married unless they are in love.	1	2	3	4	5
19. Most people truly love only once during their lives.	1	2	3	4	5
20. Somewhere there is an ideal mate for most people.	1	2	3	4	5
21. In most cases, you will "know it" when you meet the right one.	1	2	3	4	5
22. Jealousy usually varies directly with love; that is, the more you are in love, the greater your tendency to become jealous.	1	2	3	4	5
23. When you are in love, you do things because of what you feel rather than what you think.	1	2	3	4	5
24. Love is best described as an exciting rather than a calm thing.	1	2	3	4	5
25. Most divorces probably result from falling out of love rather than failing to adjust.	1	2	3	4	5
26. When you are in love, your judgment is usually not too clear.	1	2	3	4	5
27. Love often comes but once in a lifetime.	1	2	3	4	5
28. Love is often a violent and uncontrollable emotion.	1	2	3	4	5
29. Differences in social class and religion are of small importance as compared with love in selecting a marriage partner.	1	2	3	4	5
30. No matter what anyone says, love cannot be understood.	1	2	3	4	5

Note: 30 = lowest possible score—the most romantic response; 150 = highest possible score—the most realistic response.
Source: D. Knox, *The Love Attitudes Inventory.* Copyright © 1983 Family Life Publications, Saluda, NC.

Strange but true, those traits and characteristics that attract us to our mate in the first place sometimes become the very traits and characteristics that cause us the most concern and trouble later in our relationship. George Roleder (1986) defines this circumstance as love's "double cross."

When we were going together, I loved my boyfriend's spontaneity. He was never boring because I never knew what to expect. There was constant excitement. He might arrive on Friday night for our movie date and tell me to get ready for a weekend ski trip to the local ski resort. I'd have to rush around, gather my equipment, break plans with others that I might have made for the weekend, and we'd rush off to the mountains within the hour.

We've been married for three years now and his constant inability to plan ahead drives me crazy. I just wish that for once, we could sit down and make plans for the next week and stick to them. When there is a plan, there is something to look forward to and that is half the fun. I used to think that his spontaneity was fun but now I realize that he is unable to make a decision and stick to it. We both work and with the arrival of our daughter, I cannot just pick up and go on the spur of the moment. He doesn't seem to understand that having a family means that you need to make plans and follow through with them

if you are to be mature and responsible. I don't think he will ever grow up.

Notice how her husband's trait of spontaneity has changed from "fun" and "exciting" to "immature" and "irresponsible." How is this possible? It is clear that dating a person periodically and living constantly with the same person are very different experiences. The personality traits and characteristics that make an evening's date enjoyable may in fact be very difficult traits with which to live. A spontaneous energetic person can certainly be a lot of fun in a short-term relationship. On the other hand, a quiet, less energetic person may be very nice to come home to after a hard day's work.

You will find that there are many such double crosses in love. You are attracted to a very physically attractive person. Yet that very attractiveness brings her or him a great deal of

attention from others, which makes you insecure and perhaps jealous. You find that the high intelligence and quick mind of your mate really attracted you when you first met. Now you find that you can't keep up mentally and often suffer from feelings of stupidity when you are with him or her. It was great fun to visit your boyfriend's apartment when he cooked one of his special gourmet meals. Now, however, with two small hungry children, he is only a nuisance in the kitchen, and you have to remind him constantly that small children prefer plain food.

Such examples should alert you to the fact that "falling in love" and "staying in love" may be two rather different processes. The first is based mainly on immediate attraction, while the second will require negotiation, compromise, and a far better understanding of both yourself and your partner. Falling in love is grand; staying in love is hard work.

CHAPTER

4

DATING, SEXUAL MORES, AND MATE SELECTION

CONTENTS

Perhaps the most unique characteristic of mate selection in the United States as compared to the rest of the world is that it is run by the participants themselves. There are no arranged marriages, no marriage brokers, no chaperones, no childhood betrothals, no family alliance marriages, and not even many marriages of convenience. One Asian female exchange student recently commented, "I want my parents to choose my marriage partner. It is far too important a decision for me to make alone." In America this important decision is made by youth themselves, for better and for worse.

Every society has a system, formal or informal, by which mates are selected and new families are started. In the United States, mate selection is carried out by relatively unrestricted dating among young persons. The selection process is fairly informal. Essentially, American youth are left to themselves to find a mate. Once a couple decides that each is indeed his or her choice for a future mate, however, the system becomes more structured and engagement and marriage usually follow.

The topic of dating has become increasingly more complex as American lifestyles have changed. More and more Americans are delaying marriage and some never marry at all. A high divorce rate means a large group of older dating single persons. As the life span increases, growing numbers of widows and widowers are rejoining the ranks of the single. Certainly, dating at age eighteen is different from dating at age forty, which is still different from dating at age seventy.

Some researchers suggest that emphasis should be shifted away from dating to the broader topic of the formation and development of romantic relationships (Surra 1991). However, the formation of any intimate relationship requires some measure of dating by the couple involved. Hence, dating plays a meaningful role at some time in most people's lives.

AMERICAN DATING

Dating developed largely after World War I when it was encouraged by both the emancipation of women and the new mobility afforded by the car. The population moved from the countryside into the cities where youth found many more opportunities to meet one another. Whereas earlier youth had met at church and spent chaperoned evenings at home, modern youth meet at parties, make dates via the telephone, and go off alone to spend time together on the town. American dating is participant run. In other words, in contrast to the closed choice of arranged marriage societies, the American system of mate selection is close to being open choice for the participants. With open choice mate selection, the ensuing marriages are totally subservient to individual needs and desires (Adams 1986, 178). Individual attraction is the main guide. There is no pure example of open choice, but America probably comes closer to it than any other country. As we saw in Chapter 3, romantic love has been institutionalized as the basis for individual choice of a mate.

Open choice of a mate does not mean that the parents of young adults have no influence at all. Parents often try to influence their children's dating choices. Children, in turn, try to predispose their parents favorably toward their dating partners. In general, parents try harder to influence a daughter's choices. The more serious the relationship, the more parents and children try to influence one another. However, such attempts at influencing appear relatively unimportant to the process of movement toward marriage by young persons (Leslie et al., 1986).

Modern youth are so accustomed to having almost free access to one another that it is difficult to appreciate just how hard it was for a young man to meet a young woman at the turn of the century. Secondary schools were not co-educational then. After elementary school, boys and girls went to separate schools, which made it hard to meet the opposite sex. An introduction of a young man to a young woman's parents had to be arranged, and this was not always easy. Even if the parents approved of the young man, the couple could spend little leisure time together since most of their time was usually occupied by activities with other family members.

■ WHY DO WE DATE? ■

We date for many reasons:

1. Dating fills time between puberty and marriage. It is often simple recreation, an end in itself.
2. Dating is a way to gain social status based on whom and how often one dates. In arranged marriage societies, the family performs this status function. The American dating system makes it possible for certain persons to be rated highly desirable and in this way to raise their status within the peer group (Adams 1986, 181). Thus, dating can change one's status in an open choice system. The classic example of a change in status is the young man who dates and then marries the boss's daughter.
3. Dating is an opportunity for the sexes to interact and learn about one another (to become socialized). Because Americans live in small nuclear families, they may have had little opportunity to learn about the opposite sex, especially if they had no opposite-sex siblings near their own age. Dating is also an avenue to self-knowledge. Interacting with others gives you a chance to learn about your own personality as well as the personalities of others. Dating allows you to try out a succession of relationships. And you learn something about marital and familial roles by relating with the opposite sex.
4. Dating meets ego needs (Adams 1986, 181). The young person needs to be understood and considered important. Being asked for a date yields importance, and a successful date usually involves understanding one another to some extent.
5. Dating leads to mate selection for most individuals. Most young people do not begin each date by asking, "Would I marry this person?" Yet sometime in the course of their dating experience, they will ask this question (Adams 1986, 182).

In early adolescence, dating is mostly considered fun. The older one gets, the more serious dating becomes, and the more concerned one becomes with mate selection. Thus, dating patterns can be placed on a continuum leading from casual dating to marriage (see Figure 4-1).

In the past, mate selection in America was viewed as movement down two paths: the path of commitment and the path of physical intimacy. At first commitments are superficial: Let's get together for an evening. At the end of the path is the deep-seated commitment: Let's spend our lives together. The intimacy road runs from casual hand holding to a full and continuing sexual relationship.

In recent years, the physical intimacy road has been traveled much faster than the commitment road. In fact, today's youth, especially women, often complain that the persons in whom they are romantically interested are unable to make a commitment. Around A.D. 1184–1186 in his book *The Art of Courtly Love*, Andrew Capellanus wrote that "the easy attainment of love makes it of little value; difficulty of attainment makes it prized" (Murstein 1986, 104). Might this old knowledge explain some of the complaints of sexually active youth about the difficulty of finding commitment? Knox and Wilson (1983) found that the dating problem most often cited by university women was "unwanted pressure to engage in sexual behavior." In fact, in the past few years the incidence of "date rape" has been widely recognized.

The emphasis on sexual intimacy in America today seems to lead to the neglect of other important aspects of a relationship that promote commitment. For example, university men report that communication is their biggest problem on a date (Knox and Wilson 1983). Social compatibility, development of shared interests, and increased knowledge of one another as well as of oneself are all important, especially if the relationship is to become permanent. If early sexual involvement overrides these concerns, it can actually work against the furthering of a relationship.

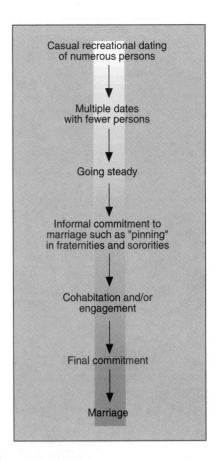

FIGURE 4-1
Dating Continuum

▨ DATING PATTERNS ▨

Adolescent boy/girl interactions have become increasingly more individualized in the past few years. This great variation makes it difficult to describe a common American dating pattern. With the fluidity of the adolescent period and the fact that dating is, by and large, participant run, each new generation redefines the dating codes and norms (Adams 1986, 185). In general, formal dating, where a boy approaches a girl beforehand and arranges a meeting time, place, and activity for them, has declined, especially in the larger urban areas such as Los Angeles and New York. Formal "going steady," where a girl and boy exchange class rings and letterman jackets, has also declined in these areas. More traditional, formalized dating is still found in many parts of America, however. For example, researchers comparing going steady in some high schools during the 1960s and the 1980s actually found no decline in the percentage of students who reported having gone steady.

> In 1960, 82 percent of the women and 71 percent of the men reported going steady while in the 1980s the figures were 81 percent and 70 percent respectively (Gordon and Miller 1984, 474).

In small towns, adolescents cruise Main Street on Friday and Saturday nights. Dates are prearranged, and afterward everyone meets at a drive-in restaurant or couples head into the countryside to have time alone. Many still go steady for a good portion of their high school years.

The first date used to be the first time a couple became acquainted. The date usually involved a function or activity, such as going to the movies. Concentrating on the activity helped the participants avoid some of the difficulties and embarrassments of getting to know one another. Today young people generally know one another better before actually dating. They have chatted with each other and perhaps done things together in the context of a larger group. Their first date comes more casually. For example, they may decide on the spur of the moment to go to a movie together. Couples still go steady, but the relationship seems less formal, more relaxed, and casual. And once they are past a period of almost total preoccupation with one another, there seems to be more group activity, going out with other couples or with friends. It is interesting that group dating has regained favor even among college-age youth. It may be that group dating acts as a barrier to sexual relations, which may be hard to refuse on an individual date.

Whereas dates in the 1950s seemed more task oriented (what will we do on our date?), dates today have become more person/relationship oriented. "Our relationship" is the most frequent topic of conversation for university students. The largest percentage of students meet their dates through a friend. Although we have stressed how free young Americans are to choose dating partners and activities, Knox and Wilson report that 60 percent of the women and 40 percent of the men in their sample indicated that some parental influence was involved in their dating patterns. Women are much more likely than men to say that it is important to date the "kind of people their parents would approve of" (Knox and Wilson 1983; Leslie et al. 1986).

Dating in high school differs from dating in college. Generally high school dating involves one's friends more than does college dating. High school friends tend to inform each other about who is interested in whom. An individual's reputation is more on the line according to who is being dated, "date a nerd, become a nerd." Cliques seem to play a more important role in high school. There is more gossiping among high school students about who is dating whom. It is harder to date casually or to date many partners in high school. This is because the gossip tends to put a couple into a steady dating relationship quickly even though their dating may not be serious. There is a lot more difficulty and embarrassment in asking for dates.

In high school there tends to be more group dating. There are several reasons for this. On a group date an individual is not so "on the spot." The whole group helps to start conversations. Group dating reduces the chances of friends assuming the couple is going steady. As noted, the chances of unwanted sexual contact is reduced in the group date situation.

In college, dating tends to be more relaxed with fewer rules. Dating partners tend to know one another less well when they first date than did dating partners in high school. Often the young person is away from parental supervision and the dating rules set by the family. There is usually a greater diversity of people in college, thus the possibility of greater dating diversity. There is less gossiping about who one is dating and less concern when couples cease dating.

Because dating patterns are so diverse, it is impossible to discuss all dating variations. We can, however, describe traditional dating since there are still some rules by which it is guided. The following description also applies to a first date or dates among the very young.

TRADITIONAL DATING AND GOING STEADY

Let's start when our hypothetical couple is first beginning to date. Age at first dating varies greatly by individual family and by social class, but in general people are dating earlier, and dating at twelve and thirteen is not unusual, especially for girls. Let us further assume that the boy has just reached the legal driving age (fifteen or sixteen).

The two will probably have known each other superficially for some time. They attend the same school and have met at various school functions. Although it requires courage, the young man asks the young woman to a movie on the coming Saturday night. A movie is usually a safe first date because it requires little interaction. Neither person has to worry about being boring or having nothing to say because the movie will occupy them. At the appointed time, he arrives (hopefully driving the family car or his own) to pick her up. Although she has been ready for some time, she is discreetly "not ready." This serves a twofold purpose: she does not appear overeager, and it gives her parents a few moments to look him over and discuss the evening's rules with him, mainly what time to return. If the girl is particularly independent, she may make a special effort to be ready when her date arrives so she can leave quickly to avoid this interaction between her parents and her date.

In the darkened theater, he often strongly feels the pressure of his friends and the anonymous larger group of peers loosely defined as "the guys" to approach her physically. He also wants to prove to himself that the girl likes him. Because of these pressures, dating often immediately embarks on the intimacy road leading to sexual contact. Since the boy generally pays for the date, the girl may feel pressure to repay him, usually with some kind of physical response. The double standard, where sexual advances are expected of him but are inappropriate for her, still operates to some degree in traditional dating. To feel masculine and proud among peers, he wants at least to try to have some type of physical contact with his date. Thus, as he sits watching the

For Better or For Worse®   by Lynn Johnston

movie, the first of many conflicts concerning sexuality arises. For example, he may notice that her hands are lying one inch in his direction on her lap. Perhaps this is a cue. Should he attempt to hold her hand? If she vigorously rejects this advance, someone in the row might notice and he'll be embarrassed. If she accepts, how will he be able to withdraw his hand when it becomes sweaty and begins to cramp? Will she take his withdrawal personally as some kind of rejection?

The fascinating characteristic of traditional American dating is what one might call *escalation*. In other words, resolution of this first minor intimacy conflict does not end the problem. If the girl accepts his first advance, then the pressure he feels to prove his masculinity actually increases. The whole interaction is designed to test just how far toward overt sexuality he can go with her. Granted, much of this pressure may be unconscious, yet he feels the need to prove himself. Once he has taken her hand, he must now consider the somewhat greater problem of attempting to place his arm around her. The reward of increased intimacy is obviously greater, but so are the risks. If she vigorously rejects his attempt, the whole audience will notice (at least it will seem this way to him). If she accepts, he faces a cramped shoulder and a new escalation level with its ensuing conflicts and insecurities.

She is having conflicts too. She does not want to lose her good reputation, yet she does not want him to think her a prude and not ask for another date. Of course, she may not want to date him again. If so, total rejection of his physical advances will give him the message. If she does like him, however, she wants to encourage him but not too much. How much physical contact can she allow without leading him to think she will eventually go all the way?

As the relationship continues, the couple gradually limit their dating to each other. They enjoy the security of knowing they have a date. They feel comfortable together and find it's a relief not to have to face the insecurity of a new date. Going together requires a higher degree of commitment than casual dating; this ability to commit oneself becomes the foundation of later marriage. Going together helps the couple understand what kind of commitments are necessary to marriage.

But going together also creates problems. It tends to add pressure to the sexual conflicts experienced by the young couple. As they see each other more frequently, it becomes increasingly difficult to avoid sexual intimacy. The couple also tends to become more possessive of one another. For example, the

young man may regard any attention or compliments paid to his girlfriend as insulting to him, so he may try to restrict her social interaction. She may resent this, and fights may result.

On the whole, starting early and remaining in a steady relationship throughout adolescence is probably disadvantageous to later adult relations. The young person who has always gone steady is unlikely to have had enough experience with a broad cross section of the opposite sex to have developed his or her interpersonal abilities to the fullest. Going steady early usually leads to earlier marriage, which tends to be less stable than later marriage. If dating is to work as a method of mate selection, it is important to date enough to ensure a good mate choice.

On the other hand, dating so many people that only brief relationships are formed is also dysfunctional. The young person never gets any practice in the give and take of long-term relationships. Ideally, then, one must date enough people to understand the many individual differences that are found. At the same time, experiencing some longer-term relationships helps a person gain knowledge of the commitments and compromises necessary to maintain a relationship over time.

GETTING TOGETHER

At the other end of the spectrum from traditional dating is "getting together" or "hanging out." Even the term *date* seems too old-fashioned to describe this more casual interaction. In "getting together" there is no orderly progression from the first parent-approved date to going steady to eventual marriage. Here meetings and even dates "just happen" as spur-of-the-moment affairs. A couple may include sexual intimacy in these casual "dates" or may never even think of sex. Much of this more casual dating involves group activities. In general, this form of dating is more egalitarian with the woman taking a more active role in initiating and helping to pay for the date than in traditional dating.

For example, a young man sees a group of young women acquaintances at a local snack bar and joins them. He is particularly drawn to one of the young women. He notices that she laughs at some of his jokes and seems attentive to him. A day or two later, he bumps into her on the street and asks if she wants to go along with him to the beach. She agrees, and on the way they find they both like the same rock groups and that both hitchhiked in Europe

American Dating

last summer. She joins him and his friends for dinner that evening. Perhaps a relationship begins to form, perhaps not.

The problems associated with this type of casual dating are almost the opposite of those connected with going steady. Rather than too limited experience with the opposite sex, there tends to be too much superficial experience and too little commitment. Neither partner is likely to feel chosen or special when she or he knows the partner is likely to have many such casual dates with others. Both may have learned to avoid conflicts or "scenes" by keeping their dating behavior at a superficial level and moving on if the relationship seems to be getting serious. If this is true, then neither learns to work things through or to compromise. Because marriage involves commitment and compromise, such persons are poor marriage prospects.

Probably most personal dating experiences will fall somewhere between traditional dating and "getting together," depending on the location, the individual's upbringing and values, and what his or her peers are doing. Regardless of dating style, everyone faces the problems of finding dating partners, coping with "bad" dates, and avoiding exploitation. The fact that American dating today is so informal and without rules compared with past mate selection processes means that each young person has to make his or her own decisions about what is best. Of course, many social and cultural pressures will influence these decisions, but these pressures vary and are not always clear-cut. With the increasing postponement of marriage and high divorce rates, it is clear that a large proportion of one's life will be spent dating.

These descriptions of American dating probably are not accurate depictions of many American young people. Most persons have dating experiences that fall between the two extremes. Sometimes a couple may just "hang around" together; at other times they may date more formally. Much will depend on the couple's circle of friends. Even within a small high school there will be different dating patterns. The important thing to remember is that any dating pattern, if it is to contribute to the courtship process, must give each person sufficient experience with the opposite sex to make good decisions about intimate relationships. Knowledge about the opposite sex comes largely through interaction with the opposite sex. Knowledge about intimate relationships in general comes through being in such relationships. Often dating couples do not recognize that the problems they are having when dating may affect their chances for successful marriage. Researchers found that high levels of premarital conflict were predictive of lower marital happiness (Kelly et al., 1988). Yet working out problems in a satisfactory way during dating is good practice for the necessary give and take that helps make a lasting intimate relationship work. Whatever its exact pattern, the courting process should give people these kinds of experiences.

DATING AND EXTENDED SINGLENESS

Thus far we have examined the dating patterns of young Americans while assuming that dating is a form of courtship that leads to marriage. Not all dating Americans want to marry, however, and not all dating Americans are young. The period of singleness before marriage is longer today than it was in the recent past. The much higher divorce rate has also increased the number of older single persons. These two factors have combined to cause a dramatic increase in the number of people living alone.

> More than one in every nine adults lived alone in 1990; 61 percent were women. Average ages of men and women who live alone differ considerably. Men tend to be much younger (median age 42.5 years) than women (median age 65.8 years) (U.S. Bureau of the Census, May 1991, 13).

The major factor increasing the number of young singles and the length of the dating period before marriage is the trend to postpone marriage. The median age at first marriage has increased to 23.6 years for women and 26.1 years for men. This represents an increase since 1970 of 2.9 years for men and 3.1 years for women.

During this same period (1970–1990), the divorce ratio (number of divorced persons per 1000 persons who are married and living with their spouse) tripled. The divorced represent about 8 percent of the adult population. Another group that tends to be forgotten in discussions of dating are the widowed singles who make up another 7 percent of the adult population. Overall then, single persons who find themselves in the dating pool make up about 35 percent of the adult population (U.S. Bureau of the Census January 1989, 3).

Postponing marriage means that the dating period of one's life will be longer. Those who divorce or are widowed may return to dating later in life. Despite the increase in singleness, it is still a transitory state for most Americans and usually ends with marriage or remarriage. Dating is more than just the young learning about and courting one another. Dating varies greatly in its purposes and patterns according to whether the single person is young and starting to date, divorced, or widowed.

Encouragement to marry remains strong in America, yet prolonged single life is becoming more acceptable. The increasing emphasis on self-fulfillment as a major life goal and society's greater tolerance of differing lifestyles both reduce the pressure to marry. Personal growth and change have become popular goals, and they conflict directly with the traditional goals of long-term commitment to marriage. The women's movement has also contributed to singleness by telling women, "There are other roles you can fulfill that do not necessarily include being a wife and mother." Greater educational opportunity also acts to postpone marriage in some cases because going to school usually postpones economic independence. Greater acceptance of sexual relations outside marriage has also removed one strong reason for marrying in the past.

There are a number of social and legal reasons why certain persons may not want to marry. For example, a woman may not want to change her name. Although she can marry and keep her maiden name, transacting daily business is often awkward and difficult if she does so. Two persons may want to keep their economic assets separate. In certain years, taxes have been higher for married couples than for unmarried people. Older people may lose Social Security benefits if they marry. If you stay single, another person does not have to sign for various business transactions; another's driving record does not affect your insurance rates; another's credit history does not affect your credit.

What effect will remaining single longer have on marriage? Obviously, both partners will be older. Older women face greater risks during pregnancy and childbirth. Couples will also be older when they have children, so the age difference between themselves and their children will be greater. Older couples will probably have fewer children, which will have effects on schools, the baby food and clothing industries, and so on. Older persons, used to a long period of singleness, may become more set in their ways. They may then find the compromises of the marriage relationship more difficult.

On the other hand, data suggest that the older one is at marriage, the greater the chances of marital success. Later marriages should also mean better economic circumstances for the couple. The maturity of older couples may also make them more willing to work toward making marriage a positive experience.

But what of the single life itself? What are the advantages? Freedom is probably the major advantage. You need only worry about yourself. Obligations are undertaken voluntarily rather than being dictated by tradition, role, or law. You have time to do what you want when you want. Expenses are lower than for a family. You can change jobs or even cities more easily. Independence can be maintained, and the conflicts about activities and lifestyle that arise in marriage don't occur. Possible loneliness, failure to relate intimately, and a sense of meaninglessness are potential disadvantages of singleness.

However, loneliness and feelings of meaninglessness depend, in part, on the attitude of the single person. Arthur Shostak (1987) suggests dividing single people into four types depending upon their attitude toward marriage. *Resolved singles* regard themselves as permanently single and express no desire to marry. A few such as priests or nuns may not be allowed to marry. They generally express few feelings of loneliness or meaninglessness. *Wishful singles* are involuntarily single. They want to marry and are actively searching for a mate. *Ambivalent singles* are voluntarily single but are open to the idea of marriage even though they are not actively searching for a partner. They are most often younger people who are pursuing an education or career. *Regretful singles* would prefer to marry but are somewhat resigned to their "fate."

CHANGING SEXUAL MORES

Puberty signals the beginning of adult sexuality. Children become biologically able to reproduce, and the male/female relationship takes on an overtly sexual nature. Adolescent years in most Western cultures are a time of sexual stress because although biology has prepared the individual for sexual intercourse and reproduction, Western society has traditionally denied and tried to restrain these biological impulses. For most people, sexual stress lasts until marriage. It is primarily in marriage that American culture allows its members to engage freely in sexual interaction. Assuming males enter puberty at about age fourteen and marry at an average age of twenty-six, they must wait twelve years after biology prepares them for adult sexuality before society condones sexual intercourse (in marriage). There is a comparable twelve-year period for females, assuming that puberty begins at approximately age twelve and that they marry at an average age of twenty-four. Thus, much dating between American young people revolves around sexual aspects of the relationship.

American society is not only more permissive than in the past but now actually encourages early contact between the sexes. Even elementary schools promote coeducational dances and parties. Makeup, adult fashions, and bras

for preteens are advertised as ways of increasing popularity. The teenage market is large, and business creates and caters to the tastes of adolescents. Much advertising is based on sex appeal, thus heightening the tensions of this period. Popular music is an especially strong influence in the lives of teenagers, and two of its major themes are drugs and sex. In "Thunder Road," Bruce Springsteen sings about Mary who is a romantic vision as she dances across the porch, listening to the songs of Roy Orbison on the radio. Sexual overtones become clear when the young man indicates to Mary that she knows just what he is there for. He exhorts her not to go back inside the house but to remain on the porch with him. Certainly, Bruce Springsteen's reputation is positive, and he is very concerned about society's problems, yet even his lyrics in this song are sexually suggestive.

Many other rock songs contain far more graphic descriptions of sexual behavior. For example, Prince and the Revolution in the song "When 2 R in Love," from the album *Prince Lovesexy*, sing about "hips moving faster than a runaway train and bodies shivering in anticipation of penetration," obviously alluding to sexual relations.

Considering Americans' concern about violence such as rape and murder, it is ironic that much of the music American teenagers listen to romanticizes violence and the degradation of people. The rock genre called heavy metal romanticizes not only sex, but bondage, sexual assault, and murder. The song "Girls L.G.B.N.A.F." by Ice-T contains the words "Girls, Let's get butt naked and f——." The lyrics in Motley Crue's album *Girls, Girls, Girls*, which has sold more than two million copies, describes the blade of the lover's knife facing away from the girl's heart but slowly turning and slicing her apart because killing her helped to keep the lover home. Crue's top-of-the-charts ballad, "You're All I Need," is about a man in a padded cell thinking about his late girlfriend: "Laid out cold / Now you're alone, / But killing you helped me keep you here." Rappers such as 2 Live Crew in their album, *As Nasty as They Wanna Be*, also pursue such themes.

The stress of emerging sexuality is compounded by the extended opportunities a young American couple have to be alone together. The automobile has not only revolutionized transportation and contributed to the highly mobile American way of life, but has also facilitated early sexual experimentation. A boy and girl can be alone at almost any time in almost any place. The feeling of anonymity and distance from social control is increased, group control and influence are lessened, and no one is present who might comment or report on their behavior.

What we find in America is a society that supposedly prohibits premarital sexual relations, yet actually encourages them through the mass media and the support of early boy/girl relations. Young people are often thrown completely on their own resources to determine what their sexual behavior will be. In the end they will make the decision about the extent of their sexual relationships based on their attitudes, peer influences, and the pressures of the moment. The days of hard-and-fast rules about sexual behavior are gone.

As we have seen, movement down the path of intimacy is a part of American dating. In the past, it has been a gradual movement characterized by escalating sexual intimacy. Traditional American dating often evolves into a sexual game of offense versus defense. With each step, the couple moves closer to sexual intercourse. Because it is the male who pressures the female for greater physical intimacy, she is put on the defensive. If her value system is vague or confused by the swiftly changing character of American society, his continuing pressure for more intimacy will often cause her to become confused and insecure.

Escalation of physical intimacy proceeds from the first cautious hand holding to necking, petting, and increasingly to intercourse. How rapidly the couple proceeds depends on the inner security of each member, the length of time and exclusiveness with which they date each other, and the dating patterns of their friends. The more insecure they are, the more they will seek security in conforming to what they believe the peer group is doing. Time is an important factor, too. Placing vigorous young adults who like one another together for long periods of time without supervision in a culture that promotes sexuality is likely to lead to sexual activity.

But it is up to the individual couple to decide how far they will go. This strategy can be called *sex-nonsex*, and it is usually the female who makes the rules. Because she must control how sexual the male becomes, she must have a personal definition of what sexual behavior is. She knows that intercourse is sex, but she may be unsure how to categorize other behavior such as kissing, necking, and various degrees of petting. If she categorizes necking as "nonsex," she can neck as much as she likes and feel no guilt. If, on the other hand, she categorizes necking as "sex," she may feel guilty when she engages in such behavior. For some young Americans, premarital sex is largely a matter of learning how to handle guilt.

When asked how they define sexual behavior a cross section of young American women will not give a single answer. One person may become upset at any action beyond kissing. Another may participate in direct genital play with little if any conflict because she has defined everything but actual intercourse as "nonsex." In the broadest sense, however, intimate physical contact of any kind is sexual behavior.

A man may not be able to judge where a woman will draw the line, and he will be insecure with a new woman until he knows the rules by which the game will be played. He also may be timid and afraid of overt sexuality, although he is obliged to hide any fears by the masculine stereotype that demands that he be the sexual initiator.

The escalation toward physical intimacy may cause young people to become centered on sex to the exclusion of most other things. And, of course, the final "solution" to escalation problems, sexual intercourse, does not end the preoccupation with sex but often exaggerates it. The preceding description of movement down the path of intimacy will seem old-fashioned to many young Americans. Jacqueline Mimenauer and David Carroll (1982) surveyed 3000 men and women aged twenty to fifty-five across the United States and found that 66 percent of the men sleep with a woman on the first to third date while 50 percent of the women sleep with a man on the first to third date. For this group of singles, movement down the path to physical intimacy is clearly faster than in traditional dating. (Current concerns about AIDS may have altered this behavior somewhat, however.)

The double standard that tacitly allowed males premarital sexual relations but forbade them to females is gradually disappearing since it was first studied by Alfred Kinsey and his co-researchers around 1950.

Ira Robinson and others (1991) found that the number of males engaging in premarital intercourse increased 12 percent during the period from 1965 to 1980. However, the increase for females attending college over the same time period was 35 percent. It is clear that young women have become more like young men in their sexual behavior. (See Clayton and Bakemeier [1980] and Darling, Kallen, and VanDusen [1984] for an overview of the many studies done on changes in premarital sexual behavior during the 1970s. See Miller and Moore [1990] for an overview of the research done on this subject during the 1980s).

Studies have also found increasing numbers of Americans approving of premarital intercourse. A national Gallup poll in 1985 found that 64 percent of the men and 52 percent of the women approved of premarital intercourse.

Data from the 1988 National Survey of Family Growth indicate that by age fifteen, approximately one-quarter of females have had sex; by age nineteen, four out of five females have had sexual intercourse (London et al. 1989; Pratt 1990). Data from the 1988 National Survey of Young Men indicate that a third of teenage males have had sex by age fifteen, as have 86 percent by age nineteen (Sonenstein et al. 1989).

The majority of teenagers who have engaged in premarital intercourse report that "it just happened," usually in the home of one of the partners. For females, the first sexual partner is, on the average, several years older. For males, the first partner averages less than one year older (Miller and Heaton 1991, 719). First intercourse is usually but not always consensual. The younger the first experience, the greater the likelihood that first intercourse was involuntary (Moore et al. 1989).

Although it is clear that American sexual mores have become increasingly liberal, some suggest that a counterrevolution is setting in. This reaction is being fueled by the increased incidence of sexually transmitted diseases (AIDS and herpes, for example); growing social concern about unwed pregnancy and the single, never-wed, female-headed family; growing female dissatisfaction with sexual exploitation by men; and the general movement toward a more conservative philosophy in America (see p. 349, "A New Sexual Revolution?" for a more complete discussion).

Although the sexual mores of American youth are becoming more permissive, middle-aged adults tends to react negatively to these changes. Most adults are still against premarital intercourse. The following are the most common reasons they give for this position:

■ Religious attitudes prohibit such behavior.
■ My upbringing and personal moral code prohibit such behavior.
■ Sexual relations before marriage lead to serious problems, such as illegitimate children, damaged reputations, and psychological problems.
■ Premarital sex contributes to the breakdown of morals in this country.
■ Sex is sacred and belongs only in marriage.
■ Premarital sex leads to extramarital sex and casual marital commitment.

It is easy for middle-aged individuals to urge young people to suppress their sex drives, but the fact remains that sexual impulses are among the most basic human needs. It is extremely difficult for young adults to accept admonitions against premarital sex. Parents need to have open and honest discussions about the sexual problems youth face. The ultimate decision about premarital intercourse will be made by the young couples themselves. Rather than giving lectures about morality, it is surely better to supply young people with as much good information as possible so that their decision will be based on a firm foundation of knowledge rather than ignorance. In a nutshell: "Knowledge breeds responsible behavior, ignorance just breeds" (Canfield 1979).

■ DECIDING FOR YOURSELF ■

A couple contemplating premarital sexual intercourse should consider four major areas: (1) personal principles, (2) social principles, (3) religious principles, and (4) psychological principles.

Every person has a set of *personal principles* that guide his or her life. The following are some personal questions you should ask yourself if you are contemplating premarital intercourse:

1. Is my behavior going to harm the other person or myself, either physically or psychologically? Will I still like myself? What problems might arise? Am I protecting my partner and myself against sexually transmitted diseases and pregnancy?
2. Will my behavior help me become a good future spouse or parent? Do I believe sex belongs only in marriage?
3. Is my sexual behavior acceptable to my principles and upbringing? If not, what conflicts might arise? How will I deal with these?

Of course, questions such as these have no general answers. Each individual will have different answers, but young adults should ask themselves such questions before they engage in premarital sexual experimentation.

Other questions arise when one considers general *social principles*. Our society has long supported certain rules about premarital sex. If enough people break these rules, pressure is placed on the society to change them. Thus, each person who decides to act against the established code adds his or her weight to the pressure for change. Before you make a decision, you should ask yourself:

1. What kind of behavior do I wish to prevail in my society? Is premarital sex immoral? Will premarital sex contribute to a breakdown of morals? Is this desirable?

2. What kind of sexual behavior do I believe would make the best kind of society? Would I want my friends to follow in my footsteps?

3. Am I willing to support the social rules? What will happen if I don't?

Questions concerning *religious principles* also need answering. Most of us have had religious training, and we have learned attitudes toward sexual behavior from that training. In a study of several hundred community college students' attitudes toward premarital sex (Cox 1978), 90 percent of those who were against it gave religion as their primary reason. In a comparison of cohabiting and noncohabiting couples, Watson (1983) found that 75 percent of the co-habiting couples never attended church, whereas only 25 percent of the non-cohabiting couples never attended church. The following are some questions you should ask yourself:

1. What does my religion say about sexual conduct? Do I agree?

2. Am I willing or able to follow the principles of my religion?

3. Do I believe there is a conflict between sexual attitudes of my church and society? My church and my friends?

Psychological principles may be the hardest to uncover. Because the socialization process begins at birth and continues throughout one's lifetime, it is difficult to remain completely unaffected by society and family. Many of our attitudes are so deeply ingrained that we are unaware of them. When our behavior conflicts with these attitudes, we usually feel stress and guilt. The following are some of the psychological questions with which you must grapple:

1. Can I handle the guilt feelings that may arise when I engage in premarital sex?

2. How will premarital sex influence my attitudes and the quality of sex after marriage?

3. What will I do if I (or my partner) get(s) pregnant? Can I handle an abortion? A child? Giving the baby up for adoption? Marriage?

◼ FREEDOM OF CHOICE AND SEXUAL HEALTH ◼

Freedom of sexual choice for the young unmarried individual can be much more threatening than for the married person. The sexual mores in many parts of American society have changed from supporting postponement of sexual intercourse until marriage to pressuring young people to engage in premarital sex. "Don't be old-fashioned." "Get with it." "Everyone does it." Especially for young women, it now seems harder to say, "No, I don't want to have sex." Or, "No, I don't want to have sex at this time." This is quite a change from the old fear of losing one's virginity. A young woman now often feels guilty and inadequate if she doesn't participate in sex. Virginity is maligned because it represents past traditions and morality, and, of course, it is supported by all the wrong people: parents, grandparents, ministers, and others who aren't "liberated."

Yet part of a healthy model of sexual behavior is the freedom to choose whether to participate in sexual relations. Being coerced into sexual relations will not lead to a healthy experience.

Healthy sexual expression is a primary part of human intimacy. As we try to make good decisions about our sexual intimacy, it is helpful to think about what we mean by healthy sex. This topic is much debated. Some maintain that no sexual involvement before marriage is healthy. Others argue that complete sexual freedom is healthy. In between are a variety of less extreme viewpoints. The following questions may help you discover foundations that promote healthy sex:

1. *Does my sexual expression enhance my self-esteem?* Behavior that adds to me, increases my self-respect and my positive feelings about myself, and helps me like myself better is behavior that is apt to be healthy. Behavior that creates negative self-feelings and causes loss of self-esteem is better avoided. Low self-esteem creates many problems, especially in intimate relationships.

2. *Is my sexual expression voluntary (freely chosen)?* Obviously, rape is neither voluntary sexual expression nor health enhancing. Other situations, however, are not always so clear-cut. Is my behavior voluntary when I have sex because I fear I'll lose my boyfriend if I don't? Perhaps it is, yet the element of fear raises a doubt. Does the fear make me think I must do it? Does the fear rob me of voluntary choice? Does the fear cause me to overlook the broader question: If I will lose him only because I will not have sex at this time, is he really someone with whom I want to have an intimate relationship? If my decision is really mine, independent of peer and social pressure, then the chances increase that my chosen behavior will be healthy.

3. *Is my sexual expression enjoyable and gratifying?* This may sound like a strange question to ask. Isn't all sex fun and enjoyable? We often find that it is not. Many people report disappointment with their early sexual encounters. A few people report that they seldom derive much joy from sex. For most, however, positive answers to the first two questions will help them answer this question positively. At times sex for its own sake is gratifying, but in general enjoyable and gratifying sexual expression tends to occur most often within intimate relationships.

4. *Will my sexual expression lead to an unwanted pregnancy?* Sexual activity leading to wanted children is healthy. Sexual relations using birth control methods and thereby avoiding unwanted children can also be healthy. Some people disagree with the latter statement for religious reasons. For them healthy sex might mean abstinence if children are not desired at a given time. For most people, though, sex leading to unwanted pregnancy is not sexually healthy. Taking steps to prevent unwanted pregnancy is an important element in healthy sexual expression.

5. *Will my sexual expression pass a sexually transmitted disease to my partner?* Obviously, healthy sex in the medical sense does not promote sexually transmitted diseases (STDs). Thus, knowledge of STDs and taking precautions against them must be a part of healthy sexual expression. The recent AIDS epidemic makes this question more important than ever (see pp. 375–383).

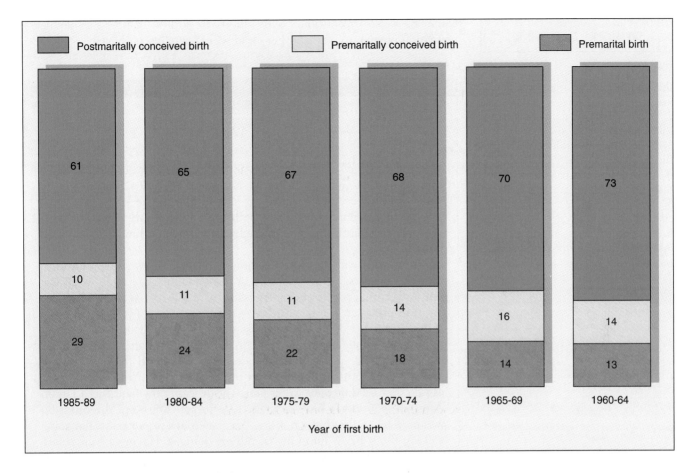

| Postmaritally conceived birth | | Premaritally conceived birth | | Premarital birth |

1985-89	1980-84	1975-79	1970-74	1965-69	1960-64
61	65	67	68	70	73
10	11	11	14	16	14
29	24	22	18	14	13

Year of first birth

POSSIBLE PROBLEMS ASSOCIATED WITH PREMARITAL SEXUAL RELATIONS

FIGURE 4-2

Marital Status of Women at First Birth: June 1960–64 to 1985–89 (Source: U.S. Bureau of the Census October 1991, 6) (Percentage distribution)

As American mores have relaxed, the distinction between premarital and marital sexual activities has blurred. However, a number of problems are clearly more closely related to premarital sex than to marital sex.

Sexually transmitted disease is more prevalent among unmarried participants in sexual activities. Their chances of having more than one sexual partner are greater than married people's. They also are more likely to have short-duration sexual encounters where communication is less open. Such encounters may lead to later discovery of an STD.

Unwanted pregnancies are also a problem. Despite the increased availability of birth control, nonmarital pregnancies have increased (Figure 4-2). The rate of pregnancy among teenage girls is now so high that, if present trends continue, 40 percent of today's fourteen-year-old girls will be pregnant at least once before they reach twenty. Of such pregnancies, 45 percent are aborted (Wallis 1985). It should be noted that the actual birthrate among teenage mothers was as high in the 1950s, but it reflected a lower age of marriage.

An unmarried pregnant woman has limited alternatives. She may marry, seek an abortion, give birth to the baby and give it up for adoption, keep the child and become a single-parent family, or let her parents care for the child

1. How will Dawn and Jim resolve their conflict? What would you advise?
2. What would you do if you were Jim? Dawn?
3. What kind of attitudes show through Jim's statements? Dawn's?
4. How would your parents react to such a situation?
5. What alternatives are open to the couple?
6. How do you feel about illegitimacy? How do you think society feels today?
7. Whose responsibility is birth control? Why?

while she works or continues with school. Regardless of how she handles a premarital pregnancy, she and her child will face many problems.

Dawn and Jim: But I Want to Keep the Baby Even If We Aren't Married

Dawn is a twenty-year-old college junior, majoring in business administration. She has gone with Jim for two years. He is a senior in premed and has been accepted for medical school. She has recently discovered that she is pregnant. In the past both she and Jim have agreed to postpone marriage until they are finished with school and Jim has established himself.

Jim is angry with her for becoming pregnant. "How stupid of you to forget to take your pill, especially in the middle of the cycle when you knew your chances of pregnancy were higher. Are you sure you didn't do it on purpose? You could have told me and I could have used something although I don't like to. It isn't natural. It is really up to the girl to protect herself, and you were plain dumb to forget after all this time."

Dawn doesn't quite agree. "You're having sex with me, too. I don't see why birth control is always just my responsibility. You know as well as I do that I didn't want to get pregnant. It wasn't my fault that I forgot. After all, you didn't have to make love to me. You were the one who was hard up and pushing, not me. But now that I'm pregnant, I'm going to keep the baby. A lot of my friends are doing it. Having a baby before you are married isn't half as bad as it used to be. I really don't care what you or our folks think; it's the modern thing to do."

Jim objects strongly. "Well, I'm not going to marry you under these conditions. We agreed to wait until I was finished with medical school and you blew it. The only thing you can do is get an abortion. They're easy to get now. There is nothing to them physically, and I'm willing to pay for it. Keeping the baby will just foul up our lives and tie us down. We'll have plenty of time to have children after we're finished with school."

"No abortion for me," replies Dawn. "I don't think they're right. Besides, I don't expect you to marry me. I wouldn't want you to feel forced into anything. I've only a year of school left and I'm sure my folks would watch out for the baby until I'm working and independent. Then, with child care, I'll be able to take care of it just fine, without you."

"Well, if you're that stupid, I'm glad to find out now," retorts Jim. "I won't be a part of such a dumb plan. Unless you do the smart thing and get an abortion, I'm through with you, pregnant or not."

Some women who are uninterested in marriage and/or are nearing the end of their childbearing years are now making a conscious decision to have a child even though they are unmarried. They became pregnant through artificial insemination or by having sexual relations with a man who has agreed not to assert his rights as father. Most of these women are older and economically successful. They do not face the same kinds of problems that a teenage mother usually faces.

Early commitment and isolation are frequent partners of premarital sexual involvement. Sex is such a powerful force in young people's lives that it can override other aspects of a relationship. Sexual involvement often reduces social, intellectual, and other areas of involvement. Sexual activity can also promote exclusivity in a relationship, thus narrowing a young person's interpersonal experiences. Such relationships may lead to sexual commitment alone rather than to a total relationship. An early commitment based on only one aspect of a relationship is usually an unstable basis for any long-term relationship.

The *quality of sex may be impaired* by premarital sexual experience. Having sexual relations under circumstances that arouse fear, conflict and/or hostility can cause sexual problems later in life. Masters and Johnson (1966) point out that these three mental states most often cripple the sex life of both men and women.

Because premarital sexual intercourse is becoming more prevalent, an increasing number of American youth may be initiated into sexual intercourse under adverse circumstances. Premarital sex in our culture is often of relatively poor quality for two major reasons: a negative environment and the sexual ignorance of the young couple. The environment of early sexual experiences is usually negative and seldom conducive to relaxed, uninhibited sexual activities. Many of these sexual encounters take place in a car. Having to duck each time another car passes doesn't help the couple relax and feel secure. Both relaxation and security are important psychological prerequisites for satisfying sex. The general environment is especially important to a woman's ability to find satisfaction.

Most young women report that their first sexual intercourse was not very enjoyable. This is not to deny that first intercourse can be pleasurable and exciting, but some young women clearly are disappointed. Such disappointment may breed later problems in their attitude toward sex. Because much modern literature, as well as movies and television, depicts sexual satisfaction for the female as a wild and violent climax, the woman may interpret her lack of enjoyment as a personal shortcoming. She may begin to think that something is wrong with her sexually, a belief that will, in turn, increase her anxiety and make her less capable of finding satisfaction. Thus, an early negative sexual experience may start a vicious circle of behavior.

In these cases, there is usually nothing wrong with the young woman. If her early sexual encounters take place in a secure, romantic environment with a man who appeals to her psychologically as well as physically and offers her intellectual rapport, warmth, and a feeling of self-respect, and if her expectations are realistic, in all likelihood she will achieve a great deal of satisfaction. Although we have mainly discussed the problems of the disappointed woman, if she shows her disappointment, the man will often feel threatened. He may react with his own feelings of inferiority because he has apparently been unable to "satisfy" her. His ability to satisfy is one of his chief masculine ego defenses, and he is highly vulnerable to insecurity in this area, yet he needs to hear and understand what his partner is experiencing.

Most young men reach orgasm very quickly compared with young women. Often the male has ejaculated before the female has even become aroused.

DEBATE THE ISSUES
DOES SEX EDUCATION PREVENT PREGNANCY
OR ENCOURAGE PROMISCUITY?

In many cultures sex education takes place in the relaxed atmosphere of the family. This was once the case in America as well. A century ago in America, many children were raised on the farm where close proximity to animals mating and giving birth was a natural part of life. Living quarters throughout most of the world and in early America were small and cramped, and children sometimes shared a sleeping room with their parents. Hence parents often did not conduct their sexual life in complete privacy. Children were initiated into the world of sex rather informally. Only with the advent of the Victorian suppression of sexuality and enough affluence to provide children with sleeping quarters separate from their parents did sex education begin to lose some of its informality. As sex education became more formalized, it became less efficient, and some parents simply avoided giving their children formal sex instruction. Some people began to advocate that the schools should do more sex education.

SEX EDUCATION REDUCES YOUTHFUL UNPLANNED PREGNANCIES

Sex education is more necessary today than ever before. Sex education must reflect a changing society. American young people are engaging in sexual behavior earlier than ever before, whether adults like it or not.

AGE AND PERCENTAGE OF FIRST SEXUAL INTERCOURSE OF AMERICAN WOMEN AGED 13 TO 18 YEARS	
AGE	PERCENTAGE SEXUALLY ACTIVE
13	4.6
14	10.0
15	12.0
16	23.5
17	27.0
18	7.5

Source: National Center for Health Statistics June 1987.

As the table makes clear, American schoolchildren are sexually active. It is equally clear from the statistics on teenage pregnancies (Chapter 11) that many of our sexually active youth are becoming pregnant.

If society is realistic, it will recognize these facts and deal with them. To pretend that young Americans are not sexually active and deny them education that will help them use their sexuality responsibly is to bury our heads in the sand. The advent of AIDS and the rapid spread of other sexually transmitted diseases add urgency to the need for sex education for America's youth.

Premature ejaculation is the major problem of the young male while failure to achieve orgasm is the major problem of the young female. The two problems are complementary and therefore contribute greatly to dissatisfaction with early sexual experiences.

The problems described above, although prevalent, do not always appear. Some couples can experience the joys of adult sexuality before marriage, but in all cases it is hard to predict just what effects premarital sexual relations will have on marital sexuality.

DATE RAPE AND COURTSHIP VIOLENCE

The term *date rape* has suddenly become popular in the mass media. A better term that encompasses rape but also speaks to the broader problems is *courtship violence*.

SEX EDUCATION PROMOTES SEXUAL ACTIVITY AMONG AMERICAN YOUTH

Providing sex education and making contraceptives available to school-age children simply encourage sexual activity. If condoms may be obtained from the school health clinic, children receive the implicit message that sex is OK.

Most young children are not sexually aware until adolescence although they may have simple questions such as, "Where do babies come from?" Giving preadolescent children thorough, explicit sexual instruction is unnecessary and may lead them to increased sexual exploration. It is certainly appropriate to answer their questions at a simple level, but it is unnecessary to provide more detail than is required to satisfy their curiosity.

Sex education properly belongs in the home where the family can present sexual information in a value context. School sex education tends to be neutral, presenting just the so-called facts. But sexual facts presented outside a value framework do not help children make sexual decisions and establish a set of ethics about their own sexual behavior. The emotional debates over pregnancy and abortion overlook the fact that there is indeed choice regardless of your position on these issues. The choice that needs to be discussed is the choice about when, where, and under what circumstances one will be sexually active. Finding oneself pregnant means that a reasonable choice has not been made.

Without a sense of values, sexual choices cannot be made. It is easy to teach sexual facts and anatomy. What is difficult is the teaching of sexual values. Too often sex education involves only the facts and anatomy.

Unless it teaches values and how to make sexual decisions, sex education is only promoting unthinking sexual activity.

WHAT DO YOU THINK?

1. Did you have sex education in school? At what age? How explicit was it?
2. Do you feel that such education encouraged you to be more sexually active?
3. Do you feel that you were able to make better sexual decisions for yourself because of the sex education you received from your schools?
4. When would you ideally start sex education for your children?
5. Do you think such education should be given by schools or do you feel it should only be given at home?

Although the figures vary, numerous studies report 15 to 40 percent of persons have been involved in receiving or inflicting violence while dating (Rouse et al., 1988; Lane and Gwartney-Gibbs 1985; Carlson 1987; Stets and Strauss 1989). Fully one half to three quarters of college women report experiencing some type of sexual aggression in a dating relationship (Burke, Stets and Pirog-Good 1988, Koss 1988). More college women report having been raped by a steady date than an acquaintance or stranger (Koss, Dinero, Seibel and Cox 1988).

Women and men initiate verbal or physical violence in about equal numbers. However, in actual date rape, it is the man who is the initiator. Women tend to react passively to courtship violence.

In a study of over 6000 students on thirty-two campuses, Moss (1987) found that about one in eight females had been a victim of actual or attempted date rape, but only 10 percent had reported it. Muren, Perot, and

Date Rape and Courtship Violence

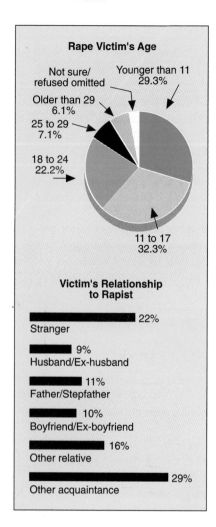

Rape Victim's Age

Not sure/refused omitted

Younger than 11
29.3%

Older than 29
6.1%

25 to 29
7.1%

18 to 24
22.2%

11 to 17
32.3%

Victim's Relationship to Rapist

Stranger — 22%

Husband/Ex-husband — 9%

Father/Stepfather — 11%

Boyfriend/Ex-boyfriend — 10%

Other relative — 16%

Other acquaintance — 29%

FIGURE 4-3
Rape victim's age and relationship to rapist.
Source: National Victim Center *Time* May 4, 1992, 15

Byrne (1989) found that 37 percent of their sample did nothing when faced with forceful sexual advances, 26 percent gave a strong verbal response, and 14 percent reacted physically. None reported the attack to the authorities, and half talked to no one about it, not even friends. Only 11 percent ended the relationship, while almost three-quarters either accepted or ignored the attack. Most blamed themselves partially or the circumstances, "We'd been drinking."

Focusing on date rape, Shotland (1989) distinguishes three different types: (1) beginning date rape, (2) early date rape, and (3) relational date rape.

It would seem that a rape that occurs on the first date, before the male "knows" his partner well or could reasonably expect to have a sexual relationship with her, has a cause quite different from a rape that occurs after the couple has had a number of dates. After a couple has been dating, but before each person has a full understanding of the other's position concerning sex, the male's misperception of his date's sexual intent can set the stage for rape. After a couple has a full understanding about each other's relative position concerning sex, misperception becomes an unlikely cause of date rape, and another explanation becomes necessary. (250)

Putting aside rape on a first date as involving a more pathological antisocial personality on the part of the male, rape later in a relationship may to some degree involve gender differences in socialization toward sex. As we shall see in the sexuality chapter, men tend to develop sexual intensity earlier than women do. Also, the sexual double standard has encouraged men to be sexually active earlier than American women. Traditionally, males have controlled dating, and the use of force may be partially the exertion of that control.

The sexual revolution has also played a role by leading both men and women to believe that sexual relations between couples regardless of marriage are now the norm. After reviewing numerous studies, Shotland (1989) concludes that "the available evidence strongly supports the proposition that males view females in more sexual terms than females view males." Men and women see the relationships among friendship, sexual interest, and love differently. Men often appear to confuse friendly and sexually interested behavior. This perceptual mismatch is important because it is structured so that if a miscommunication around sexual intent occurs within a couple, a likely outcome is that the man will perceive sexual intent when the woman feels that she communicated none. Combine this scenario with alcohol or drugs and the stage is set for an episode of date rape.

Researchers have found that males who engage in date rape have different characteristics than those who do not. They place a higher value on sexuality and feel great sexual deprivation. They tend to be more traditional in their sexual values, perhaps believing more in the sexual double standard, viewing women as property, and so on.

Shotland concludes:

Misunderstandings about sex are likely to arise between dating couples because (1) many men and women do not discuss their sexual intentions openly and frankly; (2) differences exist in perceptions of sexual intent; (3) the use of token resistance by some women may create a belief in some males that protest encountered is of a token nature; and (4) there are differing expectations concerning the stage of the relationship when sexual intercourse is appropriate. Until the couple honestly discuss their sexual wants and desires, or until a sufficient history is in place by which future behavior is predictable from past behavior, miscommunication and misperception are likely to occur. (1989, 258)

Other researchers point out that dating partners who experience aggression either in the dating situation or in other situations, such as at home, are more apt to be aggressive themselves. Sexual aggressiveness in one's peer group tends to make all of the group members more aggressive. To some degree people learn to be aggressive as well as to be victims by observing parents and peers. However, their own personal experiences as victims or aggressors is a strong influence (Gwatney–Gibbs et al. 1987).

We have not said much about victims, but it may be that women with higher self-esteem and assertion levels are less often victimized than women who do not display these characteristics. Amick and Calhoun (1987) studied successful resistance to rape and found few, if any, personality or behavioral differences. The differences that emerged were situational in nature. Also, most persons tend to view all violence between dating couples as damaging to a further relationship. Yet the relationships often continue even after episodes of date rape. For example, researchers have consistently found that physical aggression is more common in cohabiting couples than in married couples (Stets 1991, 669).

Courtship violence and date rape are far more complex relational interactions than we thought in the past. Such behavior is probably related to traditional romantic ideas of man-woman relationships, especially while dating, where the man has the power and the woman tends to be somewhat dependent (Lloyd 1991). Individuals can protect themselves to some degree from such episodes by clearly explaining their expectations and limits to potential dating partners.

FINDING THE ONE AND ONLY: MATE SELECTION

Chapter 3 pointed out that "love" is the major reason Americans give for marrying. Yet is love really the magic wand that directs our mate selection? Certainly, we fall in love or think we do at the time. Yet why we are attracted to a particular individual is a complicated process that is not completely understood. Critics who argue against using love as a basis for marriage believe that Americans are seduced by the romantic ideal into ignoring practical considerations that help ensure a successful marriage. Such factors as compatible social and economic levels, education, age, religion, ethnicity, prior marital experience, race, and so forth may be ignored. Yet this is not really true. Our social system does take these factors into consideration, and a close inspection of love finds that it does indeed incorporate some of these factors. You don't fall in love with just anybody; on the other hand, there are a great many "one and onlys."

First of all, there is a field of "desirables," or people to whom you are attracted. Within this field is a smaller group of "availables," those who are free to return your interest. You can meet them, they are not in love with someone else, they are unmarried, and so forth.

Availability is closely related to how we live. Communities are organized into neighborhoods according to social class, and in America this generally means by economic level. So the people who live nearby will be socially and economically like us. We very often marry someone living quite close geographically. This marital choice variable is called **propinquity.** Actually, it is broader than just residential propinquity. Institutional propinquity exists as well; people meet in the workplace, in social organizations, and at school and church.

Propinquity
Nearness in place or time

We also tend to choose individuals similar to ourselves; this tendency is termed **homogamy.** Thus, middle-class whites tend to marry middle-class whites; lower-class whites tend to marry lower-class whites; Catholics tend to marry Catholics; blacks tend to marry blacks; and so on. Similarly, we tend to marry within our own group, which is called **endogamy.**

Homogamy
Choosing to be with those similar to ourselves

Endogamy
The inclination or the necessity to marry within a particular group

There are exceptions to the rule of endogamy, but generally society aims us toward loving and marrying someone similar to ourselves. If you don't marry the girl or boy next door, you are likely to marry someone you meet at school. The American system of neighborhood schools and selective college attendance makes education one of the strongest endogamic factors directing mate selection. Or you may find your future mate through your family's social circle, your job, or your church. All of the groups you join tend to some degree to limit their membership to people who are similar in socioeconomic status. Strange are the ways of love, but even so a banker's college-educated daughter seldom falls in love with the uneducated son of a factory worker.

There are many theories of marital choice, but none seems totally satisfactory or predicts with much success who will make a good marital partner. Bernard Murstein (1986) lists nine major marital choice theories. One theory (Kerckhoff and Davis 1962) suggests that we select a mate by passing her or him through a series of successive filters (see Figure 4-3). Orientation to marriage is the first filter. A person must start dating with an eye to marriage rather than just for fun and recreation. Proximity (propinquity) and "suitability" of background act as the next filter. Two people are likely to meet if they live or work close to one another, and they will be interested in further exploration if they seem suitable to each other. Suitability is determined by one's values, most of which are learned from one's parents and peers. The third filter is a more thorough exploration of attitudes and values. For example, the two persons question each other about mutual friends, activities, and interests: "Where do you go to school?" "I know some people who go there, do you know Jim Black and Sally Brown?" "What classes are you taking?" "Really, I'm taking French next semester" "Do you ski? I'm going next week." If the couple's attitudes and interests prove compatible, they progress toward more subtle personality exploration, finding out whether their needs for affection, independence, security, and so on are also compatible. Or the relationship may end at any of these filters.

This kind of model is useful in understanding that mate selection is an evolving process. However, such an exact, fixed set of filters or processes has yet to be proved.

Theoretically, two principles guide mate selection: endogamy and exogamy. As we have seen, endogamy is marriage within a certain group. Race, religion,

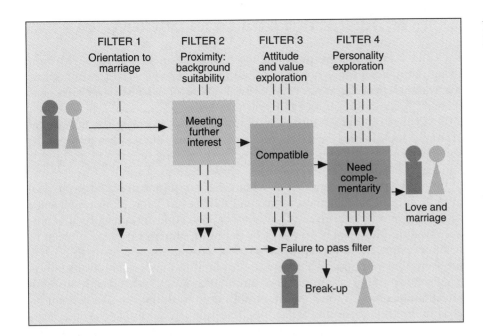

FIGURE 4-4
Mate Selection as Successive Filters

ethnicity (nationality), and social class are the four major types of groups. The mores and taboos against crossing groups vary in strength. For example, only about 2 percent of Americans cross the racial black-white line when marrying, but 20 to 25 percent of them cross religious lines.

Until recently, most states had prohibitions that enforced racial endogamy. These prohibitions were generally termed **miscegenation** laws because they prohibited interracial marriages. Most of these laws were originally aimed at preventing white-Indian marriages, but they were also used to prevent white-black and white-Asian marriages. As recently as the end of World War II, thirty states had such laws. Gradually, some states declared them void; and in 1967 the U.S. Supreme Court finally declared all such laws unconstitutional. By chance the defendant's surname was Loving, so the name of the case, *Loving v. Virginia*, fits in well with the American romantic ideal.

Exogamy, on the other hand, is a requirement that people marry outside their group. In our culture requirements to marry outside your group are limited to incest and sex; that is, you may not marry a near relative or someone of your own sex. All states forbid marriage between parents and children, siblings (brothers and sisters), grandparents and grandchildren, and children and their uncles and aunts. Most states forbid marriage to first cousins and half-siblings, although some states do not. About half the states forbid marriage between stepparents and stepchildren, and about the same number prohibit marriage between a man and his father's former wife or his son's former wife.

The other rule of exogamy, which until quite recently was taken for granted, is the requirement that we marry someone of the opposite sex. This helps ensure reproduction and continuance of the species. In the past few years, attempts by homosexuals to obtain more rights have led to some "marriage" ceremonies for homosexuals. So far, though, such marriages have no legal standing.

Miscegenation
Marriage or interbreeding between members of different races

Exogamy
The inclination or the necessity to marry outside a particular group

Finding the One and Only: Mate Selection

Let us look more specifically at the mate selection process for you, the individual. First impressions are usually belittled as superficial and unimportant. Yet without them the process cannot begin. A favorable first impression must be made or no further interaction will take place.

Physical attractiveness, although subjective, tends to create the first appeal (Hatfield and Walster 1978; Hatfield and Sprecher 1986). This seems to be true for people of all ages, from children to the elderly, but it appears to be a stronger factor for males (Nevid 1984; Murstein 1986, 35–39).

It is interesting, too, that there is a **halo effect** operating in regard to physical attractiveness. The halo effect is the tendency for first impressions to influence succeeding evaluations. Physically attractive persons are imbued with other positive qualities that may not actually be present. Attractive persons are seen to be more competent as husbands and wives and to have happier marriages. They are seen as more responsible for good deeds and less responsible for bad ones. Their evaluations of others appear to have more impact. Other people are more socially responsive to them and more willing to work hard to please them.

Thus, to be physically attractive is usually an advantage at the first-impression stage of a relationship (Nevid 1985; Mall 1986). This is not always true, however. Some persons tend to avoid highly attractive individuals in order to enhance their own chances of acceptance and to reduce the chances that their mate will be sought after by others.

The importance of attractiveness is no doubt the reason that so many Americans express dissatisfaction with their body images. Table 4-1 shows the results of a body image survey conducted by the magazine *Psychology Today*.

Your impressions of *cognitive compatibility* (how the other thinks, what his or her interests are, and so forth) are also important in first impressions. In general, similarity seems to go with attraction because (1) another's similarity is directly reinforcing, (2) another's similar responses support the perceiver's sense of self-esteem and comfort, and (3) such responses indicate the other's future compatibility (Huston and Levinger 1978). When values differ, the dissimilarity often signifies not just difference but wrongness. Knowing that another believes as we do tends to reinforce the correctness of our own viewpoint, which makes us feel good (Murstein 1986, 25).

We usually try to further a relationship by various attraction-seeking strategies. To attract a potential partner's attention, we may attempt to buoy the other person's esteem by conveying that our regard is high. We probably try to do things for the person. We tend to agree with her or him and attempt to make ourselves look good. In our efforts to further a relationship, we may overgeneralize and exaggerate, which may lead to later misunderstandings and disappointments if the relationship progresses.

Attraction tends to lead to self-disclosure. Intermediate degrees of disclosure may in turn lead to greater attraction, but this depends on the desirability of the information disclosed. Self-disclosure tends to lead to reciprocity. This phase occurs early in a relationship when a lot of exciting mutual sharing takes place. "Is that the way you feel about it? That's great, because I feel the same way." As more is disclosed, excitement increases because the potential for a meaningful relationship seems to be increasing rapidly. However, the speed with which one discloses personal aspects is also important. Disclosure that seems overly quick may arouse suspicion rather than trust.

Halo effect
The tendency for a first impression to influence subsequent judgments

TABLE 4-1
PERCENTAGE OF PERSONS DISSATISFIED WITH BODY AREAS OR DIMENSIONS

	MEN	WOMEN
Height	20%	17%
Weight	41	55
Muscle tone	32	45
Face	20	20
Upper torso	28	32
Middle torso	50	57
Lower torso	21	50
"Looks as they are"	34	38

Source: Adapted from Cash, Winstead, and Janda 1986, 33.

Chapter 4
Dating, Sexual Mores, and Mate Selection

118

Although much research has been done on interpersonal attraction, our efforts to predict the evolution of a given individual relationship based on the personal characteristics of the partners have been primitive and unsuccessful. In fact, it is still almost impossible to determine in advance whom one should marry to ensure a successful relationship.

As an example of this complexity, let us look at two marriages, one built on similar needs and one on complementary needs. In a marriage of similar needs, the partners begin with similar interests, energy levels, religion, socio-economic background, age, and so on. They share many characteristics and hence seem well selected for each other. Ideally, their relationship will lead to mutual satisfaction, but this is not always the case. If, for example, the partners are competitive, the results can be disastrous. Consider the case of Bruce and Gail:

Bruce and Gail are alike in most respects, including being computer programmers, but Gail has advanced more rapidly. Bruce is competitive, feels like a loser, and begins to resent his wife. He subtly puts her down and gradually becomes more critical of women in general. The more success Gail has, the poorer their relationship becomes because Bruce cannot accept, let alone find joy in, her success. To him it only points up his weaknesses.

By contrast, in a marriage of complementary needs, each partner supplies something that the other lacks. For example, an extrovert may help an introvert become more social; an organized partner may help bring structure to the life of a disorganized partner; or a relaxed partner may create an environment that helps ease the stress of a tense partner. Such complementarity can be very beneficial, but it cannot be counted on to happen because such differences often polarize the partners rather than drawing them together. For example, consider Carol and Greg:

Carol is so organized that Greg counts on her to pay the bills, make social arrangements, find the nail clippers, and so on. The more Greg depends on her for these things, the more organized Carol feels she needs to be, and she begins to try to organize Greg. For his part Greg resents this pressure and becomes passively resistant (procrastinates and becomes forgetful and careless). Polarization has occurred.

Unfortunately, there are no entirely satisfactory techniques for selecting marriage partners for lasting relationships. As we will see, even cohabitation trial marriages have proved relatively ineffective.

THE DESIRE TO SPEND TIME TOGETHER: A CHARACTERISTIC OF STRONG RELATIONSHIPS AND FAMILIES

WHAT DO YOU THINK?

1. What is your favorite childhood memory?
2. What do you think your siblings' favorite memories would be?
3. Are they the same or different from yours? Why do you suppose this is so?
4. What do you suppose your parents' favorite memories are?
5. If you have children what do you suppose your children's favorite memories are?

Most Americans build their intimate relationships on a foundation of "love." And persons who are deeply in love have an almost insatiable desire to spend time with the object of their affections. In fact, it can be agonizing for the partners to be apart for any length of time. The desire to spend time together is thus found in most intimate couples' relationship, at least in the early part of the relationship when the couple is dating and courting. The desire to spend time together is also one of the major characteristics of the strong, resilient family.

Stinnett (1985) and his colleagues do an exercise with their subject families entitled, "The Journey of Happy Memories." They direct their subjects to close their eyes and spend five minutes wandering through childhood memories and then ask them to tell the happiest. The researchers found that the memories recalled almost always involved family activities.

> My favorite memory is climbing the big rocks that were in the campground where my grandfather would take me and my cousins camping for two weeks each summer.

> It's hard to believe, but I'll never forget my grandmother coming into the bathroom to scrub me whenever I was in the tub. I'm sure she'd be doing it to this day if she was still alive.

> The family would go to the sand dunes by the beach and dad would always be disappearing, making us play hide and seek with him. We'd be walking along and suddenly he wouldn't be there and we'd run off to find him. We'd try to keep an eye on him but he was very good at disappearing.

> At Christmas time, dad and mom would always get out the old 8mm family movies and although we'd all say, "Oh, not the movies again," we always loved to see mom and dad as little kids and especially ourselves growing up.

Couples "in love" want to spend as much time together as possible. It is also clear that family time together is of great value at least in retrospect. Yet as time passes and the relationship becomes more enduring, as romantic love turns into companionate love, spending family time together seems to become increasingly difficult. Perhaps the major revolution in family structure in recent years has been the advent of the dual-earner family, the family in which both partners are employed outside the home. It is obvious that in such a home, family time together will be at a premium. Indeed, Curran (1983, 135) goes so far as to state, "Lack of time might be the most pervasive enemy the healthy family has." *Time* magazine reported (1989, 58) that its Louis Harris poll on time available to Americans concluded, "Time may have become the most precious commodity in the land."

> The amount of leisure time enjoyed by the average American has shrunk 37% since 1973. Over the same period, the average workweek, including commuting, has jumped from under 41 hours to nearly 47 hours.

As family time has become scarcer, many have argued that it is not the quantity but the quality of time together that counts. There is certainly truth in the argument. I may be with my partner physically but does that do much good if I am not there mentally? The stereotypical picture of the husband hidden behind his newspaper at breakfast while his wife tries desperately to get his attention comes immediately to mind. On the other hand, the argument often seems to ignore the fact that quality and quantity of time together are interrelated. There must be enough time for quality to surface. It seems, too, that the argument is sometimes used to soothe the guilty conscience of a spouse or parent who is spending very little time with the family.

When we examine the daily pattern of many dual-earner families, the difficulties become clear.

Jane and Murray have two children, aged five and seven. Jane remained home with the children until the second child started preschool at age two and has worked since that time. Jane arises about 6:30 A.M. to get everyone organized. The first child leaves for school at 8:00 A.M., and Jane drops the second child off at preschool in time to get to work at 9:00 A.M. Murray leaves about 7:45 to commute to his 9:00 A.M. job. The hour and fifteen minutes that they are all together in the morning passes quickly and with little communication since everyone is preoccupied with getting ready for his or her day. A neighbor watches the oldest child in the afternoon after school is out, and Jane picks up the second child about 5:15 P.M. Murray arrives home about 6:00 P.M. After a long day, the family members are tired, yet they must prepare the evening meal and do other family chores. The youngest child is in bed by 8:00 P.M. and the oldest child follows around 9:00 P.M. Thus, the whole family is together for a maximum of two to three hours at the end of the day, and there is clearly little quality time to communicate in the midst of household chores. Besides everyone is already fatigued from a long day. Only after 9:00 P.M. do Murray and Jane have time for themselves. It is little wonder that the family feels that time is their most sought after commodity.

Whether there can be quality family time with such a daily routine is open to serious question.

The description of Jane and Murray's routine fails to take into account the many other kinds of activities that may drain a family's time together. Most families spend time on such things as Little League baseball, PTA meetings, children's music lessons, church socials, and money-raising events such as school newspaper collections. Certainly for some families, the children's school years make great time demands on the parents.

Curran (1983, 143) points out that a family needs time to play together just as the courting couple played together before they married. Periodically, the family needs to get away from work and responsibility and simply play and enjoy life. The couple needs to do this alone away from the children as well as with the children. The family must be careful not to "work" at playing. Some families plan and organize their play time to such a degree that it turns into work rather than play. Happy couples do not hide behind "Someday we will . . . ," "When we get time . . . ," or "When we have the money . . . ." They deliberately make the time to play.

Strong families seem to have the ability to work, play, and vacation together without smothering one another. During the 1950s there was a great deal of criticism of the idea of "togetherness" in marriage. Too much togetherness between partners meant individuality was lost. Yet today the opposite problem is more prevalent. There seems to be too little togetherness to maintain family strength. The emphasis on individuality too often overrides commitment to the family as a team. Thus, the time a family spends together should be balanced between the needs of the family and the needs of individual family members.

Spending time together allows a family to develop an identity, a group unity, and a sense of family history. This feeling of belonging helps family members find an identity. The need for adolescents to turn to their peer group for support and identity is reduced if they have a strong sense of family.

Although strong families spend time together doing many different kinds of activities, almost all strong families indicate that at least one meal a day is reserved as a time of family togetherness (McCubbin et al. 1986, 123–30). It is usually the evening meal, and everyone in the family living at home is expected to attend on a regular basis.

Perhaps the importance of spending enough quality time together is best summed up by a recent student comment:

> My brother and two sisters are my best friends and my mom and dad are not only my mom and dad but my pals as well. I always look forward to doing things with the family because we have so much fun together. We have fun but I also know that if I need help they will all pitch in and give me the help I need.

It is clear that the desire to spend time together felt by all couples newly in love must somehow be maintained as the relationship becomes permanent. If it can be maintained and expanded into marriage and into the growing family, if and when children arrive, then a key element to maintaining family growth and stability is in place.

The A. C. Nielsen Company estimates that the average American television set is on approximately forty-four hours per week. With scarcity of time being one of the American family's major problems, it is clear that television often usurps what little togetherness time a family may have.

COHABITATION: UNMARRIED-COUPLE HOUSEHOLDS

A courting couple's desire to spend more time together may lead them to cohabit. The increase in the single lifestyle is, in part, directly related to the

INSET 4-1
"SHHH, I'M WATCHING TV"

Television is a powerful force in the lives of most American families. Many families report that they spend time together, but further questioning reveals that much of that time is spent silently watching television. Although a television program might foster discussion and debate among family members, this is not often the case. In fact, many families now have multiple television sets so that each family member may watch television separately from the rest of the family.

Curran (1983, 40) lists family control over television as her second major point in successful family communication patterns. The term "television widow" is no joke to many families. A woman remarked on a talk show, "I can't get worried about whether there's life after death. I'd be satisfied with life after dinner in our home."

It is interesting to note that many families place the television in the "family room." Family room is a misnomer since talking and communicating among family members are usually discouraged when the television is being watched. A "family room" containing a television set might more aptly be named the "antifamily room."

Many families simply have the television on whenever anyone is in the house. It serves as background noise. The only problem is that because television activates two senses, hearing and sight, paying no attention to it is far more difficult than ignoring noise alone. We've all had the experience of visiting someone who leaves the television on during our visit. Communication is next to impossible even though one tries to converse. Eyes keep wandering to the television. In a sense, leaving the television on when someone comes in to converse is the not-so-subtle message, "Television is more important than your communication."

---

increasing of heterosexual cohabition. The number of unmarried-couple households has grown from 523,000 in 1970 to 2.9 million in 1990, an increase of over 400 percent (U.S. Bureau of the Census May 1991, 14). Although the increase is dramatic, such households make up only 3 percent of all households in the United States. The rate of increase slowed dramatically during the 1980s when there was only an 80 percent increase.

Looking at the figures in a cumulative sense, approximately 30 percent of never-married women twenty to twenty-nine years old report having cohabited at some time (Tanfer 1987). Not all such households involve sexually intimate relationships, however. Although seldom reported in the mass media, these figures reflect a variety of living arrangements, including the elderly woman who rents a room to a male college student or the elderly man who employs a live-in female nurse or housekeeper. Another change in this statistic is noteworthy. In 1970 a sizable majority (73 percent) of the cohabiting couples without children were over forty-five years of age. By 1990 the number had dropped to 12 percent. People under twenty-five now account for 23 percent of unmarried households, while those aged twenty-five to thirty-four account for 41 percent (U.S. Bureau of the Census May 1991, 14). This probably reflects the later age of marriage plus more acceptance by society of cohabitation by young and never-married people (never-married people account for 56 percent of cohabiting couples). One last statistic is pertinent. Children are present in 30 to 40 percent of cohabiting couple households, and this percentage has remained fairly constant over the past ten years (U.S. Bureau of the Census May 1991; Bumpass et al. 1991, 913).

Cohabitation
A man and woman living together in an intimate relationship without being legally married

Cohabitation: Unmarried-Couple Households

123

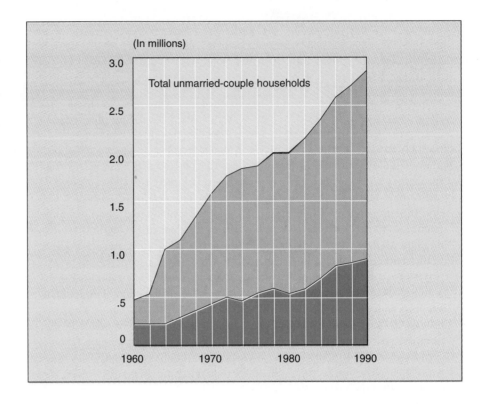

Paul Glick and Graham Spanier (1980) characterize this data by stating: "Rarely does social change occur with such rapidity. Indeed there have been few developments relating to marriage and family life which have been as dramatic as the rapid increase in unmarried cohabitation." This statement is perhaps misleading in that it overlooks the fact that historically (the nineteenth century) many young couples lived together without being married. There was a difference, however, in that most of those couples expected to marry their live-in partners, and even if they did not marry, most states legally recognized them as married after a set number of years (seven in most states). This legal change of status from cohabiting to married was called **common law marriage.**

Enough couples are now openly living together in intimate relationships that some theorists consider living together to be an ongoing part of the mate selection process for a growing minority of couples. If cohabiting couples are thought of as families, then the postponement of marriage we are witnessing doesn't really mean a longer period of premarital singleness. Young cohabiting couples actually make up for the lowered marriage rate (Bumpass et al. 1991).

Graham Spanier (1986) suggests a number of reasons for the increase in nonmarital cohabitation:

■ The increasing average age at first marriage tends to correlate with cohabitation increases.

■ Society's increased tolerance toward premarital sexual relations also makes intimate cohabitation more acceptable.

■ Higher education, especially for women, and the increasing entry of women into the work force have both lessened women's dependence on marriage as a way of economic survival.

Common law marriage
Legal recognition of a cohabiting couple as being married after a given number of years (usually seven) of cohabitation

■ Increasing urbanization leads to increased anonymity and less restrictions on individuals.

■ The high levels of divorce may make young people more wary of rushing into a marital relationship.

THE NATURE OF COHABITING RELATIONSHIPS

People choose to live together for many reasons, some of which may not be true for every cohabiting couple:

1. It is clear that many consider these experiences to be no more than *short-lived sexual flings* and only gradually drift into a cohabitation relationship.

2. Some couples live together for *practical reasons*. They are essentially no more than opposite-sex roommates. In this case the couple live together without necessarily having a deep or intimate relationship. Having a member of the opposite sex as a roommate affords certain advantages. A woman who lives in a high-crime area may feel safer living with a man. They can learn to share skills; for example, she might teach him computer skills while he teaches her automobile maintenance. Generally, the couple simply lives together as two same-sex roommates would; they date others, generally keep their love lives out of their living quarters, and react to one another as friends. Each gains something from living together in partnership rather than separately. The reason most often given for such an arrangement is "to save money." This is especially true of elderly and/or retired cohabitants.

3. Some couples see cohabiting as a true *trial marriage*. As one young woman explained, "We are thinking of marriage in the future, and we want to find out if we really are what each other wants. If everything works out, we will get married." Some of these couples go so far as to set a specific time period.

4. Other couples view cohabiting as a *permanent alternative to marriage*. They often say they have philosophically rejected the marital institution as being unfavorable to healthy and growing relationships. They are especially critical of the legal constraints imposed on partners' rights in marriage. Many couples live together to avoid what they perceive to be constraining, love-draining formalities associated with legal marriage. They say, "If I stay with my mate out of my own free desire rather than because I legally must remain, our relationship will be more honest and caring. The stability of our relationship is its very instability."

5. Some couples, especially where one or both have been divorced, live together out of *fear of making the same mistake again*. In 1990 the divorced made up 34 percent of cohabiting households (U.S. Bureau of the Census May 1991, 14). These couples also have the vast majority of children in such relationships.

IS THE WOMAN EXPLOITED IN COHABITATION?

Obviously, the answer to this question will depend on the individual relationship. However, some interesting statistics bear on this question in a general way. A number of studies indicate that males seem less committed than their female partners to living-together relationships (Risman et al. 1981; Macklin 1983). Tanfer (1987, 490) reports that a significantly larger proportion of

Cohabitation: Unmarried-Couple Households

cohabiting women than noncohabiting women want to get married, yet only 19 percent of men surveyed in one study report marrying the woman with whom they cohabited (Browder 1988).

In one study, couples living together were compared with couples going together. No significant differences were found between the groups in level of trust and reported happiness, both of which were high. A difference was found, however, in the reported degree of commitment to marriage. The couples who were going together, both males and females, were committed to future marriage. But the men in the living-together couples were by far less committed than the women. The researchers' tentative conclusions were, in part:

> To a striking degree, living-together couples did not reciprocate the kinds of feelings (of need, respect, involvement, or commitment to marriage) that one would expect to be the basis of a good heterosexual relationship. The question of whether such a lack of reciprocity is typical of such relationships and thus reflects the difficulties of bringing off a successful nonnormative relationship or whether it is merely typical of those who volunteered for our research cannot be answered. (Lyness et al. 1972, 309).

Many cohabitation relationships are short-lived and seem to revolve around the sexual part of the relationship. In fact, men tend to list "sex" as their major reason for cohabiting. If the man tends to be less committed to the relationship than the woman, it seems to be a reasonable assumption that he is often the one who ends the relationship, if not directly then indirectly by refusing equal commitment.

Researchers (Glick and Spanier 1980; Spanier 1986) also point out that cohabiting men are much less likely to be employed than married men, but cohabiting women are much more likely to be employed than married women. This might suggest that men are using women economically to help themselves get through school or pursue their own interests, which at the time may not produce much, if any, monetary return. Blumstein and Schwartz (1983, 126) report: "We notice that as a rule male cohabitors reject the economic responsibilities they would have as husbands. They do not want to become the sole supporter or breadwinner."

Many cohabiting couples share expenses equally when, in fact, the woman's earnings are usually less than the employed man's. A man earning $30,000 a year who shares expenses equally with his live-in girlfriend earning $15,000 a year is at a distinct monetary advantage.

Although cohabitation appears to be avant-garde, suggesting that those who are involved are liberated, the division of labor in the household tends to be traditional (Macklin 1983; Risman 1981; Bowe 1986); that is, the woman does the cooking, cleaning, and other household work. If she is also in the work force, it is clear that she is often overburdened in the cohabitation relationship.

The *New Woman* magazine sex survey (Browder 1988) found that live-in males are less considerate than husbands. Forty percent of the cohabiting women surveyed had had a kind of sex experience that they didn't want or enjoy with their partner. This percentage was larger than the proportion of divorced and separated women who felt they had been mistreated or intimidated sexually.

Perhaps a couple considering cohabitation should carefully examine the nature of the intended relationship before entering it. One way that couples can do this is to answer the questions posed in Inset 4-2. Note that other than question 10, these are also good questions for couples contemplating marriage.

THE RELATIONSHIP BETWEEN COHABITATION AND MARRIAGE

Many young people argue persuasively that living together provides a good test for future marriage. Living together, they say, is like a trial marriage without the legal framework required to end the relationship if it doesn't work. Cohabitors embrace a variety of other arguments in support of cohabitation:

- It provides an opportunity to try to establish a meaningful relationship.
- It can be a source of financial, social, and emotional security.
- It provides a steady sexual partner and companionship; thus providing some of the central pleasures of marriage without so much commitment and responsibility.
- It provides a chance for personal growth, a chance to increase self-understanding while relating to another person on an intimate basis.
- It enables cohabitors to develop a more realistic notion of their partners and generally less-romanticized ideas about the relationship.
- It gives cohabitors a chance to get beyond typical courtship game playing.
- Long periods of intimate contact provide an opportunity for self-disclosure and concomitant modification and/or realization of personal goals. (Jacques and Chason 1979, 37)

Although these arguments are logical and reasonable, research to date on the quality of marriage after cohabitation experiences has found little, if any, relationship between cohabitation and the degree of satisfaction, conflict, emotional closeness, or egalitarianism in later marriage (Macklin 1983). Watson and DeMeo (1987) found that the marital adjustment of couples who had cohabited was lower than that of couples who had not cohabited. Thomson and Colella (1992) also report lower quality marriages and greater likelihood of divorce for couples who cohabit before they marry. These effects were generally stronger for couples who had cohabited for longer periods before marriage. Watson (1983) found that it was mainly the women in his sample who reported greater marital dissatisfaction. Bennett et al. (1988) found the same trend among Swedish women. Premarital cohabitation appeared to raise the risk of subsequent marital dissolution. DeMaris and Leslie (1984) found that previously cohabiting couples reported lower marital satisfaction. Thinking that such a result might be due merely to the duration of time the cohabiting couple had been together (marital satisfaction tends to fall with length of relationship), the researchers correlated length of cohabitation with marital satisfaction but found no relationship. They did find that cohabitors' feelings of permanent commitment to their marriage were significantly lower. DeMaris and Leslie finally concluded that:

Rather than acting as a filter that effectively screens out the less-compatible couples, cohabitation appears to select couples from the outset who are somewhat less likely to report high satisfaction once they are married. This may be due to the fact that these individuals expect more out of marriage from the beginning.

Cohabitation: Unmarried-Couple Households

1. How did you make the decision to live together?

■ *Good signs:* We gave considerable thought to the decision, including the advantages and disadvantages of living together.
■ *Concern signs:* We kind of fell into it. We didn't really talk about the advantages and disadvantages of living together.

2. What do you think you will get out of the relationship?

■ *Good signs:* We are concerned about learning more about ourselves and each other through intimate daily living. We want to test our commitment to the relationship.
■ *Concern signs:* It's nice to be free of our parents. It is convenient in many ways including having easy sexual access. It makes me feel like an adult.

3. What roles will you and your partner fulfill in the relationship?

■ *Good signs:* We've thought a lot about our roles—how we'll divide the housework, contribute food money, and so on—and agree on the roles each of us will fulfill.
■ *Concern signs:* We'll just naturally fall into the proper roles. I love my partner and will do what is necessary to make our life together pleasant. We do disagree rather often about our expectations of one another.

4. What were your earlier dating experiences, and what have you learned from them?

■ *Good signs:* We have both dated and feel we have had a variety of rich experiences with others. We have positive perceptions of ourselves and of the opposite sex and

are aware of what we have learned from previous relationships.
■ *Concern signs:* I've never dated much. I feel more secure just being with one person. I have some negative perceptions of myself or of the opposite sex. I don't feel that I learned much from dating others.

5. What are your partner's primary physical and emotional needs, and to what degree do you think you can fulfill them?

■ *Good signs:* I think I have a clear understanding of my partner's needs, and I want to try to meet these needs.
■ *Concern signs:* I really don't know my partner's needs, but I'll find out about them when we move in together.

6. What are your own physical and emotional needs, and to what

---

Alternatively, these may be individuals who adapt less readily to the role expectations of conventional marriage. In either case it is most probably the difference between the kinds of people who do and do not choose to cohabit before marriage, rather than the experience itself, that accounts for our findings.

One inexplicable phenomenon found among cohabitants who do marry is those couples who divorce shortly after marrying even though they may have a long cohabitation history. To live together for several years, finally marry, and shortly thereafter break up seems to make no sense. Although no data are currently available on this behavior, there are some hypotheses that might explain it.

1. Cohabitation teaches the couple to withhold total commitment. One of the reasons for cohabitation is to postpone or avoid the total commitment of marriage. Thus, when a cohabiting couple do marry, they may find themselves unable to live with the commitment imposed by marriage.

degree do you think your partner will be able to satisfy them?

■ *Good signs:* Most of my needs are currently being met and are likely to continue to be met in a cohabiting relationship.
■ *Concern signs:* Although my needs are not being met in the present relationship, I'm sure they will be met when we live together.

7. To what degree can you and your partner honestly share feelings?

■ *Good signs:* We can be open and honest with one another without difficulty.
■ *Concern signs:* We do not believe expressing feelings is important. We have difficulty expressing feelings to each other.

8. What are your partner's strengths and weaknesses? To what

extent would you like to change your partner?

■ *Good signs:* I am usually able to accept my partner's feelings. I can accept my partner's strengths and weaknesses.
■ *Concern signs:* I have difficulty understanding my partner. I can accept the strengths but not the weaknesses, but I'll probably be able to change him or her when we live together.

9. How do you each handle problems when they arise?

■ *Good signs:* We express feelings openly and are able to understand and accept our partner's point of view. We are able to solve problems mutually.
■ *Concern signs:* We have difficulty expressing feelings openly or accepting our partner's point of view.

It is better to avoid problems since we often fail to solve them mutually.

10. How will your family and friends react to your living together.

■ *Good signs:* We are aware of the potential repercussions of family and friends when they learn of our cohabiting relationship. We have considered how we will handle them. Our family and friends are supportive of the cohabiting relationship.
■ *Concern signs:* We don't know how our family and friends will react to our living together. They probably won't support our cohabiting relationship, so we won't tell anyone about it.

Source: Adapted from Ridley, Peterman, and Avery 1978, 135–36.

2. The partners may still retain the stereotypical romantic ideals that most Americans have about marriage; so they marry after perhaps some years of cohabitation and then wait for the magic to happen. But since they have already done everything that married couples do, the anticipated excitement of a new status fails to materialize. As one disappointed newly married couple who had lived together for the previous three years said: "Many of our friends wondered what the big to-do about a wedding was even though we were excited. We then went to a romantic spot for our honeymoon but nothing really seemed any different. In fact, it was all kind of boring."

Larry Bumpass (1989) analyzed data from a federal survey of about 13,000 individuals and found that Americans who live together before marriage separate and divorce in significantly greater numbers than couples who go directly to the altar. Within ten years of their wedding, 38 percent of those who had lived together before marriage had split up, compared with 27 percent of those who simply married.

Cohabitation: Unmarried-Couple Households

Studies of cohabitors who remarried after divorce or widowhood have found slightly different results. DeMaris (1984) found that cohabitation did not seem to have a negative effect on marital satisfaction of remarried couples. Another study of remarried families found that cohabitation before marriage was positively related to marital quality (Hanna and Knaub 1981). Remarried couples who lived together before marriage reported significantly higher degrees of happiness, closeness, concern for the partner's welfare, and positive communication, and they perceived more environmental support than remarried couples who had not cohabited. In general, the remarried are older and more experienced than the never married. They have also gone through a marriage, not just a cohabitation experience.

Perhaps cohabitors may unknowingly be creating a self-fulfilling prophecy. They enter a relationship partly to see if it will last, and, by keeping the possibility of discontinuing the relationship in mind, they actually help cause the breakup. It is possible that some relationships might turn out differently if the partners entered them with an unshakable determination to succeed, but the cohabiting experience may teach them to withhold this kind of total commitment. Leslie (1979) suggests that living together can be a way for young people to avoid responsibility. It is easier to play house than to be married. Such an attitude might be carried into a subsequent marriage and contribute to marital dissatisfaction.

Couples who come to marriage without cohabiting experience a real change in their life situation when they marry. They are suddenly independent of their parents, established in a relationship where sex is condoned, and responsible for themselves economically, they are setting up their own living quarters, planning their activities without interference, and so forth. It is a new and exciting world. Nothing really changes for the cohabiting couple, but unconsciously they share the social idea that marriage is a new and exciting happening in life. When the excitement doesn't materialize, they express disappointment: something is missing.

Despite such criticisms, cohabitation, especially among college students, seems to be finding more acceptance in our society. Schoen (1992) found that in recently cohabiting couples who marry the risk of marital disruption was less than that found in past studies. He concluded that as cohabitation becomes more acceptable, perhaps the higher risks of marital disruption that have been found in the past will diminish. However, the decision to cohabit should not be taken lightly. The ramifications of such a decision should be considered carefully. Legal ramifications, which we will discuss in a coming section, must also be considered, now more than ever.

■ BREAKING UP ■

Cohabiting relationships have a median duration of 1.3 years. The relationships end in marriage for 23 percent of men and 37 percent of women. Within two years 40 percent of men and 23 percent of women in cohabiting relationships break up (Surra 1990).

Society, including the cohabiting couples themselves, has largely ignored one of the philosophical foundations of cohabitation: that it is easy to break up if the relationship fails. Yet for partners who are highly committed to a relationship, a breakup can be as emotionally devastating as a divorce. Moreover, society has support systems for divorced people, but no such support systems exist for persons leaving a cohabitation relationship.

Since ease of leaving a cohabiting relationship is one of the reasons for being in such a relationship, friends of the couple who break up often feel little sympathy. "Why are you making such a big deal out of breaking up?" Yet the breakup rate among cohabiting couples is high. Thus, the number of people who must cope with the trauma of breakup by themselves or perhaps with only a friend's shoulder to cry on will increase as the number of cohabiting couples increases.

■ LIVING TOGETHER AND THE LAW ■

Many readers may be surprised to learn that cohabitation is illegal in some states. Indeed, sexual intercourse between unmarried persons (fornication) is still a crime in some states. Such laws are seldom enforced, but when they are, the penalties can be stringent. Many states set a maximum fine of $500 and six months in jail. Such laws may be unconstitutional, however, because they violate the right to privacy.

In states where such laws are in effect, there are numerous ramifications for the cohabiting couple. For example, living together can be grounds for losing one's job. Because membership in professional associations and licensing may be conditional on demonstration of moral fitness, such privileges could be denied to someone cohabiting outside of marriage. In some states a divorced person who is receiving alimony may lose it for cohabiting. A divorced woman and her children who have been given the right by the court to remain in the family home until the children are eighteen years old (at which time the home is to be sold and the proceeds divided) may lose that right if the woman cohabits (Weitzman 1985, 44, 88).

Laws making cohabitation a crime are so seldom enforced, however, that they are not nearly as meaningful to the cohabiting couple as several recent court decisions concerning property distribution and the obligation of support. Perhaps the best-known case involved actor Lee Marvin and his live-in friend, Michelle Triola. Out of this case came the term *palimony*, coined to describe settlements made to a nonmarried live-in partner. The term has no legal significance but is descriptive of what Michelle Triola was first awarded.

Triola and Marvin lived together for seven years. During this period Triola acted as a companion and homemaker. There was no pooling of earnings, no property was purchased in joint names, and no joint income tax returns were filed. They often spoke proudly of their freedom as unmarried cohabitors and went to some length to keep property separate. Eventually, Marvin asked Triola to leave the household. He continued to support her for two years after the separation and then refused further support. Triola then brought suit against Marvin and asked the court to determine her contract and property rights and to award her half of the property acquired during the period of their relationship.

The trial court dismissed the action as inappropriate; Triola then appealed to the California Supreme Court, which ruled:

> The fact that a man and woman live together without marriage and engage in a sexual relationship, does not in itself invalidate agreements between them

relating to their earnings, property, or expenses. . . . Agreements between non-marital partners fail only to the extent that they rest upon a consideration of meretricious sexual services. (*Marvin v. Marvin* [1976], as reported in Myricks 1983, 210)

A *meretricious relationship* is essentially that of a prostitute to her customer; that is, sexual services are being paid for. This ruling enabled Triola to pursue her claim for support payments and established a precedent for unwed couples by allowing such persons to sue for property settlements. Triola became the first unmarried person to win compensation from a former lover in a U.S. court (*Marvin v. Marvin* [1979]. She was awarded $104,000 for:

rehabilitation purposes so that she may have economic means to reeducate herself and to learn new, employable skills or to refurbish those utilized . . . during her most recent employment, and so that she may return from her status as companion of a motion picture star to a separate, independent but perhaps more prosaic existence. (*Marvin v. Marvin* [1979], as reported in Myricks 1980, 211)

The award was primarily for retraining, yet some of the funds could be used for living expenses. Such equitable relief is similar to rehabilitative alimony, hence the term *palimony*. In effect, the judge gave Triola disguised alimony. However, this award was later thrown out by the California appellate court, and the California Supreme Court has refused to reinstate it (*Marvin v. Marvin* [1981]).

Numerous other cases have been litigated both before and after the Marvin case. In cases where the courts see the union as meretricious, any implied contracts are illegal. The bottom line is that a given court will have the final word about a cohabiting couple's obligations to one another if they break up. After a review of many palimony cases, Noel Myricks (1983) draws the following conclusions:

1. Distributions of property acquired during cohabitation remains subject solely to judicial decision.
2. Courts should enforce express contracts between cohabitors except where the contract is explicitly founded on payment for sexual services.
3. If there is no express contract, courts should inquire into the nature of the relationship to determine if there is an implied contract.
4. Courts may compensate a person for the reasonable value of services regardless of any agreement about the value of such services. In *McHenry v. Smith* (1986), a woman who cohabited was awarded $16,000 because she had supported her partner while he was writing a book.
5. Generally, sexual services must be separated from other domestic services to make a valid argument. However, Oregon has ruled more liberally and is willing to disregard the lifestyle of the parties (*Latham v. Latham* [1976]).
6. An implied contract may be inferred entitling a cohabitant to one-half of the accumulated property where parties have held themselves out as husband and wife (*Carlson v. Olson* [1977]). On the other hand, the Illinois Supreme Court turned down such a claim in a similar case, saying that the woman's claims to property were against public policy (*Hewitt v. Hewitt* [1986]).
7. A cohabitant may be awarded palimony for rehabilitation purposes.

INSET 4-3
COUPLE WED SO THEY KNOW WHAT TO CALL EACH OTHER

This piece will use names of two people, Pietro and Tess.

For three years Pietro and Tess lived together without marrying. Such an arrangement had ceased to be scandalous when they took it up, had even become fashionable. It expressed the partners' reevaluation of the culture, or their liberation from tired old values, or something. It doesn't matter what. Pietro and Tess did it.

They were married a few weeks ago.

The canker in the love nest was the English language. Though English is the world's most commodious tongue, it provided no words to define their relationship satisfactorily to strangers. When Tess took Pietro to meet her parents, the problem became troublesome. Presenting Pietro, she said, "Mommy and daddy, this is my lover, Pietro."

Pietro was not amused. "It made me sound like a sex object," he said.

A few weeks later they were invited to meet the president. Entering the reception line, Pietro was asked by the protocol officer for their names. "Pietro," he said. "And this is my mate."

As they came abreast of the president, the officer turned to the President and said, "Pietro and his mate."

"I felt like the supporting actress in a Tarzan movie," said Tess. It took Pietro three nights of sleeping at the YMCA to repair the relationship.

Back to the drawing board, on which they kept the dictionary.

For a while they tried "my friend." One night at a glamorous party Pietro introduced Tess to a marrying millionaire with the words, "This is my friend, Tess." To which the marrying millionaire replied, "Let's jet down to the Caribbean, Tess, and tie the knot."

"You don't understand," said Pietro. "Tess is my *friend*."

"So don't you like seeing your friends headed for big alimony?" asked the marrying millionaire.

"She's not that kind of friend," said Pietro.

"I'm his *friend*," said Tess.

"Ah," said the matrimonialist, upon whom the dawn was slowly breaking, "Ah—your—*friend*."

As Tess explained at the wedding, they couldn't spend the rest of their lives rolling their eyeballs suggestively every time they said "friend." There was only one way out. "The simple thing," Pietro suggested, "would be for me to introduce you as 'my wife.'"

"And for me," said Tess, "to say, 'This is my husband, Pietro.'"

And so they were wed, victims of a failure in language.

Russell Baker
New York Times

8. Lawsuits may be kept to a minimum if cohabitants draw up written agreements concerning the nature of their relationship, although the court may change or invalidate such agreements.

Despite the fact that courts are slowly giving unwed cohabitants some legal rights, cohabitation still offers few legal safeguards for either partner. As Lenore Weitzman summarizes (1981), a sanctioned marriage has legal rules and forums that provide otherwise unprepared married couples with an efficient system for dealing with the unexpected; thus, the legal system helps a married couple minimize hardships resulting from unforeseen events. For example, if a spouse is killed, the state has rules that allocate that person's property in the absence of a will and guarantee a share of the property to the surviving spouse. By contrast, if one member of a cohabiting relationship dies without a will, the surviving partner has no legal rights at all. Legally, cohabiting couples are at

Cohabitation: Unmarried-Couple
Households

a distinct disadvantage compared with married couples. Couples who regard the marriage license as simply another piece of meaningless paper do not understand the legal ramifications of the marriage contract.

ENGAGEMENT

Marriage is the culmination of courtship. Traditionally, the final courtship stage has been engagement. Until recently, this has been a fairly formal stage. But with the increased age at first marriage, higher number of remarriages, and greater cohabitation among unmarried couples, engagement has become much less formal for some people.

Engagement means that simple dating is over and the couple have decided upon one another to be their future wife and husband. Qualities that were important in a date have gradually changed into qualities that are desirable in a spouse.

In a typical engagement, the couple make a public announcement of their intention to marry and begin active marriage preparation. Once the engagement is announced, the couple usually begin to make concrete plans for when the wedding will be, what type of wedding they will have, who will be invited, where they will live after marriage, what level of lifestyle they can afford, and so forth.

During the engagement the couple often spend more time with each other's families and begin to be treated as kin. The families may also arrange to meet. Marriage is, after all, the union of two families as well as two individuals. Above all, the two people begin to experience themselves as a social unit. Families and friends as well as the public in general react to them as a pair rather than as separate individuals.

■ TYPES OF ENGAGEMENTS ■

The *short, romantic engagement* lasts from two to six months. Time is typically taken up with marriage plans, parties, and intense physical contact. Normally, such a short engagement period fails to give the couple much insight into one another's personalities. Indeed, so much time is taken up with marriage preparation that the couple may not have enough time for mutual exploration of their relationship.

The *long, separated engagement*, such as when one partner is away at college, also presents problems. There are two distinct philosophies of separation: "Absence makes the heart grow fonder" and "Out of sight, out of mind." In reality the latter often prevails. Prolonged separation tends to defeat the purposes of the engagement and raises the question of exclusivity in the relationship. Does one date others during the separation? Dating others may cause feelings of insecurity and jealousy, whereas separation without dating is lonely and may cause hostility and dissatisfaction. In general, the separated engagement is usually unsatisfactory to both members of the couple because they can't spend time together, which as we have seen is a major component in strengthening a relationship.

Another possibility is the *long but inconclusive engagement*. Here the couple puts off the marriage because of economic considerations, deference to parental demands, or just plain indecisiveness. When a couple is engaged for years but the engagement never culminates in marriage, it is probably a sign that all is not well between them.

About one in four engaged couples break up temporarily while some couples break their engagement permanently. The causes of breakups appear to be simple loss of interest, recognition of an incompatible relationship, or the desire to reform the prospective mate. Sometimes the parents of one or both engaged persons work to break up the relationship and avoid a marriage. The major areas of disagreement tend to be matters of conventionality, families, and friends. Broken engagements can be considered successful in the sense that during this formal commitment period the couple had the time to look more closely at one another and to realize that marriage would not succeed.

■ FUNCTIONS OF ENGAGEMENT ■

What should an engagement do? How can engagement help the couple achieve a better marriage? Basically, the couple should come to agree on fundamental life arrangements. Where will they live? How will they live? Do they want children? When? Will they both work?

TABLE 4-2
RANK ORDER OF DESIRABLE QUALITIES IN A DATE AND IN A SPOUSE FOR 1,135 COLLEGE STUDENTS

MOST IMPORTANT QUALITIES OF A DATE

1. Physical attractiveness
2. Congenial personality
3. Sense of humor
4. Intelligent
5. Manners/being considerate
6. Sincere, genuine
7. Compatible interests
8. Conversational ability
9. Fun to be with

MOST IMPORTANT QUALITIES OF A SPOUSE

1. Loving and affectionate
2. Honest
3. Congenial personality
4. Respectful
5. Intelligent
6. Mature/responsible
7. Ambitious
8. Loyal and trustworthy
9. Physical attractiveness

From Jorgensen, S. R. (1986). *Marriage and the family.* New York: Macmillan, 260. Copyright © 1986 by Stephen R. Jorgensen. Used with permission.

Engagement

"If you keep bugging me about getting married, I'm gonna break off our engagement."

The couple needs to examine long-range goals in depth. Do they want similar things from life? Are their methods of obtaining these things compatible? Do their likes and dislikes blend? What role will religion play in their lives? How will each relate to the other's family? Friends? Work associates? They may not be able to answer such questions completely, but they should at least agree on some tentative answers. In fact, the most important premarital agreement may be an agreement about how answers to such questions will be worked out in the future. A couple with a workable, problem-solving approach to life is in a good position to find marital success.

An important part of the engagement is the premarital medical examination, which serves several useful functions. For instance, one of the partners may have a general health problem that will require special care by the other partner. Marrying a diabetic, for example, means that the partner will have to understand and participate in careful control of diet and periodic administration of insulin. Both persons need to be checked and cured of any possible sexually transmitted disease. The Rh factor in each partner's blood should be determined, since it will be of major importance in future pregnancy. Information on mutually acceptable methods of birth control can be obtained at this time if the couple has not already chosen such methods. And each partner will have the opportunity to talk over questions about the coming marriage with the physician.

Premarital counseling is good because of the blindness that comes with "being in love." It can be helpful to discuss ideas and plans with an objective third person such as a minister, marriage counselor, or mutual friend. Various instruments are available that a couple can use to assess their relationship. For example, PREPARE (The Pre-marital Personal and Relationship Evaluation) by Olson, Fournier, and Druckman (1986) and STARTING YOUR MARRIAGE by Roleder (1986) both help guide couples contemplating marriage to a meaningful examination of their relationship. The Catholic church has long made premarital counseling a prerequisite for marriage in the church.

A truly successful engagement period leads either to a successful marriage or to a broken engagement. An unsuccessful engagement in all likelihood will lead to marital failure.

SUMMARY

1. *American dating has been a unique form of courtship and mate selection.* In a sense dating has been America's contribution to the world's various mate selection systems. American dating has become increasingly less formal, especially in the last twenty years when it can perhaps better be termed "getting together" or "hanging around."

2. *Mate selection and sexuality for the young are handled mainly through the American invention of dating.* Although dating varies greatly from person to person and place to place, there is some recognizable pattern to traditional dating, especially outside large metropolitan areas. American dating is controlled by the youth themselves and involves relative freedom for the young man and woman to be alone together. This intensifies the pressure for the pair to move toward premarital intercourse as a means of handling their sexual drives.

3. *Marriage is being postponed, thus increasing the length of time during which a person dates before marriage.*

4. *The onset of puberty signals the beginning of adult sexuality.* In America the age of sexual maturity does not coincide with social acceptance of overt sexual behavior, especially sexual intercourse. Marriage is the socially accepted vehicle for sexual intercourse. Because marriage for most Americans does not occur until they are in their late teens or early twenties, there is a period of several years during which there is conflict between the dictates of biology and of society.

5. *Acceptance of premarital intercourse appears to be increasing in the American society.* However, because there are still social mores against premarital intercourse, those engaging in it often face conflict within themselves. Questions about social, personal, religious, and psychological principles should be answered by anyone contemplating premarital intercourse.

6. *Mate selection is an involved process that is not yet fully understood.* However, it is fairly clear that similar socioeconomic backgrounds and energy levels help to increase the chances of marital success.

7. *Cohabitation has increased in the past twenty years to such an extent that some theorists now consider it to be a stage in the courtship process.* Cohabitation has legal and psychological drawbacks compared with marriage. It appears that the cohabiting woman is at more of a disadvantage than the cohabiting man. The law is becoming increasingly interested in the cohabitation relationship, but the relationship remains legally precarious.

8. *Spending time together is important to a lasting relationship and is one of the foundation blocks supporting strong and growing relationships and families.*

9. *Mate selection usually leads to engagement, a formal expression of marital intentions.* The engagement period is used to make wedding plans, make philosophical decisions about the relationship, make practical decisions about where and how to live, and so forth. A successful engagement leads to marriage or to the couple's breakup.

Judith Krantz, novelist and commentator about modern American women, wrote a popular article entitled "Living Together Is a Rotten Idea." Her general thesis is that from the woman's standpoint cohabitation is a losing proposition. The cohabiting woman loses her independence, her freedom to make choices, her privacy, all of her mystery, any practical bargaining position in the power structure of love, an opportunity to make a meaningful change in her life by taking a genuine step toward full adult status, the prospect of having a child other than an illegitimate one, and the protection of the law. This is a disturbing list of losses to say the least.

Living together is not a true commitment. It is only a commitment that says, "I can leave anytime I wish." As Krantz says, "[It is] not the sink or swim of marriage, but a mere dog paddle at the shallow end of the pool." In essence the lack of commitment makes the relationship at best only "playing house."

Women are making a series of compromises with themselves that rest on a number of falsehoods that they devise to rationalize their behavior:

■ *Falsehood number one: "He is not yet ready to make a total commitment, but once we are living together, I know it's only a matter of time until we marry."* Unfortunately, as was pointed out earlier in this chapter, most cohabiting men do not share this assumption. In fact, moving in with a man gives him many reasons not to marry. Looking at the data on the division of housework and the

proportion of cohabiting women working to support the relationship monetarily compared to their married sisters, it is clear that the man has a gold mine. He has a built-in housekeeper whom he not only doesn't have to pay, but who pays him for doing the work. Marriage means moral and financial obligations. Why marry when one can have a bedmate-companion-housekeeper for free?

[This is the] only time in recorded history when women

who are not literally slaves have made themselves totally available to men without expecting something concrete in return. Who can blame men for taking advantage of such sappy, soft-minded, pseudo-idealistic stupidity?

Also, deep within many men are the remnants of the "double standard," which said, "It's great to have sex with this woman, but I wouldn't want to marry her."

■ *Falsehood number two: "How can you really get to know a person unless you live with them?"* This belief is very popular among cohabitors who equate their relationship with a "test marriage." The idea seems rational and makes good sense in light of the high divorce rate among married couples. Unfortunately, cohabiting seems to be just as prone to error as marriage. To date research on the relation of cohabitation with a spouse prior to marriage and the permanence of the marriage seems to show no difference between the cohabitors and the noncohabitors. It is also interesting to note that many who live together feel that their problems with their partner will go away after they marry. Yet as we shall see in Chapter 5, expectations that a person will change in marriage are usually disappointed. The fact that a cohabiting couple is only "playing house" means that it is possible that one's behavior will not be the same in marriage as it is in the cohabiting relationship. That marriage asks of both partners a strong, true, lasting commitment changes the basic relationship greatly from the dating, cohabiting relationship. Usually, the two relationships simply aren't similar enough to assume that what is true of one will automatically be true of the other.

■ *Falsehood number three: "We're in love, and I trust him completely. Why bring marriage into it? It's just a piece of paper."* But what a piece of paper it is. The legalities of marriage provide protection to both partners. Protection that, no matter how much we are "in love," may be needed if the great love evaporates as America's high divorce rate indicates it often does. Of course, both in cohabitation and marriage one assumes that the legalities will never be needed. How could this loving couple do anything to hurt one another? Yet experience tells us that loving couples more often than casual couples do hurt one another. The bitterness of many divorced spouses toward one another years after the divorce attests forcefully to this fact. As we saw in the "Living Together and the Law" section of this chapter, cohabiting couples are still open to legal entanglements. However, at this time these entanglements are unpredictable and subject to the whim of a given state or judge. At least in marriage, the rules of breaking up are spelled out, giving each spouse fair consideration and protection.

A story may clarify the impact of the lack of that piece of paper (marriage certificate) in cohabitation. The couple in question were mature, in love, yet reasonable about their relationship. He was divorced and under the settlement had retained ownership of the family home; she lived in a small apartment. When they decided to live together, it seemed only sensible that she move into his home. This she did, and over the next seven years she worked hard to make his house into their home. She had a good job and earned as much as he did, and much of the home improvement was done with her money, which she felt was only fair since he made the house payments. However, she did in fact occasionally make the house payment when for some reason he was a little short on cash in a given month.

She wallpapered, painted, and gardened over the years, and the house took on much of her personality and became her home as well as his in every way but legally. In the seventh year of their relationship, she began to feel increasing distance between them. Finally, she confronted him with her feelings. With some reluctance he told her that he had fallen in love with one of his colleagues whom he now wished to marry. Naturally, since the house belonged to him, she would have to move out to make room for his soon-to-be new bride. She was free to take the furniture she had bought and all of the things that she had brought with her into the relationship. But how do you take hung wallpaper, wall-to-wall carpeting, and an attractive garden? Had she put these things into her own home, they would remain even if he didn't. At least with marriage, there would have been some division of property, some possible reimbursement for her years of work. As it was, she had to move and return to a small apartment because she had not bothered to save during the seven-year relationship. After all, why should she? She had a home with her beloved partner.

■ *Falsehood number four: "I'm simply not ready to get married yet, but I don't like being alone and need someone to give my love to."* For the young woman who hasn't been away from her family, this rationalization is particularly dangerous. As we have seen, in the past many young women left their parental homes only to enter marriage. Later in their lives when the marriage failed and they were on their own for the first time, they were helpless and afraid. The young woman who is robbed, by entrance into a cohabitation relationship, of her early years of independence, living alone and learning about her own individuality, is also robbed of experiences that she may never again be able to recapture. To be learning about independence and one's own strengths and weaknesses at age forty after a marriage failure is difficult. The best time to learn about oneself is before one takes on the responsibility of marriage. It is a short but precious time and should never be given away lightly. Young adulthood is an exciting time of testing one's wings, reaching for the sky, looking for the limits. To hide from this time in an early marriage is bad enough, but to hide from it in a possibly meaningless cohabitation experience is even worse.

How sad to forfeit the freshest years of life—a time of un-bounded freedom and opportunity that will never be repeated—for the lukewarm comforts of premature domesticity.

It is true that some of these things we have been discussing could also apply to men. But it is the man who marries approximately two years later than the woman; it is the man who is most apt to go on an adventure with a friend to far-off places; it is the man who is most likely to enter the military and be forced to test himself and find out who he is; it is the man who in his work world is most likely to have a career as opposed to only a job. The cards, unfortunately, are still stacked in his favor. Living with a free companion-housekeeper who also shares her body with him is much less dangerous for him than for her. If she wants to give these things to him for little in return, why shouldn't he accept?

In the past, it was the woman who controlled sex because she had the most to lose. Today it is the woman who must control cohabitation and not enter into it lightly because she still has the most to lose.

WHAT DO YOU THINK?

1. Do many of your friends cohabit? What kinds of problems do they experience in the cohabitation relationship?
2. Does the man or the woman usually seem most committed to the relationship?
3. In cohabitation relationships that have broken up, has the man or the woman initiated the breakup?
4. Who benefits more from cohabitation, the man or the woman? Why? What are the benefits?
5. Would you cohabit? If so, why? If not, why not?

CHAPTER
5

MARRIAGE, INTIMACY, EXPECTATIONS, AND THE FULLY FUNCTIONING PERSON

CONTENTS

Marriage is the most intimate of all human interactions. At its heart, marriage is an interpersonal relationship between a man and a woman. Most adults try to fulfill their psychological, material, and sexual needs within marriage. To the degree that they are successful, the marriage is successful. America's high divorce rate tells us just how difficult it is to achieve success.

Among the primary functions of the contemporary American family are providing emotional gratification to members, helping family members deal with emotional crises, and helping them grow in the most fulfilling manner possible. Marriage and the family ideally act as a haven from which individual members can draw support and security when facing the challenges of our rapidly changing, technological society. A fully functioning family helps its members grow, mature, and become self-actualized individuals. Ideally, a good marriage acts as a buffer against mental health problems such as alienation, loneliness, unhappiness, and depression. In a word marriage can be therapeutic, a curative to the problems of its members.

In this chapter and the next, we will explore marriage as an interaction between two individuals who desire to create a marriage that is nurturing and supports self-fulfillment and growth for all family members. Although we will be discussing interpersonal relations in the context of marriage, the insights are applicable to any kind of human relationship: boyfriend/girlfriend, employer/employee, parent/child, and so forth.

REASONS FOR MARRIAGE

As we examined dating and mate selection in the last chapter, it became clear that many factors affect both. The reasons one finally chooses a mate are varied and not always clear. What is clear is that some reasons for marrying improve our chances of success, while others work against it.

FACTORS THAT TEND TO INCREASE THE CHANCES OF MARITAL SUCCESS

1. *Similar socioeconomic backgrounds:* Social research has clearly demonstrated that a similar socioeconomic status improves the chances of success in marriage.

2. *Similar energy levels:* Similar activity levels are fundamental to every other aspect of the relationship. For example, consider a marriage where the energy levels are dissimilar:

Brian is a quiet person who needs eight to nine hours of sleep to function well the next day. His tempo is slow and deliberate, but he finishes everything he starts. His slowness causes him to be habitually late. Amy, his wife, needs little sleep and appears to be a bundle of energy. She does many things, finishing most of them quickly. When they are going out, she is always ready before Brian and often waits for him and nags him to hurry. She likes companionship in the evening and dislikes going to bed before midnight. Brian usually wants to go to bed around 10 P.M. and is annoyed if she doesn't accompany him. Over several years, the conflicts caused by their differing energy levels have grown.

3. *Openness to growth or desire for stability:* A good relationship can occur between two partners who want stability or between two partners who want growth or change. However, differences between partners in these respects are extremely difficult to overcome. For example, consider this marriage where the partners differ:

Cassie is comfortable with routine and stability . She feels safe and secure when she knows exactly what is going to happen today, tomorrow, and next week. In contrast, her husband, Greg, is spontaneous and dislikes committing himself to any plan of action too far in advance. He says that this allows him freedom and flexibility, which he feels are necessary if a person is to grow and avoid stagnation. Their differing philosophies about growth and stability cause Cassie and Greg to continually disagree.

FACTORS THAT TEND TO DECREASE THE CHANCES OF MARITAL SUCCESS

1. *Love at first sight:* It is easy to understand falling in love at first sight, but it is hard to justify selecting a marriage partner on this basis alone. Generally, marriages based on initial attraction take place after very short acquaintance and with little mutual understanding. This is not to say that strong feelings of attraction cannot occur early in a relationship, they do. But such feelings alone provide a weak foundation for a long-lasting relationship.

2. *Escape from home:* Rather than dealing with a current relationship, many persons run away, hoping a new person or a new environment will be better. Any alternative seems better than remaining in the current unpleasant situation. A marriage so conceived is often the first of a series of failures. The failures are engendered because the person is driven by the negative present situation and often fails to assess the results of changing the situation. A person in an unpleasant relationship often finds it hard to believe that a new relationship could be worse.

3. *Avoiding loneliness:* Loneliness can sometimes drive a person into a hasty marriage. To seek companionship in marriage is a proper goal. If overcoming loneliness is one's only motivation for marriage, however, chances are high that this reason alone will not sustain a long-lasting relationship. Marriage for this reason is most prevalent among the divorced and widowed.

4. *Sexual attraction:* Unfulfilled sexual attraction and guilt over sexual involvement are popular but weak reasons for marriage. An unusually fulfilling sexual relationship alone is not sufficient reason to marry. Chemical attraction is certainly a part of romantic love and of mate selection, yet as we saw in the last chapter, the strong sexual emotions of a relationship can blind the partners to other important relational aspects.

Finding "the one and only" is a romantic myth. In fact, any number of persons can become satisfactory and long-lasting partners, for the building and maintenance of a relationship are more crucial to the relationship's success than the selection of the imaginary perfect mate. The marriage ceremony is really a beginning, not a culmination. The key to successful relationships is not the initial mate selection process so much as it is the couple's learning to compromise and communicate with one another.

YOU AND THE STATE:
LEGAL ASPECTS OF MARRIAGE

Every society has some kind of ceremony in which permanent relationships between the sexes are recognized and given status. The society (or the state) sets minimum standards for marriage in the interests of order and stability. In Western societies, the state is interested in supporting a monogamous marriage; assuring the *legitimacy of issue,* or that children are born of legally recognized relationships; protecting property and inheritance rights; and preventing marriages considered unacceptable, such as those between close relatives.

In the United States, marriage laws are established by individual states. Although the requirements differ, all states recognize marriages contracted in all other states. California law is typical of many state laws relating to marriage:

> Marriage is a personal relation arising out of a civil contract, to which the consent of the parties capable of making that contract is necessary. Consent alone will not constitute marriage; it must be followed by the issuance of a license and solemnized as authorized. (West's Annotated California Codes 1989, volume 12A, section 4100)

Marriage in the United States is a contract with the rights and obligations of the parties set by the state. Like all contracts, the marriage contract must be entered into by mutual consent, the parties must be competent and eligible to enter into the contract, and a prescribed form must be followed. All states set minimum age requirements, and most require a medical examination and a waiting period between the examination and the issuance of a license. Unlike most contracts, which are between two parties, the marriage contract involves three parties: the man, the woman, and the state. The state prescribes certain duties, privileges, and restrictions. For example, the contract can only be dissolved by state action, not by the mutual consent of the man and woman.

In a few instances a couple may be exempt from the marriage license law. For example, section 4213 of the California Civil Code (West's Annotated California Codes 1989) allows couples living together as man and wife to marry without applying for a license, provided they are eighteen or older. Some states recognize common law marriage if a couple can prove they have lived as husband and wife for seven years or more.

States set a number of other standards, such as how closely within family relationships one may marry. The state may also consider a marriage invalid under certain circumstances: for example, if consent to marry was obtained by fraud or under duress, or if either party is already married, suffers from mental incapacity, or is physically unable to perform sexually.

No specific marriage ceremony is required, but the parties must declare, in the presence of the person solemnizing the marriage, that they take each other as husband and wife, and the marriage must be witnessed, usually by two persons. Although some states are quite specific, there is a general trend away from uniform marriage vows. Traditional vows reflect the permanence society expects of marriage: ". . . to have and to hold from this day forward, for better or worse, for richer, for poorer, in sickness and in health, to love and to cherish, till death do us part."

Up to this point we have discussed the legal aspects of marriage established by the state. However, it must be remembered that most faiths regard marriage as a sacrament. About 75 percent of all marriages in the United States take place in a church. The state vests the clergy with the legal right to perform the marriage ceremony. God is called on to witness and bless the marriage: "Those whom God hath joined together let no man put asunder." Some religious feel so strongly that marriage is a divine institution that should not be tampered with by humans that they do not recognize civil divorce (the Roman Catholic church is the best example).

The marriage ceremony commits the couple to a new status. It sets minimum limits of marital satisfaction. Typical of these directives are the following:

■ A husband is required to support his wife and family. It is his duty to support his wife even though she has an estate of her own.
■ A husband has no duty to support his wife's issue (children) from a previous marriage.
■ Married persons' "conjugal rights" include enjoyment of association, sympathy, confidence, domestic happiness, comforts of dwelling together in the same habitation, eating meals at the same table, and profiting by joint property rights as well as intimacies of domestic relations.
■ One of the implied conditions of the marriage contract is that the wife shall give her husband companionship and the society of home life without compensation.

The laws and statutes of the state of California concerning marriage and divorce cover approximately 1000 pages of the civil code. Marriage, then, is much more than "just a piece of paper." It commits the couple to a new set of obligations and responsibilities. In essence, the couple in many ways marries the state, and it is the state to which they must answer if the prescribed responsibilities are not met.

A BRIDE'S TRADITIONAL WEDDING BUDGET WORKSHEET

Wedding parties

Engagement party	$_____
Bridesmaids' lunch	$_____
Rehearsal dinner	$_____
Out-of-town guests' brunch	$_____

Wedding consultant $_____

Stationery

Invitations	$_____
Announcements	$_____
Thank-you cards	$_____
At-home cards	$_____
Stamps	$_____

Bridal attire

Wedding dress	$_____
Headpiece and veil	$_____
Shoes	$_____
Accessories (gloves, jewelry, etc)	$_____
Dresses for wedding parties	$_____
Undergarments	$_____
Trousseau	$_____

Photo/videography

Formal portraits	$_____
Engagements	$_____
Wedding and reception	$_____
Wedding album	$_____
Parents' albums	$_____
Extra prints	$_____
Videography of wedding and wedding parties	$_____

Flowers

Ceremony arrangements	$_____
Bride's bouquet	$_____
Groom's boutonniere	$_____
Bridesmaids/groomsmen	$_____
Mothers' corsages	$_____
Reception arrangements	$_____

Reception

Food	$_____
Drink	$_____
Wedding cake	$_____
Groom's cake	$_____
Rental of facility	$_____
Rentals of tableware, furniture, tents	$_____
Place cards	$_____
Tips and fees to food servers, doormen, coat check, valet parkers restrooms, etc.	$_____

Music

Ceremony (organist, soloist, choir, other musicians)	$_____
Reception (band, deejay, pianist)	$_____

Transportation

Limousines	$_____
Parking	$_____

Gifts

For your groom (optional)	$_____
Maid/matron of honor	$_____
Bridesmaids	$_____
To your parents (optional)	$_____
Your groom's ring (NOT optional)	$_____

Fees

Church/synagogue/other location	$_____
Officiant	$_____
Officiant assistants	$_____

Odds and ends

Guest favors	$_____
Birdseed or confetti	$_____
Monogrammed napkins	$_____
Hotel accommodations	$_____
Guest book and pen	$_____

THE WEDDING

About 70 to 75 percent of couples opt to marry in church. Indeed the traditional and often large wedding seems to have made a comeback. Weddings of any size are expensive. Checking with local wedding consultants (1992), your author found the following approximate costs for a wedding with 150 guests:

Bride's dress	$500–700	Invitations	$200–250
Rehearsal dinner	$300–400	Bridal Attendants' clothes	$400–500
Flowers	$300–400	Clergy	$100
Music	$300–400	Attendants' gifts	$200

You and the State:
Legal Aspects of Marriage

Photography	$500–600	Men's formal wear	$300
Rings	$1000	Miscellaneous	$400
Reception	$2000–3000		

As you can see, the costs run upwards of $6000 and can easily reach $10,000 to $15,000 for a wedding this size.

■ WRITING YOUR OWN MARRIAGE CONTRACT ■

Marriage contract
A written engagement between married partners outlining the responsibilities and obligations of each partner

As we have seen, marriage is a formal contract between the couple and the state and has a set form in each state. The standard state contract does not meet every couple's needs, however, and an increasing number of couples are writing their own **marriage contracts.** Such a personal contract cannot take the place of the state marriage contract, nor can it legally reject any of the state contract obligations. However, as a supplement to the state contract, it can afford a couple the freedom and privacy to order their personal relationship as they wish. It can also enable them to escape to some degree from the sex-based legacy of legal marriage and to move toward an egalitarian relationship. The couple can formulate an agreement that conforms to contemporary social reality. Personal contracts can also be written by couples who wish to have a relationship but not one of marriage (for example, a cohabiting couple or a couple barred from marriage such as a homosexual couple).

As Lenore Weitzman (1981) suggests, in addition to its legal advantages, a personal contract facilitates open and honest communication and helps prospective partners clarify their expectations. Once the contract agreement has been reached, it serves as a guide for future behavior. Contracts also increase predictability and security by helping couples identify and resolve potential conflicts in advance.

Personal contracts must be constructed carefully if they are to be legal. For example, when one partner brings to a marriage a great deal of wealth that has been accumulated before the marriage, the couple may want to sign a contract that keeps this property separate from the property that accumulates during the marriage. This is particularly difficult to do in community property states. Such a contract needs to be drawn by an attorney who understands the state laws governing community property. Any topic may be handled in a personal contract, but such contracts generally cover the following:

■ Aims and expectations of the couple
■ Duration of the relationship
■ Work and career roles
■ Income and expense handling and control
■ Property owned before and acquired after the contract
■ Disposition of prior debts
■ Living arrangements
■ Responsibility for household tasks
■ Surname
■ Sexual relations
■ Relations with family, friends, and others
■ Decisions regarding children (number, rearing, and so forth)
■ Religion

- Inheritance and wills
- Resolving disagreements
- Changing and amending the contract
- Dissolution of the relationship

The list of items that could be included is endless. It may seem unromantic to sit down before marriage with your intended partner and work out some of the details of your future relationship. Some people feel it demonstrates a lack of trust in your future mate. But it is a worthwhile exercise even if you don't plan to have a written legal contract. People's expectations about one another and their relationship are important determinants of behavior. If one partner's expectations differ greatly from the other's and are left unexpressed and unexamined, the chances are great that the couple will experience conflict and disappointment. By going through the steps of working out a personal contract, the couple can bring their attitudes and expectations into the open and make appropriate compromises and changes before major problems arise.

THE TRANSITION FROM SINGLE TO MARRIED LIFE

Married life is indeed different from single life. Marriage brings duties and obligations. Suddenly, one is no longer responsible just for oneself but shares responsibility for two people and perhaps more if children are planned.

Furthermore, one's very identity changes with marriage. No longer are you simply you, you are now Brian's wife or Margie's husband, and you may become a mother or father if you decide to have children. You become interdependent with the others in your family and lose the independence you had when you were single.

The transition from dating to establishing a home and family is often a large step for both partners. The couple may have cooked some meals together during the courtship, but preparing 1095 meals a year for two on an often tight budget is a far greater challenge. Planning a month's finances is certainly more difficult than raising money for a weekend of skiing. In fact, living within some kind of family budget is a difficult transition for many newly marrieds. Before marriage they were used to spending their incomes as they wished. Now another person must be consulted, and what they earn must be shared.

Leisure time activities, which are often spontaneous and unplanned when one is single, now must be planned with another person. Compromises must be worked out. As we shall see with Mark and Tanya, conflicts over leisure time pursuits can be difficult to resolve.

New relationships must be developed with both sets of parents after marriage. Your primary relationship is now with your spouse rather than with your parents, and you must learn to relate with your in-laws. Failure to build a satisfactory in-law relationship makes married life more difficult inasmuch as the relationship with one's parents is important to each spouse.

The sexual relationship may also involve a transition. Premarital sexuality may have been restrained, covert, and only partially satisfying. Ideally, the marital sexual relationship will become fully expressive and satisfying to both partners. However, this may not occur if one or both have been taught excessive control and repression of sexual impulses. The many sexual technique manuals and increasing interest in sex therapy attest to the problems in this area of the relationship and to the need for greater understanding about sex.

There are many other transitions that must be made if a marriage is to be successful. All are transitions from the self-centeredness of childhood to the other-centeredness of adulthood. To consider the likes and dislikes of one's partner, to compromise one's desires at times in favor of the others, to become a team that pulls together rather than in opposing directions, to become a pair that has more going than the sum total of the two individuals making up the pair—these are a few of the things necessary for a successful marriage. If one or both partners cannot make a majority of the transitions, the chances for a successful marriage are slim.

Mark and Tanya: Married Singles

Both Mark and Tanya were active singles until they met, fell in love, and married in their mid-twenties. Mark's single-life pattern had involved a great deal of time for sports, especially trips to the desert to ride his motorcycle with other dirt bike enthusiasts.

Tanya had spent a great deal of time with her office colleagues, going to picnics, bowling on the office team, and window shopping on Saturdays. Sunday was reserved for church.

As the newness of marriage begins to wear off, both Mark and Tanya find themselves somewhat bored and uncomfortable with the other's activities. Tanya did go to the desert twice when Mark went motorcycling, but she found it dirty, boring, and lonely because she didn't know the other women and the men were away from camp riding all day.

Mark doesn't like bowling although he tried once or twice. He doesn't like being alone at night either, so he pressures Tanya to give up the bowling team. "After all, why am I married if I'm going to be alone in the evening?" he complains.

Gradually, each falls back into old single-life patterns, and they spend less and less time together. Although they are still married, they do almost nothing together. Mark spends more time on motorcycle trips, and Tanya has joined a second bowling team. Their friends wonder if they ever see one another.

The transition from single to married status does not end the need for change. As time passes, the marriage will change and require both partners to make further transitions. The coming of children, for example, places a whole new set of demands on the married couple.

In general, the couple contemplating marriage seldom realize the extent of the changes necessary to make a successful marriage. They often believe "love" will take care of all the transitions from single to married life. "We get along now; of course, we'll get along after we marry." Not necessarily so.

MARRIAGE: A MYRIAD OF INTERACTIONS

Each day we interact with numerous people. On the job we talk with colleagues, receive instructions from superiors, and give orders to those who work for us. At stores we talk with salespeople. On the way home we interact with other drivers or with people on the bus. All of these interactions are relatively simple. For example, when buying things at a store, I simply want to make my purchases. I don't need to know how the salespeople are feeling, how their children are doing in school, how their sex lives are, or how they feel about their jobs. I need only relate to them as a customer. The interaction begins and ends at a superficial level.

Not so with marriage. Perhaps more than any other institution, the family is an arena of intimate and complex interaction. Literally hundreds of interactions take place within a family each day, and they vary in infinite ways. We can think of these interactions as ranging from purely intellectual to strongly emotional. Note in the following conversations how the interactions move from superficial and distant to caring, committed, and emotionally involved:

"Good morning. How are you feeling?"
"Morning. Fine. How are you?"

"Good morning. How are you feeling? Did you sleep well?"
"So, so. But I hope you slept well."

"Good morning. I'm really happy to see you looking so well this morning! I'm glad that headache went away."
"Morning. I feel better. Thanks so much for reminding me to take those aspirins; they really did the trick! Don't know what I'd do without you!"

"Good morning! You know, it's always wonderful to wake up in the morning with you!"
"It makes me feel so good when you say that! I'm so happy with you!"

The first interaction is superficial, a general morning greeting. The next, though still superficial, demonstrates more concern and awareness of the other person. The concern deepens in the next interaction: The first speaker remembers the other's headache of the previous day and is happy that the partner is out of pain. The partner expresses gratitude for the concern and for the aid. And the last interaction demonstrates a deep emotional level of sharing between the partners.

Let's also look at some of the role interactions that go on in a marriage:

husband	↔	wife
man	↔	woman
lover	↔	lover
friend	↔	friend
provider	↔	provided-for
provider	↔	provider

1. What kind of marital role expectations do you think you have learned?
2. Are they similar to the roles your parents fulfilled in their marriage?
3. What do you think are the two most important roles your spouse should fulfill?
4. What would you do if your spouse disagreed with you and didn't wish to fulfill one of these two roles you consider important?

provided-for	↔	provider
spendthrift	↔	budgeter
budgeter	↔	spendthrift
father*	↔	child*
child*	↔	mother*
child*	↔	child*
taker	↔	giver
giver	↔	taker
teacher	↔	learner
learner	↔	teacher
learner	↔	learner
worker	↔	employer
employer	↔	worker
worker	↔	worker
colleague	↔	colleague
leaning tower	↔	tower of strength
tower of strength	↔	leaning tower

Obviously, the list of possibilities is endless! And think of the complications that can arise when children enter the picture. Remember also that cross-interactions can occur, such as between lover and friend or lover and teacher. For example, the friend can interact with the woman, the lover, and so on down the list. Thus, when I wake up in the morning and say to my wife "How do you feel?" it means far more than saying the same thing to a passing acquaintance. It could mean, "I am concerned about you" as a friend; "I'd like to have sex with you" as a lover; "Will you be able to work today?" as an employer; and so forth. To further complicate matters, the spouses may not agree on what the meaning is. The wife may take the husband's question to mean he'd like to make love before getting up, whereas he really meant to inquire how she was feeling because she had been sick the day before. Complicated, isn't it?

To manage successfully the hundreds of interactions that occur daily in marriage would be a miracle indeed. But to manage them better each day is a worthy and attainable goal. If people can be successful in marriage, chances are they will also be successful in most other interpersonal relations because other relationships will almost certainly be simpler than the marital relationship. The next chapter will discuss communication and some of the ways in which interpersonal relations can be improved.

▨ FULFILLING NEEDS IN MARRIAGE ▨

Marriage can supply love and affection, emotional support and loyalty, stability and security, companionship and friendship, sexual fulfillment, and material well-being. This is a big order to expect of any relationship and explains in part why there is a high rate of marital disruption in American society. Americans ask a great deal more of marriage than they have in the past and a great

*These are not interactions between real children and real parents, but rather interactions in which one partner acts like an authority or parent and the other partner reacts as a dependent child. In the child-child interaction, the partners act like children with each other.

deal more than do many other people in the world. Such high expectations must certainly lead to disappointments. Society recognizes that fulfilling sexual, material, and psychological needs is a valid responsibility of the marriage institution. In fact, so important is the meeting of these needs for individuals that all states recognize failure to do so as a legitimate reason for divorce.

SEXUAL NEEDS

Marriage is the only legitimate outlet for sexual energies recognized by American society. Indeed, sexual intercourse is a state-mandated part of marriage. If sexual needs are not fulfilled in a marriage, the marriage can be dissolved. Thus, American spouses must function as lovers to their mates.

MATERIAL NEEDS

"Room and board" is a part of every marriage. Breadwinning and homemaking are essential to survival. Material needs also affect how successfully psychological and sexual needs are met. Marital disruption is considerably higher among families in economic trouble than among families satisfactorily meeting material needs.

PSYCHOLOGICAL NEEDS

As you may remember from Chapter 2, one of the basic assumptions of this book is that the strong family becomes increasingly important to its members as social stability decreases and people feel more isolated and alienated.

Mobility, increased anonymity, ever-larger and more bureaucratic institutions, and lack of social relatedness all contribute to feelings of loneliness and helplessness. Because of these feelings, our psychological need for intimacy has increased greatly, and most people hope to find intimacy in marriage.

Today men and women seek not only love but emotional survival within the context of their intimate relationships. A loving spouse and/or family can supply personal validity and relevance, a confirmation of one's existence. This becomes especially important in a large, technological, anonymous society.

NEED RELATIONSHIPS

It is obvious that psychological needs are closely related to both sexual and material needs. As was pointed out, marital disruption tends to be highest among the materially least well-off.

The relationship between sexual and psychological needs tends to be more complicated than the relationship between material and psychological needs. A satisfying sexual relationship certainly fulfills many of one's psychological needs. However, a satisfying life often reflects a relationship's general success at meeting needs, not just its sexual success. For example, in their study of successful marriages, Lauer and Lauer (1985) found that agreement about and satisfaction with one's sex life was far down the lists of reasons the respondents gave for a good marriage. Fewer than 10 percent of the respondents felt that a good sexual relationship kept their marriage together. However, unhappy couples or those from broken marriages often list sexual relations as one of their major problems. When other psychological needs are not being met, the sexual relationship is often the first place in which trouble appears. A couple's sexual relationship often acts as a sensitive indicator of the health of their relationship. Couples having serious marital problems seldom find that their sex life is unaffected.

DEFINING MARITAL SUCCESS

Marital success is difficult to define, partly because it is often confused with marital adjustment, permanence, and happiness, and the three concepts are not necessarily the same. For example, Bohannan (1984) points out that a neurotic relationship of mutual misery (as found in the play *Who's Afraid of Virginia Woolf?*) may be just as binding as a healthy relationship of mutual support, esteem, and love. Thus, a couple may be said to have marital adjustment although the adjustment has not led to happiness or marital success in the broadest sense. On the other hand, if marital success is defined as permanence only, it might be said that this miserable couple has marital success as long as their misery does not lead to destruction of the marriage. And if success is defined as happiness only, no marriage could be considered successful because no family is happy all the time.

Over the years, many factors, such as socioeconomic level, years of schooling, presence of children, length of premarital acquaintance, role congruence, and communication patterns, have been studied and related to marital success (Glenn 1990). Yet the results of such research remain vague and inconclusive.

For our purposes, marital success will be defined broadly to include adjustment, happiness, and permanence. Thus, a successful marriage is one in which the partners adjust to the relationship; are in relative agreement on most issues of importance; are comfortable in the roles that they assume; and are able to work together to solve most of the problems that confront them over time. Each partner expresses satisfaction and happiness with the relationship, and the marriage lasts.

Unfortunately—and despite all of the research—it remains impossible to give a definitive list of factors that influence a couple's ability to attain marital success. Research does pinpoint age at marriage and the presence of children as two factors closely related to marital satisfaction and success. In general, the younger the age at marriage, the greater the risk of marital dissatisfaction and failure. Also, a great deal of research finds that marital satisfaction is lower when children are present than in pre- or postparental stages of marriage (Glenn 1990, 823–24; 1991). Marital satisfaction appears to follow a U-shaped curve over the course of the marriage. Satisfaction starts to fall shortly after marriage and drops to a low point when children reach adolescence. Satisfaction then rises through the latter stages of marriage. Just how much these changes in satisfaction are related to the presence or absence of children or to the simple passage of time is difficult to determine. These same trends are also found in remarriages (Vemer et al. 1989). Couples probably vary so much (just as individuals do) that an important factor for one couple may be unimportant to another. This is especially true in a society such as ours where individuals not only have great freedom in mate selection but also great freedom to build the kind of relationship that they desire. Of course, as always this freedom is accompanied by responsibility. If you are free to build the marriage you want and it does not work, you alone are responsible for the failure.

Because there are no longer any hard-and-fast rules about what a marriage should be, about the roles that each partner will play, or even about the primacy of the relationship, the expectations that one brings to the marital relationship play an important role in the success of the relationship. Thus, an examination of the role that personal expectations play in marital success is perhaps more important than an examination of a long list of factors that may or may not affect a particular couple's marital success.

MARITAL EXPECTATIONS

In a very real sense, humans create their own world. The wonderful complexity of the human brain allows us to plan, organize, and concern ourselves with what we think should be as well as with what is. We predict our future and have expectations about ourselves, our world, our marriages, our spouses, and our children. In a way expectations are also our hopes about the future, and hope is an important element to our well-being. We often hear about the person who has given up hope, and we know that this can be dangerous to both physical and psychological well-being. The average American certainly enters marriage (at least the first marriage) full of high hopes for success and happiness. Who can be more hopeful than the couple newly married, in love, and off on their honeymoon?

In our earlier discussion of love, we noted that love often acts like the proverbial rose-colored glasses in that we don't see the people we love as they really are, but as we wish or expect them to be. The spouse's failure to meet these expectations often leads to disappointment in marriage.

In essence the world is as we perceive it, and our perceptions are based in part on the input of our senses and in part on what we personally do to accept, reject, interpret, change, or color that input. The study of how people experience their world is called **phenomenology.** It is important to realize that most people react to their perceptions of the world rather than to what the world really is. A simple example may clarify this point. If we insert a straight metal rod halfway into a pool of clear water, the rod appears bent or broken because of the refraction of the light waves by the water. How would we react if we knew nothing about light refraction and had never seen a partially submerged object before? We would see the rod as bent and would act on that perception. But we have measured and examined the rod, and we know it is straight. Moreover, most of us have learned that light waves will be refracted by the water and appear bent, so we assume that the rod is straight even though our eyes tell us it is bent. In other words, we know that our perceptions do not always reflect the objective world. We have learned that appearances can be deceptive.

How does this relate to marriage? In our interactions with other people, we often forget that our perceptions may not reflect "reality" or that our spouse may have different perceptions.

Tracy, newly married to Rob, feels that Rob spends too much of his free time with his friends. She suggests that he spend more time with her.

"After all, you are married now and your wife should come first." Rob feels put upon by Tracy's request because he spends much less time with his friends now than he did before he was married.

Rob's perception is that he has greatly reduced the time he spends with his friends and that he spends much more time with Tracy. Tracy feels he spends too much time with his friends and too little time with her. Who is right? Certainly, their perceptions of the situation differ, but is one right and the other wrong? This is probably one of those situations in which both partners are "right," at least in their own mind.

THE HONEYMOON IS OVER: TOO HIGH EXPECTATIONS

One morning, after Peter and Holly have been married for about a year, Holly awakens and "realizes" that Peter is no longer the same man she married. She accuses him of changing for the worse: "You used to think of great things to do in the evenings, and you enjoyed going out all the time. Now you just seem to want to stay home." Peter insists, of course, that he has not changed; that he is the same person he has always been; and that, indeed, he has always said he looked forward to quiet evenings alone with her.

This interaction may be signaling that *the honeymoon is over* for Peter and Holly. This stage is very important in most marriages. It usually means that the partners are reexamining their unrealistic, overly high expectations about marriage and their mate created by "love." In a successful relationship, it means that subjective perceptions are becoming more objective, more realistic. It also means that the partners are at last coming to know each other as real human beings rather than as projections of their expectations.

Unfortunately, some people throw away the real person in favor of their own idealizations. In essence they are in love with their own dreams and ideals, not with the person they married. Originally, their mate became the object of their love because she or he met enough of their expectations that they were able to project their total set of expectations onto the mate. But living together day in and day out forces the partners to compare their ideals with the flesh-and-blood spouses. The two seldom coincide exactly.

Jeffry H. Larson has developed the "Marriage Quiz" (1988) to measure people's beliefs in myths about marriage and family relations. He states:

> One explanation for the current high divorce rate and the prevalence of marital dissatisfaction is that Americans have high and unrealistic expectations of marriage—expecting a spouse to simultaneously be a friend, a confidant, a fulfilling sex partner, a counselor, and a parent (1988, 3)

Larson defines *myth* as a belief held uncritically and without examination. Hence a myth might well lead to an unexamined, perhaps even unconscious set of expectations. If the myths that one holds are untrue, only partially true, or not the same as the myths held by one's intimate partner, problems will arise as the reality of a relationship is discovered. By listing the myths, the reader can discover if he or she also holds these popular American beliefs. The purpose here is to raise questions about these myths so that they can be examined. Once examined, the myth will be replaced by a conscious belief or set of beliefs that can be discussed and shared with one's partner. Data on many of these myths will be found throughout the book.

1. A husband's marital satisfaction is usually lower if his wife is employed full-time than if she is a full-time homemaker. (False)

2. Today most young, single, never-married people will eventually get married. (True)

3. In most marriages, having a child improves marital satisfaction for both spouses. (False)

4. The best single predictor of overall marital satisfaction is the quality of a couple's sex life. (False)

5. The divorce rate in America increased between 1960 and 1980. (True)

6. A greater percentage of wives are in the work force today than in 1970. (True)

7. Marital satisfaction for the wife is usually lower if she is employed than if she is a full-time homemaker. (False)

8. If my spouse loves me, he/she should instinctively know what I want and need to be happy. (False)

9. In a marriage in which the wife is employed full-time, the husband usually assumes an equal share of the housekeeping. (False)

10. For most couples, marital satisfaction gradually increases from the first year of marriage through the childbearing years, the teen years, the empty nest period, and retirement. (False)

11. No matter how I behave, my spouse should love me simply because he or she *is* my spouse. (False)

12. One of the most frequent marital problems is poor communication. (True)

13. Husbands usually make more lifestyle adjustments than wives. (False)

14. Couples who have cohabited before marriage usually report greater marital satisfaction than those who did not. (False)

15. I can change my spouse by pointing out his or her inadequacies, errors, and so forth. (False)

16. Couples who marry when one or both partners are under the age of eighteen have more chance of eventually divorcing than those who marry when they are older (True)

17. Either my spouse loves me or does not love me; nothing I do will effect the way my spouse feels about me. (False)

18. The more a spouse discloses positive and negative information to his or her partner, the greater the marital satisfaction of both partners. (False)

19. I must feel better about my partner before I can change my behavior toward him or her. (False)

20. Maintaining romantic love is the key to marital happiness over the life span for most couples. (False)

Larson has found that students responded to almost half of the items incorrectly.

Romantic ideals and expectations lead us to expect so much from our mates and from marriage that disappointment is almost inevitable. How we cope with this disappointment helps determine the direction our marriage will take when the honeymoon is over. If we refuse to reexamine our ideals and expectations and blame our mates for the discrepancy, trouble lies ahead. On the other hand, if we realize that the disappointment is caused by our own unrealistic expectations, we can look forward to getting to know our mates as real human beings. Further reflection also makes it clear that recognizing our mates as real human beings with frailties and problems rather than as perfect, godlike creatures greatly eases the strain on our marriages and ourselves. Realizing the humanness of our partners allows us to relax and be human as well. But consider what can happen if we are unwilling to give up our expectations of an ideal mate:

WHAT DO YOU THINK?

1. Why does Carol seem to find so little satisfaction with her husbands?
2. Why did Carol's romance with her first husband persist so long before marriage whereas all of her earlier relationships dissolved quickly?
3. What are the qualities of your dream spouse?
4. How does your relationship with your parents influence your marriage ideals?
5. How can Carol find satisfaction in marriage?

Carol: The Perpetual Seeker

Carol's father died when she was eight years old. Her mother never remarried because she felt no other man could live up to her dead husband. Through the years, she told Carol how wonderful and perfect her father had been, both as a man and as a husband.

As a teenager, Carol fell in love often and quickly, but the romances also ended quickly, usually, she said, because the boy disappointed her in some way. The only romance that lasted was with a young man whom she met while on a summer vacation in Florida. Even though they knew one another for only a month, they continued their romance via mail the following year. They met again the next summer. Carol was now nineteen. Three months after they parted, after school had resumed, and after many letters declaring their love and loneliness, Carol's friend asked her to come to Florida and marry him. Carol assured her mother that he was the right man—strong, responsible, and loving just as her father had been.

They married and everything seemed to go well. By the end of the first year, however, Carol was writing her mother letters complaining that her husband was changing for the worse, that he wasn't nearly the man Carol had thought him to be. She questioned whether he would ever be a good father, and she noted that he didn't have the drive for success that her father had had at his age.

Two years after marrying, Carol divorced her husband. She had met an exciting, wonderful man who had given a talk to her women's sensitivity group. He was all of the things her husband wasn't and, incidentally, all of the things her father had been. She married him not long after her divorce was final.

Carol is now thirty years old and married to her third husband, about whom she complains a great deal.

It is clear that Carol is in love with her idealized image of her father. Since she never was or will be able to know her father, she has no way to correct her idealized image of him. A real live husband has no chance to live up to her expectations because they are based on someone who can't make mistakes. The chances of Carol ever being happy with a spouse are low unless she can stop comparing her spouse with her romanticized images of her father.

Note that when our expectations are unconscious, uncommunicated, or unrealistic, we can feel betrayed even when we haven't been. We feel betrayed because our spouse has not recognized our needs as we feel he or she should have. Yet betrayal implies that a promise has been made and then broken. If we have not clearly communicated our expectations, how can our spouse break a promise that was never made? A wife expects her husband to take her out to dinner this coming Friday. Her husband sees them having a romantic dinner at home. Neither shares their expectation with the other. What do you think will happen on Friday night?

■ ROMANTIC LOVE OR MARRIAGE? ■

We can see why disappointment with marriage is almost inevitable if we consider that our prevailing cultural view of marriage as expressed in the mass media is one of everlasting romance. One of the greatest disappointments newly married couples face is the fading of romantic love. Romantic love depends on an incomplete sexual and emotional consummation of the relationship. Physical longing is a tension between desire and fulfillment. When sexual desire is fulfilled, romantic love changes to a feeling of affection that is more durable, though less intense and frenzied, than romantic love. Because we have been flooded with romantic hyperbole by the media, we are often unprepared for this natural change in the emotional quality of the relationship. For example, let's look at a typical couple:

Allison fell in love with Mike when she was sixteen and he was seventeen. Neither of them had ever been in love before. After two years they were still deeply in love, and Mike persuaded Allison to marry him because he was tired of dealing with their guilt about premarital sex, worrying about pregnancies, and hiding their intimacy from their parents. After two years of marriage, Allison finds that she is not nearly as excited by Mike as she was earlier. The couple is struggling to make a living, and she feels that "the bloom is going from the rose." One day, as Allison listens to a lecture by her art history teacher, she feels a lump in her throat, a thumping in her heart, and a weakness in her knees. This was the way she felt about Mike two years ago, and she suddenly realizes that she doesn't have these feelings for Mike any more. She can't tell Mike, and she is afraid of her feelings for the teacher, so she drops the class and tells Mike it's time for them to have a baby.

It's clear that Allison is confusing feelings of sexual attraction with love. Since American folklore says you can't love more than one person at a time, she must either suppress these feelings of tension and longing, as she does, or decide that she is no longer in love with Mike and perhaps consider a divorce. Defining love narrowly as only "the great turn-on" means that all marriages will eventually fail because that intense feeling usually fades with time.

■ DIFFERING EXPECTATIONS ■

Even if their expectations about marriage are realistic, spouses may have different expectations about marital roles, especially the roles that each expects the other to play. Traditional gender roles are no longer clear-cut. For example, the husband is no longer the sole breadwinner and the wife the homemaker. However, many of our expectations about role behavior come from our experience with our parents' marriage, and often we are unaware of these expectations. For example, consider the possibilities for conflict in the following marriage:

Randy and Susan: Who Handles the Money?

In Randy's traditional midwestern family, his father played the dominant role. His mother was given an allowance with which to run the house. His father made all of the major money decisions.

In Susan's sophisticated New York family, both her mother and her father worked hard at their individual careers. Because they both worked, they decided that each would control his or her own money. Both contributed to a joint checking account used to run the household, but fulfilled individual desires from personal funds. There was seldom any discussion about money decisions because each was free to spend his or her own money.

Randy and Susan marry after Susan has been teaching school for a year, and Randy gets a good position with a New York bank. Randy believes that because he has a good job, Susan no longer needs to work; he can support them both, which he believes is the proper male marriage role. He sees no reason for Susan to have her own bank account. After all, if she wants something, all she has to do is ask him for it.

When roles are not clear-cut and accepted by everyone, the chances of conflicting role expectations increase greatly. A man and a woman from a culture in which roles are clearly specified find it easy to define what a good spouse is. If the spouse is fulfilling the assigned roles well, he or she is automatically a "good" spouse. Where role specification is not socially assigned but is left up to the individual couple, confusion may occur. For example, each spouse may want to fulfill a specific role and compete with the other to do so; or each may automatically think the other is fulfilling a role and come to realize later that neither is.

80 PERCENT I LOVE YOU—
20 PERCENT I HATE YOU

Many people expect that their partner will meet all of their needs; indeed, they believe it is the partner's duty to do so. To the extent that partners fail to live up to this expectation, they are "bad" spouses. But, human beings are complex, and it is probably impossible for any two people to meet one another's needs completely. If a couple could mutually satisfy even 80 percent of each other's needs, it would be a minor miracle.

The expectation of total need fulfillment within marriage ruins many marital relationships. As time passes, the spouse with the unmet needs will long to have them satisfied and will accuse the partner of failure and indifference. Conflict will grow because the accused spouse feels unfairly accused, defensive, and inferior. Life will revolve more and more around the unfulfilled 20 percent rather than the fulfilled 80 percent. This is especially true if the partners are possessive and block each other from any outside need gratification. Unless such a pattern of interaction is broken, a spouse may suddenly fall out of love and leave the mate for someone else. These sudden departures are catastrophic for all the parties. And the ensuing relationship often fails because of the same dynamics. For example, the dissatisfied spouse finds a person who meets some of the unfulfilled needs and, because these needs have become so exaggerated, concludes that at last he or she has met the "right" person. In all the excitement, the person often overlooks the fact that the new love does not fulfill other needs that have long been met by the discarded spouse. In a few years the conflicts will reappear over different unmet needs, and the process of disenchantment will recur.

Carl and Jane: A Good Spouse Will Meet All My Needs

They are very much in love. Their friends are amazed at how compatible and well suited to one another they are. Each expects total fulfillment within the marriage. Jane enjoys staying up late and insists that Carl, who likes to go to bed early to be fresh for work, stay up with her because she hates to be alone. At first Carl obliges, but he gradually returns to his habitual bedtime. But, of course, he can't sleep well because he feels guilty leaving Jane alone, which, she reminds him, demonstrates his lack of love and uncaring attitude. She tries going to bed earlier but also can't sleep well because she isn't sleepy; so she simply lies there resenting Carl. She begins to tell him how he has failed her, and he responds by listing all the good things he does in the marriage. Jane acknowledges these good things but dismisses them as the wrong things. He doesn't really do the important things that show real love, such as trying to stay up later.

Naturally, sex and resentment are incompatible bed partners, and Jane and Carl's sex life slowly disintegrates. Each begins to hate the other for not fulfilling their needs, for making them lose their identity in part, and for making their sex life so unsatisfactory. Then Carl, working overtime one Saturday, finds himself attracted to a co-worker and is soon "in love."

Sex is good, reaffirming his manhood, and the woman loves to go to bed early. He divorces Jane and marries his new "right" woman. Unfortunately, they also divorce three years later because Carl can't stand her indifference to housekeeping and cooking. He reminds her periodically during their marriage that Jane kept a neat house and prepared excellent meals.

Such dynamics are prevalent in "love" marriages. This is true because "love" blinds, reducing the chances of realistic appraisal and alternative seeking. To the person who believes that love is the only basis for marriage, the need to seek realistic alternatives is a signal that love has gone. But there is another way, as Lederer and Jackson point out:

> The happy, workable, productive marriage does not require love or even the practice of the Golden Rule. To maintain continuously a union based on love is not feasible for most people. Nor is it possible to live in a permanent state of romance. Normal people should not be frustrated or disappointed if they are not in a constant state of love. If they experience the joy of love for ten percent of the time they are married, attempt to treat each other with as much courtesy as they do distinguished strangers, and attempt to make the marriage a workable affair—one where there are some practical advantages and satisfactions for each—the chances are the marriage will endure longer and with more strength than so-called love matches. (1968, 59).

▪ LACK OF COMMITMENT: TOO LOW EXPECTATIONS ▪

We have looked at the problem of too high expectations because in a society that believes in romantic love as a basis for marriage, this is the most common difficulty associated with expectations. However, it is also possible to have expectations of marriage that are too low.

The expectation of permanence is important to making a marriage last. Even though it is clear from divorce statistics that American marriages do not necessarily last forever, it is important that the couple bring to the marriage the expectation that *their* marriage will last "until death do us part."

All of the studies done on successful marriage find that the couple's expression of commitment to the permanence of the relationship is high on the list of reasons for marital success (Stinnett 1979; Curran 1983; Lauer and Lauer 1985). Some of Lauer and Lauer's (1985, 24–25) respondents expressed their commitment to the relationship as follows:

"I'll tell you why we stayed together, I'm just too damned stubborn to give up."

"You can't run home to mother when the first trouble appears."

"Commitment means a willingness to be unhappy for awhile. You're not going to be happy with each other all the time. That's when commitment is really important."

cathy®

This kind of total commitment is often withheld in the cohabitation relationship. Since one purpose of cohabitation is to have a relationship that is easy to get out of, clearly total commitment cannot be offered. It may be this element of cohabitation that makes it less than good training for marriage.

THE EXPECTATION OF COMMITMENT: A CHARACTERISTIC OF STRONG AND SUCCESSFUL FAMILIES

The expectation that a relationship will grow, be strong, and last—that is, commitment to the relationship and to your partner—is the single strongest factor influencing the success of a relationship.

Commitment in the strong family is multifaceted. First of all, there is commitment to your partner. The expectation that the relationship will endure despite any problems leads to a commitment to work with your partner in finding ways to cope with life's problems. If you are committed to a relationship, problems become something to be surmounted, not something that will destroy your relationship. Overcoming the problems will strengthen the relationship. Loyalty to your partner, to the relationship, and to your family is a characteristic of committed, enduring, successful families (McCubbin et al. 1988).

Commitment to the family unit itself is also important. Support is offered to other family members because the family recognizes that if one member is in trouble and hurting, all members will be in trouble and hurting. One way each family member experiences commitment is by trusting that the family can be depended upon for support, love, and affirmation. Commitment is also experienced as willingness to support the family if trouble arises. The well-being of all family members is a major goal of the family. In fact, the commitment is so strong that it may be described as "irrational" (Curran 1983, 71). Both the squeaky concert presented by the third-grader just learning a musical instrument and the professional-quality playing of the college student both receive enthusiastic support.

It is not just parents who are committed to offer support; all members of the family offer support to one another. Olson (1983; 1986) suggests that the strong family has a high degree of cohesion and togetherness, though not so much that individuality is lost. Thus, another facet of commitment is that family members are committed to each other as individuals as well as to the family as a whole. Overworked parents may experience this commitment as the children pitching in to help them clean up the house and yard. Perhaps a brother or sister will give up plans in order to help a sibling in need. All members of the strong family accept the general idea that the family is a team of individuals working together to achieve individual as well as family goals. Cooperating as a team is often the most efficient way to achieve individual as well as group goals.

Another facet of commitment is that it is long-lasting. It is this quality that creates family stability (Barnhill 1979). Family members can count on support today, tomorrow, and next year. "I love you today" is a wonderful sentiment, but it is not worth much if the people to whom it is said have no idea whether you will love them tomorrow. If they cannot be reasonably sure about your feelings tomorrow or next week, they can only feel insecure and fearful of what tomorrow may bring. The relationship can have no stability, only fear of instability. Commitment that isn't long-lasting really isn't commitment at all because it robs people of their enthusiasm for the future; their ability to plan for the future; their future stability; and, most important of all, their ability to commit to the relationship. A person who is robbed of his or her ability to commit will be robbed of all possibility of an enduring intimate relationship.

Another facet of commitment for the strong family is that the commitment to family overrides all other commitments, even the commitment to work. Stinnett and Defrain relate the following story told by a member of one of the 3000 strong families they studied:

> I was off on my usual weekly travel. Business took me away from home three or four days a week. I'd left a teenager disappointed because I would miss her dance recital. My wife felt swamped. She'd described herself as a "de facto" single parent. I had a growing sense of alienation from my family; sometimes I missed chunks of their lives. Indignantly, I thought, "Yeah, but they don't mind the money I make. I have work to do. It's important!" Then the flash of insight came. What frontier was I crossing? I wasn't curing cancer or bringing world peace. My company markets drink mixer. Drink mixer! Granted we sell it all over Ohio and are moving into other markets, but how many gallons of mixer for my family? I didn't quit. I enjoy sales and it's a good job. I make good money. I did learn to say "no" to some company demands. And I plan my travel to leave more time at home. Sometimes now I take my wife or a child along. In a few years I'll retire and within a few months I'll be forgotten in the mixer business. I'll still be a husband and a father. Those will go on until I die. (1985, 27–28)

This does not mean to imply that other things can't, at times, take precedence over the family. The key phrase is "at times." As important and necessary as work is to family well-being, a parent married to his or her job will have a difficult time being married to his or her family. Everyone understands that at times something else will be more important than a given relationship. But if these times become all times, others in the relationship will begin to feel secondary and question the depth of commitment. Knowing what your mate or parent always puts other things ahead of you can only erode your self-esteem and confidence.

Strong commitment to one's family should not be confused with loss of individuality and "belonging to" others. The healthy family is committed to helping family members maintain their individuality. Barnhill (1979) suggests that strong families support individuation of their members. *Individuation* refers to independence of thought, feeling, and judgment of individual family members. It includes a firm sense of autonomy, personal responsibility, identity, and boundaries of the self.

In her interviews with family professionals, Curran (1983, 186) found that healthy families exhibit a sense of shared responsibility. Family members help each other recognize the responsibilities that commitment creates. They may, at times, help each other shoulder these responsibilities. At other times, they will allow a family member to live with the consequences of irresponsibility. Without responsibility, commitment becomes meaningless. "If I can't depend on myself, if others can't depend on me, then protestations of commitment aren't helpful."

In summary, commitment has many sides. Basically, the members of a strong family experience commitment to the family as trust, support, affirmation, acceptance, belonging, love, and enduring concern about their personal well-being as well as that of the family.

THE EXPECTATION OF PRIMARINESS: EXTRAMARITAL RELATIONS

In large part because American marriage is rooted in Judeo-Christian principles, one's sexual and emotional outlet is limited to one's spouse. The ideal of monogamy is an important part of American marriage. It is interesting to note that in Murdock's (1950) study of 148 societies, 81 percent of them maintained taboos against adultery, so America is not alone in its expectation of primariness in marriage. Although approximately 50 percent of married Americans do engage in extramarital sexual relations at least once, over 80 percent of all Americans believe such behavior is wrong (Lawson 1988).

Despite the strongly stated expectation of primariness in sexual relations, the sexual revolution seems to have increased the amount of extramarital sexual interaction as well as premarital sexual relations. In fact, premarital intercourse correlates with extramarital affairs (Thompson 1983; Bell 1981). Research data indicate that younger wives (under thirty) in marriages contracted since 1970 now engage in extramarital relations slightly more often than their husbands (Lawson 1988). This may relate to the greater numbers of women entering the work force. Research indicates that working wives of all ages have an incidence of extramarital relations about twice as high as that of housewives (Tavris and Sadd 1977; Hunt 1974). One of the reasons that married men (considering all ages) tend to have more extramarital affairs than married women is the overabundance of available single women. In *The New Other Woman* (1985), Richardson indicates that some single women actually prefer to have an affair with a married man because it requires less commitment, leaving the woman more time to devote to her career. For some women, the unavailability of single men makes an affair with a married man the only alternative to celibacy. In the case of career women, the object is often not marriage, but simply companionship and a sexual relationship. Since most married people have the expectation of primariness, obtaining accurate figures on extramarital sexual experiences is difficult because study participants tend to conceal such experiences. There is little doubt, however, that this expectation is being disappointed more and more often.

A number of factors correlate with greater acceptance of extramarital sexual relations (Bell 1981):

- Being male
- Being young
- Being nonreligious
- Being highly educated
- Believing in the equality of the sexes
- Being politically liberal
- Being unmarried
- Being premaritally sexually permissive

The long-time extramarital affair must be distinguished from the short-term or one-night stand extramarital experience. The long-time affair usually includes a strong emotional attachment as well as sexual involvement. Such relationships are more likely to lead to the breakdown of a marriage.

Generally speaking, men tend to take their extramarital affairs more lightly than women and center more on the sexual aspect than on the emotional aspect. They tend to associate their affairs with an increase in marital satisfaction due to a decrease in boredom and tension. Older women tend to have affairs that last longer, be more emotionally involved, and associate their affairs with decreasing marital satisfaction. Grosskopf (1983, 195) reports that 72 percent of women having an extramarital affair give "emotionally dissatisfied with husband" as their major reason for engaging in the affair. The women often report that the companionship and emotional support derived from the affair are of greater importance than the sex.

The reasons for extramarital sexual affairs are many and varied. Some engage in an affair out of simple curiosity and the desire for some variation in sexual experience. Others yearn for the romance that has been lost in their marriages or search for the emotional satisfaction they feel is missing in their lives. Some simply fall into an affair out of friendship for someone of the opposite sex. An adulterous affair can also be a rebellion or retaliation against the spouse. Most threatening to a marriage is an affair that stems from falling in love with the new partner. The experience of many marriage counselors indicates that it isn't so much the notion of the spouse having sex outside the marriage that causes a rift between couples as the idea that the spouse is emotionally involved with someone else along with the sex (Masters et al. 1988, 405).

We tend to equate extramarital relationships with sexual relationships. Yet many kinds of extramarital relationships with the opposite sex do not include sex. How do people feel about such relationships? Little research has been done to answer this question. David Weis and Judith Felton (1987) showed a written set of activities with the opposite sex to a sample of college women and asked which of the activities would be acceptable in a spouse. They found that their subjects' attitudes varied greatly. For example, 82.3 percent felt that it would be all right for their spouse to go to a movie or the theater with a friend of the opposite sex. Only 30.5 percent felt it would be all right for their spouse to dance to the stereo when they weren't present. As soon as the activities took on a directly sexual nature such as necking or petting, very few accepted the behavior (3.7 percent). The researchers concluded that the diversity of attitudes would create great potential for marital conflict over the issue of exclusivity. Some persons are more afraid of nonsexual emotional extramarital ties than they are of extramarital sex without emotional interaction. Others are afraid that nonsexual extramarital relationships will lead to sexual involvement.

Extramarital affairs are often difficult for a spouse to combat. Early in the affair, the couple is very aroused and can usually manage only a very limited time together. The partners are on their best behavior and make special efforts to be attractive and appealing. Expectations and excitement are high because of the clandestine nature of the affair. This kind of excitement is hard to bring back into a long-standing marriage.

Although the expectation of primariness is often broken, it remains an important expectation. Breaking it for whatever reason often causes the spouse to become very upset and may even end the marriage. We have seen that mutual trust is one of the cornerstones of strong and enduring relationships. The discovered clandestine affair damages this trust. Even the undiscovered affair damages trust. The spouse engaging in the affair tends to project his or her behavior onto the partner; that is, "I lie to my partner about my affair, therefore my partner probably lies to me." Once basic trust in your partner is damaged, it is very difficult to regain. Feelings of inadequacy and self-doubt often arise in the spouse who discovers the other's extramarital affair.

Such reactions may not be the case when the extramarital relationship is consensual, that is, when both spouses agree to it. During the 1970s, the media reported a great deal of consensual adultery. Estimates ranged from 15 to 26 percent of married couples having some kind of understanding that allowed sex outside the marriage under limited circumstances. Blumstein and Schwartz (1983) found that 28 percent of cohabiting couples and 65 percent of gay male couples also reported such agreements. Some surveys indicate an increasing rejection of such activity. For example, Wallenberg (1984) found hat 86 percent of his sample welcomed more emphasis on traditional family ties and only 23 percent favored more sexual freedom. In one study, 66 percent of those involved in consensual extramarital sexual activities who had divorced indicated that they would avoid such openness in their next relationship (Watson 1981). Again such research is difficult to validate since the general society does not accept the practice (see Thompson 1983 and Sponaugle 1989 for reviews of the research on extramarital relations).

■ THE SELF-FULFILLING PROPHECY ■

Some evidence suggests that the expectations you hold about another person tend to influence that person in the direction of the expectations (for a more extensive discussion, see Rosenthal and Jacobson 1968). Thus, holding slightly high expectations about another person is not totally unproductive as long as the expectations are close enough to reality that the other person can fulfill them. Remember, though, that expecting something different of a person implies that you don't approve of the person at the present time. Expectations that are clearly out of another's reach tell that person that he or she is doomed to failure because the expectations can't be met. This often happens to children. Sometimes children feel so frustrated by their inability to meet their parents' expectations that they deliberately do the opposite of what their parents desire in an effort to free themselves from impossible expectations. "All right, since you are never satisfied with my schoolwork, no matter how hard I try, I'll stop trying."

Such dynamics are also often found in marriage. If your mate constantly expects something of you that you can't fulfill, you may begin to feel incompetent, unloved, and unwanted. On the other hand, positive and realistic expectations about the spouse, or anyone else for that matter, may be fulfilled because they make the other person feel wanted and valuable, and the person then acts on this positive feeling.

Clearly, the closer to objective reality, our expectations and perceptions are, the more efficient our behavior will generally be. If we expect impossible or difficult behavior from our mates, we doom both our mates and ourselves to perpetual failure and frustration. If, on the other hand, we accept ourselves and our mates as we are, we have the makings for an open, communicative, and growing relationship.

THE SELF-ACTUALIZED PERSON IN THE FULLY FUNCTIONING FAMILY

How can we be realistic in our expectations of others and of marriage? Perhaps we can never be totally realistic, but we will be on the right road if we can accept ourselves basically for what we are, respect and genuinely like ourselves, admit error and failure and start again, accept criticism, and be self-supportive rather than self-destructive. Of course, if these steps were easy, we would all be living happily ever after. Although much is known about helping people live more satisfying lives, a great deal remains to be learned. Individuals are complex and vary greatly; no single answer will suffice for everyone. We need many paths by which people can travel to self-actualization. We will try and map some of these paths by examining common marital conflicts and possible solutions to these conflicts throughout the book. Our first step will be to set up ideal yet realistic goals toward which we may move in our quest for maturity and mental health.

CHARACTERISTICS OF MENTAL HEALTH

The National Association for Mental Health has described mentally healthy people as generally (1) feeling comfortable about themselves, (2) feeling good about other people, and (3) being able to meet the demands of life.

FEELING COMFORTABLE ABOUT ONESELF
Mature people are not overwhelmed by their own fears, anger, love, jealousy, guilt, or worries. They take life's disappointments in stride. They have a tolerant, easygoing attitude toward themselves as well as toward others, and they can laugh at themselves. They neither underestimate nor overestimate their

abilities. They can accept their own shortcomings. They respect themselves and feel capable of dealing with most situations that come their way. They get satisfaction from simple everyday pleasures.

Notice that this description recognizes that people's lives have negative aspects: fear, anger, guilt, worries, and disappointments. Mentally healthy people can cope with such negative aspects. They can accept failure without becoming angry or considering themselves failures because of temporary setbacks. Moreover, they can laugh at themselves, which is something maladjusted people can seldom do.

FEELING GOOD ABOUT OTHER PEOPLE

Mature people are able to give love and consider the interests of others. They have personal relationships that are satisfying and lasting. They expect to like and trust others, and they take it for granted that others will like and trust them. They respect the many differences they find in people. They do not push people around or allow themselves to be pushed around. They can feel part of a group. They feel a sense of responsibility to their neighbors and country.

As you have probably noticed, this description includes a great deal of common sense. Certainly, we would expect people who are considerate of other people's interests to have lasting relationships. As we noted before in our discussion of self-fulfilling expectations, if we approach people in an open, friendly manner, expecting to like them, they will be warmed by our friendliness and will probably feel friendly toward us. If, on the other hand, we approach people as if we expect them to cheat us, the chances are that they will be suspicious of us and keep their distance.

Another aspect of this description is that it recognizes that we are gregarious or, as the song says, "people who need people." Mature people recognize this need and are also aware of the responsibilities that people have toward one another.

FEELING COMPETENT TO MEET THE DEMANDS OF LIFE

Mature people do something about problems as they arise. They accept responsibilities. They plan ahead and do not fear the future. They welcome new experiences and new ideas and can adjust to changed circumstances. They use their natural capacities and set realistic goals for themselves. They are able to think for themselves and make their own decisions. They put their best effort into what they do and get satisfaction out of doing it.

▓ SELF-ACTUALIZATION ▓

Abraham Maslow (1968) spent a lifetime studying people, especially those he called self-actualized people. These were people he believed had reached the highest levels of growth, people who seemed to be realizing their full potential, people at the top of the mental health ladder. Let's take a look at some of the characteristics they share:

1. *A more adequate perception of reality and a more comfortable relationship with reality than average people have.* Self-actualized people prefer to cope with even unpleasant reality rather than retreat to pleasant fantasies.

The Self-Actualized Person
in the Fully Functioning Family

169

2. *A high degree of acceptance of themselves, of others, and of the realities of human nature.* Self-actualized people are not ashamed of being what they are, and they are not shocked or dismayed to find foibles and shortcomings in themselves or in others.

3. *A high degree of spontaneity.* Self-actualized people are able to act freely without undue personal restrictions and unnecessary inhibitions.

4. *A focus on problem-centeredness.* Self-actualized people seem to focus on problems outside themselves. They are not overly self-conscious; they are not problems to themselves. Hence they devote their attention to a task, duty, or mission that seems peculiarly cut out for them.

5. *A need for privacy.* Self-actualized people feel comfortable alone with their thoughts and feelings. Solitude does not frighten them.

6. *A high degree of autonomy.* Self-actualized people, as the name implies, are for the most part independent people who are capable of making their own decisions. They motivate themselves.

7. *A continued freshness of appreciation*. Self-actualized people show the capacity to appreciate life with the freshness and delight of a child. They can see the unique in many apparent commonplace experiences.

Sidney Jourard sums up these qualities as follows:

> Healthy personality is manifested by the individual who has been able to gratify his basic needs through acceptable behavior such that his own personality is no longer a problem to him. He can take himself more or less for granted and devote his energies and thoughts to socially meaningful interests and problems beyond security, or lovability, or status. (1963, 7)

■ LIVING IN THE NOW ■

Marriages are constantly troubled because one or both spouses cannot live in the present. Are the following remarks familiar? "I'm upset because Christmas now reminds me of how terrible you were last Christmas." "This is a nice dinner, but it doesn't compare with the one I want to fix next week." "This never happened in my last marriage."

All phrases of time—past, present, and future—are essential for fully functioning people. The ability to retain what has been learned in the past and use it to cope with the present is an important attribute of maturity. The ability to project into the future and thereby modify the present is another important and perhaps unique characteristic of humans. The healthy person uses the past and future to live a fuller, more creative life in the present.

But while retention and projection of time can help us cope with the present, they can also hamper present behavior. In the preceding comments, the present Christmas is being ruined because of a past Christmas. The spouse may now be perfectly pleasant, yet the other is unhappy because he or she is dwelling on the past rather than enjoying the present. People who do not learn from the past are doomed to repeat mistakes, yet people must develop the capacity to learn from the past without becoming entrapped by it. Much the same can be said of the future. Planning for the future is an important function. Yet people may also hamper their behavior by projecting consequences into the future that keep them from acting in the present. For example, look how a husband's performance fears create a lonely night for him and for his wife:

James knows his wife is in a loving mood, but he is too tired to make love. When she approaches him, he says he doesn't feel good and goes to the guest room to sleep.

James may or may not have been correct about his wife's desires and his ability to satisfy them. But by avoiding the situation, he ensured his wife's dissatisfaction. Of course, he could have been honest and simply said, "Let's just cuddle for a while and then go to sleep. I'm really bushed."

The Self-Actualized Person
in the Fully Functioning Family

171

As we have seen, some people live frustrated lives because their expectations of the future are unrealistic. Remember Carol and her three husbands? Carol projects idealized expectations onto her husbands. Rather than letting them be the persons they are, she expects them to act in a certain manner (as she imagines her father did). She is so preoccupied with expecting her husband to behave as she thinks he should that she derives no satisfaction from his actual behavior. As the author of the book *Love Is Letting Go of Fear* suggests, "Love is letting go of past guilts and future fears." (Jampolsky, 1989)

■ THE GOALS OF INTIMACY ■

Clearly, building a satisfying intimate relationship is a difficult and complex task yet such relationships are much sought after.

> Given one wish in life, most people would wish to be loved—to be able to reveal themselves entirely to another human being and be embraced, caressed, by that acceptance. People who have successfully built an intimate relationship know its power and comfort. But they also know that taking the emotional risks that allow intimacy to happen isn't easy. Preconditioned on the sharing of feelings, intimacy requires consummate trust. (Avery 1989, 27)

Many factors will influence the success of such relationships. Certainly, we can prepare ourselves to meet the problems so often found in intimate relationships of all kinds and learn the skills of open communication and problem solving. If we don't let hostilities and inability to communicate stand in our way, we have a better chance of maintaining and fulfilling intimate relationships. Marriage can be treated as a complex vehicle to personal happiness; as with any vehicle, preventive maintenance and regular care will minimize faulty operation.

Marriage counselors see many couples whose marriages are so damaged that little if anything can be done to help them. But most American couples begin their marriages "in love." They do not deliberately set out to destroy their love, each other, or their marriage. Yet it is often hard to believe that the couples in the marriage counselor's office or the divorce court ever felt love and affection toward each other. Too often they are bitter, resentful, and spiteful. Their wonderful "love" marriage has become a despised trap, a hated responsibility, an intolerable life situation. They seem to have forgotten the positive characteristics that led them to fall in love in the first place (see Scenes from Marriage, p. xxx).

Why? Marriages often become unhappy because we are not taught the arts of "getting along" intimately with others or the skills necessary to create a growing and meaningful existence in the face of the pressures and problems of a complex world. Far more could be done to handle marital difficulties intelligently and successfully, and failure to teach these skills, both before and after marriage, is a shortcoming of contemporary treatment of the subject of marriage.

To get along intimately with another person and create a fully functioning family, we need to be clear about ourselves, our expectations, and the basic goals of intimacy. In their most general terms, the goals of intimacy are identical to some of the functions of the family that we discussed in Chapter 1. In particular, they involve (1) helping family members deal with crises and problems, (2) helping members grow in the most fulfilling manner possible, and (3) providing emotional gratification to members. The following examples show how a marriage can fulfill these functions.

Dealing with Crises

When Pete has a crisis in the office, he tells Gail about it, and she listens, offers support, asks questions, and, very occasionally, offers advice. When he is through telling her about it, Pete often understands the situation better and feels more ready either to accept or to change it.

Growing in a Fulfilling Manner

Gail wants to be less shy, and Pete encourages her to be more assertive with him and to role play assertiveness with others. Gradually, she finds she can overcome her shyness, in large part because Pete encourages and supports her.

Providing Emotional Gratification

Pete loves to tinker with things, and he feels important and emotionally gratified if he can fix something in the house for Gail. Gail loves to knit and Pete loves sweaters, so she feels worthwhile and appreciated when she knits him a sweater. Gail knows she can sound off when she gets angry because Pete understands and doesn't put her down. Pete feels emotionally supported by Gail because she backs him when he wants to try something new. Both partners are having their own emotional needs met as well as meeting many of the needs of the other.

Certainly, it does not seem to be asking too much of a marriage to help the partners deal with crises that arise, to encourage the partners to grow in a personally fulfilling manner, and to supply emotional gratification to the partners. Yet marriage often fails this assignment or, to put it more accurately, marriage partners often fail to create a marriage in which these positive elements thrive.

The Self-Actualized Person
in the Fully Functioning Family

SUMMARY

1. Marriage is the generally accepted mode of life for most Americans. *Legally, marriage is a three-way relationship that involves the man, the woman, and the state.* The state sets certain eligibility requirements that a couple must meet before they can marry. The state also prescribes certain obligations that each partner must fulfill in marriage.

2. *The marriage ceremony commits a couple to a new status, with certain privileges, obligations, and restrictions.* In addition to state-mandated marital obligations, some couples are writing their own marriage contracts, stating goals, obligations, and responsibilities that they wish to be a part of their marriage. If properly written, such contracts are considered legal as long as they do not disregard state-mandated duties and obligations.

3. *Marriage involves constant interaction between family members and fulfillment of many roles within the family relationship.* How does one interact with another person at the intimate level of marriage? Basically, how we interact will be determined by our attitudes and expectations about marriage and our partners. We assimilate these attitudes and expectations of the larger culture from our parents. When our expectations and attitudes differ from our spouse's, there will be conflict in the marriage.

4. *Expectations that are too high or too low can lead to relationship problems.* Both the expectation of permanence (commitment to the relationship) and the expectation of primariness (monogamy) are important building blocks of strong, enduring relationship.

5. *The basic goals of intimacy in marriage are providing emotional gratification to each partner, helping each deal with crises, and helping each grow in a fulfilling manner.* The ideal goal of a family is to provide an environment in which each family member is encouraged and free to become the most actualized person that he or she is capable of becoming. Each family member will have to work toward maintaining his or her own balance and growth while at the same time contributing to the well-being of all the other family members. This is a large order and requires self-understanding and common sense from all family members.

6. *Self-actualizing people essentially are people who feel comfortable about themselves and others. They are able to meet most of the demands of life in a realistic fashion.* Self-actualizing people tend to use their past experiences and ideas about their future to enhance the present rather than to escape from it. They are not prisoners of their past but are free to use it to improve the present. Intimacy includes the commitment to help each other realize to the fullest possible degree all of the human potential inherent in each individual family member. This is a difficult and at times impossible task, yet it is a worthy goal toward which to strive.

We tend to think of an intimate relationship as one between two people. The two people build the relationship and make a go of it, or they don't. Yet in reality intimate relationships are influenced by the couple's friends, their parents, and the society in which they live. Does reading about the apparent misdeeds of numerous politicians, crime and drug-related violence influence our intimate relationships? Indeed it does. As was pointed out, intimate relationships rest on a foundation of commitment and trust. Caryl Avery (1989, 27) suggests that

Few adults under forty can remember a world without cynicism. Faith is no longer fashionable, and a quarter-century of double-dealing in high places has eroded our confidence in institutions we once revered. The personal realm seems similarly shaky. With one in two marriages ending in divorce and countless others existing in name only, trusting someone to be honest and committed over the long haul is increasingly difficult.

The fact that the mass media tends to dwell on these negatives helps us forget about the many positive things that happen in our society. For example, divorce rates never tell us about the marriages that endure and last for many years. Articles and books are written for couples having personal problems rather than for couple's celebrating their 50th (golden) wedding anniversaries.

Since the mass media tend to dwell on the negative, we may also get into the habit in our own personal relations of concentrating on the negative, on the 20 percent of our needs left unmet rather than on the 80 percent that our spouse is successfully meeting (see p. 161).

Ayala Pines, a psychologist in private practice, suggests that one way to combat this kind of negativism is to ask a couple, "Why were you attracted to your mate in the first place?" In other words, rather than concentrating on the often long list of things that the partners feel are wrong with their relationship, get them thinking and talking about the characteristics that brought them together in the first place. "You feel a change in the atmosphere when they start reminiscing about the good times they had at the beginning of their relationships," Pines says

(1985). By going back to the beginnings of the relationship when "love" made all seem positive and the rose-colored glasses masked out all of the social and personal negatives, couples may be able to restart a positive cycle in their relationship.

However, care must be used in doing this. Comparing that idyllic beginning to their current situation, couples may criticize each other with the accusation, "You used to do this. You don't anymore." Moreover, what a person found attractive about his or her partner in the beginning may be what is causing stress today. In other words, an attractive trait may turn to a negative trait with the passage of time. (See "The Double Cross," p. 89.) For example, a woman may tell you she fell in love because he was the tall, dark handsome, silent type, and then what's causing her problems is that he doesn't communicate. At first the silence was mysterious and attractive, but as time passed, it became frustrating and irritating.

A man may say he was attracted to his spouse's energy but now finds her manipulative, hysterical, and bossy. Pines suggests that when you show the couple that the same thing that is causing the trouble in the relationship is what they found attractive at the beginning, it takes away the feeling of helplessness. They recognize that although they feel changes have taken place in their partner, the characteristics that drew them together still exist.

Although Pines suggests focusing on the positive, it is not always easy. Friends tend to support one's complaints about a spouse. Friends may also increase negativism when they complain about their own relationships. Mass media adds its negativism via the news and the soap operas. Does anything positive ever happen to people's relationships on the soaps? Most couples come in with a laundry list of complaints. What they ever found attractive or interesting about each other is submerged beneath a tidal wave of negative feelings.

Couples seem to have their judgments cast in concrete. "She's bossy." "He's so cold and uncommunicative." "She's demanding." "He just wants to party all the time." Pine asks such couples questions such as "Was there ever a situation in which he was warm and communicative?" No matter how awful the relationship has gotten, she says there is always at least one positive example. And it is much more exciting to figure out what in a situation made him warm and communicative, than

it is to list all the situations in which he isn't. It also starts the couple looking at what has been good in the marriage rather than dwelling only on what is now bad.

Pines feels that concentrating on what has been and may still be right about a relationship helps a couple realize that much of their trouble may stem from unrealistically high expectations and the negative inputs of society. It may also help a couple be more tolerant of each other's faults.

To find out why a couple came together and why they have stayed together as long as they have focuses on the couple's strengths. The counselor who concentrates on their problems only emphasizes the negative aspects of the relationship and lends his or her authority to the awfulness of their situation.

A song from the 1940s tells us to "accentuate the positive, eliminate the negative." Since few of us can be a 100 percent perfect spouse, expect-

ing perfection can only lead to disappointment. Accentuation of the positive may best be found in a comment made by one of the persons interviewed in the Lauer and Lauer (1985, 24) study of successful marriages. A husband of twenty-four years said, "She isn't perfect but I don't worry about her weak points, which are very few. Her strong points overcome them too much."

To take periodic inventories of what's good in one's marriage is a helpful step to counteract negative societal input and the all-too-natural tendency for people to dwell on what seems wrong in a relationship. Remembering what drew you together, why you fell in love, what excited you about your mate in the first place will help you rekindle the spark of romance that too often is buried under unrealistic expectations of perfection, the mundane chores and stresses of everyday living, and the constant negativism fostered by the mass media.

CHAPTER

6

COMMUNICATION IN INTIMATE RELATIONSHIPS

CONTENTS

I see communication as a huge umbrella that covers and affects all that goes on between human beings. Once a human being arrives on earth, communication is the largest single factor determining what kinds of relationships he/she makes with others and what happens to him/her in the world.

Virginia Satir

Communication is the sending and receiving of messages, intentional and unintentional, verbal and nonverbal. Communication is basic to every human relationship. Without it, there could be no relationship. The more intimate the relationship, the more important communication becomes. Good communication skills are always evident in strong families. Curran (1983, 34) identified communicating and listening as the primary traits of healthy families. This finding is echoed throughout the research on strong, healthy, successful families.

Although most Americans are now well aware that communication is important to successful relationships, this awareness is quite new. As David Mace indicates, before 1970, we really had little understanding of how communication processes affect family relationships:

> I once made a survey of what I considered to be the twenty-six best books on marriage published between 1930 and 1970, in order to find out how they treated the subject of communication. Most of them scarcely mentioned it at all. Of those that did, only a few had any real perception of its importance. (1980, 10–11)

By contrast, Touliatos in the 1990–91 volume of *Inventory of Marriage and Family Literature* (1991) lists 107 articles under the general heading "Communication in the Family." (This heading includes the subheadings, "Conflict Resolution," "Power in the Family," "Technology and Human Systems," and "Decision Making.")

The importance of communication skills was probably overlooked for so long because in the past families were largely developed around gender roles. The definition of a good wife was clear. She cleaned, cooked, bore and cared for the children, and supported her husband emotionally. A good husband protected his family, supported them economically, did the heavy work around the house or farm, and assumed full responsibility for the family's physical well-being. A "good" wife, a "successful" husband, and a "strong" family resulted when all family members including children fulfilled their clearly specified roles.

Gender roles are no longer clear-cut. The family's major function has become relational rather than role fulfilling. The meeting of emotional needs in families has become more important than the meeting of physical needs. Because emotional needs are so individual, they are much harder to define and understand than physical needs. A proper role for a family member cannot be easily prescribed when that role is judged by the nebulous standard of "meeting emotional needs."

Stating that meeting emotional needs is more important than meeting physical needs in the modern American family assumes that the family is affluent enough to meet those physical needs. For families in real poverty, the meeting of day-to-day physical needs is still most important. It is much more difficult to communicate well and live happily with your partner and your children if your stomach is continually empty. Traditional gender roles have not changed nearly as much for families in the lower economic class as they have for economically better-off families. In essence, communication skills become more necessary as the individual seeks emotional and psychological intimacy, happiness, and fulfillment in marriage rather than simply successful fulfillment of socially prescribed family roles.

A marriage that supplies emotional gratification to both partners and helps them deal with crises and grow in a fulfilling manner can only be achieved by supportive interaction between the partners. Talking, listening, negotiating, and problem solving are necessary skills for building a strong relationship.

In a successful relationship, each partner's viewpoint is appreciated. The ability to compromise is also essential since seldom, if ever, can one person always have his or her own way in a relationship.

GOOD COMMUNICATION: A BASIC STRENGTH OF SUCCESSFUL FAMILIES

Successful communication is the cornerstone of any relationship. Such communication must be open, realistic, tactful, caring, and valued. Developing and maintaining this kind of communication is not always easy unless all family members are committed to the belief that good communication is important to life satisfaction. This may sound simple, yet couples in marital trouble almost always list "failure to communicate" as one of their major problems.

Good communication is both especially important and especially difficult in marriage because an intimate relationship arouses such intense emotions. High emotional levels, especially when these emotions are negative, tend to interfere with clear communication. If you have ever had trouble communicating when you are calm and collected, imagine the potential problems when you are excited and emotionally aroused. Yet only through clear communication can each partner hope to understand the needs and intentions of the other. When conflicts arise, the partners can resolve them only if each is able to communicate fairly about the problem, define it clearly, and be open to alternative solutions. Good communication also helps minimize hostilities. For example, unexpressed dissatisfaction tends to create hostility, but fairly expressed dissatisfaction allows the other partner to understand the problem and act to reduce the first partner's unhappiness and deflate the hostility.

Conflict management is essential to all intimate relationships. Considering that when two people marry, they have already experienced many years of socialization and have learned multiple—and perhaps quite different—attitudes, the surprising thing is that they can get along at all on an intimate day-to-day basis! What each person has learned about handling interpersonal relationships will be, to a large extent, particular to that individual. For example, one partner may have learned early that you do not talk about problems until everyone is calm and collected. As a consequence, sometimes a problem has not been discussed for several days. The other partner has learned that you always speak your mind immediately. She or he has been taught that waiting only makes things worse. These differing beliefs about when and how to communicate will probably cause difficulties in the relationship.

Communication is also affected by the general society. For example, American men are taught to disclose less about their feelings than are American women. The traditional American masculine role is to be strong and silent. Expressiveness, sensitivity, and tenderness are considered feminine traits. But obviously these traits are important in good communication even if the traditional masculine role denies them to males. Thus, marital communication is certainly affected by general social values about masculinity and femininity as well as by the individual communicative skills of the partners.

It is important to emphasize the influence of the general society and its institutions on intimate relationships. Most people encountering marital problems tend to believe that their difficulties are strictly personal; that is, they believe that the problems are unique to their partners, their families, themselves, or the immediate circumstances. Placing the source of the problems solely upon the partners and their marriage reinforces the myth that marriage to the "right" person will solve all problems and result in a constantly happy family life. Certainly, many problems are unique to a given family, but it is equally true that many family problems arise because of social pressures. For example, stereotypical sex roles may lock a family into rigid patterns of behavior that not only cause problems for individual family members but also create stress for the entire family.

The myth of the "right" partner sometimes leads a troubled couple to attempt to end their problems by changing partners when, in fact, it is their relational skills that need changing. A person whose lack of communication skills finally leads to the demise of his or her marriage will soon find that any new relationship is also in trouble.

Part of good communication is a couple's ability to relate to one another in a manner relatively free from cultural influences. In other words, partners should attribute meaning to each other's communications based on their personal knowledge of one another rather than on traditionally accepted interpretations.

Jane calls her husband Jim "pigheaded," but instead of becoming angry at a traditionally accepted put-down, he laughs and hugs her. Calling him pigheaded is Jane's special way of complimenting him for being properly assertive.

As this example also makes clear, for good communication, the partners must know and agree on the unique meanings of each other's communications. To react with a hug rather than with anger, Jim needed to know that his wife's use of a traditionally negative label had a positive meaning. This example also indicates that successful communication takes time to develop. It requires a learning process between two people and only develops gradually. The ultimate

Good Communication: A Basic
Strength of Successful Families

outcome of successful communication is the achievement of interpersonal understanding.

Such understanding between people in close relationships also implies a certain "richness" in their communication. Richness means that they have many ways of communicating with one another, even many ways of conveying the same thing (Galvin and Brommel 1986). Research indicates that happily married couples have more communication styles than unhappily married couples (Honeycutt et al. 1982).

Stinnett and DeFrain (1985) report on an enlightening research study during which couples were wired with portable microphones that recorded all their verbal communications. The average couple spent only seventeen minutes a week in conversation (McGinnis 1979).

As we shall see in the next chapter, one of the real changes in the American family has been the widespread entrance of wives and mothers into the work force. The dual-earner family has now become the norm rather than the exception. When both partners work outside the home, two important factors underlying strong and successful families—time spent together and conversation—tend to be weakened. Strong families do spend a lot of time conversing, both about trivial aspects of their lives and about deeper, more important issues.

Communication of support, affirmation, appreciation, caring, respect, and interest in other family members is the lifeblood of the successful family system. McCubbin et al. (1988, 123–30) found many factors that related to communication skills:

- Trusting and confiding in one another
- Trying new ways to deal with problems
- Working together to solve problems
- Expressing caring and affection for each other daily
- At least one family member talking to his or her parents regularly
- Sharing feelings and concerns with close friends
- Parents spending time with teenagers for private talks
- Checking in and out with each other

Almost all couples who come in for counseling, start divorce proceedings, or indicate serious problems in their relationship begin by describing their inability to communicate well. "He never listens to me." "All she does is nag." "I never know what he is feeling." "She expects me to read her mind." "He never talks to me." All these are common complaints of troubled couples.

A husband who doesn't listen when his wife talks about her day or a parent who doesn't listen when a child talks about his or her problems at school seems to be expressing disinterest, which signals a lack of respect and appreciation. The wife, husband, or child who doesn't share his or her thoughts and feelings also seems to be expressing a lack of trust in other family members. Parents who do not attend to the day-to-day activities of their children shouldn't be surprised when their children choose not to discuss major problems, such as drugs or sex, with them. Parents frequently say, "Why didn't you come to me with this before it became a problem?" Yet when parents turn a deaf ear to a child's day-to-day trivia, such as who said what to whom or how the tennis class or history exam went, the child may easily conclude that they probably won't listen to problems either.

Poor communication within a family is manifested in a number of ways. First, the family members suffer from a constant feeling of frustration, of not being understood, of not getting their message across. This frustration usually leads to preoccupation with escape—the need to go out, to be constantly on the phone, to have the television set on all the time, or to keep Walkman headphones in place during family time. Poor communication leads to this oft-quoted parent-child interaction:

"Where are you going?"

"Out."

"What are you going to do?"

"Nothing."

Poor communication is often evidenced in sharp words, quarrels, and misunderstandings. The poorly communicating family tends to bicker and engage in conflict frequently. Sometimes this behavior becomes so unpleasant that family members simply cease to talk, and silence becomes the norm. Some people confuse silence with lack of communication, but silence certainly sends messages and can be a devastating form of communication. Think back to the last time someone gave you the "silent treatment." How did you react?

WHAT CAUSES COMMUNICATION FAILURE?

Communication failure means communication isn't accomplishing what it is intended to accomplish. It doesn't convey what a person wants to convey. This is not always an accident. The failure is often intentional, though not overtly or consciously so. People sometimes choose not to communicate.

Often when a marriage is disintegrating, the partners say, "We just can't communicate" or "We just don't talk to each other any more." They identify a deficiency of talk with a lack of communication and believe the failure to talk is the cause of their problems. Actually, the nontalking is not a lack of communication but a form of communication that sends a surplus of negative or aversive messages that hasten the disintegration of the relationship. Remember silence also communicates.

Failure to communicate well with others sometimes begins with a breakdown of intrapersonal (internal) communication. Anger, emotional maladjustment, stress and strain, and faulty perceptions can all lead to blind spots and overly strong defenses that interfere with good interpersonal communication. When individuals' self-images become unrealistic, they tend to filter all communications to fit the faulty self-picture. Under such circumstances, communication that accomplishes shared meaning is not likely to occur.

AVERSIVE COMMUNICATION

One basic principle of human behavior is that people seek pleasure and avoid pain. But actually people first avoid pain and then seek pleasure, because in the hierarchy of human needs pain avoidance is basic to survival. This point is crucial to understanding communication failure because motivation to communicate will be most urgent when the intention is to avoid pain. Unfortunately, the quickest means of changing the behavior of the partner who is giving us pain is to threaten him or her; that is, to combat pain with aversive communication. But this threat causes pain to the spouse and is counterproductive, because the threatened partner will most likely respond at the same or higher level, creating a "vicious circle." This kind of communication is a power struggle in which the winner is the person who generates the most aversion. The loser feels resentful and may engage in typical loser behavior, such as deceit, procrastination, deliberate inadequacy, sarcasm, and sullenness. Any verbal input by the loser thereafter is likely to be an emotional discharge of the resulting resentment. Generally, the loser stops talking because communication has become so painful. Or the loser may deliberately attempt to mislead the winner. Often the loser will begin to seek fulfillment outside the relationship, at which point noninteraction will become an intentional goal.

An example of aversive communication is one that starts out dealing with one conflict but soon turns into a confusing kaleidoscope of other marginally related disagreements that are connected only by the pain each partner causes the other:

"Where did you put my socks?"

"You mean the socks I have to crawl under the bed to find every time I do the laundry?"

"Yes, every time you do the laundry—the second Tuesday of every month."

"With the machine that's always broken, that nobody fixes."

"Because I'm so busy working to pay for tennis lessons and ladies' luncheons."

"And losses at Tuesday night poker bashes."

"I'm sick of this argument."

"Well, you started it."

"How?"

"Well, I can't remember, but you did."

It is important to remember that negative thoughts must be communicated, but there are positive ways by which to communicate them (see Table 6-1). Note that in Table 6-1, most of the positive responses are ways of saying to the partner, "Yes, I'm listening." Other explicit listening indications are "I see," "Tell me about it," "This seems important to you," and "Okay, let's work on it together." As you become aware of negative responses in your interactions with your partner, substitute more positive responses to show that you care about your partner and about your relationship.

Inappropriate reassurance may be received negatively when the other person has shared a problem. Your attempt to make him or her feel better by downplaying the problem may backfire. For example, saying "Don't worry about it, everyone has that problem at some time in their lives" when a person tells you of a problem may effectively stifle further discussion. On the other hand, reassurance and praise after the partner has sufficiently explored all the feelings that are associated with the problem are appropriate and will have positive outcomes.

Remember that communication serves many purposes and takes many forms. Communication among intimates and family members will include both

TABLE 6-1

NEGATIVE AND POSITIVE RESPONSES IN COMMUNICATION

NEGATIVE		POSITIVE	
1. Ordering, directing, commanding	"Stop ordering me around." "You can't buy that." "Don't talk to me like that."	1. Providing self-direction and choice	"You appear very disappointed." "Let's discuss whether that would be a good purchase." "When you talk like that, I feel frightened."
2. Warning, admonishing, threatening	"Listen to me or else." "If you won't, then I'll find someone who will."	2. Seeking causes for differences	"What did I say that turned you off?" "Help me understand why you don't want to. . . ."
3. Exhorting, moralizing, preaching	"You should tell your boss you want that raise."	3. Choosing one of several alternatives	"Which do you think would be best for you, . . . for us, . . . for all involved?"
4. Advising, giving solutions or suggestions	"Why don't you try. . . ." "You ought to stay home more."	4. Exploring possibilities	"What could you try?" "Would it help you if. . . ."
5. Lecturing, teaching, giving logical arguments	"It makes more sense to do it this way." "The Browns are happy, and they don't have a new car."	5. Considering consequences	"Which way seems to get better results for you?" "Let's think about what would result from each decision."
6. Judging, criticizing, blaming	"You are wrong." "It's all you fault." "What a stupid idea!"	6. Sharing responsibility	"Those two statements seem to conflict." "Let's do what we can to solve it." "Let's see if that idea will work."
7. Praising, agreeing, evaluating	"I think you are absolutely correct." "You do so many good things."	7. Expanding openness	"This seems like a difficult decision for you to make." "You sound discouraged. I'll listen."
8. Name calling, ridiculing, shaming, categorizing	"You're no good." "You're just like all the other men/women." "You're a liar."	8. Enhancing self-esteem and uniqueness	"I love you." "I appreciate your understanding." "Your interpretation is different from mine."
9. Interpreting, analyzing, diagnosing	"If you weren't so tired, you could see my point." "You don't care what I think."	9. Increasing sensitivity	"If you prefer, we can discuss this at another time." "Right now, I'm feeling so alone and left out."
10. Reassuring, sympathizing, consoling	"Don't worry about it." "All men/women go through that at some time."	10. Expressing care and concern	"What worries you about that?" "This is an especially difficult time for you."
11. Probing, questioning, interrogating	"Where have you been?" "Now, tell me the real reason you feel that way."	11. Giving freedom and privacy	"I've missed you a lot." "You don't need to explain if you would rather not."
12. Withdrawing, distracting, humoring, diverting	"You're funny when you're mad." "Why don't you tell me something new!"	12. Accepting, giving attention to the other person	"I understand that you are feeling mad because. . . ." "That point is something you haven't mentioned before."

Source: From Richard Hunt and Edward Rydman, *Creative Marriage* (Boston: Holbrook, 1976), pp. 50–51.

content and relationship dimensions. "Go to your room," spoken by a parent to a child is both content (requesting an action) and relational (I am your parent and have authority over you).

Communication is also both expressive and instrumental. "Let's go out for a romantic dinner tonight, I just love you so much." In this case the spouse is expressing feelings (affection toward his or her spouse) while at the same time suggesting task-oriented behavior (going out to dinner).

COMMUNICATION CAN BE USED FOR GOOD AND BAD PURPOSES

This chapter is based on the popular assumption that improved communication is always healthy and helpful to personal relationships. Mass media and popular authors recommend communication as the cement that holds relationships together. USA Today reports that communication makes a healthy family. Shere Hite's Women and Love: A Cultural Revolution in Progress identifies communication as essential to marital satisfaction. Marriage and family therapists recommend improved communication to help troubled families.

Before proceeding further, however, we must remind ourselves that communication is a double-edged sword. It can be used to express honest feelings, convey facts and observations, share helpful information, or enhance another person, ourselves, or a relationship, as well as for other positive purposes. Or it can be used to manipulate feelings, convey falsehoods, hide information, or degrade another person, oneself, or a relationship, as well as for other negative purposes.

We see communication being used to mislead. We hear lies being told. We observe language being misused to persuade people to buy something they don't need or to destroy something or someone. A good "con" artist is usually a good communicator who can lie with sincerity and twist the truth with conviction. We see communication used as propaganda to hide or distort realities. We are bombarded with meaningless slogans designed only to arouse us emotionally. Just exactly what does "Power to the People" mean?

Merely learning better communication skills does not necessarily mean that the improved skills will be used to further a relationship. They could just as easily be used to destroy a relationship.

Hence our discussion of communication is set within the context of creating improved personal and family relationships. Good communication skills are one of the major strengths of strong, successful families and other important relationships.

THE FOUNDATION BLOCKS OF SUCCESSFUL COMMUNICATION

Three general conditions must be met to achieve the kind of communication that builds strong, positive relationships:

1. *Commitment:* The partners must be committed to make their relationship healthy and strong.
2. *Growth orientation:* The partners must accept the fact that their relationship will always be dynamic and changing rather than static.
3. *Noncoercive atmosphere:* The partners must feel free to be themselves, to be open, and to be honest.

These three conditions represent the foundation blocks of successful communication, but they are difficult to attain.

■ COMMITMENT ■

Simply stated, commitment means making a pledge or binding yourself to your partner and includes the idea of working to build and maintain the relationship. As we know, commitment to others is one of the characteristics of strong, successful families. Couples often fail to seek marriage counseling until so much pain and suffering have occurred that the commitment of one or both marital partners has been destroyed. At that point there is little hope of resolution. Often one partner is still committed enough to want counseling, while the other has covertly given up hope and commitment and resists counseling for fear of being drawn back into a painful trap. Sometimes an uncommitted partner will seek therapy only in the hope that a dependent spouse will become strong enough to survive without the marriage. This situation adds complexity, especially if the dependent partner, sensing abandonment, avoids getting stronger in the hope that the noncommitted partner will stay in the marriage.

Many uncommitted partners allow the other spouse to plan activities, anticipate problems, make necessary adjustments, and so on. Sometimes this kind of relationship works. More often than not, however, the partner with the greater commitment becomes resentful of the uncommitted partner's noninvolvement. Paradoxically, the one who cares the least controls the relationship. This is termed the *principle of least interest.*

Alice is more committed to their marriage than Roger. For their summer vacation, she wants to go to San Francisco, whereas he wants to go backpacking. Because Roger is not as committed to the relationship, it is easy for him to say, "Go to San Francisco if you want, but I'm going backpacking and you can come along if you like." Alice can plead with Roger to consider her desire but, more likely, she will resign herself to going backpacking.

Although commitment is a precondition to effective communication, each partner's commitment to the relationship can be increased through use of the five communication skills, to be discussed later.

The Foundation Blocks of Successful Communication

WHAT RESEARCH TELLS US ABOUT SELF-DISCLOSURE: IS HONESTY ALWAYS THE BEST POLICY?

It is a popular notion that the more open and honest the self-disclosure, the better the communication and thus the better the relationship. "Being truthful is, in my opinion, the only choice in a relationship that means to be long-lasting, intimate, and committed" (Steiner 1986). Yet research has produced mixed findings about this idea. Certainly, there is a correlation between openness and satisfaction (Jorgensen and Gaudy 1980; Noller 1985; Hanson and Schuldt 1984), but some researchers suggest that both too much and too little self-disclosure can reduce satisfaction with a relationship (Galvin and Brommel 1986). In addition, Schumm and his colleagues (1986) suggest that simply increasing disclosure does not necessarily increase marital satisfaction. Instead it is selective disclosure that seems to increase marital satisfaction (Sillers et al. 1987).

As time passes in a relationship, restraints tend to be released, so that manners are sometimes forgotten, frankness overrides tact, and hostility may result. If the hostility and frankness become too overwhelming, the partners tend to limit their self-expression and to withdraw from each other. Their communication has become so aversive, they choose not to continue it.

Eckman (1985) asks his readers to:

Consider what life would be like if everyone could lie perfectly or no one could lie at all. If we could never know how someone really felt, and if we knew we couldn't know, life would be more tenuous. Certain in the knowledge that every show of emotion might be a mere display put on to please, manipulate, or mislead, individuals would be more adrift, attachments less firm.

And if we could never lie, if a smile was always reliable, never absent when pleasure was felt, and never present without pleasure, life would be rougher than it is, many relationships harder to maintain. Politeness, attempts to smooth matters over, to conceal feelings one wished one didn't feel—all would be gone.

Many nonadjustive responses for both husbands and wives come as a result of open sharing of feelings about violated expectations. Contrary to popular belief about the benefits of such sharing, this open communication did not lead to improved relations. For example, disclosure of an extramarital affair is almost always destructive to a marriage yet not disclosing the affair can also have negative consequences. Disclosure that is negative in affect, is hostile or nagging, and/or expresses excessive concern about oneself is also counterproductive. In these cases less may be better (Sprecher 1987).

■ GROWTH ORIENTATION ■

Individuals change as time goes on. The needs of a forty-year-old person usually differ from the needs that person had as a twenty-year-old. Marriage must also change if individual needs are to be met within the ongoing, dynamic marriage framework. And yet change is often threatening. It upsets comfortable routines and may therefore be resisted. Such resistance will be futile because relationships do not stand still. Thus, it is wise to accept and plan for change. An individual oriented to growth incorporates the inevitability of change into her or his lifestyle. This implies that one would be wise not only to accept change but also to create intentional and orderly change in a chosen direction.

These research findings suggest that open communication offers both pros and cons. An unequivocal relationship between self-disclosure and satisfaction in human relationships doesn't exist. Schuman and his colleagues (1986) suggest that the quality of the self-disclosure is an important variable that has been overlooked. They found that when there was high regard for the partner and this regard was apparent in the self-disclosure, the more disclosure the better. When low regard for the partner is being disclosed, greater openness seems to create less marital satisfaction.

The real question is *how* to disclose rather than *whether* to disclose. What is said (the content), how positive or negative it is, and the levels on which it is said (superficial to deeply meaningful, intellectual to emotional) all have to be taken into account.

Certainly, both partners must share a willingness to converse. But equally important, they must learn how to communicate successfully and remain aware of each other's weak and sensitive points. For example, people who are insecure often feel inferior and worthless and tend to be self-deprecating. They also tend to be fearful of open communication and usually react with hostility to what they perceive as unfair criticisms. On the other hand, people with a high level of self-esteem tend to be comfortable with open communication and are willing to disclose their own thoughts and feelings and to accept their partner's.

Thus, how one discloses thoughts and feelings, especially negative ones, strongly influences how the communication will be accepted. Those who believe it is important to keep everything out in the open and to always express themselves to the fullest must also concern themselves with how this expression is conveyed and with the feelings of their partner. Otherwise they may find such openness backfiring and actually weakening communication rather than enhancing it.

There is a fine line between inviting disclosure or encouraging openness in one's partner and invading his or her privacy. Respect of each other's privacy is an important element of a successful relationship. Each couple has to work out the appropriate balance between openness and privacy in the relationship. Unilaterally crossing over this line will usually be offensive to one's partner. Rather than becoming more open, the offended partner may withdraw (becoming cool and distant) or attack (becoming sarcastic and resistant to ideas) Strong 1983, 240). In these cases, openness reduces rather than enhances the chances for successful problem solving.

Generally, however, the more openness a couple can tolerate and agree upon between themselves, the better the relationships chance of success.

Gina enjoyed attending large social gatherings, but her husband Art dreaded them. Both were oriented to growth, however, and Art wanted to become more comfortable in social situations. They decided to work on helping Art change his dread of social interaction to enjoyment. At Art's suggestion, Gina began to invite one or two couples for evenings at their home, because Art felt more comfortable at home. He began to enjoy these small get-togethers, which Gina gradually expanded. Although Art is still not perfectly at ease in large groups, he is more comfortable and accompanies Gina frequently.

Had Gina and Art not been growth oriented, their differing social needs might have caused them to grow apart or become resentful of one another. Gina might have chastised Art for his social inabilities and gone out without him, leaving him home to brood and resent her. On the other hand, Art might have been dictatorial and forbidden Gina to go to large social gatherings, which would probably have made her feel trapped and rebellious. Because neither was afraid of change and they agreed that a change in Art's attitude would be beneficial, they set out deliberately to encourage this process. Notice that both were committed to the change. If only one partner desires a change, particularly in the other partner, and the other disagrees, conflict can result. Successful communication requires noncoercion and a positive regard for the other.

■ NONCOERCIVE ATMOSPHERE ■

The goals of marriage will usually be lost if either partner is subjugated by the other. Free and open communication cannot exist in a one-sided totalitarian relationship. When any two people share a common goal, the issues of responsibility and authority arise. The situation in marriage is not unlike that in government. A marriage can be described as *laissez-faire* if both partners have total freedom of choice and action; *democratic* if responsibility is shared and authority is delegated by equitable agreement; or *autocratic* if both have responsibilities but authority is assigned to a single leader.

Most Americans say they want to establish a democratic marriage. In reality, this pattern is the most difficult to maintain, although it is ultimately the most satisfying. Most marriages end up being some mixture of all three types.

When power is invested in a single authority, a coercive relationship is usually the result. At least one partner, and often both, feels a loss of freedom. The subjugated person feels unfree and coerced by the partner with the power. But the person with authority may also feel unfree since he or she may be held responsible for all of the couple's decisions. Free and open communication usually cannot coexist when either or both partners feel coerced.

Mike and Daphne have been married six months. She pleads with him to give up his weekly evening handball game because she is afraid to be alone. He feels unfairly restricted and calls her a child. She in turn calls him an immature "jock" who can't give up playing with the boys. One thing leads to another, and Mike walks out of the room and slams the door. Daphne tearfully runs to the bedroom and locks herself in, leaving him to nurse his guilt. Although he apologizes profusely, she won't come out. So Mike stays home—his physical coercion (walking out and slamming the door) has been overpowered by her emotional coercion. He is resentful, and she is resentful and frightened. The intimacy that they experienced in their courtship is being dissolved by the acid of resentment created by their coercive acts.

At this moment, it is difficult to say just who has the power in this relationship. However, it is clear that successful communication will not survive long in such an environment. Sharing responsibilities, giving up control voluntarily, and feeling relatively free in a relationship greatly facilitate positive communication.

Instead of the foregoing sequence, Mike and Daphne might have worked out a compromise that would have satisfied them both. For example, knowing how much Mike enjoys his weekly handball game, Daphne might have supported him in this pleasure in the hope that he would then respond to her fear of being alone. He might reduce the number of times he plays handball; she might plan to visit her parents or a friend that evening. If each saw the other as noncoercive and supportive, compromise solutions would be far easier to work out.

▪ DEVELOPING A SMOOTH FLOW OF COMMUNICATION ▪

These three conditions for successful communication—commitment, growth orientation, and a noncoercive atmosphere—all contribute to creating a sense of order in which messages flow back and forth smoothly between sender and receiver. The first step in a communication flow is to *encode* the message and send it to the receiver via some verbal, nonverbal, or written *communication channel*. The receiver then *decodes* the message and, to ensure that it has been correctly received, must *feed back* what has been decoded to the sender. The sender either verifies the message or through *correction*, *negotiation*, and *problem solving* resends the message, and the process is repeated. This circular pattern may have to be repeated several times before the sender's intention and the receiver's interpretation coincide (see Figure 6-1).

COMMUNICATION SKILLS

When all is going well with couples, they usually don't think about their communication skills. Yet the best time to build communication skills is when disruptive forces are minimal. If problems arise later, the skills will be there. Conflicts that appear irreconcilable destroy relationships. In most cases conflicts become irreconcilable because the partners have failed to develop the communication skills that would help them solve conflicts.

▪ IDENTIFYING PROBLEM OWNERSHIP ▪

Clarifying responsibility or problem ownership is an important first step in problem-solving communication. This step is not always easy to accomplish. A problem can belong to either partner, or it can be shared jointly. The key question in determining ownership is, "Who feels tangibly affected?" To own

FIGURE 6-1
Communications flow chart, showing the three conditions necessary for successful communication

or share ownership of a problem, a person must know and openly admit that he or she is personally disturbed by it. For example, let's look at the following situation:

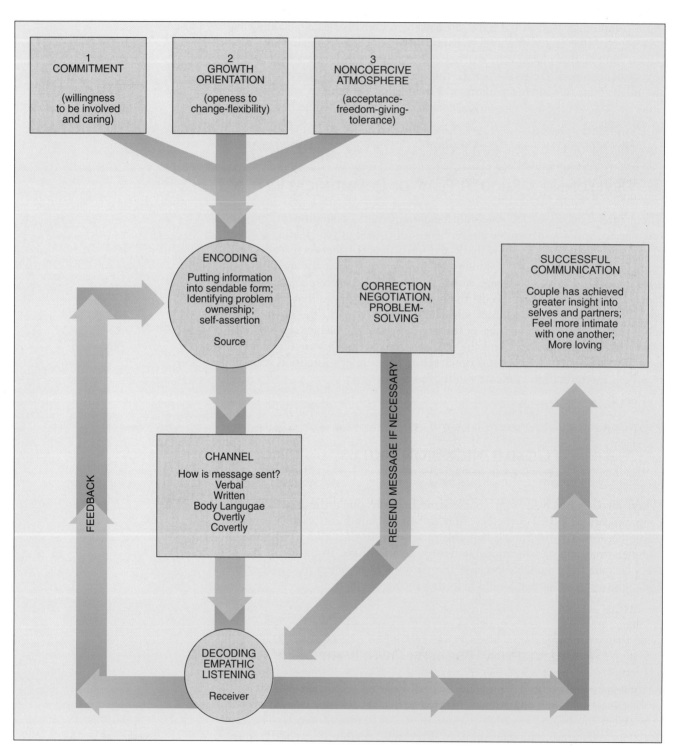

192

Jane thinks that her husband Ray is losing friends because he drinks heavily and becomes belligerent. But Ray isn't concerned about his behavior. He thinks people like him even when he's drinking, so he refuses ownership of the problem. Since he doesn't think he has a problem, he believes no change is necessary.

To own a problem, one must be tangibly affected by it. In the preceding situation, if Ray's behavior does not interfere with Jane's life, her friendships, or her sense of self, it does not tangibly affect her. However, if Jane is tangibly affected by Ray's behavior, she then shares ownership of the problem. For example, if their friends stop calling, her needs are being tangibly affected. If she communicates this to Ray and he refuses to admit to it, as paradoxical as it may seem, only Jane owns the problem. If, however, Ray acknowledges that his behavior is affecting Jane, then the problem is jointly owned. In most intimate relationships such as marriage, problems are jointly owned.

Assuming ownership of a problem is extremely important, yet we often shun the responsibility. Some people think that if they pay no attention to problems, the problems will lessen or disappear, but the reverse is generally true. In the long run, unattended problems usually become worse. Denial effectively cuts off communication and prevents change.

Modern American society too often encourages individuals to "cop out" of problems by supplying scapegoats on which responsibility can be erroneously placed:

"I'm unaffectionate because my parents rejected me as a child."

"My father beat my mother when he drank: now I can't relate to men because of my deep hostility toward him.

"The establishment controls everything, so why bother to change?"

"American society is racist. I am African American (or Jewish or Hispanic or . . .) and therefore all my problems are caused by society."

The list could go on and on, but these examples and the "Bloom County" cartoon on the following page give an idea of what must be avoided if you are to solve personal problems. For instance, it may be true that you have problems because your parents rejected you, but they are still *your* problems. Rejecting parents are not suddenly going to become loving parents in order to solve your problems. Obviously, your parents have problems of their own, but you can't make them solve their problems; you can only work to solve your own. The first step toward solution is assuming ownership and responsibility for your problems.

We must add an important caution to this discussion of problem ownership. Forcing problem ownership on your partner through "blaming" is highly destructive. Some people use problem ownership—an aspect of good communication—in a negative manner; that is, they lay blame on the other person,

saying that he or she is responsible for the trouble. "It's your problem!" We can make the same kind of comment about the next skill we will discuss, self-assertion. In essence, one partner may attack the other under the guise of being self-assertive, thus perverting a positive communication skill into harmful communication.

If the problem is mine, then I will use the skill of self-assertion. If my partner owns the problem, then I will try to use the skill of empathic listening. If we both own the problem, we will alternate these two communication skills.

SELF-ASSERTION

Self-assertion is the process of recognizing and expressing one's feelings, opinions, and attitudes while remaining aware of the feelings and needs of others.

Some people are nonassertive. They fail to make their feelings and thoughts known to others. This makes full, successful communication almost impossible.

Mary thinks Jim is becoming less affectionate toward her. He doesn't hug her and touch her as much as he used to. Mary always liked the close physical contact and misses it. But she finds it hard to talk about her physical desires with anyone, much less a man, so she says nothing. Her anxiety and discomfort grow. She believes that if Jim really loved her, he would recognize how miserable she feels and give her more physical contact. She becomes increasingly hostile to him until one day he asks, "What's the matter?" She replies, "You ought to know, it's your fault."

Jim is completely in the dark. Mary's nonassertive behavior has precluded successful communication and thus has foreclosed solving the problem.

Some of the personal reasons for nonassertive behavior are fear, feelings of inferiority, lack of confidence, shyness, and embarrassment. Society and its traditional role expectations may also influence nonassertive behavior. For example, Mary may have accepted the earlier traditional American feminine role expectation of passivity and nonassertiveness, of expecting the man to solve her problems. Whatever the reasons, if needs go unexpressed, they will not be magically recognized and fulfilled by others.

In contrast to nonassertive individuals, aggressive individuals completely bypass tact and recognition of others' needs in expressing their feelings. They demand attention and support and insist on having whatever they want at the moment, often overriding the rights and feelings of others in the process. In fact, aggressive individuals often seem unaware that other people have rights and feelings. Consequently, they may hurt other people without even being aware that they are doing so. Not all aggression is destructive, however. Used in a constructive manner, aggression can offer emotional release, let a partner know how intensely the other partner is feeling, and help both partners learn how to cope with all kinds of offensive and emotional behavior.

Self-assertive people feel free to express themselves but are aware of the feelings and needs of others. They will comment on their own observations and feelings rather than criticize another person's actions. For example, contrast the statement, "This kind of behavior is hard for me to handle and makes me angry, even though I don't want to be" with "You make me so mad." The second statement is almost useless to successful communication. It judges and places blame on the other person. Such a statement usually provokes a defensive comment on the part of the listener. This, in turn, elicits yet another aggressive comment from the first person and so on, until the situation spirals out of control.

I-statements locate the feelings or concerns inside the person who is making the statement rather than placing the problem on the partner. Gordon (1970) suggests that I-statements are less apt to provoke resistance and are less threatening than statements about the other person and therefore promote openness. Good I-messages may include "feeling," "when," and "because" parts: "I feel upset when the living room is in a mess because then guests may think I'm a sloppy housekeeper."

Wesley Burr (1990) suggests adding We-statements to the communication process. We-statements place the problem in the group or relationship rather than on one of the individuals in the relationship (see Scenes from Marriage, p. 210).

It may seem surprising that people building a relationship often need special help with self-assertion. Many people believe that what is needed is less self-assertion. In their view, self-seeking assertions and selfishness are the basis of marital difficulty. Remember, though, that our definition of self-assertion includes awareness of others' feelings and needs. We certainly need to be less destructively aggressive in our relations, but we must not confuse that with being nonassertive.

It is important to be aware that recognition and expression of needs do not necessarily lead to their fulfillment. For example, I may recognize and express my desire to smoke, which is self-assertive. If other people in the room find cigarette smoke unpleasant and tell me so, they are also being assertive. This conflict can be successfully resolved in a couple of ways. I may go outside to smoke, thus satisfying my needs without interfering with the needs of other people; or I may recognize that smoking would be more unpleasant for them than pleasant to me and decide to forgo smoking in their presence. In either case, I have been assertive: I have recognized and expressed my need, though I may not have fulfilled my desire. Self-assertion does not mean getting your way all the time.

The definition of self-assertion includes recognizing needs and inner feelings. This recognition is not always easy.

Alice has to conduct a PTA meeting tomorrow morning, and she is both anxious and resentful about it. She has put off planning the meeting until there is almost no time left. Harry comes home and says, "How about going to the movies tonight? Alice blows up and says irritably, "I still have dinner to cook and dishes to do. As the old saying goes, 'Man works from sun to sun, but woman's work is never done.'" Harry responds, "If women have it so tough, why do men have all the ulcers and heart attacks?"

And so the argument spirals on without chance of solution, at least partially because Alice has not recognized the real source of her irritation: namely, her anxiety about the PTA meeting. But why doesn't she? Perhaps she doesn't want to admit to herself that she is afraid of conducting the meeting. She avoids thinking about the meeting and thereby avoids the fear that arises when she does. Or maybe she knows she is afraid but doesn't want Harry to see this weakness, so she covers it by starting an irrelevant argument.

Self-assertion requires self-knowledge; that is, successful communication depends in large part on knowing oneself. Any relationship will have known and unknown dimensions. One way of diagramming and discovering these dimensions is called the *Johari window* (see Figure 6-2). You do not know everything about yourself or about your partner. And you do not necessarily share everything that you do know about yourself with your partner. As a relationship grows and becomes increasingly intimate, however, you usually learn more about both yourself and your partner.

Let's see how to use the Johari window. When you begin a new relationship with another person, one in which you both are committed to helping the other grow, you might both draw Johari windows. The easiest square to fill in is common knowledge. At the beginning of the relationship, common knowledge might include only such things as physical appearance, food preferences, political persuasion, and family composition. As the relationship continues, you will be able to fill in some of the other's blind spots, perhaps helping him or her become aware of such things as insensitivity, selfishness, nervous laughter, bad breath, snoring, and so forth. Your partner can do the same for you.

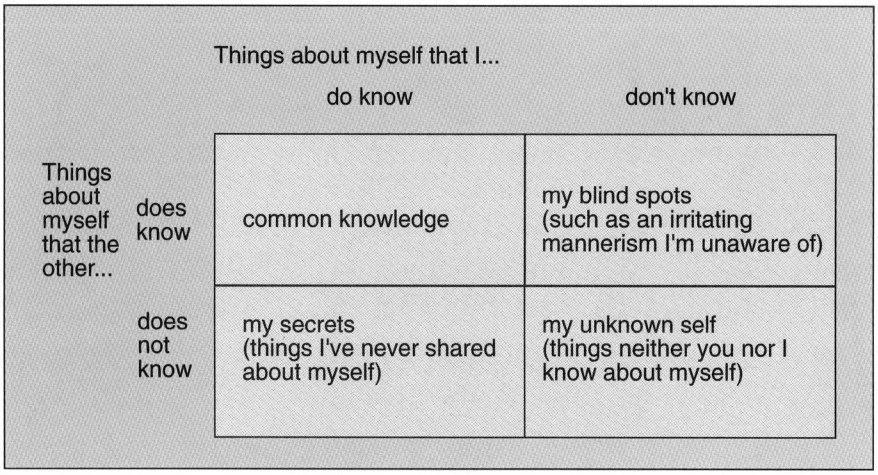

FIGURE 6-2
Johari window

Figure content:

Things about myself that I...

		do know	don't know
Things about myself that the other...	does know	common knowledge	my blind spots (such as an irritating mannerism I'm unaware of)
	does not know	my secrets (things I've never shared about myself)	my unknown self (things neither you nor I know about myself)

As you continue to develop trust in each other, you can begin to fill in your secrets, such as feelings of inferiority or being afraid to be alone at night. By now you may be discovering aspects of each other's unknown selves; these may be hidden potentials, talents, or weaknesses that the interaction between the two of you has uncovered. As you get to know each other better, the blind spots and secret areas will become smaller; more information is moved into the common knowledge window for you both.

Of course, the Johari window is not just for new relationships. It can also illuminate behavior and knowledge in ongoing relationships. In fact, the process of exploring new dimensions of the self and the other person is exciting and never ending. Unfortunately, many couples share little common knowledge because each partner has little self-knowledge. People who are afraid to learn about themselves usually block communication that might lead to self-knowledge. As we saw earlier, aversive reactions are excellent ways to stifle communication. For example, consider the following interaction:

Jim thinks his wife Jane looks unusually good one evening and says, "I really feel proud when men look at you admiringly."

Jane replies angrily, "When you say that, I feel like a showpiece in the marketplace."

"Why don't you get off that feminist trip?" he retorts.

Jane's aversive reply to Jim's statement will probably make him more reluctant to express his feelings next time. In essence, her aversive response punished him for expressing his feelings. But why did she respond aversively. She may simply have been in a bad mood. Or perhaps she has negative feelings about her appearance and thus needs to deny Jim's statement because it is inconsistent with her self-image. Her attractive appearance might be a blind spot in her Johari window. However, another interpretation of Jim's statement makes Jane's reaction more understandable. She may be objecting to his implied sense of ownership—to his describing her as if she were a shiny new sports car envied by all his friends.

So we can define the communication skill of self-assertion as learning to express oneself without making the other person defensive. Neither Jim nor Jane is particularly good at this aspect of self-assertion.

■ EMPATHIC LISTENING ■

Of all the skills we have been discussing, none is more important—and often more difficult—then that of being a good listener. We are all ready to offer our own thoughts and opinions but are not so ready to listen to those of others. Often we are so preoccupied with our own thoughts or with preparing our replies that we are unable to hear what the other person is saying. Being a good listener is an art and is much appreciated by most people. It is surely one of the most important ingredients of intimate relationships. The research on strong, healthy families finds that members of these families are listened to by other family members. They feel understood and accepted because family members not only listen well but also recognize and respond to nonverbal messages. Good listening implies a real empathy for the speaker. Empathy means not only understanding what the speaker is saying but also being able to respond to and feel the speaker's nonverbal communications and emotions.

Real listening keeps the focus on the person who is talking. The empathic listener actively tries to reduce any personal filters that distort the speaker's messages. Most listeners usually add to, subtract from, or in other ways change the speaker's message. For example, someone says, "I wrapped my car around a tree coming home from a party last night." You might hear these words and think, "Well, you probably were drinking (inference), and no one should drive when drinking (value judgment)." Although you have no evidence the speaker was drinking, you have immediately assigned your own meaning to the statement. If the speaker recognizes your nonverbal signals, he or she may react with anger or cease talking.

In contrast, empathic listening is nonjudgmental and accepting. To the degree that we are secure in our self-image, we can listen to others without filtering their message. When we really listen to and understand another, we open ourselves to new self-knowledge and change. This can be frightening to persons who feel insecure and unsure of themselves.

George is unsure of Gloria's love for him and fears she may one day leave him. At dinner she comments, "I really like tall men with beards." George rubs his clean-shaven chin and begins to feel insecure. He doesn't hear much of the ensuing conversation because he is busy trying to decide whether Gloria would like him to grow a beard or if she has a crush on another man. He has completely filtered out the part about tall men because he is tall and was therefore not threatened by her comment.

George has put his own inferences on Gloria's comment and becomes increasingly upset as he ponders not what she actually said, but what he thinks she meant by what she said.

It is interesting to note that it is sometimes easier to listen empathically to a relative stranger than to someone with whom you have a close relationship. Married people sometimes say that some other person understands them better than their spouse does. This may well be true because emotions often get in the way of listening. For example, when George's co-worker says she likes tall men with beards, George doesn't even think about her comment, he simply says, "That's nice." Also, when a couple has spent years together, each partner often assumes that "of course, we understand one another," so there is no reason to listen carefully.

Empathic listening tells the speaker that the listener hears and cares. In essence, the speaker feels nonthreatened, noncoerced, and free to speak—some of our preconditions for successful communication.

Empathic listening has several components. Obviously, the listener must feel capable of paying close attention to the speaker. If we are consumed by our own thoughts and problems, we cannot listen empathically to another. But when we know that we cannot listen well, we should point that out (self-assertion) and perhaps arrange to have the discussion at another time. For instance, family members sometimes bring up problems at inopportune times, perhaps at the end of a busy day when others are likely to be tired and hungry. They then become upset when no one is willing to listen. Most of us need time, a quiet environment, and a peaceful mind to be good empathic listeners.

We also need to want to listen fully. Instead we often use *selective attention* to filter out what we do not want to hear. This means we hear only what we want to hear. Teenagers are often particularly good at not hearing something a parent has told them. *Selective retention* also plays a role. People may attend to something at the time of communication, but later will remember only what they want to remember.

We may also need training and practice to become good listeners. As children we receive plenty of training to improve our verbal skills, but we seldom receive training for our listening skills. Just as our verbal skills can be improved through training and practice, so can our listening skills.

Communication Skills

NONVERBAL COMMUNICATION

If we are to be good listeners, part of our attention needs to be directed to the nonverbal communications of the speaker, often referred to as *body language*. Emotions are reflected throughout the body. A hand gesture, a frown, a hug, and a smile are all meaningful communications. Although bodily communication generally is culturally based, certain gestures are more idiosyncratic (personal and unique) than verbal communications. Nonverbal communications are also often more descriptive of a person's feelings. For example, Mary habitually uses her hands in an erasing motion to wipe away unpleasant thoughts. Ralph pulls at his ear and rubs the back of his neck when being criticized. The nonverbal message usually represents a more accurate picture of how a person is feeling emotionally than do her or his verbal communications. Pearson (1989, 74) cites many research findings in concluding that when nonverbal and verbal communications conflict, most adults believe the message conveyed nonverbally. For example, I am late for my date. My girlfriend says that's all right, she understands, she is not angry. Yet when I go to hug her, she pulls back and rejects my touch. Her face is set and unsmiling. Do I believe her words or her actions? Strong (1983, 65) suggests that we process the emotional messages first, since we cannot reach agreement on content unless we know each other's feelings about the content. It takes time to learn what an indi-

Janet Pearson (1989, 281–82) suggests six behaviors that facilitate feedback in the family context:

1. *Provide clear verbal feedback.* Responses that are ambiguous, overly complex, or overly simple do not help communicators. Family members may feel that you are talking down to them or purposely trying to mislead them.

2. *Rely on descriptive statements.* Descriptive statements comment on what is observable (behavior and appearance) and tend to be neutral or supportive. Contrast this descriptive statement, "Your shoulders are slumping, you're walking heavily, and your eyes are bloodshot—you look tired" with this evaluative statement, "You're sure tired, impatient, and grumpy today." Evaluative statements tend to encourage defensiveness.

3. *Provide reflective statements.* Such statements tend to mirror or reflect back to the communicator what he or she has stated. Such statements do not judge content but serve only to check whether one has understood the speaker's communications accurately.

4. *Demonstrate bodily responsiveness.* When we move in a responsive way, we suggest nonverbally that we are actively listening and concerned about the other person's message. If we are physically impassive, we appear disinterested. If we simply move randomly, we appear distracted.

5. *Use a sincere, warm voice.* Tone of voice can convey a variety of emotions. A sincere, warm voice suggests support and understanding.

6. *Establish eye contact.* When we look at the person who is speaking, we demonstrate interest.

vidual's personal nonverbal communication patterns mean, but an empathic listener will notice and interpret such patterns.

Distance between people is also a nonverbal communication indicator. The more intimate our relations with another person, the closer we can physically be with that person and feel comfortable. I put my arm around my wife or girlfriend but not around the store clerk who is a stranger. Each of us has a sense of our personal space, but this space varies both according to the culture and to the intimacy of the relationship. Americans tend to prefer a greater distance between people in their casual personal relations than do South Americans. An interesting personal experiment is simply to halve the normal distance between you and people with whom you interact and watch their reaction. They'll almost always back away.

FEEDBACK

Feedback is another key component of empathic listening. Empathic listeners periodically check their perceptions with the speaker by rephrasing the speaker's words. This rephrasing reassures the speaker that she or he is being listened to and interpreted accurately. It also provides the speaker with an opportunity to correct the listener's perceptions, if necessary, and to hear his or her ideas from the listener's perspective. Some examples of feedback are:

SPEAKER: You're always working.

LISTENER: You're right, I do work a lot. Is it interrupting something we need to do?

SPEAKER: Why don't we get out of this town?

LISTENER: You feel like leaving. I guess you don't like it here.

Communication Skills

Note that empathic listening involves an effort on the listener's part to pick up feelings as well as content. Feeding back feelings is, however, more difficult than feeding back content.

The desire to give advice is one of the major deterrents to empathic listening and clear feedback. Advice—especially unsolicited advice—always has a negative side. It says to your partner, "You don't know what to do and I do," which could be interpreted as, "Boy, are you stupid." There is no better way to turn off communication than to stir up someone's defenses. Instead of giving advice, offer alternatives. This approach increases the speaker's options, but leaves the responsibility of making the decision with the speaker. Simultaneously, it indicates respect for the speaker's intelligence (Strong 1983, 137).

Remember, though, that we are discussing how to enhance good problem-solving communication. Much communication is for play and fun, to establish contact, or to impart information. Using problem-solving skills in inappropriate situations can actually create problems. For example, if someone says "Please pass the butter," it would be inappropriate to reply (feedback), "Oh, I understand that you'd like to have some butter on your bread." Such a remark will probably invoke a muttered comment like, "There you go using that dumb psychology talk again." Knowing how to listen and give feedback are invaluable skills, but they can be misused. Knowing *when* to use these skills is just as important as knowing *how* to use them.

◾ NEGOTIATING ◾

If a problem is jointly owned, the situation calls for negotiation. In negotiation the partners alternate between self-assertion and empathic listening. Usually, the more distressed partner starts with self-assertion. But because the problem is jointly owned, the listener's feelings are also involved, and it is imperative to switch roles relatively often to be sure that each person's communications are understood by the other. Set a time period, say, five to ten minutes, for each partner to speak. Remember that in these situations listening will take extra effort in order to avoid the temptation to think about your side of the problem while your partner is speaking, which interferes with empathic listening.

When roles are exchanged, the partner who was listening should first restate the assertive partner's position (feedback) so that any necessary corrections can be made before going on to his or her own assertions. Knowing that you must restate the speaker's position to his or her satisfaction before you can present your own position works wonders to improve listening ability.

This simple procedure of reversing roles and restating the other's position before presenting your own is also amazingly effective in defusing potential emotional outbursts. Frustration usually builds up because partners do not listen well to one another and therefore often feel misunderstood. But if the negotiation process is used, even when you and your partner strongly disagree, at least you will both be assured that your partner has heard and understood your position.

◾ PROBLEM SOLVING ◾

When you have established ownership of the problem, begun to clarify the problem, and discharged some of the emotion surrounding the problem, you are ready to solve the problem. Of course, by now the problem will have been greatly diminished and may even have disappeared. If you and your partner still think you have a problem, however, you can now apply the seven steps to scientific problem solving:

1. Recognize and define the problem.
2. Set up conditions supportive to problem solving.
3. Brainstorm for possible alternatives (establishing hypotheses).
4. Select the best solution.
5. Implement the solution.
6. Evaluate the solution.
7. Modify the solution if necessary.

The first two steps have already been accomplished if you have used the skills discussed. Step 3, brainstorming, broadens the range of possible solutions. The purpose of brainstorming is to produce as many ideas as possible within a given time period. In other words, you select a time period, such as half an hour, and during that time you and your partner suggest or write down possible solutions to the problem without pausing to consider whether they are ridiculous or realistic. Negative judgments stifle creative thinking, so it is important to suspend any evaluating until both of you have run out of ideas or reached the end of the time period. Just jot down ideas as they occur, don't judge them.

Once you have run out of ideas or time, you can begin to select the best solution. Be sure to consider all ideas. Then use the skills of self-assertion and empathic listening to evaluate the likely ideas. Setting an amount of time for defending and judging each idea can be helpful.

Once you agree on the best idea, you must implement it. If the problem has been serious, it is a good idea to schedule future discussions about how well the solution is working. If the solution works well, you will not need to use Step 7. If the two of you continue to experience difficulties, you may have to modify the solution, using the information that comes from your evaluation sessions. Or you may have to go back to the possible alternatives generated during the brainstorming session and select another solution to test.

MEN AND WOMEN: DO THEY SPEAK THE SAME LANGUAGE

From the earliest ages through adulthood, boys and girls create different (language) worlds, which men and women go on living in. It is no surprise that women and men who are trying to do things right in relationships with each other so often find themselves criticized. We try to talk to each other honestly, but it seems at times that we are speaking different languages—or at least different genderlects. (Tannen 1990, 279)

Deborah Tannen and other sociolinguists suggest that some misunderstandings between men and women arise out of differences in communication styles.

There are gender differences in accepted behavior and communication styles just as there are cultural differences. Boys and girls grow up in different psychological worlds, but men and women usually think they are in the same world and tend to judge each other's communications by their own standards.

In general Tannen suggests that men grow up in a competitive world. To men, life is a challenge, a confrontation, a struggle to preserve independence and avoid failure, a contest in which they strive to be one up on their colleagues. In their conversations, men attempt to establish power and status. In the world of status, *independence* is the key.

Women, on the other hand, approach the world seeking connection and intimacy, close friendships, and equality with their friends. In their conversations, they try to give confirmation and support and to reach consensus. For women, *intimacy* is the key in the world of connection.

The stereotype is that women seek marriage in order to find intimacy and commitment, whereas men try to avoid marriage in order to preserve their independence. In America, weddings are often depicted in terms of the woman dragging the fighting, kicking, unwilling man to the altar.

If women emphasize connections and intimacy and men emphasize independence and status, conflicts and misunderstandings are bound to arise. For example, many women feel it is natural to consult their partners at every turn, while men automatically make more decisions without consultation. Women expect decisions to be discussed first and to be made by consensus. They appreciate discussion itself as evidence of involvement and caring. But many men feel oppressed by lengthy discussions about what they see as minor decisions. They feel unfree if they can't act without a lot of talking first. Women may try to invite a freewheeling conversation by asking "What do you think?" Men may take the question literally and think they are being asked to make a decision when in reality their partner only wanted conversation.

Wives often accuse their husbands of being noncommunicative: "He never talks." In a Dagwood comic strip, Blondie complains, "Every morning all you ever see is the newspaper! I'll bet you don't even know I'm here!" Dagwood reassures her, "Of course, I know you're here. You're my wonderful wife and I love you very much." With this, he unseeingly pats the paw of the family dog, which Blondie has put in her place before leaving the room.

Yet research does not support the idea that men are less communicative than women. It depends on the situation. Men actually talk far more than women in meetings and in mixed-group discussions. They are quicker to offer advice and direction, even when it is not desired by the other person. In a public situation, they more often talk about themselves than women do. In fact, many women complain that when they go out with a new male acquaintance, all he does is talk about himself. He never seems interested in what she has to say. To women, much of this talk seems to be bragging and one-upmanship. The man talks about his achievements, his interests, sports, and politics. He often seems to be telling her how to do something, giving directions, teaching, or preaching. Of course, if Tannen is correct, this conversational style fits in with men's emphasis on independence and the achievement of status.

If the woman is more interested in intimacy and connection, then her conversation will not emphasize her status or how she is better than others. Instead it will emphasize fitting in, being equal with others, sharing, and giving support to those with whom she is talking. For women, talk is the glue that holds relationships together. Women tend to be more tactful than men and are less direct in their conversations so as not to offend. Men may mistake this indirectness for weakness and lack of power.

For example, a woman complains to a woman friend about something going on in her life. Her friend may then share something negative in her own life in an effort to show that she understands the problem and is supportive of her friend's feelings. Men, however, on hearing the complaint usually offer answers and solutions. They take the complaint as a challenge to their ability to think up a solution. Many men feel that women often complain without taking action to solve the problem that is bothering them. Women think that men are often insensitive to their problems and are therefore unsupportive. This different approach to problems may explain why men are occasionally frustrated when their sincere attempts to help a woman solve her problems are met not with gratitude but with disapproval. As one man commented, "Women seem to wallow in their problems, wanting to talk about them forever. Most men I know want to get them out of the way, solved and be done with them."

For many men who work in competitive positions, the comfort of home means freedom from having to prove themselves and impress others through verbal display. At last, they are in a situation where talk is not required and they are free to remain silent. But for a woman, home is the place where she and her partner are free to talk. Especially for the traditional housewife, the return of her husband from work means they can talk, interact, and be intimate. In this situation, the woman is likely to take her husband's silence as a rejection while he takes her need to talk as an invasion of his privacy.

Although the communication styles of men and women differ in many respects, it is a mistake to think that one style is better than the other. What is important is to learn how to interpret each other's messages and explain your own in a way your partner can accept. There is no one right way to listen, to talk, or to have a conversation—or a relationship. Although a woman may focus more often on intimacy and rapport and her partner more on status, this difference need not lead to misunderstanding if the couple accepts that such differences do not imply that one partner's communication style is correct and the other's is wrong.

COMMUNICATION AND FAMILY CONFLICT

Every intimate relationship will have periods of conflict. Families, however, view and handle conflict in different ways.

> In some families it is avoided; in others, it is a common occurrence. Conflict may lead to destruction of one family unit; it may be the manner by which problems are solved in another, and thus be viewed as essential for the continuation of a satisfying family life. . . . (Pearson 1989, 287)

Some families thrive on conflict, others use conflict constructively, and still others view it as a necessary evil. (305)

Research suggests that conflicts are equally present in happy and unhappy marriages. The difference is that in successful marriages the partners have learned how to handle their conflicts and even use them to improve their relationship. If conflict is suppressed, it can cause stagnation, failure to adapt to changed circumstances, and an accumulation of hostility that may erode the couple's relationship.

Conflict occurs when two or more family members believe that what they want is incompatible with what one or more other family members want (Galvin and Brommel 1986). Realistic conflicts result from frustration over specific needs, whereas nonrealistic conflicts are characterized by the need for tension release by at least one of the partners. By exploring the process of conflict and how it can be used constructively, we can better manage it. Successful management of conflict solves problems and helps a good relationship evolve into an even better one. Recognizing nonrealistic conflict and successfully coping with it can reduce tensions and change the nonrealistic conflict into realistic conflict. Realistic conflict is usually easier to handle.

Conflict becomes damaging to a relationship when it is covert or hidden. If we can't confront and work with real conflict, it is nearly impossible to resolve the problem. Hidden conflict generally relies on one of the following communication strategies (Galvin and Brommel 1982; 1986):

■ *Denial:* One partner simply says, "No, I'm not upset; there is no problem," when in fact he or she is upset and there is a problem. Often the person's body language contradicts the words.

■ *Disqualification:* A person expresses anger and then discounts it. "You make me angry! Sorry, I am not feeling well today." Of course, this discounting could be true. It only becomes disqualification when the person intends to cover an emotion and deny that a real conflict exists.

■ *Displacement:* The person places emotional reactions somewhere other than the real conflict source. For example, John is really angry at his wife, but he yells at the children. Thus, the source of the conflict is kept hidden.

■ *Disengagement:* Family members avoid conflict simply by avoiding one another. This avoidance keeps the conflict from surfacing. Unfortunately, the conflict remains below the surface, creates anger that can't be vented, and increases the tension in the relationship.

■ *Pseudomutuality:* Family members appear to be perfectly happy and delighted with each other. In this style of anger, no hint of discord is ever allowed to spoil the image of perfection. Only when one member develops ulcers or a nervous disorder or acts in a bizarre manner does the family reveal a crack in its armor of perfection. Anger remains so far below the surface that the family members lose all ability to deal with it directly. Pretense remains the only possibility.

We also need to note the relationship of sexual behavior to these covert strategies. For many couples, sex becomes a weapon in their guerrilla warfare. Demands for, or avoidance of, sexual activity may be the most effective way to express covert hostility.

Overt conflict can also be destructive to a relationship even though the chances of dealing with it are greater than with covert conflict. This chapter cannot cover the many destructive patterns of overt conflict. In general, however, attacking one's partner verbally or physically is devastating to the relationship and will make it extremely difficult to ever establish a fully healthy relationship.

We've all heard the old saying, "Sticks and stones may break my bones, but words will never hurt me." Unfortunately, verbal abuse often does hurt. Verbal abuse like "You idiot," "Liar," or "I hate you" attacks a person's self-respect and integrity. Verbal abuse can cause real psychological damage if it is continued for an extended period. Most people can forgive an occasional verbal attack during an outburst of anger, but if the attacks come often or become the norm for handling conflict, the partner and the relationship will be damaged.

Whenever Kimberly becomes frustrated with her husband Mark, she heaps verbal abuse on him: he has no drive, he is too dumb to get ahead in his job, and he is a lousy lover. The name calling greatly affects Mark's self-esteem, and he slowly loses self-confidence. He doubts himself, which in turn causes him to act in ways that are self-defeating. What began as name calling and negative labeling has gradually become his reality.

Physical violence seldom solves a conflict; instead it tends to lead to more violence. Physical violence generally occurs in families that lack communication skills. One member may be increasingly frustrated in the relationship and be unable to communicate with the partner or the children about the conflict. The frustration finally becomes so great that the family member loses

INSET 6-3
TOPICS OF CONFLICT OVER TIME

Edward Bader and his colleagues (1981) gathered data about topics of conflict over a period of five years. They first interviewed sample couples just before marriage. They reinterviewed them after six months of marriage, after one year, and again after five years. The table shows the ranking of conflict topics for the couples at each interview time.

Before marriage the man's job and time and attention were the two topics (tied for first) that aroused the most conflict. Six months after marriage, household tasks had become number one, with handling of money second, while time and attention had fallen to third place. At the end of one year of marriage, household tasks were still the number one topic of conflict. Time and attention was second, and handling money was third. At the end of five years, household tasks and time and attention were tied for first, while sex had moved all the way from thirteenth to third. The table makes it clear that the basic job of living together (how we divide the household tasks, how and how much time and attention we give one another, how we handle our money, and so forth) creates the most conflict for couples.

PERCENTAGE OF COUPLES WHERE ONE OR BOTH PARTNERS INDICATED ANY DISAGREEMENT IN FOURTEEN SPECIFIED AREAS

DISAGREEMENT AREAS	PRE-MARRI-AGE (N63) %	RANK	SIX MONTHS (N63) %	RANK	ONE YEAR (N63) %	RANK	FIVE YEARS (N56) %	RANK
1. Husband's job	74	1	75	4	68	6	76	4
2. Wife's job	56	8	63	6	62	10	53	10
3. Household tasks	66	3	87	1	91	1	88	1
4. Handling money	62	6	79	2	76	3	72	6
5. Husband's relatives	49	11	52	10	67	7	72	6
6. Wife's relatives	64	5	56	9	71	4	72	6
7. Husband's friends	61	7	63	6	51	12	52	11
8. Wife's friends	54	10	50	12	46	13	42	12
9. Affection	56	8	65	5	67	7	76	4
10. Children	44	12	48	13	54	11	42	12
11. Religion	25	14	21	14	19	14	28	14
12. Social activities	66	3	51	11	71	4	65	9
13. Time and attention	74	1	76	3	86	2	88	1
14. Sex	41	13	62	8	64	9	78	3

control and strikes out physically. Anything that lowers one's inhibitions and/or frustration tolerance, such as alcohol abuse, increases the possibility of physical violence.

Successful conflict management can be described as follows (Galvin and Brommel 1986; Strong 1983):

1. Communication exchange is sequential; each participant has equal time to state his or her view.
2. Participants express rather than suppress feelings.
3. People listen to one another with empathy and without constant interruption.

4. Participants remain focused on the issue and do not get sidetracked into other previously unresolved conflicts.

5. Family members respect differences in the opinions, values, and wishes of one another.

6. Members believe that solutions are possible and that growth and development will take place.

7. Participants have evolved some semblance of rules from prior conflicts.

8. One or more family members do not try to control the conflict or the other participants.

9. Family control over television is important if communication is to be improved. The television-dominated family is not likely to have good communication skills. Interaction time is necessary to develop communication skills, and television can be a major deterrent to family interaction (see Chapter 13).

SUMMARY

1. *Good communication is one of the major characteristics of strong, successful families.* Couples having marital trouble almost always report communication failure as a major problem. Communication failures occur because one or both partners choose not to communicate verbally or lack basic communication skills.

2. Although communication problems are often the result of personal problems of the partners, *society can also facilitate or hinder good communication.* Society's support of stereotypical sex roles, especially that of the strong, silent male, restricts good communication.

3. *When most people talk about failure in communication, what they mean is that communication has become so aversive that it causes discomfort.* In other words, the problem is too much negative and hurtful communication rather than no communication. If the aversive communication continues too long, however, the couple may indeed stop communicating verbally.

4. *Three basic conditions must be met before good communication can be assured.* There must be a commitment to healthy communication. The partners must be oriented to growth and to improving the relationship. Neither partner must try to coerce the other through communications.

5. When these basic conditions are met, problem-solving skills can be called into play. *Basically, five skills are involved in successful problem-solving communication.* The partners must identify the ownership of the problem; each partner must be willing to speak up and state his or her position and feelings (self-assertion); each must be a good listener (empathic listening); each must be willing to negotiate; and each must be willing to use problem-solving methods if needed.

6. *Fighting fairly and using problem-solving skills will enhance any relationship and keep it alive and growing.* Failure to communicate clearly and to fight fairly will usually cause disruption and the ultimate failure of intimate relationships.

Wesley Burr (1990), in a provocative article, suggests the addition of We-statements to people's communication skills. An example of the three different ways of defining problems in families will help to illustrate the differences between You-, I-, and We-statements. If members of a family are having difficulty with the amount of affection in their relationships, they might say:

- *You-statement:* "You're not giving me enough affection."
- *I-statement:* "I'm not getting enough affection."
- *We-statement:* "We don't show each other enough affection."

In intimate relationships, You-statements are probably least effective in problem-solving situations. They tend to create distance between people by placing blame on the other. Placing blame usually arouses defensiveness and resistance on the part of the person blamed. You-statements also tend to create and maintain an adversarial "I versus you or them" relationship. As a result, You-statements often start or expand conflicts and controversies rather than moving the family toward peaceful, loving, harmonious solutions to problems.

Most of the time, I-statements are more effective and helpful than You-statements. I-statements locate the problem with the person who is suggesting there is a problem. They subtly communicate a warmer, and more accepting concern for the individuals whom the "I" person views as the focus of the problem. Thus, I-statements tend to reduce defensiveness and resistance. I-statements

may, however, create a problem for the other person, because they make that person aware that he or she is central to something that creates a problem for the "I" person.

We-statements center the problem in both persons or in the group. They emphasize mutuality and connectedness. This emphasis tends to reduce emotional and relationship distance rather than exaggerate it. We-statements place the responsibility for doing something about the problem on both people or in the group but do not imply that any one person has more responsibility than another. Such statements also reduce the power imbalance in the relationship. Rather than implying that "I have power over you," they suggest that "We are in this together." "I'm bringing up the problem, but it is something that *we* need to deal with rather than a situation where I already know what the problems and solutions are."

We-statements are more useful when someone wants to enhance the *togetherness* aspect of the relationship or family and wants to build a sense of cooperation. Like all communication principles, however, We-statements can also be used in negative ways. For example, a parent who says something like "We don't believe that in our family" may stifle differences of opinion. By combining simple I-statements and We-statements, such a problem can be avoided. For example, by saying "I don't think we believe that in our family," the parent will introduce a subjective quality that allows others to disagree but still keeps the focus primarily on family belief.

How you say something is often more important to good communication than what you say. I- and We-statements are usually more likely to produce problem solutions than are You-statements.

210

CHAPTER

7

ROLE EQUITY: THE CONVERGING OF THE SEXES

CONTENTS

The past twenty-five years have brought many changes to our traditional definitions of man and woman, husband and wife, mother and father. Much of the feminist agenda has been fulfilled despite the failure of the Equal Rights Amendment (ERA) to become law. More women than men now earn college degrees. Professions long closed to women are now open. Women—married and unmarried, with children and childless—have entered the work force in vast numbers. Pay inequity between the sexes is decreasing. Maternity and parental leaves no longer cost women their jobs. Flexible work schedules to help parents better cope with family and child responsibilities are increasingly finding favor. Good child-care facilities are finally being recognized as important adjuncts to the working family. Women's sports are finding equality with men's sports. Relationships between men and women are becoming more equitable. The list goes on.

AND YET, the largest single group in poverty is the family headed by a single mother. Women's pay still lags behind men's pay in many occupations. Few companies offer on-site child care. Husbands of working wives do not do their fair share of family and housework. Few women have reached the top levels of power in large corporations. Sexual exploitation of women continues. Men and women continue to conflict over their appropriate roles in marriage and family.

Male and female, man and woman, boy and girl, masculine and feminine—this duality is easily recognized in the human species. Almost everyone's first thought upon meeting another human is "he or she." Radical feminists of the 1970s chided us for automatically making this differentiation. Others said, "Vive la difference."

We all recognize this duality, but where did it come from? Are men and women really different biologically? Psychologically? Intellectually? Socially? If so, are such differences inborn (based on a different biological foundation) or learned? Are men the stronger sex because on the average they are physically stronger? Are women the stronger sex because they generally live longer than men? Can a woman really be like a man? Can a man really be like a woman? Why have men traditionally been breadwinners and women homemakers? Is the relationship between men and women one of equality? One of dominance and submission? One of independence and dependence? Complementarity? What would happen if a society did away with gender role differentiation (if it could) and we all became "unisex"? By **gender role,** we mean the behaviors based on a person's sex assigned to males and females by a culture.

Such questions have been increasingly asked over the past three decades. Controversy about the answers swirls around us. Regardless of how we answer the questions, it seems clear that the meanings assigned to man and woman and the relationships between the sexes are undergoing change. Essentially, women's roles are moving closer to men's roles, and men are reacting to the changes being made by women. The sexual revolution has changed women's sexual behavior, making it more like men's. The feminist revolution demands legal and economic equality for women. The movement of women, especially married women, into the labor force has created the most important changes of all in the family. This revolution is so important to intimate relationships that we have devoted an entire chapter to it (Chapter 9). What all this means is that the differences between the sexes are lessening and the similarities are increasing.

Gender
Attitudes and behavior associated with each of the two sexes

213

When men and women are freer to choose gender roles for themselves, especially within intimate relationships like marriage, their chances for success and fulfillment seem to increase. If intimate partners can share the decisions and responsibilities of their relationship in ways that feel right for them, their satisfaction will be greater than if they are forced into stereotyped behaviors that may not fit. Free choice should help reduce the feelings of oppression and dissatisfaction that so often appear over time in intimate relationships. Doing away with gender role rigidity and stereotyping does not eliminate gender roles but does promote freedom to choose a personally and socially fulfilling lifestyle. Freedom to choose is a proper goal of a free society.

ROLE EQUITY

Instead of new roles for the sexes, we need acceptance of the concept of role equity. With *role equity*, the roles one fulfills are based on individual strengths and weaknesses rather than on a set of preordained stereotypical differences between the sexes (granted, there are some biologically influenced differences between the sexes). Equity implies the fair distribution of opportunities and restrictions without regard to gender. For example, one spouse may have more interest or better skills in arithmetic and bookkeeping, so he or she manages all the family finances. If such an arrangement is freely chosen and believed to be fair by the individuals concerned, it is an equitable arrangement.

Equity between the sexes in family life embraces variation—many relationship models, not just one. True equity between the sexes implies freedom to establish roles within the relationship that accent the unique personality of each partner. Each is free to fulfill his or her own capabilities to the greatest possible degree. "Constructive liberation" takes into account the fact that people vary; a relationship that is good for one person may be restrictive for another. Rhona and Robert Rappaport (1975) suggest that those who rigidly extol the virtues of a "liberated" relationship are really only suggesting that we move from one prison (traditional prescribed roles) to another (any and all roles acceptable). As Betty Friedan (1986) chides her feminist sisters, "The time has come to acknowledge that women are different than men. There has to be equality that takes into account that women are the ones who have the babies." In other words, radical positions that simply push women to accept new rigid gender roles (copying male gender roles, for example) are as imprisoning as the traditional rigid gender roles.

It is true that when roles are tightly prescribed by society and few if any deviate from them, people tend to feel safe and secure. Some people feel threatened by too many alternatives. But American society encompasses a great deal of diversity. People may find that their neighbors have different lifestyles. Children may point to imperfections in their parents' marital life and question whether people need to get married. Couples may find the mass media criticizing a relationship they have never seriously questioned. They may read articles praising alternative living arrangements that they were taught were immoral. Such experiences often lead to confusion, insecurity, anxiety, resentment, and an even firmer commitment to the status quo. Indeed, the extreme attacks on the "traditional American marriage" mounted by radical feminists, gay liberationists, sexual freedom leagues, and others may have undercut a thoughtful and constructive approach to change within the family structure. At the least, such influences contributed to the failure of the Equal Rights Amendment in 1982. The average American woman simply failed to understand how some feminists could fight against maternity leaves or how the great amount of energy expended on behalf of lesbian rights could help her improve her marriage, do a better job in the work world, or ease her parental burdens.

To think of intimate relationships in terms of role equity opens each relationship and each individual within a relationship to the highest personal fulfillment. Past or future stereotypes need not become the only models of proper gender roles. Increased freedom to choose fulfilling and equitable individual roles within intimate relationships should lead to both increased personal satisfaction and longer-lasting, more fulfilling marital and family relationships. Whether the roles chosen are contrary to past traditions or incorporate those traditions is immaterial as long as the roles are freely chosen and felt to be fair and acceptable by each family member.

MALE = MASCULINE AND FEMALE = FEMININE: NOT NECESSARILY SO

Simply stated, whether one is male or female is biologically determined. The behaviors or roles that go along with being male or female (gender roles), however, are largely learned from one's society. For example, French males may cry in public over a sad event; American males generally repress tears in public. The social behavior assigned to their sex differs. We call this socially assigned behavior in a given society "masculine" for the male and "feminine" for the female.

An individual's sex is determined by the various chromosomal and hormonal influences that lead to the anatomical differences between the sexes. One's gender includes not only one's sex but all of the attitudes and behaviors (masculine and feminine) that are expected of that sex by a given society. Thus, sexual identity includes both physiologically prescribed sex behaviors and socially prescribed gender behaviors.

▨ NORMS AND ROLES ▨

Before we discuss gender development, it is important to define the terms *norm* and *role*. **Norms** are accepted and expected patterns of behavior and beliefs established either formally or informally by a group. Usually, the group rewards those who adhere to the norms and punishes those who do not. Note that the sanctions against cross-gender behavior are greater for boys than for girls (Archer 1984; Archer and Lloyd 1985, 277). Those sanctions start at an early age and operate through the influence of parents, peers, and others in the child's environment.

Norm
Accepted social rules for behavior

Role
Particular type of behavior one is expected to exhibit when occupying a certain place in a group

Roles involve people doing the activities demanded by the norms. For example, a husband working to support his family is fulfilling his role as husband and fulfilling the social norm of a husband as supporter of the family. Because there are many norms in a society, a person plays many roles. For example, a married woman may fulfill the roles of sexual partner, cook, mother, homemaker, financial manager, psychologist, and so on. If she works outside the marriage, she also fulfills career roles. A married man may fulfill the roles of breadwinner, sexual partner, father, general repairman, and so on. The point is that all people play a number of roles at any given time in their lives. Conflict between roles is frequent because so many roles are necessary to live successfully in a complex society. For example, in our society a woman's mother and wife role may interfere with her career role (see Chapter 9).

The expectation that people will fulfill their roles and meet social norms is strong. Because roles are so taken for granted, most of us are probably not aware of the pressure to conform. In fact, the expectation that people will behave in prescribed ways probably makes much of life simpler for us. But what happens when people behave in unexpected ways? To find out how unconscious expected role behavior is, try stepping out of an expected role and observe the reactions of those around you!

Norms and roles obviously play important parts in marriage as well. Each of us brings to a marriage, or any intimate relationship, a number of expectations about what our roles and those of our partner should be. Many disappointments in marriage stem from frustration of the role expectations we hold either for ourselves or for our spouses. For example, a man may assume that the role of wife is restricted to caring for him, the house, and the children. His wife, however, may believe that the role of wife can also include a career and the role of husband can include household duties and care of children. Such conflicting role expectations will undoubtedly cause difficulty for this couple.

Accepted norms and roles tend to smooth family functioning. Problems occur when roles and norms are not accepted or when they are unclear. In many societies, marriage involves very definite goals, such as increasing the family's land holdings, adding new workers (children) to the family, or even bringing new wealth into the family in the form of the wife's dowry. But our society does not set definite goals other than the vague "living happily ever after" we see in the movies and romantic fiction.

In societies where roles and norms are stable, people enter marriage with clear ideas of each partner's rights and obligations. In our society, though, almost all norms and roles are being questioned and none more than those associated with masculinity, femininity, and sexuality. Because the classification of behavior by gender is so central to human society, and to the concept of marriage as we have known it, this chapter will take a closer look at division according to gender and at the expectations, roles, and norms that arise from such a division.

HOW SEX AND GENDER IDENTITY DEVELOPS

Three factors determine sex identity:

1. Sex is genetically determined at conception.

2. Hormones secreted by glands directed by the genetic configuration produce physical differences.
3. Society defines, prescribes, and reinforces the gender role aspect of sex identity.

Problems with any of these factors can cause faulty sex identity.

■ BIOLOGICAL CONTRIBUTIONS ■

Every normal person has two sex chromosomes, one inherited from each parent, which determine biological sex. Women have two X chromosomes (XX), men an X and a Y (XY). If the man's X chromosome combines with the woman's X, the child will be female (XX). If the man's Y chromosome combines with the woman's X, the child will be male (XY).

Although the Y chromosome has few functional genes, the X chromosome has a number of them, including some responsible for such unwelcome conditions as color blindness and hemophilia. Most of the harmful genes are recessive, which means that when they pair with another gene that is dominant, the negative characteristic will not appear. In the female, the possession of two X chromosomes usually results in the harmful gene in one chromosome being overridden by the dominant gene in the other chromosome. In the male, however, the harmful condition will usually appear because the Y chromosome is ineffective in counteracting the harmful sex-linked gene on the X chromosome (Archer and Lloyd 1985, 30). Hence a problem like hemophilia is found only in men.

At first all embryos have the potential to become either sex; that is, the already existing tissues of the embryo can become male or female (see p. 439). In order for a male to be produced, the primitive undifferentiated gonad must

How Sex and Gender Identity Develops

217

develop into testes rather than ovaries. The male hormone (a chemical substance) testosterone spurs the development of testes, while another chemical (Müllerian-inhibiting substance) simultaneously causes the regression of the embryonic tissues that would otherwise become the female reproductive system. In the absence of male hormones, the female organs develop. The hormones have already started working by the time the embryo is 6 millimeters long (at about two weeks). By the end of the eighth to twelfth week, the child's sex can be determined by observation of the external genitalia (see Chapter 12 for a further description of embryonic development).

Note that the male appears to develop only with the addition of the male hormones, which are stimulated by the Y chromosome. Without that stimulation a female develops. This occurrence has led some researchers to conclude that the human embryo is innately female (Kimura 1985).

By puberty, hormonal activity has increased sharply. In girls estrogen (one of the female hormones) affects such female characteristics as breast size, pubic hair, and the filling out of the hips. Estrogen and progesterone (another female hormone) also begin the complicated process that leads to changes in the uterine lining and subsequently to the first menstruation, followed about a year later (or sometimes immediately) by ovulation. (The cycle mediated by these hormones causes an egg to mature each month. See the section in Appendix A on female sex organs for a fuller discussion of the menstruation and ovulation processes.)

In boys the active hormone is testosterone. At puberty it brings about the secretory activity of the seminal vesicles and the prostate and the regular production of sperm in the testes. (See the section in Appendix A on male sex organs for a fuller discussion of this process.) Testosterone also affects such male characteristics as larger body size, more powerful muscles, and the ability of blood to carry more oxygen. Castration (removal of the testicles) generally leads to obesity, softer tissues, and a more placid temperament in the male because it reduces the quantity of testosterone.

Note that both sexes produce male and female hormones. The direction of development is determined by the relative balance of these hormones.

In lower animals, these hormones have been found to cause differences between the sexes other than sexual differences. In rats and mice, the hormones seem to influence brain development, which in turn influences such activities as fighting, exploration, and play (Goy and McEwan 1980; Blizard 1983; Archer and Lloyd 1985). These findings have led some to suggest that hormonal differences also cause personality differences between human males and females.

Because every human starts with the potential of becoming either male or female, as a fully differentiated adult each still carries the biological rudiments of the opposite sex. For example, the male has undeveloped nipples on the chest, and the female has a penislike clitoris. In a few rare individuals, even though gene determinants have set the sexual direction, the hormones fail to carry out the process. Such persons have characteristics of both sexes (though neither is fully developed) and are called **hermaphrodites.** Hermaphrodites are rare and should not be confused with transsexuals or transvestites. A **transsexual** is a person who believes that he or she is actually of the opposite gender and who may have undergone a sex-change operation as discussed in Inset 7-1.

Hermaphrodite
A person who has both male and female sexual organs, or organs that are indeterminant, such as a clitoris that resembles a penis

Transsexual
A person who has a compulsion or obsession to become a member of the opposite sex through surgical changes

A **transvestite** is a person who gains sexual pleasure from dressing like the opposite sex.

The strength of the sex hormones can be seen when pregnant rhesus monkeys are injected with testosterone for twenty-five to fifty days. The genetically female offspring of the injected mothers have malformed external genital structures, which include a scrotum, a small penis, and no external vaginal orifice. In addition, the behavior of such pseudohermaphroditic females is altered in the direction of normal male behavior.

The early adaptability of the tissues that grow into mature sexual organs is also quite amazing. Ovaries and vaginas transplanted into castrated male rats within the first twenty-four hours after birth will grow and function exactly like normal female organs. This plasticity of the sex tissues quickly vanishes as the hormones cause further differentiation. Transplants of female organs into male rats more than three days old are unsuccessful.

Despite the strong hormonal influences on behavior, the environment continues to play a role even in lower animals. When Ingeborg Ward, a professor of psychology, subjects pregnant rats to high levels of stress, their male fetuses are deprived of developmental testosterone; later, most of these "stressed sons" show marked female sexual responses. However, the degree to which the stressed sons' conduct is atypical depends largely on their socialization. Those raised with normal males or with other stressed sons showed much more male behavior than those raised with females. Ward says, "Gender-related behavior depends on how much androgen is floating around at what particular time in development, and on prepubertal social factors" (Gallagher 1988).

■ ENVIRONMENTAL CONTRIBUTIONS ■

Once a baby is born, society begins to teach the infant its proper gender role and reinforce its sexual identity. In the United States, we name our children according to their gender; we give girls pink blankets and boys blue blankets; and at Christmas and birthdays boys receive "masculine" toys and girls "feminine" toys.

In keeping with cultural prescriptions, we exhibit different attitudes toward children of different sexes, and we expect and reward different behaviors. For example, we encourage boys to engage in rough and tumble activities and discourage girls from engaging in similar activities. (This may explain, in part, men's greater interest in contact sports.) Parents provide guidance to help the child assimilate the proper role. Parents say to little girls:

"Be nice!"

"Stay clean."

"Be gentle."

"Think of others."

"Be kind."

"Be thoughtful."

"Be a lady."

Transvestite
A person who prefers to dress as the opposite sex and derives sexual satisfaction therefrom

Dr. Richard Raskind, a successful physician, was an avid tennis player (well over six feet tall) who was ranked thirteenth nationally in the amateur men's thirty-five-and-over division. In 1977, after undergoing sex-change therapy to become Dr. Renee Richards, she was ranked tenth among professional women players in the United States, an unbelievable accomplishment for a forty-two-year-old woman who had never played tennis professionally. For several years she was a coach to the tennis star Martina Navratilova. Such quick success may also speak to physical differences between men and women.

Another transsexual example may be found in Jan Morris's autobiography Conundrum:

I was three or perhaps four years old when I realized that I had been born into the wrong body, and should really be a girl. I remember the moment well, and it is the earliest memory of my life.

I was sitting beneath my mother's piano, and her music was falling around me like cataracts, enclosing me as a cave. . . .

What triggered so bizarre a thought I have long forgotten, but the conviction was unfaltering from the start. (Morris 1974, 3)

Morris attended Oxford and then obtained a glamorous position as correspondent for *The Times* (London). He scored one of the world's historic journalistic coups by climbing 22,000 feet up Mount Everest with Edmund Hillary and Tenzing Norgay and flashing the first word of their conquest of the peak. The lean, stubble-chinned Morris, whose "manly" stamina made such a feat possible, became a Fleet Street legend. By this time, in spite of his inner contradictions, he had married, and he and his wife, the daughter of a Ceylonese tea planter, had five children. Eventually, he resigned from *The Times* to write books and distinguished himself in this as well.

For all of Morris's outward appearance of normalcy, however, his inner anguish remained. He consulted physicians and was advised either to wear gayer clothes or to "soldier on" as a male. His quest for help led him to New York City where he was counseled by Dr. Harry Benjamin, an endocrinologist who has specialized in the study of gender confusion. Dr. Benjamin prescribed female hormone treatments to prepare the way for Morris's sexual changeover. For men,

Parents say to boys:

"Be strong."

"Be competitive."

"Be tough."

"Be assertive."

"Be sportive."

"Be a man."

Nothing inherent within the child will give rise to the socially sex-appropriate behaviors. Each child must learn—from parents, relatives, teachers, and friends—the appropriate behaviors for the culture.

Some people argue that because gender roles are learned, it is possible for a society to change masculine and feminine behavior (see Inset 7-2). One in-

such treatments involve estrogen and progestin to soften the skin and enlarge the breasts. Morris underwent the treatment for eight years and estimates that he swallowed 12,000 pills.

In July 1972, Morris took the final, irreversible step. He checked into a Casablanca clinic that specializes in transsexual operations and submitted to the surgery. The male-to-female procedure involves amputation of the penis and castration, followed by the creation of an artificial vagina, using scrotal or penile tissue or skin grafts from the hip or thigh. Because the penile tissue is still sensitive, male-to-female transsexuals may experience orgasm, though, of course, pregnancy is impossible.

Today the former James Morris is in virtually every respect a woman, with a new name, the properly an-

drogynous Jan since it is used by both males and females; a new relationship with her former wife (divorced, they regard each other as unofficial "sisters-in-law"); and a new relationship with her children, who now call their father "Aunt Jan."

James Morris was a very conventional male, who did all of the things that a man was supposed to do. He has turned into a very conventional female, who does the things that a woman is traditionally supposed to do. The new Jan Morris enjoys having men open doors for her, flirt with her, and kiss her. She says, "Women who like to feel cherished by a stronger man have every right to their feelings."

Such cases are extremely rare. It is estimated that about 5,000 individuals in the United States have

altered their sex by surgery. For them, biology and the environment had failed to work together to produce a stable sex identity.

When it was active in the sex-change field, Johns Hopkins Medical Center received about 1,500 applications for sex-change operations each year but only performed about six operations annually. Researchers there found that the vast majority of persons who think they are transsexual are not and can be helped with psychotherapy. It is interesting to note that Johns Hopkins Medical Center ceased doing sex-change operations in 1979. The follow-up studies of sex-changed persons indicated that the psychological and other gains were minimal and not worth the risks associated with the extensive surgery necessary to accomplish a sex change.

teresting piece of evidence they offer is the few babies whose ascribed sex differs from their biological sex. Some of these babies have been studied over a twenty-year period, and one researcher concludes:

> In virtually all cases, the sex of assignment (and thus of rearing) proved dominant. Thus, babies assigned as males at birth and brought up as boys by their parents (who were unaware of the child's female genetic and hormonal makeup) thereafter thought of themselves as boys, played with boys' toys, developed boys' sports, preferred boys' clothing, developed male sex fantasies, and in due course fell in love with girls. And the reverse was true for babies who were biologically male but were reared as girls; they followed the typical feminine pattern of development. (Weitzman 1975, 108)

In one case one of two identical twins was reassigned as a female following a surgical mishap. At seven months the twin boys were to be circumcised by electrocautery. Due to an electrical malfunction, the penis of one twin was totally destroyed. Following the recommendations of the doctors, the boy's parents elected to have his sex reassigned. At seventeen months the boy was

How Sex and Gender Identity Develops

In the country of Oman, there is a class of men known as the Xanith. Over their lifetime they may change gender roles several times.

The Xanith are biologically men. They sell themselves in passive homosexual relationships, but they also work as skilled domestic servants where they are in great demand and earn a good wage. Their dress is distinctive, it resembles the long tunic worn by men but is made of pastel-colored cloth. Although they retain men's names, the Xanith violate all of the rules that govern female seclusion. They may speak intimately with women in the street without bringing the women's reputation into question. They sit with the segregated women at a wedding, and they may see the bride's unveiled face. They may neither sit nor eat with men in public. Their manners, perfumed bodies, and high-pitched voices make them appear effeminate even though, unlike Jan Morris, their bodies have not been changed medically (see Inset 7-1).

Since the feminine gender of the Xanith is socially selected, several possibilities are open to them. Should they wish to become men again, they need only marry and prove themselves able to perform heterosexual intercourse with their brides. Some Xanith never choose this path and remain women until they grow old, at which time their anatomical sex places them in the category of "old men." Some actually become women, then men, then women again until old age places them in the "old man" role.

Since Omani women are off limits to all men but their husbands, the Xanith offer a sexual outlet for the single men in the society. Since Xanith are socially women, to have intercourse with them (as long as the man purchasing their services penetrates) in no way casts a man in an unfavorable light. His manhood remains unquestioned.

The ease with which these transformations can be made clearly points out the strength of the society in determining gender roles.

Source: Adapted from Archer and Lloyd 1985.

---

taken to the Johns Hopkins clinic for the necessary surgery to give him female external genitals. John Money and Anke Ehrhardt report that since the surgery, the parents have made every effort to raise the twins in accordance with their assigned sex as one male and one female. According to the parents' reports, the two children are developing to fit the role expectations of their assigned sex. The mother described her "daughter's" behavior this way:

> She likes for me to wipe her face. She doesn't like to be dirty, and yet my son is quite different. I can't wash his face for anything. . . . She seems to be daintier. Maybe it's because I encourage it. (Money and Ehrhardt 1972, 119)

Occasionally, children fail to learn the role that traditionally accompanies their biological sex. This failure can lead to the unusual situation in which a person is one sex biologically but the opposite sex psychologically; the result is sexual identity confusion (see Insets 7-1 and 7-2).

■ A THEORY OF GENDER ROLE DEVELOPMENT ■

The old argument about whether environment and learning or genetics and biology determine sex role behavior should not be stated in this either/or form. In truth, of course, it is the interaction of these two great molders of behavior that determines one's actual behavior. The following theory tries to take both into consideration (Ullian 1976). In the early years (Stage 1), biological influence is most clearly seen. Children aged ten through thirteen (Stage 2) demonstrate behavior that is much more socially influenced. During adolescence (Stage 3), a more personal psychological orientation seems to direct sex role behaviors.

STAGE : BIOLOGICAL ORIENTATION

■ *Level One (six years)*: Differences between masculine and feminine are expressed primarily in terms of external bodily differences, such as size, strength, length of hair, and so forth. Social and psychological differences are recognized but are assumed to be the consequence of these external physical differences. Conformity to sex differences is viewed as necessary to maintain gender identity and to allow for the expression of innate gender differences.

■ *Level Two (eight years)*: There is a growing awareness that masculine and feminine traits can exist independently from biological and physical features. Emphasis is placed on the ability of the individual to act according to choice, since he or she is no longer limited by physical or biological constraints. Also, the role of training and social conditions begins to be recognized. Children become less demanding about conformity to stereotypical sex roles than they were at Level One.

STAGE : SOCIETAL ORIENTATION

■ *Level Three (ten years)*: Masculine and feminine traits are seen as inherent in the requirements of a system of social roles and are viewed as fixed and unchangeable. The traits associated with certain adult social roles are assumed to be characteristic of the members of the sex expected to fill those roles. Conformity to masculine and feminine standards is based on the need to satisfy external demands of the social system.

■ *Level Four: (twelve years)*: There is a growing awareness that the system of social roles is arbitrary and variable and may function independently of the sex of the individual. Stress is put on the individual's freedom to act according to his or her self-interest. Conformity is no longer expected.

STAGE : PSYCHOLOGICAL ORIENTATION

■ *Level Five (fourteen to sixteen years)*: Masculine and feminine traits are based on the adoption of an appropriate psychological identity by males and females. Adolescents admit that sex differences are not biologically based and may not be the result of social necessity, but they see traits as central to men's and women's identities. They view deviation as "sick" or "abnormal" and believe conformity to external standards is required for maintenance of marriage and the family.

■ *Level Six (eighteen years)*: There is an awareness that masculinity and femininity may exist independently from conformity to traditional standards, roles, and behaviors. Sex-stereotyped traits are not assumed to be crucial aspects of personal identity. Principles of equality and freedom are proposed as standards for behavior and are used to define an ideal model of personal and interpersonal functioning.

Studies of the human brain indicate that gender-related differences may affect how certain mental processes are controlled and the location of the control area (Goleman 1978; Kimura 1985; Gorman 1992). The physical size, structure, and biochemical components of brains do exhibit a few commonly

TABLE 7-1
STEREOTYPICAL SEX ROLE DIFFERENCES COMPARED WITH RESEARCH FINDINGS

STEREOTYPE	FINDINGS

Perceptual Differences

Men have:	better daylight vision	Mild but in direction of stereotype.
	less sensitivity to extreme heat	"
	more sensitivity to extreme cold	"
	faster reaction times	"
	better depth perception	"
	better spatial skills	"
	more ability to rotate three-dimensional objects in their heads	"
Women have:	better night vision	"
	more sensitivity to touch in all parts of the body	"
	better hearing, especially in higher ranges	"
	less tolerance of loud sound	"
	better manual dexterity and fine coordination	"
	more ability to read people's emotions in photographs	"

Aggression

Males are more aggressive.	Strong consistent differences in physical aggression.
Females are less aggressive.	

Dependency

Females are more submissive and dependent.	Weak differences that are more consistent for adults than for children.
Males are more assertive and independent.	

Emotionality

Females are more emotional and excitable.	Moderate differences on some measures; overall findings inconclusive.
Males are more controlled and less expressive.	

Health

Females suffer more depression and phobic reactions.	Moderate differences.
Males have more heart disease.	Strong differences.

Verbal Skills

Females excel in all verbal areas including reading.	Moderate differences, especially for children.
Males are less verbal and have more problems learning to read.	

Math Skills

Males are better in mathematical skills.	Moderate differences on problem-solving tests, especially after adolescence.
Females are less interested and do less well in mathematics.	

Source: This table has been constructed using several sources:

1. Maccoby, E., and Jacklin, C. "The Psychology of Sex Differences. Palo Alto, Calif.: Stanford University Press, 1974.

2. Goleman, D. "Special Abilities of the Sexes: Do They Begin in the Brain?" *Psychology Today*, November 1978.

3. Frieze, I., et al. *Women and Sex Roles*, New York: W. W. Norton, 1978.

4. McGuiness, D., and Pribram, K., "The Origins of Sensory Bias in the Development of Gender Differences in Perception and Cognition." in *Cognitive Growth and Development*, edited by M. Bortner, New York: Brunner-Mazel, 1979.

5. Kimura, D. "Male Brain, Female Brain: The Hidden Difference." *Psychology Today*, November 1985.

6. Archer, J., and Lloyd, B. *Sex and Gender*. Cambridge, England: Cambridge University Press, 1985.

7. Durden-Smith, J., and DeSimone, D. "Is There a Superior Sex?" *Playboy*, May 1982.

8. Gallagher, W. "Sex and Hormones." *Atlantic Monthly*, March 1988.

9. Caplan, P. J., et al. "Do Sex-Related Differences in Spatial Abilities Exist?" *American Psychologist*, July 1985.

10. Hines, M., reported in Adler, T. "Early Sex Hormone Exposure Studied." *Monitor*. American Psychological Assoc., June 1989.

11. Adler, T. "Sex-based Differences Declining, Study Shows." *Monitor*. American Psychological Assoc., March 1989.

12. Gorman, C. "Sizing Up the Sexes." *Time*, January 20, 1992, pp. 42–51.

accepted, observable differences. However, the degree to which gender-related differences in the brain influence behavioral differences is difficult to determine. Table 7-1 lists some of the stereotypical differences between the sexes and compares them to scientific findings. Some of these differences appear to be lessening (Adler 1989; Moses 1991). The belief that there are many strong and consistent differences between males and females seems to receive little support. The studies that have been done on the subject of sex differences do support some mild differences. In every case, however, the differences between persons of the same sex on a given characteristic can be greater than the average differences between the sexes.

Reduction in the use of gender role stereotypes—or any behavioral stereotypes—is a worthy goal. Furthermore, to argue endlessly over the relative influence of biology versus environment is a waste of energy. Because we know that culture does influence gender roles to a great extent, it is certainly possible to modify them.

Sweden has moved in the direction of reducing gender role differences. Boys and girls are now required to take identical subjects in school. All jobs are open to both sexes. Laws are applied equally. Perhaps in the future gender roles will become flexible enough that individuals will be able to choose roles that maximize their own unique capabilities. Yet this flexibility will not destroy the basic duality of the sexes.

▓ THE ANDROGYNOUS PERSON ▓

An **androgynous** person exhibits both male (*andro*) and female (*gyno*) behavioral characteristics. This does not mean that the person exhibits biological characteristics of both sexes. Rather, the individual is open to all aspects of his or her personality, regardless of whether the society defines them as masculine or feminine. Abraham Maslow's (1968) self-actualized person (see pp. 169–170 for a fuller discussion of Maslow's ideas) comes close to being such a person. The self-actualized person has no need to assert only those characteristics of personality assigned by society to his or her sex. He or she is free to build individualized gender roles that best fit his or her own attributes.

To create such adults, society would have to train children for competence in many areas without regard to sex. Whether this is an ideal that most Americans want to strive for remains to be seen.

Androgynous
The quality of having both masculine and feminine characteristics

> In an androgynous society children strive for competence in many areas without regard to sex. They develop motor skills through running and jumping, and hand-eye coordination through needle work, art work, and handling of tools. They learn the skills necessary to take care of themselves, such as cooking, sewing, and household repairs. They play with friends of both sexes, in school as well as out. They engage freely in games of competition as well as games of cooperation with friends of the other sex and friends of the same sex. They learn to respect (or to dislike) each other on the basis of individual differences, not according to sexual category.
>
> Children, learn not only self-confidence and a sense of mastery but also attitudes of caring and concern for others. Both sexes are held and touched often as infants and after. They learn to understand and express their own feelings and to recognize the needs and feelings of those around them. Verbal and physical displays of emotion are encouraged as long as they are not harmful to other people. (Lindemann 1976, 185–86)

How Sex and Gender Identity Develops

TRADITIONAL GENDER ROLES

The depth of most people's belief in gender role stereotypes is often overlooked. Most people simply take the various traditional gender role behaviors for granted. To the degree that our behaviors are dictated by stereotypical thinking about gender roles, we close ourselves to potential growth and broader expression. A husband may have a need to express his emotions, yet the masculine stereotype forbids him to do so. A wife may be a natural leader, yet she may suppress her leadership behavior because the stereotype says it is not feminine.

Traditional roles historically reflected the woman's childbearing functions and the man's greater physical strength and need to defend the family. A male's status today is still partially determined by his physical prowess, especially during the school years. The traditional role stressed masculine dominance in most areas of life, in the society as well as within the family. The traditional role also allowed men sexual freedom while severely limiting women's sexuality (the **double standard.**)

Double standard
Role orientation in which males are allowed more freedom, especially sexual, than females

The traditional feminine role was essentially the complement of the masculine role. Man was active, so woman was passive and submissive. Wives helped their husbands and took much of their personal identity from them, ran the home and family, and worked outside the home only if necessary. Women were the source of stability, strength, and most of the love and affection within the home.

The traditional role for women is found in almost all societies. For example, in the *Koran* (A.D. 630) Muhammad wrote:

> Men have authority over women because Allah has made one superior to the other, and because they spend their wealth to maintain them. Good women are obedient. They guard their unseen parts because Allah has guarded them. As for those from whom you fear disobedience, admonish them and send them to beds apart and beat them. Then if they obey you, take no further action against them.

The main reason that the traditional role for women has been found in almost all cultures and throughout history is that *women bear the children*. Even today in modern America, this fact tends to color thinking about women. For example, many businesses still regard women as temporary workers, who work until they decide to bear children or their husband changes jobs. Even though most mothers are now in the work world, the fact that they still bear most of the responsibility for the children in their families means that they will be absent from work more often than their partners (Collins and Thornberry 1989). These two facts, as well as other influences, combine to hold down women's pay compared to men's. Women tend to follow their husbands if they change jobs because the husbands can earn more. This fact also tends to make a woman a less reliable long-term employee than her male counterpart.

In sociological terms the traditional masculine character traits are those labeled "instrumental." Such traits enable one to accomplish tasks and goals. Aggressiveness, self-confidence, adventurousness, activity, and dominance are examples. "Expressive" character traits—gentleness, expressiveness, lovingness, and supportiveness—tend to be used in describing feminine behavior. Notice how the traits often complement one another. For example, the man exhibits aggressiveness, and the woman provides the opposite, gentleness.

We find relative agreement between American men and women when they assess the advantages and disadvantages of their gender roles. Essentially, the perceived advantages of one sex are the disadvantages of the other:

> Masculine disadvantages consist overwhelmingly of obligations with a few pro-hibitions while the disadvantages of the female role arise primarily from prohi-bitions, with a few obligations. Thus females complain about what they can't do, males about what they must do. Females complain that they cannot be athletic, aggressive, sexually free, or successful in the worlds of work and edu-cation; in short, they complain of their passivity. Males complain that they must be aggressive and must succeed; in short, of their activity. The (sanctioned) requirement that males may be active and females passive in a variety of ways is clearly unpleasant to both. (Chafetz 1974, 58)

Such a description is no longer as valid as it once was. Just ten years after this passage was written, a poll that asked people to describe their ideal man and woman found that the descriptions did not correspond to the stereotypes (Tavris 1984). Men and women generally listed similar ideal characteristics for both sexes, which suggests that androgyny is something both sexes would like to seek even though it is difficult to achieve.

IDEAL WOMAN	
As Men Describe Her	As Women Describe Her
1. Able to love	1. Able to love
2. Warm	2. Stands up for beliefs
3. Stands up for beliefs	3. Warm
4. Gentle	4. Self-confident
5. Self-confident	5. Gentle
IDEAL MAN	
As Women Describe Him	As Men Describe Him
1. Able to love	1. Able to love
2. Stands up for beliefs	2. Stands up for beliefs
3. Warm	3. Self-confident
4. Self-confident	4. Fights to protect family
5. Gentle	5. Intelligent

The five highest-rated traits for the ideal woman and ideal man as described by each sex are strikingly similar. And all of the lists contain some of the positive traits of each sex as seen traditionally (see Table 7-2).

Unfortunately, the attempt to free each gender from stereotypical role be-haviors is at best limited. Gender roles are so deeply embedded within society that they are probably impossible to escape completely. A man who is taught to be competitive and dominant may easily stand up for his beliefs yet have a difficult time being warm and gentle. On the other hand, a woman who is taught to be warm and gentle may have trouble standing up for her beliefs. A man who is only warm and gentle and not aggressive will probably have dif-ficulty succeeding in our highly competitive work culture. Successful men in our culture must still be aggressive and often must make their work their first

TABLE 7-2
POSITIVE AND NEGATIVE ASCRIBED CHARACTER TRAITS AS SEEN BY A CROSS SECTION OF AMERICANS

Women		Men	
POSITIVE	NEGATIVE	POSITIVE	NEGATIVE
Gentle	Passive	Strong	Tactless
Tactful	Nonassertive	Aggressive	Rough
Loving	Cunning	Brave	Egotistical
Social	Talkative	Objective	Unemotional
Sensitive	Moody	Logical	Socially unaware
Caring	Subjective	Adventurous	Inconsiderate
Warm	Dependent	Selfconfident	Domineering
Communicative	Illogical	Decisive	Insensitive
Sympathetic	Insecure	Independent	Loud
Socially aware	Submissive	Cool under stress	Lacking empathy
Modest	Shy	Self-reliant	Uncaring

priority, leaving the family in second place in their lives. Most women still bear children and retain the day-to-day responsibility for their upbringing.

The conflict between the idea of androgyny, the ideal masculine and feminine traits, and the real world of our culture causes each of us to feel confusion, ambiguity, and frustration as we attempt to mold our lives. For example, women are told to expand themselves by seeking careers outside the home, but are made to feel guilty if they do not devote themselves to their families. Many young women who opted for careers in the 1970s are now having children and are often abandoning their career at least temporarily to fulfill the motherhood role.

> The fertility rate for women thirty to thirty-four years old was 80.4 births per 1000 women in 1990 up from 60 per 1000 in 1980. The fertility rate for women 35 to 39 years old rose to 37.3 births per 1000 in 1990, up from 26.9 in 1980 (U.S. Bureau of the Census October, 1991, 1).

The number of women having their first babies after age thirty was quadrupled in the last sixteen years. Women who have concentrated on their careers but find the biological clock ticking down and decide to have a child are often caught in a "catch 22" or "no win" situation. They must have a child while they still can biologically but doing so usually means putting their career second at least for a short time.

GENDER ROLES AND THE FEMININE LIBERATION MOVEMENT

If people do succeed in becoming freer from past gender role stereotypes, much credit must be given to the women of the United States. As feminist author

Betty Friedan puts it:

> At the moment, I feel like women are ahead of men, and it's a lonely thing. We still have to deal with men who want to control us in the old way . . . . Is the new man going to come soon enough for us? . . . It's not women versus men any more—the anger's gone. But there can't be that flow between us until men stop playing games, too. Women have made the big leap; men are still stuck. Men have to break out of the mold next. (1981, 122)

The women's movement has contributed much toward focusing our attention on gender inequalities and thereby has energized our desire to change these inequalities and ourselves. It has brought about profound changes in the relationships between men and women and within the American family.

As women have changed their roles, the masculine role has also changed. Women's liberation, to the extent that it has succeeded, has also meant men's liberation. For example, as more and more women have entered the work force, more families have become two-paycheck families. No longer is the husband solely responsible for fulfilling the role of breadwinner for the family. Shared economic responsibility means more freedom for men and more power within the family for women. Economic participation by women also means that they have become more independent.

Some believe that a male revolt against the economic burdens of being the sole source of family support actually predated the feminist movement (Ehrenreich 1983). Postponement of marriage, increasing divorce, fewer children, a decreasing percentage of men in the work force, and failure to pay child support after divorce are all cited as evidence of this revolt by men against the breadwinner role. As men became less willing to assume the economic burdens of a family and less committed to the total support of their families, women were forced onto the labor market to survive. Even if this view is accurate, it was the women's movement that focused public attention on stereotypical gender roles and the harm that such stereotypes can do to both men and women.

All of the changes fostered by the women's movement and its allies have not been readily accepted. The failure of the ERA (Equal Rights Amendment)

to win ratification, the strength of the prolife attack on abortion, and the antifeminist movement all bear witness to the conflicts that are stirred up when traditional gender roles are challenged.

▨ WOMEN AND THE ECONOMY ▨

The major restraint to freer role choice is women's inferior economic position in our society. (See Chapter 9 for a complete discussion of women in the work force.) In general, men earn more than women regardless of their individual skills. This economic differential in earning power locks each sex into many traditional roles. For example, a father who would prefer to spend more time at home caring for his family usually cannot afford to do so. In most cases this would mean giving up a portion of his income that his wife cannot completely replace.

Although more and better job opportunities for women are now available, the male/female earnings gap has remained. Over the years women have earned approximately 58 to 71 percent of what men earned. The real stumbling block to freer role choice for both men and women is comparable pay for comparable work. For most of the time since women entered the work force in large numbers, they have been America's best source of cheap labor. Often they have done work comparable to men's but have been paid less for it. Ehrenreich (1983, 7) points out that the stereotypical idea of the man as sole breadwinner (earning enough to support a family) is also used in reverse to say that a woman does not need to earn enough to support herself (a man will do it for her).

The Equal Pay Act of 1963 and the creation of the Equal Opportunity Commission (EOC) under Title VII of the Civil Rights Act of 1964 have greatly helped women to move in the direction of equal pay for equal work,

Chapter 7
Role Equity: The Converging of The Sexes

■ In 1972 Sally Priesand was ordained the first woman rabbi. Since then sixty others have been ordained.

■ In 1977 Dr. Olga Jonasson was named the first woman head of a major surgical department at Chicago's Cook County Hospital.

■ Lauded for her eloquence during the 1974 Watergate hearings, Texas Congresswoman Barbara Jordan appeared at the Democratic National Convention two years later and became the first woman ever to deliver the keynote address.

■ Janet Guthrie is the first woman to have driven in the Indianapolis 500. Guthrie took part in the 1977, 1978, and 1979 Memorial Day classics and had her best race in 1978 when she finished in ninth place. She is now automotive editor for *Working Woman*.

■ In 1981 Sandra Day O'Connor became the first woman justice on the U.S. Supreme Court. Said O'Connor, "Women have a great deal of stamina and strength. It is possible to plan both a family and a career and to enjoy success at both."

■ In 1984 Congresswomen Geraldine Ferraro became the first woman vice-presidential candidate of a major party when she was picked as running mate to Walter Mondale, the Democratic candidate.

■ In 1985 Sally K. Ride became the first American woman astronaut in space. "I was not an active participant in women's liberation," Ride once said, "but my career at Stanford [where she earned a Ph.D. in physics] and my selection as an astronaut would not have happened

without the women's movement."

■ In 1986, Nellie Speerstra, became NATO's first female fighter pilot.

■ In 1990, 11 women were candidates for governor, 87 for the U.S. House of Representatives, 8 for the U.S. Senate, and hundreds more for local office (Carlson 1990, 16).

■ During the Persian Gulf War in 1991, women served in many military capacities. Major Marie Rossi appeared on television during the war indicating that national defense had become sex-blind and later became the best known of the women killed in combat.

■ In 1992, the number of women elected to the United States Senate increased to six, the highest ever.

but there is still a long way to go. In fact, the pay differential between men and women is so great that some seriously question whether the economy can afford true comparable pay. An overall increase in women's pay to the level of men's would be an inflationary shock the economy could not easily absorb. The courts consider the potential shock to be so great that thus far they have been very reluctant to rule in favor of comparable worth legislation. (See pp. 314–315 for a further discussion of comparable worth).

It is interesting to remember that women's rights advocates fought hard during the earlier part of this century for protective legislation to help women avoid exploitation in the workplace. Today many women consider those same protective laws to be discriminatory.

■ CHILD CARE AND PARENTAL LEAVE ■

As more and more families become dual-worker families, parental leave for pregnancy, elder care, and child sickness as well as child-care options become increasingly important. In the past mothers (especially of young children)

Gender Roles and the Feminine
Liberation Movement

stayed home to raise the children. Today only one in three mothers stays home and provides full-time care for her children. One-half of all preschoolers spend part of the day in the care of adults other than their parents (Catton 1991, 3). In just 27.5 percent of married couples with children under eighteen is only the husband employed (U.S. Bureau of the Census August 1989, 18).

The quality of care provided for children of working mothers is a matter of both public and private concern. (Lamb, et al. 1992) When both the mother and father work outside the home, other arrangements must be made. Children must be left with babysitters, with relatives, or at child-care centers. Although professionally run child-care centers might seem to be the best solution for working mothers, many families cannot afford the $10 to $20 per day ($200 to $400 per month) that good private centers charge. Consequently, in recent years women have argued and worked for family leave legislation and for government funding of day-care centers.

Prior to 1987, neither the federal government nor any of the states had a family leave policy in place. Since that time, some states have established family leave policies and have also passed legislation to encourage employers to provide day-care opportunities. For example, California encourages employers to establish child-care centers by offering tax incentives. The state reduces taxes by fifty cents for each dollar that employers spend on child-care facilities.

In 1992 137 private companies and organizations banded together to support an initiative called the *American Business Collaboration for Quality Dependent Care*. They donated $25 million to fund 300 programs to help families. Programs range from training for dependent care providers and in-home programs for the elderly, to the development and expansion of child-care facilities and school vacation programs (GenASCI, 1992).

At the federal level, there are two competing philosophies about helping parents with child care. The Act for Better Child Care Services (ABC) would encourage low-cost child care by paying monetary subsidies to the states. The other idea is to offer monetary subsidies directly to parents in the form of tax credits. The credit system would allow parents to select whatever type of child care they consider most beneficial to their families. In fact, formal day-care facilities care for only a small proportion of young children of working parents. Most children are cared for by neighbors, relatives, and other babysitters who care for other people's children in their homes.

The major objection to government funding of child care is that it gives the government too much control over childrearing practices. One provision of the ABC bill would require states that receive federal money to institute health and safety standards. Although day-care centers should certainly meet minimal fire and health standards, regulations established by the government might be extremely detailed and extend beyond necessary safety measures. With federal funding, child-care services would obviously become much more formal, and smaller child-care providers who operate in their homes might be eliminated because they would be enable to meet the higher standards. Senator Robert Dole summed up the reaction of many to increased federal control of child care when he remarked:

American families do not want big government telling them their children cannot stay with grandma because she does not meet certain standards or that their local synagogue or church is off limits for child care because it flunked some bureaucrat's test. (Santa Barbara News Press, June 23, 1989)

A second objection to government funding, especially from a feminist viewpoint, is that it provides a substitute for adequate pay for women workers. In effect, the government is giving a subsidy to employers. Because the government is paying for the child care that employees cannot afford, employers can keep wages low and still find workers. Although such government funding benefits the workers, it limits their options at the same time. If parents do not like the kind of care provided in the government-funded centers, they have little recourse. They often cannot afford to send their children elsewhere, and they would have little influence on the center's policies although legislation could make parental participation in running child-care centers mandatory.

A third objection to government funding is that the quality of child care may be poor. Consistency and predictability are crucial to the development of young children. In the past parents provided this guidance. Profamily groups argue that the chances for good care are still best with the child's own parents: they know the child best and are ego-involved with the child. (See Debate the Issues, pp. 236–237). In day-care centers, the quality and philosophy of child care and the sort of person interacting with the children are often unknown to the parents.

If working mothers were paid adequate wages, parents would be more likely to have a choice of private or public child care and could choose the type of care that best meets their needs and those of the child. If women were paid adequate wages, the resulting demand for quality child care would make it profitable to establish child-care centers, and a variety of centers would be opened with differing educational philosophies. Even if parents had little direct influence over the programs offered, they would have some indirect control because they would not have to patronize centers whose practices were inconsistent with their own values.

Gender Roles and the Feminine
Liberation Movement

233

In spite of these arguments, in the immediate future, government help for early child care would be an improvement over the present situation in which children of working mothers often receive only minimal care. In the long run, however, wage scales for women's jobs must be raised to levels comparable to those for men's jobs. That is the best way to help families choose quality child care that will meet their needs.

Family leaves including maternity leaves, elder care, and child-care leaves should be a normal fringe benefit of all jobs and should be available to men as well as women. More than one hundred countries have laws that protect pregnant workers and allow women to take job-protected maternity leaves at full or partial wages.

Most people supporting parental or family leave legislation suggest that it should include the kinds of options listed in Table 7-3. Recent bills that have come before Congress have proposed up to ten weeks of unpaid parental leave in a twenty-four month period and up to thirteen weeks of unpaid medical leave in a twelve-month period. An employee's job, benefits, and seniority would be protected during the leave period. The proposed legislation also included safeguards against abuse. Under the proposal, small businesses with few employees would be exempt from the requirements (Trzcinski and Finn-Stevenson 1991; Wisensale and Allison 1989).

Employers also need to reconsider their position on maintaining child-care facilities at the workplace. In a survey of approximately 10,000 businesses and government agencies, the Labor Department found that only about 2 percent sponsored day-care centers for their workers' children while another 3 percent offered some financial assistance with child-care expenses. However, about 43 percent of the employers offered indirect help in such forms as flexible work schedules and liberal leave policies (Hayghe 1988, 38–44).,

An employer who provides child-care facilities offers a number of advantages for working parents. No extra time must be taken to deliver and pick up the child because the child is at or close to the workplace. Because the child is nearby, the parents may be able to visit or perhaps have lunch with the child during the day, thus maintaining a higher level of parent/child contact. The company also gains a number of benefits (MaCadam and Meadows 1985). Companies that supply quality child care for their employees also dramatically reduce worker turnover and absenteeism (often a parent must miss work if child-care arrangements fail to work out for some reason). Recruitment problems diminish because the selection of employees is increased.

The Merck pharmaceutical company helped start a day-care center near its headquarters and permits employees to start work any time between 7:00 A.M. and 9:30 A.M. so they can meet family obligations. Procter & Gamble offers its workers unpaid child-care leave for up to one year and guarantees they will not lose their jobs. American Express conducts seminars on such topics as pregnancy planning and elder care. Capital Cities/ABC contributes up to $3000 when an employee adopts a child (*Time* 1988, 47) These are but a few examples of what employers can do to help their employees work and manage family responsibilities at the same time.

In addition to better child care, more part-time jobs at good pay could be created. For example, two people could share one job. They could alternate days, or one could work a morning shift and the other an afternoon shift.

TABLE 7-3
OPTIONS FOR PARENTAL AND FAMILY LEAVE LAWS

Type of Leave
    Pregnancy: recovery from birth and pregnancy-related conditions
    Parental: leave for birth or adoption of child or child's illness
    Medical: Illness or disability of employee
    Family: employee attends to urgent family matters
    Family medical: employee cares for ill family member

Gender
    Mother only or gender neutral
    Length of Leave
    Specified number of weeks in a total period of months (e.g., sixteen weeks in
       twenty-four months)

Employer
    Public (federal, state, or local government)
    Private
    Both public and private
    Size of company, measured in number of employees (e.g., law applies only to employers
       of fifty or more)

Benefits
    Paid versus unpaid
    Medical, other benefits protected
    Job protection; upon return, employee will be assigned to same or equivalent job
       without any discrimination or retaliation
    Protection of seniority

Protections against Misuse
    Prohiited use for unauthorized purposes (e.g., vacation, job searching, working at
       another job, failure to return when leave expires)
    Advance notice of several weeks when possible
    Certification of illness of self or family member
    Leave does not accrue
    Does not affect use of other types of accrued leave
    Is not cumulative for spouses if both are covered
    Minimum period of service prior to use of benefit
    Notice of anticipated duration of leave when possible

Source: Monroe and Garand 1991.

Some companies offer mothers shortened shifts within school hours. These shifts allow mothers time to be with their children and maintain their home and yet contribute economically to the family. Such mothers can participate in the world outside the home and maintain a career without becoming exhausted as so often happens when a woman works all day and then returns to her homemaking job at night. Flexible time schedules can also help working parents cope with the demands of the home while at the same time maintaining high productivity on the job.

With these suggested changes, parents would have more alternatives and would derive more satisfaction from their work. Businesses would have better workers because employees who feel worthwhile and productive in all areas of life do a better job and are less prone to quit. Fair pay and a humane work system that supports rather than hinders home life are worthwhile social goals.

YES

As more and more mothers with small children enter the work force, there has been an increasing call for child-care centers to help them cope with their children. Certainly, from the adult perspective, day care is the most obvious answer to the child-care quandary. But is it an answer that works for the child?

A great deal of research and theory supports the idea that the young child needs meaningful adult attention for proper development (see pp. 491–492). Although such attention need not come from a parent, it is clear that the adult who gives it must be around the child enough for a meaningful relationship to develop. What is "enough" is not yet clear. It seems obvious, however, that the two-year-old child who is placed in a day-care center at 7:30 A.M. and picked up at 5:30 P.M. by a tired, overworked parent will have less chance to form a meaningful intimate relationship than a child not so treated. Even in an excellent facility, the child-care workers will have to divide their time and attention among many children, rather than devoting it to just one or two children as a nonemployed parent can. At least in a child-care center, there are adults to interact with the children. Older children are often "latchkey" children (children who have no supervision except perhaps at school and must await the return of their working parents alone).

In the book *The Day Care Decision*, the Dreskins, who for several years ran a day-care facility, describe their progressive disenchantment with the system. "The problem was not with our facility," they wrote of their decision to close down their center.

The amount of toys and educational materials far exceeded the supplies of most centers. The problem was not our well-trained, credentialed staff; all staff members were qualified people who really liked and cared about young children. After two years of doing child day care, it was obvious that there was a problem inherent in day care itself, a problem that hung like a dark storm over "good" and "bad" day-care centers alike. The children were too young to be spending so much time away from their parents. They were like young birds being forced out of the nest and abandoned before they could fly, their wings undeveloped, unready to carry them into the world.

Although numerous studies indicate that good day-care centers do not harm the children, Dr. Burton White, author of the classic *The First Three Years of Life*, suggests that such studies ask the wrong question, "Is there any damage involved?" rather than the right question, "What is the best way to raise a child?"

Perhaps most troublesome is the possibility that many American children simply are not getting enough parenting to become socialized, to internalize the ethics, values, and mores that make it possible for a society to operate smoothly. The high level of violence among some segments of American youth, the drug and alcohol use, and the sometimes frightening lack of conscience and empathy for their neighbors make one wonder if perhaps a segment of our youth is becoming socio-

WOMEN AND THE LAW

Another restraint on freer gender roles has been the legal structure. Our laws are extremely complicated and have often worked to the detriment of both sexes. (It is important to remember that most of the laws governing marriage and gender roles are state laws and hence do not apply throughout the country.) In the past laws have considered females to be weaker and less responsible than men and therefore in need of protection. For example, in one state a married woman had to use her husband's home as her legal address, and until a recent change in the law, she could not buy or sell stocks or

pathic from lack of parenting. Has neglect perhaps become the worst child abuse of all? (See Scenes from Marriage, Chapter 13).

There are obligations involved in having children. Too often child-care facilities seem to be created to help the parent avoid these obligations rather than to provide for the good of the child. No one ever claimed that having children was convenient.

No

It might be wonderful for all parents to stay home with their children until the children are grown. The fact is that most parents must work to support their families, and as the statistics show in most families both parents are now required by economic necessity to work. Criticizing outside child care is unrealistic. Such energies would be better spent on being realistic, realizing that increasingly both parents must work and that with the high divorce rate in America, the number of single parents will grow. Hence improving child care, not denying that we need it, is the real issue.

Research reported by Dr. White and others supporting his position has focused on older studies and animal research. Studies of children separated from parents during World War II found that the separated children suffered more than the children who remained with their parents and endured bombings. Yet such wartime studies don't seem relevant to the discussion of child care for working parents. The appropriateness of animal parenting studies to human parenting is questionable.

Studies examining the effect of day care on the mother/child emotional bond generally contrast children reared exclusively at home with groups of children receiving daily substitute care. Of some ten studies done through the 1970s, eight reported no significant differences between the two groups of children. The similarities between the groups far outweighed the differences, thus leading to the conclusion that the mother/child bond was not weakened by day care.

Early intervention projects such as Program Headstart show that day care for preschool children from low-income homes can greatly enrich the children's environment and improve later school performance.

Studies of day care have discovered that the maternal attitude toward work and day care has an effect on the child's adjustment to day care. Farel (1980) found no evidence that a mother's working interferes with the development of her child. There was no significant relationship between a child's successful school adjustment and whether or not the mother was employed outside the home. Children whose mothers were working and *wanted* to work scored significantly higher on several measures of adjustment and competence than children whose mothers were working but did not want to do so.

In reviewing the research evidence about day care, O'Connell concludes (1987): "No consistent adverse effect of out-of-home day care has been found by over one dozen child development investigators."

Sources: Adapted from Stein 1984; Walsh 1987; White, 1984

property unless her husband consented and thus accepted responsibility for her actions. The current Georgia code (written in 1856) states:

> The husband is head of the family and the wife is subject to him; her legal and civil existence is merged in the husband . . . either for her own protection, or for her benefit or for the preservation of public order.

This may sound archaic, but recent attempts to change this wording were defeated in the Georgia legislature.

Although many laws remain in effect that are unfair to one or the other sex, the 1970s, 1980s, and 1990s have been a period of change. These changes

Gender Roles and the Feminine
Liberation Movement

have been precipitated mainly by women challenging laws they believed discriminated against them. As a result, the laws on living together, divorce, child custody, support, and Social Security have been modified as have those on crimes such as rape and sexual harassment.

Changing a law to make the sexes more equal sounds like a worthy goal. Yet some critics believe new inequities will result. For example, divorce laws that require equal division of property may leave older women who have little work experience much worse off than their former husbands (Weitzman 1985). Indeed the growing number of female-headed, single-parent families falling beneath the poverty level has resulted in what many researchers are now calling the "feminization of poverty" (see p. 606). The divorced woman may receive half of the property and still be unable to support herself. *Rehabilitative alimony* is one legal response to this new problem created by changing laws. The idea is that the former husband should provide financial help to his ex-wife so that she can retrain herself to become self-supporting.

Many changes are making work and economic participation fairer to women. One example is the California statute enacted in 1978 that makes it an unfair employment practice to discriminate on the basis of pregnancy, childbirth, or medically related conditions. This law also requires employers who provide disability insurance for their employees to include disability for normal pregnancy as a benefit.

In the criminal courts, women have successfully strengthened rape laws. Punishments for rapists have been made more stringent. For example, California now prohibits the granting of probation to any person who has been convicted of rape by force or violence (California SB 1479, Deukmejian, Chapter 1308, Statutes of 1978). More important, many states have eliminated the humiliating defense tactic of cross-examining the victim about her previous sexual conduct. In 1977 Oregon passed a statute that made it a criminal offense for a husband to rape his wife. This is a complete departure from earlier marital law where there was no such thing as rape within marriage.

Sexual harassment is another area in which the law is helping women (and even some men). Women have won numerous cases against employers who used the woman's need for work to obtain sexual favors. A few men have also won such cases. The highly publicized sexual harassment charges brought by Anita Hill against Judge Clarence Thomas at his Supreme Court appointment hearings in 1991 greatly increased the public's awareness of this problem. Unfortunately, men tend to view the sexual harassment problems of women more lightly than do the women.

◼ GENDER ROLE STEREOTYPES ◼

Intimate relationships built on stereotypical gender roles tend to limit freedom and impair the growth of both the individuals and the relationship. Although many married couples function well fulfilling traditional gender roles (i.e., husband-provider, wife-homemaker), such roles may limit a couple that adheres to them too rigidly. A woman who limits herself to a child-centered, home-centered, husband-centered life may come to feel isolated and restricted. She may have to repress other aspects of herself to conform to this role. Her husband may find himself married to someone who depends on him for the fulfillment of all of her needs, for all decisions, and so on. What began as an

ego trip (the helpless idolizing wife and strong responsible husband) quickly becomes a heavy burden. Few honest men today would deny that such overwhelming responsibility is unpleasant and restricts their own lives.

A husband may also be limited by conforming to stereotypical gender roles. In our competitive society, where success is measured by individual productivity and achievement, a husband must often manage two marriages: the first to his career and the second to his wife and family. When conflict arises between the two, he may have to place his work first and become "career oriented." This can be difficult for his wife to accept, especially if she is "family oriented." She may feel cheated and rebuffed by her husband because so much of his energy is expended outside the family. She wants him to be successful, but by encouraging his efforts outside the family, she also loses some of his interest and presence in the family. Many men locked into the traditional provider role early in their lives later complain that their emphasis on work deprived them of family life; they missed the children growing up and lost out on the benefits of close emotional family ties.

As long as the economic system is partial to men, it will be difficult for them to escape the provider role. In the middle classes, the unfortunate antagonism between male economic success and marital life is difficult to resolve. One step that can be taken to limit this conflict is for the wife to participate as much as she can in her husband's life outside the family. He can encourage this by sharing his career experiences and encouraging her interest in his work world. This is especially important if the man's work demands almost total commitment, as in medicine or the ministry. In such cases, if the wife does not participate, she may risk sharing little with her husband. Here important factors in marital satisfaction will be the wife's acceptance of and respect for her husband's commitment, as well as how comfortable she is with her own role. On the other hand, the man must make efforts to find time to spend with his family.

A similar conflict exists for the increasing numbers of married career woman. To succeed, she may have to put even more energy into her career than her husband puts into his because she must overcome prejudice in addition to doing her job. Her husband may become jealous of the attention she gives her career, or he may resent her encroaching on his domain. Unemployed men who are dependent on their wife's earnings are likely to suffer feelings of failure and guilt. Some may respond to these feelings with hostility.

Most of our discussion thus far has focused on the middle-class family. In many ways the traditional working-class family has even more rigidly stereotyped marital roles. The wife is expected to be in the home most of the time unless she is working. The husband finds much of his social life in his relations with his male friends. Thus, sharing activities and joint participation in family matters seem much less important than in middle-class families. Although shared conjugal roles may offer greater potential for mutual satisfaction, they may also lead to conflict, however. Segregated roles may leave husband and wife with little to say to one another and yet give each a sense of competence and independence.

Rubin (1983) suggests that the lower-economic-class male may be threatened when his wife works because she will contribute a much higher proportion of the family income than her middle-class counterpart. By maintaining rigid traditional roles in marriage, he is better able to maintain control and a sense of pride and importance. Working wives in these families express satisfaction with their jobs; often their husbands do not. The wife's working broadens her world and opens choices for her. Her husband may feel trapped and oppressed by his work. His choices may be limited by low pay and low prestige. Often his own lack of skills entraps him, and he is unable to think about moving ahead economically. He feels as though he is in a dead-end situation and often blames his family responsibilities for his unfavorable circumstances.

On the surface a marriage based on stereotypical gender roles may give a couple security and reduce conflict, yet in the long run such a marriage will probably create resentment in both partners. The rigidity of the marriage also tends to make it fragile and unable to adjust to new strains and pressures.

A traditional marriage that is based on stereotypical, but understood and accepted, gender roles may work perfectly well for a couple. It need not be restrictive; equity of roles can apply, and flexibility can remain a part of such a relationship. The key is that the traditional roles are understood and freely accepted by the partners. Traditional marriage has long been criticized, but any relational pattern has both positive and negative aspects. If suddenly all marriages took on some new form, it would not be long before new criticisms would arise. Traditional marriages in which the husband was the primary breadwinner and the wife had primary responsibility for the home and family worked well for some people. Who knows exactly what problems will arise with other marital relational forms? Perhaps one day we will return to the traditional marriage if we find that problems generated by new marital designs are, in fact, greater than the problems we are trying to escape.

In a relationship based on equity (see p. 214), both members are freer to create their marital roles. By becoming aware of the roles society now expects us to fill and by understanding the role expectations that we have learned, we can begin to choose roles for which we are best suited and that will yield the most satisfaction. Such freedom of choice can cause problems. Certain tasks must be accomplished to make marriage viable. Who will do the necessary tasks that neither partner wants to do? For example, neither partner may want to be tied to a nine-to-five job, yet in most families someone must earn money. The bills must be paid, the children raised, the car fixed, the house cleaned, the in-laws telephoned, and so forth.

For a relationship to foster growth, each mate must be committed to the idea of seeking equity in the relationship and to communicating openly any feelings of inequity. This philosophy requires that the couple be willing to experiment and change if first solutions fail.

After several years of marriage, Sally and Jim find that their dissatisfactions with themselves, their marriage, and each other are growing dangerously large. They decide to take an adult education class called Creative Marriage together. The class examines many facets of marriage and family living, first analyzing common marital problem areas and then suggesting creative ways to approach problems.

Sally and Jim decide that they will rearrange family responsibilities so that each can have more time to do things as individuals. They hope that by being freer as individuals, they will also find more joy in doing things together. Because both Sally and Jim work, each felt put upon by the children and the household chores. Sally did most of the chores, but was angry at Jim for doing so little. Even when he did help, he did not do it happily, and then Sally felt guilty for not properly fulfilling her role as housewife. Now they make a list of all the things that have to be done each month to keep the family running smoothly. They each pick out the four things they think they are best at. In one case they picked the same thing. Jim thinks he is good at handling money and Sally thinks she is. They decided that each will handle the money in alternate months. They divide the chores neither wants. They agree to try the new arrangement for two months and then reevaluate.

At the end of the two months, they decide to change how they did the chores neither had wanted to do. Both felt burdened by the chores even though they did not feel unfairly put upon. They decide that rather than dividing the unwanted chores, each will assume responsibility for the chores in alternate weeks. In this way each is free of the chores for one week and then responsible for them the next week.

To date, this arrangement is working well for Jim and Sally. Each feels freer and less resentful toward the other; at the same time the family is running efficiently.

This kind of exploring can lead to a great deal more satisfaction than limiting oneself to prescribed roles that may or may not fit. However, seeking equity in marriage requires that the partners be willing to explore and compromise. Each couple will have to sort their responsibilities in order to obtain the greatest freedom while maintaining love and intimacy. This is no small task, but the rewards can be large. The Couple's Inventory (see Inset 7-4) can help you explore your own and your partner's gender role attitudes.

Even with such equity a couple may be encumbered by the stereotypical gender roles held by society. For example, Sally and Jim may agree that she is to handle the investments but find that the banker or stockbroker always asks

INSET 7-4
COUPLE'S INVENTORY

■ *Personal goal:* To look at how sex role behavior influences decision making, autonomy, and intimacy in your relationship with your partner.

■ *Directions:* Both partners fill out separate inventories and then compare statements.

1. I am important to our couple because _____

2. What I contribute to your success is _____

3. I feel central to our relationship when _____

4. I feel peripheral to our relationship when _____

5. The ways I show concern for you are _____

6. The ways I encourage your growth are _____

7. The ways I deal with conflict are _____

8. The ways I have fun with you are _____

9. I get angry when you _____

10. I am elated when you _____

11. The way I get space for myself in our relationship is _____

12. The ways I am intimate with you are _____

13. The ways I am jealous of you are _____

14. I have difficulty being assertive when you _____

15. You have difficulty being assertive when I _____

16. The strengths of our relationship are _____

for Jim. Be that as it may, each couple can work to realize more freedom within marriage. As one student of changing gender roles suggests:

A society that has gone beyond narrow ideas of femininity and masculinity to the ideal of the self-actualized person offers the widest possible range of choices to its members. It is a society that has reached a level of material comfort that allows it to put resources into human rather than only material development.

17. The weaknesses of our relationship are _____

18. Our relationship would be more effective if you _____

19. I feel most masculine in our relationship when I _____

20. I feel most feminine in our relationship when I _____

21. I trust you to do/be _____

22. I do not trust you to do/be _____

23. I deal with stress by _____

24. You deal with stress by _____

25. The division of labor in household tasks is decided by _____

26. Our finances are controlled by _____

27. The amount of time we spend with our relatives is determined by _____

28. Our vacation plans are made by _____

29. Our social life is planned by _____

30. Taking stock of our relationship is done by _____

31. I am lonely when _____

32. I need you to _____

Source: Sargent 1977, 87.

The real issue is not the liberation of women so much as the liberation of humanity, the establishment of a society where men and women have equal opportunity to fulfill their hopes and dreams unhampered by oppressive and irrelevant sexual stereotypes. (Lindemann 1986)

The idea described here seems at last to be more acceptable to many Americans.

Gender Roles and the Feminine
Liberation Movement

THE MOVEMENT TOWARD
GENDER EQUALITY: SOME LOSSES

When the Equal Rights Amendment died in 1982, many people felt that the women's liberation movement had accomplished its goals and the amendment was unneeded. The amendment reads:

> Equality of rights under the law shall not be denied or abridged by any state on account of sex. The Congress shall have the power to enforce, by appropriate legislation, the provisions of this article.

Yet despite the gains, some feminists find that women are still often at a disadvantage compared to men (Faludi 1991). For example:

■ More job opportunities are available to women than ever before, and yet the pay differential between men and women remains.
■ More women are in the labor force than ever before, and yet they are concentrated in low-level jobs.
■ Single-parent families headed by women have increased greatly in number and make up the largest group of families below the poverty line.
■ Women are freer sexually than they were when the double standard was strong, but the number of children born out of wedlock and not supported by their fathers is larger than ever.
■ More women than in the past are working in upper management, yet they seem to encounter a "glass ceiling" that bars them from the highest levels of management.
■ Women have become more economically independent and have increased their economic responsibility for the family, but at the same time men have reduced their economic support of the family.

Other writers echo this mixed evaluation of the movement toward gender role equality. Among them is Betty Friedan, whose book *The Feminine Mystique*

(1963) helped set the women's movements in motion. In 1981, much to the dismay of ardent feminists, Friedan wrote *The Second Stage*, a critique of the movement that pointed out both failures and successes but emphasized the need to move in new directions and to abandon some of the dead ends of the first twenty years of women's struggle for equality.

> Though the women's movement has changed all our lives and surpassed our dreams in its magnitude, and our daughters take their own personhood and equality for granted, they—and we [the founders of the movement]—are finding that it is not so easy to live, with or without men and children, solely on the basis of the first feminist agenda. I think, in fact, that the women's movement has come about as far as it can in terms of women alone. (26–27)

Friedan points to the strident militancy of the women's movement that turned off many American housewives who also yearned for greater fulfillment but who loved and cherished their families as well. What did the hue and cry about lesbian rights mean to these women and their families?

The supposed belittling of motherhood by the radical feminists also served to turn away many American women. Sylvia Ann Hewlett in her book *Lesser Life: The Myth of Women's Liberation in America* (1987) describes how many of the feminists attacked her and other women who wanted to gain equality in the work world and yet share the joys of family and motherhood at the same time. She is reminded of the writings of Charlotte Perkins Gilman, a nineteenth-century feminist:

> We have so arranged life that a man may have a house, a family, love, companionship, domesticity and fatherhood, yet remain an active citizen of age and country. We have so arranged life, on the other hand, that a woman must "choose"; she must either live alone, unloved, uncompanioned, uncared for, homeless, childless, with her work in the world for sole consolation; or give up world service for the joys of love, motherhood and domestic service.

Hewlett goes on to state that there is no doubt in her mind that American feminism has had a strongly antichild bias. The overall thrust of the movement has been to stress equal rights for both sexes and to pretend that men and women are identical. Women can function successfully as male clones in the marketplace only if they never have children, and to demand this of most women is to thwart their deepest biological need. A movement that looks

Gender Roles and the Feminine
Liberation Movement

away from the central fact of most women's lives—motherhood—will never win widespread support (412).

"The men still have the power," "ERA has lost so we must fight even harder," "We haven't won yet," suggest some of the feminist leaders. But perhaps winning isn't the point. Perhaps the first stage of the women's movement was cast too much in "win or lose" terms. The result was polarization rather than cooperation: gain for me, loss for you, instead of gain for both. Friedan suggests that we have to begin talking about a second stage, a new stage that unlocks us from obsolete power games and irrelevant sexual battles that we may *lose by winning*. Personal liberty and equality cannot be won by one sex at the expense of the other. They can be won for each sex only by both sexes working in partnership. The women's movement must now become the "women's and men's movement" if a full measure of liberty and equality of sexes is to be realized.

We must make sure that the feminist image does not harden into a confining and defensive radical *feminist mystique* where personal truths are denied and questions unasked because they do not fit the new image of woman.

In discussing the second stage of the movement, Friedan suggests:

The second stage cannot be seen in terms of women alone, our separate personhood or equality with men.

The second stage involves coming to new terms with the family—new terms with love and with work.

The second stage may not even be a women's movement. Men may be at the cutting edge of the second stage.

The second stage has to transcend the battle for equal power in institutions. The second stage will restructure institutions and transform the nature of power itself. (1981, 28)

Perhaps the questions of the second stage that must be asked today are more difficult than earlier questions. Yet the new questions are eminently more important to the successful quest for personal equality and liberty. The very success of the movement is now forcing other questions on women and indirectly on men:

■ Has my increased equality really made me freer? Or have men simply let me take on more responsibility while they have reduced their own?
■ How can I have the career I want, and the kind of marriage I want, and be a good mother?
■ Can I make it in a man's world, doing it the man's way? What other way is there? But what is it doing to me? Do I want to be like men?
■ Will the jobs open to me now still be there if I stop to have children?
■ Does it really work, this business of "quality, not quantity" of time with my children? How much time is enough?
■ Do men really want an equal woman? Do I really want an equal man?
■ If I put off having a baby till I'm thirty-eight and can call my own shots on the job will I ever have kids?
■ Am I really freer sexually, or have I gained the right to say "yes" only to have lost the right to say "no"?

■ How can I remain free while at the same time my partner and I make loving, caring, responsible commitments to one another and to our children? (Some of these questions are from Friedan 1981, 34–35.)

These and many other questions must be answered by women seeking broader and more fulfilling roles in American society. Yet, after twenty-five years of concern with self-actualization, self-improvement, and self-awareness, can American men and women make the compromises necessary to build a successful and happy intimate relationship with a person of the opposite sex?

Trying to answer all of the questions above would be presumptuous. Yet the answers to such questions will determine the future of intimate relationships between the sexes and therefore will direct the kind of families Americans develop in the future. The answers are complex at best. Each change in the feminine role brings about changes in the masculine role and brings some gains and some losses. In some cases losses may outweigh the gains, especially during the transitional period. Certainly to some extent the questions raised by the women's movement have contributed to feelings of discontent and dissatisfaction among women and thereby have caused problems in intimate relationships. Moreover, as their increasing economic freedom has decreased their dependence on men, women have been freer to leave unsatisfying relationships.

The gains of equality for women are well discussed, but the losses engendered by these gains are seldom mentioned. What are some of women's losses? The most important seem to revolve around sexuality, childbearing, and childrearing.

Hand in hand with the women's movement came the sexual revolution, but the latter moved at a faster pace than the former. "The pill" brought reliable contraception to women and allowed couples to separate sexual intercourse from procreation. The gains for women were significant. A woman could reliably plan pregnancies and thereby participate in the working world on different terms. She found new sexual pleasures as the fear of unwanted pregnancy was reduced. She became sexually more equal as the double standard broke down. Above all, she gained the freedom to say "yes" to her own sexuality.

Her sexual freedom came so fast that within a few years, young women were as embarrassed to admit to virginity as they had formerly been to admit to premarital sexual relations. And men loved the change! No more lengthy coaxing, cajoling, necking, and petting. No more need to promise love and commitment to get sex. The female who refused sex wasn't "liberated," "free," or "with it." To say no to sex was to say no to the sexual revolution, to the women's movement, to modern society. Hence many young women, having won the right to say yes to sex, found that they had lost the right to say no. And the sex they were saying yes to was often sex without love and commitment.

The practical result of the combination of the sexual revolution and the women's movement was to *liberate men, not women.* It was as if men encouraged women's liberation so that they could gain unhindered access to women's bodies without making any kind of commitment. Today's young women do not complain about the double standard, or about being unfree sexually. Instead they complain about finding men who care, who will make commitments, who will respect them, who will share responsibility for birth control and pregnancy.

And what of unwanted premarital pregnancy? Men had long been morally obligated to provide for children they helped to conceive. The shotgun wed-

Statutory rape
Sexual intercourse with an underage female

ding had traditionally forced the man to provide if he tried to dodge his obligation. Today the term *shotgun wedding* sounds prehistoric. The enlightened parents of a premaritally pregnant girl wouldn't think of such a thing. "They made a mistake. Let's help them get out of it." **Statutory rape** (sexual intercourse with an underage female) is seldom prosecuted and seems as out of date in today's society as the shotgun wedding. As Deidre English (1981, 28) says: "If a woman gets pregnant, the man who twenty years ago might have married her may feel today that he is gallant if he splits the cost of an abortion." Legally he is obligated to support the child, yet if he will not acknowledge the child as his, a woman can do little aside from a paternity suit, which is costly, painful, and often unsuccessful.

Even the expectations for child support are far from the legal norm, which holds that both parents are responsible for supporting their children. Many women who are awarded child support from the fathers receive such monetary help only spasmodically or not at all. Only about half of single mothers who were supposed to be receiving child support payments from their ex-husbands received any money at all (Faludi 1991, 24).

Thus, a combination of the pill, free-choice abortion, the sexual revolution, the women's movement, and unenforced child support laws has freed (liberated?) American men from responsibility for their sexual behavior. Of course, failure to assume responsibility may leave a man isolated and alienated from what could have been a loving family.

And what have these liberating changes brought the American woman? She has been freed to say yes to her own sexuality. She no longer uses her sexuality as a bargaining chip, offering it in return for commitment. She now assumes full responsibility for her sexual behavior, and she is often solely responsible for birth control, for any pregnancy that may occur, and for the support of her children.

In *Sex and Destiny* (1984), Germaine Greer goes so far as to include a chapter entitled "Chastity as a Form of Birth Control," in which among other things she suggests:

> Chastity endows sexual activity with added importance by limiting its enjoyment to special persons and special times. . . . Chastity may actually serve to stabilize marriage unions by maintaining a constant level of sexual interest in a wife who is often unavailable. . . . It may sustain sexual interest over a long time period rather than allowing interest to burn out through unbridled indulgence. (Greer 1984, 114)

Single-parent, female-headed families fall disproportionately below the poverty line and cost society a disproportionate share of public monies via various welfare programs that help them survive. Poverty is being feminized as the responsibility for children has shifted more and more to women and away from men. Most of these single-parent families are headed by divorced mothers (50 percent plus). Another 20 percent are headed by unwed mothers, while the remainder are headed by separated mothers. In today's economy a mother alone with her child or children generally has a difficult time economically. Families with a female head of house represent 53 percent of all poor families (U.S. Bureau of the Census August 1991, 7).

Examined in these terms, the movement toward sexual equality for women appears to have freed the American man, not the American woman. When

we look at the American woman today in terms of sexuality, childbearing, and childrearing, a good case can be made that she has lost status and freedom although she has gained in many other areas of her life.

It seems that it is now time to take stock. We need to reevaluate past gender roles so that we can keep those parts that were positive (rather than simply throwing out all traditional roles as bad), and we need to evaluate honestly some of the changes already made so that we can keep the beneficial ones and rectify those that have proved damaging.

It is now time for "people liberation." Only when men and women work together in mutual respect and with love, care, and commitment to one another will the American family again be strong. This does not mean that it will be the American family of old or some rigidly idealized new family form of the future. It means any family form in which men and women can realize their individual abilities and work together to rear children who become responsible adults willing to make commitments and assume the responsibilities that make a society great.

SUMMARY

1. *Equity between the sexes, not sameness, is the goal to seek.* Yet achieving such a goal is not easy. First, one is born male or female, though this is not always as clear as it may at first seem. Second, one learns from society the roles (masculinity and femininity) that go with one's gender. If a society holds hard-and-fast stereotypes of gender roles, individuals will find it difficult to achieve equitable roles because variation will be discouraged. For change to occur, individual couples must strive to create equitable roles in their own marriages and at the same time join with others to fight cultural stereotypes.

2. *Two important stumbling blocks to people's liberation caused by stereotypical gender roles are the economic deprivation of women and laws that discriminate between the sexes.* Until women are able to earn the same wages as men for the same work, it will be difficult for couples to change the traditional roles of "man the provider" and "woman the homemaker." In addition, many kinds of discrimination are built into our legal system. For example, in the past women were not able to establish their own credit if married, though this law has recently been changed. Our criminal laws discriminate against men as did the armed forces draft system.

3. *The elimination of gender role stereotypes from society means that a couple are free to establish the most satisfying relationship they can.* It means that they can select the gender roles that best fit them. It also means freedom of choice within the marriage. Some individuals may choose older, traditional roles. In such traditional marriages, the roles may be rigid, yet the tasks necessary to maintain the marriage are clearly spelled out, and each partner knows his or her responsibilities. Some persons may prefer specific role assignments because they provide efficiency and security. Some may choose a radical alteration of traditional roles into new but equally rigid roles. Others may opt to change roles periodically and to maintain a flexible system. The concept of reduced gender role stereotyping does not dictate the kind of relationship a couple will have. Instead it frees couples to explore options and encourages them to make their own choices. As you'll remember from Chapter 2, one of the basic suppositions on which this book is based is that a free and creative society offers many structural forms by which family functions can be fulfilled. The best marital roles are those that fit you best.

4. *As positive as the movement toward gender equality has been, it has also caused some losses especially among women.* For women these losses center around sexuality, pregnancy, and childrearing. Both sexes have experienced the loss of commitment, security, and stability within intimate relationships. It is hoped that such losses are transitional. As women's liberation moves on to a second stage, such losses may disappear as the sexes cooperate and work together to improve and enhance commitment, caring and loving within the man/woman relationship.

American feminism late 1980s style could be defined, cynically, as women's rush to do the same foolish and benighted things that have traditionally occupied men. And why not? The good and honest things that have traditionally occupied women—like rearing children and keeping husbands in clean shirts—are valued in the open market at somewhere near the minimum wage. And whatever one thinks of investment banking or corporate law, the perks and the pay are way ahead of those for waitressing and data entry. So, every time a woman breaks a new barrier the rest of us tend to cheer—even if she's running a pollution-producing company or toting a gun in some ill-considered war.

Two cheers, anyway. Because this is not the revolution that I, at least, signed on for. When the feminist movement burst forth a couple of decades ago, the goal was not just to join 'em—and certainly not just to beat 'em—but to improve an imperfect world. Gloria Steinem sketched out the vision in a 1970 *Time* essay titled "What It Would Be Like If Women Win." What it would be like was a whole lot better, for men as well as women, because, as she said right up front, "Women don't want to exchange places with men." We wanted *better* places, in a kinder, gentler, less rigidly gendered world.

We didn't claim that women were morally superior. But they had been at the receiving end of prejudice long enough, we thought, to empathize with the underdog of either sex. Then too, the values implicit in motherhood were bound to clash with the "male values" of competi-

tiveness and devil-may-care profiteering. We imagined women storming male strongholds and, once inside, becoming change agents, role models, whistle-blowers. The hand that rocks the cradle was sure to rock the boat.

To a certain extent, women have "won." In medicine, law and management, they have increased their

participation by 300 to 400 percent since the early 1970s, and no one can argue that they haven't made *some* difference. Women lawyers have spearheaded reforms in the treatment of female victims of rape and of battering. Women executives have created supportive networks to help other women up the ladder and are striving to sensitize corporations to the need for flexible hours, child care and parental leave. Women journalists have fought to get women's concerns out of the "style section" and onto the front page. Women doctors, according to physician-writer Perri Klass, are less paternalistic than their male counterparts and "better at listening."

But, I'm sorry, sisters, this is not the revolution. What's striking, from an old-fashioned (ca. 1970) feminist perspective, is just how *little* has changed. The fact that law is no longer classified as a "nontraditional" occupation for women has not made our culture any less graspingly litigious or any more concerned with the rights of the underdog. Women doctors haven't made a dent in the high-tech, bottom-line fixation of the medical profession, and no one would claim that the influx of executive women has ushered in a new era of high-toned business ethics.

It's not that we were wrong back in the salad days of feminism about the existence of nurturant "feminine values." If anything, women have more distinctive views as a sex than they did twenty years ago. The gender gap first appeared in the presidential election of 1980, with women voting on the more liberal side. Recent polls show that women are more likely to favor social spending for the poor and to believe it's "very important" to work "for the betterment of American society."

So why haven't our women pioneers made more of a mark? Charitably speaking, it may be too soon to expect vast transformations. For one thing, women in elite, fast-track positions are still pathetically scarce. *Fortune* magazine found that in the highest echelons of corporate managers, fewer than one-half of 1 percent are female. Then there's the exhaustion factor. Women are far more likely to work a "double day" of career plus homemaking. The hand that rocks the cradle—and cradles the phone, and sweeps the floor, and writes the memo and meets the deadline—doesn't have time to reach out and save the world.

But I fear, too, that women may be losing the idealistic vision that helped inspire feminism in the first place. Granted, every Out group—whether defined by race, ethnicity, or sexual preference—seeks assimilation as a first priority. But every Out group carries with it a critical perspective, forged in the painful experiences of rejection and marginalization. When that perspective is lost or forgotten, a movement stands in danger of degenerating into a scramble for personal advancement. We applaud the winners and pray that their numbers increase, but the majority will still be found far outside the gates of privilege, waiting for the movement to start up again.

And for all the pioneering that brave and ambitious women have done, the female majority remains outside, earning 70¢ to the man's $1 in stereotypically female jobs. That female majority must still find a way to survive the uncaring institutions, the exploitative employers and the deep social inequities the successful few have not yet got around to challenging.

Maybe, now that women have got a foot in the door, it's time to pause and figure out what we intend to do when we get inside. Equality with men is a fine ambition, and I'll fight for any woman's right to do any foolish or benighted thing that men are paid and honored for. But ultimately, assimilation is just not good enough. As one vintage feminist T shirt used to say, IF YOU THINK EQUALITY IS THE GOAL . . . YOUR STANDARDS ARE TOO LOW.

Source: Barbara Ehrenreich, *Time,* Fall 1990, p. 15.

CHAPTER

8

THE FAMILY AS AN ECONOMIC SYSTEM

CONTENTS

As a marketing research consultant earning more than $40,000 a year, 34-year-old Dave Smith could be your typical affluent yuppie. Unfortunately, his income does not go as far as one might expect and he finds himself increasingly frustrated by his inability to provide for his family as he would like.

After paying rent on their apartment and other expenses, he, his wife, and two young children have little money left over to enjoy the good life. They can afford to eat out only about once a month. And he has little left over to save or invest in stocks or bonds or what he really wants—a house.

"I'm making more money than my dad ever did in his life, but I can't afford the home he could." Noting that his car payments of $280 a month were more than his dad's house payments, he said, "It's frustrating. I've got a good and stable job with potential for upward mobility, but yet with just one income, getting a nice home will be difficult."

Dave and his family are experiencing the frustrations felt by many Americans as they try to cope with the economic realities of providing a living and finding economic satisfaction. The married single-earner family has been replaced by the dual-earner family as over half of all wives are now in the labor force. Although few people directly ascribe difficulties in their marriages and families to money problems, the fact is that work, money, and intimacy are closely intertwined for most families. So closely are they related that trouble in one area almost guarantees trouble in the other two. The spouse who works two jobs to earn enough money to make ends meet almost certainly comes home overtired and perhaps somewhat disinterested in his or her relationship. Time for togetherness, sharing, play, enjoying the children, making love, and other intimate family activities is limited for the family in which both partners work full-time. On the other hand, unemployment within a family brings worry and stress as bills accumulate and money dwindles. Worry and stress are particularly troublesome enemies of successful intimate relationships. Although economic success certainly does not guarantee family success, economic failure almost always leads to family problems and breakdown. Divorce, separation, and desertion, for example, are highest among the poor.

Most couples today pay almost no attention at first to each other's financial values. Money is often a more taboo subject than sex. Courting couples may discuss their prior sex lives but never raise the question of economic histories. After all, talking about one's potential income, use of credit cards, or feelings about indebtedness is not very romantic. Yet, money matters are the topics most commonly discussed by married couples. In their popular book *American Couples*, Blumstein and Schwartz (1983) focus on just three aspects of couples' lives—money, work, and sex—because these areas are so crucial to a successful, enduring relationship.

What should we buy? When should we buy? Who should buy? Who should make the spending decisions? Who will pay the bills? Should we pool our money or maintain separate accounts? Such questions become particularly troublesome if the partners have divergent attitudes about money. For example, consider a person who comes from a background of thrift and practicality and takes pleasure in making a good buy. This individual becomes excited about buying a used car at wholesale rather than retail prices and will probably brag about the purchase. Any minor problems with the car will not be upsetting

Finding the right job and being secure from unwanted job loss are important to a person and his or her family. One way to ensure work security is to select a vocation that will grow in the future. The Bureau of Labor Statistics has prepared projections of the U.S. economy through the year 2005. By this time the bureau expects the labor force will have expanded by 21 percent and will have become increasingly minority and female. Careful review of the accompanying tables will indicate where the bureau expects job expansion. All of the following tables come from the *Monthly Labor Review*, November 1991.

because it was such a "good buy." Suppose this person's partner comes from a luxurious environment where emphasis was placed on obtaining precisely what one wants and success was often measured in economic terms. He or she believes in buying a new car of the appropriate model and considers a used car, especially a "steal," a mark of poor taste and economic failure. The married life of such a pair may be filled with conflict over money matters because of their different monetary attitudes.

Money and work affect everything we do, both as individuals and as family members. We are involved with work and money on a daily basis. Even the retired and those who are sufficiently wealthy not to have to work must attend to money matters on a daily basis. (How are my investments doing? Will my retirement check arrive today? Can we afford a new car or should we repair the old car?) Successful work and efficient money management are the foundations of family success. Whether individuals are poor or rich, work and monetary decisions play all-important roles in their lives.

As we think about the characteristics of strong healthy families, it is clear that economic stability is necessary for the development of family strength. Economic stability and security enable families to turn their attention from issues of basic survival to enhancing the quality of life. Family strengths can evolve only if economic survival is assured. Given the complexity and uncertainty of the economic climate in which families must make decisions, families obviously need to learn all that they can about the economic system in which they live if they are to be successful.

Work also produces by-products other than money. Both personal and family status are derived from occupation. A medical doctor and his or her family enjoy high status (at least in America; the status of occupations varies among cultures), and this, in turn, influences the family's lifestyle. Individuals' sense of self-esteem also relates closely to their work. Self-esteem is one of the first things threatened by unemployment. Furthermore, one's sense of identity is based largely on what is done in the workplace. Often the first question asked of a new acquaintance is "What do you do?" A person's (family's) circle of friends is often drawn in part from the work world. Thus, the work world and the family world are intimately related, and each influences the other in many ways.

TABLE 8-1
PERCENTAGE OF EMPLOYMENT CHANGE
IN SELECTED INDUSTRIES, 1990–2005

INDUSTRY DESCRIPTION	ANNUAL PERCENTAGE CHANGE	INDUSTRY DESCRIPTION	ANNUAL PERCENTAGE CHANGE
Fastest Growing		**Most Rapidly Declining**	
Residential care	4.5%	Footwear, except rubber and plastic	−4.3
Computer and data processing services	4.4	Ammunition and ordnance, except small arms	−3.8
Health services	4.0	Luggage, handbags, and leather products	−3.5
Management and public relations	3.9	Tobacco manufactures	−2.5
Water and sanitation, including combined services	3.3	Agricultural chemicals	−2.5
Libraries, vocational and other schools	3.3	Private households	−2.4
Offices of health practitioners	3.1	Stampings, except automotive	−2.3
Passenger transportation arrangement	3.0	Metal cans and shipping containers	−2.3
Individual and miscellaneous social services	3.0	Forgings	−2.3
Legal services	3.0	Petroleum refining	−2.2
Nursing and personal care facilities	2.9	Small arms and small arms ammunition	−2.1
Miscellaneous equipment rental and leasing	2.9	Guided missiles and space vehicles	−2.0
Accounting, auditing, and services	2.8	Household appliances	−1.9
Elementary and secondary schools	2.8	Motor vehicles and car bodies	−1.9
Automotive rentals, without drivers	2.8	Office and accounting machines	−1.9
Research and testing services	2.7	Soft drinks and flavorings	−1.8
Miscellaneous publishing	2.7	Photographic equipment and supplies	−1.8
Business services	2.7	Tires and inner tubes	−1.8
Photocopying, commercial art, photofinishing	2.6	Apparel	−1.8
Nondepository; holding and investment offices	2.6	Communications, except broadcasting	−1.8

TABLE 8-2
FASTEST GROWING OCCUPATIONS, 1990–2005

OCCUPATION	PERCENTAGE CHANGE	OCCUPATION	PERCENTAGE CHANGE
Home health aides	91.7%	Flight attendants	58.5
Paralegals	85.2	Computer programmers	56.1
Systems analysts and computer scientists	78.9	Occupational therapists	55.2
Personal and home care aids	76.7	Surgical technologists	55.2
Physical therapists	76.0	Medical records technicians	54.3
Medical assistants	73.9	Management analysts	52.3
Operations research analysts	73.2	Respiratory therapists	52.1
Human services workers	71.2	Child-care workers	48.8
Radiologic technologists and technicians	69.5	Marketing, advertising, and public relations managers	47.4
Medical secretaries	68.3		
Physical and corrective therapy assistants and aides	64.0	Legal secretaries	47.4
		Receptionists and information clerks	46.9
Psychologists	63.6	Registered nurses	44.4
Travel agents	62.3	Nursing aides, orderlies, and attendants	43.4
Correction officers	61.4	Licensed practical nurses	41.9
Data processing equipment repairers	60.0	Cooks, restaurant	41.8

TABLE 8-3
PROJECTED GROWTH OCCUPATIONS,
BY LEVEL OF EDUCATION REQUIRED

Group I: Occupations generally requiring a bachelor's degree or more education

- System analysts and computer scientists
- Physical therapists
- Operations research analysts
- Psychologists
- Computer programmers
- Occupational therapists
- Management analysts
- Marketing, advertising, and public relations managers
- General managers and top executives
- Teachers, secondary school
- Teachers, elementary school
- Accountants and auditors
- Lawyers

Group II: Occupations generally requiring some post-secondary training or extensive employer training

- Paralegals
- Radiological technologists and technicians

- Medical assistants
- Physical and corrective therapy assistants and aides
- Data processing equipment repairers
- Medical records technicians
- Surgical technicians
- Cooks, restaurant
- Respiratory therapists
- Licensed practical nurses
- Maintenance repairers, general utility
- Teacher aides and educational assistants
- Registered nurses
- Legal secretaries
- Medical secretaries

Group III: Occupations generally requiring high school graduation or less education

- Home health aides
- Human service workers
- Personal and home care aides
- Correction officers

- Travel agents
- Flight attendants
- Salespersons, retail
- General office clerks
- Cashiers
- Food counter, fountain, and related workers
- Truckdrivers, light and heavy
- Nursing aides, orderlies and attendants
- Janitors and cleaners, including maids and housekeeping cleaners
- Waiters and waitresses
- Food preparation workers
- Receptionists and information clerks
- Gardeners and groundskeepers, except farm
- Guards
- Child-care workers
- Secretaries, except legal and medical
- Cooks, short order and fast food
- Clerical supervisors and managers
- Stock clerks, sales floor

Per capita income (the gross national product [GNP] divided by the total population of men, women, and children) for each American was $21,700 for the year 1990. Of the major countries of the world, only Switzerland ($32,790) and Japan ($25,430) have higher per capita incomes. In many nations per capita income is much lower. For example, Bangladesh and Nepal have per capita incomes of less than $200. The average per capita income in the sixteen countries making up western Africa is only $440 (Population Reference Bureau 1992).

In 1992, the U.S. government began to use another economic indicator, the gross domestic product (GDP), in addition to the GNP to measure the economic health of the United States. *GNP* measures all goods and services produced by workers and capital supplied by U.S. residents regardless of location. *GDP* measures all goods and services produced by workers and capital only in the United States. In the long run, the change will not have much effect on the economic statistics.

Despite Americans' apparent wealth, dissatisfaction with money matters remains high. Almost all families, regardless of their actual income, feel that if they could earn $5000 to $10,000 more per year everything would be fine. In fact, in most families, needs and desires are increasing even faster than income. Thus, monetary dissatisfaction may be as high for families earning $50,000 per year as it is for families earning $25,000.

TABLE 8-4
MEDIAN ANNUAL EARNINGS BY OCCUPATION
AND LEVEL OF EDUCATION, 1987

OCCUPATION	TOTAL, ALL LEVELS	LESS THAN HIGH SCHOOL	HIGH SCHOOL	ONE TO THREE YEARS COLLEGE	FOUR YEARS COLLEGE OR MORE
Total, all occupations	$21,543	$15,249	$18,902	$21,975	$31,029
Executive, administrative, and managerial	30,264	22,306	23,286	27,255	37,252
Professional specialty	30,116	19,177	23,233	27,458	31,311
Technicians and related support	24,489	16,207	21,358	23,830	28,004
Marketing and sales	22,220	13,746	17,654	22,546	32,747
Administrative support occupations, including clerical	17,120	15,535	16,554	17,491	20,823
Service occupations	13,443	10,764	13,093	16,937	21,381
Precision production, craft, and repair	24,856	20,465	25,140	27,042	30,938
Operators, fabricators, and laborers	18,132	15,365	19,303	21,627	22,114
Agriculture, forestry, fishing and related workers	11,781	10,571	12,730	16,331	17,130

Americans may earn more money than others, but they also spend more and are more deeply in debt. Most money is spent by family units to support family members, so family income is an important measure of family function.

In 1990 real median family income (adjusted for inflation) rose to $35,353, the eighth consecutive year it had increased (see Figure 8-1). In 1973, median family income had reached $30,820, then an all-time high. In 1974, however, family income began to decline due both to a series of recessions and to an increase in the number of single-parent families. The decline continued until 1982 when median family income began to turn upward again; by 1987 it had returned to the level reached in 1973. Gains continued through 1990, but family income declined in 1991 as a result of the recession.

Not all Americans share equally in the wealth. For example, married couples do considerably better than average. Table 8-5 indicates some of these differences by various groups. In general, female-headed families, those with little

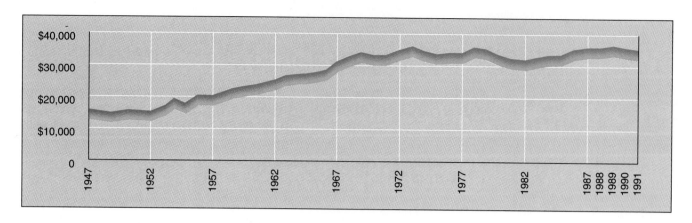

FIGURE 8-1
Median family income, 1947–1991 (in 1987 dollars) (Source: U.S. Bureau of the Census)

education, Hispanics, and black Americans all tend to earn less than the average median family income.

The modern American family is the basic economic unit of society because it is the major consumption unit. In the early years of our country, the family was also the major production unit. Then 90 percent of the population worked in agriculture on family-owned farms. Over the years, however, most farm workers became factory workers. Thus, today's average family is not directly involved in economic production in the home or on their own land.

As a consuming unit, the family exerts great economic influence. A couple anticipating marriage and children is also anticipating separate housing from their parents. This means a refrigerator, stove, furniture, dishes, television, and so on. And how will this new family acquire all of these items? Probably by using credit, not an American invention perhaps but certainly an American way of life. According to a Federal Reserve study, some 85 percent of all American households owed money at some time in 1990. Credit and debt are directly associated with bankruptcy.

Total household debt represented 83.5 percent of disposable personal income in December 1990, up from 65.4 percent in 1980. How much did Americans owe at the beginning of 1991?

■ Consumer debt includes automobile loans and credit cards. Americans owed approximately $800 billion, or about $3,200 per person for outstanding personal credit.
■ Home mortgage debt includes home-equity lines of credit. Americans owed approximately $2.6 trillion.

A record 944,000 American individuals and businesses filed for bankruptcy in 1991, a 21 percent increase over the year before. This is the highest number since the current U.S. Bankruptcy Code took effect in 1979 and the seventh consecutive increase nationally (Skidmore 1992). Ninety-two percent of these filings were by individuals, the rest by businesses.

"Buy now pay later!" "Why wait? Only $5 per week." These and many others like them are the economic slogans of modern American society. The extension of credit to the general population has produced a material standard

TABLE 8-5
COMPARISON OF INCOME BY
SELECTED CHARACTERISTICS, 1990

CHARACTERISTIC	MEDIAN INCOME
Type of family	
All races:	
All families	$35,353
Married couples	39,895
Female householder, no husband present	16,932
White:	
All families	38,915
Married couples	40,331
Female householder, no husband present	19,528
Black:	
All families	21,423
Married couples	33,784
Female householder, no husband present	12,125
Hispanic	
All families	23,431
Married couples	27,996
Female householder, no husband present	11,914
Education	
8 years or less	13,353
High school: 1 to 3 years	18,191
4 years	28,744
College: 1 to 3 years	35,724
4 years	50,549
5 years or more	54,636

Source: U.S. Bureau of the Census. "Money Income of Households, Families, and Persons in the United States: 1991," ser. p-60, No. 174.

of living the likes of which the world has never seen. On the promise of future payment, we can acquire and use almost anything we desire: material goods, travel, education, and services such as medical and dental care. If the credit system were suddenly abolished, the degree to which it supports the economy would become glaringly clear. Traffic congestion would end as the majority of autos disappeared from the roads. Many buildings, both business and residential, would become empty lots or smaller, shabbier versions of themselves. Thousands of televisions would disappear from living rooms. If debtors' prisons were reestablished at the same time, practically the entire population would be incarcerated!

If we think back over the economic events of the past few years, it is clear that the economy goes through drastic changes to which we all must adjust. For example, in 1979 and 1980 inflation was rampant, running as high as 13 percent per year. Yet by 1982 and 1983, inflation had dropped to less than 5 percent per year in the face of higher unemployment rates and a deepening recession. By 1984 the recession was over, inflation remained low, but the dollar was so strong against foreign currencies that the U.S. balance of trade suffered and steps had to be taken to lower the value of the dollar. Recession returned in 1991–1993, and median family income dropped for the first time in nine years.

Such economic uncertainties make it imperative that individuals plan their economic destiny carefully. Those who do not are doomed to lose control of their economic lives. Knowing how to budget, spend, save, borrow, and invest are important skills for personal and family stability and happiness.

Even in good economic times and with good economic planning, however, married couples often argue about money. As we shall see later, quarrels over money essentially revolve around allocation of resources and control of the allocation. And these decisions stem mainly from the attitudes about money that each brings to the partnership (see Inset 8-2).

CREDIT AND LOSS OF FREEDOM

Credit buying has allowed the average American a higher standard of living than most people in the past ever dreamed possible. The ability to buy only on the promise of future payment is a relatively modern invention. Credit has given Americans the means for a healthier, more fulfilling life, but it can also enslave people subtly at great psychological cost. This entrapment and loss of freedom usually occur because people are ignorant of the system and blindly accept persuasive and seductive advertising urging them to use credit to purchase everything they want. An understanding of economics and the relationship of debt to personal freedom will enable you to make the system work for you instead of against you.

Credit and debt are directly opposed to personal freedom. When you contract to pay for a new automobile over a period of sixty months, for example, you gain the use of the automobile but lose a degree of personal freedom. Regardless of the circumstances or what you do with the car, you have promised and have legally made yourself responsible to pay a certain amount each month for the next five years. If at the end of one year, you wish to take a lower-paying but more satisfying job or return to school to improve your skills, you may not be able to do so unless you can find a way to continue the payments. Returning the car does not cancel your debt. Even if the finance company sells the car and gives you credit for the money it receives, chances are that you will still owe because during the first year or two the car depreciates in value faster than the debt is reduced. Although the remaining debt may be small, it still exists, and so does your obligation.

If you cannot at least partially resist the temptations of credit buying, you can become so obligated as to lose almost all freedom. This modern economic slavery is far more seductive than historical systems of slavery based on power. In real slavery, slaves know who the enemy is and where to direct their hostility. But in the American economic system, you place yourself in the slavery of debt and thus have no one else to blame for your predicament. No one is forced to keep buying on "easy" installments. Unfortunately, too many small, easy payments can add up to debts that are often too heavy for the individual or family to bear.

Answer the following questions without discussing them with your partner. Then have your partner answer them. If you answer the questions differently, it may indicate points of attitudinal difference and possible conflict. You should discuss the reasoning behind your answers and how your two positions can be reconciled.

1. Are you comfortable living without a steady income?

2. Did your parents have a steady income?

3. Do you consider yourself to come from an economically poor, average, or wealthy background?

4. Do you think that saving is of value in America's inflationary economy?

5. Do you have a savings account? Do you contribute to it regularly?

6. In the past have you postponed buying things until you had saved the money for them, or did you buy immediately when you desired something?

7. In the past have you often bought on installment?

8. Do you have credit cards? How many? Do you use them regularly?

9. Do you have money left over at the end of your regular pay period?

10. Do you brag about making a really good buy or finding a real bargain?

11. If it were possible to save $100 a month for a year, what would you do with the money?

12. Possible answers to question 11 are listed below. Rank them in order of importance using 1 for what you would most likely do with the $100 and 10 for what you are least likely to do:

a. Save it for a rainy day.

b. Save it to buy something for cash rather than on credit.

c. Invest it.

d. Use it for recreation.

e. Use it for payments for a new car.

f. Use it for travel and adventure.

g. Use it to buy a home or property.

h. Use it to improve your present living place.

i. Divide it in half and let each spouse spend it as he or she chooses.

j. Use it for an attractive wardrobe, eating out, and entertaining.

RICH AND KIMBERLY—SLOWLY DROWNING IN A SEA OF DEBT

Let's look at the economic life of a hypothetical, newly married young couple and follow them through their first years of marriage. We'll see how they handle work decisions, allocate their monies, and cope with increasing economic pressures as children arrive. How do they react when they realize that today's average family must have two earners if it is to enjoy many of the benefits of the American economic system? This analysis will make clear the slow and often insidious process by which so many families lose their freedom and become economically entrapped.

For many young couples, marriage actually means a drastic reduction in their standard of living. Accustomed to living at home and sharing their parents' standard of living (usually created by thirty yeas of their parents' earnings), the newlyweds are now on their own economically. Entry-level jobs may be scarce, and the pay is low compared with their parents' earnings. If the newlyweds fail to understand this and attempt to maintain their parent's standard,

Credit and Loss of Freedom

they are likely to be trapped in the economic system to such a degree that they will never be able to regain their economic freedom.

WHEN DOES RICH'S ENTRAPMENT BEGIN?

Kimberly and Rich's actual entrapment begins before marriage. Rich finds he is not as popular as some of his friends. Like many Americans he has always been interested in automobiles. In the United States in 1991 approximately 180 million cars were registered for a population of approximately 250 million. (Information Please Almanac 1991) He figures that a good car would probably make him more popular. He also observes that his parents often judge their friends by the cars they drive. Thus, he believes that his car should be one of the better ones. He has a job as a stockboy at a local supermarket and can use his earnings to pay for the car because he lives at home and doesn't have any living expenses. It seems so simple. His parents don't object to his buying a car but make it clear that they are in no financial position to help him. So Rich contracts to pay $200 a month for the next three years. Of course, in addition to the $200, he now has all the expenses of an automobile: tax, license, insurance, gas, upkeep, and, quite likely, modifications (lowering it, turbocharging it, adding mag wheels, a CD player, or whatever is popular at the time). The costs of car ownership are much higher than many people realize. Hertz Corporation reports yearly on per mile costs for its fleet of rental vehicles. For example, a typical compact car such as a Ford Tempo costs about 40 to 50 cents per mile to operate or $4000 to $5000 every 10,000 miles. This sum includes all costs such as insurance, depreciation, gas, and maintenance.

With his new car, Rich soon attracts a wonderful young woman. Although she first noticed him because of his car, Kimberly finds Rich to be a nice person, and they are soon going steady. The pressures of the American dating game build up, and they decide they are deeply in love. Rich is near the end of his senior year in high school and will soon be able to work full-time. If he stays at the supermarket and becomes a checker, he will be earning $1200 a month to start, with the possibility of increasing to as much as $3000 a month over time. This seems like a fortune compared with the $400 a month he now receives as part-time help. Both Rich and Kimberly have always heard that two can live as cheaply as one—another of the great modern myths.

SETTING UP THEIR APARTMENT

After graduation, Rich and Kimberly wed and set up housekeeping. At first they are the envy of their friends. They are now independent, free of parental domination, and can participate in many things that were previously taboo. Soon, however, Rich finds that his salary isn't going as far as he anticipated. Somehow rent, food, and basic necessities are eating huge chunks of his new, large (?) salary. Before his marriage he thought he would have enough to update his car a bit, go on some trips, and model their apartment after those on television. But now Kimberly says they need a new washing machine; it is something all young married couples must have. When they look at washing machines, the salesperson convinces them that they should buy the deluxe model with five speeds and three water temperatures. Of course, it costs $70 more than the ordinary machine, but according to the salesperson, it's far superior and the payments are the same, just stretched over a longer time period. The salesperson forgets to tell them that the motor and all the basic parts are the same in both models. But the salesperson does add that there's a special this week on the matching dryer—they can get it for $30 off, plus free installation. It's a great opportunity and would only add $2 per week to their payments. Rich and Kimberly are a little nervous about adding more payments to the $200 Rich is still paying on the car, but the washer and dryer will make life easier for both of them. Rich still wishes he could fix up his car, though.

Gradually, Rich finds his salary is claimed before he receives it. The couple reach the point where they no longer have any freedom of decision over their income. One problem is that they are starting off with large purchases, some of which they don't need. A washer and dryer, for example, are unnecessary for a young couple without children.

CREDIT TO COVER CREDIT

A year after their marriage, Rich and Kimberly's first child is born with accompanying hospital, doctor, and general care bills. A surprising number of salespeople come knocking at their door to help them get their youngster started off right. First are the disposable diapers, a must for the modern mother. Then there is a photographer who will take regular pictures of their child so they will have a permanent record of the child's growth. There are toys that will help their child's intellectual development. And, of course, they now need a set of encyclopedias???

One month the couple discover that Rich's paycheck doesn't quite cover their monthly expenses. At first they panic, but then Kimberly remembers an ad that said "Borrow enough money to get completely out of debt." At the time the ad didn't seem to make sense, but now it does. They can wipe out all of their small debts by combining them into one large package loan that reduces their total monthly payments. With a sigh of relief, they go to the finance company and soon have their finances under control again. The interest rate is 15 percent, but they don't care as long as they can meet the payments. Rather than continue the story, suffice it to say that five years after their marriage, Rich and Kimberly are in bankruptcy court. They didn't gamble on a big investment speculation; they slowly drowned in a rising sea of debt.

Contrary to popular opinion, most people who go bankrupt are not speculative investors who get into financial trouble. Rather they are lower- and middle-class families like Kimberly and Rich who slowly become overburdened with increasing debts. Moreover, going through bankruptcy procedures does not seem to help people become more prudent. Of those who file for bankruptcy, 80 percent use credit and are in debt trouble again within five years (Miller 1984, 249–50). Hence it is crucial for all of us to know as much as possible about credit and borrowing so that we can control our use of credit rather than being controlled by it.

Consumer counseling agencies help clients who are having financial troubles by guiding them toward better money management. These counselors say that many who find themselves insolvent didn't even realize they were getting into financial trouble. How can you tell if you are headed down the road to bankruptcy?

■ You are spending more than you make. Bills are piling up, and creditors are sending second and third notices.
■ You find that you are tucking away nothing for a rainy day. You have no regular savings plan.
■ You are making no plans for retirement (even if you are just starting work).

TABLE 8-6
COMPARATIVE COSTS OF CREDIT

LENDERS	TYPE OF LOAN	ANNUAL PERCENTAGE RATE[a]	REMARKS
Banks	Personal loans (consumer goods) Real-property loans General loans	10–18[b]	60% of all car loans, 30% of other consumer good loans; real-property loans have lower interest rates because property retains value, which may cover defaulted loans.
Credit cards	Personal loans Cash loans	17–21[b]	Used as convenience instead of cash; credit is approved for the card rather than individual purchase; no interest charged if bills are paid in full each month; cash in varying amounts, depending on individual's credit rating, may also be borrowed against the approved line of credit.
Credit unions	Personal loans Real-property loans	8–15	Voluntary organizations in which members invest their own money and from which they may borrow.
Finance companies	Pesonal loans Real-property loans	12–40	Direct loans to consumers; also buy installment credit from retailers and collect rest of debt so that retailers can get cash when they need it.
Savings and loan companies	Real-property loans	9–15[b]	Low interest rates because real property has value that may cover defaulted loans.

[a]Interest rates vary because of pressures of inflation and recession.

[b]If the institution charges interest on the *face amount* of the loan over the entire period of the loan, double the listed interest rate to estimate the actual interest rate.

■ You have many credit cards, all of which run a considerable balance.
■ Your assets are not liquid. All of your money is tied up in your home or business, and you cannot easily come up with any cash.
■ You can never say no to yourself when you find something you want to buy.
■ You think your financial problems will take care of themselves and somehow magically disappear.

CREDIT, BORROWING, AND INSTALLMENT BUYING

People borrow for two basic reasons: to buy consumer goods and services and to invest in tangible assets. Consumer debt is high-priced money because it is used for consumable goods, such as cars, furniture, and clothing, whose value diminishes with time. *Discount interest* is usually charged for consumer debt. This kind of interest is charged on the total amount of the loan for the entire time period.

Investment debt, or real-property debt, is lower-priced money because it is used for tangible assets, such as real estate or businesses, where value is more permanent. If for some reason the debt is not paid, the creditor may assume ownership of the asset and sell it to regain the loaned money. *Simple interest*

TABLE 8-7
DISCOUNT INTEREST PAYMENTS

ORIGINAL LOAN ($1000)	PAYMENTS			
	INTEREST PAYMENT	PRINCIPAL PAYMENT	TOTAL PER MONTH	BALANCE
1st month	$8.33	$27.77	$36.20	$972.23
2d month	8.33	27.77	36.10	944.56
3d month	8.33	27.77	36.10	916.79

is charged for investment debt. This kind of interest is charged only on the unpaid balance of the loan. (See Table 8-6 for comparative costs of consumer credit.)

EXAMPLES OF ACTUAL INTEREST COSTS

DISCOUNT INTEREST: CONSUMER PURCHASES

If you borrow $1000 for three years at 10 percent interest per year, you must pay $100 interest each year for the use of the money ($0.10 \times \$1000 = \$100$). Each month you will pay $8.33 interest ($100/12 months = $8.33). In addition, you will pay back the principal of $1000 in thirty-six equal monthly installments so that it is all paid off at the end of the three years. The monthly principal payment will be $27.77 ($1000/36 = $27.77). Thus, your total monthly payment is $36.10; that is, your interest plus your principal payment ($8.33 + $27.77 = $36.10). (Interest rates now vary so rapidly that the rates used in these examples may not accurately reflect the rates in effect when you are reading this text. The general principles hold, however.)

Although you will pay $100 interest each year on your $1000 loan, you do not actually have the use of the full $1000 for the entire three years. Each month you pay back $27.77 of the loan. As Table 8-7 shows, at the end of a month (after one payment), you only owe $972.23 ($1000 minus your principal payment of $27.77 = $972.23) on your loan. Each month what you actually owe on the loan is reduced by your principal payment until at the end of the three years (thirty-six payments) your loan is paid off.

All you have to remember is that on a discount interest loan, you pay interest on the full amount of the loan each year even though you have paid back part of the loan. Such interest is usually figured for the full term of the loan and is added to the face amount of the loan at the time you receive the loan. Thus, in our example you would sign for a $1300 debt ($1000 principal + $300 interest = $1300) but only receive $1000. As a rule of thumb, to figure the actual interest rate on this type of loan, simply double the stated interest rate. When computed accurately, however, the interest rate will slightly exceed the doubled figure.

CREDIT CARD USE

If you maintain a balance on your credit card rather than paying promptly at the end of each month, you are charged interest at a very high rate. The interest rates charged by the top ten credit card lenders range from 17 to 21

Credit, Borrowing, and Installment Buying

percent. No interest is charged if you pay for your credit card purchases within thirty days. Thus, if used properly, your credit card gives you thirty days of "open credit"; that is, you can use the funds without having to pay interest. On the other hand, carrying a large balance on your credit card is extremely costly.

To give you an idea of the actual monetary cost, consider what a $1000 balance on your credit card for thirty-six months will cost at 21 percent interest per year: 0.21 × $1000 = $210 per year or $630 for three years. Because the actual amount of interest charged in credit transactions was often difficult to determine, Congress passed the Truth in Lending Law in July 1969. Under the terms of this law, lenders must clearly explain the credit costs of a transaction.

The National Foundation for Consumer Credit estimates that about 2 percent of Americans using credit cards are mired in credit card debt while another 4 percent face some difficulties. The average person counseled had about $17,000 in accumulated debt with credit card debt the fastest growing component of overall consumer debt (Marino 1989).

> When Rich first got a credit card, he often went on buying sprees. Using the credit card didn't seem the same as spending real money. Just after he married, he had a total of $2500 outstanding balances on all of his credit cards combined. Try as they might, Kimberly and Rich just couldn't seem to reduce this debt. In fact, it gradually increased because both of them now used the credit cards.

Credit card companies target college students because they represent the future. It is estimated that about one-half of all full-time four-year college students have and use credit cards.

SIMPLE INTEREST: HOME LOANS

Since home loans are invested in a tangible asset, the interest charged is usually at a lower percentage rate and is simple interest (that is, charged only on the outstanding balance).

You decide to buy a $100,000 home (home prices vary greatly from area to area; see p. 290). You put $20,000 down and receive a loan of $80,000 for thirty years at 10 percent simple interest (interest rates for fixed home loans have varied dramatically in the past few years from lows of 8.0 percent to highs of 18 percent). For example, to pay off your $80,000 loan and interest in thirty years, your payments will be $702.06 per month. Each month you will pay less interest and more against principal. At the end of thirty years when you have paid off the $80,000 loan, you will also have paid about $172,735 in interest!

> Actually $666.67 of your first payment will be for interest, and $35.39 will be credited against the principal. Thus, for your second payment you will owe interest on a principal of $79,964.61. Of your second payment, $666.37 will be for interest, and $35.69 will apply to the principal. (At present you can deduct home mortgage interest charges from your taxable income, which somewhat reduces the actual cost of the interest to you.)

Table 8-8 shows what monthly payments would be at different rates of interest on a $100,000 house when $20,000 is put down ($80,000 owed) or $50,000 is put down ($50,000 owed). The term of the loan is thirty years.

TABLE 8-8
THIRTY-YEAR MORTGAGE ON A $100,000 HOUSE

	EXAMPLE A	EXAMPLE B
Down payment	$20,000	$50,000
Amount borrowed	80,000	50,000

INTEREST RATE	MONTHLY PAYMENTS	
8%	$587	$365
9	644	402
10	702	439
11	762	476
12	823	514
13	885	553
14	948	592

FINANCIAL PROBLEMS AND MARITAL STRAIN

▓ BUT WHAT ABOUT RICH AND KIMBERLY? ▓

Constant worry about overdue bills and whether their savings are sufficient to cover a medical emergency, disappointment because they are unable to take a vacation or buy a new dining set, the wide gap between their marginal economic survival and the plush lifestyles shown on television, and discontent with work or the way their income is spent all combine to lower Rich and Kimberly's marital satisfaction. It is clear that their financial difficulties are affecting all the other areas of their relationship, not just the economic realm.

Under the court-supervised payment plan (remember the couple declared bankruptcy), Rich and Kimberly are slowly paying off their debts, including those incurred by the birth of their second child. They resent not being able to buy new things, including a new car now that their car is so "out of date," but every cent of Rich's salary seems to be earmarked for the old debts. Kimberly keeps asking why he doesn't get a better job. At one time he investigated going back to school to qualify for a market manager position. But he would need to spend two years in school, and Kimberly cannot earn enough to support the family during those two years. Instead, Rich has taken a second job as a night watchman. He is so tired when he comes home that the smallest noise is painful, and he constantly yells at the children to be quiet or at Kimberly to make them be quiet. He is usually too tired to make love at night. At work he envies the younger, unmarried men who are driving new cars. Why, he wonders, did he get married in the first place? Kimberly sometimes wonders the same thing herself.

It is obvious that financial pressures have put a great strain on this marriage. In view of this pressure and the fact that they married in their teens, it is quite likely that Rich and Kimberly's marriage will end in divorce.

Are Rich and Kimberly solely to blame for their predicament? Why couldn't they make the system work for them? Why didn't they wait before making major purchases? Why didn't they postpone children for a year until they were on their feet economically? In one of the wealthiest nations in the world, how could this couple have been economically strangled?

THE SEDUCTIVE SOCIETY:
CREDIT AND ADVERTISING

Certainly, Rich and Kimberly must shoulder much of the responsibility for their economic predicament. However, American society in general puts great pressure on all Americans to BUY NOW!!! and pay later (if you can).

As so often happens, actual behavior in our society bears little resemblance to the truisms we learn in the family or at school. Buying and spending have

quietly replaced thrift and saving. Traditional values, though still preached, are often no longer practiced. And in a productive, inflationary economy such as ours, they are no longer even virtues. Spending is important in a credit-oriented, inflationary society. Goods must be kept moving. The failure of consumers to buy can immediately have dire consequences for the economy. Hence the financial section of the newspaper includes such statements as "Strong growth in consumption reflects rising income and bodes well for the economy." Such attitudes encourage individual and family spending for the good of the overall economy.

A slowdown in consumer spending in any of the basic industries affects the whole economy, not just the particular industry. For example, a slowdown in the sale of cars affects literally hundreds of subsidiary industries, as well as many other major industries such as steel, rubber, and aluminum. If consumers fail to buy, production must be cut back, which means laying off workers; the problem is then compounded by the loss of these workers' buying power as consumers. Therefore, to keep goods flowing, a new field of endeavor has emerged, namely, stimulation and creation of wants and desires in the consumer.

In his classic work *The Affluent Society* (1958), John Kenneth Galbraith observed that the theory of consumer demand in America is based on two broad propositions:

1. The urgency of wants does not diminish appreciably as more of them are satisfied.
2. Wants originate in the personality of the consumer and are capable of indefinite expansion.

These two propositions go a long way toward explaining why actual income bears little resemblance to a family's feeling of economic satisfaction and also why Kimberly and Rich got into financial difficulty. Although Americans command a better standard of living than most people, many Americans are dissatisfied with the amount of money they make. As a group, the most dissatisfied are professionals, whose incomes are generally high, but so are their aspirations. Economic contentment appears to be more closely related to one's attitudes and values than to one's actual economic level.

Advertising and need stimulation have become essential parts of the American economy. A family or individual has to be made to want new material goods for more than rational, practical reasons. For example, though a well-made automobile can last ten years with care, such longevity for the average car would greatly upset automobile production. The auto industry has met this problem by changing models and promoting the concept of built-in obsolescence, often under the guise of improvement. In all fairness to the auto industry, it should be noted that many model changes are improvements, but change has often been made simply so that older models will appear less desirable.

Today's youth are growing up in a different economic atmosphere from that of their grandparents. The society they know is an affluent society. Even the recent period of relative job scarcity and recession has had little effect on spending habits. Buying, spending, credit, and debt are now familiar accompaniments of marital life. The advantages of such a system cannot be denied. Yet you must also be aware of the dangers in order to use the system to your fullest advantage. Rich and Kimberly became trapped and lost their economic freedom because they never had a chance to stand back from the system and analyze its negative aspects.

The power of advertising and the ability to satisfy one's needs or desires immediately are formidable and seductive forces for even mature adults. How well can a young couple resist the invitation to use a store's credit again when they have almost paid off their bill? An official-looking check arrives in the mail announcing that they can obtain an additional $500 worth of merchandise for nothing down and no increase in the monthly payments that were otherwise about to end. If they thoroughly understand what exercising their desires in this manner means, they can make use of some or all of the offer with no danger. On the other hand, another purchase could be the straw that breaks the camel's back when it is added to the rest of their financial debt.

You must remember that personal freedom and indebtedness vary inversely. The more debt you assume, the less personal freedom you have. Some experts suggest that families make sure that their debts total no more than 20 percent of their spendable income.

In *The Affluent Society* (1958, 155), Galbraith points out that a

> direct link between production and wants is provided by the institutions of modern advertising and salesmanship. These cannot be reconciled with the notion of independently determined desires, for their central function is to create desires—to bring into being wants that previously did not exist.

Vance Packard in *The Hidden Persuaders* (1958) exposed the extent to which advertising influences the public's attitudes, values, and behavior. He questioned the morality of advertising techniques that manipulate the consumer into buying regardless of the consequences. In concluding his book, he asked a series of provocative questions that young married couples might well consider (143):

1. What is the morality of the practice of encouraging people to be irrational and impulsive in buying family food?
2. What is the morality of manipulating small children even before they reach the age where they are legally responsible for their actions?
3. What is the morality of playing upon hidden weaknesses and frailties—such as our anxieties, aggressive feelings, dread of nonconformity, and infantile hangovers—to sell products?
4. What is the morality of developing in the public an attitude of wastefulness toward national resources by encouraging the "psychological obsolescence" of products already in use?

Approximately $128 billion was spent on advertising in 1990 (see Table 8-9 for the top fifteen advertisers). The majority of this sum went toward creating wants and desires that will add new frustrations to American families, many of whom are already monetarily unhappy even though they live at one of the highest material levels in the world.

TABLE 8-9
FIFTEEN LEADING NATIONAL ADVERTISERS, 1990*

RANK	COMPANY	ADVERTISING DOLLARS (IN MILLIONS)
1.	Procter & Gamble	$2,284.5
2.	Phillip Morris, Inc.	2,210.2
3.	Sears, Roebuck & Co.	1,507.1
4.	General Motors	1,502.8
5.	Grand Metropolitan	882.6
6.	PepsiCo, Inc.	849.1
7.	AT&T Co.	796.5
8.	McDonald's Corp.	764.1
9.	K-Mart Corp.	693.2
10.	Time Warner	676.9
11.	Eastman Kodak Co.	664.8
12.	Johnson & Johnson	653.7
13.	R. J. Reynolds/Nabisco	636.1
14.	Nestlé SA	635.9
15.	Warner-Lambert Co.	630.8

*Based on measured media expenditures only; does not include local advertising coupons, direct mail, premiums, trade shows, and product sampling.

Source: *Advertising Age*, September 25, 1991.

EFFECTIVE MONEY MANAGEMENT

Few dimensions of family life are as important, yet as difficult, as the management of family financial resources (Godwin 1990, 221). Financial matters have long been one of the most widely reported causes of family discord (Hogan and Bauer 1988). Almost 80 percent of young couples who divorce by age thirty report that financial problems were a primary cause of the divorce (Burkett 1989).

The most important step in effective money management is to determine ahead of time how most monetary decisions will be made. A family can handle monetary decisions in at least six ways: (1) the husband can make all the decisions, (2) the wife can make all the decisions, (3) they can make all decisions jointly, (4) one spouse can control the income but give the other a household allowance, (5) each spouse can have separate funds and share agreed-on financial obligations, and (6) the spouses can have a joint bank account on which each can draw as necessary. Once a couple reaches an agreement on the system by which they will handle family finances, most day-to-day monetary decisions can be handled automatically.

TO POOL OR NOT TO POOL FAMILY MONEY?

The question of whether money should be pooled seems to have no right answer. In *American Couples*, Blumstein and Schwartz found that couples who favored pooling their money were neither more nor less satisfied with their money management than couples who insisted on keeping money separate. Nevertheless, both types of couples felt that their system was the right way to handle money (1983, 108).

Both systems have advantages and disadvantages. The newly married couple often finds it difficult to avoid pooling. If one partner suggests separating the money, the other is apt to interpret the suggestion as a lack of commitment to the relationship. The same kinds of suspicions may arise when one prospective marriage partner suggests a prenuptial economic agreement.

Pooling is simpler than having separate funds because there are fewer accounts to balance. Also, each spouse knows what the other spouse is doing monetarily. On the other hand, they may lose their feeling of independence. Pooling can also lead to confusion; for example, a joint account can be overdrawn if each partner writes a check unknown to the other. Despite how a couple may feel about pooling their funds when they first marry, pooling tends to become the method of choice as the relationship persists.

Pooling is more highly favored by married couples than cohabiting couples, probably because married couples feel more "permanent" than cohabiting couples.

People who remarry after divorce are more apt to maintain separate funds, probably for two reasons: (1) They may feel less permanence in the new relationship due to the divorce trauma. (2) They are very apt to bring to the new marriage assets that were accumulated prior to the relationship and therefore seem to belong not to the new relationship but to themselves as individuals (and perhaps to any children of the first marriage).

ALLOCATION OF FUNDS: WHO MAKES THE SPENDING DECISIONS?

The decision about whether to pool funds influences the decision about who is responsible for spending those funds. If funds are separate, some kind of joint responsibility for family spending must be established. Does one partner assume monetary responsibility for rent or house payments while the other pays for food? Do they both contribute from the separate funds to a single household account that is used to make family payments? If so, who controls the account? Are both partners free to spend their separate funds in any way they wish? If one partner has greater income or assets than the other, does that partner assume more of the responsibility for family expenses?

The answers to such questions are related to power and control within a relationship. Generally, the partner who supplies the primary monetary support also claims the majority of the power in a relationship. "After all, it is my money and I can spend it any way I please!" "Remember that I earn the money in this family, and you will spend it the way I want you to!" Power through monetary control is greatest in the single-earner family. Obviously, in the past the power most often accrued to the male partner since it was he who worked outside the home to supply the necessary funds. As women have entered the work world, however, the number of dual-earner families has increased. The rapidly growing contribution of wives to family finances has wrought a revolution in the family power structure (see Chapter 9).

Effective Money Management

FIGURE 8-2
Annual expenditures for a four-person, medium-income family

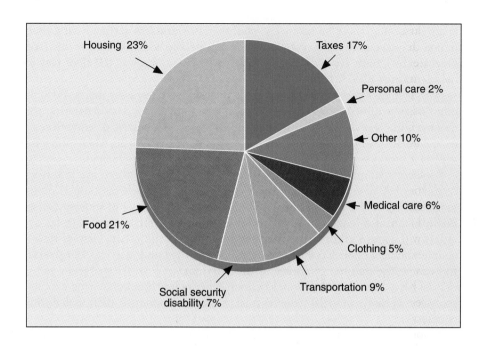

Answers to the questions posed above will vary greatly between single-earner and dual-earner families. In either case, the answers must be satisfactory to both partners if the family is to function smoothly and efficiently. No evidence suggests that a particular manner of monetary allocation is most desirable. What is important is that the partners agree and are comfortable with the manner of allocation chosen.

BUDGETING: ENLIGHTENED CONTROL OF SPENDING

The next step in reducing monetary conflict is to agree on a budget. A budget is actually a plan of spending to assure that what is needed and wanted is attained. For example, a family's income must cover such basic necessities as housing, food, clothing, and transportation and leave some money for discretionary expenditure such as vacations and recreation. How Americans spend their money is shown in Figure 8-2.

Certainly, to many people budgeting sounds like a boring and uninteresting task. Yet we all budget at least informally. If you want to buy a new stereo system but do not have the money to do so and choose not to buy it on credit, then you are budgeting. To budget formally, however, is to gain control over your financial life. Considering the number of people who have monetary problems, it is clear that budget control is imperative for most of us. Without it, it is easy to lose monetary control and to slip into economic entrapment as Rich and Kimberly did. Budgeting and long-term monetary planning lead to financial independence. Financial independence means having the economic wherewithal to say to yourself: "I may not be rich, but I am financially free to do what I want." *In a word financial independence means "freedom."*

The first step is to allot money for necessities. Whatever money is left over can be divided among the family's other wants. The fluctuating economy we have been experiencing has made planned spending more important than ever. For example, it is estimated that the spontaneous food shopper spends approximately 10 to 15 percent more for food than the shopper who has a planned food budget and a shopping list of needed items.

By living within a budget (see Inset 8-3), you can avoid many of the problems that defeated Rich and Kimberly. In addition, by allotting even a small amount to savings, you can also make investments. Saving is really only deferred spending. If immediate spending is deferred, it becomes possible to use the money to earn additional income.

A budget should only be used for a specified time, and then it should be updated to reflect changing family circumstances. For example, a newly married couple who both work may feel well off. They have two incomes and minimal expenses. But danger lies ahead if they become accustomed to using up both incomes. For example, if they decide to have children, the wife may have to give up her income, at least for a while. Expenses also increase when children are added to the family. The combination of lower income and rising expenses can throw a family into an economic crisis unless they have planned economically for both eventualities.

Another eventuality that some families must plan for is college education for the children. College usually means a drastic rise in expenditures. The cost of putting a child through college, including room and board, will be between $30,000 and $70,000.

After children become independent, a couple can usually enjoy a comfortable period of relative affluence. They must, however, plan carefully for their coming retirement. Without such planning they may spend their older years in a state of poverty, especially if inflationary pressures exist. Thus, good budgeting remains important across the life span.

As dull and uninteresting as budget planning may seem, the family that does not put time into planning its finances may face increasing monetary strain, even destruction. This is especially true when the inflation rate is high.

■ SAVING THROUGH WISE SPENDING ■

When many families think of saving, they think only of putting money into a savings account. Yet wise spending is another important way of saving. Wise spending means buying when an item is "on sale," seeking out bargains, buying used instead of new, being aware of consumer traps in marketing, studying seasonal price fluctuations in order to buy at the best time (see Table 8-10), and simply being an astute consumer.

Being a wise shopper is not as easy as one might imagine. Salespeople may be more interested in making a sale than in the exact needs of you or your family. Also, since salespeople are not necessarily highly knowledgeable about the products they sell, they may not be able to help you decide whether the product is right for you. Naturally, wise salespeople will learn about their merchandise and will take their customer's needs into consideration. By doing so, they assure themselves of satisfied customers and repeat business.

TABLE 8-10
WHEN TO BUY SELECTED ARTICLES AND FOOD ITEMS

SALES MONTHS	CONSUMER ARTICLES	FOOD ITEMS
January	Linens, baby things, men's and women's clothing, home furnishings, luggage, lingerie, furs, diamonds, cosmetics, and nonprescription drugs	Citrus fruit, cauliflower, potatoes, onions, and turkeys
February	Housewares, hosiery, and fabrics	Citrus fruit, potatoes, greens, celery, snap beans, apples, and canned fruit
March	Hardware, paint, gardening tools, made-to-order slipcovers and drapes, china, glass, women's shoes, and rain gear	Texas carrots, Florida lettuce, oranges, and green peas
April	Paint, wallpaper, building supplies, air conditioners, and tires	Asparagus, artichokes, snap beans, cabbage, carrots, onions, Maine potatoes, and fish items
May	Jewelry, candy, housewares, gardening tools, bed linens and towels, vacation gear, and cleaning supplies	Eggs, Florida corn, and onions
June	Gifts for brides, grads, and dads; men's clothing; sporting goods; and small appliances	Apricots, cantaloupes, cherries, and eggs
July	Furniture, bedding, bed linens and towels, and major appliances	Raspberries, blackberries, blueberries, limes, mangoes, peaches, beets, and okra
August	School supplies, summer clothing and equipment, and fall fashions	Corn, peaches, watermelon, cabbage, tomatoes, and seafood
September	Home improvements, sporting goods, china, glassware, major appliances, children's shoes, and auto batteries	Grapes, cucumbers, melons, squash, and lamb
October	Furniture, lamps, outerwear, and furnaces	Apples, cauliflower, grapes, pears, eggplant, and pumpkins
November	Rugs, men's clothing, furnishings, linoleum, liquors, toys, and games	Gourmet foods, avocados, cranberries, persimmons, sweet potatoes, turnips, raisins, and nuts
December	Post-Christmas cards, wrappings, lights, and decorations; toys; games; and housewares	Coconuts, flour, shortening, sugar, spices, and early citrus fruit

You should do extensive research before purchasing "big ticket" items such as household appliances and automobiles. For example, you can find objective test reports on various household items (as well as other things) in the magazine *Consumer Reports.* The various automotive magazines describe car tests each month. Knowing exactly what you want before approaching a salesperson is an important part of wise buying. If you know what you want, you will not be sold an item that is inferior, fails to meet your needs, or is more than you want or need.

Avoiding consumer traps is also important to wise shopping. Although not every trap can be discussed here, the following are some of the more common ones:

1. *Bait and switch:* An ad describes a certain product, such as a washing machine, with a very low price. When you go to make the purchase, the

salesperson claims that the product is inferior or that the store is out of the advertised machine and guides you to a more expensive machine.

2. *Low ball:* This technique is often used in car sales. The salesperson offers you the car at a good price, you think you have a deal, but then a higher authority (sales manager) countermands the salesperson's offer. By now you may be psychologically committed to buying, and the few hundred extra dollars added to the price may seem acceptable.

3. *High ball:* Again this technique is mainly found in car sales. Here the salesperson offers you an inflated trade-in allowance on your old car. The manager reduces this offer once you are psychologically committed to buying.

4. *Telemarketing:* The telephone seems to be used increasingly in sales schemes that range from offering you a low-cost vacation to notifying you that you have won some wonderful prize. Of course, there's always a catch. Some warning signs of a scam: "Just dial 1-900 . . ." (calls to 900 numbers are usually very costly). "Just send $_____ and you'll receive . . ." "All we need is your credit card or checking account number." "The offer is only good today."

5. *Contest winner:* In this case, you are told that you have won a contest that you didn't enter, but it turns out you must buy something in order to receive your prize.

6. *Free goods:* If you buy this carpeting, the installation will be free. You are actually paying for the free(??) extras by paying a higher price for the other goods.

7. *Off-brand items:* If you are knowledgeable about the goods you want to purchase, it may be perfectly all right to purchase a product that is new to the market or is not a well-known brand. In general, however, well-known brands, although usually higher priced, do offer certain advantages (especially to the ignorant buyer). The quality usually varies less, warranties are often better— you know that the company will be there to honor the warranty—and the company usually has a wider repair network.

Effective Money Management

Once you decide to do some positive money management, you must figure out a budget and try to stick to it. The budget is a planning tool to help you reduce undirected spending.

STEPS IN BUDGET MAKING

Create a spending plan by following these four basic steps:

1. Analyze past spending by keeping records for a month or two.
2. Determine *fixed expenses* such as rent and any other contractual payments that must be made—even if they are infrequent, such as insurance and taxes.
3. Determine *flexible expenses,* such as food and clothing.
4. Balance your fixed plus flexible expenditures with your available income. If a surplus exists, you can apply it toward achieving your goals. If there is a deficit, reexamine your flexible expenditures. You can also reexamine fixed expenses with a view to reducing them in the future.

Note that so-called fixed expenses are only fixed in the short run. In the longer run, everything is essentially flexible or variable. Fixed expenses can be adjusted by changing one's standard of living, if necessary.

THE IMPORTANCE OF KEEPING RECORDS

Budget making, whether you are a college student, a single person living alone, or the head of a family, will be useless if you don't keep records. The only way to make sure that you are carrying out your budget is by keeping records of what you are actually spending. the ultimate way to maintain records is to write everything down, but that becomes time-consuming and therefore costly. Another way to keep records is to write checks for everything. Records are also important in case of problems with faulty products or services or the Internal Revenue Service.

GENERAL BUDGETING

The following is a monthly general budget form that encompasses both estimated and actual cash available and fixed and variable payments.

You will note that the savings category is located under the *Fixed*

CASH FORECAST MONTH OF _____	ESTIMATED	ACTUAL
Cash on hand and in checking account, end of previous period		
Savings needed for planned expenses		
Receipts		
Net pay		
Borrowed		
Interest/dividends		
Other		
Total cash available during period		

8. *Hard sell:* Beware of the salesperson who says you must buy this sale item today because it is the last one or because the price will go up tomorrow. There is always time to buy, and an attempt to rush you usually is a signal that something is wrong.

9. *Home repairs:* People agree to make repairs on your property and ask for money in advance to buy the necessary materials. Once they have the money, you never hear from them again.

Payments heading. This is because the money in your savings account may be used to pay such fixed annual expenses as auto, fire, and life insurance, and it is necessary to plan to save in advance for these expenses.

The key to making a budget work for you is to review your figures every month to see how your monthly estimates compare with your spending.

Fixed Payments

Mortgage or rent
Life insurance
Fire insurance
Auto insurance
Medical insurance
Savings
Local taxes
Loan or other debt
Children's allowances
Other
Total fixed payments

Flexible Payments

Water
Fuel
Medical
Household supplies
Car
Food
Clothing
Nonrecurring large payments
Contributions, recreation, etc.
Other
Total flexible payments

Total All Payments

Recapitulation

Total cash available
Total payments
Cash balance, end of period

10. *Magazines:* The caller claims to be doing a survey: Which magazines do you like best? You find yourself billed for subscriptions you don't really want.
11. *Credit repair:* An ad guarantees that your bad credit record will be erased. You are told that for a fee, often several hundred dollars, bankruptcies and judgments against you can be removed from your records. They can't. If information in your record is wrong, you can contact the credit company and have corrections made at no charge.

Effective Money Management

12. *Travel:* You receive an announcement that you have won a free vacation or are entitled to large travel discounts on your next vacation. To qualify, you have to join a travel club for a fee or purchase a "companion ticket" at an inflated price.

13. *Advance fee loans:* A company offers to find a loan for you for an advance fee of several hundred dollars, but often the loan never materializes.

If you find yourself victimized by one or another of these consumer traps, be sure and fight back by lodging complaints with the proper authorities. For example, if you have bought something by mail order and it is defective or not as advertised, you can lodge a complaint with the postal department if the company does not remedy the situation. The Better Business Bureau is also a strong consumer advocate and has offices in almost every city.

THE ECONOMY AND THE AFRICAN-AMERICAN, HISPANIC, ASIAN-AMERICAN AND SINGLE-PARENT FAMILY

Table 8-5 on page 261 compared median family incomes for various groups of people. If we look only at averages, we find that certain family groups do better economically than other groups. For example, married couples in various groups have a median family income as follows:

White	$40,331
Black	$33,784
Hispanic	$27,996
Asian American	$35,000 (estimated)

Unemployment rates also vary among the various groups (Table 8-11).

Both median income and unemployment are related to educational achievement. Table 8-4 (p. 259) also highlights the fact that years of education are closely associated with economic success.

Education	Median Family Income
8 years or less	$13,353
4 years high school	$28,744
4 years college	$50,549

As Table 8-12 indicates, educational attainment varies among the groups. Those groups with the highest percentages of both men and women graduating from high school also tend to be the groups with the lowest percentage below the poverty level.

Female heads of households of all races earn considerably less than others. Early out-of-wedlock pregnancy, dropping out of school, and employment difficulties appear to be significantly related. School-age women who have a child are much more likely to drop out of school. When schooling is incomplete, high-paying employment is much harder to obtain. Poverty rates decrease dramatically as years of schooling completed increase.

| TABLE 8-11 |
| SELECTED LABOR FORCE INDICATORS BY SEX, AGE, RACE, AND HISPANIC ORIGIN (JANUARY 1992) |

CHARACTERISTIC	PERCENT
Total	
Civilian labor force (percentage of population working)	66.1%
Unemployed	7.1%
Men, 20 years and over	
Percentage of population working	77.0%
Unemployed	6.9%
Women, 20 years and over	
Percentage of population working	58.2%
Unemployed	5.9%
Both sexes, 16 to 19 years	
Percentage of population working	51.6%
Unemployed	18.3%
White	
Percentage of population working	66.6%
Unemployed	6.2%
Black	
Percentage of population working	62.9%
Unemployed	13.7%
Hispanic	
Percentage of population working	66.3%
Unemployed	11.3%

Source: *Monthly Labor Review*, March 1992, 56

| TABLE 8-12 |
| HIGH SCHOOL GRADUATES AMONG WHITE, BLACK, HISPANIC, AND ASIAN-AMERICAN ADULTS (PERCENTAGE OF PERSONS AGED 25–29) |

POPULATION	PERCENTAGE GRADUATING FROM HIGH SCHOOL
White	86%
Black	83
Hispanic	61
Asian American	91 (estimated)

Sources: Gardner et al. 1985; Knouse et al. 1992; O'Hare et al. 1991; Jackson et al. 1991.

The poverty rate in 1990 was 22 percent for heads of house who had not completed high school, 9.3 percent for those who had graduated from high school but not attended college, and 3.8 percent for those who had completed one or more years of college. Families headed by young single women make up the single largest group below the poverty line. Families with a female head of house and no husband present account for 53 percent of poor families (U.S. Bureau of Census August 1991, 2, 9).

The large proportion of black families below the poverty level tends to be a result of the large number of single-parent families in the black population. Most of these families have female heads. At the same time, it should be noted that the intact black family in the United States has greatly improved its position economically.

As noted in Chapter 1, the real economic story of the last forty years for blacks has been the emergence of the black middle class, whose gains have been real and substantial (Smith and Welch 1986, ix). Although the media emphasize those in poverty, over one-third of black families have an annual income at or above the national median (Willie 1988, 221; Lacayo 1989, 58). In 1989, nearly one in seven black families had an income of $50,000 or more, up from one in seventeen in 1967 (O'Hare et al 1991, 29). These families tend to have well-educated members with 32 percent being college graduates.

The Economy and the African American, Hispanic, Asian-American and Single-Parent Family

TABLE 8-13
EDUCATIONAL LEVEL AND PERCENTAGE OF HISPANIC FAMILIES BELOW THE POVERTY LEVEL

	PERCENTAGE COMPLETING HIGH SCHOOL	PERCENTAGE BELOW POVERTY
All Hispanic	62%	26%
Non-Hispanic	89	10
Mexican	54	26
Puerto Rican	67	38
Cuban	83	14
Central and South American	70	19

Source: U.S. Bureau of the Census August 1988.

TABLE 8-14
TRENDS IN INCOME AND POVERTY, 1960–1990

YEAR	MEDIAN INCOME (IN 1987 DOLLARS)	PERCENTAGE OF PERSONS IN POVERTY
1990	$35,353	13.5%
1985	29,302	14.0
1980	28,996	13.0
1975	28,970	12.3
1970	28,880	12.6
1965	25,059	17.3
1960	21,567	22.2

Source: U.S. Bureau of the Census August 1991.

In 1940, 75 percent of intact black families were poor. That proportion had dropped to 32 percent by 1990 (O'Hare et al. 1991, 27). The income disparity between white married-couple families and black married-couple families is dropping. In 1990, the ratio of black married-couple median family income to white married-couple median income was .84 compared to .76 in 1975. In contrast, the income disparity between white and Hispanic married couples is widening. The ratio of Hispanic married-couple family income to white married-couple income was .69 in 1990, lower than in 1984 (.75) (U.S. Bureau of the Census August 1991, 2).

Many Hispanic families also fall below the official poverty level. Closer analysis, however, reveals large educational differences between various Hispanic groups, which create large differences in the percentage of each group having economic problems (see Table 8-13). In addition, persons of Hispanic background who have been in the United States for a long period of time are much better off economically than newly arrived immigrants.

Overall the poverty rate for all Americans has fluctuated from a high of 22.4 percent in 1959 to a low of 11.1 percent in 1973. Since that year the poverty rate has varied between 13 and 16 percent of all persons (see Table 8–14).

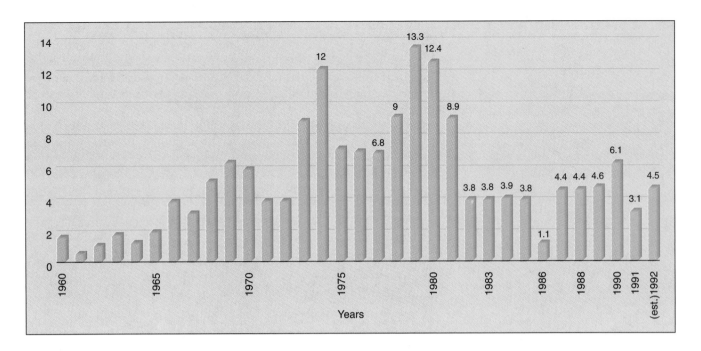

FIGURE 8-3
Inflation rates: The figures cover each
full year; the highest gain was in
1979 when the Consumer Price
Index soared 13.3 percent.

INFLATION AND RECESSION

Normally, the economy alternates between relatively long periods of inflation and shorter periods of economic downturn or recession. Not many years ago economists thought that inflation and recession were opposites and could never occur together. Yet this combination has occurred at times during both the 1970s and 1980s. Therefore, effective money management must take into consideration inflation, recession, and a combination of the two. In an inflationary-recessionary economy, every possible bad thing is happening at once. Production is falling, unemployment is rising, and inflation continues. Fortunately, such conditions seldom last for long.

This book is not the place for a detailed discussion of inflation and recession, although some understanding is necessary if you are to make the economy work for you rather than against you. Inflation, recession, economic growth, and employment are all related, so a change in one tends to produce changes in the others. The successful money manager must understand these trends.

■ INFLATION ■

Since World War II, the United States has experienced almost constant inflation. Although the rate has varied, inflation has averaged 5 to 6 percent a year (see Figure 8-3). Inflation tends to hurt those families on fixed incomes, retirees, disabled persons, and female-headed families more than others (Aldous et al., 1991). We are constantly being surprised, dismayed, or angered at the increased *nominal cost* (absolute price for an item) of almost everything we buy. Bread is more than a dollar a loaf, yet it seems only yesterday that it was fifty cents. A new car ten years ago cost about $5000, tax and license included. Today, the same model is priced closer to $12,000. "Buy now before the price increases," is an often-repeated advertising slogan that feeds our fears about inflation. Public opinion polls show that inflation is a constant concern of most people.

Prices do not always rise. The *Consumer Price Index (CPI)* is calculated on a fixed market basket of goods and services as measured in ninety-one urban areas across the country. Declines in the index have occurred during recessions or depressions in the economy. Overall, however, the CPI has risen over 700 percent in the past seventy-five years (U.S. Department of Labor October, 1992). It should be noted that the CPI does not include taxes. As of January, 1992, federal, state, and local taxes consumed 37.9 percent of incomes, the highest levels ever (Cunniff 1991).

> Another way of looking at inflation is to compare the value of today's dollar with its past value. Using 1982–1984 as the base, a dollar as of January 1992 is worth 73.5 cents. Using 1967 as the base, the dollar is worth 24.7 cents.

Inflation rates by themselves tell only half the story of the American economy. Inflation simply indicates that nominal prices have risen. However, income has also risen during this time. If income rises at the same rate as prices, buying power remains the same. Thus, a more important measure of the economy than the inflation rate is *real per capita income*. This is computed by subtracting the inflation rate from the percentage increase in per capita income. If my income increases 10 percent in a year in which inflation is only 5 percent, my real income (buying power) has increased 5 percent. The real income (buying power) of most people has actually increased since World War II. In some years, however, the real per capita income has declined.

The CPI is the most common indicator used by the popular media to measure price fluctuations. Because it is an average, the CPI tends to mask actual price fluctuations for a specific item. Thus, it is important for the consumer to look at the relative price of a product rather than just its nominal or absolute price. Although the nominal prices of most goods have increased greatly, some relative prices have actually declined. Television sets, for example, have become much cheaper. So, although overall prices as measured by the CPI are going up, the prices of some goods are rising more slowly than others, making these goods relatively better buys. Sometimes, too, nominal prices have declined as technological breakthroughs have lowered production costs in certain industries such as computers.

Another way to see the relationship between price inflation and income is to compare the actual amount of income needed to produce the same purchasing power between 1967 and 1991. A family that earned $20,000 in 1967 needed to earn approximately $85,000 in 1991 to be able to purchase as much as $20,000 purchased in 1967.

■ LIVING WITH INFLATION ■

Even though severe inflation was controlled in 1982, some degree of inflation is likely to influence the economy for the foreseeable future, and Americans

TABLE 8-15
AMOUNT OF WORK TIME NECESSARY TO PURCHASE VARIOUS GOODS AND SERVICES

This table shows how long the average American had to work, before taxes, to earn enough to purchase the goods and services listed. For our calculations, we used the actual prices of items in 1962, 1972, 1982, and 1992 and the average hourly wages in each of those years. For simplicity's sake, we show the inexpensive items in the top third of the list in minutes of work, the more costly goods and services in hours, and the big-ticket items at the bottom in days.

	1962	1972	1982	1992
Small Items	Minutes of work			
Postage (first class, 1oz.)	1.1	1.6	1.7	1.6
Newspaper (New York Times, daily)	1.4	2.4	2.3	2.8
Long-distance phone call (3 min., N.Y. to L.A.)	60.8	23.5	13.4	4.3
Apples (Red Delicious, 1 lb.)	3.1	2.9	3.3	4.7
Gasoline (1 gal.)	7.5	5.2	9.1	6.4
Chicken (whole, cut, 1 lb.)	13.5	8.7	7.4	7.4
Milk (1/2 gal.)	12.5	9.6	8.8	7.8
Ground beef (chuck, 1 lb.)	15.3	13.9	13.0	11.1
Film (Kodak, 35mm, color prints)	60.0	37.9	27.7	27.2
Barbie doll	81.1	60.8	33.2	31.3
Medium items	Hours of work			
Record album	1.8	2.2	1.2	[1] 1.6
Consumer Reports (1-yr. subscription)	2.7	2.2	1.8	2.1
Electricity (500 kwh)	4.6	3.3	4.2	3.9
Theater ticket (Broadway, best seat)	3.4	4.1	5.2	5.7
Television (RCA, 19-in.)	85.1	121.6	42.6	21.7
Dishwasher (GE, midpriced model)	112.2	64.9	55.3	35.5
Washing machine (Sears, midpriced model)	92.3	52.7	58.3	37.8
Refrigerator (Frigidaire, top-freezer)	168.0	99.2	83.7	59.8
Mattress (Simmons, with box spring)	71.6	59.5	44.0	60.7
Large items	Days of work			
Auto insurance [2]	7.1	7.8	7.3	11.3
Income taxes (Federal) [3]	50.0	48.3	63.8	49.0
Child delivery [4]	15.5	37.2	33.3	62.2
College (public) [5]	61.7	64.1	68.9	99.2
Car (average, new)	203.1	131.0	161.0	197.8
College (private) [6]	129.5	140.4	144.0	251.4
House (3-bedroom ranch, Matawan, N.J.)	1125.5	1330.7	1530.0	1777.3

[1] Compact disc.
[2] National average.
[3] Includes Social Security.
[4] Normal delivery (hospital and doctor fees).
[5] University of Michigan (room, board, tuition; 1 yr.).
[6] Colgate (room, board, tuition; 1 yr.).
Source: *Consumer Reports*, June 1992, 393.

must take it into consideration if they are to be successful economically. Even a 5 percent inflation rate each year means that a dollar will lose over half its value in ten years. You can combat mild inflation in a number of ways:

1. *Minimize your cash holdings.* Cash obviously loses value at the rate of inflation. If I bury $1000 cash to protect it from theft for a year when the inflation rate is 10 percent, inflation robs me of $100. At the end of the year, I have only $900 purchasing power.

2. *Select high-yield savings accounts whenever possible.* The longer-term accounts often impose substantial penalties if you withdraw your funds before the end of the term. Hence you should spread your savings over a number of different kinds of accounts. For instance, keep a small balance to cover unexpected expenses in a regular passbook account where you can make withdrawals at any time without penalty. You may also want some money in a six-month to one-year term account on which you may earn higher interest, although the higher yields may require larger minimum deposits. If you have enough funds, you can place more money into longer-term, higher-paying savings certificate.

3. *Try to include a cost-of-living clause in your employment contract.* Many unions have been successful in gaining automatic cost-of-living raises for their members. If inflation increases the CPI by 10 percent, cost-of-living clauses take effect, and the worker's income is automatically increased to match. Unfortunately, such raises also help to maintain inflation.

4. *Try not to let inflation panic you into buying before you are ready.* We are constantly told to buy now before prices increase. Yet as we pointed out, some prices may actually decline relative to the CPI even though they go up in absolute terms. Even with large items, such as automobiles, that have risen in cost as fast as the CPI, you may want to postpone buying. If your present auto has two more years of trouble-free life, drive it those two additional years, and you will probably save money even though a new car in two years will cost you more in absolute terms.

5. *Learn about investments.* Money earns money. The wise investor can stay ahead of inflation. For example, real estate in some parts of the country has stayed ahead of inflation. In other words, its price has risen more rapidly than the CPI has risen. Unfortunately, inflation is accompanied by a certain amount of irrationality. Thus, property in other parts of the country has not kept up with inflation. Small investors should study carefully the particular investments that interest them.

6. *Understand that inflation tends to favor the borrower.* During a period of inflation, money borrowed today is paid back in cheaper dollars in the future. For example, I borrow $10,000 at 10 percent interest per year for a five-year period. During that period, inflation is 10 percent per year. In essence I am paying nothing for the use of the money. I will have paid $1000 per year or $5000 in simple interest at the end of five years. However, at the end of five years, the $10,000 I pay back is worth only $5000 in purchasing power because of the accumulated 50 percent inflation, which has halved the value of my dollars.

7. *Try to buy wisely.* Watch for bargains such as year-end sales and seasonal price reductions.

8. *Have more members of the family work.* This suggestion is discussed in more detail in Chapter 9. Higher inflation rates are partially responsible for the increasing number of married women seeking employment.

9. *Conserve and save to accumulate investment funds.*

PERIODS OF REDUCED
INFLATION AND MILD RECESSION

Recessions cause people a great deal of hardship. Unemployment rises, production declines, and government income falls, while the costs of social programs (unemployment benefits and so forth)`rise. Because such economic problems are much more obvious than the negative effects of creeping inflation, the government comes under great pressure to support at least a mild form of inflation despite its long-term negative effects. In the face of recession, people quickly tend to forget about their problems with inflation.

Most likely, you will experience mild inflation more frequently than recessions; therefore in this book emphasis has been placed on how to cope with inflation. At times, however, the economy will experience slumps. As protection against such times, the prudent money manager will want to do the following:

1. Maintain enough liquidity to cover emergencies.
2. Beware of investments with a large balloon payment due in the near future.
3. If you are able to foresee a slowing of inflation and resulting economic downturn, try to maintain a larger percentage of your assets in cash so that you can take advantage of good buys that may result.
4. Make sure that your financial position is flexible enough that you can ride out short-term economic downturns. Judging from the inflation history of the United States during the past century (see p. 283), we can probably safely assume that some amount of inflation will remain for the foreseeable future. But there will also be periodic short-term economic downturns that must be planned for in advance.

A WORD ABOUT INSURANCE

Proper use of insurance can protect a family from catastrophic financial setbacks. Every family must have medical insurance, automobile insurance if they own a car, and fire insurance if they own their own home.

Medical coverage is an absolute necessity. Medical costs have become so high that no average family can sustain the expense of a prolonged illness. For a young, healthy couple, coverage can be limited to catastrophic illness with a large deductible, perhaps as high as $500 to $1000. This is the least expensive type of medical coverage. When children arrive, a policy that covers everyday medical problems and has a lower deductible should be sought. A family of four may have to pay $100 to $400 per month for medical coverage depending on how comprehensive it is. In addition to insurance plans such as Mutual of Omaha and Blue Cross, prepaid foundation plans such as the Kaiser Permanente plan are available; these provide full medical coverage at a certain facility, hospital, or clinic for a specified monthly fee.

Many employers offer group medical plans as part of their fringe benefits; such plans help reduce health coverage costs for their employees. In such cases the family will not need to supply its own medical coverage.

The government is also playing a larger role in the health field with Medicare plans of various kinds, Social Security disability programs, and Workers' Compensation insurance. Many analysts suggest that health services will one day be a branch of government, but for the time being, unless you are very poor, you must plan for health emergencies or face potential financial ruin. A ten-day stay in the hospital for major surgery can cost anywhere from $10,000 to $20,000.

Automobile coverage is also essential. In fact, in many states, it is illegal to be uninsured. Property damage and liability are the crucial elements. Covering one's own car for damage is less important unless, of course, it is being purchased through an installment loan. In that case the lender will require coverage for collision damage.

If you own your own home or other real property, you must have fire coverage. This is a mandatory condition for obtaining a mortgage. Because of inflation, you should increase the coverage periodically to keep up with rising construction costs. Homeowner's package policies give much more protection than just fire coverage. Usually, they include coverage for such contingencies as theft, personal liability, and wind and water damage.

Even if you do not own your own home, it is a good idea to have a personal belongings insurance policy. Such items as stereo equipment, cameras, furniture, and clothing are surprisingly expensive to replace if they are stolen or lost in a fire. Insurance, on the other hand, is relatively inexpensive.

Life insurance is also important, although it is not an absolute necessity. Essentially, individuals must protect their earning power, which is their most valuable asset. This asset should be insured against two potential hazards:

1. *Premature death:* This risk is about 30 percent before age sixty-five. It is especially important for married persons with young children to protect themselves against this risk.
2. *Long-term disability:* This means economic death and can be worse than death itself because the victim usually faces large medical costs in addition to being unable to produce income.

There are basically two types of life insurance plans: term life and cash value. Remember that the purpose of life insurance is to protect one's estate and provide for the family until the children are independent. The best protection for the least money is term insurance. With term insurance, a given amount of insurance is bought for a set period of years, usually five. Every twelve months the premium is increased slightly to take into account increasing age (increasing risk). For a typical $100,000 policy, the first-year premium for a nonsmoking male, age twenty-five is $160 with a waiver of premiums benefit (a small extra charge that covers the premium payment in case the insured is disabled).

Cash value or whole life insurance has two parts: death benefits and the cash value or savings part of the policy. The annual cost for a $100,000 policy on a nonsmoking male, age twenty-five, is around $838 per year. Although such a plan is considerably more expensive than term life insurance, the policy builds savings or a cash value. In recent years the saving aspects of such policies have paid such high returns that for some couples whole life may now be a better long-term value (if the couple can afford the higher premiums) than straight term insurance. In general, the best policy for a young family is one that insures for a substantial part of the economic loss that would occur at an early death and also fits into their budget. The appropriate insurance may be all term or all whole life or a combination of the two (Anderson 1988).

Basically, the amount of life insurance a couple needs depends on the number and ages of their children, their standard of living, and their other investments. What life insurance must do is protect the family if the major monetary contributor should die. It should cover death costs, taxes, and outstanding debts and should supply enough money to enable the family to continue functioning. Just how much this will be depends on the individual family.

YOUR OWN HOME

The home ownership rate in the United States is about 64 percent for all households (Associated Press 1992, A4). Home ownership has been a way of life for most Americans. Their home is a major source of savings for many retired Americans. Depending on the state of the economy and the location of the home, however, one can argue that the costs of home ownership make the investment less attractive than is commonly believed. If the money spent on home ownership were saved and invested wisely, it would probably make more money than would accrue through appreciation of a home. This is especially true if rents continue to rise more slowly than the general inflation rate as they have in the past. A person's home, however, yields many personal satisfactions beyond the possibility of economic gain. The American dream of one day owning a home is more than merely an economic dream.

For some young couples, the dream may not come true. The costs of home ownership have risen so drastically in the past ten years that a home is now out of reach of many Americans.

Home prices, mortgage interest rates, property taxes, and utilities costs have all risen at a much faster rate than the overall Consumer Price Index increase. As of October 1992, the overall CPI stood at 141.8 (1982–1984 base year); homeowners' costs were at 156.8.

Mortgage interest rates are extremely volatile. For example, at the beginning of 1982, they were at record highs (16–18 percent), but in 1992 they were much lower (7–10 percent). To give some idea of what these fluctuations mean to prospective home buyers, Table 8-16 shows the amount of pretax income necessary to qualify for a thirty-year, $50,000 mortgage at various interest rates.

Housing prices have risen dramatically over the past twenty years. In 1977 the national median home price was $44,000. By 1989 the median price had increased to $92,900 (a 111 percent increase). Local areas vary greatly from these national statistics (see Table 8-17). In areas of the country in economic trouble or losing population, home prices have actually declined. Considering inflation and the increased number of luxuries built into new homes, however, looking only at the median home price can be misleading. In addition, home prices in most parts of the country dropped 10 to 20 percent during the recession that began in 1991.

TABLE 8-16
PRETAX INCOME NEEDED TO QUALIFY FOR A **THIRTY-YEAR, $50,000 MORTGAGE**

INTEREST RATE	MONTHLY PAYMENTS[a]	MONTHLY INCOME	ANNUAL INCOME
10%	$439	$1,752	$21,024
12	514	2,056	24,672
13	553	2,212	26,544
14	592	2,368	28,416

[a]Principal and interest payment.

TABLE 8-17
Median Home Prices in 1977 AND 1989

AREA SURVEYED	1977	1989	PERCENTAGE CHANGE
National	$44,000	$ 92,900	+111%
San Francisco	72,000	265,700	269
Los Angeles	65,000	218,000	235
New York	48,500	182,200	275
Washington, D.C.	68,000	139,900	105
Chicago	50,900	105,000	106
Philadelphia	45,000	108,000	140
Minneapolis	47,250	87,000	85
Baltimore	47,000	95,100	102
Colombus, Ohio	42,000	76,700	83
St. Louis	37,000	75,300	102
Miami	48,500	88,000	81
Milwaukee	42,900	81,200	89
Houston	46,900	68,700	46
Portland	35,500	68,800	94

Source: Scripps Howard News Service 1989.

The economy has reacted in a number of ways in an effort to keep home ownership within reach of the American family. Smaller homes, modular homes, mobile homes, condominiums, and cooperatives have all increased in popularity. Government funding of lower-interest mortgages has also been made available. Shared ownership is another way to move into home ownership. Two families can pool their funds and buy a large home, a duplex, or a triplex. With a triplex, the families can rent out the extra apartment, and the income can help with the monthly homeowner expenses.

AN ALTERNATIVE: INVESTMENT

According to popular belief, one's chances of earning $1 million are much less than they were for one's grandparents. But the number of millionaires today

Common knowledge insists that buying a home is always more advantageous than renting. Rent is money lost forever, but a house payment helps increase one's equity in the home while inflation increases the value of the home. Although this is often true, in some circumstances rent makes more economic sense. For example, in some areas of the country, home prices have not been inflated. Recently, in states dramatically affected by lower oil prices, such as Texas and Oklahoma, homes have actually lost value over the last several years.

Figures from an analysis by the Joint Center for Housing Studies at Harvard University (1989) indicate that the real cost of home ownership has risen much faster than the cost of rent over the past twenty years. In 1980 the total cost of purchasing a home for first-time home buyers was 16.8 percent of their median income after tax benefits and equity buildup were factored in. Renters in 1980 spent 27.6 percent of their income on housing including fuel and utilities. Hence home ownership made more sense than renting.

By 1988, however, the picture was different. The cost of purchasing a home had risen to 33 percent of income while renters on the average were paying about 29.5 percent of their incomes for housing. Hence the cost of home ownership doubled during this time while the cost of renting increased only 2 percent. In the South and Midwest, rents adjusted for inflation have actually fallen in recent years.

Another study (Bond and Stillblower 1988) found that renting was more advantageous than home ownership depending on the cost of the home and one's tax bracket. For example, a family earning $30,000 would be better off paying rent of $710 per month than buying an $85,000 house. The researchers reasoned that the family would have to make a 10 percent down payment—$8500—and that if they invested that money for thirty years, the compound interest at an average of 8 percent per year would put them ahead by almost $140,000 compared to what they would gain as homeowners even after considering the homeowners' tax advantages and home appreciation. The figures worked out in favor of home ownership if a family was in the 28 percent or higher income tax bracket and if they bought a $175,000 home with 10 percent down.

The point is that each family must examine their own economic position and the area of the country in which they live to determine whether it makes economic sense to buy or rent housing.

actually far exceeds the number in your grandparents' time. Granted, $1 million may be worth considerably less in purchasing power today, but it is still a healthy mark of affluence. A gradually inflationary economy is also an economy in which money is more easily accumulated. For most young people gathering the first small amount of capital is particularly crucial because the system has a tendency to work against them. In the early years, they must stay alert to keep the system from entrapping them and thereby canceling their attempt to accumulate initial investment capital. If they can win this battle and start on the road to financial success, they will be using the system to their advantage rather than being used by it. When costs of living in the United States are compared with those in other countries (see Table 8-18), it is clear that the United States offers a great deal economically to its citizens. (The Moscow figures in Table 8-18 predate the breakup of the USSR).

Some people can become millionaires by working in certain jobs and businesses (Inset 8-5). Figure 8-4 shows the broad range of investment opportunities from which to choose. They range from the very conservative bank savings account to highly speculative gambles for high return on such things as mining

An Alternative: Investment

TABLE 8-18				
COMPARATIVE STANDARD OF LIVING IN MINUTES, HOURS, OR MONTHS OF WORK NEEDED TO BUY THE ITEM				
COMMODITY	WASHINGTON	MOSCOW	LONDON	PARIS
Weekly food basket (family of four)	18.6 hrs.	53.5	24.7	22.2
Lipstick	30 mins.	69	60	76
T-shirt (cotton)	19 mins.	185	66	53
Panty hose	18 mins.	366	18	17
Levi jeans	3 hrs.	46	6	6
Color television	65 hrs.	701	132	106
Small car	5 mos.	53	11	8

Source: National Federation of Independent Business Research and Education Foundation.

FIGURE 8-4

The investment continuum: Note that the percentage return in successful investments increases as the risk increases—the chances of striking gold are slim, but if you do, the return is great; percentages also change with economic conditions.

and oil exploration. You might ask: How can the average newly married couple even consider investments? It's all they can do to set up housekeeping. This is a legitimate question. However, the couple who plan on investing, even if only at a later date, have the greatest chance of economic prosperity and freedom. A positive attitude toward investment is actually more important than the investment itself. Such an attitude recognizes that "money makes money," that there is value in budgeting and staying free of consumer debt, that controlling one's desires in early years can lead to greater rewards later, and that the American economic system can free one from economic worries if used properly. Even if a couple can put aside only a few dollars a month toward future investments, they stand a chance of improving their economic position compared with that of their friends who have no interest in or knowl-

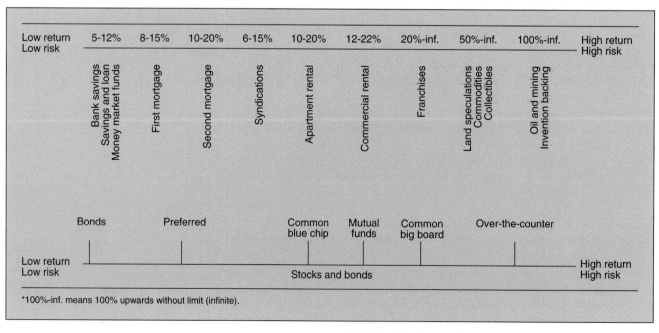

*100%-inf. means 100% upwards without limit (infinite).

292

These stories demonstrate that a person can become wealthy with hard work and creativeness, but the point is not necessarily to explain how to become wealthy. Rather it is to demonstrate that economic security leading to increased freedom is a possibility for any American.

Debbi Fields has done very well indeed with chocolate chip cookies. Mrs. Fields, a native of Oakland, California, couldn't have started smaller: baking cookies for meetings held by her wealthy financial-consultant husband. She couldn't help but hear the munches as her homemade cookies were devoured. So she opened a little cookie shop in Palo Alto. "Not a single customer showed up," she says. "I began walking up and down the block with my cookies asking people to try them." Today, Mrs. Fields has more than three hundred company-owned stores, with a thousand employees and annual sales of about $50 million.

"I never expected it to grow to these proportions," she says. She maintains a hands-on, people-oriented style of management (every worker gets a handwritten Christmas card from the boss), stringent quality controls, and winning recipes. "I'm driven to perfection," she says, adding that she's still not through after her usual twelve-hour day at her headquarters in Park City, Utah.

To the computer industry, Bill Gates was always a young man in a hurry. The inventor of the operating system now built into every IBM (or clone) home computer, Gates became a business legend before his twenty-first birthday. He founded his company, Microsoft, with money he earned as a teenage programming consultant and has never had to borrow from a bank. The company's sales exceeded $1.8 billion in 1991. *Forbes* magazine listed him as the wealthiest single American in 1992 estimating his worth to be approximately $6 billion.

Gates has been the model entrepreneur. He has hired good professional managers and constantly adds innovative products to the company. "We wanted to be a leader in the goal of putting a computer onto every desk in America. It would be a great failure not to see that through."

William Hewlett (estimated wealth about $1.2 billion), the co-founder of the $7.1 billion Hewlett-Packard Company, started in a garage with $538 in capital. His favorite invention is the pocket calculator. Although the company is involved in many fields, about 50 percent of its energy is devoted to the computers.

Although there are only about one million millionaires in the United States, such stories as these are possible in this country, and that really is the beauty of the economic system. America's handful of young millionaires rely less on luck than on talent, tenacity, and creativity. They display enormous energy, patience, and resolve in getting what they want, which often is the personal satisfaction of having done something profitably and well.

WHERE ARE THE MILLIONAIRES?

Small business owners represent most of America's millionaires. Although money can be made in almost any business field, certain industries show a relatively higher number of very profitable small firms:

- Manufacturers of specialty apparel accessories such as belts and bows.
- Manufacturers of optical, medical, and ophthalmic goods.
- Manufacturers of meat products, especially those producing specialized meats for ethnic and regional preferences.
- Manufacturers of industrial machinery.
- Wholesalers of farm products and raw materials.
- Accounting, auditing, and bookkeeping.
- Wholesalers of motor vehicles and automotive parts and equipment.
- Computer and software development.

Salespeople, especially at the wholesale level, also earn well. And where do all these millionaires live? Five states account for over half of them: California, New York, Texas, Illinois, and Florida.

Source: Adapted from David Rosenthal, "You Can Still Make a Million Dollars," *Parade*, January 26, 1986, 4; Steve Wilstein, "Electronics Pioneer Hewlett Reflects on Career," *Santa Barbara News Press*, February 15, 1987, G-3; Robert Dietsch, "Some Small Businesses Spawn More Millionaires," *Santa Barbara News Press*, March 12, 1989, F-4.

Despite the diversity of today's households, the subjects you have to consider in devising a workable financial plan for your family remain the same for everyone. The following table gives you a master-plot of the basics—the chief concerns you need to address—at a glance.

	SAVINGS AND INVESTING	INSURANCE	COMMENTS
Single	To guard against emergencies, build a cash reserve equal to three months of your after-tax income. Put other savings in aggressive investments, such as growth-stock mutual funds.	Your top priority: a disability policy that will replace 60 to 70 percent of your income in case of prolonged illness. Also buy homeowner's or renter's protection for your property.	Financial flexibility is crucial. If you are young, don't automatically lock away savings in a 401(K) or IRA, because you will probably need that money before you retire.
Living Together	Consider a joint checking account for common household expenses. Keep all other bank accounts, as well as credit card and investment accounts, completely separate.	Some life insurance companies may be reluctant to allow you to name the person you live with as beneficiary, unless he or she has some degree of dependence on your income or assets.	Put all of your arrangements in writing, including how the two of you intend to share living expenses and how you would settle financial matters if you separate.
Dual Income No Kids (DINKs)	With so few fixed expenses, DINKs should aim to save as much as 20 percent of their income. To meet long-term goals, invest aggressively in growth assets.	Coordinate company benefits so that you do not pay for overlapping coverage. Comprehensive health and disability coverage is a must; life insurance is optional.	Impulse spending is the scourge of DINKs. Cut back by devising a disciplined budget that sends dollars to your savings plan before you spend on your favorite frills.
Single Parent	Use money-market funds to shore up a cash reserve of at least three- to six-months'	As sole provider, you need ample health, life, and disability coverage. If you are divorced	If your company benefits are not comprehensive, supplement them with outside coverage. To

edge of investing. (See "Gaining Freedom through Investment" on p. 299.)

For example, putting away $20 each month starting at age twenty-five is the same as putting away $200 each month starting at age forty-five with retirement at age sixty-five Table 8-19 shows how money grows at 6 percent and at 12 percent compounded daily interest. The figures are predicated on putting aside $100 per month initially until you have $12,000.

	SAVINGS AND INVESTING	INSURANCE	COMMENTS
	expenses. Start contributing to a college fund through bank and mutual fund automatic savings plans.	and get alimony or child support, take out a life insurance policy on your ex-spouse.	ease a cash crunch, think about trading down to a smaller home.
Two Careers	Start building funds for your children's education. Your best investments: Growth-stock funds, zero-coupon bonds, and Series EE U.S. Savings Bonds.	Dovetail company benefits to make sure your family is adequately but affordably insured. Pick the best, most economical parts of each package, and decline overlapping coverage.	Neglecting to save for retirement is the most common mistake made by dual-career couples. So try to contribute the maximum to your company 401(K) through automatic payroll deductions.
Married One Income (Traditionals)	To safeguard against layoff or other set-back, keep six months of living expenses in a money fund. Invest for retirement with pretax dollars through the wage earner's 401(K) plan.	A life insurance policy whose proceeds would generate enough interest to replace 75 percent of the wage earner's salary is a must. Insure the homemaker with a small term policy.	The biggest danger is the loss of the household's single income. Your insurance policies must be up to date; both spouses must have access to the family's investments.
Blended Family (Remarried)	Make sure that your combined portfolio is adequately diversified. Responsibilities to kids from two marriages will multiply college costs, so start saving for tuition now.	Life and disability are a must. Update beneficiaries to protect your new family. Review health coverage for gaps or overlaps, making sure that all of the kids are covered.	Draft a legally binding agreement spelling out apportionment of property, investment strategies, estate plans and each parent's responsibilities for childrearing and education costs.

Source: *Money* March 1989, 56–57.

In recent years, the government has added greatly to the incentive to save toward retirement by offering several different savings plans in which the money saved and the interest earned by that money are tax-free until the money is withdrawn at a later age. The best known of these plans is the Individual Retirement Account, better known by its initials IRA. The 1986 revisions in the income tax law changed the IRA provisions so that contri-

An Alternative: Investment

	TABLE 8-19 $100 PER MONTH INVESTED AT 6 PERCENT AND 12 PERCENT			
YEARS	AMOUNT INVESTED	6 PERCENT	12 PERCENT	DIFFERENCE
10	$12,000	$ 16,766	$ 23,586	$ 6,820
20	24,000	46,791	96,838	50,047
30	36,000	100,562	324,351	223,789
40	48,000	196,857	1,030,970	834,113

butions are now deductible only to a certain level depending on income. Interest on your contributions remains tax-free until withdrawn.

In simple terms a young person and/or family can make investment a part of their planning by following these steps:

1. Use the credit system wisely to avoid economic entrapment.
   a. Avoid buying consumer goods on credit.
   b. Avoid running balances on credit card accounts.
   c. Pay bills promptly in order to maintain a good credit rating.
2. Develop the habit of saving regularly even if at first you can only save a small amount.
3. Learn about the many types of investments available to individuals in the United States, some of which are described in "Gaining Freedom through Investment" on page 299.

Such steps can lead to successful investments, which can in turn lead to economic freedom.

SUMMARY

1. *The family is the major unit of consumption in the United States.* A family must have the economic ability to provide food, shelter, and transportation and meet the needs of its members. Ideally, it will also have money for pleasurable and recreational activities. The family that is economically successful stands a much better chance of staying together than the family that fails economically. The poorest segment of American society has the highest rate of divorce.

2. Credit use in the United States has allowed Americans to maintain one of the world's highest standards of living. Yet this easy availability of credit can also curtail individual and family freedom when it is abused or misunderstood. *Agreeing to make future payments for present goods or services can lock a person into an inflexible life pattern.* Money must be earned steadily to meet the payment schedule. For many families the debt burden is so large that almost all funds are allocated automatically to make the many payments due each month. The family has little or no monetary flexibility to meet unforeseen emergencies or to act quickly if a good investment opportunity arises.

3. On the other hand, *a thorough understanding of credit, installment buying, interest costs, and budgeting can work to a family's benefit,* allowing them to invest and perhaps to achieve not only economic security but also economic freedom.

4. *The day-to-day handling of money can be a problem in a family if the partners have different values about money.* Conflict can be minimized if the couple decides ahead of time how monetary decisions will be made. They have several options: to let the husband make all decisions, to let the wife make all decisions, to make all decisions jointly, or to let both have separate funds and share agreed-on obligations. Budgeting will also allow them to plan for necessities and to see how their income is spent. Deciding together how to use income left over after meeting necessities is another way to reduce monetary conflict.

5. *Inflation is the primary economic enemy of the newly married couple.* Inflation rates have remained fairly stable (4–6 percent) in recent years, as have wages. At times, however, wages do not keep up with inflation, and many people find that their real income actually goes down. It is important for families to understand inflation so that they can take steps to guard against it. Proper budgeting and good investments are two steps that a family can take to reduce the unwanted effects of inflation.

6. *Insurance should be considered a necessity.* A family with a car and a home needs medical, automobile, and fire insurance. Life insurance is also important, though not a necessity. Couples should start with a medical policy that protects them against catastrophic illness and then change to broader coverage as children arrive. They should also follow this pattern with life insurance. The cou-

ple should buy term insurance, increasing the amount of the coverage as needed to protect family members.

7. *The American dream of home ownership for every family may be fading in the face of increased housing prices.* Smaller homes, condominiums, and cooperatives will probably be the housing of the future.

8. *Investments are a means of supplementing income and making money work to produce more money.* The family able to save and invest even a small portion of their income is freer of possible economic entrapment and stands a better chance of survival than families who cannot control wants and desires and spend their entire income.

9. *Investments can be plotted along a continuum from low risk, low return to high risk, high return.* Examples of low-risk, low-return investments are bank savings and savings and loan accounts. Risk and return increase with such investments as first and second mortgages, syndications, apartment houses, commercial property, and franchises. While the rate of return can be very high for such speculations as land, commodities, oil and mining, and invention backing, the risk is too high for young couples with limited funds. The stock market is another investment outlet. Here again there is a continuum from low risk, low return to high risk, high return.

Note to reader: *Many readers of this book have little experience with investments. Most students don't have the money or the time to invest. However, education is an investment in oneself, and for most people this investment will pay monetary dividends over the years. If the ideas in this section seem foreign to you, if you are not interested in investments, if you think that investments only come later in life when you contemplate retirement, then this section is definitely for you. The individual who thinks in investment terms early in life stands the best chance of monetary success. Over the years, many students who claimed disinterest in investing have learned about it and suddenly become enthusiastic. And a good number of these students went on to monetary success far beyond what they had envisioned. The next Bill Gates or Mrs. Fields is sitting right in your class. It could be you.*

We cannot give more than a cursory description of some of the many investment opportunities that abound in America. You can learn about investing by reading such magazines as Forbes, Fortune, Business Week, *and* Money. *In addition, many money management and investment books are designed for the beginner.* Marshall Loeb's Money Guide, The Power of Money Dynamics *by Venita VanCaspel,* Personal Finance *by E. T. Garman and R. E. Forgue, and* The Complete Guide to Investment Opportunities *by Marshal Blume and Jack Friedman are all worthwhile.*

The world of investment has undergone drastic changes in the past decade. Investment opportunities for the small investor have

greatly expanded. Perhaps the best example is the revolution in banking that occurred with the passing of the Depository Institutions Deregulation Act of 1980. For years checking accounts earned no interest, and bank savings accounts earned only minimal interest, 3 to 6 percent per year, which did not even offset inflation.

SAVINGS ACCOUNT

Starting in 1982, gradual deregulation allowed banking institutions to offer a greater variety of investment and savings opportunities with much higher interest returns to their customers. Because most investors must start by first saving some investment capital, the many types of accounts now available allow those savings to start working immediately. Table

8-19 shows the difference in interest earned over time between a 6 percent return and a 12 percent return. Using these savings opportunities can thus pay the investor big dividends. Note that interest rates on all types of savings accounts dropped greatly during the 1991–1993 recession.

Banks and savings and loan associations offer a variety of money-market accounts that pay between 4 and 12 percent depending on the market. Investors with a great deal of money, say, $100,000 or more, have always been able to invest in a variety of money instruments, such as certificates of deposit, where interest was not limited by law. Money-market funds make higher yields available to everyone by pooling the monies of a number of small investors and investing them in high-yield certificates as well as Treasury bills and other securities. Money-market savings accounts are offered by all savings institutions. Checking accounts also now earn interest on the average balance. Because of the partial deregulation of the banking industry, consumers must shop more carefully to maximize their savings and possible checking account returns because there are almost as many plans as institutions.

Once they have instituted a savings program and accumulated some capital, individuals can begin to investigate a broader range of investments. Space allows only a superficial discussion of a few of the many investment opportunities available. Each person must make her or his own decisions about saving and investing. For example, a young family with small children should lean toward conservative investments that require little personal time because they probably have little free time at this stage in their lives. Each couple must consider their personal interests and their financial goals. For example, the family in which the husband or wife has flexible time (perhaps they own their own business, do freelance work, teach and have considerable vacation time, and so on) might consider apartment ownership and management. Where time is rigidly structured, the family might investigate the stock market, real estate or business syndicates, mortgage purchases, house trading, and so on.

It is also important to review investments often. The economy shifts so quickly that an excellent invest-

ment one day may become a poor investment the next.

FIRST MORTGAGES

With a first mortgage, money is loaned with real estate as security for the debt. If the debt is not paid, the lender takes over the land and/or building. First mortgages are quite safe as long as no more money is loaned than the property is worth. For example, most savings and loan institutions lend 80 percent or less of the selling or appraised price of a property, thus assuring that they can recover their loan in the event that the property must be sold to recover the debt. Buying first mortgages is expensive; for example, 80 percent of an $100,000 house is $80,000. In addition, the money is usually tied up for a long time, twenty to thirty years in most cases. For these reasons, first mortgages usually are not appropriate investments for young couples.

SECOND MORTGAGES

Second mortgages can be potential investments for young couples because often less money is required than for first mortgages. Like a first mortgage, a second mortgage is secured by real estate but it is a more speculative investment because it is given after a first mortgage has already been placed against the property. (The first-mortgage holder has first claim on the property in case of default.) A second mortgage is often made when the buyer of a property doesn't have enough cash for the down payment or when money is needed to make up the difference be-

tween the price and the first mortgage. For example, a buyer with only $5000 for a down payment buys a house for $65,000 with a $55,000 first mortgage. The buyer is therefore $5000 short of the sales price. A short-term second mortgage of $5000 will make up the difference.

Second mortgages are usually for only a few years, seldom more than seven and more often for only two to three years. They can be in any amount, which makes them investment possibilities for young couples. They may be purchased from real estate agencies and money brokers. Ads for both first and second mortgages may also be found in the classified newspaper sections. In general, one should not invest more in a second mortgage than the buyer has put down on the property. One should also be sure that the property is worth the price paid, so that in case of default, the property can be sold for enough money to cover both the first and second mortgages.

Although the standard interest rate for most second mortgages is 10 to 15 percent, one can often earn more by buying the mortgage at a discount. Let's say that the previous owners of the $65,000 house took the second mortgage of $5000 from the new buyer, but find that they need cash before the mortgage is due. To make the second mortgage more attractive, they offer to sell the mortgage at a 10 percent discount. Perhaps $4000 is still due on the mortgage. The discount means that the new investor will get the mortgage of $4000 for $3600, thus effectively increasing his or her profit margin.

SYNDICATES

In a syndicate, a group of individuals form a partnership and raise money for investment, usually to buy real estate or a business. A young couple may be able to join such a venture as a limited partner. A few general partners will actually put the deal together and run the investment on a day-to-day basis. They will also assume the risks beyond each limited partner's investment. All the limited partner does is contribute a minimum amount of money. For example, the limited partner's shares might cost $1000 each. The limited partners have no responsibility in the management and no risk other than their initial investment. If the venture is profitable, they share in the profits. Such syndicates are often advertised in the financial pages, but more often one learns about them from other investors or from professional money managers. Under state law, syndicates must provide information so that investors know how the money will be used, what liabilities will be assumed, and what profit will be paid if the venture prospers.

APARTMENT AND COMMERCIAL RENTALS

Apartments and commercial rental real estate require time as well as money because the rentals must be managed and maintained continually. However, managing an apartment complex for other owners is a good way for a young couple to get started. They not only make money but learn the fundamentals of property management before actually investing in apartments themselves.

Commercial rentals are generally beyond the economic means of young couples, so they won't be discussed here. If a couple has time and are handy at minor repairs, buying and living in a duplex or triplex can be a good start toward property ownership. The rents help with the payments and maintenance, and in addition the value of a well-located property tends to follow the upward inflationary trend.

FRANCHISES

With a franchise, an investor buys a business such as McDonald's, Radio Shack, or Colonel Sanders' Kentucky Fried Chicken. The advantage is that one starts a business supported by a large company's reputation, experience, backing, and advertising. The new owner must use the parent company's products and maintain a given standard of service. The price for good franchises is high, but many of the larger companies have loan funds that can help the new owner get started.

LAND SPECULATION AND COMMODITIES

Land and commodities are really speculations rather than investments and should be avoided by the small investor because the risk of loss is high. Both involve gambling on the future desirability of land or the future price of commodities (commodities are farm products, such as corn, wheat, cattle, or oats, or raw materials, such as copper, silver, gold, or timber).

Let's look at one commodity speculation. Suppose a cattle producer

needs money or decides to avoid the risk of changing prices by entering into a future's account. The cattle producer purchases calves at today's prices and then sells them to a futures' account at the going rate for year-old steers. (The cattle producer still has to feed the calves for a year but has been assured of a moderate profit.) The speculator who buys the account hopes, of course, that the price of beef will be higher when the steers are actually ready for market. Risks are high because unpredictable developments such as the weather, governmental policies, and the international situation may affect commodity prices. Actually, a number of speculators may be involved over the life of the steer.

OIL AND MINING AND INVENTION BACKING

Investments in oil and mining ventures or inventions are even more speculative and should not be considered by a young family entering the investment market.

STOCKS AND BONDS

Another major form of investment is the stock market, or stocks and bonds. We will consider these investments in some detail, starting at the low-risk, low-return end of the continuum and proceeding to investments that involve more risk but also potentially more return.

In general, stocks, bonds, and notes of various kinds are bought through brokerage firms. These firms are members of various stock exchanges through which they buy and sell. The customer pays a small fee to the brokerage house to buy or sell.

BONDS

Bonds are a form of IOU or promissory note that companies issue when they need funds. Bonds are usually issued in multiples of a thousand dollars. The issuing company promises to pay the bondholders a specified amount of interest for a specified amount of time, at the end of which the bond will be redeemed for the face amount. Because the risk is generally low, bonds usually offer low interest rates. Several kinds of bonds are available: U.S. savings, corporation, and municipal bonds. U.S. savings bonds are the safest investment but are also long term and pay low interest. In periods of inflation, an investor can actually lose money over the term of the bond. Corporation bonds are relatively safe because the company pledges properties it owns as collateral. Municipal bonds are similar except that a government unit offers the bonds, usually to complete a building or park project. They are relatively safe, but as city finances have become strained in recent years, it is possible that some municipal bonds may not be repaid at the expiration date. An advantage of municipal bonds is that their interest is exempt from federal income taxes.

STOCKS

A stock is a piece of paper (stock certificate) that gives the owner the right to a portion of the assets of the company issuing the stock. Like bonds, stocks are issued when companies need money, usually for expansion. Unlike bondholders, stockholders are part owners of the company they have invested in and can vote at stockholders' meetings. The stocks of large companies are usually listed on stock exchanges, either regional ones around the country or the two largest, the New York Stock Exchange and the American Stock Exchange. These organized exchanges set minimum requirements that a company must meet to have its stock listed. For example, the New York Stock Exchange specifies that a company must have at least $10 million in tangible assets, at least $2 million in annual earnings, and at least 1 million shares divided among 2000 or more shareholders. Stocks are also sold over the counter in markets that are less organized than the exchanges. These stocks are usually not traded as often as those listed on the exchanges and are issued by smaller and less well known companies (over-the-counter stocks offer the highest risk and highest potential return). In general, two types of stocks are available:

1. *Preferred stocks:* These are called preferred because when earnings are distributed or when a company is liquidated or becomes bankrupt, holders of preferred stock are paid first.
2. *Common stocks:* Most stocks are common stocks. They may pay dividends but only after the dividends on the company's preferred stock are paid. Normally, common stocks fluctuate more than bonds and preferred stock. Although common stocks usually pay dividends, most investors hope to buy the stock at a low price and sell it at a higher price. Blue Chip stocks are those of strong companies such as General Motors or IBM. The stronger the company, usually the safer the stock.

MUTUAL FUNDS

Mutual funds are companies that buy and sell large blocks of stocks. The investor can buy shares in such companies rather than shares in individual companies which issue their own stock. Each mutual fund stock represents a share of the large, diversified group of shares the fund owns. There are two kinds of mutual funds, closed end and open end. Closed-end funds usually do not issue stock after the initial issue. Many closed-end mutual funds are listed on the New York Stock Exchange, and their shares are readily transferable in the open market and can be bought and sold like other shares. Open-end funds, on the other hand, usually issue more shares as people want them and are not listed on the stock exchange.

The young family should consider diversified investments rather than placing all of their capital into one venture. For example, in the stock market a mutual fund is safer than a single stock because the fund represents a widely diversified holding of stocks. Before considering any investment, though, the family should be sure it has enough insurance for basic security (see "A Word about Insurance" on pp. 287–289).

CHAPTER

9

THE DUAL-WORKER FAMILY: THE REAL AMERICAN FAMILY REVOLUTION

CONTENTS

The American family: Two jobs, two paychecks, paid child care, more precooked meals, and less time.

The feminist movement and the sexual revolution have both brought changes to the American family and to the ways that men and women relate to one another. Far more meaningful to our relationships, to our lifestyles, and especially to the American family, however, has been the work force revolution. The large-scale entrance of American women, especially married women, into the work force has wrought the most significant changes in the American family.

Because of this migration of women into the labor force, the relationship between work and family is now more complex. Work and family intersect more intimately. Partners grapple with more of the same problems. Sex roles are less clear and more overlapping. Power within the family is redistributed as both partners contribute monetarily to the family's support. Family activities and time schedules are more restricted. The care of children is more variable, ranging from full-time parental supervision to none at all in the case of the *latchkey child*, who returns to an empty home after school because both parents are working. Mothers try to become "supermoms" as they cope with both family responsibilities and an outside career. Fathers may become "house husbands" if their wives' careers blossom.

The many changes in family life really represent the reaction of society in general and families in particular to the woman-wife-mother entering the work world and sharing the breadwinner role. This has wrought a revolution in the family and in the overall relationship between the sexes.

WOMEN IN THE WORK FORCE

The relationship of work and family in the United States has undergone a profound change since World War II. More and more women have entered the labor force (see Table 9-1 and Figure 9-1). The U.S. Department of Labor (1989, 2) predicts that one-half of labor force entrants between 1986 and 2000 will be women. In the past, most women in the American labor force were single. Now married women, often with children under eighteen, are entering the labor force in unprecedented numbers. This has created what the U.S. Bureau of the Census now describes as a "husband–primary earner, wife–secondary earner" family, more popularly known as the "two-career," "two-earner," or "dual-worker" family.

Almost 58 percent of all American women over age twenty are working. Among married women with a spouse present, 68 percent are working. (see Table 9–2). Sixty-seven percent of all mothers with children under eighteen are in the labor force.

TABLE 9-1 WOMEN AS A PERCENTAGE OF THE EMPLOYED CIVILIAN LABOR FORCE	
YEAR	PERCENTAGE
1950	31.4%
1960	33.3
1970	37.7
1980	43.5
1986	44.0
1988	45.0
1991	45.6
2000 (est.)	47.0

Sources: U.S. Bureau of the Census, *Statistical Abstract of the United States: 1984,* 104th ed. (Washington, D.C.: U.S. Government Printing Office, 1983), no. 683, p. 413; U.S. Department of Labor, *Monthly Labor Review,* December 1985, p. 58; *Monthly Labor Review,* March 1989 pp. 65, 67; conversation with Bill Demming, Bureau of Labor Statistics, April 30, 1992; Schwartz 1992, 137.

305

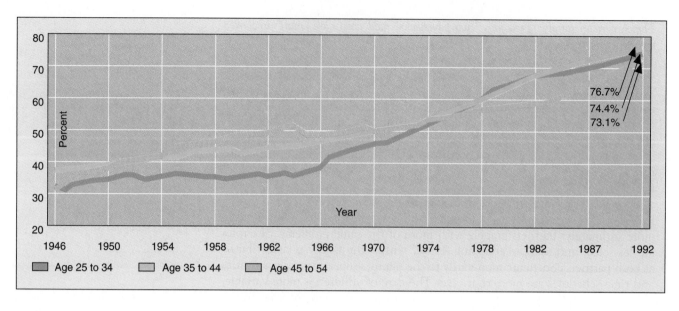

80
70
60
Percent
50
40
30
20

1946   1950   1954   1958   1962   1966   1970   1974   1978   1982   1987   1992

Year

76.7%
74.4%
73.1%

■ Age 25 to 34   □ Age 35 to 44   □ Age 45 to 54

FIGURE 9-1

Civilian labor force participation rates for women, by age, 1946–1992 (Source: U.S. Department of Labor, *Monthly Labor Review*, March 1988, p. 5, conversation with Bureau of Labor Statistics Personnel, San Francisco office, August 4, 1992)

In years past, the working woman in general and the working wife-mother in particular were unusual phenomena. Before 1900 the labor force included few women. Married women were full-time wives and mothers and were considered negligent in their family duties if they worked outside the home. If we consider the strong past attitudes about the importance of the mother being at home when her children were young, the fact that in June 1990, 53.1 percent of mothers with children under one year of age were in the labor force (U.S. Bureau of the Census October 1991, 1) is an amazing change in behavior and social mores. The number of children at home is no longer strongly related to work force participation by women. Clearly, the role of the woman as homemaker-mother only is passing, and the traditional marriage in which the husband works to support the family while the wife remains home caring for the children has become a minority pattern.

> In 1976, 43.2 percent of married couples fit this "traditional" pattern. By 1993, only 23 percent of married couples fit this pattern, and this percentage is projected to drop even further by the year 2000 (U.S. Bureau of the Census, January, 1993).

More and more married women are working outside the home for a number of reasons:

1. The inflationary pressures of the American economy and expectations of a rising standard of living have combined to bring many women into the work force. The majority of working wives work to help make ends meet. Thus, economic need is the major reason most women go to work.
2. Since World War II, real wages for both men and women have increased dramatically. (*Real wages* have been adjusted for inflation.) Because a woman can now earn much more than in the past (though still less than men), the relative cost of staying home with her family all day has increased, and more women are drawn into the labor force. One might think that increased real

TABLE 9-2
CIVILIAN LABOR FORCE PARTICIPATION RATES OF
WOMEN, BY AGE AND MARITAL STATUS, MARCH 1988

CHARACTERISTIC	AGE 25–54	AGE 25–34	AGE 35–44	AGE 45–54
Marital Status				
Never married	81.5	82.9	81.8	68.5
Married, husband present	68.1	67.5	71.7	64.0
Married, husband absent	70.9	68.2	76.0	67.6
Widowed	65.7	52.7	68.7	66.5
Divorced	84.7	83.3	87.3	82.7

Source: U.S. Department of Labor, *Monthly Labor Review*, March 1988, p. 6.

family income would encourage women to stay home because they would have less economic pressure to work and greater financial means to enjoy leisure pursuits, but this has not been the case. One reason may be that desires for increasingly higher standards of living have outpaced the increase in real income. Another reason may be that in years of high inflation, real income has not increased rapidly. Indeed, in some years it has actually declined. Thus, despite generally increasing real income, women have not remained home to enjoy it but have entered the labor market to participate in the higher wages. Increased income also enables families to reduce the amount of unpaid labor in the home because they can purchase labor-saving devices and domestic help.

3. The number and kinds of jobs available to women have increased tremendously. The importance of physical strength in many industrial jobs has diminished. Service jobs, such as clerical and sales work, have expanded greatly. The opportunity for part-time work has also increased. Equal opportunity legislation has created demands for women in jobs previously closed to women.

4. Declining birthrates have certainly contributed to the increased numbers of women working outside the home. By postponing children, having fewer children, or having none at all, women have reduced the demands of family work and have thus become free to enter the labor force.

5. Increasing education has contributed to women's working outside the home. Over half of all college graduates are now women. The same holds true of recipients of master's degrees. Better education certainly opens job opportunities. More importantly, an educated person tends to become more aware of his or her potential and, as a result, seeks fulfillment and the chance to make a broader contribution to society. The role of wife and mother becomes only one of many roles for the educated woman as she becomes more aware of her potential.

6. Attitudes about the role of the woman in the family have changed greatly during this century. Today most women believe that working outside the home is important for personal satisfaction rather than just for earning additional money. The desire to work outside the home is not universal, however.

> In a *Family Circle* survey of 50,000 American women, more than two out of three said they would prefer to stay home with their children. Only 45 percent of women with full-time jobs indicated this desire, however (Jacoby 1987, 83–84).

Nevertheless, although some women long to remain at home, the family of the future is likely to conform more and more to the dual-worker pattern. **7.** In the future the lower birthrate will reduce the number of workers available. Thus as the supply of male workers shrinks, women will become more and more important in maintaining a sufficient work force (Schwartz 1992).

Although the surge of women into the work force is slowing, few experts believe that women who have tasted the freedom, satisfaction, and added affluence of a paycheck will return to being full-time housewives in great numbers. Many employed wives appear to be working less because of financial need (although this has become increasingly important) than because of interest in their jobs. They simply enjoy their employment and derive satisfaction and self-esteem from their work.

Rich and Kimberly Revisited

In the last chapter, we left Rich and Kimberly trying to pay off their debts under a court-supervised bankruptcy payment plan. Kimberly was busy at home with her second baby. In another, more common scenario for this story, Kimberly goes back to work to help make ends meet. In this way Rich and Kimberly are able to avoid the drastic step of bankruptcy, at least for a while and probably indefinitely.

THE WORKING WIFE

The woman entering the work world is faced with more complicated and, often, more limited choices than her husband. Basically, she must choose from four major work patterns:

■ *Pattern A:* She works for a few years before she marries or has children and then settles into the homemaker job for the rest of her life. This was the predominant pattern for white, middle-class women until World War II. Although many women still follow this pattern, their proportion is declining. Today such women are apt to be mothers of more than three children, wives of affluent men, or women who have meager opportunities in the job market because they do not have a high-school education.

■ *Pattern B:* She follows the same career pattern as men; that is, she remains in the paid labor force continuously and full-time through the years between school and retirement. Women most likely to follow this pattern are women without children, African-American women, and women in professional and managerial jobs.

■ *Pattern C:* She works until she has children, then stays home for a certain amount of time (perhaps five to ten years), and returns to the labor force on a basis that will not conflict with her remaining family responsibilities.

■ *Pattern D:* She remains in the labor force continuously with short time-outs to have children. She combines family duties equally with work responsibilities.

Most men follow Pattern B, and more and more women are also following this pattern. Patterns A and C are limited by the job opportunities available. Many employers hesitate to place young, unmarried or newly married women in jobs with long-term advancement potential or higher-level jobs that require extended training. They fear that such women will soon leave the job by choosing one of the other two patterns. Pattern C presents special difficulties for the woman returning to work after a long absence. She often finds that her skills are outdated. A woman who takes a break to have children often earns less after she returns (Myers 1992, D-1). Higher-level jobs may also demand too much of her attention, causing conflict with her second job as mother, homemaker, and wife. Partly because of these difficulties, increasingly women are choosing Pattern D. This pattern, however, involves so much responsibility that it may lead to overwork, stress, and strain. The woman tries to be a superwoman, both running the family and home and holding a job outside the home. Yet this pattern, which allows women to combine work with family, will be the most satisfying in the long run. It is also the pattern that most women desire (Schwartz 1992, 88). Business must begin to recognize that a partnership between work and the family will yield the most benefit both to the worker and to the business.

Job Opportunities for Women

The vast majority of working women are not in the glamorous professions, the upper management levels of corporate America, or the government leadership roles. The work world for women is much the same as it is for most men: eight-to-five days, two-week vacations each year, and often mundane duties. Unlike her husband, though, the working wife must usually shoulder a second job, that of running her home and family.

Women have gained access to a greater variety of jobs as well as to higher-level employment in all areas. More women are doctors, lawyers, corporate executives, and managers than ever before. But these are the exceptions just as they are among men, and women are still far less represented than men in these occupations. Although opening all types and levels of jobs to women is

a worthy goal, the reality is that most women and men will not achieve lofty occupational positions. The vast majority of women (and men) in the labor force are more concerned with general nondiscriminatory job availability and good pay than with obtaining top management positions.

The mass media have reported that "Women executives are on the move and taking over top jobs in corporations" (*Time* 1985, 64), but have also called attention to the "glass ceiling" blocking women from upper management. The glass ceiling is not a barrier deliberately created by business. Rather it is the cumulative effect of various practices that place work and family in opposition to one another (Schwartz 1992, 226).

Despite the "glass ceiling," some women are breaking through to high positions in corporate America. Although the names and salaries will undoubtedly change, as of January, 1992, the following were the ten best paid women in corporate America (Working Woman 1992, 52):

1. LINDA WACHNER
   President, CEO, Warnaco $2,455,600
2. JILL E. BARAD
   President, Mattel USA $1,375,211
3. ROBIN BURNS
   President, CEO, Estée Lauder ....$1,300,000†
4. WENDY L. SIMPSON
   Senior Vice President, CEO,
   American Medical International $1,202,957
5. LINDA ALLARD
   Director of Design, Ellen Tracy ....$1,000,000†
6. HELAYNE SPIVAK
   Creative Director, Young & Rubicam/NY ....$ 750,000†
7. MARION O. SANDLER
   President, CEO, Golden West Financial ....$ 724,646
8. ELLEN MARRAM
   President, CEO, Nabisco Biscuit ....$ 700,000†
9. LUCIE SALHANY
   Chairman, Twentieth Television (Fox Inc.) ....$ 700,000†
10. KAREN ANDEREGG
    President, Clinique (Estée Lauder) ....$ 650,000†

*Numbers include salary, bonus and other cash compensation. Excluded are women on Wall Street (where compensation often includes huge bonuses), woman proprietors and those whose companies are owned by their families. †Denotes an estimate.

Women's employment opportunities are expanding greatly as they successfully penetrate historically male-dominated fields.

For example, the percentage of law degrees awarded to women rose from 2.5 percent in 1960 to 40.8 percent in 1990. In 1965, only 0.4 percent of women earned bachelor's degrees in engineering. By 1990, that percentage had risen to 13.6 percent (U.S. Department of Education 1991).

More important than these professional degrees, however, are the many categories of jobs now filled by women. From insurance adjusters to real estate brokers to production line assemblers, women make up more and more of the work force. Although one might be tempted to dismiss such jobs as less important, the opening of these jobs to women will have far more impact than the acceptance of women into the glamorous high-level jobs discussed by the media.

cathy®

by Cathy Guisewite

Despite these gains, most women still work in the jobs and occupations that have historically been open to them. These jobs for the most part are low on the pay scale. The following occupations (partial listing) have more than 60 percent female workers:

- Secretaries
- Stenographers
- Typists
- Receptionists
- Licensed practical nurses
- Teacher aides
- Textile sewing machine operators
- Bank tellers
- Financial records processing
- Dietitians
- Information clerks
- Librarians
- Elementary school teachers
- Cashiers

Despite the concentration of women in certain jobs, the variety and levels of jobs open to women are clearly improving. Because education level and employability go hand in hand, the fact that so many young women are attaining higher educational levels than in the past means that they will find a greater variety of higher-level jobs available. Remember that it was not until 1980 that women earned as many bachelor's degrees as men. These better-educated women will find the labor market friendlier and will help break down the remaining job discrimination against women.

Job Opportunities for Women

TABLE 9-3
MEDIAN ANNUAL EARNINGS OF FULL-TIME WOMEN WORKERS AS A PERCENTAGE OF MEN'S EARNINGS

YEAR	PERCENTAGE
1955	63.9%
1960	60.8
1970	59.4
1980	60.2
1984	64.5
1988	68.0
1990	71.0
1991	74.0

Source: U.S. Bureau of the Census August 1991; *Working Woman* 1992, 53.

PAY DIFFERENTIALS BETWEEN MEN AND WOMEN

As Table 9-3 shows, a definite earnings gap exists between male and female full-time workers. The gap varies slightly from year to year. In 1991 it was the smallest it has been historically.

Why does such an earnings gap exist, and why does it persist? The debate over this question is loud and often emotional. Some say the gap is due to discrimination against women, pure and simple. Others suggest that at least in the past men have been better trained (had more schooling and experience) and have therefore been more productive. Still others suggest that men are the primary breadwinners and are therefore more committed to their work. Many companies have been reluctant to invest in long-term training for women because the companies fear women employees will get married and/or pregnant and quit work periodically.

Much research has been conducted on this question, but the findings are mixed. Hours worked, amount of past experience and/or length of job tenure, occupation and/or industry (all real productivity measures) account for 30 to 40 percent of the pay differential (Madden 1985, 83–85).

One might conclude from this that the remaining difference is indeed discrimination against women in the labor force. Again, however, such a conclusion can be disputed. In light of civil rights laws and general societal disapproval, discrimination is not always easy to discover. If women freely make different choices about their work than men and these choices result in a pay differential, has discrimination occurred?

According to one argument against the existence of job discrimination, family and housekeeping duties frequently lead women to make different choices about work hours, type and amount of work experience, and occupation or industry than men. Because of their home responsibilities, women work fewer hours and thus accumulate less experience than men. Furthermore, because women anticipate lower levels of lifetime employment and lower returns, they devote less effort to acquiring skills and choose jobs that require less training, experience, and so on (Madden 1985, 87).

Lois Shaw and David Shapiro (1987, 12) discovered that the wages of women who had consistently made plans to work from the time they were in school were nearly 30 percent higher than those of working women who had never planned to work. The women who expected not to work or planned to withdraw from the labor force when they had children had less incentive to invest in work-related skills early in their working lives. They tended to look for jobs that paid high initially but offered few prospects for on-the-job training and advancement. Shaw and Shapiro concluded:

If young women underestimate their future employment and have lower wages as a result, this factor contributes to male-female earnings differences among adults. To the extent that this is the case, it suggests that young women need to be provided with better information about the likelihood of future employment and the importance of planning ahead for their working lives. (7)

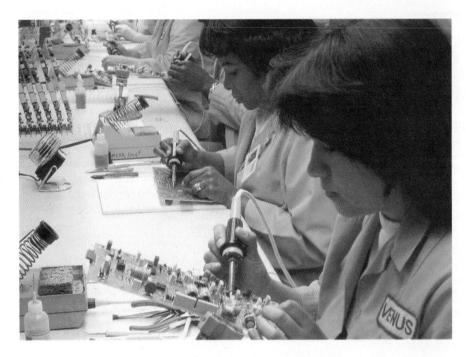

An alternative argument suggests that as a result of labor market discrimination, women have more difficulty finding jobs that are full-time, offer opportunities for training and advancement, or are in "male" occupations. Sex barriers to high-paying jobs account for significantly more of the pay differential than does differential pay between men and women for doing the same job. Thus, women do not freely choose the less remunerative jobs, but are forced into such jobs because of discrimination.

Regardless of which argument you accept or what the real reasons are for the pay differential, it does exist, and it does influence family life. For example, when Kimberly goes out to work to help with family expenses, her earnings will probably be lower than Rich's. As a result, perhaps Rich and Kimberly would be better off if Rich took a second or third job since he could earn more. The ramifications of such a decision for their relationship are great. If society can narrow the pay differential between men and women, families will have more economic choices. With more choices comes greater freedom for the family to meet both family and individual needs successfully.

Recently, the rallying cry against the pay differential has been for government intervention to mandate "equal pay for equal work" in the form of "comparable worth" legislation. *Comparable worth* takes as its premise that certain elements of dissimilar jobs may require a similar amount of training, effort, and skill; involve similar responsibility; be carried on in an environment having a similar impact on the worker; and have similar dollar value to a firm. This premise makes it possible to compare dissimilar jobs. Hence, a librarian's work may be of equal value to a truck driver's job. This idea has not been swiftly accepted by the private sector although the public sector has reacted more favorably. To date most state governments have taken some action to address pay inequities between male and female employees, but only a few states have actually taken steps to adjust salaries. Colorado Springs was the first city government to approve a comparable worth policy in full and readjust all city

DEBATE THE ISSUES
COMPARABLE WORTH (PAY EQUITY) LEGISLATION

THE ONLY WAY TO END
PAY DISCRIMINATION AGAINST WOMEN

As the data in Table 9-3 indicate, women overall have consistently earned only between 59 percent and 74 percent of what men earn. The concept of "comparable worth" has been suggested as a remedy for this pay differential. Essentially, comparable worth means "equal pay for equal work." Although neither Title VII of the Civil Rights Act of 1964 nor the Equal Pay Act of 1963 specifically mentions comparable worth, both acts do mention hiring and discharge, compensation, conditions of employment, and the limiting of opportunities for employment. Those proposing comparable worth as a solution to the pay differential problem suggest that the concept can be justified and is at least implicit in these acts.

To make the concept work, jobs must be evaluated on a point system that takes into account training, skill, responsibility, and effort needed to do the job. Most companies have already done job evaluation studies to produce the "job specifications" used to assist in hiring and wage determination. Thus, the basis for comparing jobs already exists. Based on this evaluation, some traditionally female jobs, such as executive secretary, might be found to be equal to a traditionally male job, such as cross-country trucker; thus, the two workers should be paid the same wage. Since women have tended to concentrate in historically low-paying jobs (clerical work, and so forth), finding that a given job for a woman actually requires comparable skills (granted, perhaps different skills) to those required for a job most often held by a man lays the basis for a fair pay comparison.

In the few cases where comparable worth has been tried, it seems to work without bringing undue hardship on employers. In Minnesota legislation has led to pay equity wage hikes for 9000 out of 29,000 state employ-ees. The state's commissioner of employee relations claims that this raised state payroll costs only about 3 percent and the total state budget less than 2 percent. Comparable worth legislation in Australia has helped to increase women's wages to 80 percent of men's from 65 percent a decade ago (*Business Week* 1985, 82–83). The fear that large wage increases for women would cause employers to stop hiring women has not been realized in Australia. Canada passed a pay equity law that took effect in 1990. It applies to government employees and private employees in companies with 500 or more employees. To reduce inflationary pressures, wage adjustments will be phased in over three years.

As noted earlier, single-parent, female-headed families are overrepresented below the poverty level. Increased wages for women will help these families survive economically. Perhaps a savings in public money will result as these families are able to get off welfare and be on their own economically.

Equal pay for women will free men of some of the financial burden they now bear for the family. For example, in Rich and Kimberly's case, Rich might have been able to return to school and make himself eligible for a better job had Kimberly been able to earn enough to support the family at least temporarily.

Perhaps the major benefit will be the greatly increased buying power higher wages will give women. The overall economy as well as the very businesses resisting the idea of comparable worth may be the real winners as women exercise their new buying power.

IT WILL COST WOMEN JOBS AND FUEL INFLATION

Economic theory can be used to predict the direction of market adjustments when there is a dramatic change in one segment of the market. Comparable worth legisla-

employee salaries (Crawford 1988). Thus far, there has been a great deal of discussion but little actual policy change or legislation. Some comparable worth legislation that has been passed has been struck down by the courts. (See "Debate the Issues" above.)

Perhaps more promising than legislation are the signs of improving employment opportunities for women that we have already discussed. Better education would substantially increase women's wages (by at least 20 percent). Other things being equal, economic theory suggests that employers will hire fewer employees in these jobs in an effort to hold down costs. At the same time, however, the increase in relative pay will make these jobs more attractive, thereby encouraging more people, particularly women, to seek positions in these already women-crowded occupations. Such wage increases will also deter some women from moving into nontraditional, male-dominated jobs, thereby slowing the pace of occupational desegregation.

In addition to labor market effects, the potential for inflationary pressure generated by comparable worth wage increases could be great. If women's wages were suddenly increased by 20 percent, the cost would be enormous. Such costs would be passed on to the consumer.

In light of the highly complex reasons for poverty among women, those who advocate comparable worth legislation as a means of improving the welfare of the poor offer a simplistic solution. It is not clear that raising wages would help many poor women for whom the constraints on employment would be unaffected. In other words, the uneducated, unskilled poor woman will be no better able to get a job just because wages for women increase. Perhaps more importantly, the advocates of comparable worth as a means of reducing poverty among women implicitly shift parental responsibility away from men to women. The case for equity surely requires that both parents support children, rather than that children be lifted out of poverty by changing their mothers' wage rates. A more equitable remedy for female poverty than comparable worth would be effective action to collect financial support from absent fathers.

Another outcome of comparable worth legislation might possibly be the lowering of all men's wages. The assumption implicit in such legislation is that a fair wage is a male wage. No one suggests lowering male wages as a way of reducing the pay differential between men and women, yet this is certainly a noninflationary alternative to raising women's wages. Although most unions support the idea of comparable worth, some male unions oppose it. For example in Minnesota, police and fire fighter unions began to lobby against comparable worth legislation when a librarian's job was classified at the same level of pay as a fire fighter's job (Wall Street Journal 1985). Some unions believe that if companies must give their women employees substantial pay raises, nothing will be left over for the male employees. Raises for men would also have to be limited or the pay differential would remain regardless of the increases in female wages.

Comparable worth theory also fails to consider the supply and demand factor of employee availability. If there is a shortage of workers, pay may have to be increased (regardless of actual job skill) just to draw workers to the job.

WHAT DO YOU THINK?

1. Are women really discriminated against in the workplace?
2. How does this discrimination occur?
3. Can one really compare jobs as diverse as librarian and fire fighter?
4. If women earn really high wages, will men further shirk their family responsibilities?
5. What would be the inflationary effect of comparable worth legislation?
6. Are there other ways that the pay differential could be reduced?

tion, more training, higher percentages of women in historically male-dominated occupations, and more women in managerial positions all should help reduce the pay differential in the long run. Perhaps most important of all is the sheer magnitude of women now in the work force (Table 9-1). As these numbers grow, so will women's power and with power comes the ability to bring about change.

Pay Differentials between Men and Women

TABLE 9-4
WOMEN'S EARNINGS AS A PERCENTAGE OF MEN'S EARNINGS BROKEN DOWN ACCORDING TO AGE

AGE	WOMEN'S EARNINGS AS A PERCENTAGE OF MEN'S
25–29	75.8%
30–34	63.6
35–39	60.8
40–44	55.3
45–49	53.5
50–54	51.6
55–59	49.8
60–64	48.6

Source: U.S. Bureau of Census January, 1993.

One very positive change is already occurring. If the pay differential is broken down according to age, as in Table 9-4, some significant developments emerge. Note that women in the youngest age group (25–29) earn considerably more compared to men than the overall average for women. It appears that the efforts to achieve equal pay for women are beginning to pay off in starting wages for women. If these starting wage gains persist, we can expect the overall pay differential between men and women to diminish with time.

Another positive change has occurred in the female-male unemployment differential. Females have historically suffered higher unemployment rates than males. This obviously contributes to lower overall earnings for women and thus to the pay differential. The unemployment gap between men and women started to narrow in 1978 and actually reversed for the first time in 1982. As of January 1992, the unemployment rate was 6.6 percent for women and 7.5 percent for men (U.S. Department of Labor March 1992, 59).

Another positive change is the rising number of wives who actually earn more than their husbands. Between the mid-1960s and the mid-1980s, the percentage of wives earning more than their husbands increased from 3 percent to 20 percent (Houston 1986).

WORK AVAILABILITY: A DOUBLE-EDGED SWORD FOR MARRIED WOMEN

Increasing work availability for women has also meant increasing independence. Not only does this independence mean increased freedom within marriage, but it can also mean increased freedom from marriage. There is little doubt that the working woman's ability to support herself has freed her to seek new roles. Part of the reason for the later median age of first marriage for both men and women may well be the greater work opportunities available to women. In addition, greater work availability allows a woman to escape from an unsatisfying marriage.

A working woman is more likely to postpone marriage because she is able to support herself. Although this seems to suggest employment as an alternative to marriage, overall marriage rates are still high, although declining somewhat since 1987.

The 1987 marriage rate of 10.2 marriages per 1000 population dropped to 9.4 per thousand in 1991 (National Center for Health Statistics, March 12, 1992).

The average age of marriage for women has risen from 20.8 in 1970 to 23.9. For men, the average age of marriage has increased from 23.2 in 1970 to 26.1 (U.S. Bureau of the Census, May 1991, 1).

In the past a woman's inability to support herself trapped her in marriage. She had to have a husband to survive. But with wider economic opportunities, this is no longer the case. Now a woman alone can survive financially even when she has children (although often her financial position is very marginal).

Not only did a woman in the past have fewer economic alternatives than her husband, but she also had to derive her status from his success. "Who are you?" "I'm the wife of a doctor." Work availability for women, then, frees women to have their own identity. Thus one edge of the work availability sword is the woman's increased economic and psychological independence from marriage.

A woman's increased independence sometimes leads to the demise of a marriage (divorce). William Johnson and Jonathan Skinner (1986) investigated this connection but concluded that the woman's participation in the work force had little direct effect on a subsequent divorce. What they did find was that women who anticipated the end of their marriages were apt to seek paying work or increase their work hours in preparation for the divorce. Julia Heath tracked 2742 women for fifteen years and found that participation in the work force did not relate to subsequent divorces. She did find that the number of hours worked correlated with divorce (1988, 16): the more hours worked per week, the higher the divorce rate.

The other edge of the sword is that work outside the home can improve and enhance a woman's family life. Her earnings can increase the family's standard of living and alleviate the family's monetary restraints. For example, when Kimberly goes to work, she reduces the pressure on Rich. This should help him feel happier and more satisfied with his family life. The family can take longer vacations together, afford better housing in a nicer neighborhood, and improve the children's education. Thus the wife's working can contribute greatly toward the family's well-being and the permanence of the marriage.

There are numerous other advantages for a wife who works outside the home in addition to the direct economic advantages of having another wage earner in the family. The working wife may derive great personal satisfaction from her work just as many men do. By interacting with other adults outside her family, she may feel more stimulated and fulfilled, especially if she has small children at home. Her self-esteem may increase with the knowledge that she is a more equal partner in the marriage.

How the increase in independence will affect a woman who enters the work force is hard to predict. Each individual will react differently. The point is that this increased independence is now a fact of life. It will enhance and improve family life for many women. It may also postpone or effectively end the marriages of some women.

THE WORKING WIFE'S ECONOMIC CONTRIBUTION TO THE FAMILY

Kimberly Decides to Go Back to Work

Rich manages to keep the family afloat financially until their second child is two and one-half years old. Kimberly and Rich realize that they simply can't live comfortably on his earnings alone. Kimberly has heard that a

Sickness and death may seem like far-fetched consequences of female employment. Nevertheless, considering that women traditionally made nurturing and family their principal concern, the loss or diminution of these services might lead to poorer health among family members. As they opt for the working world, women are exposing themselves to job tensions, commuting accidents, and occupational hazards; consequently, their mortality may rise. Given the overwork and strain that often occur in households with two full-time earners plus children, it seems possible that less attention might be given to the proper diet and rest. Parents cannot afford to take the time to relax or be ill, so their physical health may deteriorate. Two-job couples may consequently have shorter life spans.

On the other hand, the higher incomes of families with employed wives may provide the wherewithal for an adequate diet and preventive medical care. Husbands who are freed from the omnipresent concern of supporting their families may enjoy lower blood pressure and fewer heart attacks. Husbands may be able to turn down overtime or leave a job that is harmful to their long-term health. These benefits from women's rising labor force participation might lengthen the average life span, particularly among men.

If increases in female employment do affect longevity and the incidence of disease, however, the ramifications are enormous. The frequency and length of widowhood would be lessened. Fewer retired people might be unmarried. Pension systems and health care services would be affected. If the strains experienced by two-earner families are reflected in the incidence of sickness and death, the importance of flexible and part-time employment becomes self-evident. Clearly, this is a topic that merits attention.

Rena Repetti and her colleagues (1989) summarize the limited available evidence:

It [the evidence to date] provides no support for overall negative effects of employment on women's health, with a few research results indicating beneficial effects. However, this general conclusion might not apply to all subgroups of women. Employment may have beneficial or harmful effects on a woman's physical and mental health depending on her marital status, her husband's contribution to home labor, her parental status, her attitude toward employment, and characteristics of her job. (1396)

Our speculation at this point is that the long-run effect of women's working may be to equalize the life span, lengthening men's lives but shortening women's. A shorter life span for women would be less likely, however, to the extent that both sexes reject the aggressive, competitive model of employment.

local company is expanding and needs new employees. She applies for a job, gets it, and suddenly finds herself a full-time working mother. Although her income is relatively small compared with Rich's, she believes her $1200 per month will not only get them out of debt but will also allow them to purchase a few luxuries they have had to forgo. She and Rich hope it will also enable them to save money toward a down payment on a house.

Kimberly is not unusual in returning to work. Families in which the husband and wife both work are now a major and growing segment of American society.

In almost 70 percent of husband-wife families, the wife works outside the home. Two-thirds of these women work full-time (Jacobs, Shipp, and Brown 1989, 18).

Unfortunately, Rich and Kimberly learn that her $1200 does not raise the family income by that amount. A number of increased costs are associated with Kimberly's return to work. Before Kimberly can go to work, arrangements must be made for child care. There are several options. Mrs. Smith, an older mother down the street, also needs some extra money and, for $10 a day, will keep both children at her house during Kimberly's working hours. Rich's mother is willing to keep them one day a week for free. A public day-care center near Kimberly's workplace will care for the children for $45–$75 a week. The center's charges are based on the family's income, so the weekly costs vary from family to family. Rich and Kimberly decide to leave the children with Mrs. Smith four days a week ($40 a week) and with Rich's mother for the remaining day (free). This way the children will be with people they know and will be staying in their own neighborhood as well. If this arrangement doesn't work out, Rich and Kimberly can put them in the day-care center. Thus the family's monthly child-care costs are $160. This leaves $1040 from Kimberly's paycheck.

Transportation must also be considered. A bus goes past Kimberly's workplace, but the route is circuitous and requires her to leave the house half an hour earlier than she would have to leave if she drove. Kimberly's going to work raises the value of time as a factor of production in household activities (Jacobs, Shipp, and Brown 1989, 15). Suddenly, time for family work and activities has become very short. Riding the bus both ways will take an hour a day and cost $22 a month ($1 a day). In addition, if Kimberly takes the bus, Rich will have to take the children to the sitter's each morning. Kimberly is unable to find a car pool or ride to work with a colleague so they decide that buying an older economy car is probably the best time-saving solution. With the car Kimberly can help deliver and pick up the children and can be more efficient generally. They borrow $2000 for twenty-four months at 12 percent interest and buy a used car from a friend. The car is in good shape and requires only a new set of tires. There are additional insurance costs, however. Kimberly and Rich purchase only liability coverage, thinking that because the car is old, it isn't worth the cost of collision coverage. The total monthly cost for the car is $158, broken down as follows:

Payment	$103*
Insurance	20
Gas and maintenance	35
Total	$158 per month

Subtracting $158 more from Kimberly's monthly paycheck leaves $882.

*Discount interest amounts to $480 for two years for a total debt of $2480. Divide by 24 months to get the monthly payment of $103.

Taxes and Social Security are also deducted from Kimberly's paycheck. She takes no deductions for the children and finds that another large bite has been taken from her paycheck. She and Rich will receive a tax refund at the end of the year because of child-care costs and other deductions, but overall the taxes and Social Security costs average about $175 per month. Thus Kimberly's monthly check shrinks further, to $707.

There are other miscellaneous costs associated with Kimberly's going to work. She doesn't have as much time for food preparation and household work. She uses more partially prepared foods such as frozen dinners that tend to be more expensive. She sends more clothing to the laundry, and she has to buy some new clothes to wear to work. These costs add up to about $100 per month.

The bottom line is that Kimberly's $1200 a month pay adds only about $607 to the family income. This amounts to about 50 percent of her gross pay. In general, the working mother must spend between 25 and 50 percent of her income in order to work, depending on the age of her children, type of work, and other factors unique to her situation (Hanson and Ooms 1991). Because women tend to hold lower-paying jobs, the actual amount of money they contribute to the family tends to be small.

> Wives working part-time increase the family income on the average of 29 percent. Full-time working wives increase family income by about 70 percent in low-income families but only about 38 percent in middle-income families (Jacobs, Shipp, and Brown 1989, 18; Hanson and Ooms 1991, 632).

In the past, the working wife was the exception, and her work was often viewed as a family insurance policy, a buffer against hard times, or a source of "play" money—money used for recreation, luxuries, and extras. Today a working wife's income has become necessary to family survival. This means that many families no longer have an economic buffer against hard times. They need both incomes to survive; if either is lost, family finances become precarious if not impossible.

HOUSEHOLD ACTIVITIES AND SUPERMOTHERS

It seems strange to hear a mother of two small children answer the question "What do you do?" with "Oh, nothing, I'm just a housewife." Obviously, a mother with two small children does a great deal of work for her family inside the home. She certainly doesn't "do nothing." Therefore when she takes a job outside the home, something has to change inside the home. Mothers with children at home average about thirty-six hours a week working in the home. Generally, their time is divided into three major household activities: (1) meal preparation and cleanup, about 30 percent; (2) care of family members, 15 to 25 percent; and (3) clothing and regular house care, 15 percent.

What happens to all of this work when mother takes an outside job? Essentially nothing. It must still be done and mother still does it. She simply cuts down the amount of time she gives to each task and donates much of her leisure time (weekends and evenings) to household tasks.

The "just housewife" role usually includes more than homemaking activities although the other aspects seldom are discussed. It is the "just housewives" who often do much of the important volunteer work for society. They attend the PTA meetings, organize the church rummage sale, help a neighbor, and raise extra money for the children's school by conducting a paper drive. They serve on community committees, help run the local Red Cross, and donate time to political campaigns (Hayghe 1991).

As more and more wives enter the formal work force, our society may experience a loss in the informal work force of volunteers. Community service may diminish because the working wife simply won't have time, or if she makes the time as many do, the energy drain may be too great. Another effect is that fewer and fewer adults are left in residential neighborhoods during working hours. Some mothers who do not work are becoming *neighborhood mothers*. They serve as temporary mothers for children of working parents until a parent returns home. These neighborhood mothers do not run day-care centers in their homes; they are simply mothers to whom school-age children can come if there is a problem while their parents are working.

If the real revolution in the American family has been the entrance of the wife and mother into the labor force, one would expect that another part of the revolution would be the necessity of the husbands helping with the family tasks, childrearing and housework. In fact, husbands are likely to agree that they should do more in the households when their wives work, but they rarely live up to their professed beliefs or their wives' expectations.

Often men report doing a large share of the housework and child care, but when it comes down to actually doing the work, they rarely take as much responsibility for it as their wives do. A husband, for example, may take out the garbage (2 minutes) while the wife does the dishes (15 minutes). Clearly, men have done little to offset the household pressures created by women's increased participation in the labor force.

Husbands actually spend between four and six hours per week doing housework, which represents about 14 percent of the total amount of time that is spent in housework (Berardo, Shehan, and Leslie 1987, 388). Benin and Agostinelli (1988) report that employed women do about twice as much housework as their husbands. Broman (1988; 1991) reports that black American working wives are twice as likely to feel overburdened than are their husbands.

Arlie Hochschild analyzed past family time distribution studies and discovered that married working women worked (paid work plus housework and child care) roughly fifteen hours longer a week than men. Over a year, they worked an extra month of twenty-four-hour days (1989, 3).

Distribution of family work (housework and child care combined) is a critical issue for most dual-worker families, yet husbands' low level of household labor compared with their wives' is not necessarily negatively perceived. Studies (Berk-Fenstermaker 1985; Suitor 1991) have found that both husbands and wives feel the division of labor is fair even when the wife bears most of the household responsibilities. Apparently, then, the perception by the spouses of the willingness of the other to shoulder responsibility for family work is more important to marital satisfaction than the actual amount of work accomplished (Lewis and Cooper 1988, 146). Thus the expressed change in men's attitudes toward more willingness to do family work is important to marital happiness even if it is not acted on.

Household Activities and Supermothers

Although husbands don't appreciably increase their share of household work when their wives go to work, overall they are sharing more household work than they have in the past, whether their wives work or not. This change stems from shifting attitudes about sex roles and the increased emphasis on egalitarian marriage in the United States.

One restraint on husbands sharing family work is their continued earning advantage over women. Because the husband can usually contribute more economically to the family than can his working wife, he may feel that this makes up in part for his share of family work. "I contribute 25 percent more economically, hence I can reduce my family work proportionately and thereby maintain an equalitarian relationship at home." Hochschild found, however, that the amount of money men earn above what their wives earn does not relate to the amount of family work the man does. In her sample, men who earned less than their wives uniformly did little or no family work. She hypothesized that since the men could not demonstrate superiority through higher earnings, making the wife do all of the family work was a way of maintaining power (1989, 221).

For many wives one result of going to work is overload and strain. They end up doing two jobs, one outside the home and one inside. Their leisure time is greatly reduced. The quality of their household work declines. Time becomes their most precious commodity, especially spending more time with the family (Blankenhorn et al. 1990, 88).

It is this overload of the working wife, especially the working mother, that families most resent. In general, working wives and mothers indicate they do not have enough time for themselves. It is interesting to note that fewer working fathers feel the same way. Both working parents mention lack of time with family and children and long hours on the job as the greatest strains placed on the family when both work. Constant complaints are made about lack of time for recreation, picnics, vacation trips, children, love making, and plain old "doing nothing."

Despite the strains reported by working wives, the triple roles of spouse, mother, and employee are linked with good health:

> Of the factors we examined, employment was by far the strongest and most consistent tie to women's good health. Marriage ranked second and parenthood third. The combination of no job and no spouse was linked strongly to poor health, especially for women aged 25 to 34. (Verbrugge and Madans 1986).

These findings may reflect the fact that unhealthy women stay out of the work force or that working outside the home is healthy. These data conflict with the ideas suggested in Inset 9-1.

The failure of husbands and fathers to react positively to their working wives' overload may be one of the major factors in America's increased divorce rate. Although the media try to portray the working supermom as the ideal, the fact is that such a role is almost impossible for anyone. The leisure gap leads women to feel resentful and put upon, which indeed they are if their husbands do not give them family help. Women try to cope with the unfair burden in a number of ways. They may try to change their husband's behavior directly so that he does more family work. Setting up work schedules and making lists to organize family time is one approach. Wives may also try indirectly to convince their husband to do more work. Or they may simply give up on their husband and try to be supermoms. When this proves impossible, they may cut back on housework and child care or try to cut back at their job (Hochschild 1989, 193–99).

Although we are discussing the stresses and strains on the women, such stresses are also felt by the men regardless of whether they share the family work burden. If a husband shares the family work, then he too may feel over-burdened. If he does not share, he may feel guilty about the wife's unfair work load. He will certainly feel her resentment.

Hochschild rightly points out that the revolution of the woman entering the paid work force has not been accompanied by a revolution in how family work is handled, either by her spouse or by society at large. And this gap between what happens to women in the workplace and in the home is causing family problems. She suggests as do others that the United States needs a Marshall Plan for the family:

> An honestly profamily policy in the United States would give tax breaks to companies that encourage "family leave" for new fathers, job sharing, part-time work, and flex time. Through comparable worth, it would pull up wages in "women's" jobs. It would go beyond half-time work (which makes it sound like a person is doing "half" of something else that is "whole") by instituting lower-hour, more flexible "family phases" for all regular jobs filled by parents with young children.
>
> The government would give tax credits to developers who build affordable housing near places of work and shopping centers, with nearby meal-preparation facilities. It would create warm and creative daycare centers. If the best daycare comes from elderly neighbors, students, grandparents, they would be paid to care for children. Traveling vans for daycare enrichment could roam the neighborhoods as the ice-cream man used to do.
>
> In these ways the American government could create a "safer environment" for the two-job family. It could draw men into children's lives, reduce the number of children in "self-care," and make marriages happier. These reforms could even improve the lives of children whose parents divorce, because research has shown that the more involved fathers are with their children before divorce, the more involved they are with them afterwards. If the government encouraged corporations to consider the long-range interests of workers AND their families, they would save on long-term costs due to higher absenteeism, turnover etc. (1989, 268–69)

Kimberly Seeks Part-Time Work

Kimberly works for seven months at her new full-time job. Although her salary enables them to pay off their debts, she finds that she is increasingly fatigued. She and Rich never seem to have fun together any more. Their sex life seems nonexistent. If she does find some free time, all she wants to do is sleep. The house looks unkempt. She hasn't had fun cooking a meal in months. She feels guilty about the little time she is able to spend with the children. She is grumpy and unhappy much of the time. Now that they are out of debt, Kimberly decides to see if she can find a part-time job. She finally does and, with a sigh of relief, quits her full-time job.

PART-TIME WORK

The conventional wisdom that all working mothers would like to reduce their work loads was refuted in a large study done by *Family Circle* magazine. Of the

TABLE 9-5

AGE AND SEX COMPOSITION OF THE PART-TIME LABOR FORCE AND RATE OF EMPLOYMENT, 1989

AGE AND SEX	PERCENTAGE OF THE TOTAL WORKING POPULATION	PERCENTAGE PART-TIME WORKING
All persons aged 16–21	10.3%	46.3%
Women aged 22 to 44	27.7	21.9
Women aged 45 to 64	11.6	23.8
Men aged 22 to 64	47.8	6.7
All persons age 65 and over	2.6	52.4
Total	100.00	18.1

Source: U.S. Bureau of the Census March 1991.

wives and mothers who held full-time jobs, 55 percent indicated that they would not want to quit to work at home (Jacoby 1987, 84).

> "I'd like my life to be less hectic," said a Chicago hospital administrator who is the mother of an 8-month girl, "but my work is so satisfying to me that I wouldn't give it up under any circumstances. We do need the money, but that isn't my main reason for working. I really love my job."

Women and young people hold most part-time jobs. Table 9-5 compares the percentage of men and women of various ages who work part-time. Overall about 18 percent of the work force are employed part-time (U.S. Department of Labor March 1991, 11).

Approximately half of all women who work part-time give "taking care of the home" as their reason for preferring part-time work. The creation of more and better part-time jobs for mothers with young children would help alleviate the overload experienced by full-time working mothers. Unfortunately, part-time work reduces the economic contribution to the family, not only because fewer hours are worked but also because pay standards are lower. On an hourly basis, part-time work generally pays only 75 percent as much as full-time work.

Those who seek part-time employment are usually assumed to be intermittent workers who are not committed to a long-term career. Therefore part-time work seldom offers fringe benefits, job protection, or opportunities to advance. Lack of fringe benefits, especially health insurance, combined with low pay in part-time jobs may keep some people on welfare. Welfare recipients are eligible for free medical care under the Medicaid program, and in some cases welfare payments may provide as much income as can be earned in a part-time job.

Ninety percent of part-time employment occurs in the service industries, the so-called pink-collar occupations where women predominate. Very few jobs are available for part-time managers, accountants, butchers, and machinists. At the same time, four out of five waitresses work less than full-time. Department store saleswork is becoming increasingly part-time, and offices are turning more to temporary help. Beauty shops have always used part-time people. In

Part-Time Work

the health field, where women make up 75 percent of the work force (except in upper-level positions), shift work and part-time arrangements are commonplace. Schools are turning increasingly to part-time substitute teachers to save money. In contrast, part-time and temporary work are seldom found in the industries dominated by men.

As a result of these patterns, most mothers will be downwardly mobile at work rather than upwardly mobile like their husbands. More and better jobs are open to women before they have families because they can work full-time. After a woman has a family, the hours when she is available for work often determine the job she finds. In the face of demands on her time, the young mother is likely to find that the scheduling of her job is the most important single consideration. Her immediate job choice is dictated in large measure by the time constraints imposed in the short run, and this in turn affects her subsequent career development. As more and more mothers enter the work force and prove to be good workers, however, part-time jobs may take on more of the advantages that come with full-time work.

An employer who hires two part-time people to do one full-time job encounters certain problems. Social Security contributions, for example, will be higher for two workers than for one full-time worker even when the rates of pay are identical. Generally, record keeping and paperwork are increased. As the advantages of part-time work are recognized, however, such inequities may be removed.

Kimberly's New Part-Time Job

Kimberly's new half-time job pays her $500 per month. With her mother-in-law's help, she is able to do away with child-care costs. Transportation costs remain the same, $100 per month, leaving her $400. Taxes and Social Security are reduced to $70 per month, leaving $330. Miscellaneous costs are also reduced to $50 per month. In the end Kimberly contributes $280 extra dollars to the family compared with the $607 she contributed when she worked full-time. This amount is just enough to keep them out of debt. The strain on Kimberly and hence the family is much less, however.

Kimberly moved from full-time employment to part-time and experienced a reduction in family conflict. However, women moving into part-time work from nonemployment (full-time housewife role) may actually experience more conflict than if they had moved into full-time employment. Perhaps this is because they bring such a small amount of extra money into the family. "It's not worth having you work. We lose more than we gain," suggest some husbands. When the wife is contemplating taking a full-time job, the couple are more apt to make a considered decision than the couple where the wife takes on a part-time job. Often a wife just slides into part-time work because it has become available. Little thought is given to the family ramifications of her part-time work.

MARITAL SATISFACTION IN THE TWO-EARNER FAMILY

As with so many areas we have discussed, the question of marital satisfaction in a two-earner family is double-edged. The family may gain satisfaction through the wife's economic contribution; the family may lose satisfaction because she is no longer able to supply all of the caring and services of a full-time wife and mother. Economic strain may be reduced when she works; psychological and physical strain may be increased.

The research evidence on marital satisfaction when the wife works is mixed. After reviewing many studies, researchers have concluded that wives who work from choice rather than economic necessity, those whose husbands view their employment favorably, and those who work part-time are happier with their marriages than full-time housewives (Voydanoff 1987, 47; Scarr, Phillips, and McCartney 1989). Smith (1985) reviewed twenty-seven research studies and, although the studies again showed mixed results, concluded that whether a wife works has little relation to marital satisfaction. How couples cope with the wife working seems to be individually determined by each couple. Once a couple works out the new routines and relationship changes, marital satisfaction seems to return to its normal level.

Although we have spoken mainly of the working wife's economic contribution to the family, it is clear that she may also receive psychological dividends from her participation in the work world. Work may allow her to use some of her skills that are unused in the homemaker role. She will meet and interact with a wider variety of adults. She will gain more power in relation to her husband by contributing economically to the family. Her feelings of integrity, self-respect, competence, self-determination, and accomplishment may increase if she enjoys her work and has successfully solved the problems of working and caring for her family.

The evidence of husbands' marital satisfaction when their wives work is also mixed but tends to indicate that they are less satisfied than the wives (Mehren 1986; Staines, Patrick, and Fudge 1986). It seems that some husbands accept their wives' work grudgingly and that some men may have more trouble than women in adapting to nonstereotypical roles. In going to work, a woman is frequently expanding into a new role, one that is higher in status than that of homemaker, while a husband who assumes homemaking functions is adopting a role of lower status, which may strain not only his sense of status and identity but his feeling of competence as well. Furthermore, a busy wife may not be able to provide the same level of physical and emotional support that a full-time homemaker can, so a husband may well come to feel he is losing out on all fronts.

On the other hand, a second income can provide the husband additional freedom. He can cut down on moonlighting or overtime work. He may be able to take a temporary reduction in pay to enter a new career or job he finds more satisfying. Increased free time may allow more family enjoyment and leisure time pursuits.

Because of the importance of expectations in human relations, what one thinks or expects about something is often as important as what actually happens. Research on marital quality in families where the wife works indicates that happiness with the relationship is more closely related to the congruence between the role expectations of one spouse and the role performance of the other spouse than to any particular pattern of roles. It is not simply a matter of whether a woman's working has an impact on marital adjustment but rather the extent to which that behavior violates her own and her family's role expectations. If a woman expects to be a housewife, if her husband expects her to stay home, and if significant others in her environment (parents, in-laws, children, and so forth) have negative attitudes about her working, the chances are great that both her satisfaction and her family's will drop when she goes to work.

On the other hand, as the working wife becomes the norm for our society, negative attitudes will diminish. Children of working mothers tend to be more supportive of the idea of wives working (Corder and Stephan, 1984). Dual-career families tend to produce children whose attitudes are more egalitarian and who prefer dual-career families themselves (Stephan and Corder, 1985, 928). This being the case, the incidence of families in which the wife works should continue to increase as should the level of marital satisfaction in such families.

Lower-class families seem to have more adjustment problems than middle-class families when the wife goes to work. One possible explanation for this is that the lower-class woman usually must work in order for the family to survive. Her working is thus a direct statement about her husband's inability to provide for his family and may be perceived by him as a threat to his status. Middle-class women are more likely to be in the labor force voluntarily. One must be careful interpreting social-class differences in marital satisfaction, however, because a variety of influences are involved. For example, differing educational levels lead to differing attitudes about a mother's entering the work world.

Traditionally, only a small minority of mothers with children under age six have been employed. Two factors have worked to keep mothers of young children out of the labor force:

1. The logistics of caring for the children are often unsolvable.
2. There has been a long-standing belief that a mother belongs with her children, especially when they are young. Because of earlier studies of the effects of prolonged separation of children from caring parents (orphanage and foster home placements, war orphans, and so forth), many people believe that the mother's absence during the early years will harm the child (see p. 236).

Yet effective child care by someone other than the true biological mother does not necessarily lead to severe problems in children. Actual effects of substitute child care are just as difficult to uncover as are the effects of natural parenting. The effects depend on (1) the quality of the substitute care, (2) the

TABLE 9-6
CHILD-CARE ARRANGEMENT FOR PRESCHOOL CHILDREN

PROVIDER	PERCENTAGE OF CHILDREN CARED FOR
Father	11.3%
Siblings	1.1
Other relative	28.8
Other person	22.3
Child-care center	18.1
Mother cares for child at work	3.0
Child cares for self	1.9
Other	13.5

Source: Veum and Gleason 1991.

characteristics of the child, (3) the mother's reasons for working and the quality and quantity of the time both parents spend with the child, and (4) the general social acceptance of substitute child care.

The quality of substitute child care can be excellent. It can provide for the child both physically and psychologically. A loving, caring baby-sitter is often an important and happy influence on a child. It would seem, however, that other family members would be more likely than strangers to give the child adequate love and attention. Thus substitute child care cannot be wholly praised or condemned but must be judged on its specific merits. It can be good or bad for a child, just as the child's biological parents can be.

About 37 percent of working mothers arrange for their preschoolers to be cared for in someone else's home. Only about 18 percent leave them in organized day-care centers. Grandparents and other relatives care for about 29 percent of the preschoolers whose parents work (see Table 9-6).

After years of debate, Congress finally passed child-care legislation in 1990. Although very modest, it is a start toward encouraging more support of the working family. The legislation allocates some monies to help states expand child-care services and establishes minimal standards to be met by day-care providers. The statute also includes a small increase in the tax credits that poverty-level workers can obtain for child care.

Individual children will react differently to the partial loss of their mother and the substitution of another type of care. Their reaction may be positive or negative. A hyperactive, disruptive child may experience much negative feedback in a large day-care center, but may thrive with an attentive baby-sitter.

If the mother is unhappy and frustrated as a homemaker and prefers the work world, her child will probably be better off with a substitute. It is perhaps not the quantity of time parents spend with their children but the quality of time that counts. A working mother may spend less time with her children, but if she makes it high-quality time, her relationship with her children may

Marital Satisfaction
in the Two-Earner Family

329

be improved. Note, however, that a generous quantity of time must be spent with children if there is to be quality. Note also that the overworked mother trying to do both her job and family work may lack the energy to offer her children quality time.

Kimberly Tries to Improve the Time She Spends with Her Children

When she was a full-time homemaker, Kimberly found that her two children were always underfoot. She never seemed to have a minute's peace. They called "Mommy, Mommy, Mommy" so often that she almost never paid attention to them. In fact, sometimes when she heard the children, she'd deliberately hide to escape their constant pressure. Now that she works part time, she finds she enjoys spending time with the children. She looks forward to the weekends so she can do projects with them and give them her undivided attention.

Daughters of working mothers tend to view women as more competent than daughters of nonworking mothers and view female employment as less threatening to marriage. These findings suggest that the working mothers provided adequate nurturance even though they worked. Although a working mother may shortchange her children, she may also be better able to provide for them.

WORK AND FAMILY:
SOURCES OF CONFLICT

Ideally, work and family should complement and support one another. Yet in reality these two arenas of life often conflict. The conflicts tend to differ for husbands and wives in large part because of the historical division of labor between the sexes. The work world tends to intrude on a husband's family life. If he is asked to work overtime, for example, he must usually do so to keep his job, regardless of what plans he may have made with his family. The family is more likely to intrude into a wife's work world. For example, if a child is sick, it has traditionally been her responsibility to tend the child. A husband's family usually must bend to his work demands; a wife's work must usually bend to her family's demands. Sanctions against a man for poor performance have traditionally been greater on the job, while sanctions against a woman for poor performance have traditionally been stronger in the family.

As more and more wives and mothers enter the labor force, however, it becomes imperative that the conflicts between job and family be reduced. The work world and the family realm must be balanced (see Hansen [1991] for a

listing of literature and resources about balancing family and work responsibilities). The work world cannot ask men and women to forgo having families. With increasing numbers of two-earner families, parenthood becomes one of the costs of doing business. Family members must work to support themselves and keep society functioning. But to enable work to proceed efficiently, employers must recognize and accept family concerns.

Time becomes a highly valuable commodity to both partners in the dual-worker family, especially to the wife, and particularly if there are children. Since the husband in the dual-worker family usually does not shoulder his fair share of household tasks (Lewis, Izraeli, and Hootsmans 1992; Benin and Agostinelli 1988; Broman 1991), it is clear that time is more of a constraint to the working woman. This is also true of the single-parent family. Returning home from a long day's work to prepare dinner, houseclean, and perform other family chores is hardly an inviting prospect. If there are children, how does one find any time for them, much less summon up enough energy to make it quality time? The increased pressure on home time due to long hours at work and inflexible work schedules means that much less of a couple's time can be devoted to their children, to one another, recreation, play, and/or self-renewal activities.

The dual-worker family with children perhaps suffers the most from lack of time, especially parenting time. Parents are working more and spending less time with their children. According to one estimate, the amount of total contact parents have with their children has dropped 40 percent since 1965 (Mattox 1990, 2). Surveys of American parents find they believe that parents spending less time with their families is the most important cause of the fragmentation and stress in contemporary family life (Hewlett 1990, 216; Mellman and Lazarus Inc. 1989).

When both husband and wife work, they will not necessarily have less time together, but the time they have together will be consumed by daily necessities. Too often the important time for self-improvement and for intimate caring and working on the relationship is lost. When a couple works exactly the same hours, they do not lose "togetherness" time. But if one mate starts work an hour earlier than the other ("off-scheduling"), then the couple loses an hour of togetherness time.

We should also note that time at home is not necessarily family time. A spouse may well bring work home, either concretely or psychologically. The dawn of computers, fax machines, and cellular phones has made it possible to work anywhere, anytime. This can be beneficial at times and harmful at other times. A career-oriented spouse is much more apt to bring work home than is a family-oriented partner. A career-oriented partner usually puts his or her career ahead of the family. This can cause family resentments because of the perceived lack of commitment to the family. "You're married to your job" is a criticism often made by other family members.

Strain on the job can cause difficulty at home or vice versa. "Don't ask your father to borrow the car the minute he gets home. Give him time to relax." This is an example of work strain causing family difficulty. Obviously, the stresses and strains of the work world take their toll emotionally on the working family member and will be felt at home as well.

Less often discussed is the effect of family strain on the job. "Jack is not very efficient today. He and his wife are probably fighting again." Many companies considering a person for promotion evaluate both job performance and family life. One might object to this as an invasion of privacy, but the job performance of a worker undergoing severe family strain (illness, divorce, and the like) will be hampered.

On the other hand, an enlightened employer will recognize that employees have legitimate family needs and concerns and will try to arrange work accordingly. The parent concerned about who is caring for the children, who will meet with a child's teacher, or who will stay home with a sick child may also falter at work. An employer who offers help with such family concerns improves the productivity of the work force.

Specific patterns of role behavior on the job and in the family may be incompatible. For example, the male managerial role tends to emphasize self-reliance, emotional stability, aggressiveness, and objectivity. Family members, on the other hand, may expect that person to be warm, nurturing, emotional, and vulnerable in interactions with them. A person must be able to adjust her or his behavior to comply with the expectations of different roles. To the degree she or he cannot adjust, conflict is likely to ensue.

Such role disparities are especially difficult to cope with when the home-oriented spouse does not share in the other spouse's work world. In the traditional husband working–wife homemaking family, failure to know and understand each other's domains causes conflict. In fact, in extreme cases the husband lives in a work world totally unknown to his wife and has little understanding or empathy for her problems with the family. A husband and

Role conflict and ambiguity are exaggerated when both partners work. Am I first a worker and then a family member or vice versa? Susan Lewis and Cary Cooper (1988) review many of the studies bearing on such questions. For example, many working mothers suffer from feelings of guilt about their children and try to overcompensate by spending every bit of spare time with their children, but such efforts contribute even more to their overload problems. Women have these feelings regardless of the type of occupation they are in whereas men tend to have such feelings only when they are in highly demanding jobs. There is a great deal of conflict between husbands and wives over their perceptions of spouse and parent roles. Often the wife feels that her husband is not fulfilling his family duties. Some husbands feel that they are not fulfilling their roles or that they are less than successful if their wife must work.

Overload is another problem faced by members of dual-worker families, especially the working mother. Because working women still perform most of the family work, they are indeed often overloaded. Whether this will be a serious problem seems to be determined not by the objective work load but rather by the perception that it is "too much" and by the perceived willingness of the spouse to share the domestic role.

Often overlooked is the employment overload. Many workers, especially those who are self-employed, have management positions, or have voluntarily taken on extra shifts or jobs work far longer than forty hours per week. Approximately 30 percent of both men and women now work on weekends (Presser 1989). The idea of Sunday as a day off was laid to rest years ago in America. Obviously, the longer the work day/week, the less time one can devote to family work.

Time magazine (April 24, 1989) discussed how many of the so-called time-saving technological marvels actually take up time. For example, the telephone paging service prevents escape from those who wish to contact you. Another example is the fax machine, which can send documents to a worker anywhere, anytime. The home computer means that work done at home can be interfaced with the office at any time.

Business also adds to family stress by forgetting to take their workers' family lives into consideration. A survey of many companies including 374 of the top 1300 *Fortune* corporations found a large gap between what the businesses stated they favored for family-oriented personnel practices and what they had actually enacted (Catalyst reported in Voydanoff 1987, 107). For example:

	FAVOR	HAVE
Flexible work hours	73%	37%
Flexible benefit plans	62	8
Monetary support for child care	54	19

Unfortunately, work and family responsibilities still too often clash, and this clash leads to stress and strain both within the family and in the workplace.

perhaps father is legally in the family but for all practical purposes is not a functioning member of the family other than supplying economic support. In general, however, the traditional family has less conflict between work and family because one spouse assumes most of the family responsibility while the other spouse assumes most of the work responsibility.

Work and Family:
Sources of Conflict

If a dual-worker family is really a two-person–single-career family, work-family conflicts will be reduced. Such a family shares the same career and works together in the work world. Obviously, the husband who comes home tired and upset after a day at the office will be better understood and supported by a wife who comes home from the same office, and vice versa. This pattern is unusual, however.

Felice Schwartz (1992, 203–4) offers a series of suggestions to companies that are trying to face up to the reality of the two-earner family and the importance of considering the family life of employees:

■ Accept that you (the business) must be flexible and must provide family supports.
■ Provide the full range of benefits to women on maternity leave and to those who return part-time after the leave.
■ Let women who have babies return when they're ready. Ready means when they feel well psychologically and physically, when they're getting enough sleep to function effectively, when they've bonded with their babies, and when they have located child care, tested it, and are satisfied with it.
■ Let women return from maternity leave on less than full-time or other alternative schedules—part-time, shared, telecommuting arrangements, and the like.
■ Permit new fathers to take paternal leaves, sequencing them with those of their wives.
■ Establish a policy that permits parents to cut back to half-time (at prorated pay) but remain on a promotion track.
■ Take responsibility—in partnership with parents, communities, and government—for making high-quality, affordable child care available for every child.
■ Provide opportunities for parents to work at home if possible.
■ Learn how to measure productivity instead of time in the office.

Although considering family needs may appear to be an unnecessary expense, such steps will benefit companies economically in the long run. High rates of turnover will be reduced since a new parent will not have to decide between family and work. High-performing men and especially women who want to be involved with their families will not be lost. Companies will be more desirable workplaces and thus will be able to recruit new workers more easily. Certainly, companies with such family-oriented policies will improve their public images and relations.

JOBS, OCCUPATIONS, AND CAREERS

Up to this point, we have been discussing women taking jobs in the labor market. However, a short- or even long-term job is not the same as a long-term career. Essentially, we can place work on an attitudinal continuum according to the degree of commitment (Kahn and Weiner 1973, 153):

Basic Attitude toward Work	Basic Additional Value
1. Interruption	Short-run income
2. Job	Long-term income; some work-oriented values (working to live)
3. Occupation	Exercise and mastery of gratifying skills; some satisfaction of achievement-oriented values
4. Career	Participating in an important activity; much satisfaction of work-oriented, achievement-oriented, advancement-oriented values
5. Vocation (calling)	Self-identification and self-fulfillment
6. Mission	Near fanatic or single-minded focus on achievement or advancement (living to work)

Most people in the labor force occupy one of the first three levels. A far higher percentage of men than women fall into the latter three categories, however. As attitudes about sex roles have changed, more and more career opportunities are opening to women. The dual-career family is becoming a more visible reality. A career may be denoted by (1) a long-time commitment, including a period of formal training; (2) continuity (one moves to higher and higher levels if successful); (3) mobility in order to follow career demands.

■ DUAL-CAREER FAMILIES ■

In the families of most career men, the man's career dictates much of the couple's life. Where and how the family lives depends on his career demands. These demands are met relatively easily if the wife is a homemaker or works at one of the first three levels. A dual-career family, however, may encounter conflict between the partners over career demands as well as the other kinds of problems that occur in any family when both partners work. For example, what happens when one spouse is offered an important promotion, but it entails moving to another location? Will moving harm the other partner's career? If the new location is not too far away, should one spouse commute? Should they take up two residences? What will this living arrangement do to their relationship? Each time one partner has a major career change, a series of such questions will have to be answered. When the couple strives for career equality, the answers are not easy.

The dean of a local community college is married to a high-level school administrator in that district. She is offered a new position as president of a college several hundred miles away. After much discussion, the couple decide that they should continue their own careers. They are now a "weekend family." Each spends the week at the job, and they take turns visiting each other on the weekends.

About one million couples in the United States are believed to have such commuter marriages. Of course, such a lifestyle is not suitable for families with small children. Couples that choose this lifestyle tend to be free of childrearing responsibilities, older, and married longer; they also tend to have established careers, high educational levels, high-ranking occupations, and high income levels.

Past literature on the dual-career family reported that the impact of dual-career stress is felt mostly by women. This is true not only in the woman's family life but also in her work. She takes more career risks, sacrifices more, and makes more compromises in her career ambitions in attempting to make the dual-career pattern work.

More recent studies (Guelzow, Bird, and Koball 1991; Thomas 1990; Schnittger and Bird 1990) suggest that dual-career families are coping better with the responsibilities of family and work. Guelzow et al. (1991) suggest that women highly committed to their professions are combining their marital-parental and employment roles without consequent high levels of stress. They find that role strain and stress are not significantly related to having younger children. This may suggest that these women are resolving some of the guilt and role conflict reported in previous research on women with young children who choose to work full-time. Number of children does relate to increased stress in these career women, however.

Stress is reduced if the career woman has a supportive husband who is willing to leave his job and relocate to advance his wife's career. Strain is also greatly reduced if the couple is free of childrearing responsibilities and each partner has a flexible work schedule. A flexible work schedule is especially important if the dual-career couple have young children.

Marjorie Smith, a trust officer at Chase Manhattan Bank, is up every morning at six o'clock. After making breakfast and laying out clothes for her five-year-old daughter Suzy, she leaves for work. At that point, her husband, Lee, takes over—getting Suzy dressed and walking her to school. At five o'clock, after her day at the office, Marjorie picks up Suzy at a day-care center. Once home, the Smiths continue their hectic schedule, doing the laundry, dashing through a supper of soup and sandwiches, and dividing up the other household tasks: grocery shopping by Marjorie, vacuuming by Lee. The only trouble is that the routine rarely works. "The norm is frantic phone calls and schedule changes," says Lee with a laugh.

The Smiths are one of a growing number of couples whose daily life is fraught with the hassle of keeping two careers and a family afloat. This short description of Marjorie Smith's day may help give some sense of the frenetic pace found in many dual-career families, especially those with children still living at home.

If both partners are successful in their careers, it usually means that major career decisions will have to be made periodically throughout the relationship. Each new decision may upset the balance that the couple has worked out.

SUMMARY

1. Many consider the number of women entering the work force to be the major revolution affecting the American family in this century. In the past, the woman's, and especially the mother's, place was in the home. This is no longer true. *In most families today, the woman is an active participant in the economic support of her family.*

2. Although now a permanent and large part of the American labor force, *women still earn a disproportionately lower income than their male counterparts.*

3. *Career opportunities are still narrower for women than for men.* Many steps have been taken to change these inequities. Although change is slow, there are many hopeful signs that the future work world will be as advantageous for women as for men.

4. *The working mother is often overburdened, carrying out her job as well as being the major worker in the home.* This situation occurs because husbands of working wives do not yet shoulder their fair share of family work.

5. *Increasing job availability has made women more independent than they have been in the past.* This independence has put pressure on many husbands because women now have a realistic alternative to a bad marriage—moving out and supporting their families themselves. But a woman's increasing independence can also reap rewards for her family. Her additional earnings may help the family invest and start the economy working for them, ease the pressure on the husband to be the only breadwinner, and generally lead to a more egalitarian relationship within the marriage.

6. *Unfortunately, the lower incomes often received by women blunt some of the possible advantages of working.* Due to the costs of working, including clothes, transportation, increased taxes, and child care, the woman's real economic contribution is often small and even "not worth it" at times. However, as women improve their skills and become an indispensable part of the work force, gain political power, and become more career oriented, the pay differential between male and female workers should decrease.

When Kathy talks about Mondays and Tuesdays at home, this efficient, down-to-earth business executive can sound quite lyrical:

It is a precious time. My little girl can get up whenever she wants—no need to bundle her up in a snowsuit, no need to rush off to the day-care center. We often go out to a long lazy 10 o'clock breakfast or just fool around in bed and watch *The Lady and the Tramp* on the VCR. It seems to be such a wonderful gift—two whole days of totally discretionary time. Of course, by the time Wednesday rolls around I am quite ready to get dressed up in a suit, go into the office and be with grown-ups, and Caroline is equally ready to be with playmates of her own age. But changing the balance of my life so that I have four days at home and three in the office instead of the standard 2 and

5, is quite simply the best thing I ever did.

Kathy works three days a week, sharing a middle-management job in the card division of American Express. Job sharing was not something she had in mind when she started out at American Express. But becoming a mother changed her priorities in unexpected ways:

When Caroline was born three and a half years ago, I just took the standard leave and was back at work full-time when my baby was eight weeks old. . . . I guess I just assumed that we modern women can "have it all" and should "do it all."

For a while things worked out—more or less. After a bad experience with an *au pair* girl who stayed only two months, Kathy put her daughter, Caroline, into a day-care center. Caroline was there 10 hours a day, five days a week. She seemed to do

well, but Kathy began to feel that her life was unbalanced:

If you figure in the commute, my job was consuming 55 hours a week. Many evening hours and much of the weekend seemed to be filled with household chores and errands. I felt I was on a treadmill: tired, harassed, and unhappy. I resented the fact that there was no time to enjoy my child, my husband, my family.

As Kathy was having second thoughts, she met Jean, another middle-level manager at American Express who had just had her second child and wanted to work part-time. Kathy and Jean put together a proposal and applied for a middle-management job in human resources. They got the job, and for the last two years, Jean has worked two-fifths time (at 40 percent of her former salary) and Kathy has worked three-fifths time (at 60 percent of her former salary). Both are entitled to full benefits for themselves, though not for their dependents.

Before Kathy goes home on Friday night, she leaves a file folder of pending work for Jean. When Jean comes into the office on Monday, she spends half an hour on the phone with Kathy going over these materials. The same routine is followed when Kathy takes over. The work gets done efficiently and smoothly. Kathy and Jean's job share has proved to be so successful that there are now nine other job shares in the same division.

According to Kathy, when they broached their plan, American Express was surprisingly open to the idea. Moreover, social attitudes were also beginning to change. For the first time in a while, it was all right to admit that you wanted to spend time with your baby, that your worth was not solely wrapped up in working. Reflecting on her decision, Kathy says:

If you're ambitious, or if your identity is mixed up with being a professional, becoming a part-timer is kind of scary. It's easy to imagine that you will become a second-class citizen, that no one will give you responsibility or take you seriously. I don't feel that has happened to me—at least not yet. My work is valued by the company.

How does Kathy see the future?

We need a whole new career track for part-timers. I know that I would feel better about my future at AMEX if I could identify the next rung on the ladder. With creativity and imagination it should be possible to create part-time or job-sharing positions up to the vice-presidential level.

Many employers feel that women with children are not as likely to make the same commitments to their careers as are men. Yet with women making up almost half of America's work force and with 67 percent of mothers with children under eighteen years of age already in the work force, women are clearly an integral and necessary part of America's labor supply. It is true that mothers bear the major responsibility for child care and thus are more torn between their families and their work than men. Yet by taking this into account rather than simply complaining about it, business can improve workers' performance and at the same time support family stability as American Express did with Kathy and Jean.

More than one hundred countries have laws that protect pregnant workers and allow new mothers a job-protected leave at full or partial wages at the time of childbirth.

The "Report on a National Study of Parental Leave" (Mehren 1986) found that 46.8 percent (currently over 50 percent) of women with children under one year of age are working outside the home, yet only 40 percent of American working mothers receive even six weeks of postpartum leave with any income or job guarantee. Of the companies surveyed, 42.6 percent offered a comparable job while only 38 percent offered the same job back after a maternity leave. Only 39 percent offered full wages during the disability leave.

If the family is to survive both parents working outside the home and if business is to have satisfied, productive workers, the obligations of family will have to be integrated with the obligations of work. Instead of setting family and work in opposition and conflict, Americans need to figure out a way to make them allies and cooperative partners in the business of life. Better leave policies, more flexible working hours, job sharing, on-site child-care facilities, and, with the advent of computer networking, increased use of the home as a workplace are all possible ways to improve the relationship between family and work (see Table 9-7). American Telephone and Telegraph (AT&T) approved a labor contract increasing parental leave to one year for fathers and mothers of newborns. The company will also permit such leaves for the care of ailing relatives. In addition, AT&T will pay up to $2000 to cover costs of adoption and set up a $5 million fund to help support and establish child-care centers. In return for these new family-oriented contract provisions, employees agreed to forgo automatic cost-of-living adjustments (*Time*, June 12, 1989, 51).

Binney and Smith, the makers of crayons, have a unique employee phase-in policy. After a birth or

TABLE 9-7
WHAT EMPLOYERS PROVIDE TO HELP FAMILIES

	PERCENTAGE OF EMPLOYERS PROVIDING
Employee assistance programs	73%
Child care	64
Flexible schedules	54
Unpaid parental leave	44
Elder care	32
Paid medical leave	23
Unpaid medical leave	21
Adoption benefits	12
Paid parental leave	5

Percentages are based on 837 survey respondents.

Source: Hewitt Associates, reported in *Los Angeles Times*, October 14, 1990, D4.

adoption, a parent may request to "Phase-In" to active work in lieu of a leave of absence. "Phase-In" allows working part time for up to three (3) months. Salaried personnel must work a minimum of 20 hours/week. Hourly personnel must work a minimum eight hour day (or a standard work shift), for at least three (3) days. Employees are paid only for the time worked but receive full benefits during the phase-in period.

Merck and Company realized impressive returns from its parenting-leave policy. The cost of replacing an employee at this large pharmaceutical firm is $50,000. But by permitting a new parent to take a generous six-month child-care leave—at a cost of $38,000, which includes partial pay, benefits, and other indirect costs— the company succeeds in retaining almost all of its new-mother employees. By doing so, the company achieves a net savings of $12,000 per employee. In addition to its parenting-leave policy, Merck offers a child-care center, child-care referral services, and a flexible time option that has increased productivity up to 20 percent in some departments.

When women ran the home and reared the children and men supported their families by working outside the home, employers did not need to concern themselves with these types of accommodations to keep their workers satisfied and productive. The days of such separation between family and work are probably gone forever. A century and a half ago, work and family were integrated on the American farm, but they were separated by the Industrial Revolution and now as women have become essential to the American work force, the family and work will have to become integrated and supportive of each other again. Once employers team up with the family instead of engaging in conflict with it, American productivity will be stimulated to reach new heights.

Source: Adapted from Sylvia Ann Hewlett, "Good News? The Private Sector and Win-Win Scenarios." In *Rebuilding the Nest*, edited by David Blankenhorn, Steven Bayme, and Jean Bethke Elshtain. (Milwaukee, Wis.: Family Service America, 1990), pp. 209–210, 213–215.

CHAPTER

10

HUMAN SEXUALITY

CONTENTS

FRIEND: What is sex?

STUDENT: Everyone knows what sex is! Sex is for having babies—you know, reproduction.

FRIEND: I know, but if sex is only for reproduction, why don't humans mate like other animals, once a year or so? Why don't human females go into "heat" to attract males?

STUDENT: Well, human females are more sexually receptive at certain times during their monthly cycle, aren't they?

FRIEND: The evidence on that is mixed, but even if it were true, why are humans interested in sex all the time?

STUDENT: Perhaps sex is for human pleasure.

FRIEND: But if sex is for fun, why are there so many restrictions on sexual behavior? Why does society try so often to regulate sexual expression? Why are there so many sexually transmitted diseases? STDs certainly aren't fun. Why does religion try to focus sexual behavior toward some higher purpose?

STUDENT: Well, then, perhaps sex is for love, and love will limit the number of sexual partners.

FRIEND: But, what is love exactly? Does sex always mean love? If masturbation is sex, does it mean I love myself if I do it? Can I love more than one person at the same time?

STUDENT: Love is emotional closeness that allows you to communicate at an intimate level. Love also makes you feel good about yourself—it enhances your ego. So if sex is love, it does all these things too.

FRIEND: Certainly, sex can be for all of the things you mention. But isn't sex sometimes just for biological release? This doesn't sound much like love or ego enhancement, does it?

STUDENT: No, but sex can and should be an expression of love.

FRIEND: Ah, yes, but what it sometimes is and what it should be are often two different things.

STUDENT: What do you mean?

FRIEND: Well, is sex an expression of love when it is used to possess another person, such as when a woman is considered to be a man's property? Or when it is used to gain status, such as when a king marries the daughter of another king to increase his holdings and thereby his prestige? Or when it is accompanied by violence, as in rape? Or when it is a business, as in prostitution? Or when it is used indirectly, as in advertising where appeals based on sex are used to sell many different products?

STUDENT: Now I'm really confused. Just what is sex?

From this short discussion, it is obvious that sex is many things and, at times, is something of a riddle. If sex were only for reproduction, or only an expression of love, or only for fun, there would be little controversy about it and no need to control it. Sex isn't for one purpose, though, but for many. It is this fact that causes people to be so concerned and, at times, so confused about the place of sex in their lives.

Marriage is society's sanctioned arrangement for sexual relations. A happy, satisfying sex life is a characteristic of the healthy family. Sex is one of the foundations of most human intimate relationships. Sex is the basis of the family—procreation—and the survival of the species. Sex is communication and closeness. It can be pleasuring in its most exciting and satisfying form. Certainly, it is proper to study marriage by viewing humans as the sexual creatures they are. And our thoughts and attitudes toward sex are the most important part of human sexuality. It is also important however, to understand the biological foundations if we are fully to understand sexuality and the male-female bond. (Sexual anatomy is presented in Appendix A for your reference.)

Because of the sexual revolution, all Americans are supposed to know everything about sexuality. See if you do by taking the Sex Knowledge Inventory in Inset 10-1 before you continue reading the chapter.

HUMAN SEXUALITY COMPARED WITH OTHER SPECIES

No society has ever been found where sexual behavior was unregulated. True, regulations vary greatly: one spouse, multiple spouses; free selection of sexual partners, rigidly controlled selection; and so forth. Actually, if one takes a cross-cultural view of sexuality, the specific regulations include almost any arrangements imaginable. Within a given culture, however, the regulations are usually strictly enforced through taboos, mores, laws, and religious edicts. Transgression may bring swift and sometimes severe punishment, as in some Middle Eastern cultures where an adulterous woman may be stoned to death.

Why do humans surround sex with regulations? Certainly, sex is controlled among lower animals, but the controls are usually identical throughout the species, dictated by built-in biological mechanisms. Humans regulate sex precisely because their biology has granted them sexual freedom of choice. Sexual behavior can occur at any time in humans. Among animals sexual behavior occurs only periodically, depending on the estrus cycle of the female in all mammals below primates. For mammals sexual behavior is for reproduction. Thus, sexual responsiveness is tied directly to the period of maximum fertility in the female. The female gives clues, such as a change in odor and genital swelling, to which the male responds.

In lower animals sexual behavior is controlled by lower brain centers and spinal reflexes activated by hormonal changes. In general, the larger the brain cortex, the higher the species and the more control the animal has over its own responses. So we come to humans with their large cortex and what do we find? Earth's sexiest animal, an animal with few built-in restraints and hence many variations in sexual behavior. Without built-in guidelines, human sexuality is dependent on learning, and because different societies and groups teach different things about sexuality, there are many variations in sexual attitudes and behavior. Sexual compatibility, in part, depends on finding another person who shares your attitudes about sex. For human beings sex is less tied to reproduction than it is in lower animals; thus, for humans sexual expression seems to serve other purposes as well. For example, Desmond Morris notes:

The vast bulk of copulation in our species is obviously concerned, not with producing offspring, but with cementing the pair-bond by producing mutual rewards for sexual partners. The repeated attainment of sexual consummation for

INSET 10-1
SEX KNOWLEDGE INVENTORY

Sex is a subject that most people think they know a lot about. Let's see if we do. Mark the following statements true or false. Answers can be found on page 348.

1. Women generally reach the peak of their sex drive later than men.

2. It is possible to ejaculate without having a total erection.

3. Sperm from one testicle produce males and from the other, females.

4. A person is likely to contract a sexually transmitted disease when using a toilet seat recently used by an infected person.

5. If a person has gonorrhea once and is cured, he or she is immune and will never get it again.

6. Certain foods increase the sex drive.

7. Premature ejaculation is an unusual problem for young men.

8. The penis inserted into the va-

gina (sexual intercourse) is the only normal method of sex.

9. It is potentially harmful for a woman to take part in sports during menstruation.

10. A woman who has had her uterus removed can still have an orgasm.

11. During sexual intercourse a woman may suffer from vaginal spasms that can trap the male's penis and prevent him from withdrawing it.

12. The cause of impotence is almost always psychological.

13. For a certain time period after orgasm, the woman cannot respond to further sexual stimulation.

14. For a certain time period after orgasm, the man usually cannot respond to further sexual stimulation.

15. Taking birth control pills will delay a woman's menopause.

16. The size of the penis is fixed by hereditary factors and little can be done by way of exercise, drugs,

and so on to increase its size.

17. If a woman doesn't have a hymen, this is proof that she is not a virgin.

18. As soon as a female starts to menstruate, she can become pregnant.

19. About 80 percent of women infected with gonorrhea show no symptoms.

20. The penis of the male and the clitoris of the female are analogous organs.

21. A woman can't get pregnant the first time she has intercourse.

22. A good lover can bring a woman to orgasm even when she doesn't want to have an orgasm.

23. Herpes is easily curable with antibiotics.

24. Thus far over one-half of persons with AIDS have died.

25. One can become infected with herpes simply by kissing an infected person.

---

a mated pair is clearly, then, not some kind of sophisticated, decadent outgrowth of modern civilization, but a deep-rooted, biologically based, and evolutionarily sound tendency in our species. (1971, 65–66)

Human sexuality differs significantly from that of other animals in several other important ways besides the greater freedom from instinctive direction. It appears that human females are the only females capable of intense orgasmic response. The sexual behavior of the human male, however, still resembles the sexual behavior of male primates; it depends largely on outside perceptual stimuli and is under partial control of the female in that she usually triggers it. Of course, in humans this trigger can be indirect, as in fantasies.

Another important difference between humans and other animals is that unlike most other animals, human females are not necessarily more sexually responsive during ovulation. There seems to be no particular time during the menstrual cycle when all women experience heightened sexual desire. A few women seem to become more sexually aroused at midcycle when they are most

WHAT DO YOU THINK?

1. What do you think is the major purpose of human sexuality? Why?
2. Do we need any controls on human sexuality? Why or why not?
3. What controls would you have if you believe they are needed?
4. If there were no controls, how would the institution of marriage be affected?

Human Sexuality Compared with Other Species

SEXUAL ADDICTION IS A PROBLEM LIKE DRUG OR ALCOHOL ADDICTION

When sex is separated from love and care, it can become addictive. Rather than bringing us close to someone, it becomes a block to intimacy. This kind of sex frequently leads to secret agendas. Addictive sex does not open up feelings but is carried out in an attempt to hide them. "It is skin touching skin in search of a 'high.' After the high, participants feel lonely, empty, and, often, disgusted" (Kasl 1989, 10).

Although there is disagreement over whether sex can be a real addiction, the fact remains that a significant number of people have identified themselves as sexual addicts: in these people sexual behavior has gone "out of control" with serious consequences (Carnes 1986).

Five basic criteria are used to determine addiction:

1. Powerlessness to stop at will.
2. Harmful consequences.
3. Unmanageability in other areas of life.
4. Escalation of use.
5. Withdrawal feelings upon quitting.

Sexually addicted men and women report being unable to control or stop sexual behaviors that lead to harmful consequences. For example, a man may compulsively expose himself to others leading to his arrest and punishment. A woman may continually pick up strange men and take them home with her, thus placing herself in a potentially harmful situation. Such a person becomes so preoccupied with sex that other areas of his or her life such as work or marriage become unmanageable.

Like many other addicts, the sexual addict needs more and more stimulation to maintain the high—more partners, more explicit pornography, more varied sexual activities. Such persons also suffer real symptoms of withdrawal when they are unable to engage in sexual behavior.

Other addictions such as alcohol, drugs, or eating disorders often accompany sexual addiction. In one study of sex addicts, 38 percent were chemically dependent and another 38 percent had eating disorders (Carnes 1986). Carnes suggests that sexual addiction may cause alcohol or drug addiction rather than the other way around.

Current addiction theory suggests that there is often a form of family intimacy dysfunction such as child abuse or neglect in the background of sexual addicts. In response to this trauma, the young person develops feelings of shame. Feelings of shame lead to low self-esteem, which blocks healthy interpersonal relating, which leads to a sense of loneliness. Sex becomes an instant way in which to create a relationship. This person wants to have sex with me; therefore I am attractive, I am loved, I am cared for, I have a relationship, I am no longer lonely. While such thoughts lead to an instant high and momentarily hide one's sense of loneliness, the relief is usually only temporary and the shame, low self-esteem, and loneliness return when the addict realizes that sex may mean none of these things. Consequently, the addict feels a need to return to the "fix," and the behavior becomes repetitive (Sprenkle 1987, 12; Earle 1990).

THERE IS NO SUCH THING AS SEXUAL ADDICTION

Sexual addiction is a myth. The notion that people can be addicted to sex represents a pseudoscientific codification of prevailing cultural values rather than a valid clinical diagnosis. There is nothing intrinsically pathological in the conduct currently labeled as sexual addiction; these behaviors have assumed a pathological status

fertile. For other women, sexual desire peaks just after the menstrual flow begins; possibly this pattern is related to a reduced fear of pregnancy. Some women peak just before the menstrual flow. Some people suggest that these differences, coupled with the development of the orgasm in females, may mean that humans are the only species to derive pleasure out of sexual behavior without becoming involved in its reproductive aspects.

only because they violate prevailing cultural standards. We believe that sexual addiction is a myth for two fundamental reasons. The first stems from the cultural relativity of sexual conduct. The very behavior that is defined as sexual addiction in our society is considered perfectly normal in other cultures. The second flows from the conceptually flawed manner in which sexual addiction is defined. As used currently, the concept is highly moralistic and subjective and violates traditional interpretations of addiction (Levine and Troiden 1989, 92).

As noted in this chapter, all cultures surround sex with certain rules and restrictions. Thus the sexual behavior one society may define as erotic deviance another culture may encourage as completely normal. For example, among the people of the Polynesian island of Mangaia, casual sex with numerous partners is seen as perfectly normal. American sexual mores term such behavior *promiscuous*. Using masturbation to help both young boys and girls sleep is normal to certain peoples in India. In America such sexual stimulation of children is considered to be one of the worst possible sex crimes. Anal intercourse is not a popular sex act in America, yet among certain peoples it is a major method of birth control. The list goes on. Almost any sexual act can be found to be acceptable in some culture.

If we examine closely the sexual behaviors cited by those proposing the idea of a sexual addiction pathology, it is clear that many of the behaviors go against the accepted norms of a Christian monogamous society. The idea of recreational sex or sex for its own sake is not popular in many segments of the American population despite the sexual revolution. Hence having many sexual partners, especially partners who are not well known and having sex outside marital boundaries, for example, are behaviors labeled pathological. The person engaging in such behaviors and unable to stop is labeled addicted.

Criticizing the concept of sexual addiction, Levine and Troiden (1989, 94) point out that strictly speaking addiction is a state of physiological dependence on a specific substance arising from habitual use of that substance. Sex, however, is an experience, not a substance.

Also, sex is the only type of "addiction" in which the so-called addict does not have to give up the abused behavior as part of the treatment. As long as sex is confined to the culturally appropriate context, i.e., marriage or a committed relationship, there is no addiction. A married couple may be so preoccupied with sex—having sex several times a day—that other parts of their life may be neglected, but such behavior is not labeled addiction because it takes place within acceptable boundaries.

Levine and Troiden (1989, 95) also point out that the so-called characteristics of sexual addiction—preoccupation, ritualization, sexual compulsivity, and despair—can just as well describe the intense passion of falling in love by conventional couples. Although these researchers do not deny the existence of people who find it hard to control and manage their sexuality, they feel that the invention of sexual addiction as a "disease" threatens the civil liberties of sexually variant peoples.

WHAT DO YOU THINK?

1. Should a person's sexual conduct be judged as long as no one is harmed?
2. Can sexual behavior be labeled normal or abnormal?
3. What standards of conduct would you use to apply such labels?
4. How many sexual partners do you personally feel a person might have before you would label him or her "promiscuous"?
5. Why and how did you choose this number?

The major difference between humans and animals is that *much of human sexuality depends on what the individual thinks rather than on biology.* Compared with other species, human sexuality is:

1. Pervasive, involving humans psychologically as well as physiologically.
2. Under conscious control rather than instinctual biological control.

Human Sexuality Compared
with Other Species

Answers to "Sex Knowledge Inventory"

1. T	6. F	11. F	16. T	21. F
2. T	7. F	12. T	17. F	22. F
3. F	8. F	13. F	18. F	23. F
4. F	9. F	14. T	19. T	24. T
5. F	10. T	15. F	20. T	25. T

3. Affected by learning and social factors and thus more variable within the species.
4. Largely directed by an individual's beliefs and attitudes.
5. Less directly attached to reproduction.
6. Able to serve other purposes in addition to reproduction such as pair bonding and communications.
7. More of a source of pleasure.

It is these differences that have led humans to create such a variety of sexual standards and practices. Because human sexuality is not totally under biological control, a free society will also experience changes in sexual attitudes and behaviors. Such changes have been occurring rapidly during the past decades in the United States.

HUMAN SEXUALITY IN THE UNITED STATES

For better or worse, sexual attitudes and behavior in American society have changed rapidly over the past twenty-five years. Generally, sexual expression has become freer, more diverse, and more open to public view. The infamous **double standard,** which promoted sexual expression for men while limiting it for women, has broken down for many Americans. Alternatives to traditional sexual relationships and practices have become more acceptable. Better understanding of one's own sexuality has become an important goal in many people's lives.

In fact, better understanding and acceptance by women of their sexuality may be one of the revolutionary changes affecting the family and all intimate relationships. As noted in Chapter 4, the sexual revolution has really been a revolution for women in that their sexual behaviors have become more like men's.

As women have become freer to initiate sexual activity and to express their desires, they have been able to set the stage for sexual expression or at least to share in the decision. Thus women too can pick times for sexual activity when they feel interested, ready, and capable. And if they can pick the times, their chances of sexual satisfaction are increased.

Women are now able to channel sexuality into their lives in their own way and at their own pace. Sexual equality between men and women should reduce sexual dysfunction in both men and women. If each person is free to express himself or herself sexually with a partner and respects that same freedom for the partner, the chances of sexual exploitation of one partner by the other are reduced. Without exploitation and manipulation, the chances for sexual fulfillment and enjoyment are greatly increased. Freedom of sexual expression also includes the freedom to say "no" to sexual interaction.

In a sense greater sexual diversity and freedom create as well as solve problems. Freedom means responsibility. I must assume personal responsibility for my actions if I am free to choose those actions. In the past when sexual expression was surrounded by mores, taboos, and traditions, responsibility was removed from the individual. One could always blame the rules for lack of

Double standard
Freer sexual expression allowed for males than for females

satisfaction, failures, and unhappiness. But in the past few years, America has rapidly removed the rules from sexual expression. Now more than ever, the decisions are up to each individual, and this can be frightening.

A NEW SEXUAL REVOLUTION?

As we have seen and will continue to see throughout this book, American sexual attitudes and practices have been considerably liberalized. Starting in the 1980s, however, a number of factors began to modify some of the changes brought about by freer sexual expression.

The most important factor has been the epidemic return of sexually transmitted diseases (STDs) that has accompanied freer sexual life (see pp. 372–384). Several years ago, with the emergence of herpes simplex virus, Type II, and a resurgence of all the historical diseases, Americans began to curb their sexual experiences and to question just how far sexual liberation could go. The appearance of the deadly acquired immune deficiency syndrome (AIDS) has had an even greater impact on American sexual behavior. Some people actually seem relieved by the threat of herpes or AIDS. It's a good excuse for them to give up a sexual lifestyle that has become increasingly unsatisfying.

A second factor may be that recreational sex alone becomes dull and boring. Boy meets girl; boy and girl have sex; they part. They never discover the excitement of the chase, the enjoyments of sex within a wider relational context, the bonding that sex can create (see "Marital Sex" on p. 362), the expression of care and intimacy that sex can be, and many of the other roles that sex can play in an intimate relationship. One young woman declared, "I have sex with a new date as soon as I can to get the hassle out of the way." Such a person has not yet discovered many of the pleasures and relational enhancements sex can provide. Many young women report that they are getting tired of dating only to have sex and express interest in doing other things on a date besides going to bed. More and more they complain that their dates seem interested only in the bedroom aspect of a date. If they say no, the date doesn't call back. If they say yes, he leaves after the sex, although he may call back. Many young women seem to be asking young men, "Aren't you interested in anything else besides my body?"

"What Role Should Sex Play in My Life?" Beth-Ann Asks

It's been a perfect evening. The moon is full and casting a soft glow on the water. The air is thick with your perfume and sea air. You and your date have just finished a wonderfully romantic dinner and you now sit on the beach. A soft kiss goodbye when he drops you home will finish the evening . . . *wrong!* Back to reality girl! This young man just bought you an expensive dinner and roses instead of putting a new stereo in his car. Now you *owe* him, or at least that's what he'll tell you when he's pleading for you to come back with him to his apartment.

So what do you do? I mean this guy's really cute, and you really want him to call again. So do you have sex with him, even if it's only your first date? It's this constant pressure that guys put on girls that really bothers me the most. If a guy takes you out on a date, why do you need to perform sexual favors to make the night worth while to him?

Males seem to feel that sex is the natural end to a date. Of course, there is the occasional sensitive man who likes you for your mind, but he's becoming a real rarity. Now when a guy calls and wants to take you out, you have to doubt his reasons. This isn't right. When two people go out, it should be to enjoy each other's company and have a good time, and this can be accomplished without getting under the sheets.

Sex is not a form of payment for a night out, sex is not a way of saying "thank you." Nowhere is it written that you have to have sexual intercourse with a guy because he spent money on you. It's your body and ultimately your word.

And as if that isn't enough, if you finally do give in and have sex with him, the next day you're known as a cheap easy "lay," and no guy wants you because you're "too easy." So ultimately you lose either way. Either you are a prude or a cheap slut.

As noted in Chapter 7 (pp. 244–249), many of the women who were early supporters of the women's movement and had more liberal sexual attitudes are starting to criticize some of the practical outcomes of freer sex for women. They feel that they have gained the right to say yes to their sexuality but lost the right to say no. They believe men are the big winners in that they can now have sex whenever they want (since the liberated woman supposedly won't say no) without the necessity of commitment to a more meaningful relationship or even the responsibility for birth control or ensuing pregnancies. Numerous young women who find themselves pregnant and approach the author for counseling indicate that the father-to-be doesn't know of their problem. When asked why, they say that they don't want to bother him with it. This attitude is leading many older women to think that they may have been conned by the sexual revolution—tricked into playing the male's game of easy sex.

Freedom to have uncommitted sex, freedom to become pregnant, and freedom to be a single parent were not exactly what women had in mind when they voiced support for freer sexual mores and women's rights. In a way, it has been the men who have been freed of the responsibilities that, in the past, went with an intimate sexual relationship. And it is the newly liberated women who now must bear the responsibilities.

Stanley Graham (1992), in his 1991 Presidential address at the American Psychological Association's 99th Annual Convention said:

> The emancipation of women was paralleled by the abandoning of responsibility by men. What I am saying is that the social and economic revolution as it pertained to women gave them a lot more work, a lot more responsibility, and sexual freedom to some degree, but it gave men much more sexual freedom at least until the spread of herpes and AIDS.

Women who have been unable to establish a long-lasting intimate relationship with a man despite their liberated ways are beginning to express bitterness. "I feel used and manipulated by the men I meet." "I really am getting tired of wondering whose bed I'm in and whether he cares who I am." "I'd like someone to at least offer to share in birth control responsibilities." As Beth-Ann asks, "Isn't there someone who cares about my head, my thoughts, my interests, who cares about me and not just my body?"

Redbook (1987) found that for many women affection, tenderness, and cuddling were more important to their happiness than sex. Many women readers wrote negatively about freer sexual interaction and said they longed for vanished intimacy and the now elusive joys of romance and commitment. For some people, then, sexual liberation may have become as much of a trap as the old Victorian constraints on sexuality. Ann Landers found similar sentiments when she asked her readers which they preferred, sex or tenderness. She was overwhelmed by responses from women who said that the latter was what they wanted.

Saying no to sex when you want to say yes, because you think you shouldn't, is sometimes heroic. But saying yes when you want to say no, because you think you should, is merely grotesque. If anything in human life should be voluntary and spontaneous, it is erotic behavior.

Another factor modifying America's liberalized sexual behaviors may be that despite all of the sex education efforts, the practical outcome of more sex is

The following letter in a student newspaper was obviously written by a coed with her tongue in her cheek (a little bit).

Editor:

Recently, a mere acquaintance presumed I'd be thrilled to have casual sex with him. I told him to buzz off. Next time I am going to be prepared. I don't know about you, but as a woman, I am forced to be exceedingly responsible about my reproductive capacities. What is casual sex for some is a headache for me. How can sex be casual when I run the risk of getting pregnant or contracting any of a variety of ghastly diseases?

Being a diehard romantic, I've got to temper my idealism with a good dose of realism. So I've devised a PRECOITAL CONTRACT to stifle any attempt by my hormones to sabotage my good intentions:

1. All prospective lovers must submit a signed medical report that proves they are free from sexually transmitted diseases.

2. All prospective lovers must submit proof of attending a sex education and contraception class and must be fully prepared to participate in preventing pregnancy.

3. All prospective lovers must post a bail of $300 in case of an accidental pregnancy because no method of birth control, no matter how diligently used, is 100 percent effective.

Presenting this PRECOITAL CONTRACT is going to be a problem. Do I slip it under the door and demand signature when a prospective lover arrives to pick me up for our first date? Do I pick him up and drive to a distant place and demand his signature and bond before I'll give him a lift back to town? Do I wait for a lull in the conversation somewhere between the peas and the prune danish to spring the contract on him? What would happen if I procrastinated until after our first embrace—would my prospective lover be so overcome by desire that he would sign anything—would I want him to be?!

Sex in the nineties demands a PRECOITAL CONTRACT—I just haven't worked out the logistics—YET.

more children. Frequently unwanted, born to young unwed women who are forced to become single parents with all the attendant drawbacks (see pp. 431–434), these children too often are neglected and/or abused (see pp. 513–516) and ultimately become unsocialized and troubled adults who cost society rather than contributing to it. In most cases, society as a whole must pick up the monetary costs as well as the social costs of "sex is fun" for the young woman and her child.

In a way, the very emphasis on sex and liberation has made sex education more difficult. Everyone is now supposed to know all there is to know about sex. Not to know is not to be "in," "with it," "liberated," and what young person doesn't want to be in? Better not to ask and feign knowledge than show ignorance by asking. As a result, sex is still a subject that is rife with misunderstanding and misinformation. How youth can remain so ignorant in such a supposedly sexually enlightened society is a question Americans have yet to answer successfully.

Such factors will not cause a return to earlier sexual mores, but they are moderating the sexual revolution. Many Americans are beginning to ask more of their intimate relationships than recreational sex alone. It is interesting to note that much of this reaction against the sexual revolution is coming from

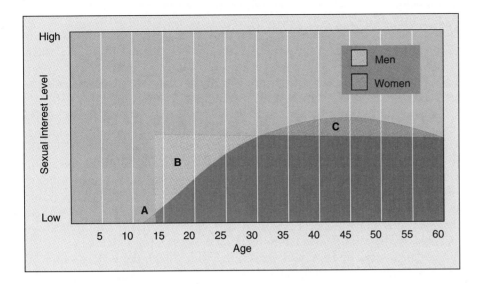

FIGURE 10-1
Intensity of sex drive across the adult life span

the young, who might be expected to favor liberalized sexuality as they have in the past. In a 1969 *Psychology Today* reader survey, some 17 percent of the men and 29 percent of the women believed that sex without love was either unenjoyable or unacceptable. In a repeat study fourteen years later, 29 percent of the men and 44 percent of the women felt this way. Of those under age twenty-two, half felt this way (Rubinstein 1983). In the past, sexual intimacy was usually accompanied by commitment to a broader relationship. As sex became more and more an end in itself, commitment, caring, and the broader aspects of a meaningful intimate relationship were lost. The new revolution (if there is one) seems, in part, to be searching for these lost relational elements.

DIFFERENCES BETWEEN MALE AND FEMALE SEXUALITY

Figure 10-1 diagrams some general differences in sexual drive between men and women across their adult life span. The source of these differences is the subject of considerable debate. Some biologists suggest that they stem from inborn differences in biological makeup between males and females. Most sociologists and psychologists believe that the differences stem from the socialization processes that teach men and women their sex roles and the place of sexual behavior in their lives. The truth probably lies somewhere between these two views, with both nature (biology) and nurture (culture) combining in some manner to create the differences between the sexes.

Because puberty begins on the average about two years earlier in females than in males, young girls develop an interest in sexuality earlier than boys do (area A of Figure 10-1). This interest is usually described as "boy craziness." During this period most boys remain essentially uninterested in girls. When

Differences Between Male and Female Sexuality

Masturbation
Stimulation of the genital organs, usually to orgasm, by means other than intercourse

puberty does arrive in young men, their sexual interests and desires soar above those of girls of similar age. From age fifteen through the twenties, males are at the height of their sexual drive. Most similar-age females perceive their male counterparts as "preoccupied with sex" during this period (area B on Figure 10-1). Often a male's major thought at this time is "I don't get enough sex." **Masturbation** is common among young men at this time in their lives.

Various studies indicate an 86 to 96 percent incidence of masturbation among men, while the same studies find only a 47 to 69 percent rate among women (Nass and Libby 1984). These studies are misleading to some degree because they look at the incidence of masturbation over the entire life span. Most men have masturbated in their early youth, whereas relatively few women have. Women's masturbation rates climb slowly over the life span to reach the levels reported, whereas the men's rates are reached early in their lives. Masters, Johnson, and Kolodny (1988, 371–72) report several studies indicating that the incidence of female masturbatory activity has been increasing.

During his teens and twenties (area B in Figure 10-1), the male is simply a much more sexual creature than the female. The female's sexual drive increases gradually, reaching its peak when the woman is between thirty and forty years of age. Because of some females' multiorgasmic capability, their sexual drive may become even stronger than the males in later years (area C in Figure 10-1).

Figure 10-1 indicates that males and females are somewhat incompatible across their sexual lives. If we consider only sexual drive, older men and younger women and older women and younger men make the most compatible partners sexually. Margaret Mead, in fact, suggested that a sexually compatible culture would be one in which older men married very young women, who on the death of their first husbands would be left economically secure. These women in turn could marry young sexually compatible men whom they could help to a good economic start. Although such an idea might solve the problem of differing sex-drive strength between men and women at different ages, it is not likely to find wide acceptance in our culture. Thus men and women will have to work out compromises as their sex drives vary over time and clash periodically.

In the early teens, males are far more genitally oriented than females, who are more socially oriented. When young males are sexually stimulated, the flow of seminal fluid increases. This buildup causes a preoccupation with the genital area and the need to ejaculate.

Men generally are aroused more easily and directly than women by visual stimuli or mental imagery caused by pictures of nude women and pornography. Women's reactions to various sexually provocative materials are more complex, depending to a large extent on the type of material. Some people suggest that there is an important distinction between pornographic material and erotica. They see pornography as based on the exploitation of women, featuring sex without emotional involvement and, all too often, violence. Erotica is sexually explicit material that has emotional and romantic overtones of sensuality and caring. Women are more apt than men to react negatively to sexually explicit pornography. Women react more positively to erotica, especially erotic romantic novels. Here again, however, women and men tend to be coming closer together in their reaction to sexually explicit materials (Masters, Johnson, and Kolodny 1988, 375).

Sexual fantasies play an important part in both men's and women's sex lives. Such fantasies can be important to sexual arousal. Gathering information on people's sexual fantasies is difficult because they are regarded as private and intimate. Fantasies are influenced by personal experiences as well as by societal mores regarding sex. Although the details of people's fantasies vary greatly, certain general themes have been found in both sexes (Rokachi 1990; Kealing 1990). Masters, Johnson, and Kolodny (1988, 350) report that the five leading fantasy contents for heterosexual men and women are as follows:

Heterosexual Male	Heterosexual Female
1. Replacement of established partner	1. Replacement of established partner
2. Forced sexual encounter	2. Forced sexual encounter
3. Observation of sexual activity	3. Observation of sexual activity
4. Homosexual encounters	4. Idyllic encounters with unknown men
5. Group Sex experiences	5. Lesbian encounters

Probably the most outstanding feature of these lists is their similarity. Their general similarity masks more specific gender differences, however. For example, women tend to surround sexual fantasies with more romantic images than men do. Masters and Johnson point out that fantasy content will change with time, personal experience, and one's culture. They also note that analysis of fantasy content for diagnostic purposes is usually nonproductive. For example, it is sometimes said that a person who fantasizes about same-sex experiences may be a "latent homosexual." Yet both heterosexual men and women report such fantasies, and both homosexual men and women report fantasizing about heterosexual relations. We do not label homosexuals who fantasize about heterosexual relations as "latent heterosexuals."

Another important difference between men and women's sexuality is that women have to learn how to reach orgasm, but men do not. This is probably where the idea that a woman must be awakened to her sexuality originated.

The capacity of females for orgasm differs more widely between individual women than it does between individual men (Calderone and Johnson 1989, 14). Some women never achieve orgasm (5 to 10 percent) and some only when they are thirty to forty years of age. At the other extreme, some women have frequent multiple orgasms. In a *Redbook* study of 26,000 women, almost half the women reported having multiple orgasms sometimes or often (1987, 149). Neither of these extremes is true for males (Masters, Johnson, and Kolodny 1988).

As was mentioned earlier, there is also an interesting difference in the reported subjective feelings of pleasure with repeated orgasm. Women who experience multiple orgasms usually find their second and third orgasmic episodes the most pleasurable. But most men report greater pleasure from the first ejaculation rather than from a repeated orgasmic experience (Masters, Johnson, and Kolodny 1988). This might be explained in part by the relatively greater volume of seminal fluid in the first ejaculation, especially following a period of continence.

Another difference is that females tend to have a cyclical increase in sexual desire related to the menstrual cycle although the pattern varies between individual women. There is no counterpart of this cyclically heightened desire in the male.

WHAT DO YOU THINK?

1. What differences between male and female sexuality have you found troublesome?
2. There has always been a double standard of sexual conduct for the sexes in America. How does this affect sexual differences between the sexes?
3. Must sex and love always go together? Why or why not?

Differences Between Male and Female Sexuality

Premenstrual syndrome (PMS) is the name given to a number of symptoms, both physical and psychological, that may accompany a woman's period. Although the numbers vary according to the studies, probably 30 to 70 percent of menstruating women notice at least one emotional, physical, or behavioral change in the week before menstruation. For most of these women, the symptoms are negative, but for about 12 percent, they may be positive (such feelings as increased energy and a general feeling of well-being). For another 5 to 10 percent of menstruating women, the symptoms are numerous and so severe that their lives are disrupted for a week or so each month (Hopson and Rosenfeld 1984; Lee and Rittenhouse 1991).

Although physical problems such as breast tenderness and water retention are troublesome, the

TABLE 10-1
PREMENSTRUAL SYMPTOMS IN BLACK AND WHITE WOMEN FROM A COMMUNITY, NONPATIENT SAMPLE

	BLACK WOMEN (N=321)	WHITE WOMEN (N=462)
Feeling depressed, sad, or blue	29%	27%
Having wide mood swings	26	21
Feeling under stress	16	18
Having cravings for certain foods	25	17
Having decreased energy	29	23
Being irritable	28	31
Feeling unable to cope	10	10

Source: From A. L. Stout, et al, "Premenstrual Symptoms in Black and White Community Samples," *American Journal of Psychiatry* 143 (1986): 1436–39. Copyright 1986, the American Psychiatric Association, Reprinted by permission.

changes in mood, depression, feelings of worthlessness, irritability, despair, unreasonableness, and lack of emotional control trouble women most. Generally, such symptoms start to occur about seven to ten days before menstruation. The symptoms abate and disappear shortly after the onset of menstruation.

At first doctors believed that such symptoms occurred due to a drop in progesterone level and prescribed daily doses of the hormone to treat the symptoms. However, research has found that placebos

The menstrual cycle in women is also related to personality changes due to the changing chemical balances in the woman's body. (See Appendix A for a description of the physiological changes that take place during women's menstrual cycle.)

MENOPAUSE

Menopause
The cessation of ovulation, menstruation, and fertility in the woman; usually occurs between ages forty-six and fifty-one

The cessation of the menstrual cycle in women is termed **menopause** or the climacteric. This is also a difference between men's and women's sexuality. Although sperm count reduces as men age, leveling off around sixty years of age, men do not entirely lose their ability to reproduce as women do. Some women find that they become even more interested sexually after menopause because the fear of pregnancy is gone. It is also interesting to note that steri-

TABLE 10-2
PROPOSED CAUSES AND TREATMENT OF PMS[a]

CAUSES	TREATMENT[b]
Psychosomatic	Exercise
Abnormality of brain neurotransmitters	Diet changes (especially restricting sugar and salt)
Hormonal	Birth control pills
Estrogen	Progesterone
Progesterone deficiency	Vitamin supplements
Antidiuretic hormone excess	Diuretics
Aldosterone abnormality	Dietary supplements (minerals, herbs, etc.)
Hormone allergy	
Vitamin A deficiency	Tranquilizers
Vitamin B deficiency	Counseling
Low blood sugar (hypoglycemia)	
Fluid retention	

Source: Masters, Johnson, and Kolodny 1988, 103.

[a]There is no current evidence that suggests that any of these treatments is superior to a placebo in producing improvement in women with PMS.

[b]Local health clinics and state health departments will have more detailed information on current treatment and follow-up.

gesterone might increase the risk of breast tumors.

Unfortunately, because researchers cannot agree on a definition of PMS, there is little agreement on its treatment. Some go so far as to say it doesn't really exist, but thousands of women strongly contest that view. Since most women can predict the time of their menstruation fairly accurately, they can also predict the onset of PMS. The ability to predict just when the symptoms might arise helps women plan ahead and prepare to cope with the symptoms.

Today's treatment uncertainties are bound to frustrate PMS sufferers in search of a quick, safe effective cure. While there are many treatments, both behavioral and biological, none has been proven safe and effective. Yet, ironically, since PMS sufferers seem to respond to almost any treatment, the chances of an individual finding relief are quite good.

(pills thought to be the hormone but actually containing no medication) also alleviated the symptoms.

Progesterone treatment has lost some popularity due to these studies and other studies that suggest pro-

---

lized women report an increase in sexual enjoyment because they too are free of the fear of pregnancy.

Menopause generally occurs between the ages of forty-six and fifty-one. Menstruation does not stop suddenly but usually phases out over a period of time not exceeding two years. As long as a woman has any menstrual periods, no matter how irregular, the possibility of ovulation and therefore conception remains.

Because of the changing hormonal balances during menopause, a woman may experience some unpleasant symptoms such as "hot flashes," excessive fatigue, dizziness, muscular aches and pains, and emotional upset. These symptoms may last considerably longer than two years.

Estrogen replacement therapy (ERT) may be prescribed to help reduce negative symptoms of menopause. Because of this use, estrogen gained a reputation during the 1960s for slowing down the general aging process although

Estrogen replacement therapy (ERT)
Supplying estrogen to menopausal women

357

this is untrue. ERT lost favor in the 1970s after a number of studies related its use to an increased risk of cancer of the uterine lining (endometrium). By adding progestin to the therapy, however, the cancer risks are apparently greatly reduced. A survey of practicing gynecologists found that 75 percent prescribed ERT for at least 75 percent of their recently postmenopausal patients (Barrett-Connor 1986). ERT is now widely used to reduce the symptoms of menopause as well as to reduce the risks of **osteoporosis**—the progressive deterioration of the strength of bones as they lose calcium (Ettinger et al. 1985). There is also evidence that ERT reduces the risk of cardiovascular disease.

Osteoporosis
Progressive deterioration of bone strength

THE PHYSIOLOGY OF THE SEXUAL RESPONSE

In the 1960s we began to understand the physiology of the human sexual response. In a series of controversial studies, Masters and Johnson (1966) pioneered research using human subjects engaged in sexual activities. Before these studies most of our knowledge was derived from animal research. Among other techniques Masters and Johnson photographed the inside of the vagina during sexual arousal and orgasm. Although controversial, this research opened a new field of study, gave us a new understanding of the human sexual response, and paved the way for programs to help people with sexual difficulties. Masters and Johnson's work has been criticized for methodological errors and careless reporting, yet their pioneering efforts finally brought scientific research to bear on human sexuality.

Masters and Johnson divide the sexual response of both men and women into four phases: *excitement*, *plateau*, *orgasm*, and *resolution*. A partial description of these phases follows. The responses in all the stages for both females and males are usually independent of the type of stimulation that produces them. In other words, the same basic physiological reactions occur regardless of whether they are produced through manual manipulation, by penile insertion, or in some other manner.

THE FEMALE SEXUAL RESPONSE

Sexual response begins with the *excitement phase*, which may last anywhere from a few minutes to several hours. The breasts swell with blood. The skin may also be flushed; the nipples may become erect; and general muscle contractions may occur in the thighs, back, and abdomen and throughout the body. The **clitoris** becomes engorged with blood (tumescent); the vagina walls begin to sweat a lubricating fluid that facilitates the entrance of the penis. The inner portion of the vagina balloons, and the uterus may undergo irregular contractions. The labia minora (inner vaginal lips) increase in size. Blood pressure, heart rate, and breathing rates all increase.

The *plateau phase* lasts from only a few seconds to about three minutes. Tumescence and the sex flush reach their peak. Muscle tension is high, and

Clitoris
A small organ situated at the upper end of the female genitals that becomes erect with sexual arousal; homologous with the penis

Previous research has shown that expert judges were unable to distinguish reliably between written reports of male and female orgasms. The sex of the person describing orgasm in the following examples from our files may surprise you.

1. Like a mild explosion, it left me warm and relaxed after a searing heat that started in my genitals and raced to my toes and head.

2. Suddenly, after the tension built and built, I was soaring in the sky, going up, up, up, feeling the cool air rushing by. My insides were tingling and my skin was cool. My heart was racing in a good way, and breathing was a job.

3. Throbbing is the best word to say what it is like. The throbbing starts as a faint vibration, then builds up in a wave after wave where time seems to stand still.

4. When I come it's either like an avalanche of pleasure, tumbling through me, or like a refreshing snack—momentarily satisfying, but then I'm ready for more.

5. My orgasms feel like pulsating bursts of energy starting in my pelvic area and then engulfing my whole body. Sometimes I feel like I'm in freefall, and sometimes I feel like my body's an entire orchestra playing a grand crescendo.

Source: Masters, Johnson, and Kolodny 1988, 91.

1. M 2. F 3. M 4. F 5. F

the woman becomes totally absorbed, both physically and emotionally, with the impending climax. The clitoris withdraws beneath its hood and can only be stimulated indirectly. (The idea that direct stimulation of the clitoris is necessary for female orgasm is untrue. Indirect stimulation is effective, and, in fact, the heightened clitoral sensitivity during this phase may make direct stimulation uncomfortable.) Muscle rigidity reaches a peak as shown by the facial grimace, rigid neck, arched back, and tense thighs and buttocks. The labia minora experience a dramatic change in color. (In women who have not borne a child, the color will be pink to bright red; in women who have had children, the color will be pink to deep wine.) Blood accumulates in the arteries and veins around the vagina, uterus, and other pelvic organs. This pelvic congestion is relieved by the orgasmic phase.

The third phase, **orgasm,** is the most intense. During orgasm, most of the built-up neuromuscular tension is discharged in three to ten seconds. Orgasm is so all-absorbing that most sensory awareness of the external environment is lost. The whole body responds, although the sensation of orgasm is centered in the pelvis.

The most dramatic of the widespread muscle responses is caused by the muscles that surround the lower third of the vagina. These muscles contract against the engorged veins that surround that part of the vagina and force the blood out of them. These contractions also cause the lower third of the vagina and the nearby upper labia minor to contract a number of times.

Although it is generally recognized that women do not ejaculate as men do, a few researchers (Addiego et al. 1980) report isolated cases in which women have experienced an ejaculatory-type phenomenon. The researchers claim to have evidence that "some women ejaculate a fluid which contains the product of the 'female prostate,' . . . which is homologous to the male prostate" (100).

Orgasm
The climax of excitement in sexual activity

The Physiology of the Sexual Response

359

Their evidence suggests that such responses occur most frequently from stimulation of the so-called Grafenberg spot (G spot), an area located on the front wall of the vagina halfway between the top of the pubic bone and the cervix. The G spot, which ranges from the size of a dime to that of a quarter, lies along the urethra, just below the neck of the bladder. This research remains suspect, however, because even the existence of the G spot is questionable at this time. Researchers Perry and Whipple (1981) report finding the G spot in 400 of the women in their sample. Masters, Johnson, and Kolodny (1982; 1988), however, were unable to replicate this finding. Because areas of the body can be eroticized psychologically, they suggest that some women may have located a psychological pleasure spot within a certain area of the vagina, but that there is no physiological basis for the increased sensation. Masters and Johnson also note that the few women in their studies who discharged considerable fluid with orgasm secreted fluid with essentially the chemical makeup of urine, although some claim the fluid is similar to prostatic fluid (Maloney 1982). The fluid bears no chemical similarity to male semen.

In the last phase, *resolution*, the body returns to its prestimulated condition, usually within ten to fifteen minutes. If orgasm does not take place, the resolution phase may last twelve hours or more. Women have the capacity of repeating the four-phase cycle immediately after resolution and can experience multiple orgasms if stimulation is continued.

▧ THE MALE SEXUAL RESPONSE ▧

The male undergoes the same changes as the female during the four stages of the sexual response cycle, but with a few differences. For example, during excitement the penis (as well as the breasts and nipples) becomes engorged with blood until it erects. Also, the sperm begin their journey from the epididymis to the penis (see Appendix A, p. A-1).

The next and major difference occurs during the orgasmic phase. The male reaches orgasm by the ejaculation of the semen and sperm through the penis. Once the male ejaculates, penile detumescence (loss of erection) usually follows quickly in the resolution phase, though complete detumescence takes longer. Unlike the female, who can experience multiple orgasms, the male usually experiences a refractory (recovery) period during which he cannot become sexually aroused. This period may last only a few minutes or up to several hours depending on such factors as age, health, and desire. Some men are able to keep an erection or partial erection after they ejaculate and continue to enjoy sex for a while (Masters, Johnson, and Kolodny 1988, 94). Because in our society the male has usually been taught that it takes time to become sexually aroused again after ejaculation, the refractory period may be psychological as well as physiological. Although orgasm and ejaculation occur simultaneously in the male, it is possible for the male to learn to withhold ejaculation even though orgasm occurs. Certain eastern yogis and others claim this ability although exactly how they acquired it is unclear.

The male who is sexually aroused for a length of time without ejaculating may experience aching in his testicles and a general tension. These sensations can last for an hour or two. Such tension can be relieved by masturbation if a sexual partner is unavailable.

■ VARIATIONS IN SEXUAL RESPONSE ■

Although Masters and Johnson's early work suggested that all persons follow the four-phase pattern of sexual response, other research indicates that there may be more individual variation than first thought (Nass and Libby 1984). This research suggests four variations on the basic pattern of sexual response described by Masters and Johnson. Some people appear to experience orgasm as they're approaching the peak of heartbeat and breathing, some as they hit the peak, and some on their way down; a few people have orgasms that are so gradual the researchers can't tell when they start, although their end is obvious.

Masters and Johnson believed that the woman's orgasm was identified by vaginal contractions and that without these the woman's sexual response was not an orgasm. They concluded that women experience only one kind of orgasm, although earlier researchers had described two kinds of female orgasms, clitoral and vaginal.

Others (Crooks and Baur 1987) suggest that there may be three kinds of female orgasms. The first is the vulval or clitoral orgasm described by Masters and Johnson. The second is a uterine or upper orgasm during which a strong contraction in the muscle at the back of the throat leads to involuntary breath holding, followed by an explosive exhalation. This orgasm is not accompanied by vaginal contractions. The researchers suggest that the third type is a blending of these two.

Although much research has been done on the female orgasm, we still do not have a definitive answer about its nature. What is clear is that females have a greater diversity of sensation and reaction to sexual stimulation than males do. Therefore when a woman reads a popular description of what she "should" be feeling and how she "should" be reacting to sexual stimulation, she must be aware that her responses may not fit the description. If they do not, she should not necessarily label them as inadequate. As Masters and Johnson point out, feeling and intensity of orgasm are matters of perception, and satisfaction is influenced by many psychological as well as physiological factors (Masters, Johnson, and Kolodny 1988, 93).

Hormonal balances play a large role in sexual interest and arousal in both male and female. A drop in a man's testosterone levels will lead to gradual loss of interest in sex. Many believe that the same will be true of a woman if her estrogen level drops. Nevertheless, although estrogens influence a woman's attractiveness by keeping her skin soft, her hair full and shiny, and her breasts firm and help sex to be pleasurable by stimulating vaginal lubrication, they seem to have little to do with desire. Interestingly, testosterone seems to influence women's level of desire just as it does in men. Long after estrogen levels drop with menopause, women remain interested in sex. But if a woman's testosterone level drops, she loses interest just as a man does. Conversely, women treated for medical disorders with synthetic testosterone typically experience a surge in sexual desire that may come as quite a surprise.

■ SOME MYTHS UNMASKED ■

Masters and Johnson's research put to rest a number of myths about human sexuality. First, it established beyond question that women can have multiple orgasms. It also established that, within normal ranges, the size of the penis and vagina has little to do with the experience of orgasm. For example, the back two-thirds of the vagina is practically without nerve endings and plays little part in orgasm. Most of the stimulation occurs in the front third of the vagina, the labia minora, and the clitoris. A larger penile circumference may increase a woman's sexual sensation by placing pressure on the vaginal ring muscles, thus causing pleasurable tugging of the labia minora. Further, a longer penis may heighten sensations by thrusting against the cervix. On the other hand, too large or too long a penis may be uncomfortable for the woman and detract from her sensual enjoyment.

Masters and Johnson also revealed that it is not essential to stimulate the clitoris directly for orgasm to occur, though such stimulation produces the quickest orgasm for most women. And they found that the myth that the female responds more slowly is not necessarily true. When she regulates the rhythm and intensity of her own sexual stimuli, the female reaches orgasm in about the same time as the male. The female's much-discussed slowness in arousal is probably due to cultural repression rather than to some physiological difference.

Partners often believe that to achieve complete sexual satisfaction, they should experience orgasm simultaneously. As pleasant as this may be, there is no reason why partners must always reach orgasm at the same time. In fact, doing so may hinder spontaneity and may prevent each person from being fully aware of the other's pleasure. The couple may find it equally satisfying to reach orgasm at different times in the lovemaking sequence.

In addition to these specific findings, Masters and Johnson's work changed our ideas about other general aspects of sexuality. For example, many sexologists now consider masturbation to be an important and necessary part of sexual expression rather than a taboo behavior. Some women who have never experienced orgasm can learn how by first learning the techniques of masturbation. Once they have learned how to reach orgasm, they can transfer what they have learned to sex with their partners. The rationale behind this is that so many emotions surround sex (for example, shame and guilt about the failure to achieve orgasm, disappointment, and perhaps insecurity on the part of the partner) that it becomes almost impossible for some women to enjoy sex or change their behavior. The direct stimulation of masturbation encourages orgasm, and being alone may ease the emotional tension associated with sex.

Americans' attitudes toward sexual expression have generally become more open as they have learned more about their sexuality. Rather than ignoring or hiding sexuality, it is important to understand it so that you can use it to enhance your life and bring greater joy and pleasure to your intimate relationships.

MARITAL SEX: CAN I KEEP THE EXCITEMENT ALIVE?

The sexuality question most often asked by married couples is: How can we maintain the excitement and interest that we had in our sexual interactions through years of marriage? Ann Landers queried her readers on the question: "Has your sex life gone downhill after marriage? If so, why?" She received over 140,000 replies from the United States as well as other countries. The respondents were nearly evenly divided between men and women. In her words: "The verdict was clear. Eighty-two percent said sex after marriage was less exciting. The adjectives that turned up most frequently were: boring, dull, monotonous, routine. The message came equally from both men and women" (Landers 1989 A and B). Her conclusion may be overdrawn because most people who respond to such public questionnaires tend to be dissatisfied and are looking to Ann Landers for answers to their problems. A couple satisfied with their sex life probably wouldn't respond to such a survey.

Certainly, many factors in married life do act to reduce sexual interaction and excitement. Monetary concerns, job demands, household chores, and children all conspire to rob a couple's sexual life of spontaneity and time. Both the quantity and quality of the average couple's sex life are diminished by the daily chores of maintaining a family. Many studies find that the quantity of sexual relations declines as time passes. However, the reduction in quantity seems less important to most couples than the reduction in quality. Quality sex takes time and concentration, both of which are lacking in a busy family, especially now when both partners are likely to be employed.

Couples with children find it especially hard to be alone together, and even when they are alone, concern about the children is very disruptive. "We don't make love until the kids are in bed and asleep. Then it's 'Be quiet,' or 'Don't make so much noise.'" Postponing sexual relations until the children are asleep often means that both parents are tired and sleepy themselves. Who wants to be romantic, build a fire, listen to music by candlelight, and spend three hours making love and attending to one another when it's 11:00 P.M. and you both must get up at 6:30 A.M. to get the children off to school and get to work on time?

Research indicates that husbands complain the most about their children interfering with their sex lives. Wives tend to dismiss the impact of childrearing as a temporary inconvenience or attribute their sexual problems to other factors such as fatigue. "Jennifer has taken a lot of time away from us. It seems like maybe on the weekend when we would normally like to sleep in, or just have lazy sex, Jennifer wakes up and needs to be fed. But I'm sure that will pass as soon as she gets a little older. We're just going through a phase," says one young mother.

It may be that for mothers the rewards of having children are so great that the costs are not recognized. Or mothers may find it so threatening to think that children disrupt their sex lives that they will not consider it. However, we do not believe that motherhood is blinding women to the truth about their sex lives. Mothers accept disruptions caused by children more readily than fathers do. Women do not feel less satisfied sexually when they have children. This makes them very different from their husbands who often feel deprived. (Blumstein and Schwartz 1983, 205)

Rather than continuing to discuss the various difficulties (jobs, housework, and so forth) that plague married couples' sex lives, let's examine a more ideal role that sex can come to play in a long-term healthy and growing relationship.

One Husband's Sexual Life

I find that after fifteen years of marriage the quality of our sex life has increased immensely even as the quantity has decreased. Sex between us seems to serve as a bonding agent. Sexual relations are embedded in our total relationship now rather than existing in and of themselves as they did at first. Perhaps I can best explain this situation by telling you what turns me on sexually now as compared to when my wife and I first met. You may be surprised.

Like most young men, I was at first attracted to her physical attractiveness, her smile, her body (wow!) her walk, and other physical qualities, and these attributes still attract me. Today, however, I can take a shower with her and not necessarily become sexually aroused. I couldn't even imagine such a thing at the start of our relationship. A tiny glimpse of her nude and I was turned on. If seeing her nude does not necessarily turn me on today, what does?

We take a ski trip with the children. I watch them happily skiing down the hill with grace and skill. Suddenly, I feel sexually aroused toward my wife. I'd like nothing better than to throw her down in the snow and make mad, passionate love to her. Why? Because she is the mother of these wonderful children. She bore them and cared for them and helped (along with me, I hope) to make them what they are. I admire and respect her and love her and want to tell her this. What better way to communicate this than to physically get close to her, feel her, share our love together?

We have a fight, and she makes the first efforts to resolve the conflict. I love her for still making the effort after fifteen years—for wanting to make the effort, for caring to make the effort. How lucky I am. How sexually attracted I am.

She is sound asleep. She looks peaceful and contented. She looks like an angel. I think back over the ups and downs of our relationship. I think of the things she really doesn't like about me but tolerates and accepts. I think about her encouragement when I tried something new or difficult. And suddenly I am sexually attracted to her and want to hold and cuddle her and tell her, "thank you."

Down inside I've been lusting for an expensive new car, which I know we can't afford and which I really won't buy. The new model that I have been reading about for three years finally is in the showrooms, and she suggests we go look at it. It is beautiful but out of our financial reach. She says, "You've worked hard, honey. Buy it, you deserve it. I'll help make ends meet." Whether I really buy it or not is immaterial. I want to take it for a drive to the hills and make love to her in the back seat because of her thought.

Of course, we have "quickie" sex. Of course, we have sex for sex. Of course, we have sex when there is no time, when we can't concentrate. But then there are times when our souls meet, when sex becomes the ultimate communication, when it stands for all the things she means to me, when it transcends all our differences, all our problems, when it becomes the ultimate expression of our love. Once you experience sex in this way, avant-garde discussions of number of orgasms, lovemaking techniques, sex as an end in itself, multiple partners, and the like pale in comparison.

Of course, I'm titillated at times by such thoughts. Of course, I'm attracted to other women at times. Of course, the sexual excitement is sometimes missing, but I wouldn't trade in our sex life. After all, it took years to build it into a meeting of our souls. Would I really trade that in on a one-night stand because I was horny? No way!

One of the dangers of the more liberal sexual practices may be that when sex becomes too casual, too taken for granted, or too available, the bonding qualities described by this husband may be lost. Many people—and especially women—who have participated to a great extent in liberalized sexual behavior now talk about the meaninglessness of sex in their lives (Chapter 4). In the *Psychology Today* follow-up sexuality study, the leading sexual problem mentioned by both men and women was "lack of desire." A whopping 40 percent of the women and 28 percent of the men felt lack of interest (Rubinstein 1982). As one sex therapist reports, "Being part of the meat market is appalling in terms of self-esteem" (Leo 1984, 78).

Therapists report that more and more often they are treating couples for **inhibited sexual desire.** This may be defined as pervasive disinterest in sex, with genital contact occurring less than twice a month, which is distressful to one partner. The problem with such a definition is that it implies some normal standard or level of sexual interaction. The only real standard is that both partners are happy and satisfied with their sexual interaction.

Inhibited sexual desire
A pervasive disinterest in sex

Many of my sexually active students report increasing dissatisfaction with their sexual relationships. Few seem to have deeply meaningful sexual relationships. Perhaps when a person knows a relationship is only transitory or fears that it may be, he or she guards against the impending loss by reserving total commitment and holding back from too much closeness. If such reservations are a constant part of one's premarital sexual life, they may carry over into one's married sexual life. In this case, premarital sexual activity may work against fulfilling, broadly meaningful marital sex.

Married couples must work to maintain a fulfilling sex life. First of all, it is imperative to find time alone together to concentrate on one another without distraction. When children are present, baby-sitting money is a couple's best expenditure in helping to maintain sexual happiness. Having a place that is comfortable, romantic, private, and, if possible, fairly soundproof will also help couples to relax. Constant worry that the children will hear is inhibiting to sexual activity.

One technique that some couples have found helpful is to start dating one another again, with the partners alternating responsibility for the dates. To add interest, some of the dates may be surprises. One partner asks the other out for a coming night but doesn't say what the date will be, indicating perhaps

Marital Sex: Can I
Keep the Excitement Alive?

365

PORNOGRAPHY IS HARMFUL TO WOMEN AND DESTRUCTIVE TO SOCIETY

Many groups in America believe pornography is harmful to women. Women's groups in particular express outrage over the constant pornographic depiction of women as sexual objects to be demeaned and brutalized. They especially abhor the increasing violence in pornographic material (Collins 1990). Neil Malamuth and Edward Donnerstein (1984) indicate that 15 percent of pornographic movies, 10 percent of pornographic magazines, and 30 percent of pornographic books convey messages of brutal disregard for the value of women as human beings. Further they found that men exposed to such materials become more tolerant of the idea of violence against women and actually become more aggressive toward women.

Many rape counselors report that rapists often expect women to like uninvited sex as is sometimes depicted in pornographic materials. Many rapists confess to being stimulated by pornographic materials. Again some researchers suggest that people become increasingly desensitized by pornographic material and that this insensitivity carries over to real life (Condron 1988). In addition, increasing desensitization leads to the need for more and more explicit and graphic pornographic materials in order "to turn" on sexually.

Another potential problem with easily available pornographic material is that people may get their sexual information from it rather than from valid sources that can supply correct knowledge. Young men viewing several men in a "gang bang" situation may come to believe that is what women want and act out these beliefs.

The high numbers of rapes and the increasing violence toward women are clear evidence of the harm that can be wrought by the easy availability of pornographic material, especially if sex is associated with violence toward women. The Meese Report (Final Report of the U.S. Attorney General's Commission on Pornography 1986) supported this conclusion and recommended numerous steps to fight the problem, such as the banning of obscene television programming and dial-a-porn telephone services. In June 1989, however, the U.S. Supreme court found that a state law banning dial-a-porn calls violated the First Amendment.

In 1992 the Canadian Supreme Court decided that pornography can cause violence against women. It concluded that when freedom of expression clashes with the rights of women and children to be protected against violent sex crimes, the rights of women and children come first. In addition to upholding the obscenity code, the court redefined obscenity to mean that which subordinates or degrades women.

PORNOGRAPHY CAN BE A SOURCE OF PLEASURE AND A STIMULANT TO AN UNSATISFACTORY SEX LIFE

Pornography is defined as any form of communication intended to cause sexual excitement. If this broad definition is taken literally banning pornography would also mean banning sex. How can people engage in sexual relations without somehow trying to cause sexual arousal? Historically, in the United States as well as in other societies, the graphic depiction of sexual interaction was an accepted art form and was indeed used to create sexual excitement. From ancient Greek vases to high relief carvings on Indian temples, portrayals of the sex act have been perfectly acceptable. The ancient Indian love manual *Kama Sutra,* dating from about A.D. 400 did not have to be hidden by its readers. Today Japanese films are notorious for their depictions of violence, bondage, and rape, often of young girls, yet Japan has one of the lowest rates of rape of any industrialized nation. Even in the United States, the government's blue ribbon commission on Obscenity and Pornography reported that it was unable to find evidence of direct harm caused by pornography. The later Meese Report, which declared pornography to be harmful to the family and society, has been taken to task by many researchers for stacking the evidence and drawing unwarranted conclusions.

In some ways, sexually explicit material can be of help to both society and to individuals. For example, poor though it may be, such material can serve an educational purpose by teaching persons who have had no sex education something about the sexes and sex.

Masters, Johnson, and Kolodny (1988, 374) list a number of ways in which sexually explicit material (erotica) can be useful. Erotica can trigger the imagination and thus helps people deal with forbidden or frightening areas in a controlled way. It gives people the opportunity to imaginatively rehearse acts that they hope to try or are curious about. It can provide pleasurable entertainment separate and apart from its sexual turn-on effect. But its most important use may be to stimulate a more active sex life between partners who have experienced some loss of interest.

Although in the past men have been thought to respond more frequently and strongly to erotica, the advent of the VCR and the availability of sexually explicit videos have increased women's participation in the use of erotic materials. Although very few women attend erotic movies in public theaters, about half of the erotic videos are now checked out by women.

Perhaps one might conclude that evil is in the eye of the beholder. What one person considers an art work and/or a reasonable adjunct to his or her sex life, another person may find unacceptable.

WHAT DO YOU THINK?

In 1987 Media General–Associated Press conducted a nationwide poll on pornography asking for opinions about the effects of pornography; attitudes toward the sexual content of advertising, novels, shows, and movies; and support for banning such material. How would you answer each of the following questions used in the Media General–Associated Press poll? Why do you agree, or disagree, with the majority in each question?

1. First, do you think reading or looking at pornography is generally harmful to adults or not?

Yes: 29 percent. No: 64 percent. Don't know, no answer: 7 percent.

2. (If yes) In what way? (Multiple answers OK)

Leads to sexual crimes: 27 percent. Causes psychological problems: 27 percent. Is against religious or moral beliefs: 23 percent. Other: 35 percent.

3. What do you think of stores that remove magazines like *Playboy* and *Penthouse* from newsstands? Do you think such action is appropriate or inappropriate?

Appropriate: 48 percent. Inappropriate: 41 percent. Don't know, no answer: 11 percent.

4. (If appropriate) Why do you feel that way? (Multiple answers OK)

Should not be accessible to young people: 45 percent. Don't like magazines: 23 percent. Seller should be al-

lowed to decide: 16 percent. Other reasons: 31 percent.

5. Are you offended by sexual content in advertising, or not?

Yes: 35 percent. No: 58 percent. Don't read or watch: 1 percent. Don't know, no answer: 6 percent.

6. Contemporary novels?

Yes: 16 percent. No: 70 percent. Don't read: 10 percent. Don't know, no answer 4 percent.

7. Television shows?

Yes: 39 percent. No: 52 percent. Don't watch: 4 percent. Don't know, no answer: 5 percent.

8. Hollywood movies?

Yes: 33 percent. No: 56 percent. Don't watch: 7 percent. Don't know, no answer: 4 percent.

9. Do you think magazines that show nudity should be banned in your community, allowed as long as they are kept out of sight or under the counter, or allowed with no restrictions?

Banned: 22 percent. Allowed out of sight: 55 percent. Allowed with no restrictions: 18 percent. Don't know, no answer: 5 percent.

10. How about magazines that show adults having sexual relations? Should they be banned from your community, allowed as long as they are under cover, or allowed with no restrictions?

Banned: 41 percent. Allowed under cover: 47 percent. Allowed with no restrictions: 8 percent. Don't know, no answer: 4 percent.

11. Should theaters that show X-rated movies be banned or allowed in your community?

Banned: 49 percent. Allowed: 44 percent. Don't know, no answer: 7 percent.

12. How about the sale or rental of X-rated home videocassettes? Should they be banned or allowed in your community?

Banned: 33 percent. Allowed: 60 percent. Don't know, no answer: 7 percent.

13. Have you ever read or looked through a magazine that features nudity?

Yes: 81 percent. No: 17 percent. Don't know, no answer: 2 percent.

14. Have you ever seen an X-rated movie or videocassette?

Yes: 61 percent. No: 37 percent. Don't know, no answer: 2 percent.

Source: Associated Press.

only the appropriate dress. Going back to places you visited when you met and fell in love, listening to music that rekindles memories, and doing things together that you both enjoy and make you laugh and relax all help to reawaken sexual interest.

Occasionally, there are physical reasons for loss of sexual desire. For example, some medicines for high blood pressure lower desire. If such a reason is suspected, the couple should check with their doctor. In general, however, the couple that makes working on their overall relationship a part of their everyday lives will stand the best chance of maintaining a satisfying sexual life.

SEX AND THE AGING PROCESS

For some inexplicable reason, the myth has grown up that for older persons sex is a thing of the past. Yet the natural function of sex endures as we age, just as other natural functions do, albeit in changing forms (Mulligan 1991). We don't expect to run as fast at age seventy or to have the physical strength we had at age twenty. Yet we accept these changes and don't give up jogging or exercise. Likewise, changes in our sexual functioning don't mean that we shouldn't still use it. In one of the few studies describing active, healthy Americans in their later years, Brecher (1984) concluded that the sexual interest and activity of older persons is one of the best-kept secrets in America. Men and women who have been sexually active early in life tend to remain so even in their eighties and nineties, although the frequency of intercourse is limited by their physical health and by social circumstances including lack of an available partner (Bretschneider and McCoy 1988).

Masters and Johnson, (1981) have found three criteria for continuing sexual activity regardless of age. First, one must have good general health. Second,

INSET 10-5
SEX AND PHYSICAL DISABILITY

The physically disabled (more than 11 million people) are sometimes thought to be uninterested in or unable to engage in sexual behavior. Generally, however, the disabled are every bit as interested in sexual behavior as anyone else. Although their disability may prevent them from engaging in certain kinds of sexual behavior, this does not mean that they are less interested in sex than they might otherwise be. The love and intimacy that can be expressed in various forms of sexual interaction are as important to the disabled person as to anyone else. In fact, sexual expression may be even more important to the disabled because it verifies their acceptability to others.

"People in wheelchairs have to stop thinking that their sex life is over," said one spinal-cord injured patient. "While your genitals may or may not be dead, your emotions are very much alive. And you can still express your emotions without your genitals—your eyes, hands, fingers, lips, and tongue still work." (Knox 1984, 394)

Various diseases can also interfere with sexual expression. For example, a person with rheumatoid arthritis, swollen and painful joints, and muscular atrophy, may experience pain when interacting sexually with a partner, depending on the positions used. The couple may have to select sexual positions carefully and choose times when the arthritis is quiescent. If the arthritis responds to heat, the individual may need to plan sex after a warm bath.

Sexual enrichment aids are also available, often from mail-order catalogs, that can help disabled persons who have difficulty sexually.

What is clear is that sexuality is important to all people and important to the building of intimate relationships. When someone is injured or has a disease that interferes with normal sexual expression, the person and his or her partner must be creative and learn different ways of expressing sexuality.

an interesting and interested sexual partner is necessary. Third, past fifty years of age, the sexual organs must be used. "Use it or lose it" is their advice to aging people, especially males.

As a man moves past his mid-fifties, he may notice four changes in his basic sexual physiology:

1. He may take longer to achieve a full erection even with overt sexual stimulation, and he may experience fewer spontaneous erections. His former pattern of rapid erective responses to real or imagined sexual opportunity becomes slowed and more dependent on his partner's direct physical approach (Masters, Johnson, and Kolodny 1988; Cross 1989).
2. He may notice a reduction in expulsive pressure.
3. The volume of seminal fluid during ejaculation may be reduced.
4. He may notice an occasional reduction or loss of ejaculatory demand. Aging men continue to have a high level of interest in the sensual pleasure specific to sex, but subjectively the need they feel to ejaculate may be reduced. Perhaps one out of three or four times that aging men have intercourse, they may not experience the need to ejaculate. It's not that they can't if they force the issue; they just don't feel the need.

Knowledge of such changes is important for both the man and his partner. If a man does not anticipate and understand the changes associated with aging,

Sex and the Aging Process

he may develop fears about his sexual performance that may rob him of his sexual desire. If his partner does not understand these changes, she may question her own sexuality when confronted by them. For example, she may interpret his slower erective response as loss of interest in her. If he doesn't ejaculate regularly, she may be concerned that he doesn't desire her.

The aging process also brings changes in the woman's sexual facility. The older woman produces less lubricating fluid and at a slower rate. Because the vaginal walls lose some of their elasticity, sudden penile penetration or long-continued coital thrusting can create small fissures in the lining of the vagina. As with the aging male, more time should be allocated for precoital stimulation. If neither partner evidences a sense of urgency in sexual interaction, erections and lubrication usually develop satisfactorily. Even with these physiological changes, it is important to remember that the psychologically appreciated levels of sensual pleasure derived from sex continue unabated.

Older men and women are losing their sexual involvement far earlier than necessary because little effort has been made to educate them to the physiological facts of aging sexual function. Older people are and should continue to be sexually responsive human beings.

SEX AND DRUGS

Aphrodisiac
A chemical or other substance used to induce erotic arousal or to relieve impotence or infertility

People have long sought the ideal **aphrodisiac,** a substance that would arouse sexual desire. Thus far, the search has failed, although extensive folklore exists about such things as powdered rhinoceros horn, "Spanish fly" or cantharis, ginseng, and alcohol. None of these claims hold up in scientific experiments (Covington and McClendon 1987; Pechter 1988).

Alcohol is the most widely used sexual stimulant in America, but in reality it is a depressant and inhibits the sexual response in males if ingested in large amounts. Long-term alcohol consumption increases the production of a liver enzyme that destroys testosterone, thereby reducing sexual desire (Klassen and Wilsnack 1986; Lang 1985;). Sexual-response times for erection and ejaculation are also increased as alcohol ingestion increases. In women the effects of alcohol are somewhat more mixed than in men. Researchers (Malatesta 1982) found that women who had drunk large quantities of alcohol had a more difficult time achieving orgasm and experienced less orgasmic intensity. Despite these findings, the women believed (self-reports) that they experienced increased sexual arousal and heightened pleasure. Alcohol's reputation as an aphrodisiac apparently stems from its psychological effects: It loosens controls and inhibitions, thereby indirectly stimulating sexual behavior. Perhaps Shakespeare's phrase about "much drink" best sums up the effect of alcohol on sex: "It provokes the desire, but it takes away the performance."

Marijuana has mixed effects on sexuality. There is no evidence that it heightens physical reactions, but it does cause some sense distortion that probably increases sexual sensitivity, especially sensitivity to touch, with a compatible partner. As a true aphrodisiac, however, it is a failure in that it appears

	N	SECONDARY IMPOTENCE	PREMATURE EJACULATION
TABLE 10-3 **MALE SEXUAL DYSFUNCTION** **AND CHRONIC MARIJUANA USE**			
Control group (no use)	225	8.4%	14.2%
Group A (less than once a week)	272	8.5	13.2
Group B (1 to 2 times a week)	342	7.3	14.0
Group C (3, 4, and 5 times a week)	117	13.7	12.8
Group D (daily use)	94	19.2	16.0

to have neither a positive nor a negative effect on sexual desire. Some evidence indicates that those who use marijuana heavily for prolonged periods have a higher incidence of impotence than nonusers, probably because testosterone levels drop. Feelings of increased sexuality probably stem from reduced inhibitions and the relaxing of tensions as in the case of alcohol.

Robert Kolodny (1981) studied five groups using different amounts of marijuana for sexual dysfunction. Table 10-3 catalogs the results. Those who used marijuana infrequently showed no effects on either secondary impotence (unable to consistently have an erection) or premature ejaculation (see Chapter 11). Chronic marijuana use, however, was clearly related to secondary impotence but apparently unrelated to premature ejaculation. Those using marijuana every day showed almost two and a half times more secondary impotence than those using it fewer than three times a week.

LSD, by distorting time, may seem to prolong the sexual experience. It is not, however, linked with enhanced sexual response. A bad "trip" (frightening hallucinations and so forth) can have disastrous effects on one's sexuality (Jones and Jones 1977; Crooks and Baur 1987, 175).

Amphetamines (speed) act as stimulants, in that the male can maintain a prolonged erection, but their long-term use destroys general health as well as sex drive and ultimately leads to impotence. Cocaine has similar effects. For the female, these drugs have a drying effect on vaginal secretions, so prolonged intercourse may be uncomfortable unless extra lubrication is supplied. Direct injection of cocaine seems to prolong a man's erection (Rubinstein 1982). Kolodny (1985) found, as did Weinstein and Gottheil (1986), that 17 percent of his sample of cocaine users had episodes of erectile failure when they used the drug, and 4 percent had experienced priapism (painful, persistent erections) at least once during or immediately after use of cocaine. Siegel (1982) reported that the dangerous practice of "free-basing" cocaine consistently leads to sexual disinterest and situational impotence. Kolodny (1985) studied 60 male crack users and found that more than two-thirds were sexually dysfunctional, while 23 of 30 female crack users reported decreased sexual interest and responsiveness. Some cocaine users believe that placing the substance directly on the end of the penis or on the clitoris heightens sensitivity, but the opposite is true. Cocaine is a local anesthetic and therefore acts to deaden the area to which it is applied. It is interesting to note that because cocaine is expensive, offering it to a person of the opposite sex is almost always secondarily an

Sex and Drugs

invitation to have sexual interaction as well. After much research on the relationship between cocaine and sex, Kolodny (1985) noted:

> Widely available at singles bars and in the economically advantaged "just-got-a-divorce" crowd, cocaine literally opens the doors of sexual access for many males and provides a convenient excuse for many females who otherwise might pass on having "instant sex" with a partner they hardly know.

The Roman philosopher Seneca knew the best aphrodisiac: "I show you a philtre [potion], without medicaments, without herbs, without witch's incantations. It is this: If you want to be loved, love." Masters and Johnson echo this when they say that intimacy—being close to another in all ways—is the best stimulant to eroticism.

Anaphrodisiacs are drugs that decrease sexual desire and activity. Perhaps the best known is saltpeter (potassium nitrate). Saltpeter acts as a diuretic, and frequent urination may deter sexual activity. However, saltpeter has no known direct physiological effect on sexual behavior.

Four groups of drugs impair sexual functioning. *Sedatives* such as barbiturates and narcotics can suppress sexual interest and response. *Antiandrogens* are drugs that counter the effect of androgen (a male sex hormone) on the brain and thus diminish sexual responsiveness. *Anticholenergic* and *antiadrenergic* drugs work to diminish sexual response by blocking the blood vessels and nerves connected to the genitals. These drugs are used to treat diseases of the eye, high blood pressure, and circulatory problems. Two drugs commonly used to treat hypertension, reserpine and methyldopa, cause loss of sexual interest and erectile incompetence (Gotwald and Golden 1981). *Psychotropic drugs* such as tranquilizers and muscle relaxants may cause ejaculatory and erectile difficulties. Some of the psychiatric drugs reported to cause erectile dysfunction include Tofranil, Vivactil, Pertofrane, and Nardil. Those reported to impair or delay ejaculation include Librium, Haldol, and Elavil (Knox 1984, 174).

Regular use of opiates such as heroin, morphine, and methodone often produces a significant drop in sexual interest and activity in both sexes. Nicotine has the same result in men (Abel 1984; Crooks and Baur 1987; Hagen and D'Agostino 1982).

As this discussion shows, there are a number of drugs with known anaphrodisiac qualities. Drugs with aphrodisiac qualities are less understood and are often surrounded by unsubstantiated folktales.

Anaphrodisiac
A drug or medicine that reduces sexual desire

SEXUALLY TRANSMITTED DISEASES

Unfortunately, no discussion of human sexuality is complete without mention of the most social of human diseases, that oft-found bedmate, sexually transmitted disease (STD) (Table 10-4). In the past, the incidence of such diseases in the United States was drastically reduced by the use of antibiotics such as penicillin. Recently, however, there has been an STD epidemic. For example, gonorrhea is the most commonly reported communicable disease in the United

TABLE 10-4
SEXUALLY TRANSMITTED DISEASES (STDs)

DISEASE	CAUSE	INCUBATION PERIOD[a]	CHARACTERISTICS	TREATMENT[b]
Primary syphilis	Bacteria	7–90 days (usually 3 weeks)	Small, painless sore or chancre, usually on genitals but also on other parts of the body	Penicillin and broad-spectrum antibiotics
Secondary syphilis	Untreated primary		Skin rashes or completely latent, enlarged lymph glands	Same
Tertiary syphilis	Untreated primary		Possible invasion of central nervous system, causing various paralyses; heart trouble; insanity	Same
Gonorrhea	Bacteria	3–5 days	Discharge, burning, pain, swelling of genitals and glands; possible loss of erectile ability in males who delay treatment, with chance of permanent sterility; 80% of infected females asymptomatic	Same
Chancroid	Bacteria	2–6 days	Shallow, painful ulcers, swollen lymph glands in groin	Sulfa drugs, broad-spectrum antibiotics
Lymphogranuloma venereum	Virus	5–30 days	First, small blisters, then swollen lymph glands; may affect kidneys	Broad-spectrum antibiotics
Genital herpes	Virus	Unknown	Blisters in genital area; very persistent	Pain-relieving ointments
Chlamydia	Bacteria	10–20 days	Men: early morning watery discharge, hot or itchy feeling within penis Women: may be similar to men or symptom free Untreated causes pelvic inflammatory disease leading to infertility	Tetracycline
Genital warts	Virus	Unknown	Observable in genital areas	Removed by freezing or ointment
AIDS	Virus	5–12 years	Many symptoms	Treat symptoms

Note: As soon as you suspect any sexually transmitted disease or notice any symptoms, consult your doctor, local health clinic, or local or state health department. Both syphilis and gonorrhea, in particular, can be easily treated if detected early; if not, both can become recurrent, with dire results.

[a]If sexually transmitted disease is diagnosed, all sexual partners during the infected person's incubation period and up to discovery of the disease should be examined medically.

[b]Local health clinics or local and state health departments will have more detailed information on current treatment and follow-up.

States (Hatcher et al. 1990, 110). In addition, the number of sexually transmitted diseases has increased to include twenty organisms and syndromes.

At least three factors have played a role in the resurgence of STDs:

1. Because the pill has become a major method of birth control, the condom, with its built-in protective barrier against STD infection, is no longer so widely used. Due to AIDS, however, its use is rapidly increasing.

2. The antibiotics themselves have lulled people into apathy. "Who cares about STDs, they're easy to cure" appears to be a common attitude. (Although this belief is partly true, cure depends on prompt treatment; furthermore, new forms of antibiotic-resistant strains of the infecting organisms are appearing.)

Sexually Transmitted Diseases

3. The increased sexual activity among the young, especially the increased number of sexual partners, has contributed to the widespread outbreak of STDs.

If you, your spouse, or a sexual partner suspects an STD, have a medical examination as soon as possible. In most cases the disease does not "go away," even though some of its symptoms may change or even disappear. If treatment is begun early, it is effective; if it is delayed, the disease may recur or become more dangerous. Anyone seeking treatment will be treated with confidentiality. If an STD is diagnosed, all persons who have had recent sexual contact with the carrier should be notified and should also be examined. With increased public awareness of STDs, it is hoped that their incidence can be cut back to earlier low levels, although that has not yet started to happen. Although we cannot discuss all of the many STDs, some of the more prevalent or dangerous will be examined here.

■ GENITAL HERPES ■

Of the various kinds of STD, AIDS and genital herpes are the most discussed. Genital herpes appears to be infecting Americans at a rate of 200,000 per year, yet the disease was practically unknown to the public just a few years ago. Of the five types of human herpes, Types I and II are at the center of the current epidemic. Type I is most familiar as the cause of cold sores; Type II causes genital lesions. The two types are similar, with Type I also being capable of causing genital problems.

The first symptom of genital herpes is usually an itching or tingling sensation. Blisters appear within two to fifteen days after infection. The moist blisters ooze a fluid that is extremely infectious. After one to three weeks, the blisters gradually dry up and disappear. The infected area is extremely sensitive and sore to the touch. For this reason sexual activity is precluded when genital herpes is in an active state. In addition, unless the herpes sores are completely healed, the friction of sexual activity can reactivate them.

Because the herpes virus remains in the body once it has been contracted, it can be activated at any time. The exact causes of reactivation are not known, but stress, sunshine, and nutritional and environmental changes are clearly involved (Francoeur 1991, 347). Indeed, herpes is so closely related to a person's moods and emotions that learning to remain calm and under emotional control is one of the most effective preventives against its reactivation.

At this time there is no cure for genital herpes, only treatment for its symptoms. Acyclovir (trade name Zovirax), a creamy salve, alleviates symptoms and speeds healing. Unfortunately, it is less effective on subsequent episodes and does nothing to reduce the frequency of outbreak. Some evidence, however, indicates that taken in oral form it reduces both the severity and frequency of outbreak.

Because no cure exists, many herpes sufferers have sought help from one another. A national group that encourages this self-help is the Herpes Resource Center in Palo Alto, California, which has chapters known as "help groups." The chapters offer group therapy sessions, where newcomers can talk about their problems and those with herpes are assured that they are not alone.

Although herpes is not as physically threatening as syphilis, its incurability is so discomforting and its incidence so widespread that it is beginning to put a damper on indiscriminate sexual contacts. In part, because herpes is not yet curable, it is especially important that infected persons share this fact with their partners. In fact, failure to do so is leading people into court. Numerous damage suits have been brought by partners of infected persons who were not apprised of the infected partner's condition. Perhaps the best-known case to date was filed against the singer Tony Bennett by a woman asking for damages of $90 million (*Time*, 1987). Such cases are also being brought by persons contracting other sexually transmitted diseases such as AIDS. In the latter case, Marc Christian, the last lover of movie star Rock Hudson, was awarded millions of dollars in damages because Hudson failed to disclose that he was suffering from AIDS.

■ WHAT IS AIDS? ■

In the newspaper, on the radio, on television, and in your friends' discussions, you frequently hear the term "AIDS." In June 1989, in an unprecedented action, the U.S. government mailed a pamphlet, *Understanding AIDS*, to all American households. Often the term AIDS is surrounded by emotion and fear because AIDS kills people and at present there is no known cure. By now you probably know that AIDS involves the most intimate aspects of your life, namely, sexual behavior. Although AIDS is closely associated with the sexual aspects of your life, it is also related to drug use, blood transfusions, and pregnancy and birth. Since there are no effective vaccines against AIDS, your best protection against this new deadly disease is information.

How can I live a full life but avoid contracting or spreading AIDS? To answer this question, you must know what AIDS is, how it is transmitted, and what steps you can take to prevent its spread. Because AIDS involves intimate aspects of your life, the answers also involve moral and ethical judgments, both about yourself and your relationships with others.

We use the letters "AIDS" to denote a deadly group of diseases caused by newly discovered viruses. The letters stand for a long name—*Acquired immune deficiency syndrome*. *Acquired* means that the conditions are not inherited but are acquired from environmental factors, such as virus infections. *Immune deficiency* means that AIDS causes deficient immunity, often reflected in poor nutrition, low resistance to infections, and to cancer. *Syndrome* means that AIDS causes several kinds of diseases, each with characteristic clusters of signs and symptoms.

The virus that causes AIDS has different names, but the preferred term that most scientists are now using is *HIV (human immunodeficiency virus)*. Although we usually speak of one AIDS virus, there are, in fact, several related viruses that can cause AIDS, AIDS-related conditions, and cancers in human beings.

Source: This AIDS information was derived from many sources. The most important are the International Conferences on AIDS, 1985–1992; *Morbidity and Mortality Weekly Report* (Atlanta, Ga.: Centers for Disease Control, June 1981–1992); *HIV/AIDS Surveillance* (Atlanta, Ga.: Centers for Disease Control); Frank Cox, *The AIDS Booklet* (Dubuque, Iowa: William C. Brown, 1992).

Sexually Transmitted Diseases

People afflicted with AIDS usually suffer with varying combinations of severe weight loss, many types of infections, and several kinds of cancer. Several of these symptoms may occur at one time. The usual result is that AIDS-afflicted persons go through long, miserable illnesses that end in death one to two years after first diagnosis. The person does not actually die from AIDS but from one of the opportunistic diseases that strike because of the damaged immune system. This general description does not apply to every person with AIDS. Some persons with AIDS alternate between periods of sickness and periods of fairly good health, at least in the early period after diagnosis. Some people die within a few months while a very few persons have now lived eight or more years after the initial diagnosis.

Varying symptoms are associated with AIDS because, as the name implies, the AIDS virus (HIV) impairs the body's ability to fight infection. HIV does this by destroying **lymphocytes,** or "lymph cells." These cells are the most common kind of white blood cells and form the basis of the body's **immune system** (its biological defense system). Lymphocytes help to prevent cancers by controlling cell growth and guard against infections by producing **antibodies** (proteins that fight infection). The AIDS virus destroys the ability of the lymphocytes to perform these functions. Consequently, persons with AIDS appear undernourished and wasted, often have cancer, and lack protection against infections.

Lymphocyte
A type of white blood cell that is active in the body's immune system

Immune system
The body's biological defense system that wards off disease and illness

Antibody
A protein produced by white blood cells that fights infection

WHAT ARE THE GENERAL SYMPTOMS?

Once the AIDS viruses get into your body, the following symptoms are likely to appear:

1. Loss of appetite with weight loss of ten or more pounds in two months or less.

2. Swollen glands (lymph glands) in the neck, armpits, or groin that persist for three months or more.

3. Severe tiredness (not related to exercise or drug use).

4. Unexplained persistent or recurrent fevers, often with night sweats.

5. Persistent unexplained cough (not from smoking, cold, or flu), often associated with a shortness of breath.

6. Unexplained persistent diarrhea.

7. Persistent white coating or spots inside the mouth or throat that may be accompanied by soreness and difficulty in swallowing.

8. Persistent purple or brown lumps or spots on the skin. They look like small bruises on fair-skinned people and appear darker than the surrounding skin on darker-skinned people.

9. Nervous system problems including loss of memory, inability to think clearly, loss of judgment, and/or depression.

10. Other problems such as headaches, stiff neck, and numbness or muscle weakness may occur.

Any of these symptoms may be caused by diseases other than AIDS, so self-diagnosis is difficult. If such symptoms persist or if several appear at the same time, exposure to HIV is a possibility, and you should immediately see a physician familiar with the disease.

THE INCUBATION PERIOD AND USUAL COURSE OF AIDS

Within a few weeks after first exposure, some HIV-infected persons develop an illness that lasts seven to fourteen days; symptoms include enlargement of the lymph glands, sore throat, fever, muscle ache, headache, and a skin rash that may look like measles. HIV can be detected in circulating blood lymphocytes at this time, but tests for antibodies to HIV seldom become positive until six weeks to six months later. This early illness usually disappears or is often so mild that it is not even remembered. *The infected person is now contagious for the remainder of his or her lifetime, however, and can transmit HIV to other persons.*

Months or years may now pass without any signs of AIDS in the infected person. However, usually five to twelve years after initial exposure, the infected person can expect to come down with one or more of the characteristic signs of AIDS. Just how long the incubation period can be for any one individual is currently unknown. Some researchers predict that an incubation period as long as twenty years may be possible. Be that as it may, once AIDS appears, death will usually follow within the next two years. At this time, 66 percent of all Americans who have developed AIDS have died (approximately 160,000 as of January 1993).

OCCURRENCE OF AIDS

The number of cases in the United States is doubling about every three years, leading the Centers for Disease Control (CDC) to predict there will be approximately 350,000 cases by 1994 (see also Figure 10-2). Researchers estimate that there are currently 1.5 to 2 million persons who have the virus present in their blood but show no symptoms of the disease. Such a person is termed **seropositive.** *A virus carrier can spread the disease, however.* At present, we do not know what percentage of those infected will actually contract clinical AIDS. Some researchers suggest that over time all HIV-infected persons will eventually develop AIDS.

AIDS cases can be divided into the following categories:

Seropositive
Blood reacts positively to a test for a disease or illness, indicating that the person is carrying the disease germ or virus

Category	Percentage of AIDS Cases
Sexually active homosexual and bisexual men (or men who have had sex with another man since 1977)	58%
Homosexual and bisexual men who are also intravenous drug users	6
Present or past users of illegal intravenous drugs	23
Persons with hemophilia or other blood-clotting disorders who have received blood-clotting factors	1
Persons who have had transfusions of blood or blood products	2
Heterosexual men and women (including sex partners of persons with AIDS or at risk for AIDS and people born in countries where heterosexual transmission is thought to be common)	5–6
Other/unknown	4

Sexually Transmitted Diseases

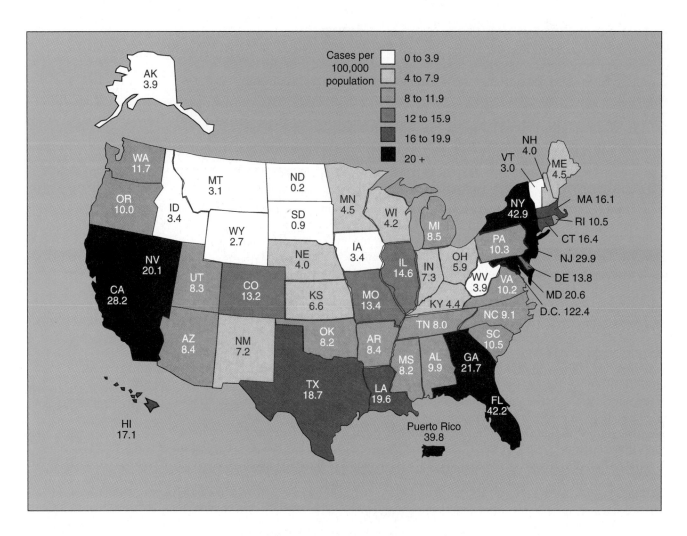

Cases per 100,000 population

- 0 to 3.9
- 4 to 7.9
- 8 to 11.9
- 12 to 15.9
- 16 to 19.9
- 20 +

FIGURE 10-2
AIDS annual rates per 100,000 population, for cases reported April 1991 through March 1992
Source: HIV/AIDS Surveillance Report, Centers for Disease Control, April 1992

Although anyone engaging in the known practices by which AIDS is transmitted can contract the disease, 89 percent of the AIDS cases in the United States are found in men between the ages of twenty and fifty. Women account for only 11 percent of all AIDS cases. Although young people (below age twenty) account for 31 percent of the American population, only 1 percent of persons with AIDS fall into this age range. Many persons with AIDS who are now in their early twenties must have become infected while in their teens, however. Because of its long incubation period, AIDS does not appear until years after exposure to the virus.

AIDS is found in all races. In the United States, approximately 54 percent of persons with AIDS are white, 29 percent are African American, and 16 percent are Hispanic. In absolute numbers, the problem of AIDS among minorities does not compare with the problem among whites. However, when we consider that African Americans represent only 12 percent and Hispanics only 8 percent of the U.S. population, both groups clearly appear to be at high risk. The statistics for women with AIDS reveal that 52 percent are African American and 20 percent are Hispanic. Although children under five years of age account for less than 1 percent of all persons with AIDS, nearly 80 percent are either African American or Hispanic.

In contrast to the United States, in some countries in central Africa, intravenous drug use and homosexuality are uncommon. *In these countries, AIDS is found equally among women and men and is spread partially by customary heterosexual relations. Such countries indicate that AIDS can infect anyone—including you—not just persons who abuse drugs or engage in homosexual activity.* However, the fact that only 5–6 percent of U.S. AIDS cases are classified as non-drug-abusing heterosexual persons means that there is still a good chance that AIDS can be stopped before it spreads throughout the general population. Most persons with AIDS categorized as heterosexual have had heterosexual contact with a person with AIDS or at high risk for AIDS or were born in African or Caribbean nations with high rates of AIDS infection.

How Do You Get AIDS?

You've no doubt read and heard about many different ways people can get AIDS. Some of the stories are true, but many are false. Unfortunately, you may be afraid of catching AIDS when you need not be. Even more unfortunately, you may not be afraid of catching AIDS when you should be. Fear is usually not very helpful when you are trying to understand and make logical decisions. Knowing the actual ways AIDS is transmitted as well as the ways AIDS *is not* transmitted is vital to your health.

High-Risk Behaviors Until now AIDS has infected very specific groups of persons in the United States. By studying these groups and their behavior patterns, we have gained a better understanding of how the causative viruses are spread and the kinds of precautions that all people must take to avoid contracting or spreading the disease. Since anyone engaging in risky behaviors can become infected with or transmit HIV, it is critical that we learn from the people infected at this time.

Essentially, such high-risk groups tell us that certain sexual behaviors and drug-related activities are the major means by which AIDS is transmitted in the United States. These groups tell us that engaging indiscriminately in sexual or drug activities with multiple partners is particularly dangerous.

Essentially, HIV is primarily spread through the sharing of virus-infected lymphocytes in *semen* (the thick, whitish fluid secreted by the male during ejaculation) and in *blood*. *Specifically the major ways AIDS is transmitted are by engaging in sexual behavior or sharing needles for intravenous drugs with different partners with little or no discrimination.* For example, if you have sex or share drug needles with two other persons, each of whom has also shared these activities with two other persons and so on, you quickly find that you have interacted with literally hundreds of people. *In other words, when you have sex with someone, you are having sex with everyone he or she has ever slept with as well as the partners of those persons and so on.* AIDS is also spread in a few other ways such as during pregnancy and birth (to the newborn), through HIV-infected lymphocytes in a mother's milk and occasionally through transfusion of blood or blood products.

Sexual Behavior *AIDS is primarily a SEXUALLY TRANSMITTED DISEASE.* Thus, it is transmitted in much the same way as other STDs such as syphilis and gonorrhea. Sexual contact with persons who have the disease or carry the virus is currently the most common way by which AIDS is transmitted. Avoidance of sexual contact (**abstinence**) is the best way to keep from being infected. The *safer sex* you have been hearing so much about, especially from the homosexual (gay) male groups fighting AIDS, involves using condoms and other methods to avoid sharing bodily fluids (semen in particular). However, so-called safer sex does not eliminate the danger completely, and avoidance of sexual contact outside of long-term mutually **monogamous** (the practice of having only one sexual partner) relationships is the only really safe sex.

Certain sexual practices are very liable to transmit AIDS and therefore should be avoided. Receptive anal-rectal intercourse (allowing the penis to enter one's rectum) appears to be the most dangerous sexual practice. Because the rectum is lined by a thin, single-cell layer, virus-infected lymphocytes in semen can migrate through the lining. This area of the body is richly supplied with blood vessels, and insertion of the penis or other objects into it is very apt to result in tearing and bleeding.

Fellatio (insertion of the penis into the partner's mouth) may also be a means of AIDS transmission. Persons with tooth or gum infections are particularly at risk. The possibility that teeth may accidentally break the skin of the penis is another risk of fellatio. Since the semen of an infected person has a high concentration of HIV, it is probably not a good idea to swallow it although there is no current evidence of transmission in this manner.

Vaginal intercourse can transmit AIDS to either men or women, although researchers currently are unsure what the mechanism for transmission is. The lining of the vagina itself is thick and difficult for the virus-infected lymphocytes to penetrate. In addition, the normally acidic (acid) environment of the vagina is not hospitable to the AIDS virus. However, the uterus is lined with only a single layer of cells, which is more easily penetrated. Semen is probably most apt to reach the uterus with prolonged or repeated acts of intercourse. It also appears that due to the high concentration of the virus in semen, HIV is more easily transmitted to the woman than from the infected woman to her male partner. Fortunately, for most females and males who enjoy regular vaginal intercourse and mutually monogamous patterns of sexual relationships, there is little or no danger of contracting AIDS. The use of condoms with a spermicide such as nonoxynol-9, attention to adequate lubrication, abstinence from sex during menstruation, and mutually monogamous relationships can all help prevent the spread of AIDS.

Drug Abuse   *Intravenous* (IV) drug users shoot drugs directly into their veins using syringes and needles. IV drug users who share syringes and needles are the second largest group of people with AIDS in the United States. In some parts of the country such as New York and New Jersey, IV drug users constitute the majority of infected persons. IV drug users are important because they represent the major bridge by which AIDS spreads to women and children and thereby enters the general population. This group serves as a bridge in three ways:

1. A heterosexual partner may be infected through sexual contact.
2. Infected blood may be shared via needles used to inject drugs.
3. Babies born to mothers infected by sexual contact or shared needles may also be infected. A baby can be infected either by lymphocytes migrating

through the *placenta* (the internal organ that develops with pregnancy and through which the fetus absorbs oxygen and nutrients and excretes wastes) or by lymphocytes in the mother's milk when she nurses the baby.

IV drug users are extremely hazardous because, unlike homosexual men who have organized to fight the spread of AIDS, drug users are engaged in illegal behavior and thus cannot openly organize to fight AIDS. Many women IV drug users resort to prostitution to support their drug habits. Thus, if infected, they add to the risk of spreading AIDS via sexual relations. Also, when under influence of drugs, people are often unaware of exactly what they are doing. Thus, they may not practice lower-risk behaviors and may use unsafe methods when **shooting up** (injecting drugs into the body with a needle and syringe). Sharing infected blood in needles is the major way AIDS is transmitted between IV drug users.

Unfortunately, drug users are difficult persons to reach. Attempts to educate this group to the dangers of AIDS and methods of prevention have not been very successful so far. As is the case with sexual transmission, *the best defense against AIDS is avoidance—simply not using drugs at all.*

Blood Supply and Transfusions   Transfusions and the use of contaminated blood products account for only 3 percent (including the hemophilia category) of AIDS cases in the United States. Fortunately, the chances of infection are small and have become smaller since the possibility of transmission through infected blood has been recognized.

Starting in 1985, blood donations have been tested for contamination by HIV. The test, which is known as ELISA (enzyme-linked immunoabsorbent assay), checks to see if antibodies against the AIDS virus have formed. If the test is positive, the blood is discarded, and the donor is notified confidentially that she or he has been infected with HIV. This does not mean that the individual has AIDS but only that exposure to the virus has occurred. ELISA has helped to reduce AIDS transmission via contaminated blood products. Unfortunately, the tests are not perfect for a number of reasons so that the chance (although small) of AIDS infection via contaminated blood or blood products still remains. The CDC suggests the chances of infection via blood transfusion are about 1 in 60,000 although some researchers suggest the chances of infection are higher.

Casual Transmission (The Transmission of AIDS without Sexual Contact or Intravenous Drug Use   One of the most important things to understand about AIDS is that the chances of casual transmission are very low. By this we mean that AIDS is transmitted in very specific and limited ways, most often involving sexual contact or the sharing of needles among drug users. Outside these specific means of transmission, AIDS does not seem to move from the infected to noninfected person easily. If AIDS were casually transmitted, it would be found in much larger numbers throughout the population by this time. Being around a person with AIDS is not considered dangerous unless you have sex or share needles and drugs. Although we cannot be 100 percent certain that casual transmission never happens, so far, nearly all cases have been traced to the sharing of infected lymphocytes in semen, blood, or blood products. In general, no one is likely to get AIDS by shaking hands, patting a friend on the shoulder, superficial kissing, drinking from the same

Shooting up
Injecting drugs directly into the bloodstream with a needle and syringe

Sexually Transmitted Diseases

381

cup, working in the same office, eating food served by infected persons, being sneezed or coughed on, using public restrooms, and other casual contacts.

PREVENTING AIDS

The following are measures that can be taken to prevent AIDS:

1. Sexual abstinence, especially when a caring relationship is not involved.
2. Sexual fidelity.
3. If you want to have sexual relations, but are not in a permanent monogamous relationship, use mechanical barriers to prevent the exchange of potentially infectious body fluids, especially blood, semen, and uterine secretions.
4. Use barriers proven to prevent pregnancy as well as STDs:
   a. *Latex* condoms approved by the Food and Drug Administration (FDA) can protect a woman and a man from sharing semen and vaginal secretions during conventional vaginal intercourse.
   b. Doctor-prescribed and fitted vaginal diaphragms or cervical caps block semen from reaching the uterus.
   c. In addition, use spermicides such as nonoxynol-9, which paralyze sperm and migrant lymphocytes that may have gotten past the barrier. A few people will have allergic reactions to specific spermicides.
5. Use barriers strictly in accordance with recommendations supplied by the FDA, as well as inserts supplied by the manufacturers. A great deal of careful research, time, and effort are embodied in these recommendations.
6. Avoid anal intercourse with or without a condom because this is the most dangerous way to share semen; condoms are not well designed for this means of sexual expression.
7. Avoid sexual relations with persons at great risk for having AIDS or other transmissible viruses, such as homosexual or bisexual persons, persons who "shoot" drugs, or persons who sell or buy sex.
8. Do not use alcohol or drugs. They interfere with your caring for yourself, as well as for other persons; and especially avoid the use of drugs that are injected into the veins.
9. Do not share needles used for injecting drugs into the veins or handle sharp instruments contaminated with the blood of other persons.
10. Donate blood to your community blood banks and encourage your healthy friends to do so as often as possible. Such donations will help save lives and protect the blood supply from possible contamination.
11. If you know well ahead of time that you might need blood during an operation, predonate, and let your caring friends of similar blood type know that their donations would be appreciated.
12. Continue to build caring, meaningful, and trusting relationships with people with whom you are intimate. Everyone will benefit.
13. Regarding persons with whom you are not intimate, who are sick with any disease, or are known to have AIDS, your sincere caring will prove to be mutually helpful.
14. Although AIDS seems destined to become one of the most deadly epidemics humans have faced, do not be afraid. Your chances of becoming infected are near zero if you apply the foregoing precautions.
15. Do not pay attention to rumors and hearsay about AIDS. Whenever you have questions about AIDS or behavior that increases the chances of exposure,

seek out answers from health professionals, medical clinics, teachers, counselors, and other knowledgeable persons.

16. Last, but not least, do not be lulled into a sense of complacency or apathy encouraged by the conflicting reports on AIDS in the news media. Although significant breakthroughs are often reported, you must do all you can to protect yourself from acquiring the virus since all real and permanent cures are still in the distant future.

POSSIBLE LEGAL RAMIFICATIONS

Several interesting legal questions arise when the blood test for detecting antibodies to the HIV virus is used on individuals. A positive reaction to the test (meaning that the individual has been exposed to the virus) indicates that the individual is a carrier of the virus and thus has the potential to infect others. If a person, knowing that he or she is a carrier of the virus, has sexual relations with another, and this partner develops AIDS in the future, can the carrier be held liable by the infected partner?

Taking this scenario a step further, what if the partner infected with AIDS by a known carrier dies? Is the known carrier then vulnerable to criminal charges such as manslaughter?

■ CHLAMYDIAL INFECTIONS ■

Chlamydial infections are caused by the bacteria *Chlamydial trachomatis* and affect an estimated three to four million persons each year. These infections are the most common bacterial STDs in the United States. Among other problems, such an infection can cause urethritis in males and is closely related to pelvic inflammatory disease in females. Fortunately, chlamydial infections are susceptible to inexpensive, readily available antibiotics so infected persons can be effectively treated. Unfortunately, many infected people, especially females, are asymtomatic and therefore fail to get treatment.

■ PELVIC INFLAMMATORY DISEASE ■

Pelvic inflammatory disease (PID) accounts for over 200,000 hospitalizations every year in the United States. More than one million episodes occur annually. Among American women of reproductive age, one in seven reports having received treatment for PID (Hatcher et al. 1990). The patient experiences pain and tenderness involving the lower abdomen, cervix, and uterus combined with fever, chills, and an elevated white blood cell count. If untreated, PID can progress to the point where the Fallopian tubes are scarred, and this in turn can lead to female infertility.

■ GENITAL WARTS ■

Researchers estimate that between 500,000 and one million new cases of genital warts caused by the human papillomavirus (HPV) occur each year. The hardest-hit group seems to be young women in their teens and twenties. According to the Centers for Disease Control, an estimated 5 to 15 percent of those with persistent warts are expected to develop cancer, usually cancer of the cervix.

▨ GONORRHEA ▨

Approximately 1.5 million cases of gonorrhea are estimated to occur each year in the United States. The symptoms in men include an increased need to urinate, some discomfort when urinating, and a purulent urethral discharge. Women may experience abnormal vaginal discharge, abnormal menstruation, and painful urination. Here again, especially women, but some men as well, may be asymptomatic.

▨ SYPHILIS ▨

Syphilis currently affects about 40,000 Americans each year, occurring more frequently in low-income heterosexual populations. Congenital syphilis (the infant becomes infected during birth) occurs in about one in 10,000 pregnancies (Hatcher et al. 1990, 122). The symptoms occur in three stages:

▨ *Primary:* The classical chancre is a painless ulcer, located at the site of exposure.
▨ *Secondary:* Patients may have a highly variable skin rash, swollen glands, and other signs.
▨ *Latent:* Patients have no clinical signs of infection.

SUMMARY

1. *Sexuality pervades the lives of humans.* This is mainly because human sex is, to a great extent, free from instinctual control. Although sexuality is a biological necessity, much of the way in which sex is manifested is learned unlike sexual behavior in lower animals, which is instinctual. For this reason, human sexual behavior exhibits far more variations than the sexual behavior of other animals.
2. *All human societies try to control sexual expression, but the controls vary from one society to another.* Because of the variability of sexual expression and the often conflicting teachings about sexuality, confusion exists both within societies and within individuals about sexuality. In all societies, human sexuality serves purposes other than procreation, such as communication, strengthening the male-female bond, increasing intimacy, pleasuring, having fun, and generally reducing tension.
3. *In the United States, sexual behavior has become freer since the 1960s.* However, the appearance of herpes and AIDS has brought about a reevaluation of Americans' sexual behavior.

4. Our understanding of sexual physiology has increased greatly as science and medicine have expanded our knowledge about the functioning of the body. *Males and females are physiologically similar, having developed their sexual organs from common structures, but they also differ in some respects.* One difference involves timing: Young males tend to have higher sexual intensity than young females, reaching the peak of sexual intensity in their late teens and early twenties. Women tend to peak sexually during their thirties and forties. Another important difference is the cyclical preparation for pregnancy that the female goes through each month, but the male does not. Males also tend to be more genitally oriented than females.

5. *Both males and females share the same basic physical responses during sexual activity.* These are called the excitement, plateau, orgasmic, and resolution stages. The major difference between the sexes takes place during the orgasmic stage: the ejaculation by the male. The male also usually goes through a refractory period after the resolution stage before he can have another erection.

6. *Satisfactory sex at older ages is much more prevalent than many people believe.* Good health and partners desirous of maintaining sexual interaction throughout their lives are necessary. Individuals who remain sexually active will continue to have sex into their later years.

7. *Unfortunately, sexually transmitted diseases too often accompany sexual activity.* All STDs seem to be on the increase, and many new STDs have appeared in recent years. This increase is attributed to use of the pill rather than the condom, the mistaken belief that modern drugs have eliminated the diseases, and, most of all, youth's increased sexual activity and variety of sexual partners. Genital herpes and AIDS have increased to epidemic proportions and may slow the sexual revolution by encouraging more careful choice of sexual partners.

SCENES FROM MARRIAGE
WHAT ARE YOUR BIGGEST PROBLEMS AND COMPLAINTS ABOUT SEX?

See if you can identify which of the following comments were made by a male and which by a female (the answers are on p. 000). These comments were made anonymously by students in my marriage and family classes in response to the following question: "What are your problems or complaints in the area of sex?" It is interesting to note that women write much more and describe many more problems than the men. That women are more expressive in answering this question may indicate that they are more troubled by their sexuality. On the other hand, they may simply be more open about it. Or maybe they just write more and better.

1. Many people just want to jump right into bed and "do it." The preliminaries are totally skipped. All my partners seem to want is a piece of the action. Is all romance dead?

2. My problems in the area of sex are the moral questions: Is it right to have sex before marriage? I will, probably, but not until I am in a lasting relationship, and some love is there. I find myself sexually attracted to members of the opposite sex before I know them emotionally. This is difficult because I'm not sure if there is any emotion in it too.

3. Many of the times when I have had opportunities to have sex, anxiety seems to set in and I back out. Too much pressure on being "good."

4. I really hate it when the opposite sex expect us to start and do everything. They want equality but

want us to start all of the seduction games.

5. After dating steadily for a while, I start to feel this pressure to go farther than just necking and petting. I have broken off a lot of relationships because of this pressure. I am amazed at how many of the opposite sex expect you to do it, like it isn't any big deal.

6. My biggest complaint about sex is that, to me, it's such a definite step toward total commitment to a person. When I do have intercourse, I want it to be with the person I marry. I want this part of me to belong to only one person. Sometimes

this bothers me, because it's such a hard thing for my dates to accept.

7. Basically, the problem of the still-existing double standard. Men are allowed to enjoy casual sex without acquiring a negative label, whereas a woman enjoying sex for the sake of sex can risk her "good reputation" unless she is very discreet in her choice of sexual partners.

8. My biggest complaint is pressure from friends. "Hey, we're doing it, why aren't you?" I'm not out for a quickie.

9. I can't get enough, can't last all night, am afraid of VD and possible pregnancy.

10. Not enough responsibility taken for birth control by my partner. Not enough communication between partners. There should be more sex education for younger men and women.

11. The hang-ups people have about sex. If both partners want it, then what's wrong? I never get enough.

12. After having sex, my partners want a commitment that I don't feel is necessary to give just because you sleep with someone.

13. I never get enough holding, cuddling, and talking before or after sexual intercourse.

14. My partner never seems interested in sex, never starts anything sexual, and seems more interested in talking about our relationship.

1. F	**2.** F	**3.** M	**4.** M
5. F	**6.** F	**7.** F	**8.** F
9. M	**10.** F	**11.** M	**12.** M
13. F	**14.** F		

CHAPTER

11

FAMILY PLANNING

CONTENTS

HAVING BABIES

Karen, age sixteen, and James, nineteen, are spending Saturday night watching television in Cottage Hospital with their two-day-old infant, Susan Marie. "When I get out we'll celebrate," says the new mother. "We're too young to go to a bar, so I guess we'll hang out at the mall." "Yesterday we were talking about how we would pay for the baby's wedding when she grows up," says James who has offered to marry Karen although she has refused his offer.

With many teenagers now sexually active, some high schools have begun dispensing birth control devices and establishing day-care facilities on the premises. Karen's solution to child care is more common: her mother will look after the baby until the high school junior graduates. "I think Karen will think twice about having sex now," says her mother, who like many parents believes offering birth control measures in the schools only encourage students to be sexually active. "A single girl Karen's age shouldn't need contraception. I don't want her on birth control—she's only a teenager."

A paradox has arisen in America during the past twenty years. Condoms, vaginal spermicides, and other contraceptives are now sold openly at the drugstore counter so that embarrassed young persons no longer must ask the druggist for them. Prescription contraceptives such as the pill or diaphragm are easily obtained from such organizations as Planned Parenthood. Yet despite the great increase in the availability of contraceptive devices, the number of unwanted pregnancies has risen from about 8 percent in 1982 to about 10 percent (National Center for Health Statistics 1990b, 1). In addition, 23 percent of all women who had a child in 1990 were not married at the time of birth.

The percentages of women in various groups who had a child in 1990 but were unmarried at the time of birth were as follows (U.S. Bureau of the Census 1991a, 3):

Asian American	9 percent
Caucasian	17 percent
Hispanic	23 percent
Black	57 percent

If present trends continue, it is estimated that fully 40 percent of today's fourteen-year-old girls will be pregnant at least once before they reach the age of twenty. Obviously, the changes in sexual mores that started in the 1960s are related to the increasing number of pregnancies. More sexual activity will lead to more pregnancies. Yet society has worked hard to get the family planning message across. What has gone wrong is a matter of growing debate (see Inset 11-1).

Because of the increased availability and effectiveness of birth control methods, friends, husbands, and lovers may pressure us to have intercourse whenever they want. We need to be assertive about our desires: Being protected from pregnancy does not always mean we want intercourse. Many of us have found that we ourselves resist using birth control. What may appear to be personal reasons are actually due to social and political factors.

■ We are embarrassed by, ashamed of, or confused about our own sexuality.

■ We cannot admit we might have or are having intercourse, because we feel it is wrong.

■ We are unrealistically romantic about sex; sex should be passionate and spontaneous; birth control seems too premeditated, too clinical, and often too messy.

■ We hesitate to "inconvenience" our partner. This fear of displeasing him is a measure of the inequality in our relationship.

■ We feel, "It can't happen to me. I won't get pregnant." We hesitate to find a medical practitioner and face the hurried, impersonal care or,

if we are young or unmarried, the moralizing and disapproval that we think we're likely to receive. We are afraid the practitioner will tell our parents.

■ We don't recognize our deep dissatisfaction with the birth control method we are using and begin to use it haphazardly.

■ We feel tempted to become pregnant to prove to ourselves that we are fertile or to try to improve a shaky relationship; sometimes we want a baby just so that we will have someone to care for.

Family planning means just that, intelligently planning one's family. It means controlling one's sexuality to avoid unwanted pregnancies and to create, when desired, an ideal family in which children can grow up in the healthiest possible manner. Family planning means, in part, responsible sex. Family planning means avoiding pregnancy through intelligent use of contraceptive methods, including abstinence. Family planning means becoming pregnant and giving birth only when one wants and is ready to have children. Thus, family planning involves both the avoidance of pregnancy and the creation of pregnancy. It involves learning about birth control and working to solve infertility problems.

The place and function of children within the family and the culture vary from culture to culture and over time. In countries with high infant mortality, women have to bear many children to ensure that at least a few children will each adulthood. For women in these countries, pregnancy may be nearly a perpetual state. In such cases, family planning emphasizes fertility and pregnancy rather than contraception.

Years ago when the United States was still an agricultural nation, it was important to have many children to help work the land; children were major economic contributors to the family. In today's urban economy, however, the costs of rearing children far outweigh their economic contributions to the family. Thus, from a strictly economic viewpoint, children have changed from assets into liabilities. In urban America then, contraception is often the major focus of family planning.

Modern contraceptive techniques give couples free choice about the number and timing of children. These same techniques also have ramifications for population control. Countries, such as India, that chronically suffer from overpopulation can initiate programs to reduce birthrates and gain some control over their burgeoning populations. Considering 2.1 to 2.5 children per woman as the population replacement rate, it is interesting to compare birthrates for some of the world's countries (see Table 11-1).

The ideal family is one that allows children to grow up to become healthy adults. Aside from environmental considerations, this requires that:

1. The children are wanted by both partners.
2. The partners are healthy enough physically and psychologically to supply love and security to the children.
3. Family economic resources are adequate to nourish the children properly and keep them physically healthy.
4. The family can supply the children with sufficient educational opportunity to enable them to acquire the skills necessary to survive and enjoy success within their culture.

TABLE 11-1
TOTAL FERTILITY RATE IN SELECTED COUNTRIES

	TOTAL FERTILITY RATE*
Germany	1.4
United States	2.0
China	2.2
Brazil	3.1
Mexico	3.8
India	3.9
Nigeria	6.5
Syria	7.1

*The average number of children a woman will have thorughout her childbearing years (15–49).

Source: Population Reference Bureau 1992.

ARE WE READY FOR CHILDREN?

Proper family planning leads to the first question a couple should answer when thinking about raising a family: Do we really want children? The answer requires the couple to resolve the questions raised above in the definition of a healthy family. More specifically: How much time do we want for just each other and establishing a home? How much more education do we want or need for the jobs and income we want? Are we ready to give a baby the attention and love it needs? Can we afford to provide it with the food, clothing, and education we want for it? Can a child successfully fit into the lifestyle we feel is best for ourselves?

Most family planning experts advise young couples to wait a while before having their first child. Waiting gives them time to make important adjustments to each other, to enjoy one another's individual attention, and to build some economic stability before adding the responsibility of a child. Yet we know that couples like Karen and James can't wait. For them, it is already too late for good family planning.

The decision to have children is one of the most important family decisions, yet it is often made haphazardly or not made at all. Karen and James hadn't even made a decision about their relationship, much less about becoming parents. "It just happened." Having children is too important to let it "just happen." Having a child generally means assuming long-term responsibilities, usually for eighteen to twenty years or more. In fact, once a parent, always a parent. We can divorce a spouse that we do not want anymore, but we cannot divorce our children. There is almost no time when children do not make heavy demands on their parents, sometimes even long after they have become adults. True, having children brings many rewards. There is joy in watching a child grow, become competent, and assume a responsible role in society. There is joy in learning to know another person intimately. And doing things together as a family is just plain fun. Responsible family planning makes it easier to experience these joys and to create a healthy family.

The chances of Karen and James creating a healthy family for Susan Marie are certainly less than if they had planned for the pregnancy and for parenthood. Responsible family planning avoids "It just happened."

BIRTH CONTROL

Modern birth control techniques, though far from perfect, have made better family planning possible. For example, reliable contraception allows couples to remain childless if they desire. Although in the recent past the mass media have emphasized reports of large numbers of American women choosing to remain childless, government population reports tend to show otherwise. Also, some women who remain childless do so involuntarily because of fertility problems.

> The highest proportion of childless women since records have been maintained occurred among women born in 1880 (22 percent). Current estimates of lifetime childlessness for the first decade of baby boomers (women born between 1946 and 1955) who were thirty-five to forty-two years old in 1990, are approximately 17 percent (U.S. Bureau of the Census 1991b, 1). In 1990, 37 percent of women between the ages eighteen and forty-four were childless, little changed from 35 percent in 1976 (U.S. Bureau of the Census 1991a, 13).

What is clear is that women are having fewer children and are postponing both marriage and childbirth. Most women are now having their children between the ages of twenty-five and thirty-four.

The idea of birth control has long been a part of human life. The oldest written records mentioning birth control date back to the reign of Amenemhet III Egypt around 1850 B.C. Women were advised to put a pastelike substance in the vagina to block male sperm from reaching the egg. Pliny's *Natural History*, written in the first century A.D., lists many methods of birth control, including potions to be taken orally, magical objects, primitive suppositories and tampons, and physical actions such as jumping to expel the semen. These early birth control methods were generally unsuccessful.

Two ancient birth control methods did evolve into the first effective contraceptive techniques:

1. The ancient attempts to block the cervix so that sperm could not penetrate to the egg eventually evolved into the vaginal diaphragm and cervical cap when vulcanized rubber was invented. The most sophisticated historical prototype of the modern cervical cap was the use of half a lemon, emptied of its contents and inserted over the cervix; the residual citric acid, which is mildly spermicidal (causing the death of sperm), provided additional protection.

2. Early attempts to cover the penis evolved into the modern condom. Starting in the sixteenth century, the penis was covered to protect it from venereal infection. Manufacturers began to make condoms of inexpensive rubber in the 1840s and later switched to latex.

Despite the long history of birth control, modern birth control and family planning have had a difficult and eventful development. The Englishman Francis Place, the father of fifteen children, was the founder of the birth control movement. In the 1820s he posted handbills advising contraception to counteract the effects of the growing industrialization and urbanization that he believed were fostering poverty. His handbills recommended that women place a piece of sponge tied with a string into the vagina before intercourse and remove it afterward by pulling the string. (Note that one of the newer birth control devices is a spermicidal sponge.)

In the United States, Margaret Sanger and others waged a long hard battle for birth control that lasted well into this century. The Puritan morality in the United States opposed birth control. Although contraceptives were recommended for the highest ethical reasons—that is, to prevent poverty, disease, misery, and marital discord—their promoters were accused of immorality and were often brought to trial and fined. In 1873 Congress passed the Comstock Law, which prohibited the distribution of contraceptive information through the mail. Numerous states also passed repressive laws. For example, physicians were forbidden to prescribe contraceptives in Connecticut until 1965 when the state law was overthrown by the U.S. Supreme Court in *Griswold and Duxton v. Connecticut*.

Of course, family planning is possible without the aid of mechanical contraceptive devices. **Infanticide** was practiced historically in many cultures. Postponing marriage acts as an effective birth deterrent, providing illegitimacy is controlled. In China today, for example, marriage is discouraged until the woman is twenty-four and the man is twenty-seven. Rigid peer group control has reduced illegitimacy to a low level.

Withdrawal and abstinence also reduce fertility rates. France, for example, has long had a relatively stable population of about 50 million. Inasmuch as contraception is prohibited by the Roman Catholic church, this population stability has been achieved mainly by withdrawal (coitus interruptus), even though it is not completely reliable. Other methods of sexual outlet, such as masturbation, oral sex, and homosexuality, also serve a contraceptive purpose.

Although various chemical and mechanical means of birth control are widely used in the United States, approval of such methods is by no means universal. The Roman Catholic and Mormon churches both have official doctrines banning "artificial" methods of birth control. Some minority group members also discourage birth control in an effort to increase their proportion of the population. Still other groups shun certain birth control methods for various other reasons. Nevertheless, the vast majority of Americans practice birth control at times, using many of the specific methods we will describe. Birth control is also advocated by people who are concerned about the world population explosion (see Table 11-2).

Infanticide
The deliberate killing of infants as a population control measure or for some other purpose

PRESENT CONTRACEPTIVE METHODS

Although family planning in itself is generally healthful, some methods of implementing it may have side effects that can be detrimental to the user's health.

Birth Control

	YEAR	YEARS TO ADD
TABLE 11-2		
WORLD POPULATION:		
NUMBER OF YEARS TO ADD EACH BILLION		
First billion reached	1800	All of human history
Second	1930	130
Third	1960	30
Fourth	1975	15
Fifth	1987	12
	Projected	
Sixth	1998	11
Seventh	2009	11
Eighth	2020	11
Ninth	2033	13
Tenth	2046	13
Eleventh	2066	20
Twelfth	about 2100	34

Source: Population Reference Bureau, based on United Nations and World Bank estimates and projections.

Table 11-3 summarizes the various contraceptive devices, indicating their effectiveness, advantages, and disadvantages (including possible side effects).

Planning a family requires couples to decide how many children they want and how far apart the children should be. The couple must also answer questions about birth control, including "Who will be responsible for using a birth control method? What method will be used? How will the method chosen affect our sex lives? What will be the cost?"

An *ideal* contraceptive—which does not yet exist, though research continues—would:

Contraceptive
Any agent used to prevent conception

- Be harmless.
- Be reliable.
- Be free of objectionable side effects.
- Be inexpensive.
- Be simple.
- Be reversible in effect.
- Be removed from the sexual act.
- Protect against venereal disease and AIDS.

Although the contraceptives shown in Figure 11-1 and Table 11-3 do not fulfill all of these goals, they do meet many of them.

THE CONDOM

Condom
A sheath, usually made of thin latex, designed to cover the penis during intercourse; used for contraceptive purposes and to control sexually transmitted disease

The **condom** has become increasingly popular with both men and women since AIDS has come upon the sexual scene. In the late 1980s, sales increased by more than 60 percent, with women buying 40 to 50 percent of all condoms sold (*Consumer Reports* 1989, 135). The role condoms can play in the prevention of sexually transmitted diseases (STDs), AIDS in particular, accounts for their sudden popularity. Former U.S. Surgeon General C. Everett Koop called

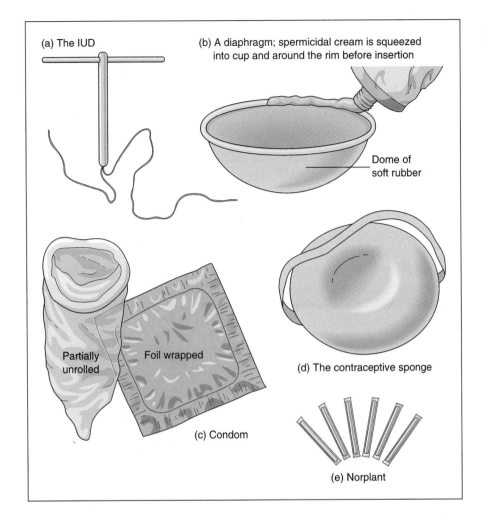

FIGURE 11-1
Types of contraceptives

(a) The IUD

(b) A diaphragm; spermicidal cream is squeezed into cup and around the rim before insertion

Dome of soft rubber

Partially unrolled

Foil wrapped

(c) Condom

(d) The contraceptive sponge

(e) Norplant

condoms the best protection against AIDS infection barring abstinence and pushed their use.

Condoms are now easy to buy. In addition to being openly displayed in drugstores, they are available from vending machines in the public bathrooms on many college campuses as well as in restaurants and bars. Studies on adolescent male condom use indicate that one-third of sexually active males, aged fifteen to nineteen, report using condoms consistently, about half use them sometimes, and about 20 percent never use them (Pleck et al. 1991, 733).

The condom is a sheath of very thin latex or animal gut that fits over the penis and stops sperm from entering the vagina when ejaculation occurs. The condom should be placed on the penis as soon as it is erect to ensure that none of the preejaculatory fluid (which contains sperm) gets into the vagina.

Care should be taken not to puncture the condom. After ejaculation, the condom should be held tightly around the base of the penis as the man withdraws so that no semen will spill from the now-loose condom.

Latex condoms used properly are close to 100 percent effective against both pregnancy and STDs. So compelling is the evidence about condom effectiveness that since 1987 the U.S. Food and Drug Administration (FDA) has allowed manufacturers to list diseases (AIDS, syphilis, gonorrhea, chlamydia, genital herpes) that condoms can help prevent.

Birth Control

TABLE 11-3
CONTRACEPTIVES

POPULAR NAME	DESCRIPTION	EFFECTIVENESS (PREGNANCIES PER 100 WOMEN USING METHOD FOR 1 YEAR)[a]
The pill (oral contraceptive; consultation with physician required)	Contains synthetic hormones (estrogens progestin) to inhibit ovulation. The body reacts as if pregnancy has occurred and does not release an egg. No egg—no conception. The pills are usually taken for 20 or 21 consecutive days; menstruation begins shortly thereafter.	Combined pills[b]
Norplant	Six slender match-sized capsules are implanted under the skin, usually on the inner upper arm. They time release progestin into the body.	1
IUD (intrauterine device; consultation with physician required)	Metal or plastic object that comes in various shapes and is placed within the uterus and left there. Exactly how it works is not known. Hypotheses are that endocrine changes occur, that the fertilized egg cannot implant in the uterine wall because of irritation, that spontaneous abortion is caused.	3–6
Contraceptive sponge	A soft, round polyurethane sponge saturated with spermicide.	10
Diaphragm and jelly (consultation with physician required)	Flexible hemispherical rubber dome inserted into the vagina to block entrance to the cervix, thus providing a barrier to sperm. Usually used with spermicidal cream or jelly.	10–16
Chemical methods	Numerous products to be inserted into the vagina to block sperm from the uterus and/or to act as a spermicide. Vaginal foams are creams packed under pressure (like foam-shaving cream) and inserted with an applicator. Vaginal suppositories are small cone-shaped objects that melt in the vagina; vaginal tablets also melt in the vagina.	13–17 (more effective when used in conjunction with another method, such as the diaphragm)
Condom	Thin, strong sheath or cover, usually of latex, worn over the penis to prevent sperm from entering the vagina.	7–14
Withdrawal (coitus interruptus)	Man withdraws penis from vagina before ejaculation of semen.	16–18
Rhythm	Abstinence from intercourse during fertile period each month.	10–29
Abstinence	Avoid sexual intercourse.	0

Advantages[c]	Disadvantages	Cost
Simple to take, removed from sexual act, highly reliable, reversible. Useful side effects: relief of premenstrual tension, reduction in premenstrual tension, reduction in menstrual flow, regularization of menstruation; relief of acne.	Weight gain (5 to 50% of users) breast enlargement and sensitivity; some users have increased headaches, nausea, and spotting. Increased possibility of vein thrombosis (blood clotting) and slight increase in blood pressure. Must be taken regularly. A causal relationship to cancer can neither be established nor refuted.	$9–$13 per month
Once implanted, no other contraceptive measures are needed. Easily reversible. Lasts for five years. Removed from sexual act.	Initial expense is high. Implantation procedure requires minor surgery. Visability may be unacceptable. Menstrual cycle changes.	$500
Once inserted, user need do nothing more about birth control. Highly reliable, reversible, relatively inexpensive. Must be checked periodically to see if still in place.	Insertion procedure requires specialist and may be uncomfortable and painful. Uterine cramping, increased menstrual bleeding. Between 4% and 30% are expelled in first year after insertion. Occasional perforation of the uterine wall. Occasional pregnancy that is complicated by the presence of the IUD. Associated with pelvic inflammatory disease. Availability limited.	$50–$100 for insertion
Does not have to be fitted. Simple to use. Allows repeated intercourse.	Disliked by some women because insertion requires manipulation of genitals, 2% of users report allergic reaction.	$1.50 each
Can be left in place up to 24 hours. Reliable, harmless, reversible. Can be inserted up to 2 hours before intercourse.	Disliked by many women because it requires self-manipulation of genitals to insert and is messy because of the cream. If improperly fitted, it will fail. Must be refitted periodically, especially after pregnancy. Psychological aversion may make its use inconsistent.	$40–$75 for fitting
Foams appear to be most effective, followed by creams, jellies, suppositories, tablets. Harmless, simple, reversible, easily available.	Minor irritations and temporary burning sensation. Messy. Must be used just before intercourse and reapplied for each act of intercourse.	$7–$9 for month's supply
Simple to obtain and use; free of objectionable side effects. Quality control has improved with government regulation. Protection against various sexually transmitted diseases.	Must be applied just before intercourse. Can slip off, especially after ejaculation when penis returns to flaccid state. May rupture (rare). Interferes with sensation and spontaneity.	50¢ each and up
Simple, free, requires no other devices.	Requires great control by the male. Possible semen leakage before ejaculation. Possible psychological reaction against necessary control and ejaculation outside the vagina. May severely limit sexual gratification of both partners.	
Approved by the Roman Catholic church. Free, requires no other devices.	Woman's menstrual period must be regular. Demands accurate record keeping and strong self-control. Difficult to determine fertile period exactly.	
Simple, free, reversible. Reduces chance of contracting a sexually transmitted disease.	May have adverse psychological effects.	

[a]Without some method of birth control, between 80 and 90 out of 100 sexually active women would get pregnant in the course of one year.

[b]If taken regularly pregnancy will not occur. If one or more pills are missed, there is a chance of pregnancy.

[c]Individuals vary in their reaction to contraceptive devices. Advantages and disadvantages listed are general ones.

INSET 11-2
CONDOM TESTING AND RATING

In its March 1989 issue, *Consumer Reports* described the results of condom tests it had conducted. The report described the various condoms in detail, listed user likes and dislikes, and indicated the bursting and breakage rates. Only latex condoms were included in the tests.

The condoms came in many configurations. Some models come with wet lubrication, Usually a water-based surgical jelly. Others come with dry lubrication, usually a silicon-based oil. Some come with no lubrication. Some condoms contain a spermicide. Some have texture such as ribbing or stippling, which supposedly increases stimulation. Others are contoured, some with a reservoir end. They also come in various colors.

Of the 42 condom brands tested, 32 had maximum failure rates of 1.5 percent or less, 8 had a maximum failure rate of 4 percent, and only 2 had a maximum failure rate of more than 10 percent. Thus, most latex condom brands proved to be reliable.

Most users listed the following characteristics that they liked about condoms:

- Easy to put on
- Thin; greater sensation
- Color
- Stays on
- Partner likes
- Right amount of lubrication
- Low cost

Most users listed the following characteristics that they disliked about condoms:

- Difficult to put on
- Too much lubrication
- Doesn't stay on
- Caused allergy
- Too expensive
- Thick; less sensation
- Odor

Reprints of this report with specific brand names can be obtained by writing CU/Reprints, P.O. Box CS 2010-A, Mount Vernon, N.Y. 10551.

Barring breakage, the risk of pregnancy with condom use is essentially zero. Most pregnancies occur because of careless removal of the condom. Some may occur because of a puncture in the condom. Both risks can be reduced by using a vaginal spermicide in addition to the condom. *Consumer Reports* (1989) conducted a large-scale study evaluating many brands of condoms (see Inset 11-2). In general, the report concluded that there are differences among the various brands. Foreign brands should be avoided as they are sometimes less reliable than domestic brands. In addition, although condoms made from animal membranes are much stronger than latex condoms and allow more natural sensation, they are permeable to very small viruses and bacteria (though not to sperm) and are therefore inappropriate for disease protection.

A new alternative is a condom that women can wear. This new device consists of a soft, loose-fitting polyurethane sheath and two diaphragm-like, flexible rings. It is inserted like a tampon and protects the inside of the vagina, with the inner ring covering the cervix and the outer ring holding it in place by pressing against the woman's body. The female condom (there are several manufacturers) offers all the advantages of the male condom and also gives the woman control over condom use. Unfortunately, it is expensive, costing up to $3 each. It can, however, be cleaned and reused (Seligmann 1992; Hatcher et al. 1990).

THE DIAPHRAGM
The **diaphragm** is a dome-shaped cup of thin latex stretched over a metal spring. It is available on prescription from a doctor. Because the sizes of vaginal

Diaphragm
A contraceptive device consisting of a hemispherical thin rubber cup that is placed within the vagina covering the cervix

openings differ, a diaphragm must be carefully fitted to ensure that it adequately covers the mouth of the cervix and is comfortable. The fitting should be checked every two years, as well as after childbirth, abortion, or a weight loss of more than ten pounds.

Once she has been fitted properly, the woman can insert the diaphragm with the dome up or down, whichever feels more comfortable. Before insertion, she should spread a spermicidal jelly or cream over the surface of the dome that will lie against the cervix.

She can insert a diaphragm just before intercourse or several hours in advance. If she inserts it more than two hours before intercourse, however, she should insert additional spermicide into the vagina before intercourse or take the diaphragm out and reapply spermicide. Spermicide should also be added before any further acts of intercourse. The diaphragm must stay in place for six hours after the last act of intercourse to give the spermicide enough time to kill all sperm.

The diaphragm is highly effective when used with a spermicide and has no physical side effects. It dampens spontaneity, however, and loses its effectiveness when fresh spermicide is not used for additional intercourse. It is avoided by some women who do not like to touch their genitals. Women using it tend to be more susceptible to urinary tract infections, probably because the front rim of the diaphragm impinges on the urethra and partially obstructs it, thus causing urination difficulty. Fitting a slightly smaller diaphragm tends to avoid this problem (Hatcher et al. 1990, 193–221).

The main causes of pregnancy with diaphragm use are inaccurate fitting and incorrect insertion. Sometimes, too, the vaginal walls expand during sexual stimulation and dislodge the diaphragm.

THE CERVICAL CAP

Similar to the diaphragm in that it blocks entrance to the cervix is the cervical cap. Although it has been in use for years, especially in Europe, it is still little known and used in the United States. The cervical cap is much smaller than the diaphragm and is made of flexible rubber. It looks something like an elongated thimble and fits over the cervix much as a thimble fits over one's thumb. Unlike the diaphragm, the cap may be left in place for up to two days. After intercourse, it should not be removed for eight to twelve hours. Also like the diaphragm, it should be used with a spermicide. Currently, only the Prentif cavity-rim cervical cap is available in the United States.

THE CONTRACEPTIVE SPONGE

Another variation on the diaphragm is the Vorhauer sponge (trade name *Today Vaginal Contraceptive Sponge*). It is a soft, round polyurethane sponge permeated with spermicide. The sponge offers numerous advantages over the standard diaphragm. It does not have to be fitted by a doctor because it automatically conforms to the woman's shape and size. It is easier to insert than the diaphragm, and it remains effective for twenty-four hours regardless of how often the woman has intercourse. It is not messy or awkward. A small polyester loop attached to the sponge makes removal easy although it should be left in place at least six hours after intercourse. It needs to be dampened with tap water immediately before insertion in order to activate the nonoxynol-9 spermicide. Each sponge costs about $1.50; thus, it is expensive in comparison with other methods. About 2 to 6 percent of the women using the sponge report an allergic reaction (Shapiro 1988, 117). Difficulty in removing the sponge has caused about 6 percent of users to discontinue use. In some cases, it appears to cause vaginal dryness (Hatcher et al. 1990, 211).

THE INTRAUTERINE DEVICE

Intrauterine device
A small object inserted into a woman's uterus to prevent conception

The **intrauterine device (IUD)** is a stainless steel or plastic loop, ring, or spiral that is inserted into the uterus. A doctor uses a sterile applicator to insert the IUD into the cervical canal and presses a plunger to push the device into the uterus. The protruding threads are trimmed so that only an inch or an inch and a half remain in the upper vagina. Usually, the threads can't be felt during intercourse. The best time for insertion (and removal) is during menstruation because the cervical canal is open widest then, and there is no possibility of an unsuspected pregnancy.

Just how or why the IUD works is still unknown. Theories include production of biochemical changes, interference with the implantation of eggs or the movement of eggs or sperm, and spontaneous abortion. The IUD is quite effective, second only to the pill in overall effectiveness. Once inserted, it can be used indefinitely without additional contraceptive measures; it doesn't interrupt sexual activity, it is fully reversible, and its long-term cost is low.

However, the IUD has numerous disadvantages. The most common is abnormal menstrual bleeding. Bleeding starts sooner, lasts longer, and is heavier after IUD insertion. Bleeding and spotting between periods are also fairly common. Women who have never been pregnant often experience uterine cramps and backache. The uterine cramps usually disappear in a few days, although they often recur with each period and may be severe enough to require removal of the IUD.

About 10 percent of the women who try IUDs spontaneously expel them, and if the woman does not notice the expulsion, an unwanted pregnancy may result. The threads can also be checked periodically to make sure the device is still in place.

A more serious complication that may occur is pelvic inflammatory disease (salingitis). About 2 to 3 percent of women using the device may develop the disease, usually in the first two weeks after insertion. Most of these inflammations are mild and can be treated with antibiotics. In rare cases, the IUD may puncture the wall of the uterus and migrate into the abdominal cavity, requiring surgery. Pelvic infection, usually caused by bacteria, also seems to be more common among IUD users (Mishell 1989; Shapiro 1988; Hatcher et al. 1990, 355–84).

Most of the risk of pregnancy occurs during the first few months of IUD use; therefore an additional method of contraception should be used during that period. The failure rate tends to decline rapidly after the first year of use. Pregnancy may occur with the device in place, but the rate of spontaneous abortion for such pregnancies is 40 percent (compared with 15 percent for all pregnancies). There is little additional risk of birth defects for babies born of such pregnancies. The device usually remains in place during the pregnancy and is expelled during the delivery.

The IUD peaked in popularity in the early 1970s when as many as 10 percent of sexually active women used it. Optimism about its use ended quickly in 1974 when the Dalkon Shield IUD was taken off the market because its users experienced an unusually high pregnancy rate and developed uterine infections at a much higher rate than nonusers. A. H. Robins, the maker of the Dalkon Shield, has been flooded with lawsuits (about 14,000). Although the makers of other IUDs had little problem with them, the continuing threat of litigation has driven most IUDs from the market. Currently, the FDA approves four types of IUDs: the copper-bearing devices (the copper 7, the copper T200B, and the copper TCu-380A) and a progesterone-releasing T-shaped device (Progestasert). Only the copper TCu-380A and Progestasert are currently available in the United States. (Boston Women's Health Book Collective 1992, 294–300).

The latest data from the Women's Health Study indicate that the relative risk of pelvic inflammatory disease among married women using an IUD who had only one sexual partner was not significantly different from that of sexually active women using no contraceptive method (Mishell 1989, 784). The IUD is widely used in other countries without widespread negative results. For example, approximately 50 million women use the IUD in China (*China Daily* 1986, 1).

From the various studies conducted on the IUD, the following facts are apparent (Mishell 1989; Shapiro 1988; Hatcher et al. 1990):

1. Not every woman can successfully use an IUD.
2. Some pain and discomfort are experienced upon insertion of an IUD.
3. The pregnancy rate for women who can use the new copper TCu-380A is very low, only 0.5 per 100 women after one year and 1.4 after four years of use.
4. Some women experience expulsion of the IUD, uterine perforation, and pelvic inflammatory disease although the latter seems more often, to be caused by the insertion procedure than by the IUD itself.

THE PILL

The **pill**, or **oral contraceptive**, is a combination of the hormones estrogen and progesterone and must be prescribed by a doctor. Daily ingestion of these hormones fools the body into thinking it is pregnant so that ovulation stops. Because no mature eggs are released, pregnancy cannot take place. In addition, the hormones thicken the mucus covering the cervix, thus inhibiting sperm entry.

The combination pill is a monthly supply of twenty or twenty-one tablets. The woman takes pill 1 on day 5 of her menstrual cycle, counting the first day of the cycle as day 1. She takes another pill each day until all the pills have been taken. Menstruation usually begins two to four days after the last pill. If menstruation does not occur when expected, a new series of pills should be started a week after the end of the last series. If a period doesn't begin after this series, the woman should consult a doctor.

During the first month of the first cycle, the woman should use an additional method of contraception to ensure complete protection. The pill should be taken at about the same time each day. If the woman forgets a pill, she should take it as soon as possible and should take the next pill at the scheduled time. If she forgets two pills, the woman should use an additional form of contraception for the rest of the cycle. If she forgets three pills, withdrawal bleeding will probably start. In this case, the woman should stop taking the pills and start using another method of birth control. She should then start a new cycle of pills on the fifth day after the bleeding starts but continue to use an additional method of birth control for the first new cycle.

Oral contraceptive
Hormonal material in pill form that suspends ovulation and prevents conception

Birth Control

Taken properly, the pill is the most effective method of contraception available today. It is relatively simple to use, does not affect spontaneity, and is inexpensive and reversible. However, irregular use does not afford protection.

The pill was once the most widely used method of contraception in this country. In 1975, as many as 8 million American women, or about 40 percent of all women using birth control, used the pill. "The pill" became almost synonymous with the "sexual revolution" because it freed sexually active women from the fear of pregnancy more efficiently and reliably than other contraceptive methods. However, use of the pill began to drop rapidly thereafter due to fear of a link between the pill and breast cancer. This fear has proven to be unsupported, however. Studies have found no link between oral contraceptives and breast cancer, regardless of the type of pill or the duration of use, up to twenty years (Hatcher et al. 1990, 243). Indeed, use of the pill appears to decrease benign breast cysts, reduce the chances of ovarian cancer, and protect against acute pelvic inflammatory disease (Shapiro 1988, 43; Hatcher et al. 1990, 242–45).

Today the pill is the second most popular method of contraception in the United States and is used by about 14 million women.

The pill's side effects range from relatively minor disturbances to serious ones. Among the former are symptoms of early pregnancy (morning sickness, weight gain, and swollen breasts, for example), which may occur during the first few months of pill use. Such symptoms usually disappear by the fourth month. Other problems include depression, nervousness, alteration in sex drive, dizziness, headaches, bleeding between periods, and vaginal discharge. Yeast fungus infections are also more common in women taking the pill. The more serious side effects include blood clots and a possible increase in the risk of uterine cancer. Although the incidence of fatal blood clots is low (about thirteen deaths among 1 million pill users in one year), women with any history of unusual blood clotting, strokes, heart disease or defects, or any form of cancer should not use the pill (for a more complete discussion of oral contraceptives, see Shapiro 1988; Mischell 1989; Hatcher et al. 1990; Boston Women's Health Book Collective 1992, 279–288).

Another form of the pill, the minipill, is taken throughout the month, even during menstruation; this eliminates the necessity of counting pills and stopping and restarting a series. The minipill also eliminates many of the negative side effects related to the estrogen component of the regular pill. Minipills contain only progestin and do not stop ovulation or interfere with menstruation. Instead, they make the reproductive system resistant to sperm or ovum transport. Should fertilization take place, they impede implantation. They are slightly less effective than the regular pill, however. Women using the minipills appear more susceptible to **ectopic pregnancy** (implantation of the fertilized egg in one of the Fallopian tubes) (Shapiro 1988, 32; Hatcher et al. 1990).

Norplant is a progestin-only implant that provides the woman with five years of protection. The six-capsule Norplant system (see Figure 11-1e) is implanted under the skin in the woman's inner upper arm. Once implanted, nothing more is needed to achieve contraception. Ovulation can be restored by removing the implants. Norplant is relatively expensive but averaged over the five-year period of effectiveness, it's a cheap form of contraception.

RHYTHM OR NATURAL FAMILY PLANNING

The *rhythm* method of contraception is based on the fact that usually only one egg per month is produced. Because the egg lives for only twenty-four to forty-

Ectopic pregnancy
Implantation of the fertilized egg in one of the Fallopian tubes

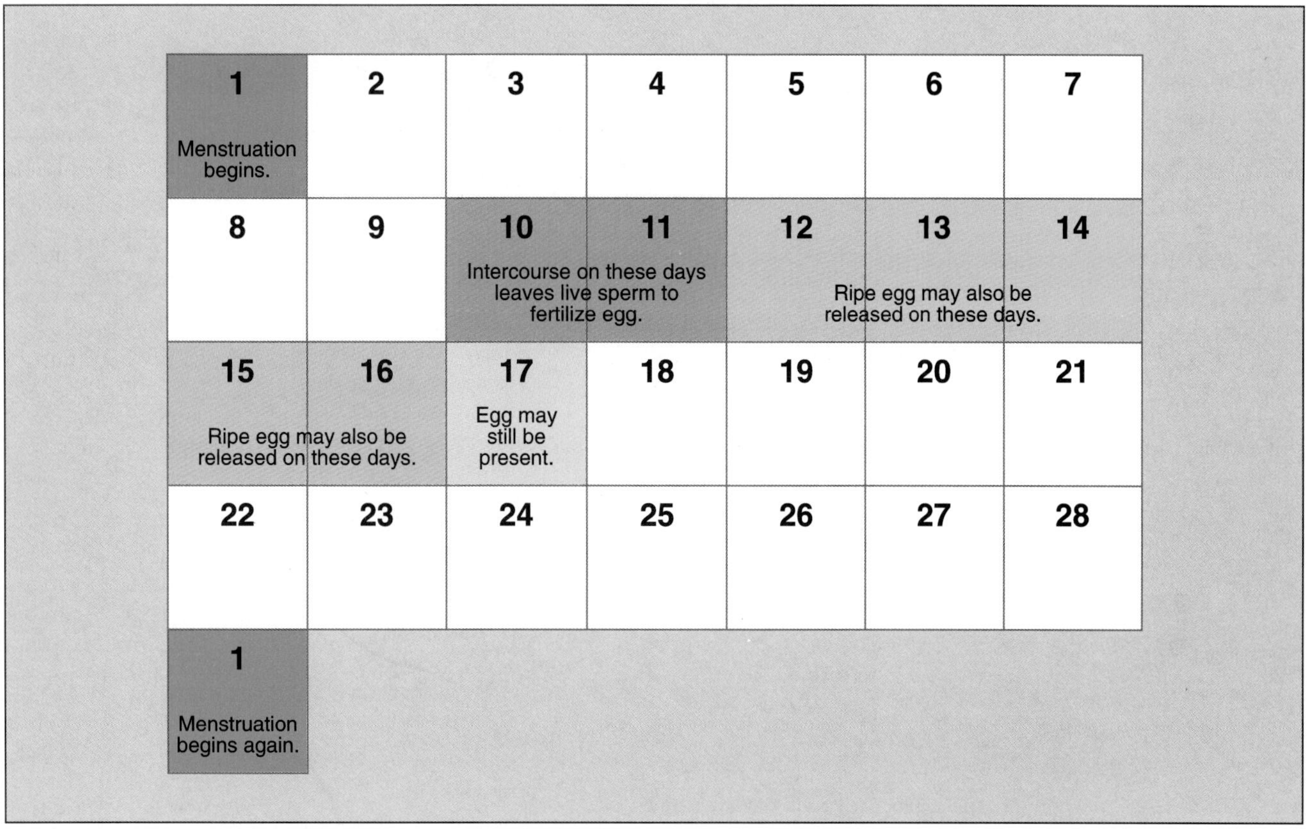

1 Menstruation begins.	2	3	4	5	6	7
8	9	10 Intercourse on these days leaves live sperm to fertilize egg.	11	12 Ripe egg may also be released on these days.	13	14
15 Ripe egg may also be released on these days.	16	17 Egg may still be present.	18	19	20	21
22	23	24	25	26	27	28
1 Menstruation begins again.						

FIGURE 11-2
The 28-day cycle

eight hours if it is not fertilized, and because sperm released into the uterus live only forty-eight to seventy-two hours, theoretically conception can occur only during four days of any cycle. Predicting this four-day period is the difficulty, however. If each woman had an absolutely regular monthly cycle, rhythm would be much more reliable than it is. Unfortunately, not all women have regular cycles. In fact, about 15 percent have such irregular periods that the rhythm method cannot be used at all.

To use the rhythm method, a woman charts her menstrual periods for a full year. Counting the day menstruation begins as day 1, she notes the length of the shortest time before menstruation starts again and also the longest time. If her cycle is always the same length, she subtracts 18 from the number of days in the cycle, which gives the first unsafe day. Subtracting 11 gives the last unsafe day. For example, a woman with a regular 28-day cycle would find that the first unsafe day is day 10 of her cycle and the last is day 17. Thus, she should not engage in intercourse from the tenth to the eighteenth day. Figure 11-2 shows the 28-day cycle.

If a woman's cycle is slightly irregular, she can still determine unsafe days by using the formula. In this case she subtracts 18 from her shortest cycle to determine the first unsafe day and 11 from her longest cycle to find the last unsafe day. Table 11-4 gives the unsafe days for periods of varying duration.

Basal body temperature (BBT) can also be charted. The BBT is by definition the lowest body temperature of a healthy person taken upon awakening. By noting this temperature daily, a woman may determine her time of ovulation. This determination is possible because BBT sometimes drops about

Basal body temperature
The lowest body temperature of a person taken upon awakening

403

	TABLE 11-4		
	HOW TO FIGURE SAFE AND UNSAFE DAYS		
LENGTH OF SHORTEST PERIOD	FIRST UNSAFE DAY AFTER START OF ANY PERIOD	LENGTH OF LONGEST PERIOD	LAST UNSAFE DAY AFTER START OF ANY PERIOD
21 days	3d day	21 days	10th day
22 days	4th day	22 days	11th day
23 days	5th day	23 days	12th day
24 days	6th day	24 days	13th day
25 days	7th day	25 days	14th day
26 days	8th day	26 days	15th day
27 days	9th day	27 days	16th day
28 days	10th day	28 days	17th day
29 days	11th day	29 days	18th day
30 days	12th day	30 days	19th day
31 days	13th day	31 days	20th day
32 days	14th day	32 days	21st day
33 days	15th day	33 days	22d day
34 days	16th day	34 days	23d day
35 days	17th day	35 days	24th day
36 days	18th day	36 days	25th day
37 days	19th day	37 days	26th day
38 days	20th day	38 days	27th day

twelve to twenty-four hours before ovulation and almost always rises for several days after ovulation.

A breath and saliva test may soon allow women to predict their optimum fertile days more accurately. Scientists have found a correlation between levels of mouth odor and saliva chemicals and fluctuations in basic body temperature during the menstrual cycle. By using simple tests on saliva samples, a woman will be able to recognize when she is ovulating and thus know exactly when to avoid intercourse if she does not want to become pregnant.

VAGINAL SPERMICIDES (CHEMICAL METHODS)

Spermicides (sperm-killing agents) come as foams, creams, jellies, foaming tablets, and suppositories. Foams are the most effective because they form the densest, most evenly distributed barrier to the cervical opening. Tablets and suppositories, which melt in the vagina, are the least effective.

Foams are packed under pressure (like shaving cream) and have an applicator attached to the nozzle. Creams and jellies come in tubes with an applicator. A short time before intercourse, the applicator is placed into the vagina (like a sanitary tampon) and the plunger is pushed. Vaginal spermicides remain effective for only about half an hour, so another application is necessary before each act of intercourse.

Vaginal contraceptive film (VCF) is the newest vaginal spermicidal agent. It is a paper-thin, two-inch-square vaginal insert containing the spermicide

Spermicides
Chemical substances that destroy or immobilize sperm

nonoxyol-9, polyvinyl alcohol, and glycerine. When placed high in the vagina five minutes to two hours before intercourse, it dissolves into a sperm-killing gel. VCF is less messy and more comfortable to insert than other vaginal contraceptives. It cannot be felt by either partner, and nothing needs to be removed since it dissolves completely (Shapiro 1988, 126; Hatcher et al. 1990, 183).

Vaginal spermicides are generally harmless, relatively easy to use, and readily available in most drugstores without a prescription. However, they are not very effective, though their effectiveness can be increased by using them with a diaphragm. Other disadvantages are that they are messy, may interrupt the sexual mood, must be reapplied for each act of intercourse, and sometimes cause a burning sensation or irritation. If this occurs, usually changing to another brand will solve the problem. If irritation persists, a doctor should be consulted.

WITHDRAWAL (COITUS INTERRUPTUS)

Withdrawal is simply what the name implies; just before ejaculation the male withdraws his penis from the vagina. Withdrawal is probably the oldest known form of contraception. It is free, requires no preparation, and is always available. However, it has a high failure rate. It requires tremendous control by the man, and the fear that withdrawal may not occur in time can destroy sexual pleasure for both partners. The woman may also be denied satisfaction if the man must withdraw before she reaches orgasm. In addition, semen leakage before withdrawal can cause pregnancy.

DOUCHE

A *douche* is a stream of water applied to a body part to cleanse or treat it. As a contraceptive method, douching involves forcing water through the vagina by use of a douche syringe. *Used as contraception, douching is probably useless and may, in fact, wash sperm into the uterus, thus increasing the chances of pregnancy.* A number of commercial douches are available, but their use should be limited. Using a substance other than water can cause a bacterial imbalance in the vagina, leading to yeast and other infections.

MORNING-AFTER PILL

Morning-after pills contain hormones that prevent implantation of the egg if fertilization has taken place. Because some pills contain a high dose of estrogen, about 70 percent of users report nausea and about 30 percent report vomiting. Users also report menstrual irregularities, headaches, and dizziness. In general, morning-after pills should be a method of last resort because the full effects that the various hormones have on the body may not be fully understood.

RU-486

Although not currently available in the United States, the drug RU-486, which is produced by the French pharmaceutical company Roussel-Uclaf, is attracting considerable publicity. It appears able to abort pregnancies of up to five weeks duration; hence, it is sometimes referred to as "the month-after" pill. Later abortions using this drug are accompanied by numerous negative side effects. These problems, plus the anti-abortionist labeling of the drug as "chemical warfare against the unborn," make acceptance of RU-486 in the United States doubtful at present.

FIGURE 11-3
Male reproductive system, showing effects of vasectomy. Note that in actual sterilization, surgery is performed on both sides of the body.

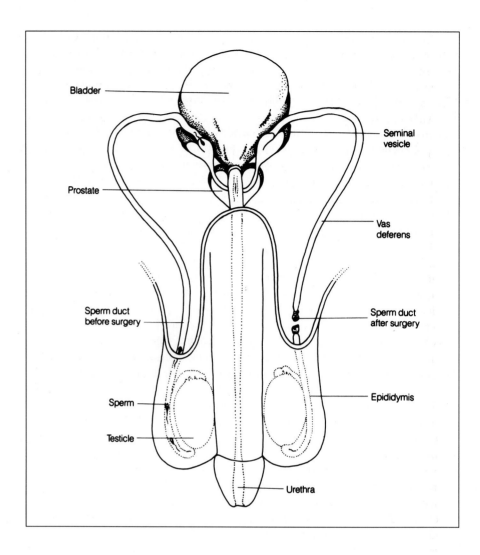

Bladder

Seminal vesicle

Prostate

Vas deferens

Sperm duct before surgery

Sperm duct after surgery

Sperm

Epididymis

Testicle

Urethra

Sterilization
Any procedure (usually surgical) by which an individual is made incapable of reproduction

Vasectomy
A sterilization procedure for males involving the surgical cutting of the vasa deferentia

Chapter 11
Family Planning

406

STERILIZATION

Sterilization is the most effective and permanent means of birth control. Despite the fact that in many cases it is irreversible, more and more Americans are choosing sterilization as a means of contraception. Female sterilization is currently the most popular method of birth control while male sterilization ranks third in popularity (Hatcher et al. 1990, 132).

Vasectomy   Although a vasectomy is safer, simpler, and less expensive than the woman's tubal ligation, only about one-third of the sterilization operations are vasectomies. **Vasectomy** is the surgical sterilization of the male. It is done in a doctor's office under local anesthetic and takes about thirty minutes. Small incisions are made in the scrotum, and the vasa deferentia, which carry the sperm from the testes, are cut and tied (see Figure 11-3).

The man may feel a dull ache in the surgical area and in the lower abdomen after a vasectomy. Aspirin and an ice bag help relieve these feelings. The man can return to work in two days and can have sex again as soon as he doesn't feel any discomfort, usually in about a week.

An additional method of contraception must be used for several weeks after the operation because live sperm still remain in parts of the male reproductive system. After about one to two months and a number of ejaculations, the man must return to his physician to have his semen examined for the presence of live sperm. If none are found, other birth control methods can be dropped.

Although the man will continue to produce sperm after the operation, the sperm will now be absorbed into his body. His seminal fluid will be reduced only slightly. Hormone output will be normal, and he will not experience any physical changes in his sex drive. Some males do experience negative psychological side effects, however. For example, some equate the vasectomy with castration and feel less sexual. Such feelings may interfere with sexual ability. Postvasectomy psychological problems occur in perhaps 3 to 15 percent of men. On the other hand, many men report they feel freer and more satisfied with sex after a vasectomy.

In about 1 percent of vasectomies, a severed vas deferens rejoins itself so that sperm can again travel through the duct and be ejaculated (Masters, Johnson, and Kolodny 1988, 181–84; Hatcher et al. 1990). Because of this possibility, a yearly visit to a doctor to check for sperm in the semen is a good safety precaution.

One of the major drawbacks of vasectomy (or any other method of sterilization) is that in many cases it is irreversible. Thus, the husband and wife should be sure to discuss the matter thoroughly before deciding on this method of contraception.

If reversal is desired, the tubes can be reconnected in some cases. Doctors at the University of California Medical Center in San Francisco have recently reported much higher success with reversal operations than in the past. In some studies, up to 50 to 90 percent of the men who underwent microsurgical vasovasotomy (reconnecting the vas) subsequently ejaculated sperm, and three-quarters of those men were able to impregnate their wives (reported in Shapiro 1988, 205; Hatcher et al. 1990, 417). However, some vasectomized men develop antibodies to their sperm, which may persist after the reversal and counteract fertilization.

Earlier concerns about later health problems, especially heart disease, seem unfounded (Shapiro 1988, 204–5). The only health problem seen significantly more often in vasectomized men in inflammation of a sperm-collecting duct near the testicles, and this minor problem is found in only about 1 percent of vasectomies.

Tubal Ligation **Tubal ligation** is the surgical sterilization of the female. Until recently, it has been a much more difficult operation to perform than a vasectomy because the Fallopian tubes lie more deeply within the body than the vasa deferentia. The operation, performed in a hospital rather than a doctor's office, requires a general anesthetic and a hospital stay of about three to four days. One or two small incisions are made in the abdominal wall, the Fallopian tubes are located and severed, a small section of each is removed, and then the two ends of each tube are tied (see Figure 11-4). Incisions can also be made through the vaginal wall; this procedure will not leave a scar and requires shorter hospitalization (however, recent pregnancy or obesity make this approach more difficult or impossible). Both procedures take about thirty minutes.

Tubal ligation
A sterilization procedure for females in which the Fallopian tubes are cut or tied

FIGURE 11-4
Female reproductive system, showing effects of tubal ligation. Note that in actual sterilization surgery is performed on both sides of the body.

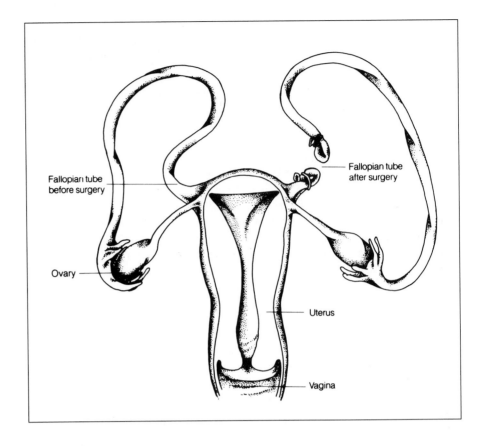

Fallopian tube
before surgery

Fallopian tube
after surgery

Ovary

Uterus

Vagina

Besides being more difficult than vasectomies, tubal ligation is also riskier. A few women experience problems after the operation, mainly from infections. Some women also experience abdominal discomfort and menstrual irregularity. Most women, however, have no after effects (Masters, Johnson, and Kolodny 1988, 180–81; Boston Women's Health Book Collective 1992, 302–304).

A more recent and now more widely used procedure is called **laparoscopy.** This too is a hospital procedure that requires a general anesthetic. However, the operation takes only fifteen minutes and does not require overnight hospitalization. A tiny incision is made in the abdomen, and a small light-containing tube (laparoscope) is inserted to illuminate the Fallopian tubes. The surgeon then inserts another small tube carrying high-intensity radio waves that burn out sections of the Fallopian tubes. The incision is so small that only a stitch or two are needed; hence, the procedure is often referred to as "Band-Aid" surgery. Most women leave the hospital two to four hours after surgery. Infection rates with this method are less than 1 percent.

Both forms of tubal ligation have a failure rate of about 0.1 to 3 percent (Shapiro 1988, 226). Attempts to reverse the sterilization have been about 70 percent successful (Hatcher et al. 1990). However, the reversal procedure is a major operation lasting several hours and as such is very costly ($10,000 to $15,000).

Women who have been sterilized tend to report an increase in sexual enjoyment because they are now free of the fear of pregnancy. A few women report reduced sexual enjoyment because of the loss of fertility, which they may equate with femininity.

Laparoscopy
A sterilization procedure for females involving the use of a telescope instrument (laparoscope) to locate the Fallopian tubes, which are then cauterized

Hysterectomy **Hysterectomy,** which is the surgical removal of the uterus, also ends fertility. This is an extreme procedure, however, and should be used only when a woman has uterine cancer or other problems of the uterus and not just for birth control reasons.

Hysterectomy
Surgical removal of a female's uterus; results in sterilization

ABORTION

In the United States, the 1960s witnessed mounting interest in **induced abortion** as a method of birth control. Although each state had restrictive legislation against abortion, many illegal abortions were performed. Expectant mothers were sometimes killed and often harmed because of nonsterile or otherwise inadequate procedures.

Abortion
Induced or spontaneous termination of a pregnancy before the fetus is capable of surviving on its own

Other countries successfully use abortion to control population and to help women avoid unwanted pregnancies. Japan, for example, was plagued by overpopulation for years until 1948 when it enacted the Eugenic Protection Act that, in essence, allowed any woman to obtain a legal abortion. In conjunction with a massive educational campaign to make the populace aware of the need to reduce family size, this measure reduced the birthrate from 34.3 to 17 per 1000 by 1956. In 1991 the birthrate was 10 per 1000 population or 1.5 children per fertile woman.

After a number of states liberalized their abortion laws, the U.S. Supreme Court (*Roe v. Wade* and *Doe v. Bolton*, January 22, 1973) made abortion on request a possibility for the entire country. Essentially, the Court ruled that the fetus is not a person as defined by the U.S. Constitution and therefore does not possess constitutional rights. "We do not resolve the difficult question of when life begins. When those trained in the respective disciplines of medicine, philosophy, and theology are unable to arrive at any consensus, the judiciary . . . is not in a position to speculate as to the answer."

More specifically, the Court said that in the *first trimester* (twelve weeks) of pregnancy, no state may interfere in any way with a woman's decision to have an abortion as long as it is performed by a physician. In the *second trimester* (thirteen to twenty-five weeks), a state may lay down medical guidelines to protect the woman's health. Most states that allow abortion by choice in the second trimester permit it only through the twentieth week. After that time there must be clear medical evidence that the mother's health is endangered or that the baby will be irreparably defective. Only in the *last trimester* may states ban abortion, and even then an abortion may be performed if continued pregnancy endangers the life or health of the mother.

The proponents of abortion on request believed they had won a final victory, yet this conclusion proved premature. Abortion has become one of the most emotional issues that the nation faces. On one side are the crusaders "for life," otherwise known as "right-to-lifers," who argue on religious and moral grounds that abortion is murder and therefore should be outlawed. On the other side are the "pro-choice" crusaders who contend that every woman has the right to control her own body, which includes the right to have an abortion if she so chooses (see Debate the Issues on p. 412).

Abortion

One reason the conflict continues is that the American public is fairly evenly divided on the question. National polls have continually shown the country is narrowly divided as to whether abortion should be legal and easily available. Figure 11-5 presents the results of just one of many polls taken on the question of abortion. On the question, "Do you favor or oppose passing laws making abortion more difficult for women?" 47 percent of Americans were in favor while 48 percent were not. On the question, "Do you personally believe having an abortion is wrong?" 50 percent answered yes while 43 percent answered no.

Although it is difficult to estimate the number of illegal abortions performed before 1973, around 1.5 million legal abortions were being performed annually by 1978. This figure has remained relatively constant since then and represents about 350 abortions per 1000 live births. It is estimated that one in five American women of reproductive age has had an abortion and that almost one-half of American women will have had at least one abortion by the age of forty-five (Johnson et al. 1992, 28).

The following statistics give some idea of which women are having abortions and when they are having them (*World Almanac* 1991; *Time* 1992;

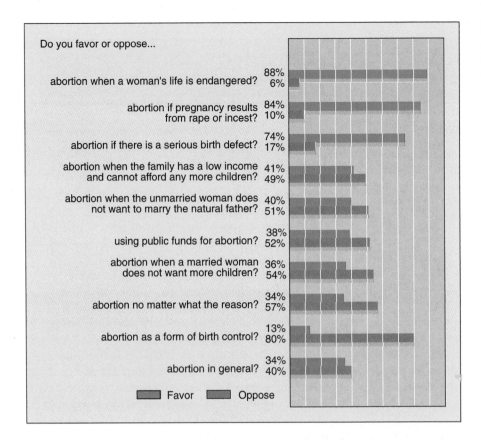

Do you favor or oppose...

abortion when a woman's life is endangered? 88% 6%

abortion if pregnancy results from rape or incest? 84% 10%

abortion if there is a serious birth defect? 74% 17%

abortion when the family has a low income and cannot afford any more children? 41% 49%

abortion when the unmarried woman does not want to marry the natural father? 40% 51%

using public funds for abortion? 38% 52%

abortion when a married woman does not want more children? 36% 54%

abortion no matter what the reason? 34% 57%

abortion as a form of birth control? 13% 80%

abortion in general? 34% 40%

Favor   Oppose

FIGURE 11-5

Abortion: Do you favor or oppose? (Source: Adapted from the *Los Angeles Times*, March 19, 1989, 26)

Kochanek 1989; National Center for Health Statistics 1991a):

■ For white women, the media age at which an abortion is performed is 23.5 years while the greatest number of abortions occur at 18 years of age. For black women, these figures are 23.9 and 21 years, respectively.

■ About 25 percent of the women having abortions are under twenty years of age.

■ The abortion ratio for black women is about 2.2 times that of white women. (Abortion ratio is the number of abortions per 1000 live births).

■ Forty percent of white and 54 percent of black women having abortions have had one before.

■ About 20 percent of the women having abortions are married. Approximately 58 percent of these women have no other children.

■ About 90 percent of the abortions take place in the first trimester (twelve weeks) of pregnancy.

The prolife movement's ultimate goal is to add an amendment to the U.S. Constitution that would reverse the Supreme Court's decision. An amendment (Human Life Amendment) has been introduced several times in Congress to do what the Supreme Court said it could not do; namely, decide when life

Abortion

ABORTION ON DEMAND IS EVERYONE'S RIGHT

Those who support legal abortion (pro-choice groups) believe that a woman's body belongs to her and that she should have the right to determine whether to pursue pregnancy to completion. They believe that laws governing abortion are an unconstitutional invasion of privacy.

When we women approach abortion from the point of view of our own experience, it does not seem to us that we are arriving at a radical conclusion when we suggest that choice is the answer. On the contrary it seems sweet reason. Surely, at least, we have the ability to control our own physical selves, surely we can make decisions from the skin in if not from the skin out. What could be more reasonable than to ask that we be allowed to make choices for our own bodies? Nothing is more reasonable than that. (Steinem 1982)

Those favoring legal abortion argue that overpopulation is a major threat to civilization and humanity. Thus, to fail to use every acceptable method to reduce population growth is immoral and shortsighted and will ultimately lead to world disaster.

They further argue that having unwanted children is more immoral than seeking abortion. The unwanted child suffers and becomes the source of many of society's problems. Problems are created both for and by unwanted children.

Abortion is not as dangerous to the mother as childbirth. The maternal death rate in New York, for example, is 29 per 100,000 births, whereas the death rate from legal abortions is only 3.5 per 100,000 abortions. Deaths from pregnancy and birth in England are about 20 per 100,000 deliveries, and the death rate from abor-

tions is about 4 per 100,000. Overall, complications are indicated in less than 1 percent of induced abortions, and there appears to be even less risk in first-trimester abortions done by vacuum aspiration (see p. 415) (Kochanek 1989; Hatcher et al. 1990, 456).

Negative psychological reactions appear to be minimal, with most women responding with relief after ending an unwanted pregnancy. A committee of the American Psychological Association studied the surgeon general's report on abortion and concluded, "severe negative reactions are rare and are in line with those following normal life stresses (such as job loss and divorce). The time of greatest stress is likely to be before the abortion" (Landers 1989b, 32).

Certainly, in many cases, abortion can be the greater good—when there is a clear threat to the life and health of the woman, in cases of rape and incest, and when there are reliable indications of serious physical or mental retardation in the child.

Women have always sought abortions and always will. By making abortion illegal, society fosters a black market in abortions and increases the woman's chances of injury and death.

ABORTION IS MURDER

Anti-abortion ("pro-life") groups believe that abortion is murder and that since murder is not condoned in our society, we should not condone abortion. To them, the life of the unborn is of paramount importance.

Abortion opponents argue that social utility is not a viable criterion in matters that involve life and death and essential liberties. Although a huge proportion of unhappy lives and a whole network of social ills can be traced to the unwanted child, no one can predict with certainty how a child will turn out. No one can say

begins. The amendment reads: "For the purpose of enforcing the obligation of the States under the Fourteenth Amendment not to deprive persons of life without due process of law, human life shall be deemed to exist from conception." The amendment would allow states to pass laws defining abortion as murder. To date, the amendment has not been passed. Congress has passed statutes cutting off most federal funds for abortions, and these restrictions have

that an unwanted child won't later be wanted and loved. How many people, even those who are unhappy or in trouble from time to time, seriously wish they had never been born? The social utility argument reduces human life to the value of a machine: How well does the life work?

Anti-abortion groups believe that easy availability of abortions will lead to promiscuity. They maintain that the Christian heritage of the United States not only bans abortion but also has implications for sexual mores. The possibility of pregnancy forces individuals to contemplate sexual intercourse in a responsible manner since the act may lead to a child for whom they must take responsibility. Making abortion freely available encourages promiscuous behavior and reduces the use of contraceptives because the consequences of the act are removed. "If I become pregnant, I can always get an abortion."

Opponents of abortion maintain that abortion can lead to severe psychological trauma. They argue that the feelings of guilt, the frustrated desire to have the child, the sense of responsibility for the death of the child, and many other psychological reactions pose as much of a threat to the mother's health as the continued pregnancy. Although those who support legal abortion quote from the surgeon general's report on abortion to refute the existence of such negative reactions, the surgeon general refused to release the report, indicating that the studies of psychological reactions to abortion simply are not good enough to tell us exactly what these reactions are or the extent of their severity (Landers 1989a).

Multiple abortions or second-trimester abortions may lead to future problems. For example, in future pregnancies, the woman may be at greater risk of having a low-birth-weight baby, a premature delivery, or a spontaneous abortion.

Improved premature birth technology (see Chapter 12) is reducing the age at which a child can be born and survive. The Supreme Court decision in *Roe v. Wade* banned abortion in the third trimester (after twenty-four weeks) because the fetus's chances of survival outside the womb are high. Improved technology is now making it possible for fetuses to survive after twenty-two weeks and in the near future perhaps after a gestation period of only twenty weeks. These developments and ultrasound pictures of eighteen-week-old fetuses moving, sucking a thumb, and so forth make the argument that the fetus is only a blob of tissue and in no way human untenable. Anyone who has observed a premature baby realizes that even though the fetus is yet to be born, it certainly is a human being long before the actual birth. Thus, to take its life is to take the life of a human being.

WHAT DO YOU THINK?

1. Do you believe that a fetus is a living person with all of his or her individual rights under the U.S. Constitution?
2. Under what circumstances would you personally have an abortion?
3. Do you think underage women should have the right to have an abortion without parental knowledge?
4. Should we think of abortion as simply another method of birth control?
5. What role should the father/husband have in an abortion decision?
6. Do you think having an abortion, giving up the child for adoption, or raising an unwanted child is harder psychologically on the mother?

been upheld by the Supreme Court. Federally financed abortions have dropped from a high of 300,000 to essentially zero.

Many states have passed restrictions controlling second-trimester abortions as allowed by the Supreme Court. In July 1989, the Supreme Court issued (5–4) a controversial decision (*Webster v. Reproductive Health Services*) upholding the right of states to restrict abortion to some degree. Specifically, the

Abortion

Webster decision upheld key provisions of a 1986 Missouri law and thus allowed the states to:

■ Refuse to let abortions be performed in public hospitals and clinics.
■ Prohibit doctors and other health professionals on public payrolls from "encouraging or counseling" women to have abortions.
■ Require physicians, where possible, to determine if a fetus at least twenty weeks old can survive outside the womb.

In June, 1992, the Supreme Court again upheld Roe vs. Wade (5–4) *(Pennsylvania Planned Parenthood vs. Casey)*. The court did, however, uphold several restrictions on abortion contained in the Pennsylvania law that makes it more difficult for women to end their pregnancies. These restrictions are:

■ Women seeking abortions must be told about fetal development and alternatives to ending pregnancies.
■ Women must wait 24 hours after receiving that information before proceeding with an abortion.
■ Doctors are required to keep detailed records, subject to public disclosure, on each abortion performed.
■ Unmarried girls under 18 and not supporting themselves are required to get consent of one of their parents or the permission of a state judge who has ruled that the girl seeking the abortion is mature enough to make the decision on her own.

One provision of the Pennsylvania law that was struck down by the court required married women in most cases to tell their husbands about their plans for abortion.

Because these decisions allow the states more freedom in setting abortion regulations, we can expect to see other states passing increasing restrictive abortion rules (see Figure 11-6). Although many people are predicting that the more conservative Supreme Court will overturn *Roe v. Wade*, only time will tell where the abortion debate will end, if it ever ends at all. One thing seems sure: the issue of abortion will remain controversial for some time.

Another aspect of the debate concerns the right of the father to participate in the abortion decision. Current laws exclude him from the decision on the ground that it is the mother-to-be's body and therefore under her control. In the second trimester of pregnancy, though, a hospital may require the husband's consent. This remains a controversial aspect of the abortion law. Should the father of an unborn child be totally barred from participating in the abortion decision? What happens if the mother-to-be and the father cannot agree on an abortion? In a nationwide survey, 66 percent of the prospective fathers said they felt guilt about the abortion as did 56 percent of the women; 33 percent of the men reported feeling regret as did 26 percent of the women. As you can see, the negative feelings about the abortion are felt more strongly by men than women (Skelton 1989a).

Improving medical technology also influences the abortion debate. In 1973 the earliest that a fetus could survive outside the womb was about twenty-eight weeks. Now that threshold has dropped to twenty-four weeks, and many doctors predict that it will soon be twenty weeks. What does this mean for a woman contemplating abortion later than twenty weeks? What happens when a saline abortion is performed late in pregnancy, but the fetus, although damaged, can survive with the new technology? Many states hold physicians to the same standard of care for fetuses born live from induced abortions as for any other premature infant. This occasionally results in the paradox of a doctor performing an abortion and then fighting to keep the infant alive.

The debate over induced abortion tends to cloud the physical act of abortion itself. First of all, spontaneous abortion occurs by the end of the tenth week in 10 percent or more of all diagnosed first pregnancies. If undiagnosed first pregnancies are taken into account, the figure is probably closer to 25 percent. A high percentage of spontaneously aborted embryos are abnormal. There is evidence that emotional shock also plays a role in spontaneous abortions.

Abortion is a fairly simple procedure, though it can be more unpleasant than some who support legal abortion claim. One method of legal abortion is **dilatation and curettage (D and C).** In this method the cervix is dilated by the insertion of increasingly larger metal dilators until its opening is about as big around as a fountain pen. At this point a curette (a surgical instrument) is used to scrape out the contents of the uterus. An ovum forceps (a long, grasping surgical instrument) may also be used. The woman is instructed not to have sexual intercourse for several weeks, and she may take from ten days to two weeks to recover fully from the procedure.

Vacuum aspiration is now the preferred method of abortion (about 96 percent of all induced abortions) because it takes less time, involves less loss of blood, and has a shorter recovery period than a D and C. In this method the cervix is dilated by a speculum (an expanding instrument), and a vacuum-

Dilation and curettage
An abortion-inducing procedure that involves dilating the cervix and scraping out the contents of the uterus with a metal instrument (curette)

Vacuum aspiration
An abortion-inducing procedure in which the contents of the uterus are removed by suction

415

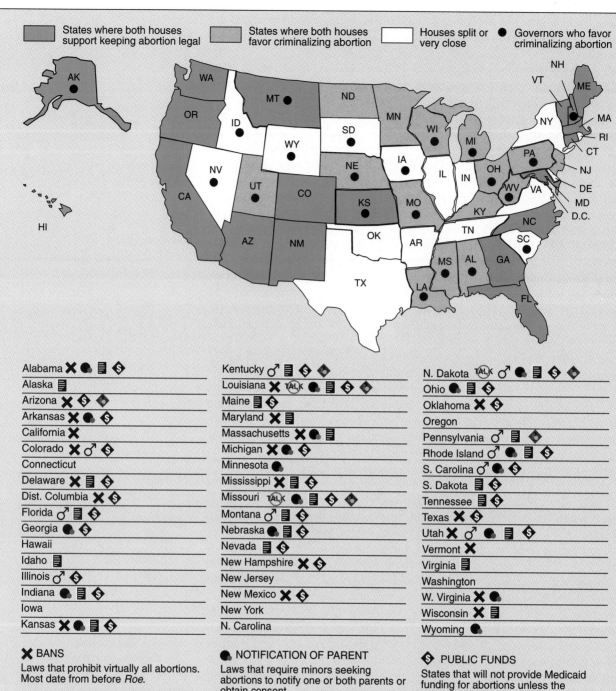

States where both houses support keeping abortion legal   **States where both houses favor criminalizing abortion**   **Houses split or very close**   ● **Governors who favor criminalizing abortion**

Alabama ✕ ● ▤ 💲
Alaska ▤
Arizona ✕ 💲 ◆
Arkansas ✕ ● 💲
California ✕
Colorado ✕ ♂ 💲
Connecticut
Delaware ✕ ▤ 💲
Dist. Columbia ✕ 💲
Florida ♂ ▤ 💲
Georgia ● 💲
Hawaii
Idaho ▤
Illinois ♂ 💲
Indiana ● ▤ 💲
Iowa
Kansas ✕ ● ▤ 💲

Kentucky ♂ ▤ 💲 ◆
Louisiana ✕ TALK ● ▤ 💲 ◆
Maine ▤ 💲
Maryland ✕ ▤
Massachusetts ✕ ● ▤
Michigan ✕ ● 💲
Minnesota ●
Mississippi ✕ ▤ 💲
Missouri TALK ● ▤ 💲 ◆
Montana ♂ ▤ 💲
Nebraska ● ▤ 💲
Nevada ▤ 💲
New Hampshire ✕ 💲
New Jersey
New Mexico ✕ 💲
New York
N. Carolina

N. Dakota TALK ♂ ● ▤ 💲 ◆
Ohio ● ▤ 💲
Oklahoma ✕ 💲
Oregon
Pennsylvania ♂ ▤ ◆
Rhode Island ♂ ● ▤ 💲
S. Carolina ♂ ● 💲
S. Dakota ▤ 💲
Tennessee ▤ 💲
Texas ✕ 💲
Utah ✕ ♂ ● ▤ 💲
Vermont ✕
Virginia ▤
Washington
W. Virginia ✕ ●
Wisconsin ✕ ▤
Wyoming ●

✕ BANS
Laws that prohibit virtually all abortions. Most date from before *Roe*.

TALK COUNSELING BANS
Laws that prevent certain health-care providers from giving advice or referrals regarding abortions.

♂ NOTIFICATION OF HUSBAND
A requirement that a woman must gain consent from or notify her husband.

● NOTIFICATION OF PARENT
Laws that require minors seeking abortions to notify one or both parents or obtain consent.

▤ INFORMED CONSENT/DELAY
Laws that require women be counseled and/or given state-prepared materials. Often they must wait up to 24 hours or more before proceeding.

💲 PUBLIC FUNDS
States that will not provide Medicaid funding for abortions unless the women's life is in danger.

◆ PUBLIC FACILITIES/EMPLOYEES
States that prohibit the use of public facilities for abortion, or that prohibit public employees from participating in an abortion.

suction tube is inserted into the uterus. A curette and electric pump are attached to the tubing, and suction is applied to the uterine cavity. The uterus is emptied in about twenty to thirty seconds. The doctor sometimes also scrapes the uterine lining with a metal curette. The procedure takes five to ten minutes. The woman may return home after a rest of a few hours in a recovery area. She is usually instructed not to have sexual intercourse and not to use tampons for a week or two after the abortion (see Figure 11-7).

After the fourteenth to sixteenth week, a different method, called the **saline abortion,** may be used because the fetus is now too large to be removed by suction, and performing a D and C now may cause complications. The uterus is stimulated to push the fetus out; in other words, a miscarriage is induced. When a fetus dies, the uterus naturally begins to contract and expel the dead fetus. In order to kill the fetus, the mother is given a local anesthetic, and a long needle is inserted through her abdominal wall into the uterine cavity. The amniotic sac (see Chapter 12) is punctured and some of its fluid is removed. An equal amount of 20 percent salt solution is then injected into the sac. The injection must be done slowly and carefully to avoid introducing the salt solution into the woman's circulatory system. She must be awake so that she can report any pain or other symptoms. Once the fetus is dead, the uterus begins to contract in about six to forty-eight hours. Eventually, the amniotic sac breaks and the fetus is expelled. In up to 50 percent of cases, the placenta does not come out automatically, and a gentle pull on the umbilical cord is necessary to remove it. In about 10 percent of cases, a D and C must be performed to remove any remaining pieces of the placenta. The saline procedure should be carried out in a hospital, and the woman should remain there until the abortion process is complete. The recovery period is longer than for other forms of abortion, and complications are more frequent.

A new chemical abortion procedure being used in France and Scandinavia may make the preceding methods obsolete. The synthetic prostaglandin RU-486, described earlier in the discussion of contraceptive methods, is placed in the vagina in suppository form. The chemical causes muscle contractions within one to five hours after a "missed period." The uterine contractions lead to abortion. This method is used early in the pregnancy.

Death from an early first-trimester abortion is rare (1.7 to 2.6 per 100,000 women). The Centers for Disease Control indicate that complications from the anesthesia, infection, and hemorrhage are the major contributing factors. The decision to have an abortion may not be easy and should not be made lightly. Whenever possible, it is wise for the woman considering an abortion to discuss the decision with the prospective father, parents, physicians, counselors, and/or knowledgeable and concerned friends. But although abortion should be a considered decision, the decision to have an abortion should be reached as quickly as possible. The later in the pregnancy the abortion, the greater the risks of complications.

Professional abortion counseling can be obtained at local Planned Parenthood chapters and in most states from the Clergy Consultation Services on Abortion. Both agencies are listed in local telephone directories. Many prolife groups also run consultation facilities.

Abortion is not recommended as a means of birth control. The sexually active, responsible man and woman who are well informed about sex and contraceptive devices usually will not be faced with having to make an abortion decision.

FIGURE 11-6
(facing page at left)
Abortion laws by state. This is a selection of the laws that affect the availability of abortion. Some, like the outright bans and husband notification, are not enforced, pending consideration by the Supreme Court. (Source: *Time*, May 4, 1992, 29)

Saline abortion
An abortion-inducing procedure in which a salt solution is injected into the amniotic sac to kill the fetus, which is then expelled via uterine contractions

Abortion

417

FIGURE 11-7
Vacuum aspiration, an abortion
method, takes only five to ten
minutes; it can be performed up to
the twelfth week of pregnancy.
(a) The vacuum aspiration process.
(b) An operating unit for vacuum
aspiration.

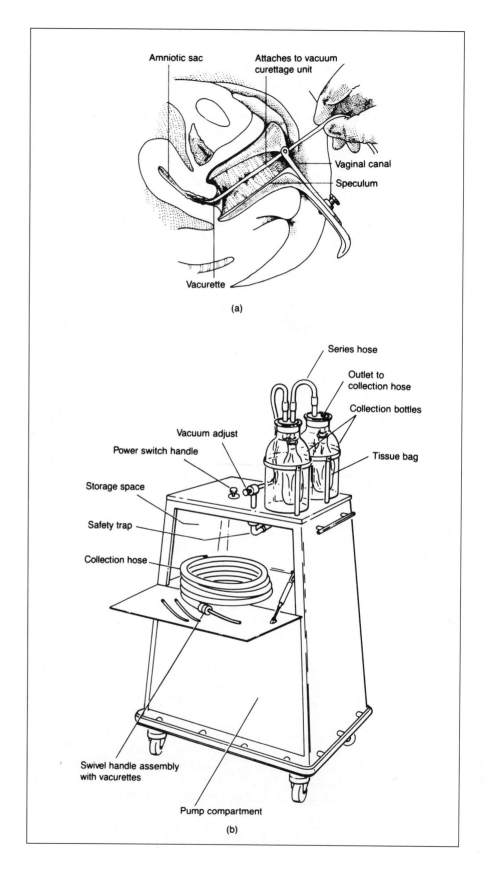

Amniotic sac

Attaches to vacuum
curettage unit

Vaginal canal

Speculum

Vacurette

(a)

Series hose

Outlet to
collection hose

Collection bottles

Vacuum adjust

Tissue bag

Power switch handle

Storage space

Safety trap

Collection hose

Swivel handle assembly
with vacurettes

Pump compartment

(b)

INFERTILITY

Although many people think only of contraception when they hear the phrase "family planning," problems of infertility are also important aspects of family planning. About one in twelve couples has problems conceiving (*Time* 1991, 56). **Infertile** means that a man is not producing viable sperm or a woman is either not producing viable eggs or has some other condition that makes it impossible to maintain a pregnancy.

Infertile
Unable to produce viable sperm if a man or become pregnant if a woman

> It is estimated that about 33 percent of all married couples conceive the first month they try and that about 60 percent conceive within the first three months. About 10 to 15 percent of couples are not able to conceive within one year (Hatcher et al. 1990, 479).

A number of factors have combined to increase infertility problems. Many more women are postponing childbearing into their thirties due to work commitments. The effects of age by itself on fertility are moderate and do not begin until the late thirties. Lowered fertility in the late thirties may be connected to the fact that a woman is born with her entire supply of eggs and produces no new ones. As she ages, the remaining eggs also age, and the number of viable eggs is reduced. In addition, as time passes, there is increased risk of exposure to sexually transmitted disease and other infections that can impair fertility. About one in seven couples in their thirties have difficulty conceiving.

The treatment of infertility involves three phases: education, detection, and therapy. Young couples should persist in trying to conceive for at least one year. If they are not successful, they should seek help from a physician. Often when couples learn more about how conception occurs and the possible reasons for failure to conceive, they will feel less tense and anxious and thus increase the chances of conception.

PREREQUISITES OF FERTILITY

For a couple to produce a child unassisted by the new fertility technology, both partners must be **fecund,** meaning they must have the capacity to reproduce. For the male, fecundity includes the following:

Fecund
Having the capacity to reproduce

1. He must produce healthy live sperm in sufficient numbers. Ordinarily, a single normal testicle is all that is required, although both usually assume an equal role in producing sperm. To function properly, a testicle must be in the scrotal sac. In the male embryo each testicle is formed in the abdomen and descends into the scrotum during the seventh month of intrauterine life. Infrequently, one or both testicles fail to descend. If they have not descended by five or six years of age, the boy is usually treated with a hormone to stimulate testicular growth. This makes the testicle heavier, which in some instances brings about descent. If hormone treatment fails, surgery is performed, usually when the boy is about eight.
2. Seminal fluid (the whitish, sticky material ejaculated at orgasm) must be secreted in the proper amount and composition to transport the sperm.

Infertility

Jonie Mosby Mitchell is three months pregnant and thrilled about it. She and her husband adopted a baby girl three years ago, and they are eager to produce a sibling for her. Nothing unusual about that, except for the fact that Mitchell is fifty-two. She went through menopause years ago.

Mitchell's pregnancy represents one of the latest and most extraordinary achievements of infertility science. By treating his middle-aged patient with hormones, Dr. Mark Sauer, at the University of Southern California, was able to essentially reverse the effects of menopause. Using an egg from a young woman and artificial insemination with sperm from Mitchell's husband Donnie, Sauer was able to establish the pregnancy. Mitchell is not even Sauer's oldest patient. He is also helping a fifty-five year-old woman, who has a thirty-year history of infertility and was too old for an in vitro fertilization when it was introduced in 1978. "She had given up hope of ever having a child, and came to me hoping for a miracle," says the sympathetic doctor.

Such miracles are now possible. Expensive, but possible. But is this an appropriate use of technology? When Sauer first used the technique, it was to help younger women who had gone through menopause prematurely. But after publishing his results last October, he was besieged by requests from middle-aged women hoping to turn back the clock. Should they be helped?

Not everyone in the field is enthusiastic. Some professionals fear that these new techniques will only encourage women to delay pregnancy. "There is a time and place for everything," says Dr. Georgeanna Jones of the Jones Institute for Reproductive Medicine in Norfolk, Va. "Women should know that their eggs age. They need to plan for their families and careers so they can have children earlier." Most in vitro clinics are reluctant to accept patients over age forty. The reason is primarily practical: the success rate for such women is minimal, though donor eggs can certainly improve the odds. Natural childbearing is also rare in this age group. Only 1 percent of the 4 million U.S. babies born in 1988 had mothers between ages forty and forty-five, and less than 0.04 percent were born to women over forty-five.

From a medical standpoint, there are two problems with very late childbearing: health risks to the fetus and to the mother. After age 40, the risk of fetal abnormalities is substantial: the incidence of Down syndrome, for example, rises to one in forty live births. (Using donated eggs from a young woman presumably reduces the risk.) The mother meanwhile faces increased risks of diabetes, obesity, high blood pressure, and other complications of pregnancy—all of which can harm the unborn child. These problems are usually manageable, however, if the woman's health is generally good.

The ethical and social concerns are trickier. Jonie Mitchell will be seventy when her child graduates from high school. She is unlikely to live to see that child's children grow up. But such considerations have not deterred men from fathering children while in their fifties, sixties, and even seventies. "If I can raise him or her until age thirty, then he should be able to make it on his own," says Mitchell. She notes that her own mother had nine children and is still going strong at eighty-six.

Psychologists point out that older parents are more likely to be emotionally and financially stable, even if they lack the stamina to chase a toddler for hours on end. "From the kid's perspective one could argue that it would be nicer to have a mother who can run faster than the kid," says Dr. Ellen Wright Clayton, a pediatrician and law professor at Vanderbilt University. But, she says, "the child's other alternative is not to exist." Not many fifty-year-olds want to be pregnant, and not many can afford the $10,000 or more it takes. Clearly, says Clayton, "if these women want to have babies this badly, then these babies are going to be loved."

Source: *Time*, September 30, 1991, 62.

3. An unobstructed seminal passage must exist from the testicle to the end of the penis.

4. The man must be able to achieve and sustain an erection and to ejaculate within the vagina.

For the female, fecundity includes the following:

1. At least one ovary must function normally enough to produce a mature egg.

2. A normal-sized uterus must be properly prepared to receive the developing fetus by chemicals (hormones) fed into the bloodstream by the ovary.

3. An unobstructed genital tract must exist from the vagina up through the Fallopian tubes to the ovary to enable passage of egg and sperm.

4. The uterine environment must adequately nourish and protect the unborn child until it is able to live in the outside world.

5. Miscarriage must be avoided, and the infant must be delivered safely (Hatcher et al. 1990, 447–78).

It is not uncommon for couples seeking fertility help to conceive before treatment begins and for adoptive parents to conceive shortly after they decide on adoption. Clearly, emotional and psychological factors are tremendously important to the process of conception.

CAUSES OF INFERTILITY

Males account for about 40 percent of infertility problems as do females. Problems with both members of a marriage account for another 20 percent of infertility problems (Hatcher et al. 1990, 478). With men, for example, **impotence** (the inability to gain or maintain an erection) precludes sexual intercourse and thus conception. Often impotence is psychological in nature, though it can be caused by alcohol, general fatigue, or a debilitating disease. Low sperm count is another possible reason for infertility. An ejaculation that contains fewer than 100 to 150 million sperm limits the possibility of conception. Alcohol, tobacco, and/or marijuana use have all been implicated in lower sperm motility and count. Infectious diseases such as mumps can damage sperm production. Sterility can also occur if the testes have not descended into the scrotum, because the higher temperature of the body inhibits the production of healthy sperm. A prolonged and untreated sexually transmitted disease can cause permanent sterility in both men and women.

If a couple consults a physician, as they should, about their apparent infertility, it is easier to test the man first because fertility tests for the male are much simpler than those for the female. Basically, the tests involve collecting a sample of ejaculate and determining the number and activity level of the sperm and checking for abnormal sperm.

Unfortunately, some men associate fertility with manhood. To them, an examination for possible fertility problems is an attack on their manhood, and they may be unwilling to cooperate. Both partners, however, must share in the search for a solution to infertility.

A woman must ovulate if she is to conceive. Almost all mature women menstruate, but in about 15 percent of a normal woman's cycle, an egg is not

Impotence
Inability to gain or maintain an erection

released. In a few women, ovulation seldom occurs, which makes them almost infertile.

A woman may have a problem conceiving if the tract from the vagina through the uterus and Fallopian tubes to the ovary is blocked. This is the most common reason for infertility in women. If the egg and sperm cannot meet, conception cannot occur. It is possible to determine if the Fallopian tubes are open by filling them with an opaque fluid and X-raying them.

Both vaginal infections and ovarian abnormalities can cause infertility. Infection probably accounts for the dramatic jump in infertility problems among young women that has occurred in recent years (Mosher and Pratt 1987). Doctors place some of the blame for this increase on more liberalized sexual attitudes. Increased sexual activity and more sexual partners have contributed to increases in genital infections, especially pelvic inflammatory disease. Such infections scar the delicate tissue of the Fallopian tubes, ovaries, and uterus. As noted, about half of these cases of pelvic inflammatory disease result from chlamydia, while gonorrhea accounts for another 25 percent of pelvic inflammatory infections (see pp. 384).

Another possible problem can arise from the chemical environment of the woman's reproductive organs. Too acid an environment quickly kills sperm. The chemical environment may also make implantation of the fertilized egg into the uterine wall difficult or impossible. In the latter case the woman may conceive and then spontaneously abort (miscarry) the embryo.

■ METHODS OF TREATMENT ■

Recent advances in the understanding of reproduction have led to a whole new technology that can be used to battle infertility (see Table 11-5). Artificial insemination, in vitro fertilization, and surrogate mothers are all used to help infertile couples. Combinations of these methods produce a dozen different patterns of parenting (see Figure 11-8).

ARTIFICIAL INSEMINATION

Artificial insemination
Induction of semen into the vagina or uterus by artificial means

When the cause of infertility rests with the husband, **artificial insemination** is sometimes used to induce conception. This consists of injecting sperm—from the husband, if possible, or from an anonymous donor—into the wife's vagina during her fertile period. Even if the husband's sperm count is low, his ejaculate can be collected and the concentration of sperm increased to bring it within the normal range necessary for fertilization. For reasons unknown, artificial insemination results in conception of a marked preponderance of males.

Sperm banks have been established where sperm is frozen and stored for later use; it seems to remain viable for long periods. Sperm that has been frozen for up to three years has been used for successful human fertilization.

Numerous controversies surround artificial insemination, especially when the sperm comes from someone other than the husband. Questions of legitimacy and parental responsibility have arisen. For example, after a divorce can a sterile husband deny financial responsibility for a child conceived with sperm from another man? Conversely, can such a husband be denied visitation rights because he is not the biological father of the child? Biologically, however,

	TABLE 11-5		
	NEW REPRODUCTIVE ALTERNATIVES		
METHOD	ADVANTAGES	RISKS	COST*
Fertility pump	Physiologic, mimics what occurs naturally	Inflammation of vein	$500 pump rental plus cost of synthetic GnRH
	No known side effects		
	Works when Clomid (fertility pill) doesn't		
	Much less costly than in vitro fertilization		
	No surgery		
	Normal incidence of multiple births		
In vitro fertilization	Best, if not only way for a couple to have their own baby if woman's tubes are irreparably blocked	Surgery and anesthetic	$10,000
		Multiple births	
	Potential for correcting genetic defects in embryo	Potential for genetic manipulation to malevolent as well as benevolent ends	
Embryo transfer	No surgery or anesthetic	Not being able to retrieve fertilized egg from donor	$6000–$8000
	Avoids genetic disorders carried by mother		
	Pregnancy possible for women who have no ovaries or ovaries that don't function		
Cryopreservation (freezing embryos for later implantation)	A second chance without surgery for a woman whose first attempt at in vitro fertilization fails	Slight increase in risk of abnormalities	Not known yet
	Banks of fertilized ova available for transfer to infertile women who are willing to bear another women's child	Potential for genetic manipulation to malevolent as well as benevolent ends	
	Potential for correction of genetic defects		
Microsurgery	Very effective in reversing female sterilization	Surgery and anesthetic	$8000
	Very effective in removing scar tissue around Fallopian tubes		
	Effective on tubes blocked at end near uterus		
Surrogate mothering	Woman whose infertility is not correctable can rear a child fathered by her husband	Wife must adopt baby	$10,000–$20,000
		Legal questions of legitimacy, inheritance, adultery, financial responsibility, and rights of the biological mother	
Artificial insemination	Best sperm can be used	Cramping	$300
	Sperm is deposited directly into uterus	Slight risk of infection	
		When sperm is donor's, not husband's, legal questions of legitimacy, inheritance, financial responsibility, adultery, and rights of biological father	
Clomiphene citrate (Clomid) (fertility pill)	Very effective in women with normal or high estrogen level	Multiple births	$50 per menstrual cycle
		Effective only 50 percent of time	
Pergonal (fertility injections)	Very effective for low estrogen levels	Multiple births	$1000 per menstrual cycle

*Costs are estimated

FIGURE 11-8
New ways of creating babies

FIGURE 11-8
New ways of creating babies

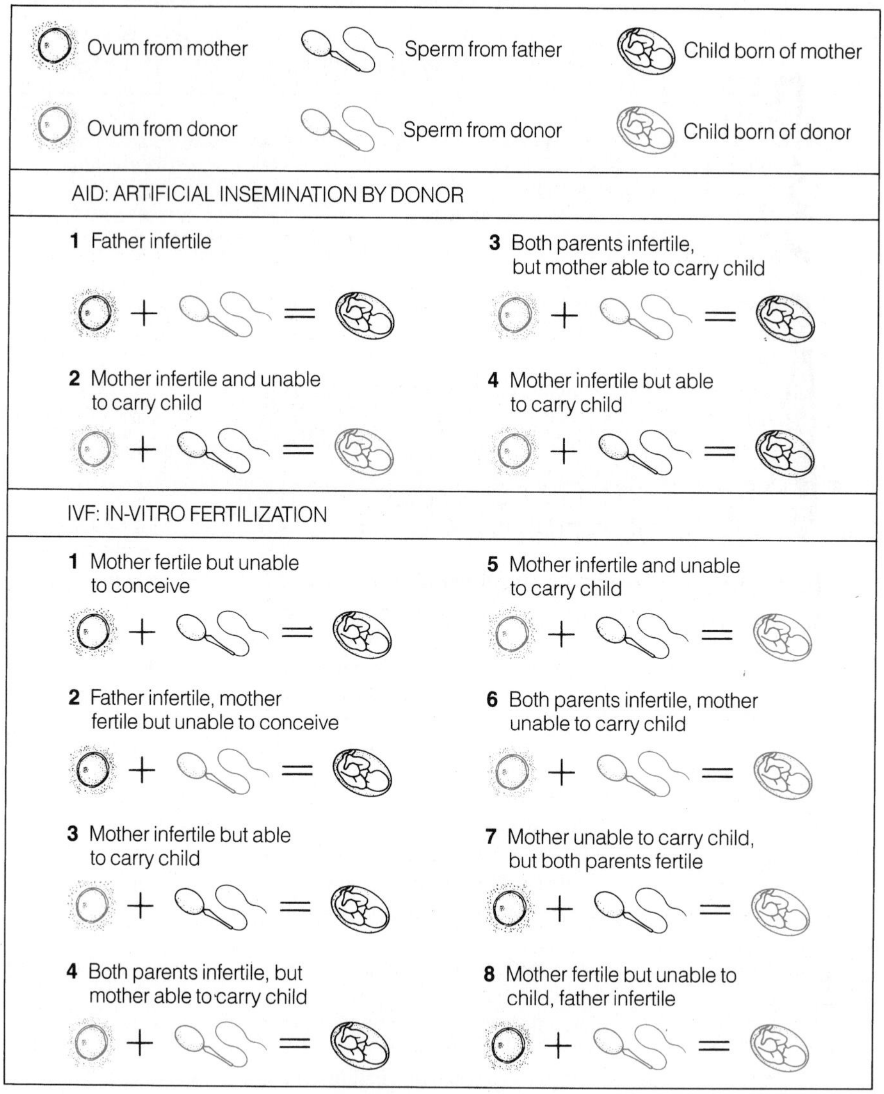

artificial insemination is a perfectly acceptable manner of overcoming a man's infertility.

FERTILITY DRUGS

When the cause of infertility is the woman's failure to ovulate, fertility drugs such as clomiphene citrate (Clomid) and menotropins (Pergonal) have been used to stimulate ovulation. The drugs often overstimulate ovulation, however, and cause multiple births.

From 1972 to 1989, triplet births increased 156 percent; quadruplet births were up 386 percent; and quintuplets and greater-number sets rose 182 percent among white women. Rates of increase were lower among black women. Increased use of fertility drugs accounts for most of this increase in multiple births (Associated Press. July 15, 1992.)

LOOK, LADY— YOU'RE THE ONE WHO ASKED FOR A FAMOUS MOVIE STAR WITH DARK HAIR, STRONG NOSE AND DEEP SET EYES...

ARTIFICIAL FERTILIZATION AND EMBRYO TRANSFER

For the woman who cannot become pregnant, it is now possible for a human egg to be fertilized outside her body and then implanted within her uterus. Louise Brown, the first such "test-tube baby," was born in July 1978 in England. The first baby in the United States conceived by the in vitro fertilization (IVF) technique was born in December 1981. There have now been over 10,000 such births in the United States (*Time* 1991, 58).

The first step in IVF is the retrieval of a mature female egg. The physician inserts a laparoscope through a small incision to see the follicle inside the ovary where the egg is being produced. Then the doctor inserts a long hollow needle through a second incision and gently suctions up the egg and surrounding fluid. The ovum is carefully washed and placed in a petri dish containing nutrients, and the dish is placed in an incubator for four to eight hours. The second step is to gather sperm from the husband and add them to the dish containing the egg. If all goes well, the egg is fertilized and starts to divide. When the embryo is about eight cells in size, it is placed in the woman's uterus.

It takes two to three weeks to know whether the pregnancy will be viable, and the chance of success was only about 20 percent five years ago. The major problem was getting the fertilized egg to implant into the uterine wall. With newer techniques such as inserting a mix of sperm and eggs directly into the Fallopian tube, success rates have doubled. In this procedure the egg is only out of the woman's body for a few minutes, and sperm are assured of reaching it. Even when pregnancy ensues, about one-third of the women will miscarry within the first three months. The cost of the IVF procedure is approximately $10,000. The procedure often has to be repeated several times before it works, thus increasing the costs dramatically.

Infertility

In 1983, the first successful transfer of human embryos was achieved. Women who were carrying fetuses had them transferred into nonfertile women at an early stage (around the fifth to sixth week).

SURROGATE MOTHERS

When it is impossible to correct a woman's infertility, another woman may be hired to bear a child for the couple. Such a woman is termed a **surrogate mother** (see Inset 11-5) and is usually paid between $10,000 and $20,000. Normally, she is fertilized via artificial insemination using the husband's sperm. Once the baby is born, it is legally adopted by the infertile couple. A number of organizations throughout the United States bring infertile couples together with potential surrogate mothers. The organizations screen and match the parties and handle the complex legal problems of adoption and payment. Because it is illegal in every state to buy or sell a child, payment must be made to compensate the surrogate mother, not for the child, but for such things as taking the risk of pregnancy and childbirth and for the loss of work because of pregnancy. The contract in each situation is unique and may include such specifications as the following:

- The surrogate agrees to terminate her maternal rights and allow adoption by the couple.
- The surrogate agrees to abort the fetus if an abnormality is discovered during the pregnancy.
- The surrogate agrees not to drink, smoke, or use drugs during the pregnancy.
- The couple will take out an insurance policy on the surrogate mother and on the biological father (husband), with the child named as beneficiary.
- The couple agree to compensate the surrogate at a reduced rate if she miscarries.
- The couple will accept all babies should multiple births occur.
- The couple will accept the child should it be born abnormal.

The potential legal problems are complex. Even though a contract is signed, what actually happens when a surrogate mother decides to keep the child? Or what happens when the parents-to-be decide they don't want the child, if, for example, the surrogate mother gives birth to a mentally defective child? If a surrogate mother contracts to bear a child, does she have the right to smoke or drink in defiance of the couple's wishes? Does she still have a right to an abortion? Does a child born to a surrogate mother have a right to know its biological mother? Surrogate mother bills defining the rights of the parties have been introduced in a number of state legislatures. The American Bar Association has approved a model set of surrogacy laws to serve as guidelines for the states. Fortunately or unfortunately, depending on one's point of view, such laws may be unnecessary in the future. Dramatic surrogacy disputes like the case of "Baby M" are leading some states and even the federal government to consider surrogacy. For example, the Supreme Court of New Jersey has ruled that surrogacy contracts are illegal. Michigan banned surrogate parenting in September 1988. On the other hand, California's legislative joint committee on surrogate parenting concluded that voluntary, unpaid, surrogate parenting arrangements should not be prohibited, although paid commercialized surrogacy arrangements should be prohibited (California legislature July 16, 1990).

On February 6, 1985, Mary Beth Whitehead signed a surrogacy contract agreeing to be artificially inseminated with sperm from William Stern (who was unable to conceive with his wife) and to turn over the child to the Sterns upon birth. Further she agreed to assume all medical risks and to submit to amniocentesis or abortion on demand. In return, she would receive $10,000 if she gave birth to a healthy baby. In March 1986 Mary Beth gave birth to a baby girl but decided to keep her.

A lengthy court battle ensued with the baby traded back and forth at first. In March 1987 the court finally terminated Mary Beth's rights to the child on the ground that she had breached a legal contract. Ten months later, the New Jersey Supreme Court upheld the grant of custody to William Stern, but granted Mary Beth visitation rights. At the same time the court declared surrogacy contracts illegal:

A surrogacy contract that provides money for the surrogate mother and that includes her irrevocable agreement to surrender her child at birth to the natural father and his wife is invalid and unenforceable. (New Jersey Supreme Court 1988)

This case reveals some of the many complications that can arise with the new technologies of reproduction. With their drama and media coverage, such cases obscure the many cases in which people have benefited from the new technologies without problem. For each "Baby M," there have been numerous surrogate relationships that have given an infertile couple a child without complications for any of the parties.

The use of a surrogate mother is a method of last resort. Informally, however, the procedure is as old as history. In days past it was not unusual for a woman to have a child and give it to another couple, infertile or not. This often happened with an illegitimate birth that was hidden from public view. For example, a daughter might have an illegitimate child who was then passed off as her new brother or sister.

In a modern twist, the mother of a daughter born without a uterus recently became a mother and grandmother at the same time. In this case, the daughter's fertilized eggs were placed in her own mother's uterus. Her mother carried the twins to term and then delivered her daughter's and son-in-law's biological twins via cesarean section. She thus became the grandmother to her daughter's children at the same time she became their mother via the birth (*Santa Barbara News Press* October 13, 1991). This is an example of the type 7 family in Figure 11-8.

One seldom-discussed problem common to all these new techniques is the potential reaction of the person who finds that he or she was born through one of these methods. Suppose a child is conceived from sperm and egg of anonymous donors, carried by a surrogate mother, and raised by a family to whom the child is not even biologically related. Should the child be told about such things? What will the child's reaction be if he or she finds out?

SEX THERAPY

Sex Therapy is being used to help couples with nonphysical problems that affect their sex lives and ability to conceive. Obviously, intercourse is necessary

Sex Therapy
Any kind of therapy designed to help persons overcome sexual problems

SURROGATE MOTHERS PROVIDE A HUMANITARIAN SERVICE

Women who carry a child for another couple where the wife is infertile are really no different from mothers of children adopted by others. It is no crime to agree to bear a child for another and then relinquish it for adoption. Adoption has long been accepted. Artificial insemination and other technological advances in fertility control are accepted. Children are often reared by non-biological parents in the case of blended families where one parent is a stepparent. What greater gift could there be than offering a child to a couple desiring parenthood but unable to produce a child themselves? Naturally, a surrogate mother must forgo certain activities and run some risks for the nine months of pregnancy and the birth. Thus, paying her a fee for her troubles and risk does not seem unreasonable.

With the increasing shortage of adoptable children, a couple may have to wait years for an adoptive child. Using a surrogate mother reduces that time to months. In addition, when an egg from the wife and sperm from the husband are used for conception, the adoptive parents are, in fact, the biological parents. Even if one mate cannot supply the sperm or egg, the child is biologically related to the couple through the biological contribution of the other parent. In one California case where the surrogate mother tried to break her contract and keep the child that was implanted into her uterus (the sperm and egg both belonged to the couple who had contracted with her to carry the child because the wife could not), the court ruled that the child belonged to the biological parents (*Time* 1990, 77).

Such an arrangement may also benefit the surrogate mother. Some women do not desire parenthood but may wish to experience pregnancy and birth. Some surrogates also take pleasure in helping another couple by giving the "gift of life."

Despite the highly publicized disputes between surrogate mothers and the couples who use them to produce a child for themselves, the majority of surrogate births have been loving, life-giving arrangements that benefit all concerned.

SURROGACY IS REALLY THE SELLING OF A BABY

In most surrogacy contracts, the infertile couple wishing a child pays the surrogate mother to have the child. Although the money is ostensibly given to the woman for her time and trouble in going through pregnancy rather than for the infant, this is simply a way around the laws prohibiting the sale of children.

In most surrogacies, the surrogate woman's egg is artificially fertilized by the sperm of the infertile couple's man. Thus, the surrogate mother is linked both biologically and through gestation with the child. In the past, the courts have upheld the rights of biological parents to the companionship of their children (Dolgin 1990, 7). When the surrogate's egg is used, such precedents give the surrogate mother maternal rights upon the birth of the child. Past decisions suggest she has a legal right to the companionship of the child even though she has signed a contract relinquishing that right.

Critics also argue that permitting surrogate motherhood for pay will create a "breeder" class of women. Will surrogate motherhood turn pregnancy into just another service industry? Is the uterus a spare room available to any boarder for a price? Is the child another product we can buy? Will this simply be a job you can do in your spare time at home with little training (Goodman 1990; 1991).

Those who say that women are intelligent enough to make the decision to be a surrogate have little understanding of economic pressures. This is why we impose limits on all medical commerce. We cannot sell a kidney. We should not be able to sell a pregnancy. There is no way to stop a genuinely altruistic act of surrogate motherhood. Giving the "gift of life" is far different from selling it. There is a way to end pregnancy as a commercial activity. Make payment illegal. Take surrogacy off the sales rack (Goodman 1990, A-17).

Before the baby came, her bedroom was a dimly lighted chapel dedicated to the idols of rock 'n' roll. Now the posters of rock stars are gone and the walls painted white. Angela's room has become a nursery for six-week-old Corey. Angela, who just turned 15, finds it hard to think of herself as a mother. "I'm still just as young as I was. I haven't grown up any faster." Indeed sitting in her parents' living room, she is the prototypical adolescent, lobbying her mother for permission to attend a rock concert, asking if she can have a pet dog, and so forth. The weight of her new responsibilities is just beginning to sink in. "Last night I couldn't get my homework done," she laments with a toss of her blond curls. "I kept feeding him and feeding him. Whenever you lay him down, he wants to be picked up." "Babies are a big step, I should have thought more about it," she says.

Childbearing out of wedlock has increased dramatically since the 1960s.

Of the first babies born to women fifteen to thirty-four years old during the period 1985–1989, 39 percent were either born out of wedlock or conceived before the woman's first marriage, up from 27 percent during the period 1960–1964 (U.S. Bureau of the Census 1991a, 1).

Although the percentage of children conceived out of wedlock may not have risen substantially between 1960 and 1990, the percentage of women marrying before the birth has dropped significantly, from 52 percent in 1969 to 27 percent in 1990. This is due in large part to society's greater acceptance of out-of-wedlock births and to the trend to postpone marriage. In 1950, for example, an out-of-wedlock pregnancy led to a quick marriage in most cases. Thus, many women indeed became pregnant before they were married, but these pregnancies did not appear to be a problem since a quick marriage kept the women from being out-of-wedlock mothers.

Teenage pregnancy has been around as long as there have been teenagers, but the dimensions and social costs of the problem are just beginning to be appreciated. In November 1985, Wisconsin passed landmark legislation designed to combat unwanted teen pregnancies.

The law provided funds for sex education in public schools, repealed restrictions on the sale of nonprescription contraceptives, and provided funds for counseling pregnant adolescents. It also took the unusual step of making grandparents of babies born to teenagers legally responsible for the babies' financial support. Other states are trying to start birth control clinics in high schools. These are just some of the attempts to combat the growing problem of teenage pregnancy.

Such strong and controversial measures reflect the magnitude of the problem (see Table 11-6). Teen pregnancy imposes lasting hardships on two generations: parent and child. Teen mothers, for instance, are many times more likely than other mothers with young children to live below the poverty level. According to one study, only half of those who give birth before eighteen complete high

431

TABLE 11-6
WOMEN AGED FIFTEEN TO NINETEEN WHO HAD A CHILD IN THE LAST YEAR AND WERE UNMARRIED

PERCENTAGE

All races	68%
Caucasian	59
Black	90
Hispanic	65
Asian American (all ages)	9*

*The percentage of women aged fifteen to nineteen was not available.

Source: U.S. Bureau of the Census 1991[a], 3.

school (compared to 96 percent of those who postpone childbearing). On the average they earn half as much money and are far more likely to be on welfare: 71 percent of females under thirty who receive Aid to Families with Dependent Children had their first child as a teenager.

As infants, the offspring of teen mothers have high rates of illness and mortality. Later in life they often experience educational and emotional problems. Many are the victims of child abuse at the hands of parents too immature to understand why their baby is crying or has developed a will of its own. Finally, these children are prone to dropping out and becoming teenage mothers themselves. According to one study, 82 percent of girls who gave birth at age fifteen or younger were daughters of teenage mothers.

Such statistics have aroused considerable debate. Arline Geronimus and her colleagues take the position that many of these disadvantages are not really the result of the early out-of-wedlock pregnancy and birth, but rather reflect the disadvantageous economic and social position occupied by the majority of unwed teenage mothers (Geronimus 1991; 1992). She goes so far as to argue that an early birth to a disadvantaged young woman might even be a rational reaction to her difficult and unrewarding social and economic place in life. Most researchers, however, take the more traditional position that an early out-of-wedlock birth does indeed cause problems for the young mother, her child, and society in general (Furstenberg 1991; 1992).

With disadvantage creating disadvantage, it is no wonder that teen pregnancy is widely perceived as the very hub of the U.S. poverty cycle. Much of the so-called feminization of poverty starts off with teenagers having babies. Teenage pregnancy ranks near the very top of issues facing African Americans in the view of many African-American leaders.

The shocking prevalence of teenage pregnancy among American teenagers was brought to light when the Alan Guttmacher Institute released the results of a thirty-seven-country study in 1985. Its findings: The United States leads nearly all other developed countries in its incidence of pregnancy among girls aged fifteen through nineteen. Looking in detail at Sweden, the Netherlands, France, Canada, and Britain, the researchers found that American adolescents were no more sexually active than adolescents in these countries but became pregnant in much greater numbers (see Table 11-7).

To understand the nature of the problem, one must look beyond the statistics and examine the dramatic changes in attitudes and social mores that have swept through American culture during the past thirty years. The teenage birthrate was actually higher in 1957 than it is today, but that was an era of early marriage when nearly a quarter of eighteen- and nineteen-year-old females were married. Thus, the overwhelming majority of teen births in the 1950s occurred in a connubial context, and mainly to girls over seventeen. Twenty to thirty years ago, if an unwed teenager should, heaven forbid, become pregnant, chances are her parents would see that she was swiftly married off in a shotgun wedding. Or if marriage was impractical, the girl would discreetly disappear during her confinement, the child would be given up for adoption, and the matter would never again be discussed in polite society. Abortion, of course, was out of the question because it was illegal at the time.

All of this has changed. Today if a girl does not choose to abort her pregnancy (and some 45 percent of teenagers do not), chances are she will keep the baby and raise it without the traditional blessings of marriage. With teen marriages two or three times more likely to end in divorce, parents figure, "Why compound the problem?"

Unfortunately, unwed motherhood may even seem glamorous to impressionable teens. The mass media show Jessica Lange, Farrah Fawcett, and Goldie Hawn all having their lover's children and expressing their happiness. Yet an out-of-wedlock pregnancy for one of these women hardly

TABLE 11-7 TEENAGE PREGNANCIES AND ABORTIONS AROUND THE WORLD (RATES PER 1000 WOMEN AGED FIFTEEN TO NINETEEN)		
COUNTRY	RATE OF PREGNANCY	ABORTION RATE
United States	96	60
Sweden	43	30
France	44	30
Netherlands	14	7
Canada	44	24
England and Wales	45	20

Source: Shapiro 1988, xii.

leads to the dire financial poverty in which most teenage unwed mothers will find themselves.

But if unwed motherhood has lost much of its notoriety, over the same period premarital sex has become positively conventional. Like it or not, American adolescents are far more sexually active than they used to be.

Social workers are almost unanimous in citing the influence of the popular media—television, rock music, videos, and movies—in propelling the trend toward precocious sexuality. It's obvious from Bruce Springsteen's lyrics in "She's the One" that each girl must be a scheming seductress chasing innocent boys. The girl in the song has "killer graces" and "secret places" that are too large for any boy to fill. Although the boy tries to resist her, he doesn't have a chance against her lovely soft French cream complexion and dreamlike qualities. Her French kisses, long falling hair, and eyes that shine like a midnight sun seduce the innocent boy into a sexual relationship. That a sexual relationship may

lead to a pregnancy or sexually transmitted disease never seems to be mentioned in most popular lyrics pushing sex.

Instead, our young people are barraged by the message that to be sophisticated they must be sexually hip. And yet for all of their early experimentation with sex, their immersion in heavy-breathing rock and the erotic fantasies on MTV, one thing about American teenagers has not changed: they are in many ways as ignorant of the scientific facts of reproduction as they were in the day when Doris Day, not Madonna, was their idol. For example, studies show that teenagers wait about twelve months after first becoming sexually active before they seek contraception. Unable to grasp the situation when they become pregnant, they often wait too long to consider an abortion. The gravity of the situation completely eludes them. "I was going to have an abortion, but I spent the money on clothes."

For many young girls, there is another, less tangible factor in the sequence of events leading to parent-

hood: a sense of fatalism, passivity, and, in some cases, even a certain pleasure at the prospect of motherhood. "Part of me wanted to get pregnant. I liked the boy a lot and he used to say he wanted a baby." For young girls trapped in poverty, life offers a few opportunities apart from getting pregnant. Pregnancy brings recognition. In Bill Moyers's television special on the black family ("CBS Reports: Vanishing Family, Crisis in Black America," January 25, 1986), all the young women either pregnant or with a child out of wedlock reported that being a mother made them someone: it gave them an identity, if not prestige. "Before I was pregnant, I was nothing. Now I'm somebody, I'm a mother." According to Guttmacher statistics, black American teenagers have the highest fertility rate of any teenage population in the entire world. One in four black babies is born to a teen mother, most of them unwed. The National Urban League has declared teenage pregnancy its primary concern. Says league president John Jacob, "We cannot talk about strengthening the black community and family without facing up to the [fact] that teenage pregnancy is a major factor in high unemployment, the numbers of high school dropouts, and the numbers of blacks below the poverty line."

Needy girls, black or white, who imagine that having a baby will fill the void in their lives are usually in for a rude shock. Hopes of escaping a dreary existence, of finding direction and purpose, generally sink in a sea of responsibility. With no one to watch the child, school becomes impossible, if not irrelevant. And despite the harsh lessons of experience, many remain careless or indifferent about birth control.

> About 15 percent of pregnant teens become pregnant again within one year; 30 percent do so within two years.

The problems faced by the children of such parents begin before they are even born. Only one in five girls under age fifteen receives prenatal care at all during the vital first three months of pregnancy. The combination of inadequate medical care and poor diet contributes to a number of problems. Teenagers are 92 percent more likely to have anemia and 23 percent more likely to have complications related to prematurity than mothers aged twenty to twenty-four.

All of this adds up to twice the normal risk of delivering a low-birth-weight baby (one that weighs under 5.5 pounds), a category that puts an infant in danger of serious mental, physical, and developmental problems that may require costly care. Speaking of cost, it is estimated that overall the United States spends $18 billion on income support for teenagers who are pregnant or have given birth (*Washington Post* 1987).

The Rand Corporation (Abrahamse et al. 1988) undertook a broad study to identify factors that predict which teenage girls will become pregnant and which will not. They found the following factors to be related to teenage pregnancy:

Parenting

■ High quality of the parent-child relationship is consistently associated with lower than expected rates of single parenthood.

■ Close parental supervision has a similar but less consistent relationship.

Religious commitment

■ The intensity of the individual's religious commitment (religiosity) can be powerfully influential, but its effect is complex and not uniform.

Willingness

■ Young women who themselves reject the idea of having a child without being married often manage not to, even when they come from backgrounds that predispose them to do so.

■ The prevailing peer milieu a respondent encounters at her school also conditions her propensity to become a single mother.

Problem behavior

■ A higher than expected proportion of young women who initially had symptoms of problem behavior became single mothers thereafter.

Opportunity costs

■ Those young women who expect to continue their education (hence have more to lose in the future by becoming single mothers) are less likely to bear a child out of wedlock than those who lack that opportunity.

Close parental supervision has the strongest influence in lowering the rate of single childbearing for blacks; for whites, a high-quality relationship with parents is the strongest influence; among Hispanics, religiosity appears strongest. The teenager is a person with newly active hormones that make sexual activity especially hard to resist. This combined with the overwhelming amount of sexual stimulation provided by the mass media and the sexual revolution means that teenagers are going to be getting pregnant unless parents and other social institutions act to help them handle their newly emerging sexuality.

Source: Adapted in part from Wallis 1985, 78–90.

WHAT DO YOU THINK?

1. If American society is now so hip about sex, why do these girls fail to use contraceptives?
2. Do you think that the mass media has much influence over teenagers?
3. What are the messages about sexuality given out in popular music and videos?
4. How are women presented in popular music and videos?
5. If you are a woman contemplating a date, do you go prepared (with contraceptive precautions) to have sex?
6. If a situation in which you could engage in sexual intercourse arose unexpectedly, would you put the behavior on hold until prepared contraceptively?
7. What do your answers to questions 5 and 6 tell you about your attitudes toward sexual activity?
8. Why do research studies of college women (not young teenagers) find that most say they will use contraception if they have sexual intercourse, but most report not using anything when they do have intercourse?

CHAPTER

12

PREGNANCY AND BIRTH

CONTENTS

Despite all the talk about effective birth control methods, zero population growth, and low birthrates, most Americans do have children, and most of the children are desired, cared for, loved, and a source of happiness (along with some heartache) to their parents. Indeed the *birthrate* has risen slightly from a low 1.8 per woman in 1975 (or 14.5 babies per 1000 population) to about 2.1 (or 15.9 babies per 1000 population) in 1992 (National Center for Health Statistics June 1992).

The government also uses a second method to measure the rate of birth. Called the **fertility rate,** it is the number of births per 1000 fertile women aged fifteen to forty-four years. Examining the fertility rate for 1990, one finds:

Fertility rate
Number of births per 1000 fertile women aged fifteen to forty-four

- 65.2 births for Caucasian women
- 78.4 births for black women
- 93.2 births for Hispanic women
- 58.1 births for Asian-American women

The overall fertility rate in 1990 was 67. (U.S. Bureau of the Census October, 1991, 2). This compares to an overall fertility rate of 123 during the peak year (1957) of the baby boom.

Relatively few American women remain childless throughout their lives. In this century the highest proportion of women having no children was 15 percent among women born between 1920 and 1924. These women reached the peak of their childbearing years during the Great Depression and World War II when many factors combined to increase the likelihood of childlessness. Although women who married during the 1950s felt a great deal of social pressure to have children, such pressure slowly disappeared, and childlessness is much more readily accepted today.

Currently, 26 percent of women in their early thirties (thirty to thirty-four years old) are childless. This proportion is somewhat higher than in 1980 when 20 percent of this age group were childless (U.S. Bureau of the Census October 1991, 13).

CONCEPTION

A mother listening to her six-foot son explain the finer points of football or a father escorting his lovely twenty-two-year-old daughter down the aisle may find it hard to remember the beginnings: the lovemaking; the missed menstrual period that led mother to think, "Maybe I'm pregnant"; the thrill of feeling a tiny, unseen foot kick; the scary feelings when labor started; the dramatic rush to the hospital; holding the red, wrinkled seven-pound newborn son or daughter and counting the fingers and toes to make sure they are all there; the long discussion over the name; the wet spot on dad's suit after hugging the baby goodbye before going to work; the first tooth, the first sickness, the first bicycle, the first day of school, the first date, high school graduation, and now marriage—and perhaps soon the new cycle when suddenly a little one hugs them and says "Hi grandad, hi grandma."

Conception
Fertilization of the egg by the sperm to start a new human life

FIGURE 12-1
Sperm wander aimlessly when no egg is present (a); all move toward the egg when it is present (b).

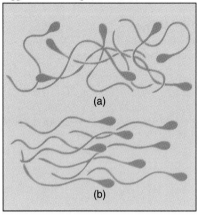

(a)

(b)

All of us, with our billions and billions of cells and complex organs, have grown from the union of two microscopic cells: the ovum, or egg cell (about 0.004 inch in diameter), and the sperm (about 0.00125 inch in diameter). We weighed only 0.005 milligram or one 20-millionth ounce at conception!

The possibility of **conception** begins with ovulation, the release of one mature egg (containing twenty-three chromosomes, fat droplets, protein substances, and nutrient fluid, all surrounded by a tough gelatinous substance or membrane) that must find its way to the Fallopian tube and begin a three-day journey to the uterus. Fertilization must occur within twenty-four hours of ovulation, or the egg will die and be expelled.

Like the egg, a sperm cell, the other necessary ingredient for conception, contains twenty-three chromosomes within its nucleus (the head), but it also has a tail that gives it mobility. There are about 200 to 400 million sperm in an average ejaculation. They are so minute that enough of them to repopulate the earth could be stored in a space the size of an aspirin tablet.

When sperm are deposited in the vagina after an ejaculation, they are affected by the presence of an egg. If an egg isn't present, sperm swim erratically in all directions. But if an egg is present, they swim directly toward it (see Figure 12-1). By using their tails, they can swim at a rate of three to four centimeters an hour. Their great numbers are necessary because the job of reaching the egg is so arduous that only a few thousand reach the Fallopian tube that contains the egg. Many die in the acidic environment of the vagina.

At left: The round egg can be seen emerging from a group of cumulus-corona cells, which at ovulation completely surround the egg. On the egg's surface are thousands of spermatazoa, which look like small needles. The egg has been fertilized, and the two round structures in the center contain the chromosomes from the mother and father. At right: Spermatozoa in early stages of penetration on the moonlike landscape of the egg's shell.

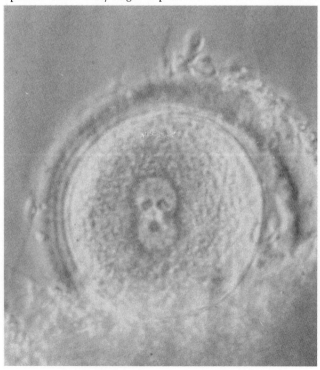

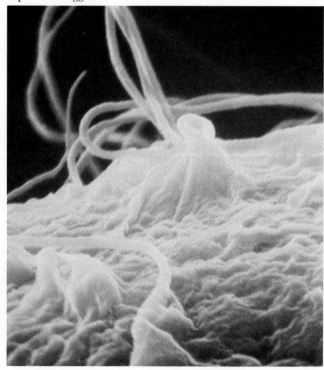

Many also go up the wrong tube or get lost along the way. Those that do reach the egg have to overcome another obstacle: the tough outer membrane of the egg. Each sperm that reaches the egg releases a bit of enzyme to help dissolve the egg's membrane. Finally, one sperm manages to enter the egg and fertilizes it. Once this occurs, the egg becomes impervious to all remaining sperm and they die.

There is increasing evidence that sperm differ in their ability to fertilize an egg. For example, we know that some men's sperm are better swimmers and can fertilize eggs more easily than other sperm (Small 1991). We also know that many of the sperm are faulty.

In addition, sperm can be harmed by environmental forces just as the egg can. Although the evidence is limited, such substances as paint solvents, lead, benzene, and various pesticides may cause malfunctioning sperm. The most publicized and most controversial evidence that chemicals may harm sperm comes from research on U.S. veterans of the Vietnam War who were exposed to the herbicide Agent Orange (dioxin) used by the U.S. military to destroy foliage that hid enemy forces. A study published by the Harvard School of Public health found that Vietnam vets had almost twice the risk of other men of fathering infants with one or more major malformations. Other research, however, found conflicting results (Merewood 1991).

Sperm remain viable within the female reproductive tract for about forty-eight hours; the egg remains viable for about twenty-four hours. Their lives may be slightly shorter or longer depending in part on the chemistry of the reproductive system of the woman at a given time. Thus conception can occur only during approximately three days of each twenty-eight-day cycle. For example, if intercourse occurs more than forty-eight hours before ovulation, the sperm will die, and if it occurs more than twenty-four hours after ovulation, the egg will have died. The rhythm method of birth control is based on this fact (see Chapter 11).

Within thirty-six hours after fertilization, the egg divides in half and then divides again. The dividing continues as the egg moves down the Fallopian tube, with the cells getting smaller with each division (see Figure 12-2). By the time the floating mass of cells reaches the **uterus** (in about three to four days), it will contain about thirty-six cells. This cluster, called a *blastocyst*, then becomes hollow at the center. The outermost shell of cells, called the *trophoblast*, multiplies faster, attaches the blastocyst to the uterine walls, and eventually becomes the placenta, umbilical cord, and amniotic sac. The inner cells separate into three layers. The innermost layer (the *endoderm*) will become the inner body parts; the middle layer (the *mesoderm*) will become muscle, bone, blood, kidneys, and sex glands; and the outer layer (the *ectoderm*) will eventually become skin, hair, and nervous tissue (see Table 12-1). On the sixth or seventh day after fertilization, the blastocyst begins to implant itself in the uterine wall, and the cells begin to draw nourishment from the uterine lining.

FIGURE 12-2
Cell division after conception

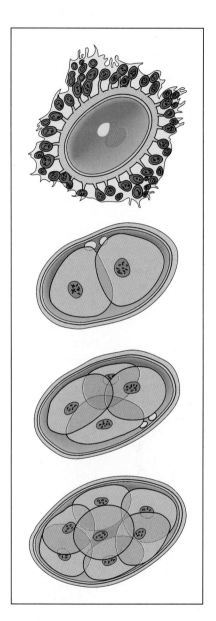

Uterus
The hollow, pear-shaped organ in females within which the fetus develops; the womb

■ BOY OR GIRL? ■

Sex determination takes place at conception. The female egg always carries an X chromosome. The sperm, however, may be either of two types, one carrying an X chromosome and the other a Y chromosome. If the egg is

Conception

	TABLE 12-1 PRENATAL DEVELOPMENT	
TIME ELAPSED	**EMBRYONIC OR FETAL CHARACTERISTICS**	**ILLUSTRATIONS**
28 days 4 weeks 1 month	¼–½ inch long. Head is one-third of embryo. Brain has lobes, and rudimentary nervous system appears as hollow tube. Heart begins to beat. Blood vessels form and blood flows through them. Simple kidneys, liver, and digestive tract appear. Rudiments of eyes, ears, and nose appear. Small tail.	
56 days 8 weeks 2 months	2 inches long. 1/30 of an ounce in weight. Human face with eyes, ears, nose, lips, tongue. Arms have pawlike hands. Almost all internal organs begin to develop. Brain coordinates functioning of other organs. Heart beats steadily and blood circulates. Complete cartilage skeleton, beginning to be replaced by bone. Tail beginning to be absorbed. Now called a fetus. Sex organs begin to differentiate.	
84 days 12 weeks 3 months	3 inches long. 1 ounce in weight. Begins to be active. Number of nerve-muscle connections almost triples. Sucking reflex begins to appear. Can swallow and may even breathe. Eyelids fused shut (will stay shut until the 6th month), but eyes are sensitive to light. Internal organs begin to function.	
112 days 16 weeks 4 months	6–7 inches long. 4 ounces in weight. Body now growing faster than head. Skin on hands and feet forms individual patterns. Eyebrows and head hair begin to show. Fine, downy hair (lanugo) covers body. Movements can now be felt.	

TABLE 12-1
PRENATAL DEVELOPMENTAL (Continued)

TIME ELAPSED	EMBRYONIC OR FETAL CHARACTERISTICS	ILLUSTRATIONS
140 days 20 weeks 5 months	10–12 inches long. 8–16 ounces in weight. Skeleton hardens. Nails form on fingers and toes. Skin covered with cheesy wax. Heartbeat now loud enough to be heard with stethoscope. Muscles are stronger. Definite strong kicking and turning. Can be startled by noises.	
168 days 24 weeks 6 months	12–14 inches long. 1½ pounds in weight. Can open and close eyelids. Grows eyelashes. Much more active, exercising muscles. May suck thumb. May be able to breathe if born prematurely.	
196 days 28 weeks 7 months	15 inches long. 2½ pounds in weight. Begins to develop fatty tissue. Internal organs (especially respiratory and digestive) still developing. Has fair chance of survival if born now.	
224 days 32 weeks 8 months	16½ inches long. 4 pounds in weight. Fatty layer complete.	
266 days. 38 weeks 9 months	Birth. 19–20 inches long. 6–8 pounds in weight (average). 95 percent of full-term babies born alive in the United States will survive.	

Human embryo in amniotic sac, approximately eight weeks old.

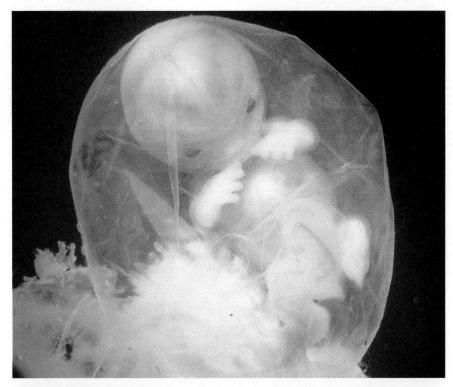

At four and one-half months (just over 7 inches). When the thumb comes close to the mouth, the head may turn, and lips and tongue begin their sucking motions—a reflex for survival.

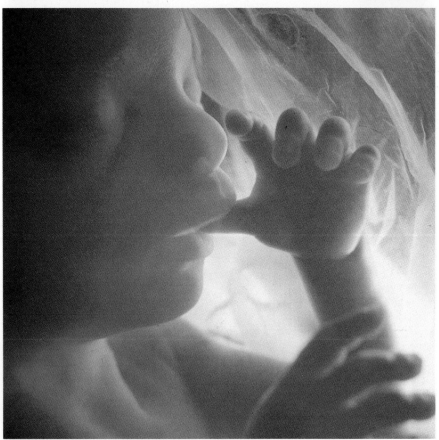

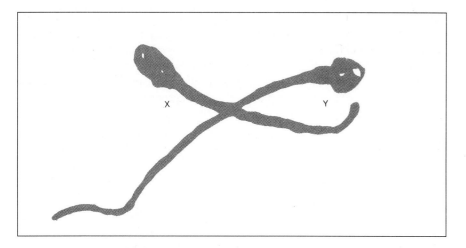

fertilized by an X sperm, the child will be female (XX). If, on the other hand, the egg is fertilized by a Y sperm, the child will be male (XY) (see Chapter 7 for a complete discussion). Researchers believe that Y sperm (androsperm) have a small wedge-shaped body with a long tail and that X sperm (gynosperm) have a larger oval-shaped head and a shorter tail (Figure 12-3), but these differences have not yet been proved conclusively.

Many more males are conceived than females. In fact, approximately 140 males are conceived for every 100 females. However, only 106 males are born for every 100 females. We do not know why this is so. Some suggest that the Y sperm move more quickly than the X sperm and thus reach the egg earlier. Perhaps it is because the male is the weaker sex as far as survival is concerned. In all age groups up to age eighty, males perish at a greater rate than females. For example, in the age bracket fifteen to twenty-four years, 277 males die for every 100 females who die; in the age bracket thirty-five to forty-four years, 161 males die for every 100 females who die.

■ MULTIPLE BIRTHS ■

The human female normally conceives only one child at a time, so multiple births have always been unusual. Twins occur about once in every 90 births, triplets once in 9000 births, and quadruplets once in 500,000 births among American whites. Twins occur once in every 70 births among American blacks (Papalia and Olds 1986, 44). Mortality rates are significantly higher for multiple births. Twins are often born somewhat prematurely and are usually smaller than normal in size.

Most twins are **fraternal,** which means they developed from two separate eggs that were fertilized simultaneously. Such twins are no more similar in physical characteristics than any other siblings (brothers or sisters). Such twins could also each have a different father if the mother had sexual intercourse with two different men at about the same time, and each egg was fertilized by a sperm from a different partner. About a third of twins are **identical,** which means they developed from the subdivision of a single fertilized egg, and usually shared a common placenta. Unlike fraternal twins, their genetic makeup is identical, so they have very similar physical characteristics and are always the same sex.

Fraternal twins
Twins who develop from two different eggs and therefore have differing genetic makeup

Identical twins
Twins who develop from the subdivision of a single egg and thus have the same genetic makeup

443

Recently, the so-called fertility drugs have contributed to the multiple birth phenomenon (see p. 424). Women who fail to ovulate properly have been given ovulation-inducing agents or gonadotropin to stimulate proper ovulation. In numerous instances the use of these hormones has caused multiple births. In one case an Australian woman gave birth to nine infants, none of whom survived. With increased understanding of the reproductive functions, the risk of multiple births from fertility drugs may be reduced.

PREGNANCY

How does a woman know if she is pregnant? Because the union of the egg and the sperm does not produce any overt sensations, the question "Am I pregnant?" isn't easy to answer in the early stages of pregnancy. What are some common early symptoms of pregnancy?

■ *A missed menstrual period*. Although pregnancy is the most common reason for menstruation to stop suddenly in a healthy female, it is certainly not the only reason. For example, a woman may miss a period because of stress, illness, or emotional upset. In addition, about 20 percent of pregnant women have a slight flow or spotting, usually during implantation of the fertilized egg into the uterine wall.

■ *Nausea in the morning (morning sickness)*. Early in the first trimester a pregnant woman often experiences nausea in the morning, although vomiting usually doesn't occur. The nausea usually disappears by the twelfth week of pregnancy.

■ *Changes in the shape and coloration of breasts*. The breasts usually become fuller, the areolae (pigmented areas around the nipples) begin to darken, and the veins become more prominent. Sometimes the breasts tingle, throb, or hurt because of the swelling.

■ *Increased need to urinate*. The growing uterus pressing against the bladder and the hormonal changes that are taking place may cause an increase in the need to urinate. Somewhere around the twelfth week of pregnancy, the uterus will be higher in the abdomen and will no longer press against the bladder, so urination will return to normal.

■ *Feelings of fatigue and sleepiness*. Because of the hormonal changes that are taking place, some women find that they are always tired during the first few months of pregnancy and need to sleep more often and for longer periods.

■ *Increased vaginal secretions*. These may be either clear and nonirritating or white, slightly yellow, foamy, or itchy. Such secretions are normal.

■ *Increased retention of body fluids*. Increased body fluids are essential to pregnant women and growing babies, thus some swelling of the face, hands, and feet is normal during pregnancy.

Some women do not experience any of these symptoms; some experience only a few; few experience them severely.

Pregnancy may also have some cosmetic effects. Skin blemishes often abate, leaving the complexion healthy and glowing. In the latter stages of pregnancy, pink stretch marks may appear on the abdomen, although most of them will disappear after birth.

PREGNANCY TESTS

Usually, a physician can tell if a woman is pregnant by a simple pelvic examination. It is possible to feel the uterine enlargement and softening of the cervix by manual examination after six to eight weeks of pregnancy. Most women, however, want to know if they are pregnant as soon as possible, so chemical tests are used to discover pregnancy earlier.

Doctors usually perform a test of agglutination, the clumping together of human chorionic gonadotropin (HCG), to assess whether pregnancy has occurred. This process takes only a few minutes and can be used seven to ten days after conception or at the missed menses. The test involves taking a morning urine specimen, placing a drop of it on a slide, and adding the proper chemicals. In a negative reaction, agglutination will be visible in two minutes. If the woman is pregnant, no agglutination will occur at two minutes (see Figure 12-4).

Several tests examine the woman's blood serum, also seeking changed levels of HCG. One is called radioimmunoassay (RIA). This test takes about one hour to complete and becomes positive a few days after presumed implantation. A newer test, the Biocept-G technique, has reduced the necessary incubation period to thirty minutes and gives accurate results within a few days after conception. In this case a blood sample is mixed with radioactive iodine with which the HCG will react if present.

The tests are considered 95 to 98 percent accurate but can give inaccurate results if they are performed too early (before enough hormone shows up in the urine) or if there are errors in handling, storing, or labeling the urine (Boston Women's Health Book Collective 1992; Francoeur 1991, 209–10; Hatcher et al. 1990). Sometimes several tests are needed to determine if a woman is pregnant because she may produce very low levels of hormone and there may not be enough in her urine to give a positive result even though she is pregnant. It is rare for a pregnancy test to give a positive result when the woman is not pregnant.

False pregnancy (pseudocyesis), in which the early physical signs are present although the woman is not really pregnant, is also possible. Inexpensive pregnancy tests clarify the situation and usually end the symptoms (unless a physical problem is causing them).

Because the menstrual cycle is easily affected by one's emotions, uneasiness about engaging in sexual activity may disrupt a woman's monthly cycle enough to delay her period or even cause her to skip a period altogether. Unfortunately, emotional reaction and physical reaction interact to increase her problems in this case. For example, if a woman has sex and worries that she might be pregnant, the worry may actually postpone her period, causing her further worry, further upsetting her menstrual timing, and so on. A pregnancy test is one way to resolve the worry over possible pregnancy.

A number of home pregnancy test kits are on the market, selling for $10 to $20. They work on the same system as the HCG tests we have already discussed and may be used from seven to fourteen days after conception. The accuracy of these tests is high if they are used correctly. The false positive rate

FIGURE 12-4
Negative and positive pregnancy test reactions. In a negative test, agglutination (clumping) will be visible within two minutes. In a positive test, no agglutination will occur at two minutes.

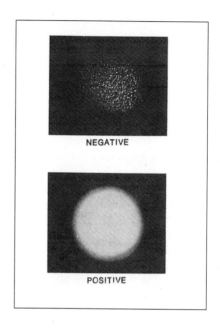

NEGATIVE

POSITIVE

False pregnancy (pseudocyesis)
Signs of pregnancy occur without the woman actually being pregnant

Pregnancy

Embryo
The developing organism from the second to the eighth week of pregnancy, characterized by differentiation of organs and tissues into their human form

Fetus
The developing organism from the eighth week after conception until birth

Congenital defect
A condition existing at birth or before, as distinguished from a genetic defect

Genetic defect
An abnormality in the development of the fetus that is inherited through the genes, as distinguished from a congenital defect

Umbilical cord
A flexible cordlike structure connecting the fetus to the placenta and through which the fetus is fed and waste products are discharged

Placenta
The organ that connects the fetus to the uterus by means of the umbilical-cord

is plus or minus 5 percent, while the false negative rate is plus or minus 20 percent (Hatcher et al. 1990, 439). Of course, misuse increases the error rate.

Doctors fear that diagnostic errors with home pregnancy tests may lead to serious health hazards. For example, the early stages of uterine cancer may produce a false positive reading and thereby delay treatment of the cancer. Assured by a false negative that she is not pregnant, a woman might continue to take drugs or smoke, thereby threatening the well-being of her unborn child. Moreover, a positive pregnancy test does not guarantee a normal pregnancy. A doctor's visit costs money, but it is well worth the precaution if pregnancy is a possibility. There are also clinics, such as those run by Planned Parenthood, that give pregnancy tests for a minimal charge or free.

The average duration of pregnancy is 266 days, or thirty-eight weeks, from the time of conception. For the first two months, the developing baby is called an **embryo;** after that it is called a **fetus.** The change in name denotes that all of the parts are now present. The sequence of its development is shown in Table 12-1.

ENVIRONMENTAL CAUSES OF CONGENITAL PROBLEMS

Although the developing fetus is in a well-protected environment, negative influences from outside may still affect it. Sometimes these outside elements cause birth defects, which are called **congenital defects.** (These should not be confused with **genetic defects,** which are inherited through the genes.)

The developing fetus gets its nourishment from the mother's blood through the **umbilical cord** and **placenta.** There is no direct intermingling of the blood, though some substances the mother takes in can be transmitted to the fetus. When you consider the extremely small size of the fetus during its early months, you can see how a small amount of a substance can do a lot of harm.

DRUGS
If the mother uses narcotics, such as heroin (and also methadone) or cocaine (see Inset 12-1), the child will be born addicted and will suffer withdrawal symptoms if it is not given the drug and then gradually withdrawn from it.

Furthermore, most common prescription drugs affect the fetus. According to the Boston Women's Health Book Collective (1992, 403), some antihistamines may produce malformations. General anesthetics at high concentrations may also produce malformations. Cortisone crosses the placenta and may cause alterations in the fetus. Antithyroid may cause goiter in infants, and tetracycline may deform babies bones and stain teeth.

Among other drugs thought to damage the human fetus are the antibiotics streptomycin and sulfonamides taken near the end of pregnancy; excessive amounts of vitamins A, D, B_6, and K; certain barbiturates, opiates, and other central nervous system depressants when taken near the time of delivery; and the synthetic hormone progestin, which can masculinize the female fetus. The most commonly prescribed tranquilizers, chlordiazepoxide (Librium) and meprobamate (Equanil and Miltown), and diazepam (Valium) may cause defects when taken early in pregnancy. (For a more complete discussion of the effects of drugs on the fetus, see Olds, London, and Ladewig 1988, 519–20.) The most widely publicized instance of drug-related birth defects came from the widespread use of thalidomide in Europe. Thalidomide, a very effective sleeping pill and tranquilizer, was believed to be safer than most other sedatives. It was widely used in Europe during the 1960s and was sampled by many women in the United States before cases of seriously deformed babies began to receive attention. Many of these children had only small, flipperlike appendages attached to their shoulders rather than arms and hands. Others had stunted arms and legs.

INFECTIOUS DISEASES

Certain infectious diseases contracted by the mother, especially during the first three months of pregnancy, may harm the developing fetus. The best known of these is German measles (rubella), which can cause blindness, deafness, or heart defects in the child. Some women who contract German measles elect to have an abortion rather than risk having a deformed child.

Sexually transmitted diseases also affect the fetus. Herpes (see p. 374), for example, can cause a spontaneous abortion, inflammation of the brain, or other brain damage. Sexually transmitted diseases can be contracted by the newborn baby. If the mother has syphilis, the baby will have the symptoms of the second and last syphilitic stages (see p. 384). Gonorrhea can affect the newborn's eyesight; as a precaution, silver nitrate or another prophylactic agent is applied to the eyes of all newborns. This safeguard has almost totally eradicated the problem. AIDS can also be passed on to the unborn child by an infected mother (see pp. 375–383). There is some evidence that AIDS may be passed on to an infant through the infected mother's milk as well.

SMOKING

Smoking adversely affects pregnancy. It increases the risk of spontaneous abortion, of premature birth, and of low-birth-weight babies carried to term. Low birth weight is one of the major predictors of infant death. A health department comparison of smoking pregnant mothers found that white mothers were more likely to smoke than black mothers and that black mothers who did smoke smoked less than the white mothers. Hispanic mothers smoked the least of all, especially mothers from Mexico, Cuba, and Central America (National Center for Health Statistics April 15, 1992b, 2–4).

ALCOHOL

Fetal alcohol syndrome (FAS), first identified in 1973, affects babies born to chronically alcoholic mothers. The U.S. Public Health Service suggests that FAS may be the leading cause of birth defects in the United States. The effects of FAS include retarded growth, subnormal intelligence, and slow motor development. Affected infants also show alcohol withdrawal symptoms such as tremors, irritability, and seizures. Even when the children are of normal intelligence, they often have a disproportionate amount of academic failure.

Although the concern over FAS relates to alcoholic mothers, drinking of any kind during pregnancy may cause problems. Mothers who reported having three drinks or more per week during pregnancy had low-birth-weight babies in 15–29 percent of births compared to 8–12 percent of births to mothers reporting up to two drinks per week and 7 percent of births to mothers who did not drink (National Center for Health Statistics April 15, 1992b, 4–5).

A pattern of abnormalities and suffering endured by cocaine babies is beginning to emerge. Many of these babies begin life in an agonizing state of withdrawal that may last up to three weeks. Such babies now make up more than one-half of the drug-associated births reported to the Los Angeles Department of Children's Services.

At eight months, Aaron is about the size of an infant half his age. Listless and uncoordinated, he has yet to sit up by himself. His eyes are red-rimmed and appear unable to focus on anything for any length of time. It may be that he is partially blind.

One study done at Northwestern Memorial Hospital in Chicago found that coke users had an extremely high incidence of miscarriage (38 percent). In some cases spontaneous abortion occurred immediately following use of cocaine (Chasnoff et al. 1985). In addition, since the drug causes dramatic fluctuations in blood pressure, it may deprive the fetal brain of oxygen or cause fragile vessels to burst, the prenatal equivalent of a stroke.

Cocaine babies seem to have higher than normal rates of respiratory and kidney troubles, and some researchers suspect a link with sudden infant death syndrome.

It is clear that with an estimated 5 million Americans using cocaine on a regular basis, more and more cocaine-addicted and/or damaged infants will be born. As one researchers warns, "For pregnant women, there is no such thing as 'recreational' drug use" (Chasnoff et al. 1985).

The emergence of crack (a cheaper form of cocaine) has exacerbated the problem. For example, in 1984 some 5 percent of newborns at Highland General Hospital in Oakland, California, were contaminated with cocaine. In 1988 about 20 percent were so afflicted.

DRUG USE DURING PREGNANCY EXACTS AN UNCONSCIONABLE TOLL FROM UNBORN

The use of cocaine by pregnant women has resulted in children who have suffered from asphyxiation, brain damage, strokes, prematurity, seizures, and profound mental retardation.

The long-term developmental outcome of most of these children is unknown, but for many the damage is irreversible. Some of these children will never face a day in their lives without being reminded by their limitations that their mother used cocaine while pregnant. A few will not have enough mental capacity to generate such a thought.

How have we responded to this attack on babies? Basically, we have not. If an adult were to injure a three-year-old child and cause brain damage or inflict an injury that placed the child at risk of dying, we would act decisively to remove the child from jeopardy and punish those who harmed him or her. But we afford the child who is not yet born no right of protection. In our community, the chance that a child exposed to cocaine will go home with his or her parents is overwhelming. This is true even if, as a result of the parent's cocaine use,

RADIATION

Radiation, of course, penetrates the mother's body, so it will also reach and affect the fetus. The worst abnormalities occur if the mother is X-rayed during the first three months of pregnancy, when the embryo's major organs are developing. Even one pelvic X ray can cause gross fetal defects during this period. Thus, if pregnancy is suspected, a woman should avoid all X rays, even dental X rays, especially early in the pregnancy.

RH BLOOD DISEASE

The Rh factor (named for the rhesus monkey, in whose blood it was first isolated) is a chemical that lies on the surface of the red blood cells in most

Rh factor
An element found in the blood of most people that can adversely affect fetal development if the parents differ on the element (Rh negative versus Rh positive)

the child needs a home heart monitor or medications. We have always protected the freedom of parents to raise their children in ways that they feel best. They have the responsibility to nurture, educate, and train their children and the autonomy to decide how this shall be done. We do not, however, extend that freedom to allow for the abuse or injury of children. Society has a responsibility to ensure that parents do not inflict harm. The child abuse laws were written for that purpose.

Children are an asset and resource to all of us. They are our hope. We will not allow the mutilation of a generation. Can we then allow severe and lifelong injuries to be set upon children merely because they are not yet born? This question always raises deep and divisive issues between the rights of the mother and of her unborn offspring. As in most situations, the answer probably does not lie in siding wholly with one or the other.

We can accept the sanctity of a woman's privacy, as well as her ability and responsibility to decide what is best for herself. Currently, this right of privacy is held prime. But it is not that simple. The private use of cocaine by a pregnant woman may physically devastate her child. This is a situation in which society's concern for the welfare of children, our responsibility to assure their physical well-being, ought rightfully to coexist with a pregnant woman's right to privacy. Indeed, it should supervene.

There must be some middle ground on which we can protect a woman's right to decide the course of events that her life and body will take, without abandoning our responsibility to protect a developing infant whom she has decided to bring to term. The responsibilities of parenthood begin with the decision to complete pregnancy, not at the time of birth. We would most wisely hold parents accountable for actions measured against this standard.

We must end the damage to children that occurs from the use of cocaine during pregnancy. We must educate every woman of childbearing age to the dangers of cocaine use to her child, although it's hard to believe that there is anyone left who doesn't know. Thus we need to find a way to get women off cocaine, at least during their pregnancy and while nursing, if we can't get them off forever.

The law must reflect our responsibility to protect children so that they cannot be abused before birth without consequence. Those charged with the protection of children must recognize cocaine-induced injuries for what they are: assaults on the totally helpless. Our children are too important to our future to allow them to be harmed or injured, even if it occurs during pregnancy. We must stop it. If we do not, we will leave behind a legacy of tragically damaged children who will be a testament to our inability to conquer our own vices and our willingness to have allowed their lives to be destroyed.

Source: Adapted from *Time* 1986; 1988; and Barkley 1989.

people. People with the chemical are considered Rh positive; those without are Rh negative. Only about 15 percent of white and 7 percent of African Americans are Rh negative. If a child inherits Rh positive blood from the father but the mother is Rh negative, the fetus's Rh positive factor is perceived as a foreign substance by the mother's body. Like a disease, it causes the mother's body to produce antibodies in her blood. If these enter the fetus through a capillary rupture in the placental membrane, they destroy red blood cells, which can lead to anemia, jaundice, and eventual death unless corrective steps are taken. Only small amounts, if any, of the child's antibody-stimulating Rh factor reach the mother through the placenta during pregnancy, so the first child is usually safe. However, during delivery the afterbirth (placenta and

Pregnancy

remaining umbilical cord) loosens and bleeds, releasing the Rh positive substance into the mother, which causes her system to produce antibodies. Once
these are produced, she is much more easily stimulated to produce them during
future pregnancies involving Rh positive children. Each succeeding child will
be more affected than the previous one. With complete replacement of the
child's blood at birth, many can be saved. An even better treatment is now
available that essentially eradicates Rh problems. An Rh immunoglobulin that
blocks the mother's immune system can be injected into the mother, thereby
preventing production of the antibodies that attack the red blood cells of the
fetus. This is done at twenty-eight weeks of pregnancy. It is often repeated
within seventy-two hours of delivery of an Rh positive baby for protection in
future pregnancies. (See Olds, London, and Ladewig 1988, 505–9, for a more
complete discussion.)

■ CONTROLLING BIRTH DEFECTS ■

Once a woman learns that she is pregnant, she should arrange for regular visits
to a physician. Regular prenatal care will help avoid birth defects and dispel
any fears she may have.

DIET

The expectant mother should eat a well-balanced diet with plenty of fluids.
Inasmuch as the mother's diet has a direct effect on the fetus, she should
consult her doctor if there is any doubt about the adequacy of her diet. Protein
and vitamin deficiencies can cause physical weakness, stunted growth, rickets,
scurvy, and even mental retardation in the fetus (Boston Women's Health
Book Collective 1992, 402–403). Poor diet can also cause spontaneous abortions and stillbirths. The pregnant women may find that she feels nauseated if
she tries to eat large meals early in pregnancy. In late pregnancy the uterus
takes up so much room that she may again be unable to eat large amounts. In
both cases she should eat small amounts more often and avoid going for long
periods without food.

An inadequate diet leaves the mother more prone to illness and complications during pregnancy, both of which may cause premature birth or low birth
weight. As we have seen, premature and low-birth-weight babies are more
prone to illness and possible death than normal-term babies. Women whose
finances are inadequate for them to eat well during pregnancy and nursing can
get help from the Women, Infants, and Children program (WIC), a supplemental food program sponsored by the government. This program provides
milk, fruit, cereal, juice, cheese, and eggs. (Contact your local public health
office for information about this program.)

In the past women have attempted to limit weight gain during pregnancy
to some specified amount such as twenty-five pounds. Since each woman's
metabolism is different, it is impossible to forecast just how much weight a
given woman should gain to remain healthy. Certainly, pregnancy is not the
time to diet because proper nutrition is so important both to the mother's
health and the baby's development.

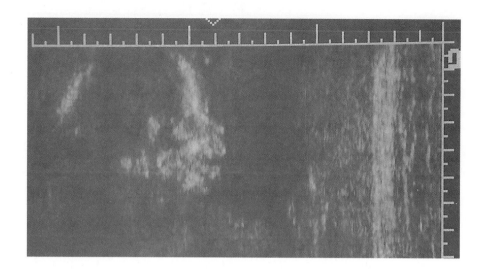

FIGURE 12-5
Sonograph of fetus

AMNIOCENTESIS

A test has been developed for detecting genetic defects, such as Down syndrome (formerly called mongolism), amino acid disorders, hemophilia, and muscular dystrophy. The procedure, called **amniocentesis,** involves taking a sample of the amniotic fluid and studying sloughed-off fetal cells found in it. Amniocentesis should be done between the fourteenth and sixteenth weeks of pregnancy. The test can be performed in a doctor's office, generally under ultrasound guidance to maximize fetal safety. The laboratory work will take another fourteen to eighteen days to complete. The test also reveals the fetus's sex.

It is well to have the test if you have already had a child with a hereditary biochemical disease, if you are a carrier of hemophilia or muscular dystrophy, if you have already had a child with a genetic abnormality, and if you are over forty because the risk of having a child with a genetic abnormality increases with age. If the test indicates the presence of a birth defect, the woman, her husband, and the doctor can discuss their options, including possible abortion.

Amniocentesis is not risk-free. The technique can induce miscarriage, but this occurs in less than 1 percent of cases. Other problems such as infection and injury to the fetus also occur in about 1 percent of cases (Olds, London, and Ladewig 1988, 552).

ULTRASOUND IN OBSTETRICS

Ultrasonography, generally considered safe and noninvasive, has become a major means of obtaining data about the placenta, fetus, and fetal organs during pregnancy. It can replace the X ray as a method of viewing the developing child in the uterus, thus avoiding radiation exposure for both mother and child (Olds, London, and Ladewig 1988). Ultrasound is also simpler than X rays because the picture is immediately available.

Ultrasound works on the principle that when high-frequency sound waves are directed at the fetus, different tissues give off echoes of different speeds. Moving a transducer (sound emitter) across the mother's abdomen creates an echogram outline of the fetus and its various organs (see Figure 12-5). Using a "real time" transducer that gives off several simultaneous signals from slightly differing sources will produce a picture showing movement of the different

Amniocentesis
A prenatal diagnostic procedure in which a long hollow needle is inserted through the mother's abdomen into the amniotic sac to obtain a sample of amniotic fluid, which is analyzed for signs of defect or disease

Ultrasound
Sound waves directed at the fetus that yield a visual picture of the fetus; used to detect potential problems in fetal development

organs, such as the heart. The echogram allows the physician to learn about the position, size, and state of development of the fetus at any time after about the first ten weeks of pregnancy. For example, the procedure can tell a physician if the fetus will be born in the normal headfirst position or in some problem position.

FETOSCOPY

Fetoscopy, a delicate procedure usually performed some fifteen to twenty weeks into pregnancy, allows direct examination of the fetus. First, an ultrasound scan locates the fetus, the umbilical cord, and the placenta. The physician then makes a small incision in the abdomen and inserts a thin tube about the size of a pencil lead into the amniotic sac. The tube contains an endoscope with fiber-optic bundles that transmit light. This light-containing tube enables the physician to see tiny areas of the fetus. By inserting biopsy forceps into the tube, the physician can take a 1-millimeter skin sample from the fetus. A blood sample can also be drawn by inserting a needle through the tube and puncturing one of the fetal blood vessels lying on the surface of the placenta (see Figure 12-6). The technique induces miscarriage in about 5 percent of cases, while the rate for amniocentesis is less than 1 percent. Since ultrasound has come into use, the need for fetoscopy has lessened (Olds, London, and Ladewig 1988, 561). Percutaneous umbilical blood sampling (PUBS) by ultrasound guidance has essentially replaced fetoscopy for blood sampling with less risk.

Fetoscopy
Examining the fetus through a small viewing tube inserted into the mother's uterus

▪ INTERCOURSE DURING PREGNANCY ▪

Although some people regard intercourse during pregnancy with suspicion, research indicates that it is usually not harmful (Olds, London, and Ladewig 1988, 391–92; Boston Women's Health Book Collective 1992, 422–423). Indeed, couples should not lose the close contact as well as physical enjoyment afforded by intercourse. There is evidence that for some women erotic feelings increase during the second trimester of pregnancy. By the third trimester, however, most women lose sexual interest to a degree.

Couples should exercise some care to avoid excessive pressure on the woman's abdomen, deep penile penetration, and infection. Because the uterine contractions of orgasm are similar to labor contractions, intercourse should be avoided during the last three weeks of pregnancy. If symptoms and signs of premature labor such as previous history, premature dilation or thinning of the cervix, or abnormal vaginal bleeding appear, sexual intercourse should be avoided. In the later stages of pregnancy, the rear entry position with the woman lying on her side is usually the most comfortable.

If a woman has miscarried or has been warned that she is apt to miscarry, she should avoid intercourse during the first three months of pregnancy, especially around the time her period would be due. In most normal pregnancies, however, intercourse poses no real threat. Indeed, some doctors suggest that the contractions of orgasm are helpful to pregnancy because they strengthen the uterine muscles. Intercourse also provides exercise for the muscles of the

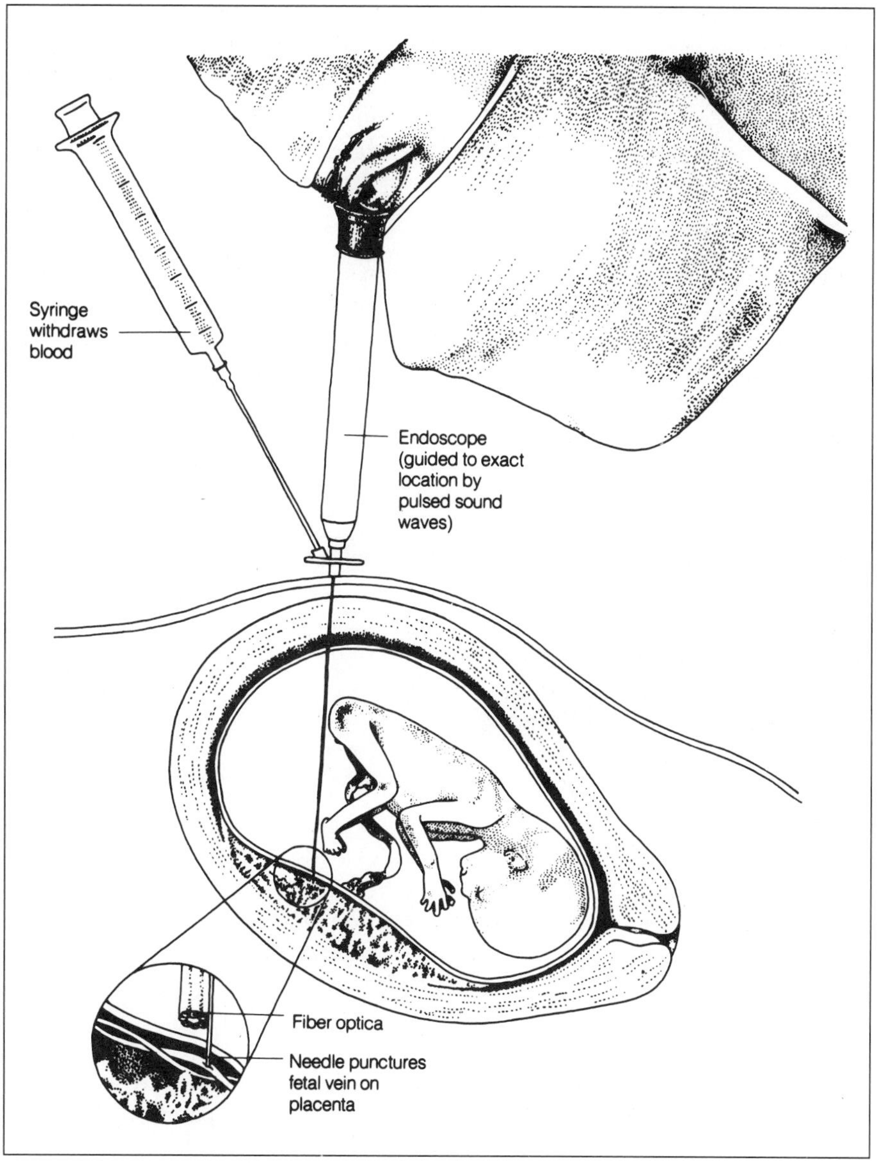

FIGURE 12-6
The fetoscopy procedure

Syringe withdraws blood

Endoscope (guided to exact location by pulsed sound waves)

Fiber optica

Needle punctures fetal vein on placenta

pelvic floor. And focusing on the feelings of complete relaxation after orgasm can help one learn to relax during labor contractions.

Many women report that sex is important to them during pregnancy. They believe that continued sexual contact maintains close emotional ties with their husbands. To them their husbands' interest shows acceptance of the pregnancy and of their changing body shape. In other words, sexual contact means tenderness, caring, sharing, and love. Many women also feel freer in their sexual behavior because they obviously no longer need fear pregnancy. To hold one another, to caress, and to be intimate are important as birth draws near. Such contact will help allay anxieties and let both partners know that they are not alone but have loving support.

Pregnancy

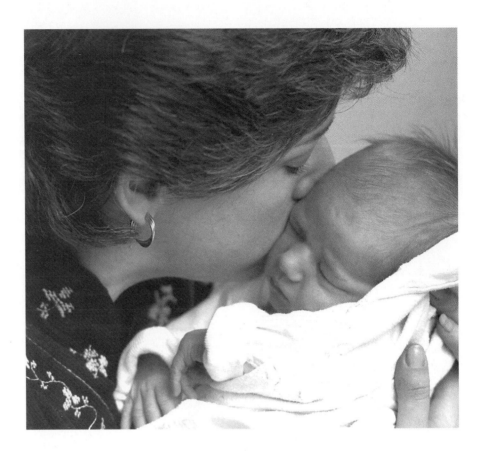

BIRTH

By the time nine months have passed, the mother-to-be is usually anxious to have her child. She has probably gained twenty to thirty pounds. This extra weight is distributed approximately as follows:

- Amniotic fluid: 2 pounds
- Baby: 7 to 8 pounds
- Breast enlargement: 2 pounds
- Placenta: 1 pound
- Retained fluids and fat: 6+ pounds
- Uterine enlargement: 2 pounds

There are several objections to gaining too much weight during pregnancy: Excessive weight can strain the circulatory system and heart, and many women find it difficult to lose the extra weight after the baby is born. Fetal weight above 9 pounds complicates labor and delivery and increases the risk of postpartum hemorrhage. On the other hand, dieting during pregnancy to remain within an arbitrary weight-gain limit is also risky because, as we pointed out earlier, good nutrition is important during pregnancy.

Guidelines issued in 1990 by the National Academy of Sciences advise an optimum weight gain of twenty-five to thirty-five pounds for women of normal weight.

Maternal weight gain has its most visible impact on the infant's birth weight. Babies born to mothers who gain thirty-one pounds or more are at considerably reduced risk of low birth weight compared to mothers gaining fewer than twenty-one pounds (National Center for Health Statistics April 15, 1992b, 5).

Although the average length of time a child is carried is 266 days, the normal range varies from 240 days to 300 days. It is therefore difficult for the physician to be exact when estimating the time of delivery. In fact, there is only about a 50 percent chance that a child will be born within a week of the date the doctor determines. In general, the expected birth date will probably come and go without any sign of imminent birth. This can be wearisome for the expectant mother, but it is perfectly normal.

▨ LABOR ▨

Three to four weeks before birth, the fetus "drops" slightly lower in the uterus (called lightening) and is normally in a headfirst position (see Figures 12-7 and 12-8). The cervix (the opening to the uterus) begins to soften and dilate (open). The uterus may undergo occasional contractions, which women pregnant for the first time may mistake for labor (false labor). These early contractions are irregular and are usually not painful.

Essentially, there are three stages of **labor.** The first two are illustrated in Figure 12-8. The *first stage* is the longest, lasting eight to twenty hours on the average for the first child and three to eight hours for subsequent children. During this time the cervix must dilate enough for the baby to pass through. (The contracted and closed cervix has held the baby in the uterus until now.) The sac of **amniotic fluid,** a salt solution that suspends, cushions, and maintains the embryo at an even temperature, will break some time during the labor process, except in about 10 percent of women who experience breaking shortly before labor begins. The uterine contractions become more frequent and longer lasting until the baby finally descends into the birth canal (vagina). During this first stage the mother can do little except rest, try to relax, and remain as comfortable as possible.

At first, the contractions may be thirty minutes apart, but gradually they will come more often until they occur every few minutes. The expectant mother should go to the hospital as soon as she ascertains that she is having regular labor pains or by previous instructions of her obstetrician.

Transition is the term used to describe the baby coming through the cervix and the commencement of the *second stage* of labor. In the second stage, the uterine contractions push the child down through the vagina into the outside world with about a hundred pounds of force. During this stage the mother can actively help the process by pushing or bearing down, thereby adding another fifteen pounds or so to the pressure created by the uterine contractions. This stage may be as short as fifteen to twenty minutes, or it can last an hour or two or, in rare cases, longer.

The *third stage* is delivering the afterbirth or detached placenta, which occurs five to twenty minutes after the birth of the child. During this time the uterus

Labor
Changes in a woman's body as it prepares to deliver a child, consisting mainly of muscle contractions and dilation of the cervix

Amniotic fluid
The fluid that surrounds and insulates the fetus in the mother's womb

Transition
The passage of the baby through the cervix into the birth canal

Birth

455

FIGURE 12-7
The position of the fetus before birth.

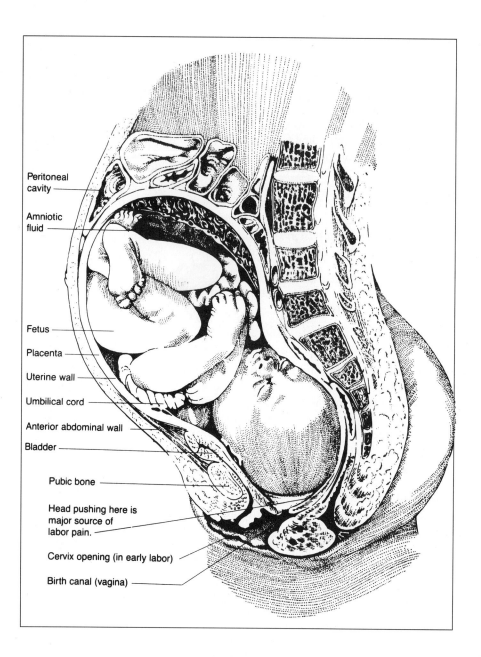

Peritoneal cavity

Amniotic fluid

Fetus

Placenta

Uterine wall

Umbilical cord

Anterior abdominal wall

Bladder

Pubic bone

Head pushing here is major source of labor pain.

Cervix opening (in early labor)

Birth canal (vagina)

contracts and begins to return to its normal size, and there is minor bleeding. Normally, this stage lasts for only a few minutes.

Although a certain amount of pain is connected with a normal birth, knowledge of the birth process and the source of labor pain and a relaxed and confident mental attitude will reduce such pain. It is wise for both expectant parents to take childbirth preparation classes. Local Red Cross units, county health facilities, and adult education programs usually offer such courses. As mentioned earlier, prenatal care from a doctor should be sought as soon as a woman becomes pregnant. Although most births are normal, a small number will be abnormal, such as when the child presents buttocks first (breech presentation) rather than head first (see Figure 12-9). In many cases the doctor can recognize the potential problem and be prepared ahead of time.

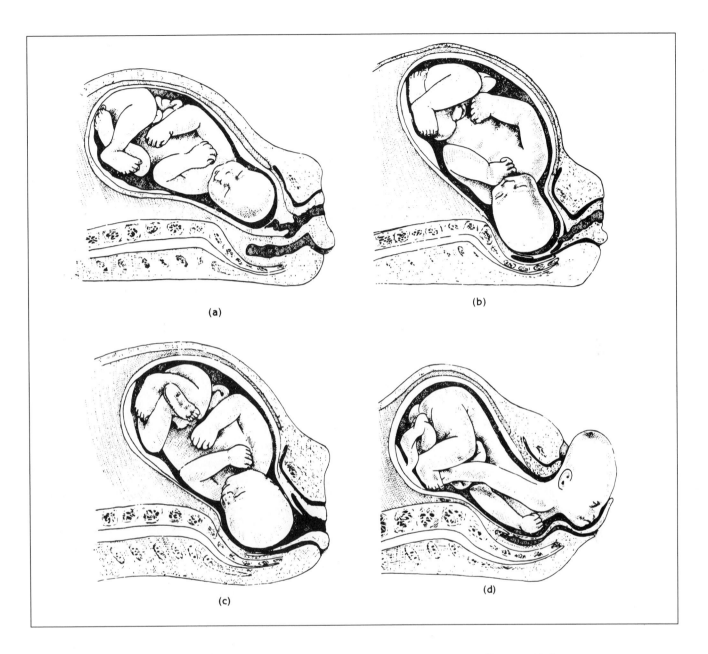

FETAL MONITORING

Within the past few years, **fetal monitoring** has become specialized.

Recently, engineers at NASA invented a new fetal heart rate monitor belt. The device uses acoustical sensors and a small microprocessor that distinguishes a healthy heartbeat from tones that may signal problems. It is worn around a woman's abdomen thus allowing constant monitoring at any time during the pregnancy. Hopefully this device will help women with high risk pregnancies who don't get adequate prenatal care (Popular Mechanics 1991, 16).

During labor electronic sensors are placed on the mother's abdomen, and in the second stage of birth, an electrode is attached to the baby's scalp. These electrodes record the baby's heartbeat as well as the uterine contractions. Ul-

FIGURE 12-8
Events in the birth process: (a) before labor begins; (b) early stages of labor, dilation of cervix begins; (c) cervix completely dilated, baby's head starts to turn; (d) late stage of labor, baby's head begins to emerge.

Fetal monitoring
Using various instruments to measure the vital signs of the fetus during the birth process

FIGURE 12-9
Atypical fetal positions at birth:
(a) breech presentation, with fetus in
buttocks-first position; (b) transverse
position, with fetus's head at one side
of the uterus and its buttocks at the
other.

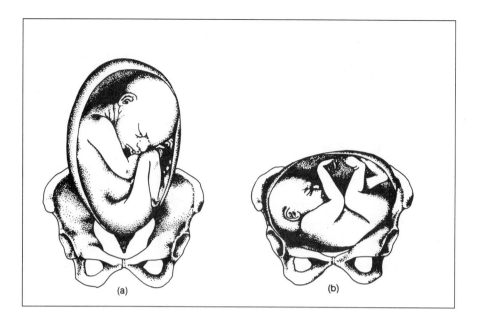

trasound techniques also display a picture of the baby and offer another measure of the heartbeat. These monitoring techniques allow the physician to
monitor the baby's condition closely. Fetal distress can be recognized more
quickly than in the past when only external monitoring methods were used.

Considerable criticism has been aimed at this kind of technical monitoring,
mainly because it is associated with increased cesarean births. However, many
claim that such monitoring has reduced infant mortality rates. For example,
in 1950 the infant mortality rate was 30 per 1000 live births. By 1991 that
rate had dropped to 8.8 (National Center for Health Statistics April 15, 1992c,
3). It seems obvious that monitoring of both mother and baby during birth
can be important to successful birth. Whether monitoring leads to unnecessary
cesarean births, as some critics claim, is a separate question that should be
investigated.

■ CESAREAN SECTION ■

From as early as 1882, under certain circumstances, such as when a baby is
too large to pass through the mother's pelvis or when labor is very long and
hard, the baby has been removed via a *cesarean section*. In this operation an
incision is made through the abdominal and uterine walls, and the baby is
removed. The recovery period is longer than for a normal birth. Contrary to
widespread belief, it is possible for a woman to have several babies in this
manner or to have one by cesarean section and the next normally. The name
of the operation derives from the popular but erroneous legend that Julius
Caesar was delivered surgically.

Recently, the percentage of cesarean section births has increased, rising to
25 to 30 percent of all births and even higher in specific hospitals (see
Table 12-2). The frequency of cesarean sections has led to controversy because
the operation is more traumatic to the mother's body than natural birth. At
the same time, it is far less traumatic to the child because there is no prolonged
pressure on the child as there is in the normal birth process.

TABLE 12-2			
HOW COMMON IS CESAREAN SECTION DELIVERY?			
	1984	**1990**	**2000***
All ages	21.1%	28.8%	40.3%
Under 20	16.5	22.2	31.4
Age 20–24	19.6	26.9	38.3
Age 25–29	20.8	29.1	40.8
Age 30–34	24.6	32.3	45.1
Age 35 and older	28.7	35.4	48.6

*Projected.

Sources: U.S. Bureau of the Census and the National Center for Health Statistics.

Hospitals contend that better monitoring of the child just before birth and throughout the procedure leads to early recognition of possible problems and that many of these can be headed off by a cesarean section. They admit that monitoring has led to a higher proportion of cesareans but point out that it has also reduced infant mortality. However, it appears that some of the increase in cesarean births stems from the desire of parents to have a "perfect" baby and the ensuing fear on the part of the delivering doctor that legal action will be taken against her or him if the baby is less than "perfect."

The incidence of infection associated with cesarean delivery is about five to ten times higher than with vaginal deliveries (Hawrylyshyn et al. 1981). Some women's groups criticize the increasing use of cesarean delivery, feeling that most are unnecessary and are not in the best interest of the mother (Boston Women's Health Book Collective 1992, 459–462).

BIRTH PAIN

The uterine contractions, which are simple muscle contractions, usually don't cause pain, though prolonged or overly strong contractions can cause cramping. The majority of pain arises from the pressure of the baby's head (the largest and hardest part of the baby at the time of birth) against the cervix, the opening into the birth canal. In the early stages of labor, the contractions of the uterus push the child's head against the still-contracted cervix, and this point becomes the major source of pain. A woman can reduce labor pain by trying to relax at the onset of a contraction, breathing more shallowly to raise the diaphragm, and lying on her side with knees somewhat drawn up.

Once the child's head passes through the cervix, the woman experiences little or no pain as the baby passes on through the vagina. Hormonal action has softened the vagina to such an extent that it can stretch up to seven times its normal size. There will be some discomfort as the baby moves through the middle and lower pelvis. An additional difficulty may occur at birth as the child passes out of the mother into the outside world. There is often a slight tearing of the perineum, or skin between the vaginal and anal openings, because the skin may have to stretch beyond its limits to allow the infant to exit. In most cases the doctor will make a small incision called an **episiotomy** so that the skin does not tear. The incision is sewn after the delivery. Some-

Episiotomy
A small incision made between the vaginal and anal openings to facilitate birth

459

What makes being born so frightful is the intensity, the boundless scope and variety of the experience, its suffocating richness.

People say—and believe—that a newborn baby feels nothing. He feels everything.

Everything—utterly, without choice or filter or discrimination.

Birth is a tidal wave of sensation, surpassing anything we can imagine. A sensory experience so vast we can barely conceive of it.

The baby's senses are at work. Totally.

They are sharp and open—new.

What are our senses compared to theirs?

And the sensations of birth are rendered still more intense by contrast with what life was before.

Admittedly, these sensations are not yet organized into integrated, coherent perceptions. Which makes them all the stronger, all the more violent, unbearable—literally mad-

dening (Leboyer 1975, 15–16). Many theorists have hypothesized that the trauma of birth leaves an indelible mark on human personality. One of Freud's early followers, Otto Rank, suggested that the birth trauma is the major source of later problems that center around insecurity, because this trauma marks humans with a basic anxiety about life.

The child emerges out of the quiet, warm, dark, secure environment of the womb into a bright, loud, cooler world, and its source of oxygen and nutrition, the umbilical cord, is immediately severed. The child is hung upside down, slapped, cleaned, and made to function immediately on its own. Little wonder that the child screams, clenches its fist, and has an agonized look on its face. The sensation of the air rushing into its lungs for the first time must be a searing experience. Add to this all of the other new experi-

ences, and life must seem a cacophony of terrifying intensity.

Frederick Leboyer simply tells us to listen to the child. Let the child guide us through the first few minutes after birth. Leboyer's four basic steps are simple.

1. Once delivery is imminent, reduce the light and be quiet. The infant's vision and hearing will then not be immediately assaulted.
2. As soon as the infant is out, place it comfortably on the mother's warm abdomen, which will serve as a nest for the child. Let the child retain the prebirth curved position of the spine until ready of its own accord to straighten and stretch.
3. Do not cut the umbilical cord until the child's own systems are functioning smoothly, six to ten minutes after birth. This way the child is doubly supplied with oxygen and there will be no period of

---

times massage can be used to stretch the skin enough so tearing will not occur, especially if the infant is small.

▨ NATURAL CHILDBIRTH ▨

Natural childbirth
Birth wherein the parents have learned about the birth process and participate via exercises such as breathing techniques to minimize pain

In recent years many women have sought an alternative to the automatic use of anesthesia and the rather mechanical way many American hospitals have handled childbirth. Many years ago Grantly Dick-Read coined the phrase **natural childbirth** and suggested in his book *Childbirth without Fear* that understanding of birth procedures by the mother could break the pattern of fear, tension, and pain too often associated with childbirth (Dick-Read 1972). Natural childbirth thus means knowledgeable childbirth, not simply childbirth without anesthesia or at home.

General anesthesia for childbirth has become much less popular, even in hospitals, because it slows labor and depresses the child's activity, making the

possible deficit and related alarm reaction and ensuing terror. During this time the mother and doctor gently massage the child, simulating the environmental contact the child has so long enjoyed within the mother.

4. Once the cord stops pulsating, cut it and bathe the baby in water similar in temperature to the familiar environment from which it recently emerged. During this time hold the baby and massage it gently. The hands make love to the child, not briskly rubbing not timidly caressing, but deeply and slowly massaging just as the child felt within the womb. The child makes contact with the world at a pace that is comfortable for it. And how long might this be? Perhaps ten to twenty minutes is all. Is this too much to ask for a child at this most eventful time in its life?

And what of the Leboyer-born children's later personalities? It might be too early to tell, but they seem noticeably different, especially in their unusually avid interest in the world around them. Does fear and terror at birth cause many of the problems felt by adult humans? Will reducing the impact of birth on the child help that child become an adult with fewer problems? Only time will tell. But shouldn't we try to reduce birth trauma and see what happens?

On the other hand, many doctors feel that the Leboyer method does nothing. A study conducted at McMaster University Medical Centre in Hamilton, Ontario, compared twenty-eight infants delivered by the Leboyer method with twenty-six who had routine deliveries. The study reported no differences between the infants (Associated Press 1980).

Water birth, pioneered by the Russian doctor Igor Charkovsky, is another method of "gentle birth."

A large tub is filled with warm distilled water. Doctors and nurses are positioned outside the tub. The water is used as a relaxation tool throughout labor. If the mother actually has the baby under water, it is lifted from the water while still receiving life-giving oxygen through the umbilical cord. Once the baby is breathing on its own, the cord is cut. Much the same after-birth treatment is given to the baby as in the Leboyer method.

Advocates of water birth claim that it significantly reduces the mother's pain, length of labor, and need for drugs. It provides the baby with a safe setting for a gentle, nontraumatic birth, free of the stress of gravity at the moment of delivery. Again there is little hard research evidence to support the advantages of such a birth method (Ehrhardt 1990a; 1990b).

birth more difficult though less painful. All systemic drugs used for pain relief during labor cross the placental barrier by simple diffusion. Although such drugs affect the fetus, so do pain and stress experienced by the mother. Withholding medication from tense, anxious laboring women may not accomplish the intended goal of reducing fetal problems (Olds, London, and Ladewig 1988, 692). Generally, however, using systemic drugs with women in labor should be minimized. An epidural block is sometimes used in both first and second stages of birth. Anesthetic injected into an area in the spinal column causes loss of feeling in the pelvic region.

Paracervical anesthesia, which involves injection of novocaine or a similar pain-killing substance into the area around the cervix is sometimes used (less often now than in the past because of concern that it will affect the fetal heart rate). This quickly deadens the area, blocking out the pain. It is similar to being injected in the gums around a tooth that is to be filled. The anesthetic action is localized and the mother is completely conscious and able to participate in the birth.

Birth

Hypnosis is also being used more frequently during labor and delivery to help relax the mother and reduce her sensations of pain. It is particularly useful for women who cannot tolerate the drugs used in anesthesia. Hypnosis cannot be used with everyone and requires a knowledgeable doctor. Those who use it report relaxed and relatively uncomplicated deliveries.

Today, more and more physicians are letting the woman decide whether she wants an anesthetic and if so, what type. It is important that the expectant mother be informed of the benefits and disadvantages of the available forms of anesthesia so that she can make her choice intelligently.

As mentioned earlier, Red Cross facilities, county medical units, and evening adult education programs often provide childbirth preparation classes. The classes provide information on the birth process, what to expect, and how to facilitate the natural processes. The woman is also taught physical exercises that will help prepare her body for the coming birth. She learns breathing techniques to help the natural processes along and to reduce the amount of pain she would otherwise experience.

We have already noted that one of the basic principles underlying natural childbirth is that knowledge reduces fear and reduced fear means less tension and pain. The other basic principle of natural childbirth is that the mother and father should be active participants in the birth of their child rather than passive spectators. For instance, controlled breathing (with the father helping to pace the breathing) supplies the right amount of oxygen to the working muscles, giving them the energy they need to function efficiently. Voluntarily relaxing the other muscles helps focus all energy on the laboring muscles. Breathing exercises also focus attention on responding to the contractions, which keeps attention away from pain.

Since the couple have decided to have the child together, it is also important that they learn together about the processes involved and that the father not be simply a spectator during labor and delivery. The couple will want to know if the hospital they plan to use will allow the father into the labor and delivery rooms so that he can give psychological support and comfort to the mother. During the early stages of labor, he will be able to remind her of what to do as the contractions increase. He can keep track of the time intervals between contractions, monitor her breathing, remind her to relax, massage her (if she finds that a help), and keep her informed of her progress. In other words, he can help by *sharing* the experience. Several birthing methods (including Bradley and Lamaze) urge the father to learn about the birth process and actively participate. This also facilitates father-child bonding.

Once the baby has passed through the cervix into the birth canal (vagina) and the doctor is present, things happen so fast and the woman is so involved with the imminent birth that the father's presence may be less important than during labor.

■ ROOMING-IN ■

Rooming-in
The practice of placing the newborn in the mother's room after delivery so that the mother (and father) can care for it

More and more hospitals are allowing **rooming-in,** in which the mother is allowed to keep her baby with her rather than having the child remain in a nursery. Rooming-in is especially helpful to the breastfeeding mother. Both mother and newborn benefit from the physical closeness, and the child will

cry less because it will get attention and be fed when hungry. Many hospitals are planning for rooming-in by connecting the nursery to the mother's room and allowing for free access to her infant. In these hospitals the baby is placed in a drawerlike crib that the mother pulls into her room whenever she wants. If she is tired, she simply places the child in the drawer and pushes the infant back into the nursery where it is cared for by nurses.

ALTERNATIVE BIRTH CENTERS

Some hospitals have created **alternative birth centers,** homelike settings for childbirth. Relatives and friends are allowed to visit during much of the childbirth process. Barring complications, childbirth takes place in the same room that the mother is in during her entire stay at the center. Couples interested in such birth centers usually must apply in advance. The mother-to-be must be examined to be as certain as possible that she will have a normal delivery. In addition, the birth center usually requires that the couple attend childbirth classes. Birth centers are a compromise between hospital birth and home birth. They are part of the continuing trend by hospitals to make childbirth less mechanical and help couples participate as fully as possible. There are also numerous out-of-hospital birth centers now operating.

Alternative birth center
A special birth center that creates a homelike atmosphere for birth

HOME BIRTHS

Some women prefer **home birth** to having their children in a hospital. At home the woman is in familiar surroundings, can choose her own attendants,

Home birth
Giving birth at one's home rather than in a hospital

463

and can follow whatever procedures soothe and encourage her (have music playing, for example). At home, birth is also a family affair. Social support, especially that of the father-partner is especially important during pregnancy and birth (Liese et al. 1989).

The immediate question that comes to mind is whether home birth is safe. In Europe where home birth is common, statistics indicate that home birth is just as safe as hospital birth (Boston Women's Health Book Collective 1984). American doctors do not agree and cite many instances of tragedy with home birth that could have been avoided in a hospital. The amount of risk can be reduced by careful prenatal screening of the mother and by providing backup emergency care. If the prenatal screening indicates conditions that might involve a complicated delivery, the woman should have her baby in a hospital that has the facilities to deal with possible problems.

The emergency backup for a home delivery should include a doctor, paraprofessional, nurse, or midwife to deal with any unforeseen problems. In the future it may be possible to set up some kind of mobile birth unit staffed by trained personnel. The unit, perhaps housed in a converted motor home, could either be parked outside the home or be summoned to the house by calling an emergency number. In case of emergency, the mother could be quickly shifted to the unit, which would contain any necessary equipment. Remember, though, that birth is a normal process; 85 to 95 percent of births do not involve any difficulties (Boston Women's Health Book Collective 1984).

The **midwife** is an honored professional used by 80 percent of the world's population to attend childbirth (Olds, London, and Ladewig 1988, 8–9). Midwives are used in home delivery in many modern countries such as Sweden and the Netherlands and were used in our country until the turn of the century, yet the organized medical profession and many others believe that delivery in the hospital by doctors is much safer. In addition, they believe that it would be difficult to enforce standards of competence if home delivery by midwives became widespread. England, on the other hand, has set high standards and has trained midwives since 1902. About 80,000 women are registered as midwives in England, and about 21,000 are actively practicing. In England the obstetrician is the leader of the birth team, and the midwife does the practical work. In Holland about 35 percent of Dutch women now choose to have their babies at home. Home birth is considered so safe that the national health insurance scheme, which pays for most births, will not pay for a hospital birth unless medically indicated (*Santa Barbara News Press* 1985).

In the United States, certified nurse-midwives (CNM) are registered nurses who practice legally in the hospital setting. Some states do not allow certified nurse–midwives to perform home births. (For information on your state's midwife regulations and a list of CNMs in your area, contact The American College of Nurse-Midwives, 1522 K Street NW, Suite 1000, Washington, DC 20005.)

As interest in home births increases and hospital costs soar (it now costs over $4000 to have a baby with standard hospitalization and delivery), the idea of midwifery is returning in the United States. Some states now have licensed training programs for midwives. Midwives delivered 2.8 percent of all babies in the United States in 1989, up from 1 percent in 1975 (Ehrhardt 1989).

Midwife
A person, usually a woman, trained to assist in childbirth or, in some countries, to perform delivery

■ BREASTFEEDING ■

Associated with the natural childbirth philosophy is a strong emphasis on breastfeeding. There are many reasons for this emphasis, including the fact that breastfeeding is more natural. The major reason that psychologists advocate breastfeeding, however, is that it brings the mother and child into close, warm physical contact, which encourages bonding. Inasmuch as feeding is the infant's first social contact, many experts, such as Erik Erikson (1963) and Ashley Montagu (1972; 1989), believe that this loving contact is necessary to the development of security and basic trust in the infant. Another advantage of breastfeeding derives from the secretion of **colostrum.** This substance is present in the breast immediately after birth and is secreted until the milk flows, usually three to four days after birth. It has a high protein content, but, most important, it is high in antibodies and helps make the child immune to many infectious diseases during infancy. Breastfeeding also causes hormones to be released that speed the uterus's return to normal. One should also count the warm, loving feelings that arise in the nursing mother as an advantage of breastfeeding.

The new mother needs to prepare for breastfeeding as well as understand the natural process if she is to be successful. Her breasts will be engorged, congested, and painful for the first few days after birth. However, mothers who have rooming-in and begin to breastfeed the baby from birth onward (the sucking reflex of a baby born to an unanesthetized mother is very strong), on the baby's demand, usually do not experience engorgement. The act of breastfeeding itself soon relieves the congestion. Before birth it is helpful if the mother massages her nipples to prepare them for the child's sucking. Otherwise, the nipples sometimes become chafed and sore. If this happens, exposing the nipples to the air will help.

Milk normally begins to flow between the third and fourth day. The baby is biologically prepared to maintain itself during these days, because it normally has a little surplus fat that sustains it until milk flow begins. Thus the mother does not need to worry that she will not be able to satisfy the infant's hunger during the first few days. (For more information on breastfeeding, contact La Leche League International, 9616 Minneapolis Avenue, Franklin Park, IL 60131.)

In the words of Ashley Montagu, women should remember that "Over the five or more million years of human evolution, and as a consequence of seventy-five million years of mammalian evolution, breastfeeding has constituted the most successful means of administering to the needs of the dependent, precariously born human neonate" (1972, 80).

Although about 60 percent of American mothers breastfeed (up from 25 percent in 1970), many new parents decide to bottle feed their newborns. With bottle feeding it is important to make sure the infant receives the holding and close bodily contact that breastfeeding supplies. One advantage is the father can participate as well, in providing holding and physical contact for the baby.

At times the father is a forgotten person immediately after birth. Not only does the mother occasionally suffer mild postpartum depression, but the father may suffer feelings of neglect, jealousy, and simply "being left out" after childbirth. The more of a partnership, the more sharing a couple can have in the

Colostrum
The fluid secreted by the breast during the first days postpartum consisting of immunologically active substances and white blood cells, water, protein, fat, and carbohydrate in a thin yellowish fluid

Birth

whole process of conception, pregnancy, and childbirth, the more satisfaction both the father and mother will receive.

POSTPARTUM EMOTIONAL CHANGES

The first few weeks and months of motherhood are known as the postpartum period. About 60 percent of all women who bear children report a mild degree of emotional depression ("baby blues") following the birth, and another 10 percent report severe depression.

> Some of us are high, some are mellow, some of us are lethargic and depressed, or we are irritable and cry easily. Mood swings are common. We are confused and a little scared, because our moods do not resemble the way we are accustomed to feel, let alone the way we are expected to feel. If this is our first baby we may feel lonely and isolated from adult society. The special attention and consideration many of us receive as expectant mothers shift to the baby and we too are expected to put the baby's needs before our own. (Boston Women's Health Book Collective 1973, 207).

From 25 to 50 percent of women experience this mild postpartum depression between the second and fifteenth day after delivery. This may be due in part to the changing chemical balance within the woman's body as it readjusts to the nonpregnant state, which takes about six weeks. For most women this depression passes quickly (Dix 1985). The general emotional reactions to parenthood, especially with the first child, continue for a much longer period. Postpartum counseling before the birth can help couples understand and cope with any normal feeling of depression that might follow birth.

SUMMARY

1. *Pregnancy and childbirth are an integral part of most marriages.* Despite the drop in the birthrate and the increasing number of couples expressing the desire to remain childless, childbearing and rearing will be a part of the majority of people's lives. Knowledge of pregnancy and the birth process is important to the act of birth itself. Those who are knowledgeable stand a better chance of having a simple, uncomplicated childbirth.

2. *Both the egg and sperm cells are among the smallest in the body, yet they contain all the genetic material necessary to create the adult human being.* Both contribute the same number of chromosomes (twenty-three), but the sperm is responsible for the sex of the child. There are two kinds of sperm, an X sperm, which creates a female, and a Y sperm, which creates a male. Many more males are conceived than females, but by the end of the first year of life, there are almost equal numbers of males and females. This is because the death rate for males at all stages of life after conception is higher than the rate for females.

3. *Pregnancy takes several weeks before it becomes recognizable, though some pregnancy tests can determine pregnancy within seven to ten days of conception.* A missed menstrual period is usually the first sign. Other signs might be breast tenderness and coloration change, slight morning sickness, and the necessity for more frequent urination.

4. *The average pregnancy is 266 days, or thirty-eight weeks.* During this time the mother should eat a good diet and be under the care of a physician. She should avoid medicines and being X-rayed, as well as stressful life events, if possible. The developing fetus can be affected by the environment. If the mother is addicted to narcotics, has an infectious disease such as German measles or an STD, or is a heavy smoker, for example, the child may be damaged. Any resulting defects in the child are called congenital defects. Genetic defects are caused by the chromosomes and genes. By removing a small amount of amniotic fluid—a process termed *amniocentesis*—doctors can analyze it to discover any genetic defects, such as Down syndrome, before birth.

5. *The birth process is generally divided into three stages.* The first is the labor stage, during which the cervix relaxes and opens and the uterus contracts periodically in an effort to push the infant into the birth canal (vagina). In the second stage these contractions, with help from the mother, push the child through the birth canal into the outside world. The third stage comes shortly after the baby has been delivered when the placenta or afterbirth is expelled.

6. *In recent years more and more emphasis has been placed on having the mother and father participate as much as they can in the birth of the child.* Natural childbirth means knowledgeable childbirth, with the use of drugs reduced to a minimum. Breastfeeding is being encouraged, as is rooming-in, or keeping the baby with the mother immediately after birth rather than removing it to the hospital nursery.

7. *Those encouraging natural childbirth believe that for a couple to share the miracle of creating life can be an emotional high point.* They suggest that care and planning be made a part of pregnancy so that the birth process will function smoothly and the parents will be able to derive the most pleasure and satisfaction from the entire process of bringing a child into the world.

Several years ago I spent a weekend with some friends in the country. Helen, my hostess, was seven months pregnant, and in the evening I would find her sitting alone in front of the fireplace, softly singing a beautiful lullaby to her unborn child.

After the birth of her son, Helen told me that the same lullaby had a magical effect on him. No matter how hard he was crying, he would calm down when the song was sung. As a psychiatrist with a special interest in prenatal experience, I was intrigued. I wondered if a woman's actions, perhaps even her thoughts and feelings, might be able to influence her unborn child.

From my investigation and search of the scientific literature a new portrait of the unborn child emerged, one fundamentally different from the passive, mindless creature of the traditional pediatrics text:

■ The unborn child is an aware, reacting being who from the sixth month on—perhaps even earlier—leads an active emotional life.
■ The fetus can see, hear, experience, and, on a primitive level, even learn.
■ Whether a child becomes happy or sad, aggressive or meek, secure or anxiety-ridden may depend, in part, on what messages the fetus receives in the womb.

■ This new knowledge has enormous implications for parents. It suggests they have a greater influence over the unborn child than ever before imagined.

Many studies suggest that the unborn child is not just conscious and aware, but sensitive to remarkably subtle emotional nuances. Precisely at what moment the brain cells acquire this ability is still unknown. However, most of what is known with some research support suggests that the child from the sixth month in utero onward has such skills.

To illustrate, consider the sensation of anxiety. What could produce a deep-seated anxiety in an unborn child, one that could have long-term effects? One possibility is his mother's alcohol consumption or smoking. Studies have shown the profound effects of maternal cigarette smoking on the fetus: a sharp increase in the heart rate, a decrease in the oxygen supply, and a reduced birth weight. It is possible that some of these effects are stress related.

Naturally, the fetus has no way of knowing the mother is smoking or thinking about it, but the fetus is developed enough to react to the unpleasant sensation it produces, which is caused by a drop in the oxygen supply. Possibly even more harmful are the psychological effects of maternal smoking. Periodic reduced oxygen might thrust the fetus into a chronic state of uncertainty and fear, never knowing when that unpleasant physical sensation will recur or how painful it will be when it does.

Another happier kind of learning goes on in utero through hearing. Our speech patterns are as distinct as our fingerprints. Apparently, the learning of these speech patterns is influenced by our mothers even before birth. In addition, acute hearing allows the fetus to react to music. A six-month-old fetus definitely responds to the sound and melody. Put

Vivaldi on the phonograph and even the most agitated baby relaxes. Put on hard rock and most fetuses start kicking violently.

Even something as mundane as the mother's heartbeat has an effect. It is an essential part of the unborn child's life-support system. The child does not know that, but it does seem to sense that the reassuring rhythm of its beat is one of the major constellations of its universe. This was demonstrated a few years ago when a hospital piped a tape of a maternal heartbeat into a nursery filled with newborn babies. The researchers assumed that if the sound had any emotional significance, the babies on the day the tape was played would behave differently than on days when it wasn't played.

And so they did, to a degree that stunned the investigators. In virtually every way the heartbeat babies did better, apparently reassured by the comforting rhythm. They ate more, weighed more, slept more, breathed better, and cried and got sick less.

Although much more difficult to assess, psychologist Monika Tomann-Specht concluded that the mother's attitude toward her child had the greatest single effect on how an infant turned out. In her study she followed 235 women through pregnancy and birth. The children of accepting mothers, who looked forward to having a family, were much healthier, emotionally and physically, at birth and afterward, than the offspring of rejecting mothers.

What about a father's influence? Few things affect the mother as deeply as worries about her partner, and his support is important to her and the child's well-being. Conversely, perhaps nothing is more dangerous to a child, emotionally and physically, than a father who abuses or neglects his pregnant wife. A study done in the early 1970s indicates that a woman locked in a stormy marriage may run a 100 percent greater risk of bearing a psychologically damaged child than a woman in a secure, nurturing relationship.

This underscores the father's important part in the prenatal equation, but studies suggest another dimension to his supportive role. It appears that a child learns to identify the father's voice in utero. There are also indications that the newborn, hearing that voice, may respond to it, at least physically. If crying, for instance, the child may stop at the familiar soothing sound of the father's voice.

Today men should be thoughtfully involved in their children's lives from the very beginning. The sooner this bonding based on love and care begins, the more each child is likely to benefit.

If, in fact, the child can respond in utero, then pregnancy becomes an important part of the environmental influence on that child in more ways than we had previously realized.

Source: Adapted from *The Secret Life of the Unborn Child* by Thomas Verny, M.D., and John Kelly (New York: Simon & Schuster, 1981).

WHAT DO YOU THINK?

1. Do you think that a fetus can respond to its environment before birth?

2. What might this mean in the case of an abortion?

3. What effect might an unwanted pregnancy have on the unborn child?

4. What effect might a parental fight or breakup have on the unborn child?

5. Since an increasing number of pregnancies occur outside of marriage where fathers are apt to be less involved with the mother, might this have an effect on the unborn child?

6. When a pregnancy occurs outside of marriage, what are the chances of the mother being happy and accepting of the baby compared to a pregnancy within marriage?

Chapter 13

THE CHALLENGE OF PARENTHOOD

CONTENTS

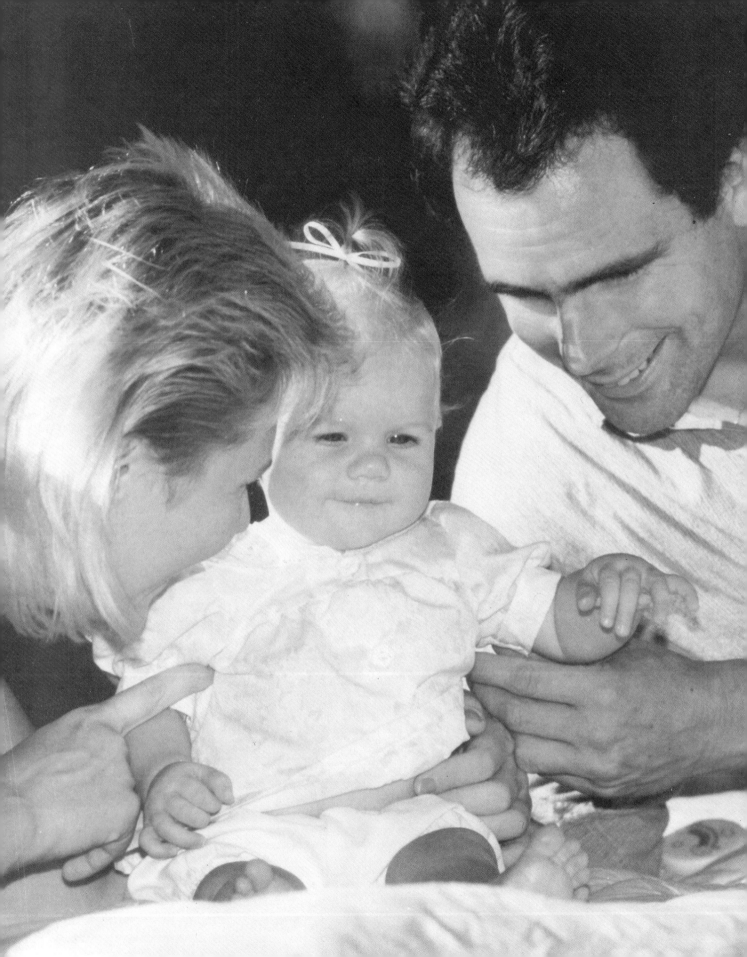

Only sentimentalists have ever considered childhood to be a kingdom of untroubled innocence. Today there is more trouble for children and less time for innocence than in past generations. The problem is not so much that children have changed. The world has changed.

It is both the best and the worst of times for children. Their world contains powers and perspectives inconceivable to a child fifty years ago: computers; longer life expectancy; the entire planet accessible through television, satellites, air travel. But so much knowledge and choice can be chaotic and dangerous. School curriculums have been adapted to teach about new topics: AIDS, adolescent suicide, drug and alcohol abuse, incest. Trust is the child's natural inclination, but the world has become untrustworthy. The hazards of the adult world descend upon children so early that the ideal of childhood is demolished.

The social messages are powerful and contradictory. Rock videos suggest orgiastic sex. Public health officials counsel "safe sex." Prudence—and morality—would recommend no sex to children, who have no clear idea of what sex is anyway.

Television pours into the imaginations of children a bizarre version of reality. But TV has a certain authority in loco parentis. It is there when the kids come home.

Every stable society transmits values from one generation to the next. That is the work of civilization. But what values do we transmit?

Children have lost status in the world. Teachers have endured a long decline in public esteem. Day-care workers rarely earn a living wage. The role of mother is being rewritten, and that of father as well. A generation of children is being raised in the midst of a redefinition of parenting. Childhood has become a kind of experiment.

Cant phrases, such as "quality time," have found their way into the vocabulary. A motif of absence—moral, emotional and physical—plays through the lives of our children. There appears to be a new form of neglect: absence. . . . Recently my six-year-old daughter exclaimed, "Look, Mom, Sarah has a new babysitter." The "babysitter" was Sarah's mother.

Growing up has always been difficult. Today it is difficult in unprecedented ways. For American children fourteen and under, the terrain is strange and forbidding. Perplexed parents, finding their own childhoods seemingly irrelevant to the task, are left to improvise. (Time 1988b, 32–33)

Children are ever the future of society. Every child who does not function at a level commensurate with his or her possibilities, every child who is destined to make fewer contributions to society than society needs, and every child who does not take his or her place as a productive adult diminishes the power of that society's future. (American Psychologist 1989).

Will children today be better or worse off than their parents? Part of the answer rests on the commitment by the public and by parents to ensure the well-being of children. Children traditionally embody their parents' hope for a better life, and their country's wish for a more resourceful and productive citizenry. They also reflect the strength and values of the society that produces them; their well-being exemplifies the country's well-being; their future is the country's future. (Bianchi 1990, 36)

Marriage and parenthood have often seemed synonymous in the past. Having children was the major goal of marriage. Many popular assumptions supported this goal:

■ Marriage means children.
■ Having children is the essence of a woman's self-realization.
■ Reproduction is a woman's biological destiny.
■ All families have a duty to produce children to replenish the society.
■ Children prove the manliness of the father.
■ Children prove the competence and womanliness of the mother.
■ Humans should be fruitful and multiply.
■ Having children is humanity's way to immortality; children extend us into the future.
■ Children are an economic asset, providing necessary labor.

The beliefs of the past often remain to encumber the present long after the original reasons for the belief have disappeared. So it is with reproduction and parenthood. For thousands of years, humans had to reproduce—had to be parents—if the species were to survive. And they had little choice in the matter because the pleasure of sexual relations often meant pregnancy.

Historically, marriage has implied having and rearing children. Indeed, the primary function of the family was to provide a constant supply of individuals so that the human species and the particular society would continue to exist.

> Society needs new individuals born into a social context that maximizes the likelihood of socially approved socialization. In order for society to survive, the new members must be committed to the society's maintenance and perpetuation. As such society must assure that new members are efficiently and economically taught values that promote these goals. As a consequence, an institution is created in all societies that is the most efficient one for socializing new members. This core socialization unit is what we call the family, and it is given the function of bringing new members into the society within a context that ensures the stable continuation of the society. (Belsky, Lang, and Rovine 1985, 15)

The dogma of the past has quietly become the liability of the present because uncontrolled reproduction today means the ultimate demise of the species, not its survival. In the past, high infant mortality, uncontrolled disease, and war meant that society had to pressure all families to reproduce at a high level in order to maintain the population. Women were pregnant during most of their fertile years. Even today in many developing countries, infant mortality runs as high as 200 per 1000 live births, and because of malnutrition and disease, many families see fewer than half of their children reach maturity.

In developed countries, however, the infant mortality rate has been cut to less than 15 per 1000 live births. The infant mortality rate in the United States has dropped from 14 per 1000 live births in 1977 to less than 9 per 1000 live births in 1992, the lowest ever recorded (Population Reference Bureau 1992).

Currently, twenty-five countries have lower infant mortality rates than the United States. For example, Finland and Denmark both have infant mortality rates of 5 per 1000 live births. Countries in Western Africa such as Nigeria and Liberia average 111 deaths per 1000 live births (Population Reference Bureau 1992).

CHILDREN BY CHOICE

Reduced infant mortality through greater control of disease and pestilence has removed the necessity for most American families to have large numbers of children. Because a much larger percentage of children now reach adulthood, a family may safely limit the number of children they produce to the number they actually desire. Hence the historical pressure on the family to reproduce continually has disappeared. The fertility rate in the United States is at or below zero population growth. If this trend continues, the population will reach a high in the year 2015 and start downward around 2020, depending on the amount of immigration.

A couple's conscious or unconscious reasons for having children strongly affect the way the child is treated and reared. Because species survival, political reasons, and economic factors are no longer relevant to the decision to have children in modern Western societies, people's personal reasons for wanting children have become much more important. Many of the personal reasons have a selfish element. It is this selfish element that so often causes the parents to feel a sense of disappointment and failure when they are frustrated by the child. Bernard Berelson (1972) lists six basic personal reasons for having children; each has a large selfish component:

1. Children give parents *personal power* in several ways. There is the power over the children, which during the early years of childhood is absolute. Having children may also give one parent power over the other. Either partner may use the children to obtain a hold over the other. Children can also lead to increased political and/or economic power, as in societies where marriage alliances are arranged to control power. In the United States the Kennedy and Rockefeller families come to mind when we think of children as potential power.

2. Children offer proof of *personal competence* in an essential human role. "Look what I can do; see how virile I am; see how fertile I am."

3. Parenthood confers *personal status*. "I have contributed to society; I can produce and achieve."

4. Children are a form of *personal extension*; they confer immortality and represent a form of life after death. "After all, my children are a part of me, both biologically and psychologically."

5. The *personal experience of having children* is rewarding. Among the rewards are the deep curiosity a parent may feel about how the child will turn out; the renewal of self in the second chance; the reliving of one's own childhood; the redemptive opportunity; the challenge of shaping another human being; and the sheer creativity and self-realization involved in childrearing.

6. The experience of having children can produce *personal pleasure*—the love involved in having wanted children, caring for them, and enjoying them.

Of course, there are many other personal reasons for having children. For example, the major reasons many teenage mothers give for having a child are "Children will make me an adult." "I'll have something of my own." Other reasons include "People will pay attention to me." "I'll have someone to help and to love." "A child will save my marriage." As we shall see in the next section, the idea that children will save a marriage is erroneous. The increased complications of parenthood usually hasten the end of a troubled marriage.

To know and understand our reasons for having children is a small step in the right direction. And to understand that the resultant child is an individual in his or her own right and that this new individual has no responsibility to fulfill our needs and reasons for producing him or her is a big step in the direction of enlightened childrearing.

▪ CHILDLESSNESS ▪

Reliable contraception allows couples to remain child-free if they so desire. Although in the recent past the mass media have played up reports of large numbers of American women choosing to remain child-free, government population studies tend to show these reports are exaggerated. What is clear is that women are having fewer children and are postponing both marriage and childbirth. About 9 percent of women between the ages of eighteen and thirty-four say they expect to remain childless (U.S. Bureau of the Census October 1991c, 1). Just how many actually will do so remains to be seen.

Remaining childless after marriage is more acceptable in the 1990s than it has been in the past. During the 1950s and early 1960s, couples who married and postponed having children (or, worse yet, decided not to have any children) experienced a great deal of societal criticism. The couple's parents dropped hints about how nice it would be to become grandparents. Friends who already had children wondered if something was wrong with one of the partner's reproductive capabilities. Others viewed the couple as selfish and preoccupied with themselves. Fortunately, such pressures on newly married couples have lessened.

Today, although these earlier pressures have declined, a new pressure has appeared. With the postponement of marriage and parenthood, age becomes a factor in pregnancy. The only group that has recently experienced in an increase in fertility is women aged thirty to thirty-nine. Many women who decided when they were young to remain temporarily or permanently child-free are now feeling the pressures of advancing age and are deciding to have children before it is too late.

> In 1976, births to women aged 30 to 34 and 35 to 39 made up 14 and 5 percent, respectively, of all births in that year to women between the ages of 18 and 44. By 1990, these age groups accounted for 23 and 10 percent, respectively, of all births (U.S. Bureau of the Census October 1991, 123).

Childlessness offers numerous advantages to a couple. The most important is increased freedom. The couple does not have the responsibilities of children. They are monetarily less encumbered. Their time and money are their own to

"RIGHT" AND "WRONG" REASONS TO HAVE A BABY

"WRONG" REASONS

1. To save or strengthen the marital relationship.
2. To please your parents or friends.
3. Because everyone you know has children.
4. To escape from the outside working world.
5. To relieve the fear of being alone in old age, the fear of what you may be missing out on, the fear of what people may think of you, and so forth.

6. Because you've been mothering your mate and think a real baby would be more fun.
7. To prove to the world you are a real woman or man.
8. To become somebody important.
9. To do a better job than your parents did with you.

"RIGHT" REASONS

1. Both you and your mate want and choose to have a child.
2. Your aim is to give, rather than to get.

3. Your relationship and lives are established so that you give from your excess and do not need to take from your lives.
4. You are going to be available to your child and not always busy and preoccupied with other things.
5. You want the challenge of rearing a child into a healthy productive adult.
6. You are looking forward with pleasure to rearing a child.

Source: Adapted from Brinley 1984.

devote to their careers, each other, hobbies, travels, and adult life in general. Often the childless couple is a two-career family (sometimes known as *DINCs*, which is short for *dual income no children*). Both partners are free to invest their energies in their work and meet during leisure times for mutual enjoyment.

WHAT EFFECTS DO CHILDREN HAVE ON A MARRIAGE?

The most often heard words from parents to couples thinking about becoming parents are, "Your life will never be the same again." "We know, we know," replies the couple contemplating parenthood. "Oh no, you don't," reply the parents. And the parents are right. Parenthood is constant. It is demanding. You can divorce a problem spouse, but you can't divorce a problem child. Parenthood lasts to the end of your life.

Russ received an urgent call from his thirty-five-year-old son living 1000 miles away. The son asked Russ to come as soon as possible because he and his wife were breaking up and he needed his dad's help and support. Fortunately, Russ was retired so he left the next day. He arrived just in time to see the wife and her brothers driving off with all the furniture that Russ had given to his son and daughter-in-law as a wedding gift. He and his son ended up sleeping on the floor in the empty house for a week until the son got things sorted out.

The point of this story is that parenting does not end when children are twenty-one years old, when they are married or when they live at some distance from their parents. Parenthood is a lifetime commitment and obligation.

The effect that children have on a marriage is complicated and involves many factors. Certainly, the readiness of the couple for pregnancy and ensuing parenthood is crucial. We have already discussed the importance of planning parenthood so that the child is wanted. Yet even parents who want a child will experience ambivalence when they near the point of actually having one. Are we really ready? How much freedom will I lose? Can we afford a child? Will I be a successful parent? Such questions will arise constantly for any expectant parent.

Unplanned pregnancies make such questions infinitely more difficult. Couples often feel trapped into parenthood by an unexpected pregnancy. They are not ready for, and have not consented to, parenthood. They are often angry and resentful, especially the prospective father because he has the least control over the pregnancy. An unwed father, for example, has virtually no legal rights in deciding what shall be done about an unwanted pregnancy. Yet he is legally responsible for the newborn child.

Men may have more trouble working out parenthood readiness questions than women because they rarely seek out support or help in dealing with such questions. They are also more prone than women to keep their concerns to themselves. They are reluctant to discuss their concerns with their pregnant spouses for fear of upsetting them and "making matters worse." Yet a man may worry about losing his wife or baby during childbirth, facing increased responsibilities, and being replaced in his wife's life by the newborn (Shapiro 1987).

Although women seem to be better at handling readiness-for-parenthood questions, they too must confront meaningful life choices. In the past women did not have much choice; the parenting/homemaking role was often the only role open to them. In those days, however, the homemaking role was much larger and more varied than it is today. Women were productive members of farm and craft teams along with their husbands. Children either shared in the work of the household or were left to amuse themselves. These mothers were usually not lonely or isolated because the world came into their homes in the form of farmhands, relatives, customers, and so on. Such women had no reason to complain of the boredom and solitude of spending ten-hour days alone with their children. In addition to being mothers, they contributed to their family and society in other important and productive ways.

Today, the scope of the homemaking role has been drastically reduced. The general affluence—especially of the American middle-class family—the small

nuclear family structure, the influence of feminism, and the transferal of economic production from the home to the factory all have combined to decrease the satisfactions derived from the now narrow and exaggerated maternal/homemaking role. The modern woman has many other choices available to her, which make the decision of whether she is ready for parenthood increasingly difficult (see Chapters 7 and 9).

Today, the idea that a mother must remain at home with her children at all times is losing credence as more and more mothers join the work force. The supposedly negative effects that absent mothers, baby-sitters, and child-care centers have on children have not been found when good child care is available (Belsky, Learner, and Spanier 1984; Cochran and Gunnarsson 1985; Clarke-Stewart 1989). The key word here is *good*. Unfortunately good child care for working mothers has not kept pace with the need. Neglected children are now more of a problem than ever before (Hechinger 1986, A-11; *Time* 1988) (see Chapter 7).

Latchkey children are children who spend part of their day without adult supervision. An estimated 10 to 20 percent of school-age children spend some time in self-care with the percentage increasing as children become older (Bianchi 1990, 27–28). Typically, these children have been portrayed as being from poor, single-parent families; living in high-risk, inner-city settings; and suffering from neglect. This is only part of the picture, however; many of these children are not from such backgrounds and appear to be growing up without suffering huge problems from neglect (Hofferth and Cain 1987, 12). Despite the stereotype of a latchkey child spending many long, lonely hours at home, most of these children are alone for less than one hour before school and less than two

Latchkey children
Children left to care for themselves some part of the day

What Effects Do Children Have on a Marriage?

hours after school. Nevertheless, teachers report that the latchkey phenomenon is a major cause of students' difficulty in school (Bianchi 1990, 29).

Regardless of the state of preparation and readiness, the actual transition to parenthood involves a number of costs to the parents:

1. The physical demands associated with caring for the child are usually far greater than the parents anticipated.

2. Unforeseen strains are placed on the husband-wife relationship. Many studies suggest that the presence of children in the family lowers the marital happiness or satisfaction of the parents (Belsky, Spanier, and Rovine 1983; Belsky, Lang, and Rovine 1985; Belsky and Pensky 1988; McHale and Huston 1985; Ruble et al. 1988). Many couples report that the happiest times in their marriage occurred before the arrival of the first child and after the departure of the last. The findings reported by these studies are not new. For example, research done during the 1960s on family stability and happiness also found that children more often detract from than contribute to marital happiness (Hicks and Platt 1970). Of course, most of this research involves group data and averages. The effect that children will have on your own marital relationship will depend on your understanding and tolerance of the natural demands and strains that the presence of children creates. The effects that children have on a marriage also vary greatly with the ages of the children (see "The Growing Child in the Family" on p. 494).

Some of the negative effects that children appear to have on the marital relationship may actually be caused by two unrelated factors. First, dissatisfaction with the marital relationship tends to increase with the length of the marriage. Marital satisfaction appears highest early in marriage, drops, and then, if the marriage survives, increases again during the latter years of the marriage (Glenn 1990, 818–31). Second, parents' expectations about the changes children cause in the marital relationship also influence the parent's relationship. Parents who anticipated the changes correctly did not experience the degree of marital dissatisfaction that other parents reported (MacDermid et al. 1990; Kalmuss et al. 1992).

3. The personal elements of the marital relationship—friendship, romance, and sex—tend to become less satisfying as the relationship becomes focused more on instrumental functions (day-to-day obligations, managing and running the family, integrating family routine and work schedules, and so on) than on emotional expression. The time that the childless couple has used to nurture their personal emotional relationship is displaced by the time demands of the child.

4. New parents complain about the limits children place on their social lives, particularly their freedom to travel or do something on the spur of the moment.

5. Parents also complain about the monetary cost of rearing children.

The Department of Agriculture estimates that in raising a child from birth to age twenty-two a family with an income of $50,000 or more will spend $265,000 on the basics—food, clothing, and shelter. The baby's first year will cost parents $10,800. The three most expensive items are medical costs at $4400, day care at $4000, and clothing at $900. Other expenses include

$600 for furniture, $400 for diapers, and $300 for accessories, including high chair, car seat, and toys. Food accounts for about $200 (*Client's Monthly Alert* 1990, 3).

Despite the negativeness of some research findings, most parents express overall satisfaction with children and the parenting role. In one large study, more than three-quarters (77 percent) of parents said that their children were "the main satisfaction in my life" (Blankenhorn, Bayme, and Elshtain 1990, 75).

Miller and Sollie (1980) have identified several positive themes in new parents' lives. Parents derive emotional benefits from the joy, happiness, and fun that accompany child care. New parents often report feelings of self-enrichment and personal development when undertaking parental responsibilities. Parents also report an increased sense of family cohesiveness and strengthened relationships between themselves and their extended family. Miller and Sollie suggest that the transition to parenthood is a good time for the couple to work to build family strengths.

At first glance parents' expression of satisfaction with their children and family life may seem to contradict the general evidence of reduced marital satisfaction when children enter the family. In fact, both the negative and positive expressions are genuine. In many ways parenthood is a paradox. On the one hand are the problems of contending with a demanding child; on the other hand are the joys of being close to and caring for another person. Parenthood exhibits this paradoxical character not only because it includes both positive and negative experiences but also because the "lows" and "highs" of parenting tend to be extreme. Children often make you want to cry one moment and laugh the next.

Colleen (Monday afternoon): I never realized that an infant could be so demanding. I never get a moment's peace when she's awake, not even to go to the bathroom. I can't even say "wait a minute" because she is too young to understand (ten months). I feel as though my whole life has been taken over by a tyrant. All she does is demand—me! me! me! I've lost my identity, my individuality, to a word—"mother."

Colleen (Tuesday morning): I'm glad I have her. It's neat to know she is part of me and of Bob. She is a real little person who is perfect and loves me and needs me. She makes me feel successful at something, helping another. It makes me feel good to know that I was able to produce a child and be a parent. (LaRossa and LaRossa 1981, 177)

The fact is that children add enormously to the complexity of family relationships. For example, a couple must contend with communication in only

two directions. Add one child and this becomes six-way communication; add two children, and there is now twelve-way communication (see Figure 13-1).

Prospective parents can become better prepared for parenthood by reading and taking classes. Yet even with a thorough preparation, bringing the first new baby home is an exciting, happy, and frightening experience for the parents. No matter how much they have read about children, they can never be sure that what they are doing is correct. If the baby cries, they worry. If he or she doesn't cry, they still worry. Parents also have to adjust to the feeding routine. As the next section explains, most couples become more traditional with parenthood, with the mother becoming the primary care giver. This means she cannot venture far from the baby, especially if she is breastfeeding. The father has to adjust to taking second place, at least for a while, in his wife's time and attention. An infant demands both of these if nothing else.

TRADITIONALIZATION OF THE MARITAL RELATIONSHIP

Examining a couple's relationship after a child enters the family provides a clear illustration of the overriding change that occurs. In almost all cases—except for two-career families that can afford to place child care almost entirely in the hands of others—the parents' relationship moves in the traditional direction (MacDermid et al. 1990). The changes in the marital relationship are more pronounced for wives. Mother assumes most of the parenting and household roles (even if she works), while the father turns toward the work world. This change occurs even in couples who believe in and work for an egalitarian homemaking relationship.

Several theories try to account for this traditionalization phenomenon. Alice Rossi (1977, 17) advances a physiological explanation in which hormonal changes in women during pregnancy, birth, and nursing establish "a clear link between sexuality and maternalism." New mothers receive "erotogenic pleasure" from nursing their infants, which means, according to Rossi, that "there may be biologically based potential for heightened maternal investment in the child, at least through the first months of life, that exceeds the potential for investment by men in fatherhood" (24). Implicitly answering the traditional-

Chapter 13
The Challenge of Parenthood

482

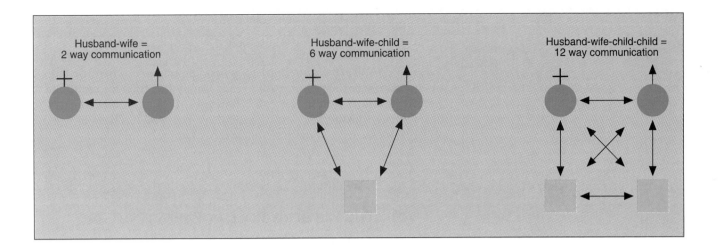

Husband-wife =
2 way communication

Husband-wife-child =
6 way communication

Husband-wife-child-child =
12 way communication

FIGURE 13-1
Adding children complicates communication

ization questions, Rossi goes on to say that "significant residues of greater maternal than paternal attachment may then persist into later stages of the parent-child relationship."

Personality theories of socialization can also be used to account for traditionalization. In particular, early sex role socialization offers an explanation. Such socialization, usually modeled upon one's parents, is deeply ingrained. Because our society provides little or no formal education for parenthood, we tend to act out these parenting models when we have our own children. As young people among our peers and early in marriage we may be egalitarian in philosophy, but when children arrive, we fall into behavior patterns to which we were early socialized, and these, in most cases, tend to be traditional.

Sociological explanations of traditionalization examine the social constraints placed on parents due to the nature of the human infant. The human infant is born in the most dependent state of any animal. A human baby is so dependent that without continuous care from an adult, it will not survive. The infant's demands are also nonnegotiable: it cannot be told to "wait until tomorrow." Thus, during the early life of the child, continual adult supervision is essential. This demand clashes with the social realities. As we saw in Chapter 9 (p. 312), economic reality for most couples is that the man can earn more money. The coming of a child increases the economic burden on the family. If the husband can earn more than the wife, who should go out to work and who should stay home to care for the child? The answer is obvious.

If the mother breastfeeds and the society frowns on breastfeeding in public, social pressure keeps her at home with her infant. If workplaces do not have infant-care facilities, as most do not, how can a mother go to work? If she does, much of what she earns is absorbed by the costs of outside child care (see p. 319).

The infant's need for continuous adult care also means that when one partner "wins" (is free to pursue his or her own interests outside parenting), the other must "lose" (forgo his or her interests for the sake of the baby). This constant time demand by the young child causes much of the conflict between parents. As Ralph and Maureen LaRossa state: "It is this basic pattern—child dependency resulting in continuous need for care—which means scarcity of time, which leads to conflicts of interest and often conflict behavior that cuts across the experiences of all couples in our sample" (1981, 47). This loss of free time is the aspect of parenthood that bothers new parents the most.

WHAT DO YOU THINK?

1. Have you ever caused trouble between your parents?
2. What could your parents have done to avoid the trouble you caused?
3. Overall, do you think that having children improved your parents' marriage?
4. Do you think having children harmed your parents' marriage? How?
5. Assuming that you have children, what do you think are some of the ways that they might positively influence your relationship with your spouse? Negatively influence your relationship?

Colleen: I do still have some time to myself, for example, when she (the baby) is taking her nap. But it isn't really totally free time for me to use any way I wish. I'm still "on call." Bob tries to give me free time by staying home with her and letting me go out. But if he has been at work all day, he also needs some free time so it is hard for him too.

THE FATHER'S ROLE IN PARENTING

Colleen touches on a basic conflict between most new fathers and mothers. How much do they share the parenting duties? The movement toward traditionalization in new parents' relations means that the ideal of sharing (if it was an ideal before birth) is slowly lost. If the new mother stops work and remains home to parent, the father assumes few of the childrearing duties once the "baby honeymoon" passes. Mothers claim that the period of help given by the father when the new baby comes home ends quickly (usually within a few months).

Studies have found that when the mother goes back to work after the birth, her employment has a negligible impact on the husband's housework and child-care responsibilities (Berk-Fenstermaker 1985; Barnett and Baruch 1983; Pleck and Rustad 1980; Blumstein and Schwartz 1983; Robinson 1988). Most fathers, even those who share childrearing obligations, fail to appreciate the everyday life of a mother with small children. They help, but as an appreciated helper who never really assumes full responsibility. In a sense mothers feel more trapped than fathers because they have no one to hand their job to, whereas fathers do—mother. Robinson (1977; 1988) found that housewives spend seven times as much time as employed men in child-care activities, and employed mothers spend twice as much. Even these statistics are misleading because 50 percent of men's care activities involve play with the child.

Many fathers indicate that their work in providing economic support for the family is the most important part of their parenting role. Accordingly, they feel that they need to do little else with the children, especially if their wives are not working.

Jean and Jim have two children, a boy age ten and a girl age eight. Jim believes that because he is at work all day, it is Jean's duty to keep the children "out of his hair" when he gets home so that he can relax and recuperate. Jean resents his attitude, believing that she, too, works all day in their home. She has also had full responsibility for the children after school. She has asked Jim to watch the children occasionally on Saturday or Sunday so that she may have a day off, but he thinks weekends should be a family time.

The successful, happy father must accept the reality of having a child and being a father. Even though he loses personal and economic freedom and some of his wife's attention, he must feel that the gains of fatherhood offset such loses. The new father must also alter his role in his extended family. He moves from being primarily a son to being a father.

Even though the American father has not shared equally in the parenting role, recent social changes indicate that he may be participating more in the future. The historical characterization of the harsh, austere, disciplinarian father is being replaced by a more humanistic, affectionate, caring father. Liberation of the woman's role also works to liberate the father's traditional role, freeing him to be more loving than he has been in the past. Paternal participation in childbirth is now more and more encouraged (Chapter 12). Fathers who participate in childbirth tend to hold and rock their infants more. The experience seems to lead to earlier bonding between a father and his newborn. As more women move into careers, more men will have to share a larger portion of the parenting role. A few men are experimenting with filling the home and parent role that used to be limited to their wives while their wives move out into the work world. Although these examples are limited, they are indicative of a trend to expand the father's role to include more parenting (Ricks 1985). Most experts agree that this would be rewarding for all concerned.

Fathering is drastically reduced when families break up. In most cases (90 percent) children go with their mother, and their father's contact with them is greatly reduced. Many former husbands are just as happy to escape their parental duties. Those who wish to maintain their father role are often defeated by the logistics of spending enough time with the children to remain effective parents. Contact with the children usually means contact with the former wife, which may be painful. The father's living situation is often not conducive to having the children stay with him. New commitments limit his time. In most cases even when the father desires to retain his role with the children, studies indicate that his contact with the children declines rapidly.

For a few fathers the breakup of the marriage means coming to know their children better. When divorced fathers have the children, they are prepared in advance and devote time to them, which they might not have done when the family was intact. More fathers (although a very small percentage) are also obtaining custody of their children, and for them parenting becomes a central responsibility. About 11 percent of families are single-parent, male-headed families. (For further reading on the father's role in child development, see Hanson and Bozett 1987.)

PARENTAL EFFECTIVENESS

Most people take on the job of parenthood assuming they will be successful: "Of course, we can be good parents." Yet raising children is an extremely demanding job. Certainly, it is time-consuming, lasting for twenty years or more. What qualifications do expectant parents have? They all have parents, and all have been children. But, as we know from our own experience as children, all parents fail in their job to some degree. Some failure, especially in the eyes of one's children, seems to be an integral part of parenting.

> There is no question but that your parents failed you as parents. All parents fail their children, and yours are no exception. No parent is ever adequate for the job of being a parent, and there is no way not to fail at it. No parent ever has enough love, or wisdom, or maturity, or whatever. No parent ever totally succeeds. (Close 1968)

Of course, much advice flows to new parents from grandparents, doctors, clergy, popular magazines, and child experts, all of whom know best how to rear children. Benjamin Spock, known to millions of parents for his advice about childrearing (*Baby and Child Care* has sold more copies than any other book except the Bible), has observed:

> A great many of our efforts as professionals to help parents have instead complicated the life of parents—especially conscientious and highly sensitive parents. It has made them somewhat timid with their children—hesitant to be firm. They are a little scared of their children because they feel as parents they are being judged by their neighbors, relatives, and the world on how well they succeed. They are scared of doing the wrong thing. (Spock 1980).

And, of course, a great deal of advice comes from the children themselves who are as yet unblessed with their own children. What fifteen-year-old doesn't know exactly how bad his or her parents are and how to be the perfect parent?

The problem with all this advice is that there is little agreement about the best way to rear children. In a sense children come to live with their parents; their parents do not go to live with them. Parents need not think they must relinquish their lives completely in favor of the child's development. Parental growth and development go hand in hand with child growth and development.

Good parents love their children but are also honest enough to know that there will be days when they are angry, unfair, and in other ways terrible with them. Secure children will survive such episodes.

There is no single correct way to rear children. If children are wanted, respected, and appreciated, they will be secure. If they are secure, they usually will also be flexible and resilient. What is important is that the parents are honest and true to themselves. Small children are very empathetic; that is, they have the ability to feel as another is feeling. They respond to their parents; feelings as well as to their actions, although the children may not be cognitively advanced enough to understand the reasons why their parents are acting or feeling as they do. Parents who are naturally authoritarian will fail in coping with their children if they attempt to act permissively simply because they read that permissiveness is a beneficial way of interacting with children. The children will feel the tension in their parents and will respond to that rather than to the parents' overt actions. Parents who attempt to be something other than what they are—no matter how theoretically beneficial the results are supposed to be—will generally fail. Thus parental sincerity is one of the necessary ingredients of successful childrearing. By and large, the pervasive emotional tone used by the parents affects the children's subsequent development more than either the particular techniques of childrearing (e.g., permissiveness, restric-

WHAT DO YOU THINK?

1. Do you want children at some time in the future? Why or why not?
2. If you want to have children, how many do you want? Why?
3. In what ways do you think your parents were successful in their parenting? In what ways were they unsuccessful?
4. How would you change the ways in which your parents raised you? Why?

tiveness, punishment, or reward) or the cohesiveness of the marital unit (whether it is stable or broken by divorce or death).

In general, studies have found that the *authoritative parenting style* relates most closely to producing competent children. This style emphasizes the development of autonomy and independence in children with reasonable parental limits. Parents who focus on cues given by the child as to his or her needs, have extensive knowledge about child development and rearing, consciously consider child-focused goals and develop plans of action to reach these goals, and provide opportunities for the child to be self-directing in some situations seem to do the best job rearing competent children (Cooke 1991, 11). Remember that the end result of good parenting is a healthy, happy, successful adult.

Overconcern and overprotection can cause problems for children. Children need increasing degrees of freedom if they are to grow into independent adults. This means that they must have freedom to fail as well as to succeed. They need to experience the consequences of their actions, unless the consequences are dangerous to their well-being. Consequences teach children how to judge behavior. Parents who always shield children from failure are doing them a disservice. The children will not be able to modify their behavior to make it more successful because they will be ignorant of the results.

Overprotection can sometimes even be dangerous. For example, children taken to beach resorts need to develop water skills as soon as possible. Knowledge and skill are the best protection against accidents. Parents who take their children to the beach and then scream hysterically at them the moment they move toward the water are doing only one thing—teaching them to fear the water. Any lifeguard knows that fear of the water may lead to panic if there is trouble and that panic is the swimmer's worst enemy. Certainly, parents need to be aware of small children's activities near water. But the parents should show their concern by helping the children learn about the river, lake, or ocean and by showing them how to have fun in the water and gain confidence in their abilities rather than by making them fearful. The best protection for children at a beach is early swimming lessons, proper information about water safety, and then unobtrusive watchfulness to make sure they are safe.

It is also important to remember that the family and the child are not isolated from the broader society. Parents are the first to be blamed for their children's faults. Yet the influences on the child from sources outside the family become increasingly powerful as the child grows older. School, peers, friends, and the mass media all exert influence on both parents and children. For example, parents will find it difficult to enforce a rule against alcohol use when their teenager's friends are using it and the media run numerous advertisements depicting beautiful young people having great fun drinking beer. But if their child has alcohol problems, the parents are often blamed, seldom the peers or the media.

Parents have the most difficult task in the world—to rear happy, healthy children to be competent, successful adults—and they must do this in an incredibly complex environment. The vast majority of parents love their children and do the best job they can. Our society puts the tremendous responsibility of childrearing almost entirely on the parents, even though parents in reality are only one among many influences on the development of children. Our economic system, schools, religious organizations, mass media, and many other

Because television plays so large a role in American family life, controversy about its effects, especially on children, has been almost continuous since television first entered the home. In February 1992 the Children's Television Act of 1990, the first federal law to regulate children's programming, went into effect. Among other things the law limits the duration of advertising in children's programming to not more than 10.5 minutes per hour on weekends and not more than 12 minutes on weekdays. In addition, the networks must broadcast some specific programs designed to serve the educational and information needs of children. The statute describes examples of acceptable programming for children.

GOOD!

In most American homes, three parents mind the child: the father, the mother, and television. Indeed, with the increasing incidence of single-parent (especially female-headed) families, television may have replaced father for a good many children. Certainly, the generations born in the 1960s and later are the product of the television age.

For some children television has become a surrogate parent. The child can be taught and entertained by television as well as by the parent. At times television can free the parent from child-care responsibilities for short periods of time, allowing the parent time for self-improvement and revitalization.

Daniel Anderson and Patricia Collins (1989) reviewed the research literature from the U.S. Department of Education and reached the following conclusions:

■ Contrary to popular assertions, children are cognitively active during television viewing and attempt to form a coherent, connected understanding of the program.
■ There is no evidence that children are generally overstimulated by television.
■ Television generally displaces movie attendance, radio listening, comic book reading, and participation in organized sports rather than general reading.
■ There is no evidence that homework done during television viewing is of lower quality than homework done in silence.

■ There is little evidence that television viewing reduces children's attention span, and some evidence indicates it may actually increase their ability to focus attention.
■ Some evidence suggests that television viewing reduces reading achievement but, if so, this effect occurs during the early elementary school years and is probably temporary.

Anderson and Collins suggest that if a problem, exists, it is not television itself but the content offered by television programming.

Jib Fowles (1992) argues forcefully that television actually acts as a mental release for people and is thus therapeutic. He feels that, on balance, children do learn from television and are not as susceptible to commercials aimed at them as adults may believe. He thinks television violence actually encourages the release of vicarious aggression, thus reducing the need for overt aggressive behavior.

Television is a wondrous medium that allows the viewer to walk on the moon with the astronauts, enjoy the wild animals via a safari though the African Serengeti Plain, watch the birth of a baby, and visit the seven wonders of the world. Perhaps we are fortunate that television programming is often inferior and second rate. If it were always as good as it could be, viewers would never turn the television off.

To blame television for society's ills is like blaming a cookbook for a poorly prepared meal. Because television viewing has a strong impact on viewers, especially children, it is important for parents to consider its place in their home. How can it be used to promote prosocial rather than antisocial behavior? How can it improve children's cognitive development rather than retarding it? A few concerned parents who object to the negative influence of television opt to have no television. Yet as their children grow and begin to visit friends, this strategy can backfire because the children end up watching at friends' houses, thus limiting parental control over television input. Inasmuch as 95 percent of American homes contain television, the best course of action for parents is to set up supervised viewing for their children. First, parents will need to consider the role of television in their own lives. For instance, if a mother has the television turned on all day for company while she is alone at home or the father watches sports all weekend, they will need to decide whether they want to continue this practice.

Once parents determine their preferences about television's role in their own lives, they will need to set appropriate ground rules for their children. These rules should include:

1. How much time per day and per week the children may devote to television.
2. The actual time of the day or evening that television may be watched.
3. The kinds of programs that may be watched.
4. The amount of adult attention and discussion to be given during and after television viewing (such parental interaction with the child has been found to mitigate the most negative effects of television).
5. Whether television will be used as a reward to influence other kinds of behavior besides television viewing.

Simply to dismiss television as harmful to children is to miss out on using one of the most powerful modern inventions for the good of children. The potential for good in television is every bit as large if not larger than its potential for harm.

BAD!

By age sixteen most children have spent more time watching television than going to school (Singer 1983). A Nielson survey in 1984 found that preschool children watched television on the average of twenty-seven hours and nine minutes each week or an average of three hours and forty minutes per day (re:act 1984). A survey of over 21,000 public school children revealed that 43.6 percent had a television set in their bedrooms (O'Hara 1989, B-1).

What effect does all of this television viewing have on children? Most researchers feel that the effects are negative, yet they have been hard-pressed to document their feelings. Essentially, they cite three major problems: the effect of commercials, the content of pro-

grams, especially violence, and the time spent in passive observation.

Small children accept commercial messages uncritically because their thinking processes are not advanced enough to make judgments about truth and fantasy. Because young children believe everything they see in commercials, they are easily manipulated into wanting everything they see. The parents are therefore placed in the position of resisting the constant demands of their children or succumbing and buying everything from expensive toys that soon become boring or broken to sugared cereals and drinks that promote tooth decay (Berger 1986, 334).

The content of television programs is even more controversial. As early as 1952, congressional hearings investigated the amount of violence on television. Over the years a great deal of research has been conducted on the violence questions, yet the answers remain somewhat clouded. For instance, research on three- and four-year-olds attending nursery school (Singer and Sherrod 1979; Singer and Singer 1981) correlated their imaginativeness, emotionality, aggression, cooperation, interaction, and mood with their parents' reports of television watching. A strong relationship was found between frequent physical aggression and frequent viewing of all but educational children's programs. Viewing of the latter programs, on the other hand, was found to be related to prosocial behavior and to using mature language in school. This example reflects the mixed findings about television viewing that often emerge from the research. Nevertheless, most researchers now conclude that there is at least a moderate causal relationship between television violence and later aggressive behavior (Pearle 1984). Certainly, all researchers agree that television is indeed an important influence on children and is as influential as parents themselves (Rubinstein 1983).

Violence aside, the content of television programming allows children access to all of the social and human problems from which they were shielded to some extent in the past. Postman (1982) suggests that television is doing away with childhood. What makes one group (adults) different from another group (children) is the knowledge they possess. When knowledge was gained through the written word, a child had to learn to read before newspaper stories of violence or corruption could be understood. Today, via pictures and words, children can understand immediately. The constant reporting of all of the negative happenings in the world leads to skepticism about the worth of adult society. Children who view a great deal of television are more likely to view the world as a mean and scary place. To what extent does viewing so much that is negative about the world undermine a child's belief in adult rationality, in the possibility of an ordered world, in a hopeful future? Without such hopes and beliefs, a person is unlikely to work to better the human condition.

Also, the way in which television content is presented presents difficulties for the child. Everything is handled quickly. For example, ten books and hundreds of research papers may have been written about AIDS, but when television does an "in-depth" study of the AIDS epidemic, it lasts forty-five seconds on each for four different nights. Thus a major social problem is condensed into three minutes interspersed among commercials. How important can the problem be? Some suggest that watching television is like attending a party populated by people you don't know. Every few seconds you are introduced to a new person as you move through the room. The general effect is one of excite-

ment, but in the end it is hard to remember the names of the guests or what they said. Whether you do or not is of no importance in any case. Tomorrow there will be another party. Why bother to concentrate on one person or one topic when by tomorrow all new people and topics will appear? The classroom teacher who must ask pupils to concentrate in order to learn is hard put to compete against the excitement and constant change of the television set. Many teachers report that holding students' attention has become their major classroom problem.

Hours of passive observation deprive the child of social interaction as well as of the physical activity necessary to grow in a healthful manner. Many children now enter school without any social skills because they have had so little social interaction. Many children also appear in poor physical condition, apparently because they have little active play time. Some families who voluntarily gave up television viewing reported that their children played and read more, that siblings fought less, that family activities became more common, and that mealtimes were longer (Chira 1984).

Because television will not disappear from family life, it is important that parents and family professionals work together to reduce the negative impact that television may have on children (Fabes et al 1989).

Calvin and Hobbes

by Bill Watterson

institutions and pressure groups impinge on the child's world. Often these influences are positive and help the parent in the task of rearing and socializing children. Unfortunately, these influences can sometimes be negative, countering the direction parents wish their children to take.

Parenting then is not something done only by parents. How parenting is accomplished and the results of the parenting are influenced both by the family and the larger society. Parents must pay attention to the society as well as to their children. To expect children to become adults reflecting only the values and behaviors of their immediate family is unrealistic. The effective parent must also be a concerned citizen and work to better the society at large.

STIMULATION AND DEVELOPMENT

Belsky, Learner, and Spanier (1984, 41–48) identify several key dimensions of mothering: physical contact, attentiveness, verbal stimulation, material stimulation, responsive care, and some restrictiveness. Note that all of these involve stimulation of the child.

Stimulation is necessary for the development of basic behavioral capacities. Early deprivation of stimulation generally leads to slower learning later in life. Early stimulation, on the other hand, enhances development and later learning. For example, various research evidence suggests that given the present state of our knowledge, the best physical environment in which to rear children is one that gives them experience with a variety of physical objects that they can manipulate and control freely with minimal restriction. Experiences will give children an opportunity to develop basic motor skills that they can later apply to more specific learning situations. However, overstimulation such as is found in some accelerated learning programs may have negative effects (Berger 1986, 192–195).

The emphasis on early childhood education and intervention, beginning with the Head Start program in the early 1960s, reflects recognition of the importance of early environmental stimulation for children. Although some controversy exists over the effects of Head Start experiences and the contribution they make to lasting changes in the child, there is little doubt that the preschool years are important to the cognitive development of the child.

Some stress in a child's life is beneficial to development of stress tolerance. This doesn't mean that parents should deliberately introduce stress into their children's lives, but rather that parents may relax and be less concerned if their children are placed in a stressful situation. Children who are secure in the love and warmth of their parents will be able to survive and, in fact, grow in the face of stress. For example, moving away from a neighborhood, from familiar places and friends, can be upsetting. Yet studies of long-distance moves find they have little negative effect on children. The children seem to make friends easily, the school change is not difficult, and any disturbance in their behavior dissipates quickly (Barrett and Noble 1973).

Belsky, Learner, and Spanier (1984) concluded from their review of infant stimulation research that parents who promote optimal cognitive development

TABLE 13-1
PERCENTAGE OF PARENTS USING VARIOUS DISCIPLINARY METHODS

METHOD	PERCENTAGE
Yelling at or scolding children	52
Spanking children	50
Making children stay in their rooms	38
Not allowing children to play	32
Not letting children watch television	25
Making children go to bed	23
Threatening children	15
Giving children extra chores	12
Taking away an allowance	9

Source: Adapted from General Mills, 1977.

during infancy function effectively as *sources of stimulation* by speaking to and playing with the infant. Parents also function as *mediators or filters of stimulation* by directing the infant's attention to objects and events in the child's world and by restricting the toddler from engaging in dangerous activities. In other words, successful parents moderate and control the amount of stimulation and stress experienced by their infants.

CHILDREARING, DISCIPLINE, AND CONTROL

Many parents accomplish control of their children in a haphazard manner. If the parents liked their own parents, they tend to copy their childrearing methods. If the parents disliked their own parents' methods, they tend to do the opposite. In either case the parents' own experiences as children influence how they themselves parent. The General Mills American Family Report indicates that most parents overwhelmingly use negative techniques to control their children. Table 13-1 shows the percentage of parents reporting use of various disciplinary methods.

Unfortunately, negative control methods tend to have negative side effects because they serve as model behaviors. A child who is screamed at tends to become a child who screams to get his or her way. A child who is treated negatively tends to become a negative child. A child who is punished violently tends to learn that violence is the way to change another's behavior. Hostility, low self-esteem, and feelings of inferiority and insecurity are frequent reactions of children who are reared by basically negative methods.

Rather than having only a few control techniques and using them automatically, parents must develop a variety of well-understood childrearing methods. Each child and each situation will be unique, and parents should try to react in accordance with the specific situation. First, the parent should try to understand the child and the problem, then to identify what changes are necessary, and finally to accomplish the changes in the best possible manner. Thus childrearing becomes a rational, thoughtful, directive process rather than an irrational, reactive process.

In general, children can be controlled by using many different methods that vary in intensity from mild to strong. Many parents use a strong method such as punishment when, in fact, a mild method such as distraction might have worked equally well. By first trying milder methods, many of the negative side effects of punishment can be eliminated or at least reduced. Table 13-2 outlines a continuum of mild to strong methods. One must consider the age of the child when using this table. Two-year-olds will not understand item 3c, an appeal to their sense of fair play, because they are too young to grasp this ethical concept.

Directing a child's behavior ahead of time is preferable to, and much easier than, being unprepared and surprised by a child's behavior and then trying to react properly. For example, if you give a child a difficult task, stay close (1b, proximity control) so you can offer help if it is needed (2a).

Firm routines (2c) reduce conflict and the number of overt decisions necessary. For example, an orderly routine at bedtime accomplishes tooth brushing, elimination, getting into pajamas, story reading, and lights off. In a sense

TABLE 13-2

MILD-TO-STRONG CHILD CONTROL METHODS

1. Supporting the child's self-control
   a. Signal interference (catch the child's eye, frown, say something)
   b. Proximity control (get physically close to the child)
   c. Planned ignoring (children often do "bad" things to get attention, and if they don't get it, they will cease the behavior because they are not getting what they want)
   d. Painless removal (remove the child from the problem source)

2. Situational assistance
   a. Giving help
   b. Distraction or restructuring a situation
   c. Support of firm routines
   d. Restraint
   e. Getting set in advance

3. Reality and ethical appraisals
   a. Showing consequences to behaviors
   b. Marginal use of interpretation
   c. Appealing to sense of reason and fair play (not useful until child is intellectually able to understand such concepts)

4. Reward and contracting
   a. Rewards (payoffs) should be immediate.
   b. Initial contracts should call for and reward small pieces of behavior (a reward for picking up toys rather than a reward for keeping room clean for a week).
   c. Reward performance after it occurs.
   d. Contract must be fair to all parties.
   e. Terms of contract must be clear and understood.
   f. Contract must be honest.
   g. Contract should be positive.
   h. Contract must be used consistently.
   i. Contract must have a method of change to cope with failures.

5. Punishment: See Inset 13-2.

I HATED THE WAY I TURNED OUT.

SO EVERYTHING MY MOTHER DID WITH ME I HAVE TRIED TO DO THE OPPOSITE WITH MY JENNIFER.

MOTHER WAS POSSESSIVE. I ENCOURAGED INDEPENDENCE.

MOTHER WAS MANIPULATIVE. I HAVE BEEN DIRECT.

MOTHER WAS SECRETIVE. I HAVE BEEN OPEN.

MOTHER WAS EVASIVE. I HAVE BEEN DECISIVE.

NOW MY WORK IS DONE. JENNIFER IS GROWN.

THE EXACT IMAGE OF MOTHER.

9-8 © 1974 JULES FEIFFER

Whether one agrees with the use of punishment as a means of teaching children, studies of parental control indicate that it is still a major method used by most parents. Unfortunately, punishment does not always work, and it causes anger and hostility.

If punishment is used, the parent needs to understand a few simple principles that help maximize its usefulness and minimize the negative side effects. If mild punishment is to be effective, an alternative behavior should be open to the child. For example, if a child is punished for turning on the television rather than dressing for school, the punishment will work better if the child knows when he or she can watch television. In this case the child knows that there is another way to do what he or she wants

that will not result in punishment. In addition, punishment works best if the child is not highly motivated. For example, a child eats just before dinner. If the child missed lunch, chances are she or he is very hungry (highly motivated), and punishment will probably not be very effective in keeping the child from eating. If there are alternatives and if the child is not highly motivated, following the guidelines based on psychological learning theory set forth here will help achieve desired goals while keeping punishment to a minimum.

1. Consider the individual child and the potential negative side effects. *Example:* Randy reacts strongly to punishment, and the reaction lasts for a considerable length of time. He is better con-

trolled by reward or distraction. If punishment is used, it is mild. Michelle is not at all sensitive to punishment. When she is punished, her behavior changes, and there are no lasting side effects.

2. Punish as soon after the act as possible. *Example:* Children are bright, but they have difficulty associating an act with punishment that comes many hours after the act. The mother who at 10 A.M. tells the child to "Just wait until your father comes home, you will get it," does little more than turn father into an ogre. By the time the father arrives home, little change of behavior will be derived from punishment.

3. If possible, let the punishment flow from the act. *Example:* If a child is constantly warned when he reaches toward a hot stove, behav-

the child is on automatic pilot, and little conflict arises once the routine is established. Such routines are only helpful in certain areas of life and probably work best with the preschool and early school child. Distraction (2b) is helpful with small children; they usually have short attention spans and are easily shifted from one focus to another. Saying "no" to a child immediately creates a confrontation: "Don't touch the expensive art book." In contrast, presenting an alternative and saying "do this" does not necessarily create such a confrontation: saying "Why don't you color with these crayons?" while handing them to the child. Parents in strong families emphasize positive behaviors, attitudes, and moral character and avoid overemphasis on minor details.

THE GROWING CHILD IN THE FAMILY

The essence of children is growing, changing, maturing, and becoming rather than sameness. Parents themselves must constantly change in their relationship

ior change takes time. The child who touches the hot stove is immediately punished by his own action, understands what the word *hot* means, and has learned in one trial. Obviously, one cannot always set up a situation where punishment flows from the act, but when possible it is more efficient.

4. Be sure that children understand what their alternatives are. *Example:* Many young children really do not understand exactly what they have done and what new behavior is desired. Mary was punished when her mother found her at the cookie jar before dinner. Later Mary found some cookies on the counter and was again punished. Mary did not understand that she was being punished for eating cookies the first time. She thought her mother did not want her around the cookie jar

for fear she might break it. Also, she did not understand that she could have cookies after dinner.

5. Keep the punishment mild and devoid of emotion. *Example:* Jimmy's mother lost her temper and spanked him. By losing her own temper, she increased the emotional atmosphere, causing Jimmy to become even more upset. She also modeled overt anger.

6. Try to punish the act, not the child. *Example:* "You are a bad boy. We don't love you when you are bad." This is a threatening and upsetting statement to a child and really is unnecessary. Generally, it is the particular act that is bad rather than the child. When the child changes the behavior, there is no longer a need for punishment, and the child's relationship should immediately return to normal.

When punishment is directed only at the act, the child will not continue to be punished by thinking he or she as an individual is bad and unworthy of love ("I don't like your behavior so please change it. I like you, however.").

WHAT DO YOU THINK?

1. What were the major methods of control used by your parents when you were a child?
2. How did you react to these methods as a child?
3. What do you think of them as an adult? Did they work? Why or why not?
4. Which methods would you use with your children? Why?
5. What will you do if you and your spouse disagree on control methods?

---

to the growing child. Just about the time they have adapted and learned to cope with a totally dependent child, they will need to change and learn to deal with a suddenly mobile, yet still irresponsible two-year-old. Then come the school years, when the increasing influence of peers signals declining parental influence. Puberty and adolescence are the launching stage when once small, dependent children go into the world on their own ultimately to establish new families and repeat the cycle. As the child grows and changes, the family also changes. For example, the mother usually remains close to the child during its infancy. During elementary school the parents often become chauffeurs, taking the child to a friend's home, music lessons, after-school sports, and so on. Thus change and growth in the child mean parental and family change.

One way of viewing these changes is to see them as a series of social and developmental situations involving encounters with the environment. These situations involve normal "problems" children must "solve" if they are to function fully. This section will focus on psychosocial stages rather than biological developmental stages, though the two are interrelated.

Erik Erikson (1963) identifies eight psychosocial developmental stages, each with important tasks, that describe the human life cycle from infancy through

The Growing Child in the Family

STAGES

Stages								
1 Infancy Oral-sensory 1st year	Trust vs. Mistrust (mothering, feeding)							
2 Toddler Muscular-anal 2 to 3 years		Autonomy vs. Shame, Doubt (toilet training, self-control)						
3 Early Child Locomotor-genital 4 to 5 years			Industry vs. Inferiority (working together, school)					
4 School Age Latency 6 to 11 years				Initiative vs. Guilt (increased freedom and sexual identity				
5 Puberty and Adolescence 12 to 18 years					Identity vs. Role-Diffusion (adult role)			
6 Young Adulthood						Intimacy vs. Isolation (love and marriage)		
7 Adulthood, Middle Age							Generatvity vs. Self-Absorption (broadening concerns beyond self)	
8 Maturity Old Age								Integrity vs. Despair

FIGURE 13-2
Erikson's eight developmental stages

old age (Figure 13-2). Erikson's stages are theoretical, of course, and there is some controversy over the exact nature of developmental stages. Nevertheless, the idea of stages is useful in helping parents understand the changing natures of the growing child and themselves. In each of these stages, children must establish new orientations to themselves and their environment, especially their social environment. Each stage requires a new level of social interaction and can shape the personality in either negative or positive ways. For example, if children cope successfully with the problems and stress in a given stage, they gain additional strengths to become fully functioning. On the other hand, if children cannot cope with the problems of a particular stage, they will, in effect, invest continuing energy in this stage, becoming fixated to some extent or arrested in development. For example, an adult who always handles frustration by throwing a temper tantrum has failed to move out of the early child-hood stage when temper tantrums were the only manner of handling frustra-tion. Such an individual is not coping successfully with the stress and problems of adult life.

Notice in Figure 13-2 that each stage can be carried down the chart into adulthood. For example, trust versus mistrust influences all succeeding stages. A person who successfully gains basic trust is better prepared to cope with the ensuing developmental stages. The reverse is also true. A mistrusting individual will have more trouble coping with ensuing stages than a trusting person. Let's now take a closer look at the first six stages.

INFANCY: THE ORAL-SENSORY STAGE— TRUST VERSUS MISTRUST (FIRST YEAR)

Human beings undergo a longer period of dependence than any other species. In the first years, children are completely dependent on parents or other adults for survival and are unable to contribute to the family because their responses to the environment are quite limited. Thus their development of trust depends on the quality of care they receive from their parents or the adults who care for them. The prolonged period of dependence makes the child more amenable to socialization (learning the ways of the society). Sometimes, however, a child will be too strongly or wrongly socialized in the early stages and thus will suffer from needless inhibitions as an adult. Such inhibitions are easily recognized by modern youth as *hang-ups*.

The first year, when the infant must have total care to survive, is a difficult adjustment for many new parents because they have previously enjoyed rela-tively great personal freedom as well as time to devote to one another. Over-night a newcomer usurps that freedom and has first call on their time. Not only does the infant demand personal time and attention, but many other considerations also arise. Going to a movie now entails the additional time and cost involved in finding and paying a baby-sitter. Taking a Sunday drive means taking along special food, diapers, car seat, and so forth. But for the couple who really want children, the challenge and fun of watching a new human grow and learn can offset many of the problems entailed in the new parental roles.

During this first year, the husband must adjust to sharing his wife's love and attention. This can be difficult for a husband who is accustomed to being the center of "his" wife's life. Now suddenly the baby takes priority. As we men-tioned earlier, it is not uncommon for a new father to feel some resentment and jealousy over this change in his position. Although most couples are fi-nancially strained at this time in their marriage, it is important for them to arrange times to be by themselves and to remember to pay attention to their own relationship. In the past this was easier to do because relatives who could watch the infant were often close by. Today, spending time together usually means paying someone to take care of the child. Such money is well spent if it gives the couple an opportunity to improve their own relationship. Their relationship is the primary one, and if it is good, the chances are greater that the parents-children relationship will be good also.

The Growing Child in the Family

Children learn trust through living in a trusting environment. This means that their needs are satisfied on a regular basis and that interactions with the environment are positive, stable, and satisfying. Parents who have a good relationship are better able to supply this kind of environment.

This is called the *oral-sensory* stage because eating and the infant's mouth and senses are its major means of knowing the world at this time.

TODDLER: THE MUSCULAR-ANAL STAGE— AUTONOMY VERSUS SHAME AND DOUBT (TWO TO THREE YEARS OF AGE)

As children develop motor and mental capacities, opportunities to explore and manipulate the environment increase. From successful exploration and manipulation emerges a sense of autonomy and self-control. If the child is unsuccessful or made to feel unsuccessful by too-high parental expectations, feelings of shame and doubt may arise. This is a time of great learning. Children learn to walk, talk, feed and dress themselves, say "no," and so forth. If parents thought the infant demanding, they learn what "demanding" really can be with their two- and three-year-olds. There never seems to be a minute's peace. The relationship between the parents can suffer during this time because of the fatigue and frustration engendered by the child's insatiable demands. On the other hand, it is exciting to watch the child's skills rapidly developing. First steps, first words, and curiosity all make this period one of quick change for child and parent alike.

During this stage parents should try to create a stimulating environment for the child. As we mentioned earlier, stimulation appears to enhance learning skills. Alphabet books, creative toys that are strong enough to withstand the rough treatment given by most two- and three-year-olds, picture books, and an endless answering of questions all help stimulate the child. Toilet training, which also occurs during this period, needs to be approached positively and with humor if it is to be easily accomplished. The achievement of toilet training is a great relief to parents since the messy job of diaper changing and cleaning is over.

The name of this stage denotes the increasing activity of the child and the toilet-training tasks.

EARLY CHILDHOOD: THE LOCOMOTOR-GENITAL STAGE—INITIATIVE VERSUS GUILT (FOUR TO FIVE YEARS OF AGE)

During early childhood, children become increasingly capable of self-initiated activities. This expansion of the children's capabilities is a source of pride for the parents and exciting to see. With each passing month, the children seem to be more mature, have more personality, and become more fun to interact with. As their capabilities and interests expand, so must the parents'. The extent of children's energy is a constant source of amazement and bewilder-

ment to often-tired parents. However, school is just around the corner and with it comes a little free time. Children who do not increase their capabilities, perhaps because of accident or illness, may feel guilty and inadequate about their chances of success in school.

Locomotor indicates that the child is now very active in the environment; *genital* refers to interest in and exploration of the sex organs.

SCHOOL AGE: THE LATENCY STAGE— INDUSTRY VERSUS INFERIORITY (SIX TO ELEVEN YEARS OF AGE)

At last the children are in school, and for a few hours a day the house is peaceful. Now the children's peers begin to play a more active role in the family's life. Relationships broaden considerably as parents also become PTA members, den mothers, or Little League coaches. This stage is often a period of relative family tranquillity as far as the child is concerned.

The children's increasing independence also affects the parents. They find that what other parents allow their children to do becomes an important influence on their own children. "Mom, everyone else can do this, why can't I?" becomes a constant complaint of children trying to get their own way.

The children have new ideas, a new vocabulary, and broader desires, all of which can conflict with parental values. Reports about the children's behavior may also come from other parents, teachers, and authorities. How the children are doing at school becomes a source of concern.

The Growing Child in the Family

Children become increasingly expensive as they grow. They eat more, their clothes cost more, and they need more money for school and leisure activities. As the latter expand, many parents find themselves juggling schedules to meet the demands of after-school sports, PTA meetings, Little League, and music lessons.

Yet for most families the elementary school years go smoothly. Children become more interesting, more individual, and increasingly independent. More important for the parents is their own increased freedom because the children are now away from home for part of the day.

During this time it is especially important for parents to work together in childrearing. Children are aware and insightful and can play their parents off against each another to achieve their ends unless the parents coordinate. Children can also cause conflict between their parents, especially if the parents differ widely in their philosophy of childrearing. Often a well-functioning supportive husband-wife relationship can buffer or inhibit the negative impact of a difficult child. Couples who do not enjoy a supportive relationship may find that fighting about the children is one of the major points of disruption in their relationship (Belsky, Learner, and Spanier 1984, 129).

Latency refers to the general sexual quietness of this stage, although there is more sexual activity than Erikson thought.

THE PUBERTY-ADOLESCENCE STAGE: IDENTITY VERSUS ROLE DIFFUSION (TWELVE TO EIGHTEEN YEARS OF AGE)

The tranquillity of the elementary school years is often shattered by the arrival of puberty. The internal physiological revolution causes children to requestion many earlier adjustments. **Puberty** refers to the biological changes every child, regardless of culture, must pass through to mature sexually. **Adolescence** encompasses puberty as well as the social and cultural conditions that must be met to become an adult. The adolescent period in Western societies tends to be exaggerated and prolonged, with a great deal of ambiguity and marked inconsistencies of role. Adolescents are often confused about proper behavior and what is expected of them. They are not yet adults, but at the same time they are not allowed to remain children. For example, an eighteen-year-old boy may enter the armed services and participate in battle, yet in many states he may not legally drink beer. The fact that prolonged adolescence is a cultural artifact does not lessen the problems of the period.

The problems of puberty and adolescence fall into four main categories:

1. Accepting a new body image and appropriate sexual expression
2. Establishing independence and a sense of personal identity
3. Forming good peer group relations
4. Developing goals and a philosophy of life.

During this stage peer influence becomes stronger than parental influence. What friends say is more important than what parents say. The major problem facing parents now is how to give up their control, how to have enough faith in the child to "let go."

Puberty
Biological changes a child goes through to become an adult capable of reproduction

Adolescence
The general social as well as biological changes a child experiences in becoming an adult

For Better or For Worse®   by Lynn Johnston

Parents, who by now are entering middle age, are also requestioning and reordering their lives (see Chapter 14). They must begin to think about coping with the "empty-nest" period of their lives as their adolescent children grow into young adulthood and leave home to establish their own families. Most research suggests that this is the stage of greatest family stress (Olson 1986).

THE YOUNG ADULTHOOD STAGE: INTIMACY VERSUS ISOLATION

Although some children leave the family in their late teens, many remain longer, especially if they choose to go on to higher education. Seeking a vocation and a mate are the major goals of this period. In the past, success in these two tasks ended children's dependence on the family. Today, however, parents often continue to support their children for several more years of schooling and may sometimes support a beginning family if a child marries during school. This can be a financially strained period for the family. In addition, studies indicate that the presence of unmarried sons and daughters over eighteen in the home can be a strain on their parents' relationship. Both husbands and wives often report that this period when older children are living at home is a dissatisfying time in their marriage (Glick and Lin 1986). Older adult children who return to live with their parents usually do so out of their own needs, not the needs of their parents. Economic worries and problems brought on by divorce are two major reasons adult children return home to live with their parents (Ward, Logan, and Spitze 1992).

More and more young adults are living at home with their parents. Between 1960 and 1990, the proportion of persons aged eighteen to twenty-four who lived in the home of their parents increased from 43 to 53 percent. Of these, 4 percent have children of their own also living in the home. Thirty-one percent of unmarried persons aged 25 to 29 lived in the home of their parents. Thirty-two percent of single men aged twenty-five to thirty-four reside with their parents, while about 20 percent of women in the same age category live at home (U.S. Bureau of the Census May 1991 1, 10; April 1992 1, 10).

The Growing Child in the Family

John is twenty, living at home with his parents, William and Jan. John works and contributes a little toward the food budget. However, his parents find that his living at home strains their relationship. John has a new car and insists that because it is new, it should have a place in the garage. His father often transports clients in the car, and though it is older, he thinks it should be parked inside so it will remain clean. Jan often intercedes in her son's behalf, "Oh, William, it's his first new car, let him use the garage." This angers William, and he sometimes feels as though it's two against one. He also has wanted a den for years and would like to convert John's bedroom into one. When he encourages John to look for his own place, Jan says that he is "just throwing John out." "We should be happy that he wants to be with us." However, Jan does find it difficult when John has his friends over. They take over the living room and television, leaving her and William with little to do but retreat to their bedroom.

Ideally, by the time their children are grown, parents like and love them and take pride in a job well done. Now, after twenty or more years, the marital relationship again concerns just two people, husband and wife. Sometimes parents discover that their relationship has been forfeited because of the urgency of parenthood. In this case they face a period of discovery and rediscovery, of building a new relationship, or of emptiness. Parents must work to maintain their relationship throughout the period of childrearing. If they fail to do this, their relationship may become simply "for the children." When the children leave, there may be no relationship between the husband and wife (see Chapter 14).

BROADER PARENTING

Perhaps the dissatisfaction and decreased marital happiness experienced by some parents result from the American nuclear family where one father and one mother are expected to give a child total parenting: all the care, love, and attention that is necessary for healthy growth. But most societies do not expect one father and one mother to supply 100 percent of a child's needs. Grandmothers and grandfathers, aunts and uncles (blood relatives or not), older siblings, and many others also supply parenting to children.

In many American suburban families, children and their parents (especially children and their mothers) are basically alone together. The parents cannot get away from the small child for a needed rest and participation in adult activities, and the child cannot get away from the parents. The nuclear family is often too isolated from friends and relatives who might occasionally serve as substitute parents.

TRY TO SEE IT MY WAY. I AM
NEARLY TWENTY AND IF I WAS
EVER GOING TO MAKE THE BREAK
NOW WAS THE TIME TO DO IT
IMAGINE HALF MY GIRL FRIENDS
WERE ALREADY SEPARATED FROM
THEIR HUSBANDS AND HERE I WAS
STILL LIVING AT HOME!

SO I TOLD MY
PARENTS I WAS
MOVING OUT

YOU CANT **IMAGINE** THE YELLING
AND SCREAMING MY FATHER SAID.
YOU'RE BREAKING YOUR MOTHER'S
HEART! MY MOTHER SAID
"WHAT WAS MY CRIME? WHAT
WAS MY TERRIBLE CRIME?

AND BEFORE I KNEW IT WE WERE IN
THE MIDDLE OF A BIG ARGUMENT
AND I TOLD THEM THEY BOTH
NEEDED ANALYSIS AND THEY
TOLD ME I HAD A FILTHY MOUTH
AND SUDDENLY I WAS OUT ON
THE STREET WITH MY RAINCOAT
MY SUITCASE AND MY TENNIS
RACKET BUT I HAD NO PLACE
TO MOVE!

SO I LOOKED AROUND DOWNTOWN
AND EVERYTHING WAS TOO EXPEN-
SIVE AND EVENING CAME AND
ALL MY GIRL FRIENDS HAD
RECONCILED WITH THEIR HUSBANDS
SO THERE WAS ABSOLUTELY NO
PLACE I COULD SPEND THE NIGHT

WELL, **FRANKLY** WHAT ON EARTH
COULD I **DO**? I WAITED TILL IT
WAS **WAY** PAST MY PARENTS BED-
TIME THEN I **SNEAKED** BACK
INTO THE HOUSE AND SET THE
ALARM IN MY BEDROOM FOR
SIX THE NEXT MORNING.

THEN I SLEPT ON TOP OF THE
BED SO I WOULDN'T WRINKLE
ANY SHEETS. SNEAKED SOME
BREAKFAST IN THE MORNING
AND GOT OUT BEFORE ANY-
ONE WAS UP

I'VE BEEN
LIVING THAT
WAY FOR
TWO MONTHS
NOW.

EVERY NIGHT AFTER MIDNIGHT
I SNEAK INTO MY BEDROOM
SLEEP ON TOP OF THE BED
TILL SIX THE NEXT MORNING,
HAVE BREAKFAST AND SNEAK
OUT

AND EVERY DAY I CALL UP MY
PARENTS FROM THE DOWNSTAIRS
DRUGSTORE AND THEY YELL
AND CRY AT ME TO COME
BACK. BUT, OF COURSE, I
ALWAYS TELL THEM NO.

I'LL **NEVER**
GIVE UP MY
INDEPENDENCE.

Susan and her mother have always disagreed, but recently, with puberty, the conflict has intensified to such a point that the entire family is in constant turmoil. Susan and her mother simply cannot communicate at this time. Susan feels that her mother doesn't understand her, and her mother feels that Susan is too defensive to talk to and won't listen. Susan says her mother is old-fashioned and behind the times. Her mother says that Susan lacks respect for her elders and is insensitive to others in general.

Susan relies on her girlfriends for advice. Yet she needs a female adult with whom she can communicate her fear and anxieties about becoming an adult and from whom she can learn. In the past Susan could have turned to a grandmother or an aunt who lived in the family or nearby.

What if parents find they can't be good parents for a particular child? The child will be trapped in the setting for years. In the past this child might have lived with relatives who were better suited to act as his or her parents. Children were sometimes traded between families for short periods, spent summers on a farm, and were assisted in growing up by numerous adults and older children. This extended family meant that no one person or couple was responsible for total parenting. Some critics of the nuclear family suggest that the nuclear family pattern of parents and children always alone together creates problems in children rather than preventing them. Inasmuch as the reality of their own nuclear family is the only reality small children may know, they cannot correct misperceptions. because they have no other basis with which to compare the actions of adults, it is difficult for them to recognize problems and reorient themselves.

Broader parenting might be supplied by trading care of children with other families, setting up volunteer community nursery schools, establishing business-supplied day-care centers for workers, and expanding the nuclear family to include relatives. Volunteering to work in a community nursery is also a way for prospective parents to gain experience with children.

PARENTS WITHOUT PREGNANCY: ADOPTION

Although accurate adoption statistics are not available, the National Committee for Adoption estimates that approximately 60,000 nonrelative adoptions take place each year (Gibbs 1989, 86). For every completed adoption, however, there are approximately three women seeking to adopt (Bachrach, London, and Maza 1991). People adopt for many reasons. Mainly, couples adopt because they want children but cannot have children of their own.

About 8 percent of women who are infertile adopt (Bachrach 1986, 246). When parents are unable to care for their children, friends or relatives may adopt the children to give them a home. Couples who feel strongly about the problems of overpopulation may decide to adopt rather than add to the population. A husband or wife may wish to adopt his or her spouse's children by a prior marriage to become their legal parent as well as their stepparent.

Most babies placed for adoption (88 percent) are born of never-married mothers. Donnelly and Voydanoff (1991) found that adolescents with the fewest economic and social resources are most likely to keep and raise their children. Better-educated young mothers with greater resources are most apt to offer their children for adoption.

Although the percentage of unmarried mothers keeping their child rather than giving it up for adoption has greatly increased, the number of premarital births has also greatly increased as we saw in Chapter 11.

> Approximately 6 percent of all babies born premaritally to women fifteen to forty-four years of age are placed for adoption. Babies born to white mothers are much more likely to be placed for adoption (12 percent) than babies born to black mothers (less than 1 percent). Prior to 1973, about 20 percent of white mothers placed their premarital child for adoption compared to 12 percent now (Bachrach 1986, 250; Donnelly and Voydanoff 1991).

To some extent the increase in the percentage of unmarried mothers keeping their child may reflect the greater availability of abortion as a way to end an unwanted pregnancy. Infants carried to term may be wanted and thus kept by the mother rather than placed for adoption.

The choice to adopt a child is just that, a reasoned decision, a choice made by a couple after a great deal of deliberation and thought. As such, the decision-making process leading to adoption makes an ideal model that all couples desiring children can follow. Adoption takes time, and the prospective

Parents without Pregnancy: Adoption

parents must meet certain requirements such as family stability, finances, and housing. Costs of adoption range from $5000 to $20,000. Although many older children and children with special problems are available for adoption, infants are in highest demand.

Adoptive parents have some advantages as well as disadvantages compared with natural parents. For example, adoptive parents may choose their child. To some degree they can select the genetic, physical, and mental characteristics of the child. They can bypass some of the earlier years of childhood if they desire. On the other hand, they do not experience pregnancy and birth, which help focus a couple on impending parenthood. Of course, some may consider this another advantage of adoption.

A unique parenting problem faced by adoptive parents is that of deciding whether and when to share the knowledge of adoption with the child. Experts believe the best course is to inform the child from the beginning, but this is sometimes difficult for parents to do. They may fear that such information will affect the child's love for them. They may want to tell them but simply keep avoiding it until it seems too late. Most adoption agencies, such as the Children's Home Society, counsel prospective adoptive parents on how to tell the child. The parent-child relationship can easily be harmed if the child finds out about the adoption from others. The child's basic trust in the parents may be weakened or perhaps even destroyed if the parents aren't the ones to tell the child about the adoption.

At some time in their lives, many adoptive children feel the need to know something about their natural parents. In the past adoption records were closed to avoid the situation in which a biological parent regrets the decision to give up the child and seeks to get the child back at some later date. The potential for heartache for both the biological and adoptive parents in such a situation is well documented. However, making adoption records unavailable to the adoptee can cause problems in getting passports and other circumstances where a valid birth certificate is necessary.

Although their situation is seldom mentioned, parents who give up their child for adoption also sometimes feel the need to know what has become of their child. Parents who give a child up to an adoption agency rather than using a direct adoption may never know if the child is actually adopted.

For many years legal adoption was a long drawn-out process in which prospective parents went through a strenuous screening process to establish their parental suitability. Recently, such screening has been minimized. In a few cases, especially with older children, single persons are being allowed to adopt.

Cooperative adoption, in which the biological parents and the adoptive parents mutually work out the adoption, is also being tried. The idea is that the child is gaining a family rather than losing a family when adoption occurs. Needless to say, cooperative adoptions must be entered carefully so that problems do not arise later between the two sets of parents.

Cooperative adoption represents one extreme in the debate over just how open adoption should be. The other extreme is represented by the historical position of the courts that all records should be sealed and availability to the biological parents blocked. The successful search for their biological parents may indeed be a positive experience for strongly motivated adopted children. But what if the biological parents do not want or fear such contact? What of their rights to privacy? What effect will a successful search have on the adoptive parents? Will they be supportive of their child's search or fearful that their child will be drawn back to the biological parents?

Most experts today agree that adoptees need to know, or at least believe, some of the basic facts about their natural parents. This is important to shaping the child's identity. Yet for adoptive parents to place too much emphasis on the biological family is as hard on the adoptee as is the denial of the natural family. The adoptive family has a difficult line to walk because there are no sure guidelines (Kaye 1988, 46–50).

Adoption gives parentless children a home and family as well as giving childless couples children. Unfortunately, not all parentless children are easily adoptable. Many minority and handicapped children are never adopted. Although those adopted into white families seem to adjust well (*Los Angeles Times* 1985, 11), in some cases, there is resistance to white families adopting minority children. Navajo Indian tribal officials are resisting such adoptions because they fear that the flow of Indian foster children to non-Indian homes threatens their survival as a people (*Time* May 2, 1988a, 65). Children with defects and health problems are seldom sought by prospective adoptive parents. For the most part, such children are reared in various kinds of institutions or in a series of short-term foster home placements.

THE SINGLE-PARENT FAMILY

The single-parent family is the fastest growing family type in the United States. The fact that the situation is only temporary for many single parents does not minimize the dramatic change in American family life brought about by this phenomenon.

Single-Parent Family Statistics

■ The proportion of children under eighteen who lived with one parent more than doubled between 1970 (12 percent) and 1991 (26 percent).
■ Mother-child families comprise 88 percent of single-parent families. In the past decade, however, the proportion of children living with only their father has risen from 9 to 12 percent.
■ More than 50 percent of all black families with children under age eighteen are mother-child families. Nineteen percent of Caucasian families with children under eighteen are single-parent families. Thirty percent of Hispanic families with children under eighteen live with one parent.
■ The fewer years of schooling a parent has completed, the greater the likelihood that he or she will be maintaining a single-parent family. Of single parents under forty-five years of age with children under eighteen,

Single-parent families derive from a number of sources (see Figure 13-3). The increase in single-parent families is due mainly to the rapid rise in divorce rates over the past decade. The number of children with divorced mothers has doubled since 1970. Although the actual number of children is far smaller, the number with never-married mothers has tripled. This dramatic change is due not to a great increase in illegitimacy but to an increase in the number of unwed mothers who opt to keep their child (94 percent of adolescent unwed mothers). The so-called teenage pregnancy epidemic of recent years turns out to be more of a teenage baby-keeping epidemic (see Scenes from Marriage, Chapter 11).

As we noted, the rising divorce rate has been the major contributing factor to the increase in single-parent families. Beginning in 1980, however, the divorce rate began to level off so we can expect the rate of increase of single-parent families also will slow. Remember that single-parent families tend to be transitional because marriage rates for single parents are high.

Although family form (single-parent, nuclear, three-generation, foster, and so forth) affects children, the old idea that only the traditional two-parent, father-mother family does a good job in rearing children is passing. Still there is little doubt that single parenting has more inherent problems than two-parent childrearing. In many ways the problems of the single-parent family are exaggerated versions of the working mother's problems.

The majority of single-parent families are women and their children. Consequently, all of the problems encountered by the working mother are present (see Chapter 9). The single mother must cope with low pay, child-care problems, and the overburden of working and continuing to shoulder household and childrearing duties. The single father may face these same problems, except that his pay is usually much better. A problem that most fathers face is that the home and child-care burdens are new and often frightening at first.

Single-parent families headed by women with small earning power suffer numerous logistic problems. Finding affordable child care is a major concern. Finding adequate housing in a satisfactory neighborhood is often impossible.

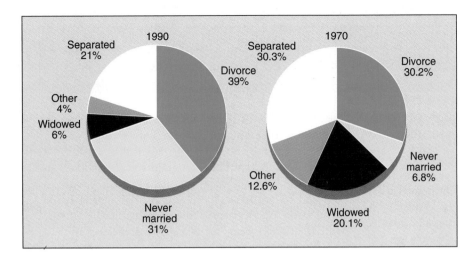

FIGURE 13-3
Children living with one parent, by marital status of parent: 1970 and 1990
Source: U.S. Bureau of the Census May 1991, 6

Even in small cities female-headed families are concentrated in less desirable blocks of the city (Roncek, Bell, and Chaldin 1980; Norton and Glick 1986), although most single mothers do not live in disadvantaged neighborhoods (McLanahan and Garfinkel 1989; McLanahan and Booth 1989). Larger amounts of welfare aid go to these families than to any others, which is indicative of the financial difficulties they face.

Social isolation is one of the problems faced by any single parent. Juggling work, home maintenance, and child-care duties usually leaves the parent little time for either social interaction or self-improvement activities. Emotional isolation is a second major problem. Having no other adult in the home with whom to interact often leads to feelings of loneliness and a sense of powerlessness. The emotional isolation of a separated, divorced, or unmarried parent may be increased by the social stigma sometimes attached to these statuses. The early widowed parent, on the other hand, will experience sympathy and support from society.

Many single parents attempt to alleviate their isolation and reduce expenses by sharing living arrangements. In one study 23 percent of the single-parent sample had a second adult (usually a relative) living in the household, whereas only 9 percent of the two-parent families shared their household with another adult (Smith 1980). This trend has been reversed, however, by black single mothers who are more often living on their own than with their families as was prevalent in the past. Remaining with her family gives a single mother support and help with the rearing of her child that are lost when she lives alone. (The October 1989 issue of *Family Relations* is devoted to child care and the family including a long section on single parents.)

It will be a long time before all of the evidence is in about the ability of the single-parent family to rear children successfully. Certainly, the job is much harder for the single parent, but whether the increase in single-parent families will result in increasing numbers of problem children and hence problem adults is still debatable. In 1965 Patrick Moynihan suggested that the American family, especially the African-American family, was in serious trouble. His views were roundly criticized. In 1986 Moynihan again reviewed the American fam-

DEBATE THE ISSUES
CAN THE SINGLE-PARENT FAMILY DO A GOOD JOB REARING CHILDREN?

THE SINGLE-PARENT FAMILY CAN DO AS GOOD A JOB REARING CHILDREN AS THE TWO-PARENT FAMILY

The single-parent family is no less a family than the two-parent family. It is simply a different family structure for carrying out family functions. As *Parents Without Partners* (America's largest self-help group for single parents) points out, "It is the quality of parenting, not the quantity of parents, that counts most in rearing children." Two-parent families in which both parents work, or in which there is a great deal of conflict, may offer little quality time to their children. Thirty minutes of quality time with a child is worth more than hours of nonattentive time such as when the parents are preoccupied with their work or with watching television. Quality time involves mutual response; the parent attends fully to the child, talks to, plays with, and expresses affection for him or her. All these elements can be offered to the child by a single parent.

Although quality time cannot be dictated, the parent needs to plan some time alone with the child. Here single parents have a decided advantage in that they are 100 percent in charge of their free time and do not have to share it with a spouse. They can direct their total attention to the child whereas in the two-parent family, each parent must reserve some attention for his or her spouse.

Choose activities that both you and the child enjoy. If you also enjoy the activity, your enthusiasm will interact with that of your child to create quality time. Again selecting an appropriate activity is easier for a single parent because the single parent does not have to find an activity that both the child and the spouse enjoy.

Don't try for quality time when you first arrive home from work. Allow yourself time to relax and be honest with your child if you are too tired for active play. You need energy to create quality time, so give yourself time to build up energy after a long day's work. Again the single parent has an advantage over the spouse in a two-parent family in that energy does not have to be shared with another adult. If the parent is tired, the little energy available can be used to create quality time with the child.

Since the single parent does not have to share emotional resources with a spouse, it is clear that with some planning and a strong commitment to making quality time available for parent-child interaction, the single parent can be an effective parent.

THE SINGLE-PARENT FAMILY FACES TOO MANY DIFFICULTIES TO DO A GOOD JOB OF CHILDREARING

The statistics on single-parent families clearly indicate that such families have too many obstacles to overcome to find success in childrearing. Most single parents must work, which means they must leave their children with caretakers for most of the day. For mother-child fami-

ily and discovered that much of what he had predicted about family problems had come true for all American families. This time his views found general acceptance among many family scholars. According to federal estimates, 8 to 10 million American youngsters age six and under are in child-care situations. The average latchkey child spends 2.5 hours a day without adult supervision (Turkington 1983, 19). A combination of divorce, births to unmarried women, dual-worker families, and a preoccupation with self may mean that more American children are indeed neglected and troubled children (see Scenes from Marriage, p. 513).

lies, simply surviving financially is a difficult task. Such difficulties make it likely that single parents will be worried, frustrated, monetarily unfree, and therefore unable to give their best to their children.

Also, the single parent must bear all responsibilities without support from another adult. The tired, depressed, financially strapped single parent has little chance of escape since there is usually no other adult to assume responsibility for the children during the single parent's free time. For the working single parent, placing the children with a caretaker during the parent's free time is difficult psychologically. After all, the child is with a caretaker all day long. The simple logistics of the single parent's situation make quality time with children almost impossible to create.

Character formation is the essential family task, for the obvious reason that children are first formed by families. If the family does not lay the needed psychic foundation, it falls to the schools to try to do so. To date, however, the schools have not been an adequate substitute for the family in the forming of basic character in the young.

For character formation, which is the educational mission of the family, active and involved parents are essential. They must be accorded sufficient time and commitment, at least during the children's formative years, especially from birth until age six but preferably until the end of adolescence. What children require above all are parents who care, educate, have a com-

mitment to parenting and the energy to back up their commitment, and have a relationship to emulate. Hence parents who are overworked, habitually tired, or consumed by their own personal problems are unable to provide effective basic parenting.

Because of the difficult logistical situation of the average single parent, basic parenting is often nearly impossible. Today, more children must fend for themselves because they have no parenting adults at home much of the time (latchkey children). Some suggest that the full impact of the dramatic changes in childrearing (working mothers, single-parent families, and the like) will become evident in increasing neglect of American children (see Scenes from Marriage, p. 513). As part of the ideology that tries to legitimate absent parenting, it has been argued that "quality" counts; that if you cannot spend much time with your child, you can make up for lost hours by making the minutes you do provide "count." Pop psychologists who promote this notion do not cite any data to show that a parent can turn minutes into quality time on order. Indeed, it is more plausible that quality time occurs when a parent has a larger "quantity" of time. Most important, there is no evidence that quality time can make up for long stretches of no time. In general, the increasing numbers of single-parent families reduce the chances for successful parenting and may soon make lack of character development in America's children the nation's number one problem.

SUMMARY

1. *Parenthood remains one of the major functions of marriage.* Despite decreasing emphasis on parenthood and more tolerance of childlessness for married couples, the majority of married couples will become parents.

Summary

511

2. Planning for parenthood, improving parenting skills, working as a parent team, and understanding the course of development a child passes through in becoming an adult are all important to successful parenting. Understanding how children will affect the parental relationship is crucial. There is no one method whereby parents can assure the successful upbringing of their children. *The fact is that parenthood is a difficult and ever-changing job that demands intelligence, flexibility, emotional warmth, stability, and a good portion of courage.*

3. *Children will affect their parents in many ways.* Bringing the first baby home immediately changes the lifestyle of the parents. Suddenly, they have a dependent and demanding person to take care of who contributes little to the family. The new family member not only takes up room in the family's living place, but requires additional funds for care. Dad and Mom will both come second to the infant's demands. Parents are legally and morally responsible for their children until they reach legal adulthood. Even then in many cases parents will still shoulder responsibility for their children (through graduate school, for example).

4. *Erik Erikson identifies eight psychosocial developmental stages that describe the human life cycle from infancy through old age.* The first six are important to parents. They are the oral-sensory stage (first year), the muscular-anal stage (two to three years), the locomotor-genital stage (four to five years), the latency stage (six to eleven years), the puberty-adolescence stage (twelve to eighteen years), and the young adulthood stage (eighteen to thirty, approximately). Each stage involves certain tasks that the child must accomplish to become a successful adult. By knowing what stage a child is passing through and the kinds of tasks that characterize the stage, parents can better understand the child and plan helpful activities.

5. *Broader parenting would help parents do a better job.* Having alternative sources of parenting available would help parents in several ways. Parents would have time away from their children. This would allow them to concentrate for a short period on themselves and their relationship and would give them a respite from the burdens and responsibilities of caring for children. The children would have a broader set of influences and greater stimulation. They would also learn to cope with new and different kinds of people. In general, their experience base would be broader.

6. *Adoption is another avenue to parenthood.* It has the advantages of contributing to population control as well as allowing parents greater choice in selecting the children they want. It does, however, involve the difficulty of having to tell the children that they are adopted.

7. *The single-parent family, although usually transitory, is more common today than ever before.* Such a family faces many problems, but with support is capable of doing a good childrearing job. Adolescent parents also face special problems, the main one being that the parents themselves are still in the process of becoming fully functioning adults and parenthood makes this job harder.

A group of boys thirteen to seventeen years old attack, beat, rape, and leave for dead a young woman jogger in Central Park, New York City. When asked about their motives, they simple said they were out for a little "fun" or "wilding" as they called it.

A fourteen-year-old pregnant teenager is shot and left brain dead by her sixteen-year-old boyfriend. He will not be immediately tried for the shooting, however, because he must stand trial first for another murder.

Two boys, fifteen and eleven years old, shoot a seventy-nine-year-old male hiker with their BB guns. He is hit in the face several times. When caught and asked about their actions, they said that it was just a joke.

These stories were all taken from the author's local newspaper over a few days. Anyone who reads is familiar with such stories. Shortly thereafter *Time* magazine brought out an edition in which the cover story pictured the 464 people killed by guns during the week of May 1 to May 7 (July 17, 1989). Many of these deaths were suicides and some were accidents. What is most frightening is that there were also numerous deaths that appeared to be perpetrated randomly, for no real reason or for "fun." What kind of American would kill someone for no apparent reason? Only a person who had not been socialized by the culture, a sociopathic or psychopathic personality, would be capable of killing for fun.

COULD IT BE THAT SOME AMERICAN CHILDREN SIMPLY ARE NOT GETTING ENOUGH "PARENTING" TO BECOME SOCIALIZED?

A child is not born knowing instinctively the mores, rules, and laws by which his or her society is governed. Each child must be taught by adults the necessary behaviors that will allow the society to function. Without learning these behaviors children will grow into adults that cannot function within the society. If society produces enough unsocialized adults, the society itself will deteriorate into anarchy and cease to function smoothly. A person who does not internalize a minimum number of social rules and mores will lack a sense of social responsibility and be unable to conform to prevailing social norms even when the norms are adaptive (that is, helpful to both the individual and the society). Such a person is termed a *sociopath*. Not all such persons run afoul of the law, although many do. They are always difficult to relate to, however, because they cannot be depended upon to behave in predictable ways. Certainly, mass murderers Ted Bundy and Randy Kraft, who each killed from 40 to 60 or more young women and men for sexual kicks, were sociopathic. They did not have a social conscience or social responsibility.

Rehabilitation programs for adult sociopaths have proven uniformly unsuccessful. It appears that a minimum amount of socialization must begin early in a person's life, probably at birth. Thus far it has been difficult if not impossible in most cases to instill a sense of social responsibility into adult sociopaths. One factor that seems to appear in the background of those sociopaths who have come to the attention of the authorities is a conspicuous lack of parenting. They have often been reared in a series of foster homes, have been in and out of detention facilities for much of their youth, come from poor or economically marginal homes and neighborhoods, and often have had little relationship with their parents if in fact they know who both their parents are (Magid and Mc-Kelvey 1987).

A number of trends that we have already examined or will examine may be combining to increase the number of sociopathic individuals in

the American society. The sexual revolution, the movement of mothers into the work force, increasing teenage motherhood, and the high divorce rate all combine to create conditions that reduce the amount of parenting given to America's children. Although actual child abuse makes the headlines, child neglect is the greater problem in modern America. It is child neglect that creates the sociopathic child and, in time, the sociopathic adult.

Perusal of the average daily schedule of a working single mother or father and/or the working couple with small children finds little if any time that might be counted as "quality time" for the children. Certainly, no quality time is available in the morning hours. Parents are getting ready for work, fixing breakfast, preparing the child for and delivering the child to a baby-sitter or day-care center, and often commuting some distance to work. Coming home in the evening, perhaps after 6 P.M., tired and in need of some peace after a long day's work, preparing dinner, doing necessary housework, paying bills, and getting the children into bed by 9 P.M. leaves very little space for any parenting at all, much less quality time. As *Time* magazine pointed out in the cover story "The Rat Race: How America Is Running Itself Ragged" (April 24, 1989a, 58–67):

Nowhere is the course of the rat race more arduous than around the kitchen table. Hallmark, that unerring almanac of American mores, now markets

greeting cards for parents to tuck under the Cheerios in the morning ("Have a super day at school," chirps one card) or under the pillow at night ("I wish I were there to tuck you in"). Even parents who like their jobs and love their kids find that the pressure to do justice to both becomes almost unbearable.

Parenting is increasingly being done by baby-sitters, day-care programs, television, and the child's peers. Baby-sitters and day-care programs can certainly care for children and can indeed work to socialize children. However, parents seldom know what the socialization is (except in the many cases where close relatives and friends are the primary baby-sitters). Few parents take the time to interview numerous child-care centers in an effort to find one that fits into their own philosophical values. Centers are usually chosen because they are physically convenient and/or fit the family budget. To use television as a surrogate parent (see pp. 488–490) is highly questionable considering the often antisocial messages of sex and violence portrayed. For older children the peer group may become the surrogate family, as it seems to do in adolescent gangs. A child cannot be socialized by other children as attested by the novel

Lord of the Flies and the many unsocialized and uncivilized activities of gangs described daily in local newspapers. Youths under eighteen now make up more than 10 per-

cent of all homicide arrests (Freiberg 1991).

Another term for a sociopathic personality is antisocial personality disorder (APD). This syndrome is caused by failure of the child to become attached or bonded to the parents. Signs of this disorder can be found as early as infancy. Magid and McKelvey (1987, 248–49) list the following high-risk signs:

■ Infant has poor sucking response, rageful crying (without tears), and/or constant whining.

■ Infant has poor clinging response and extreme resistance to cuddling and close holding (fights to get free). Infant arches back when picked up (after first six weeks of life) and seems stiff as a board.

■ Infant maintains weak contact in eye-following response. Infant

strongly resists close face-to-face eye contact and consistently averts gaze.

■ Baby doesn't motivate to approach mother for receiving nurturance.

■ Infant resists smiles even when tickled or played with lovingly. There is no reciprocal smile response.

■ Infant is extremely passive and lifeless and seems to be in another world with no positive response to humans. Later this passivity will give way to rage. Baby looks and feels "as if something is wrong."

Magid and McKelvey (250–51) also list high-risk signs in parents:

■ Parent withdraws and assumes negative psychological and physical posture regarding baby at birth.

■ There is minimal touching, stroking, or talking to or about the baby unless in a negative manner. "Be quiet." Parent may hold infant tensely.

■ Parent has emotionless and flat affect or is depressed and angry.

■ Parent overstimulates the baby by too much talking and touching or plays in inappropriate or hostile ways (cruelly teasing infant).

■ Parent doesn't establish eye contact except when angry and rarely smiles or does so inappropriately (when infant is in pain).

■ Parent leaves infant, when awake, for long periods in isolation and doesn't show the ability to comfort the baby when needed. Handles baby roughly or in a detached manner and may be abusive and neglectful.

■ Parent fails to provide basic supplies for baby care and is angry at most baby behaviors.

TABLE 13-3
SYMPTOMS OF ANTISOCIAL PERSONALITY DISORDER (APD) CHILDREN

1. Lack of ability to give and receive affection
2. Self-destructive behavior
3. Cruelty to others or to pets
4. Phoniness
5. Stealing, hoarding, and gorging
6. Speech pathology
7. Extreme control problem
8. Lack of long-term childhood friends
9. Abnormalities in eye contact
10. Unreasonably angry seeming parents
11. Preoccupation with blood, fire, and gore
12. Superficial attractiveness and friendliness with strangers
13. Learning disorders
14. Crazy living

Source: Adapted from Cline 1979; Magid and McKelvey 1987, 80.

■ Mother is unhappy, frustrated, and angry at being a mother and primary caretaker.

Such behaviors on the part of parent and infant signal future problems and the possible development of antisocial personality disorder in the child. Table 13-3 lists the symptoms of APD children.

CBS News (February 9, 1987) reported the top seven public school problems listed by teachers in the

1980s and compared them to the top seven problems listed in 1940. The comparison is frightening because our children are the future of America.

1940
1. Talking out of turn.
2. Chewing gum.
3. Making noise.
4. Running in the halls.
5. Cutting in line.
6. Dress code infractions.
7. Littering.

1980s
1. Drug abuse.
2. Alcohol abuse.
3. Pregnancy.
4. Suicide.
5. Rape.
6. Robbery.
7. Assault.

Charles Krauthammer in an essay about the attack on the young woman jogger in Central Park entitled "Crime and Responsibility" (*Time* May 8, 1989, 104) concluded: "Children must be taught (by adults). If not taught, they grow up in a moral vacuum. Moral vacuums produce moral monsters." Are American families turning out moral monsters because of lack of parenting?

CHAPTER
14

FAMILY LIFE STAGES: MIDDLE-AGE TO SURVIVING SPOUSE

CONTENTS

BLUSH—BLUR—BACKLASH—BALANCE: SAME COUPLE—DIFFERENT MARRIAGES

- *Blush*. Donna and Bill spend a great deal of time romancing each other. They enjoy candlelight dinners, evenings at concerts or the theater, and lots of hugging and loving. They have been married two years and are still in the honeymoon stage.
- *Blur*. Donna and Bill spend a great deal of time talking about Little League baseball, driving children to music lessons, hearing about each other's work experiences, and wondering if they will ever find time to hug and love again. They have been married fifteen years (childrearing stage).
- *Backlash*. The travel folders and maps are out, and Donna and Bill are planning their first vacation alone together in twenty years. Goodness, they even hugged and loved last Sunday morning without fear of interruption. You guessed it, they have been married twenty-five years and the last child has left home. They are reawakening to one another (middle-age stage).
- *Balance*. Donna and Bill love and respect one another and are enjoying their lives, children, grandchildren, and retirement. They often look at one another and say, "What do you know, we really survived all of the ups and downs and made it." They have been married forty years and are 90 percent sure that health permitting, they will reach their golden wedding anniversary (retirement stage).

Donna and Bill may be the same people (at least in name) as when they first married, but they have clearly been through a number of different marriages, even if each marriage was to one another (Mooney 1986).

The flush of love and the excitement of exploring a new relationship effectively keep most newly married couples from thinking about the later stages of their relationship. After all who can think about children leaving home when no children have yet arrived? What possible relevance can retirement have for a twenty-three-year-old man receiving his first job promotion? And what newly married woman can be thinking about the very real likelihood that she will spend the last ten to twenty years of her life as a widow, alone and without this man she now loves so much?

Yet these are important questions with which almost all married couples must come to grips at some time in their lives. The young adult reader may find it difficult even to think about such questions because the answers will not be needed until far in the future. Perhaps one way you can make such questions relevant is to consider them in the context of your parents' and grandparents' lives. Our lives will not be identical to theirs because we are different and live in changing times. Yet their experiences may serve as a preview for some of the changes that will come into our own lives.

If you have children, for example, eventually your children will leave home. Couples who think about and prepare for these inevitable family life changes before they occur stand a better chance of adapting to them in a creative and healthy manner.

Marriage and family relationships change, just as individuals within the relationship can and do change. Change does not mean the end of the relationship. Indeed, lack of change over time is usually unhealthy and may ultimately lead to the demise of the relationship.

This chapter deals with later-life families. These are families who are beyond the child-rearing years and have begun to launch their children, families who are facing retirement or are retired, families who are in the grandparenting stage of the life cycle, and families who are experiencing the death of one of the partners. As the American population ages, later-life families are becoming the subject of more and more research. (For an overview of research during the 1980s, see Brubaker 1990; see also the "Special Issue: Intergenerational Relationships," *Journal of Family Issues* December 1992.)

Families can change for better or worse. If too much of the change is for the worse, the marriage may end. On the other hand, individuals and families can grow in positive directions to become stronger, more intimate, more communicative, more fulfilling of needs, more supportive, and more loving. Because change cannot be avoided, the real question becomes, "Can I (we) deal with the changes, crises, and stresses that occur in all lives and families in a positive and healthful manner?"

ABILITY TO DEAL WITH CHANGE AND STRESS IN A POSITIVE MANNER: ANOTHER CHARACTERISTIC OF THE STRONG FAMILY

Even strong, lasting families have problems and must, of course, face change as the family passes through the life cycle. Where they seem to differ from weak, unsuccessful families is in their ability to deal with the problems and crises that come their way. Strong families deal with difficulties from a position of strength and solidarity. They can unite and pull together as a team to cope with problems. They do not squander energy on intrafamily differences and conflicts but focus on the problem at hand. Each family member's attitude seems to be, "What can I do to help?" By planning and working together, strong families often head off crises, so life runs smoothly and is generally free of emergencies.

Strong families also seem to remain flexible, and this adaptability helps them weather the storms of life and the inevitable changes that occur in every family and every relationship (Stinnett and DeFrain 1985, 35; McCubbin et al. 1988). Strong families bend and adapt; when the storm is over, they're still intact. A crisis is a turning point for such a family rather than a disaster. Because the family is strong it not only solves the crisis but also learns and emerges stronger than before as a result of having dealt with the situation successfully.

It is clear from perusing the data on strong families that such families have a pool of resources on which to draw when times become difficult (McCubbin et al. 1988). In contrast, unhealthy families are worn out and depleted by the daily stress of poor relationships. When a crisis comes along, the unhealthy family must add the new problem to the burden they already carry. It is no wonder that a crisis sometimes destroys such a family.

Curran (1983, 292) finds that the strong family expects problems, anticipates changes, and considers them to be a normal part of family life. Strong families seem to have the ability to find the positive even in the most negative situations and do not expect the family to be perfect. Unlike families of yesteryear, today's strong families do not often write off problems and/or family members as lost causes.

How did our ancestors cope with the problems we know they had? They coped in a way modern parents can't and don't want to use. They wrote off the people owning the problem as different. They used the term "black sheep" and this flock of sheep came in many forms. The spouse who was unfaithful or alcoholic was labeled "ne'er-do-well" by the community, thus sparing the family both responsibility and shame for his/her behavior. The depressed woman was "going through her time" or "in the change" and her family was thus alleviated from blaming itself for her problem. The teenage boy who wanted a slice of life bigger than his local community had to offer had "itchy feet," and if he decided to go off for a year or two to find himself, his parents weren't castigated for pushing him out. Always he was the problem not they. Old people got "ornery," children who were heard as well as seen were dismissed as "young upstarts," and women that wanted more out of marriage than cooking and children were considered suspect. A child with an emotional or learning problem was "not quite right," and those who questioned approved mores and customs were "just plain crazy." In sum, the problems of the family of the past were attributed solely to the individual, never to the family. (Curran 1983, 293)

Thus the family of the past only seemed perfect because family problems were blamed on the individual rather than the family. Of course, individuals do have problems, but strong families tend to see the problems of their individual members as family problems too.

Because the strong family recognizes that problems and change are a normal part of life, they tend to develop problem-solving skills. They also recognize when they may need outside help and are able to seek assistance (Chapter 18).

Although our discussion has focused on major family problems, small day-to-day frustrations often cause as much trouble in a family as major crises. No spouse will complain if her or his partner occasionally leaves a little toothpaste on the sink, but if there is toothpaste to clean up everytime the partner brushes, tolerance will soon turn to anger. Successful families work out ways to cope with the minor irritations before they grow into major confrontations. Naturally part of the solution is the respect and appreciation that each family member has for the others in the family. Obviously the family that learns to cope with stress, frustration, and day-to-day irritations is likely to have the greatest chance of dealing successfully with all kinds of changes and therefore remaining intact.

As we describe changes across the life cycle, it is important to remember that changes take place not only within the family, but in the society as well

Ability to Deal with Change and Stress in a Positive Manner: Another Characteristic of the Strong Family

(Glick 1989). Many of the adjustments that successful families must make are adjustments to outside societal forces. Women becoming better educated and entering the work force in great numbers is just one example of social change to which the family has had to adapt.

AN OVERVIEW OF FAMILY LIFE STAGES

As we saw in Chapter 13, a development stage approach has long been used in studying children. The prenatal stage, infancy, preschool, school, prepuberty, puberty, adolescence, and young adulthood are all well-known developmental stages in the life of the maturing human. Similarly, dividing family life into stages or cycles will help us gain a better understanding of the changes that people go through as they move from birth to death.

What are the stages in the life of a maturing marriage? If we examine the general kinds of problems faced at various marital stages, we find that the average American couple goes through six important periods in a long-term marriage: (1) newly married, (2) early parenthood, (3) later parenthood, (4) middle age (empty nest), (5) retirement, and (6) widowed singleness.

The problems of the *newly married* stage revolve around adjusting to each other, establishing a home, setting directions for the relationship, learning to confront the world as a pair rather than as individuals, and learning to work together to achieve mutually acceptable goals. These problems have already been discussed in various preceding chapters.

With the arrival of children, the couple enter the parental role. This change will compound the problems of a newly married couple, especially if they have children shortly after marriage, before they have had much time to work out the challenges of the first stage.

Early parenthood covers pregnancy, birth, infants, toddlers, preschoolers, and elementary school children. When puberty arrives and the children move into junior and senior high school, college, and the young adult world, the problems parents face change dramatically. So drastic are these changes that it is worthwhile to examine this period in marriage separately; hence the third stage, *later parenthood*. As we saw in Chapter 13, adolescence is actually a combination of puberty—the biological maturing of the child—and the social expectations that the child will behave in an adult manner. Like many Western cultures, American society does not sharply define entrance into adulthood. In fact, the adolescent period in America is nebulous, conflicting, and confused because it extends well beyond the achievement of biological maturity. As a result, many parents find later parenthood a trying time. Children become increasingly independent, yet parents are still legally and ethically responsible for their children's actions. Finances can be strained, especially if the children go on to higher education. Parents also have to begin adjusting to their children's adult sexuality and mate selection process, which culminates in the acceptance of an extended family as the children marry and reproduce.

THE GRAYING OF AMERICA

The remaining three stages—middle age, retirement, and widowed single-ness—have all been greatly affected by increased life expectancy.

In 1900 life expectancy for white males was 48.2 years and for white females 51.1 years. Now the figures are 72.3 years and 79 years, respectively (National Center for Health Statistics March, 1991, 11). The percentage of the population over age sixty-five is also increasing rapidly as Figure 14-1 shows. The median age in the nation is now at an all-time high, thirty-three years, as compared to twenty-three years in 1900 and thirty years in 1950 (Schmid 1988).

Peter Uhlenberg (1980) suggests that the combination of increased life expectancy and declining mortality have a number of effects on the family:

■ Decreased infant and childhood mortality encourages a stronger emotional bond between parents and children and reduces fertility since it is no longer necessary to have two babies to produce one adult.
■ The number of living grandparents is greatly increased for children, and three-, four-, and even five-generation families are more common.
■ Marriages potentially can last much longer so that more couples experience middle age and prolonged retirement together or divorce.
■ Greater survival advantages for women relative to men have increased the period of widowhood at the end of the life.
■ The number of elderly persons depending on middle-aged children is increasing.

FIGURE 14-1
Growth of U.S. population over age 65

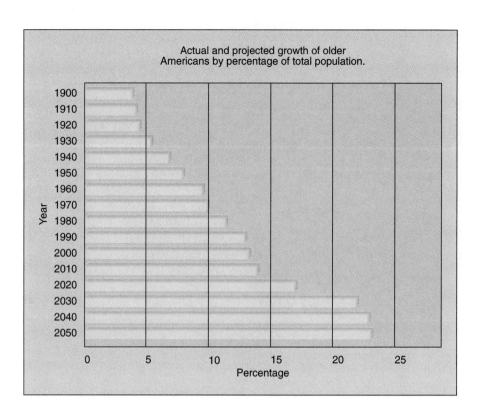

The final three family life stages take on a new and greater significance as life expectancy increases and an ever-larger percentage of the population enters these stages.

Middle-age, or the *launching stage*, begins when the last child leaves home. In many families, this stage is being postponed because many young adults are remaining in the parental home longer than in the past. The increasing number of years of schooling and the high costs of living independently are combining to keep many children at home well into their twenties. Even when the children do leave home (sometimes after they start their own families), many parents continue to provide monetary and psychological support. For other parents, especially traditional child-centered mothers, the departure of the last child can mean feelings of loneliness and loss, especially if the children move far away or reject continued parenting. New interests and goals must be developed to replace the lost parenting functions. The husband may need to help his wife reorient her life away from the children, and this in turn will usually influence his own life. Fathers or career-oriented mothers survive this stage more easily than traditional mothers because many of their goals and fulfillments lie outside the family. Their feelings of loss when the children leave are usually less severe.

The husband and wife may draw closer during the middle-aged stage. In earlier marital years, when many wives devote their energies to the children and their husbands devote themselves to their work, husband and wife may well grow apart emotionally. When the children are gone, a couple may renew their life together, reinvest in one another, and lay the foundation for the next marital stage, retirement.

Increasing life expectancy, automation, and America's emphasis on youth have combined to almost double the length of retirement in the average worker's life during this century. People now spend at least a quarter of their adult lives in retirement. In fact, early retirement has become so widespread that far fewer individuals are working beyond age sixty-five than in the past. Early retirement is affected by the state of the economy. For example, during recession, many businesses offer retirement bonuses to employees in an effort to reduce their work forces. On the other hand, many people who are eligible for retirement continue to work out of fear that they would be unable to survive financially in a recessionary economy.

> Seventy-five years ago, about 66 percent of men over sixty-five were drawing wages; today, less than 20 percent of our male senior citizens are in paid employment (*Monthly Labor Review* February 1988, 75.)

The retiring worker faces the problem of adjusting to leisure after years of basing much of his or her self-worth on working and income production. Under our work ethic stature is gained by work not leisure, so retirement equals obsolescence in the view of American society. For the productive worker, retirement presents a choice: adjust or be miserable.

In a sense retirement for a worker is similar to the empty-nest or launching stage for the traditional child-centered wife. The retiree must cope with a lack of purpose and feelings of uselessness. Those who cannot develop substitute goals find retirement an unhappy period. For some it is literally a short-lived period; death often arrives shortly after retirement for those who cannot adjust. For others, however, especially those who have been financially successful, retirement may mean rebirth rather than death. It may signal a new beginning, expanding interests, and rediscovery of the marital partner (see Scenes from Marriage, "Older—But Coming on Strong").

Inevitably, one of the marital partners dies, so the final marital stage is usually a return to singleness in *widowhood*. There are approximately six times more widows than widowers in the United States. Thus widowhood is a far greater possibility for women than for men. Although the percentage of widowed persons in the general population has dropped during this century, the number of years that widowed singleness may be expected to last has risen dramatically. For example, half the women widowed at age sixty-five can expect fifteen more years of life. Thus this final marital stage can be especially lengthy for women.

Being widowed is predominantly an older person's problem. Younger widowed persons tend to remarry, but remarriage becomes increasingly remote with advancing age. In 1988 only 1 percent of brides and 2 percent of grooms were sixty-five or older (National Center for Health Statistics 1991b, 15). These percentages will rise as the population over sixty-five increases. For the widowed person who does remarry, being widowed may not be the last stage of marriage. Remarriage will reinstate an earlier marital stage.

Because we have discussed the first three family life stages—newly married and early and later parenthood—in earlier chapters, we will devote the remainder of this chapter to the last three stages, middle age, retirement, and widowhood.

MIDDLE AGE (THE EMPTY NEST)

For most couples middle age starts when the children become independent and ends when retirement draws near. Although these figures are arbitrary, most people are in the middle-age stage between the ages of forty and sixty-five.

The U.S. Census Bureau uses the age of forty-five to denote the onset of middle age. It is better, however, to define this stage by the kinds of changes and problems that occur. For example, a very young mother might face empty-nest changes by the time she is thirty-five.

Historically, middle age is a relatively new stage in marriage. Owing to the much shorter life spans before 1900, most wives buried their husbands before the last child left home. As Paul Glick (1955, 4) points out, "In 1890 women bore their last child at thirty-two, buried their husband at age fifty-three and attended their last child's wedding at age fifty-five". Thus, for most marriages before 1900, there was no period of return to being simply a couple again. Yet today such a period is very likely, and the chances are great that it will last for fifteen to twenty-five years.

Men and women may face somewhat different changes during middle age. For most women who have not had a career, adjustment centers on no longer being needed by their children. This, of course, is not true for childless women. Men's problems usually revolve around work and their feelings of achievement and success.

For both partners, however, middle age reactivates many of the questions that each thought had been answered much earlier in their lives. Indeed, many of the questions that arise resemble those adolescents struggle with: Who am I? Where am I going? How will I get there? What is life all about? How do I handle my changing sexuality? The term **middlescence** has been coined to describe this stage.

Middlescence
The second adolescence, experienced in middle age, usually involving re-evaluation of one's life.

Not all writers and researchers agree that there is a midlife crisis (Skolnick 1983). Those suggesting that a midlife crisis does exist describe the changes and pain that middle-aged people experience in reexamining their identities as similar to a lobster's periodic shedding of its shell: It makes the lobster vulnerable, but allows it to grow (LeShan 1973).

Some people, however, use their marriages as an escape from facing the existential challenges of middle age. They do not want to ask the important questions because it is safer to assume that marriage is answer enough.

Who am I?
I am Mr. or Mrs. Jones.

What is my life all about?
I am a wife or husband.
I do my duty to the family and help keep it running smoothly.

Where am I going?
We hope to take a trip to Cape Cod next summer.

What is life all about?
My marriage is the answer to all existential questions.
My marriage is my existence.

But for the couples who take the risk, the problems of middle-age transition can become a vehicle for growth. Marriage enrichment for the middle-aged couple is not focused so much on improving the marriage as on improving the humans in it. What really counts is not so much what actually happens to us in middle age as our attitude toward it. We all experience some kind of changes in this stage as in other stages, but how do we use these changes? If we use them for further growth and expansion, our lives, our marriages, our relationships, and ourselves may all benefit, and the second half of our lives may be even more fulfilling than the first half.

There is infinite variety in the way individuals face the questions that arise when they realize that life is finite. Some people simply look the other way and avoid the questions. Others try to change their external world by relocating, finding a new spouse, or starting a new job. Others seek internal changes such as a new set of values or a new philosophy of life.

Obviously, a person's life circumstances influence the questions and their answers. A child-centered mother out of the work world for twenty years may feel panic as she realizes that she will soon be unneeded by her children. Another mother who has always worked in addition to raising her children may be happy that her children will no longer need her and she will thus be free to pursue long-neglected interests. Because of these individual differences, our discussion of the midlife changes must remain general. Some individuals will undergo the experiences we discuss, others may not, and still others may experience things that are not discussed. Despite these limitations, examining the middle years of life is worthwhile because we will all pass through them.

For the traditional wife and mother, the midlife transition may indeed be a crisis. She has to face her partial failure as a parent (all parents fail to some degree as we saw in Chapter 13) and her feelings of loss and uselessness. She

Middle Age (The Empty Nest)

Five years ago Jane and Bill Wyzinski and their older children left their home in Santa Barbara where they were a mathematician and a teacher, respectively. Now they're back as a lawyer-to-be and as a physician. Bill, an internist with a local medical group, used to be a systems analyst with a large research and development firm. Jane is scheduled to take her bar exam early this year after having taught elementary school for years.

"I read about a program at the University of Miami where they retrain people with Ph.D's in the biological sciences to become M.D.'s," said Bill. "There was at the time a plethora of Ph.D.'s and a lack of M.D.'s. Then they let a few people in with degrees in the physical sciences"—he has a doctorate in math—"and discovered that they did just as well."

He spent two years in the accelerated medical school program, which he calls the time of "learning the language," then three years in a Veterans' Administration hospital for his internship and residency, "where I really learned to be a doctor."

Bill said he'd never had much exposure to the hospital environment until he began singing in a barbershop quartet, which was often invited to entertain in rest homes and hospitals. He said he'd had the field of medicine "in the back of my mind" for a long time before he applied. He thought that medicine would be a more self-sufficient career than computers.

"I enjoy the work itself. I never took math home. Nobody cares about the answers except people in the field. However, I never get tired of medicine. When I get home, I get out the medical journals and the texts."

"I knew there'd be 700 applicants and only 28 selected so I didn't get my hopes up. They called for an interview, and three weeks later called again to say that I was 29th, the 'first alternate.' I figured that they told this to many people, so we bought a ping-pong table and settled back into our old routine."

Classes begin in Miami on July 1. On July 5, after an afternoon of tennis, the couple arrived home to a telephone call from Miami asking, "Can you come tomorrow?" A student had dropped out making room for the first alternate. Making a quick decision, Bill packed up and left the next day, leaving Jane to sell the house and furniture and complete a summer job that she had undertaken.

Bill said the only courses he had in undergraduate school that applied to medical school were a year of chemistry and a course in physiology. But based on his medical school test scores, the lack of preliminary courses wasn't an insurmountable problem. "Math training involves more rational thought and medicine is simply more memorization at first."

During Bill's residency, Jane took the opportunity to go to law school. When they returned to Santa Barbara she did some volunteer work in the consumer fraud division of the district attorney's office. "Now I'm spending all my time studying for the bar," she said.

As a teacher, Jane said she "had always been interested in the political side of teaching. I'm interested in educational law—children's rights, parents' and teachers' rights. I don't think anyone is working in that area here." She said that she was considering this career change even before Bill made his decision.

For both spouses to make such dramatic midlife changes is certainly unusual. Yet this true story illustrates that families can make major and dramatic changes and survive and be rejuvenated.

may have general feelings of dissatisfaction with her marriage and her life and periods of increased introspection as she seeks new life goals. Her feelings are somewhat akin to a worker's feelings on retirement, although she often faces reentry into the work world. Today, women must face the questions of changing identity and roles aroused by the women's movement. As more and more women become career oriented (Chapter 9), the launching of the children will probably denote release and freedom rather than a sense of loss and uselessness.

Any wife, whether traditional or not, faces the biological boundary of the end of her childbearing years. "No more children even if I wanted them." This and the accent on youth in America will cause her to reevaluate her sexuality. "Am I still attractive to men? Is there more to sex than I have experienced?" Some women may welcome the end of their reproductive capacities because it frees their sexuality from the constant worry about possible pregnancy. Many women report renewed and intensified sexual appetite once they have completed menopause.

A wife and her husband as well will become aware of death in a personal way as their parents die one by one. These events cause many people to direct their thoughts for the first time to the inevitability of death and the realization that their lives are finite.

Thus the midlife changes faced by women are broad and profound. Furthermore, both the woman and her husband also experience the turmoil the other feels during this stage.

The typical husband's midlife crisis revolves around his work rather than his family. This is particularly true for highly successful men. In our competitive economic society, a person must devote a great deal of energy to his or her work to achieve success. The male is often forced to handle two marriages, the first to his work and the second (in importance also) to his family.

America's emphasis on youth presents problems for the man. Competitive younger men become a threat to his job security. Subtle comments about retirement may take on a personal significance.

A husband's midlife transition centers around letting go of some of the dreams of his youth. He begins to recognize that he may not achieve all of his dreams. For the few men who have fulfilled their dreams, the midlife question becomes, What do I do now? Most men, however, must cope with some disillusionment: the sense that the dream was counterfeit, the vague feeling of having been cheated—that the dream isn't really what they thought it would be—and the growing awareness that perhaps they will never ever achieve all of their dreams.

Unfortunately, this disillusionment usually carries over into the man's family. He doubts himself and doubts his family as well. He may even blame them for his failure to achieve the dreams of his youth.

Along with general self-doubts come doubts about sexuality. Unlike his wife's, though, these doubts usually revolve less around physical attractiveness than around performance. His wife's sexuality is at its peak, and she may be more aware and assertive of her own sexuality. Her assertiveness can heighten self-doubts. Self-doubt can be a man's greatest enemy in achieving satisfactory sexual relations. The "other woman" may become a problem at this time as the man seeks to prove his sexuality (see Inset 14-2).

In some cases a rather interesting partial exchange of roles takes place at this time of life. The woman becomes more interested in the world outside her family and more responsive to her own aggressiveness and competitive feelings. She returns to the work world or to school or becomes interested in public affairs and causes. Her husband becomes more receptive to his long-repressed affiliative and loving urges. He renews his interest in the family and in social issues outside his work. He becomes more caring in the way that his wife has been caring within the family. Unfortunately, the children are not very receptive to his newfound parental caring since they are busy seeking their own independence. A mother's new interest in the world outside her

The wives of men in midlife crisis are usually enraged at the "other woman" who may enter their husband's lives at a vulnerable point. For many of these wives, the midlife crisis has only one meaning: a married man having an affair, usually with a younger woman.

Although the midlife crisis is much broader than that, it is important that the voices of distressed wives and former wives be heard. After reading an article on the problems of single women dating married men, an irate woman wrote:

I am greatly annoyed at your considerable sympathy for the single woman involved with the married man. What about the wife, after twenty or more years of marriage, having this turbulence thrust upon her? No matter how good the marriage, living with another person is never perfect. When he meets a new woman it builds his ego to know that she finds him interesting and attractive. The wife has probably already gone through her midlife crisis with little or no support from him, and now he is shattering their marriage and creating emotional havoc for her and the children. Invariably the man is looking for change and is not open to counseling.

Six months ago my husband left our twenty-year marriage to have space to work out his problems. Of course, there's more to it than that: including an eighteen-month extramarital relationship. It's a shame that he couldn't put more effort into his marriage.

Others wrote of their self-doubts: "Did I do something wrong? Did I care too much? Did I overprotect and let him get away with too much? Did I nag?" And many talked of their dismay at having to face a future so different from the one they had envisioned: "Now at fifty-plus I must find a new way of life and a job to support myself in the manner I have been accustomed to. Great way to start my senior years!"

The letters from single women who are dealing with men in their midlife crisis proclaim that it's no picnic for them either. One such woman wrote that the man she had a "flirtation" with suddenly ended his marriage. He told her he had been unhappily married for years. He then pursued her ardently and had her give up her apartment and move into a house for the two of them. After she moved in, he decided to reconcile with his wife and moved her out again.

But none of the single women addressed the questions frequently asked by angry wives: "Don't these women care that they are entering a man's life when he's extremely vulnerable, and that they are breaking up a longstanding marriage and family? Aren't they at all concerned about the wife?"

"Other women" seem to care a little and feel somewhat guilty, but not enough to end the relationship. They have several reasons for this behavior:

■ The "other woman" often does not enter the relationship wanting the man to leave his wife and commit himself to her. This is particularly true now, when affairs with married men are much more common than they were in the past (Richardson 1986).

■ The "other woman" usually knows the wife only through the husband's words, and she often hears how bad things are, that he hasn't loved his wife in years, and that his wife is terrible.

■ The man tells her how much he values her, that she makes him happy, and so forth. The "other woman" begins to think of his wife as the past and herself as his future.

■ She truly feels that she is good for the man and believes that it would be a tragedy for herself and for him if he went back to his wife.

Because of these beliefs and feelings, her own powerful attachment to the man and the "all is fair" attitude that seems to exist because of the scarcity of single men, the "other woman" is not usually deterred by sympathetic feelings for the wife.

Source: Adapted from Halpern 1986.

family may be impeded by the fact that the empty nest is increasingly refilled by returning adult children or the couple's elderly parents.

THE SANDWICH GENERATION: CAUGHT IN THE MIDDLE

Young adults (eighteen to thirty-four years old as defined by the U.S. Census Bureau) in 1990 were more likely than young adults in 1970 to be living in the homes of their parents. A number of factors probably contribute to the higher proportion of young adults living with their parents. Marriage is being postponed, increasing emphasis is being placed on advanced education, and housing costs are high in many areas of the country. The high divorce rate among young couples also prompts increased numbers of adult children to return home, at least temporarily, after a divorce.

Research indicates that a young adult in the home contributes to a high level of parental dissatisfaction as we saw in Chapter 13. With more young adults remaining or returning home, the parents find themselves having to share their home and lives with other adults rather than being alone and able to concentrate on themselves and their relationship. The continuing lack of privacy and their children's failure to contribute monetarily or share in the day-to-day running of the home are parents' major complaints about having adult children living at home. In turn, the young adults complain about lack of freedom and parental interference.

Young adults remaining or returning home represent one side of a "sandwich." Longer life expectancy has also increasingly led to a middle-aged couple's empty nest being refilled by aging parents (Beck and Beck 1984), the other half of the sandwich. Even if elderly parents do not actually live with the couple, the couple must concern themselves with caring for and helping their parents. The number of persons over sixty-five years of age doubled between 1950 and 1980 and is predicted to double again by 2020. In addition, modern medicine is keeping older people with chronic illnesses like Alzheimer's disease alive for years longer. Thus the likelihood that a couple will have to help care for aging parents will continue to increase.

Caring for the elderly has traditionally been women's work, a natural extension of their role as homemakers and nurturers. Numerous studies find that daughters rather than sons are the primary caregivers to aging parents (Finley 1989; Brubaker 1990, 973–975; Spitze and Logan 1990; Mancini 1989). One representative study found that 33 percent of the elderly surveyed received help from a daughter, compared to 17 percent who received help from a son (Hull 1985).

It must also be noted that distance plays a large role in the amount of care provided by adult children to aging parents. Children who live far away from their parents obviously cannot give as much personal care to aging parents as children who live close by.

Today the average American woman can expect to spend more years caring for her parents than she did caring for her children (Clabes 1989). Although most of the literature discusses the stress put on adult children by care for aging parents, the problems of adult children also cause distress to their parents. Parents whose adult children experience serious problems report increased stress and depression in their own lives (Pillemer and Suiter 1991).

Middle Age (The Empty Nest)

From the time we are young, we soak up a pervasive myth and accept it meekly: People used to care for their elders but we, callously, will abandon our parents in old age, just as our children will abandon us. The persistence of this myth is remarkable because the evidence is overwhelming that the opposite is true. Not only are more people—many of whom are old themselves—caring for their aged parents, but they are providing care for more difficult problems and for longer periods than ever before.

A recent congressional study reported that family caregivers provide between 80 and 90 percent of medically related care, personal care, household maintenance, and assistance with transportation and shopping needed by older people. What's more, the duration and extent of care have changed since "the good old days." Whereas people typically used to care for parents during an acute, ultimately fatal illness, people today live long after chronic disease and disability

set in. It is long-term parent care that has become the norm—expectable, though usually unexpected.

Some researchers equate parent care with other developmental stages that occur in the normal course of life. It differs, however, in that parent care is not linked to specific age periods. Need for parent care may arise as adult children rear their own young, as they enter and advance through middle age, or as they adjust to the realities of their own old age.

Unfortunately, despite benefits such as companionship, feelings of usefulness, and an improved sense of self-worth, many people find that stress is a tiresome companion to their care-giving responsibilities. Studies repeatedly identify emotional strain as a widespread and deeply felt consequence. Shifting roles and competing demands for time disrupt comfortable balances in both the caregiver's workplace and at home. Relationships between husbands and wives, among adult siblings, and between adult

caregiver and younger offspring must be adjusted, often for long and indefinite periods during which the needy relative is likely to grow ever more dependent.

Sociologist Samuel H. Preston of the University of Pennsylvania reports that for the first time in American history, the average married couple, by the time they are 40 years old, has more parents than children. While many men, particularly spouses of the care recipient, readily fulfill care-giving roles, the job overwhelming falls to women. Authorities believe this reflects acceptance by both men and women of traditional sex roles rather than the sons' deficient sense of responsibility. Daughters are twice as likely as sons to become primary caregivers, and when the son is the official caregiver, the daughter-in-law often assumes the care-giving tasks.

The potential for conflict is especially great for "women in the middle" who are squeezed between dramatic demographic shifts and

Many times the care given by adult children to their aging parents is reciprocated by the parents so care giving by the adult children is not a one-way street. Monetary aid and/or advice is often given back to the adult children by the cared-for parents (Walker, Pratt, and Oppy 1992).

For the woman joining the work force (Chapter 9) or renewing her interest in the world outside the family, shouldering the burden of caring for elderly parents can be particularly frustrating. One study found that 28 percent of nonworking women had quit their jobs to care for their parents (Hull 1985).

Most children, however, are loath to put their aging parents into institutional homes. Despite the public stereotype of the elderly living in nursing homes, only a very small percentage actually live in institutions. Indeed, mak-

INSET 14-3

A GUIDE TO CAREGIVING FOR THE ELDERLY							
CAREGIVERS		**WHO RECEIVED HELP**		**KINDS OF ASSISTANCE**		**AVERAGE AGE OF CAREGIVERS**	
Women	72%	Women	60%	Personal hygiene	67%	Under 65	65%
Daughters	29	Men	51	Administer medication	50	65–74	25
Wives	23	Widowed	41	Financial matters	50	75 plus	10
Husbands	13	Lived with spouse	40	Household tasks	80		
		Lived with spouse and children or children only	36	Indoor mobility	46		
		Lived alone	11				

Source: Simon 1988.

changes in women's lifestyles. Many women in this generation are mothers and are employed in addition to their responsibilities as primary caregivers. Given the sex differences in life expectancy, experts say that many of these women will care for dependent husbands in the future.

As family caregivers mete out untold hours of parent care, why don't they feel they are doing enough? Why do they continue to believe that most elderly parents are abandoned and that their children, in turn, will abandon them? Why does the "myth of abandonment" persist?

The myth does not die because at its heart is a fundamental truth.

At some level, members of all generations expect that the devotion and care given by the young parent to the infant and child should be repaid in kind when the parent, now old, becomes dependent.

But that level of devotion is not possible for most adult caregivers, and consequently they feel guilty. The good old days may not be an earlier period in our social history but an earlier period in each individual's and family's history to which no one can return. Not only does the myth persist because the guilt persists, but the guilt persists because the myth persists."

ing the decision to intervene with frail elderly parents is extremely difficult for most children. How do you tell a parent or parents that their home is now too much for them to care for, or that it might be wise for them to move into a retirement home (Hansson et al. 1990)?

Thus middle age may mean an empty nest and a renewed emphasis on the primary couple, or it may not. For both men and women, however, midlife usually means rethinking and reevaluating life. It is a time of restructuring. The resulting turmoil may threaten the marriage and family, or it may result in a revitalized marriage. By recognizing and squarely confronting the issues of midlife, the chances increase that the results will be positive and growth enhancing rather than negative and destructive.

Middle Age (The Empty Nest)

RETIREMENT

Retirement can be a wonderful time of catching up on all the activities that a person or couple have put off during the early part of their lives. Findings vary about the relationship between retirement and marital satisfaction, however, some studies suggest marital satisfaction increases in later years while other studies find little or no relationship. Some older couples may experience a "honeymoon" phase after retirement because they are no longer hampered by the demands of work and can spend more time with one another (Brubaker 1990, 962).

Differing patterns of retirement between a couple affect a family's adjustment to retirement. For example, Lee and Shehan (1989) found that an employed wife with a retired husband experiences lower marital satisfaction than a wife who retires first or at the same time as her husband.

In part, retirement signals the beginning of disengagement. In many non-industrialized societies, this is a gradual process. The hardest physical labor is performed by young men and women at the peak of their physical condition. As they age and their offspring grow to maturity, the parents assume more administrative and supervisory duties while the children take on the harder physical labor. This gradual tapering off of duties with a smooth transition of tasks from one generation to the next was also to some extent the practice on the farms of rural America.

By contrast, in American urban areas, retirement is usually abrupt; it occurs when the worker reaches a certain arbitrary age or has worked for a specified number of years. This abruptness of retirement can cause severe adjustment problems for the newly unneeded worker. The woman in the traditional mothering role who faces her retirement at the earlier empty nest stage, finds that it comes gradually as her children gain independence one by one. In contrast, working spouses are suddenly placed in a totally new role. After forty to fifty years of going to work, they receive a gold watch and are told to go fishing and enjoy their new leisure time. They are thrust into a new lifestyle that for most retirees is characterized by less income, declining health, and increasing loneliness. Of course, they are now free to travel and catch up on the activities they missed because they were working but they also miss their colleagues and the status derived from their job. Now when a new acquaintance asks "What do you do?" the former worker answers, "Nothing, I'm retired." Because so much of a career person's self-image is defined by work identity, retirement often brings a kind of identity crisis.

Because retirement comes abruptly for many Americans, it is necessary to prepare ahead, both economically and psychologically. The Scenes from Marriage at the end of this chapter points out that for many retirees, the scenario just described is not accurate. Numerous retirees leave their job but take on so many new activities and responsibilities that their life becomes even busier than it was when they were working full-time.

A few retirees seem able to find happiness in "doing nothing." "It's great not to have to get up every morning and go to work." Yet most cannot "do

TABLE 14-1 REACTION OF HOUSEWIVES TO THEIR HUSBAND'S RETIREMENT			
POSITIVE ASPECTS OF RETIREMENT	PERCENTAGE OF WIVES MENTIONING	NEGATIVE ASPECTS OF RETIREMENT	PERCENTAGE OF WIVES MENTIONING
Time available to do what you want	81%	Financial problems	36%
Increased companionship	67	Husbands not having enough to do	31
Time flexibility	33	Too much togetherness	22
Increased participation of husbands in household tasks	28		
Decrease in own household responsibilities	22		
Husbands happier	22		

Source: Hill and Dorfman 1982.

nothing" easily and happily after years of working. Many retirees continue to do odd jobs or work part-time if their occupation permits. For example, a retired school teacher may occasionally do substitute teaching. Some retirees change activities entirely and take up a new vocation or avocation. They may decide to open their own business or actively pursue some long-suppressed interest such as writing or painting. Perhaps they busy themselves with volunteer work. There are numerous examples of people retiring and then returning to the work world. Konrad Adenauer assumed the leadership of postwar West Germany at the age of seventy-three and actively guided Germany to a powerful world position for fourteen years until he was eighty-seven.

Making specific plans for one's newly acquired leisure time is of great help psychologically to the new retiree. A person who wakes up each morning with something to do rather than wondering what to do is more likely to make a successful adjustment to retirement.

Those who have always had broad interests or are able to develop new interests generally make the quickest and best adjustment to retirement. People who age optimally are those who stay active and manage to resist shrinkage of their social world. They maintain the activities of middle age as long as possible and then find substitutes for the activities they are forced to relinquish: substitutes for work when forced to retire and substitutes for friends and loved ones lost to death.

Elizabeth Hill and Lorraine Dorfman (1982) investigated the reactions of housewives to the early years of their husbands' retirement. Table 14-1 lists some of the positive and negative aspects mentioned by these wives.

In addition, when the researchers asked what suggestions these wives had for other women whose husbands were soon to retire, the wives mentioned the following most frequently:

- Wives should try to keep their husbands busy in retirement.
- Wives should try to continue their own preretirement activities.
- Couples should do more together.
- Wives should plan to maintain some privacy.

Although most of the literature on retirement concerns men, questions of retirement are becoming more important for women as well. As we saw in Chapter 9, more and more women are entering the work force. Past research (Lowenthal, Thurnher, and Chiriboga 1975) has indicated that retirement does not hold the same significance for women as for men even when the woman has worked full-time for most of her life. One possible reason for this is that many women experience several other roles (wife, mother, homemaker) that they perceive to be as important as the role of worker. This pattern may well change, however, as more and more women seek lifelong careers. Just as men must prepare for retirement, so must working women.

Money and health seem to be the two most important factors influencing the success of both retirement and general adjustment to old age. It takes a great deal of money to live free of economic worries. Generally, a person's income is more than halved on retirement. The stereotype of the older retiree fighting off poverty has largely disappeared since Social Security and many pension plans have been indexed to the inflation rate. Moynihan (1986, 94) points out that in the late 1970s and early 1980s, poverty among America's elderly was largely defeated. *Fortune* magazine reported that median real family income for seniors had increased 54 percent between 1970 and 1988 (see Figure 14-2). The average annual gain for seniors was 2.6 percent a year. No other age group came close to this gain. For example, the income of nonelderly married couples increased only 1.5 percent per year during the same period (*Fortune* 1988, 156).

For those who still suffer financially in retirement, however, it is ironic that when they finally retire and have free time for the activities they want to pursue, they have little money available for more than subsistence. Financial status is directly related to the quality of life for the retired couple. Can they travel, indulge their hobbies, and satisfy their interests? They can, but only if they are financially well off.

Retirees must not only prepare economically for retirement but must also plan for a potentially long retirement due to the increased life expectancy. As we saw earlier, people may now live up to 25 percent of their lives in retirement. Inflation is the retired person's greatest enemy. Those retired on an essentially fixed income fall further and further behind with each passing day of inflation. A couple financially well off at retirement may have dropped into poverty ten years later due to continued inflation and the shrinking value of the dollar. Indexing retirement income to the inflation rate works to cancel this trend, but unfortunately, such indexing also fuels inflation.

Health is the other major influence on people's adjustment to retirement and old age. About 40 percent of those over sixty-five have chronic conditions. Although government programs such as Medicare help the elderly cope finan-

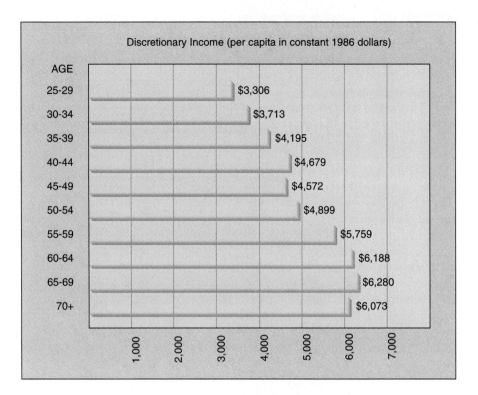

FIGURE 14-2
The old have more to spend (Source: Conference Board)

Discretionary Income (per capita in constant 1986 dollars)

AGE	
25-29	$3,306
30-34	$3,713
35-39	$4,195
40-44	$4,679
45-49	$4,572
50-54	$4,899
55-59	$5,759
60-64	$6,188
65-69	$6,280
70+	$6,073

1,000 2,000 3,000 4,000 5,000 6,000 7,000

cially with health problems, most retirees find they need private medical insurance as well. Thus lack of money may compound health problems and further reduce the quality of life for the retired. Given the high costs of medical care, few people can be completely safe from financial disaster brought on by prolonged or severe health problems.

The health problems of seniors are often viewed as hypochondria by the general public. Objective studies of medical use by elderly persons, however, indicate that they do not make disproportionately large numbers of visits to physicians (National Center for Health Statistics March, 1991a) Considering the physical problems that accompany increasing age, elderly persons do not seem to be any more prone to hypochondria than the general population (Costa and McCrae 1985). Half of all people aged seventy-five to eighty-four report no health limitations (Neugarten and Neugarten 1987, 30).

Assuming that monetary and health problems are not overwhelming, many couples report that the period of retirement is one of enjoyment and marital happiness. They are able, often for the first time, to be together without jobs and children making demands on them. They can travel and pursue hobbies and long-neglected interests. They can attend to one another with a concentration not available since they first dated. In some ways a successful retirement is like courting. After years of facing the demands of work and family and growing apart in some ways, retirement provides the time needed to renew the relationship, make discoveries about each other, and revive the courtship that first brought the couple together. In addition, most retirees express general satisfaction with family relationships and do not feel neglected or abandoned by their relatives (Brubaker 1990, 960).

Indeed, the increasing longevity of Americans has created the phenomenon of the four-generation family. An estimated half of all persons over sixty-five with living children are members of four-generation families. This does not mean that they live with their families, but that they are great-grandparents. This role is relatively new in society. Great-grandchildren can be as great a source of joy and fulfillment as grandchildren. At the same time, the generational gap is so large that great-grandchildren can also be a source of bewilderment because their lifestyles are so different from those of the oldest generation.

Elderly parents (or a parent in the case of widowhood) who live with their children may put their children in the position of "parenting their parents." This role reversal is difficult for both the elderly parents and their children. The frustration that often occurs when elderly parents live with their children creates the possibility of elder abuse (see Chapter 15).

Since children no longer automatically care for their aging parents, government agencies have had to be created to help the elderly. Government-regulated retirement programs and Social Security have been established to help economically. Medicare and nutrition programs such as Meals on Wheels assist in the area of healthcare. The National Council on Aging publishes a directory of special housing for the elderly. Licensing and supervision of institutional facilities for the aged are being tightened. The elderly themselves are organized as a power bloc (American Association of Retired Persons and the Gray Panthers, for example) to work to improve care and opportunities for people in their later years. Programs such as the Retired Senior Volunteer program, which pays out-of-pocket expenses to those involved in comunity activities and projects, and the Senior Corps of Retired Executives, which pays former managers to counsel small businesses, are springing up to keep the elderly active and useful. All of these developments bode well for us as we move into the later years of our lives.

Yet the question remains: If possible, isn't the bosom of the family—the center of inmate relationships—the place to age gracefully and die with dignity and care? Fortunately, current research supports earlier work that reported that older persons are not abandoned by their families. In fact contact between older parents and their adult children, especially daughters, is often frequent and supportive (Sanders et al. 1985, 93; Brubaker 1990; for an overview of literature and resources about family care giving for the elderly, see Blieszner and Alley 1990; Coward, Mullens, and Christopherson 1990).

WIDOWHOOD AS THE LAST STAGE OF MARRIAGE

One can be faced with the death of a spouse at any stage of marriage. A spouse can die of disease or accident at any time. But the problems of the young widower or widow are much different from the problems spouses face when they lose their partner near the end of their lives and find themselves alone after many years of marital partnership. The young person who loses a spouse

America's population is aging (often referred to as the "greying of America"). In 1900 approximately 5 percent of the U.S. population was over age sixty-five while today that group is closer to 14 percent and is projected to be more than 20 percent by 2030. With the low birthrate, fewer young people will be available to support the aging population. Paul Chance (1987) discusses some provocative ideas in the following essay:

In China, the old lean upon the young. Only one worker in four is covered by a pension, and there is no social security system. Old people are cared for by their children, a long-standing tradition now backed by law. The system has worked well for hundreds of years, it is possible that the system may break down in the decades ahead.

China has a young population, with a much smaller proportion of old people than the United States and most other Western nations. This means that there are lots of young workers to provide for a few elderly. but with the one-child policy and improved medical care, China is expected to age rapidly. There will be fewer and fewer workers to care for more and more old people.

Caring for the elderly is expensive. In the United States the cost of caring for an old person is more than ten times the cost of caring for a child. Though the cost of oldsters may not be so great in China, it will place a considerable burden upon young workers. This will require sacrifices that the young may be unable or unwilling to make.

China's alternatives are few. And each solution seems to bring with it new problems. With the current one-child policy, the population is expected to continue to rise until the year 2000, after which it will remain stable at 1.2 billion. Allowing more births at that point would relieve the elderly care problem, but would relight the fuse on the population bomb. Raising the retirement age would reduce the period of dependency on offspring, but it would also block the career paths of those offspring. Implementing a social security system would lessen the burden by making children without dependent parents pay, but we have seen in this country that the system may not work well when old people survive more than a few years after retirement. Improving productivity may lessen the burden, but increased productivity is likely to lead to rising expectations.

generally remarries, but only about 2 percent of men and 1 percent of women over sixty-five remarry although these percentages seem to be increasing.

Regardless of age, the death of a spouse arouses all the emotions that occur whenever one loses a loved one. Grief, feelings of guilt, despair, anger, remorse, depression, turning away and at the same time toward others are all normal reactions. Given time, most of us can overcome our emotional distress at losing a spouse and go on with our lives. But, for a few long-married couples, death of one precipitates the death of the other. This often occurs when a woman has derived most of her self-identity from her husband (see Inset 14-5).

As we saw in the overview of family life stages, the last stage of marriage is overwhelmingly one of widowhood.

Of women between the ages of sixty-five and seventy-four, 62 percent are widowed compared to only 2.1 percent of men in this age range (U.S. Bureau of the Census July 1985, 49).

Widowers generally exhibit more severe problems of disorganization than widows. The men have higher rates of suicide, physical illness, mental illness,

Widowhood as the Last Stage of Marriage

My grandmother died only a few months after my grandfather even though she was in good health and had seldom been sick in her life. My grandfather was a strong independent man who worshipped my grandmother and took especially good care of her. He never allowed her to work or to want for anything and remained deeply in love with her, often publicly displaying his affection, until he died.

He was an old-fashioned family doctor who made house calls and regarded his patients as his family. My grandmother's entire identity revolved around being "doctor's wife" (that is how she often referred to herself). Her life was his

life, and in hindsight I realize she never developed any interests of her own. In fact, she seemed to have no interests apart from his interests. As "doctor's wife" she took care of him, the family, and the house. When the children became independent, she became even more attentive to him and didn't develop any other interests to replace the missing children.

With the arrival of grandchildren, she became the happy mother all over again, caring for the grandchildren as often as she could. When grandfather died, we all tried to visit her often and invited her to visit our families. She told us to give her a little time to adjust and

said that for the present she preferred to stay home. About three months later, I found her lying in grandfather's bed having passed away from an apparent heart attack. In retrospect I think that she had died in spirit when grandfather passed away. The death certificate records "heart attack" as the cause of death.

When I think about it, I had no grandmother. My grandmother was "doctor's wife." When he died, her identity died and soon thereafter her body. I prefer to substitute "broken heart" for "heart attack" on the death certificate.

alcoholism, and accidents although in part these differences are characteristics of all males. One study also showed that widowers' overall mortality rate was 26 percent higher than for married men with the same traits (age, schooling, smokers, nonsmokers, and so forth). In contrast, the mortality rates for widows was only 3.8 percent higher than for married women with similar traits. Widows appear to have better support systems than widowers (more friends, companions, interaction with children and grandchildren). This may stem from the fact that wives generally pay more attention to the couple's social relationships, and this social activity simply extends into widowhood (Brubaker 1985, 100; 1990).

There is no evidence that either men or women are significantly more likely to die in the early months of bereavement. Death occurs later and seems to be a product of the stressful life situation of the widowed person rather than an immediate reaction to the death of the spouse. Another interesting discovery is that remarriage by widowers dramatically lowered their mortality rates.

> In men under the age of fifty-five who remarried (about half of them did), the death rate was 70 percent lower than for those who did not remarry. In men aged fifty-five to sixty-four, the death rate was 50 percent lower (*Time* 1981).

Although parallel statistics for widows are not available, such data tend to support our assumption that marriage can promote health, at least for men

(Chapter 2). Both widowers and widows experience a dramatic rise (three to four times) in mortality rates when they move into a retirement or nursing home because of illness or inability to live with other family members (*Time* 1981).

Despite the negative findings about the problems of widowers, the social problems caused by aging center on the much greater numbers of widows in the American society. As we saw earlier, widows outnumber widowers over sixty-five years of age by about six to one. About 74 percent of men but only 40 percent of women over age sixty-five still live with a spouse. The problems of widowhood are for the most part the same problems faced by the elderly in general, but the problems are compounded by the fact that the widow faces them alone without a spouse.

In rural America a century ago, many retired parents, especially those who were widowed, received some support from their grown children. People tended to grow old on the farm within the family setting. Grandparents gradually turned the farm over to their children, but remained on the farm, giving advice, fulfilling the grandparent role, and being active family members until they died. Thus much of the widowed person's normal role in the family remained intact.

As America urbanized, however, children tended to move away from their parents and establish independent households within the cities. Often both partners worked at jobs that took them out of the home. Living space diminished so that room was available for only the immediate nuclear family. When the children who had moved to the cities grew older, there was no farm to which they could return. Thus urbanization slowly moved the care of the elderly out of the children's reach.

Today many Americans own their homes, which often gives them refuge and a major asset in their later years. More than two-thirds of the elderly remain in their home until death. Remaining in the home reduces the impact of spousal loss since the widowed person is not forced to adjust to new living quarters at the same time that he or she must cope with the loss. Another 25 percent of persons over sixty-five live with a child. The remaining elderly live in a variety of circumstances: with relatives other than children, with roommates, in nursing homes, and in rented quarters (see Table 14-2). Perhaps half a million are well enough off monetarily to buy or lease living quarters in exclusive retirement communities such as Arizona's Sun City or California's Leisure World.

THE ADJUSTMENT PROCESS AND REMARRIAGE

We pointed out earlier that most people do finally make an adjustment to the death of a loved one. Generally, the surviving spouse goes through three stages in the grieving process. First is the *crisis-loss phase* when the survivor is in a state of chaos. Fortunately, the survivor usually has a lot of support from friends and family immediately after the loss of the loved one. The second stage is the *transition phase* when the survivor attempts to create a new life. The final stage entails the establishment and continuation of a new lifestyle. The reorganization may result in a new life as a single widowed person (particularly for surviving wives) or a remarriage may occur (particularly for surviving husbands) (Brubaker 1985, 91–92).

TABLE 14-2 LIVING ARRANGEMENTS OF PERSONS AGED SIXTY-FIVE AND OVER

LIVING ARRANGEMENTS	PERCENTAGE OF MEN	WOMEN
Alone	16%	42%
With spouse	74	40
With other relatives	8	16
With nonrelatives only	2	2

Source: U.S. Bureau of the Census May, 1991, 12.

Widowhood as the Last Stage of Marriage

Jim was only twenty-eight when Jane was killed in an auto accident while returning home from her job. He was left with his son, Mike, who was four years old. Jim tells his story.

"At first, everyone rushed over and wanted to keep Mike for me. Some of our friends almost couldn't accept 'no' for an answer. Yet I felt that Mike needed to be with me and certainly I needed him.

"It is also amazing to remember who came over the first few days. People whom we had hardly known brought food. At first when they asked what they could do, I replied, 'Nothing.' Yet they were so obviously disappointed that I finally tried to think of something for them to do. This seemed to make them feel better, although I'm not sure it helped me. In a way I needed things to do, things to distract me from my grief at least for a short time.

"Although I certainly mourned at first, I found that I was often too angry to mourn. I wanted revenge on the other driver, and I was particularly mad at the city for allowing such a dangerous intersection to exist without stop signs. At times I was even angry at my wife for driving so poorly, but this always made me feel guilty. Actually I think I was angry at the whole world. Why did events conspire to take her away from me?

"I had a lot of remorse for things I had put off doing with and for Jane. We really should have spent the money and gone home to see her parents last Christmas. Why hadn't I told her I loved her more often? In many ways at first I felt I had failed her.

"As time passed, however, I realized that perhaps she had failed me just a little also. At first I could only think of the good things. To think of bad things between us when she wasn't there to defend herself just seemed terrible. Gradually, though, I have been able to see her and our relationship as it really was, with both good and bad. I want to preserve her memory for myself and our son, but I want it to be a realistic memory, not a case of heroine worship. I do fantasize about her, especially when I'm alone, and it really helps me to relive some of the memories, but I know that they can't substitute for the present. I must keep living and carrying forward for myself and our son.

"Although I'm not dating yet, I will in the future. She'd not want me to remain alone the rest of my life. Right now, though, I prefer to be alone with our son, with my thoughts and memories. I need time to understand what has happened, time to be sad. I need time for grief, time to adjust to my new single-parent role, time to ease the pain. I'll be ready for a new relationship only after I have laid the old one gently and lovingly to rest. When the time comes, I will look forward to marrying again."

In her study of elderly Chicago widows, Helena Lopata (1979) reported the figures for adjustment periods shown in Table 14-3. A few widows reported that they would never be able to establish a new life, but only time will tell if their belief is correct. Lopata makes several interesting points about her sample that probably hold true for many widows. Many of the women had never been alone in a home, having gone from the home of their parents directly into the home they established with marriage. Many of them had no occupational skills, never having worked except perhaps in a few odd jobs before marriage. Their traditional socialization was to be passive about the world outside their home environment. They had always depended on a family support system. Thus their socialization and consequent life experiences did not adequately prepare them to start a new life alone.

These difficulties will diminish as more and more women enter the work force and establish a more independent lifestyle. The emphasis of the women's movement on individual identity for all women, even when married, should also help negate the problems Lopata found.

The upsurge of interest in death and bereavement has helped both widows and widowers cope with their new roles. More understanding and empathy have been extended to them. For example, programs in which widows counsel other widows have been helpful in reducing the adjustment period.

Remarriage is perhaps the best solution for the widow or widower. Most elderly who do remarry face a more complex marriage because the children and grandchildren of each newly married spouse often play roles in the new marriage. Children may be concerned that a parent's new spouse will take away their inheritance, or worry that the new spouse is a con artist preying on the widowed. The children will also have to interact with a whole new set of relatives. Despite these potential problems and the complexity of remarriage, most elderly report high levels of satisfaction with their new marriages (Brubaker 1985, 43–44; 1990).

For widows, the lack of available older men is the major obstacle. Some researchers (Lasswell 1973; Duberman 1977) suggest that polygyny might be an appropriate solution. If the few available older men were allowed more than one wife, older widows would have more opportunities to remarry. Another way to alleviate the problem would be for women to marry men eight to ten years younger than themselves, but this would require a change in the long-standing American tradition of women marrying men one to two years older than themselves. Nevertheless, marriages in which the woman is older seem to be on the increase.

In 1970 about 3.7 percent of brides were five years or more older than their husbands. By 1983 that number had increased to 6.2 percent. As women grow older, they show an increasing tendency to marry younger men, Table 14-4 indicates (Wilson 1987, 13):

Regardless of one's age, it is important to plan ahead against the loss of a spouse. Yet few of us do—probably because it means contemplating the death of someone we love, and this is always unpleasant and often avoided.

Nevertheless, married people need to be able to answer a number of practical questions if their spouse should pass away.

■ Is there a will? If so, where is it, and what are its contents?
■ Is there life insurance? If so, how much is it, and what must the survivor do to collect it?
■ What are your financial liabilities and assets?
■ Do you have access to safety deposit boxes and where are the keys?
■ How much cash can you raise in the next sixty days to keep the family going?

Satisfactory answers to these questions can greatly ease the practical transition to widowhood. This, in turn, allows the surviving spouse more time to deal with the emotional and psychological transition.

TABLE 14-3
TIME NECESSARY FOR ELDERLY WIDOWS TO ADJUST AND BEGIN DEVELOPING A NEW LIFE AFTER THE DEATH OF A SPOUSE

TIME NEEDED	PERCENTAGE
2–11 months	25%
1 year	20
2 years	23
Over 2 years	16
Other	16

TABLE 14-4
PERCENTAGE OF WOMEN MARRYING YOUNG MEN

BRIDE'S AGE	PERCENTAGE WITH YOUNGER HUSBAND
Under 20	3.4%
20–24	13.4
25–34	31.3
35–44	39.1
45–64	32.5
Over 65	37.1

Widowhood as the Last Stage of Marriage

THE GRANDPARENTING ROLE

Many people speak nostalgically of the extended family of rural nineteenth century America. Parents, grandparents, and grandchildren happily living and working together on the farm is a wonderful romantic ideal, yet the short life expectancy of the nineteenth century meant that this arrangement was relatively rare. Between 1900 and 1980, the probability of three or four grandparents being alive when a child reaches age fifteen increased from 17 to 55 percent (Uhlenberg 1980).

Greater life expectancy has also drastically changed the image of grandparents. Grandparents are no longer the little white-haired couple sitting contentedly in their rock chairs. (The author's seventy-two-year-old mother, grandmother of two, recently eloped.) Grandparents are often still actively employed, living full and active lives of their own. In fact, the term "young-old" seems an appropriate way to describe many grandparents. With the high rate of teenage pregnancy, many persons will become grandparents in their thirties. With the increasing emphasis on maintaining healthful activity, many elderly persons remain youthful both in appearance and attitude.

For some retired, widowed, and elderly persons, fulfilling the role of grandparent can bring back many of the joys and satisfactions of their own early family life. Grandchildren can mean companionship, renewal of intimate contact, the joy of physical contact, and a sense of being needed and useful. One source of family strength reported by older couples was the support offered to them by their children and grandchildren (Sanders et al. 1985, 89). This is especially true of divorced or single people with children (Denham and Smith 1989, 347–348).

Like the retirement and widowed stages of marriage, grandparenting has been greatly extended by increased life expectancy. Most children have a relationship with one or more grandparents throughout their youth. It is quite possible today for people's period of grandparenting to be longer than the period in which their own children were at home. Of course, younger grandparents still married, employed, and living in their own homes do not have the same need to grandparent as older, retired, and perhaps widowed grandparents.

For older grandparents the role might be described as "pleasure without responsibility." They can enjoy the grandchildren without the obligations and responsibilities they had to shoulder for their own children. The grandparenting role gives people a second chance to be an even better parent: "I can do things for my grandchildren that I could never do for my own kids. I was too busy to enjoy my own, but my grandchildren are different." Association with grandchildren can also yield a great deal of physical contact for the widow or widower. Such contact is one of the things most often reported missed after a spouse dies.

Physical contact (other than sexual) is an important source of intimacy and emotional gratification, regardless of age. Much physical warmth can be had with grandchildren. Hugging, kissing, and affection gained from grandchildren

can go a long way toward replacing the physical satisfaction found earlier in marriage.

Many grandparents also report feelings of biological and psychological renewal from interacting with their grandchildren: "I feel young again." "I see a future."

This picture of grandparenting is only one of many. The kinds of relationships that grandparents have with their grandchildren vary considerably. Much of the relationship depends on how close grandparents and grandchildren live to one another. If a grandchild lives far away, there may not be a relationship. If one set of grandchildren lives nearby and all the others live at some distance, the grandparents may have a relationship only with those nearby. Some grandchildren may live with parents who don't get along with their own parents and as a result there may be little or no relationship.

After interviewing 510 grandparents Cherlin and Furstenberg (1985, 102) identified three styles of grandparenting: detached (26 percent) where there was little or no contact; passive (29 percent) where the grandparents saw their grandchildren once or twice a week but the relationship was shallow and ritualistic; and active (45 percent) where grandparents and grandchildren enjoyed a deep, meaningful ongoing relationship. It is obvious from the figures that only a portion of grandparents derive the pleasures and satisfactions from their grandchildren that we have described.

Cherlin and Furstenberg point out that there is often selective investment in grandchildren (1985, 110). Even active grandparents may be only selectively relating to one or two of many grandchildren, remaining detached or passive with the others. In addition, the kinds of relationships established by grandmothers and grandfathers tend to differ.

We have discussed the kinds of satisfactions grandparents can derive from their grandchildren. At the same time, grandparents can give a great deal to their grandchildren and to the overall family as well. Bengtson (1985, 21) suggests that just "being there" is an important grandparenting function. Family members can draw support and feelings of well-being just by knowing that their grandparents are alive and available. The grandparents can provide a buffer against family mortality; act as a deterrent against family disruption; serve as arbitrators in family disputes; and provide a place to go to escape marital difficulties. Children whose parents divorce can seek support and permanence with their grandparents (Troll 1983). Grandparents can become surrogate parents for grandchildren who don't get along with their parents or are missing a parent because of death or divorce. Since grandparents normally are not responsible for grandchildren and therefore do not have to set the rules and administer punishment, they can become friends and sometimes allies of their grandchildren.

The grandparenting role differs by ethnicity or subculture. Among Mexican-Americans relations between grandparents and grandchildren tend to remain close. The families often reside nearby, and there is considerable contact between generations. While 66 percent of Mexican-Americans answered the question, "Would you like to live in the same neighborhood as young children?" affirmatively, only 33 percent of blacks and 20 percent of whites did so (Bengtson 1985, 19).

Another striking contrast between groups is that 47 percent of blacks over the age of sixty, reported raising children other than their own or "fictive" grandchildren. Only 8 percent among whites reported having raised children other than their own (Bengtson 1985, 19).

Increasing life expectancy and the high divorce rate have combined to add a number of new dimensions to the grandparenting role. The increasing life expectancy means that more and more grandparents have their own elderly parents still living and perhaps will have to shoulder some responsibility for them.

Divorce of grandparents or death of one and remarriage of the other may lead to new stepgrandparents for grandchildren. Also, especially when a grandfather remarries, it could mean new children for the grandparents. Of course, remarriage of the grandparents' own children may mean the grandparents must relate to a new set of stepgrandchildren.

Divorce also raises the question of visitation rights for grandparents as well as spouses. Since children go with the mother in 90 percent of divorces, it is the paternal grandparents who usually lose contact with their grandchildren. Detached or passive grandparents may not be distressed by this situation, but it can be devastating for active grandparents. At the behest of grandparents, all fifty states now have statutes granting grandparents legal standing to petition for legally enforceable visitations with their grandchildren-even over parental objections (Thompson et al. 1989).

It is clear that with increased longevity the grandparenting role is becoming more important and complex. Fortunately, as more and more people become

AGING NO LONGER HAS TO MEAN SICKNESS, SENILITY, AND SEXLESSNESS

D___ __ who specialize in treating ol___ ople delight in telling the story of a ninety-year-old man named Mo___ who has a complaint about his l_t knee. Says his exasperated physi___n: "For heaven's sake, at your age w___ do you expect?" Rejoins Morris __ily: "Now look here, Doc, my righ__ __ee is also ninety and it doesn't ___ t." It is an apocryphal tale with a p___nted message. As long as anyone c___ remember, old age and disability ___ __en paired as naturally and i___ __ as the horse and carriage or ___ _ taxes. After all, most people ___ garded advancing years as an i___ __ble slide into illness, impoten___ __nd immobility.

No longer. ___ wadays America's seniors are giv___ the lie to that grim vision. Accordi___ to surveys, fully half of all people ___ow seventy-five to eighty-four are fr__ of health problems that require s___cial care or curb their activities. Say___ ociologist Bernice Neugarten of N__hwestern University: "Even in ___ very oldest group, those above eig___ ___e, more than one-third report n___ __itation due to health."

That more cheerful vie__ of growing old is gaining currency mainly because of the rapidly expanding scientific discipline of gerontology. Modern studies of the aging process involve everyone from laboratory researchers examining brain tissue to nutritionists interviewing nonagenarians to physicians specializing in treating the elderly. The goal of gerontology is not to extend the upper limit of human life—now about 115

to 120 years of age—but to make the lives of the elderly less burdensome physically and more rewarding emotionally.

How long and how well one lives, of course, depend in part on heredity. The chances of blowing out eighty-five candles go up 5 percent with each parent or grandparent who has passed that milestone. A family history of certain ailments, such as breast or colon cancer, heart disease, depression, or alcoholism, extends the risk of developing such problems. Increasingly, though, researchers believe personal habits and environmental influences may hold the key to why some people are more "successful" at aging than are others.

Many of the fears people have about aging are greatly exaggerated. Senility is probably the most dreaded of all debilities, yet only about 15 percent of those over sixty-five suffer serious mental impairment. Alzheimer's disease, now considered the scourge of old age, accounts for more than half that total. For many of the remainder, mental impairment from conditions such as heart disease, liver or thyroid trouble, and dietary deficiency is either reversible or preventable.

Another frequently overlooked culprit is overmedication. Nearly 80 percent of people sixty-five and older have at least one chronic condition (top four: arthritis, high blood pressure, hearing impairment, heart disease); about one-third have three or more. To combat their problems, they rely on a battery of over-the-counter and prescription drugs. The majority of people in this age group use more than five medications, and 10 percent take more than twelve. Interactions among drugs, as well as too much of some drugs, can cause a host of complications, from mental confusion to slowed blood clotting to disturbance of the heart's rhythm.

Flagging libido and sexual ability have also been wrongly equated with advancing years. Women supposedly lose interest in sex after menopause; in fact, desire normally remains strong throughout life. The dampening of sexual urges often results from physical problems, such as hot flashes and vaginal dryness, which may be alleviated by estrogen therapy, lubricants, and attention to nutrition and exercise. Older men, for their part, routinely accept continued impotence as normal. It is not. As a man ages, he does need more time to achieve an erection. But almost all impotence, whether psychological or physical, is reversible. Among the common physical causes: diabetes, heart disease, and chronic alcohol abuse.

Yet another widely held fear is that wear and tear on the joints inevitably leads to painful and immobilizing arthritis. Yes, there is a wearing down of the cartilage pads that cushion bones, but less than half of those over sixty-five whose X rays show degenerative arthritic changes suffer symptoms. Many of the aches and pains attributed to acute arthritis, doctors say, have more to do with weakening muscles than creaky joints. People with some joint damage fare better when they engage in regular moderate exercise, such as walking or swimming.

Some striking physiological changes accompany age. Among them:

■ The immune system starts to decline at around age thirty, which makes it harder to stave off illness.

■ Metabolism begins to slow at around age twenty-five. For each decade thereafter, the number of calories required to maintain one's weight drops by at least 2 percent. Muscle mass gradually shrinks. As a result, people tend to get fatter.

■ Lungs lose on the average of 30 percent to 50 percent of their maximum breathing capacity between ages thirty and eighty. Blood vessels lose elasticity, though the heart remains astonishingly well preserved.

■ Bone mass reaches its peak in the thirties for both men and women, then begins to drop by about 1 percent a year. Brittle bones are the major cause of the fractures, particularly of the hip, that cripple many of the elderly. Alcohol and tobacco use accelerate bone thinning.

■ The senses flag. Taste diminishes as the nose loses its sense of smell (odor accounts for about 80 percent of overall flavor sensation). The loss of taste can lead to lack of appetite and sometimes to serious nutritional deficiencies. Hearing fades, particularly in the high-frequency range, and processing of information slows. Vision begins deteriorating at about forty. The pupil shrinks, reducing the amount of light reaching the retina.

■ Changes occur in the skin. The topmost layer, or epidermis, becomes dry and blemished. The middle layer, or dermis, thins dramatically, making the skin seem translucent, and becomes much less elastic and supportive. These changes, along with loss of fat from the underlying subcutaneous layer, cause the skin to sag and wrinkle.

■ The need for sleep gradually diminishes. Newborns sleep sixteen to eighteen hours a day; by age sixty-five, three to six hours a night, perhaps with a nap during the day, is typically all that is necessary. The quality of sleep changes, becoming lighter and more fitful. Shorter, restless nights lead many who recall the easy slumber of youth to complain of insomnia. As a result, half of elderly women and one-quarter of elderly men take largely unneeded sleeping pills.

So far, gerontologists have no surefire prescription for staying healthy longer, but they do make some strong recommendations: stay out of the sun, cut back on drinking, and stop smoking. They stress that it is never too late to adopt better habits. A person of seventy who stops smoking immediately reduces the risk of developing heart disease. The elderly should follow general principles of a sound diet: avoid foods rich in cho-lesterol or saturated fat, such as eggs and beef, and eat more chicken and fish. Seniors should stress high-fiber foods, including whole-grain cereals and many fruits, and items rich in vitamins A and C, such as broccoli and cantaloupe. Exercise, at least half an hour three times a week, is an important aid to controlling weight, keeping bones strong, building muscle strength, conditioning the heart and lungs, and relieving stress. Declares physiologist William Evans of the U.S. Department of Agriculture–Tufts University center on aging: "There is no group in our population that can benefit more from exercise than senior citizens. For a young person, exercise can increase physical function by perhaps 10 percent. But in an old person you can increase it by 50 percent." The advice is catching on: A Gallup poll taken at the end of 1987 found that 47 percent of those sixty-five and older regularly engage in some form of exercise.

Resignation exacts as heavy a toll on the road to old age as disease or poor habits, warn gerontologists, who stress the importance of cultivating new interests and staying mentally engaged. That view is shared by no less an authority than comedian George Burns. "People practice to get old," he avers. "The minute they get to be sixty-five or seventy, they sit down slow, they get into a car with trouble. They start taking small steps." Burns stays young by taking fearless strides. He plans to play the London Palladium on his 100th birthday.

Source: Adapted from "Older—but Coming on Strong." *Time*, February 22, 1988, 76–78.

CHAPTER
15

FAMILY CRISIS

CONTENTS

One of the characteristics of all strong families is the ability to handle crises. A *crisis* is any event that upsets the smooth functioning of a person's life. It may be an emotionally significant event or a radical change of the person's status. It is a turning point. the birth of a child, unemployment, moving to a new location, divorce, remarriage, illness, natural catastrophes, injury, and death are all turning points in life. Developing crisis management skills is a top priority for all individuals as well as all families because we all will face periodic crises as we go through life. Although a crisis may directly affect only one individual in a family, it will indirectly affect the entire family. In a strong family, family members rally to help each other in times of crisis.

Most people think of crises only as negative events, but a positive event can also be a crisis if an individual or family is upset by it. Certainly, the marriage of a grown child is a positive and happy event. But, perhaps this is the last child living at home. Thus, when he or she marries and leaves home, the parents will have to adjust to being alone again. If the adjustment to this change is smooth and problem-free, there is no crisis. But if the parents are upset and have difficulty adjusting, then the happy event can also become a crisis.

Not all turning points are crises. Whether a change is a crisis depends on the family—its crisis management skills, its resources, and the way it views the turning point. Short-term unemployment may be highly disruptive to one family and become a severe crisis. Another family may have planned for the unemployment and saved enough funds to last until the parent is reemployed; this family, which views unemployment as an opportunity to do other important things for a short time, may not consider the change a crisis.

Some families seem to experience many crises. When such families are studied, the researchers often discover that the families lack some of the six qualities found in strong families. Crisis-prone families are often troubled families long before a crisis arises. A poorly functioning family—one having day-to-day problems they can't resolve—is in an already weakened condition. When a crisis arises, such a family may simply not have the resources and energy available to cope with it.

Whatever crises families may face, keep in mind the six characteristics of strong families: (1) commitment, (2) appreciation, (3) good communication patterns, (4) liking to spend time together, (5) a strong value system, and (6) the ability to solve problems constructively. By working to build these characteristics into your own family, you are taking the first and most important step toward successful crisis management. A strong family can survive crises well because the family members have the resources, the sense of unity, and the sense of direction that enables them to work together to overcome problems.

COPING WITH CRISES

Depending on a family's viewpoint and resources, many different kinds of events are apt to become crises. We term such crisis-provoking situations as

TABLE 15–1
TYPES OF STRESSOR EVENTS

Internal
Events that arise from someone inside the family, such as getting drunk, suicide, or running for election.

External
Events that arise from someone or something outside the family, such as earthquakes, terrorism, the inflation rate, or cultural attitudes toward women and minorities.

Normative
Events that are expected over the family life cycle, such as birth, launching an adolescent, marriage, aging, or death.

Nonnormative
Events that are unexpected, such as winning a lottery, getting a divorce, dying young, war, or being taken hostage. Often but not always disastrous.

Ambiguous
The facts surrounding the event are uncertain. They are so unclear that you're not even sure that the crisis is happening to you and you family.

Nonambiguous
Clear facts are available about the event: what is happening, when, how long, and to whom.

Volitional
Events that are wanted and sought out, such as a freely chosen job change, a college entrance, or a wanted pregnancy.

Nonvolitional
Events that are not sought out but just happen, such as being laid off or the sudden loss of someone loved.

Chronic
A situation that has long duration, such as diabetes, chemical addiction, or racial discrimination.

Acute
An event that lasts a short time but is severe, such as breaking a limb, losing a job, or flunking a test.

Cumulative
Events that pile up, one right after the other, so that there is no resolution before the next one occurs. A dangerous situation in most cases.

Isolated
An event that occurs alone, at least with no other events apparent at that time. It can be pinpointed easily.

Source: From Pauline Boss, *Family Stress Management*, page 40. Copyright © 1988 Sage Publications, Inc., Newbury Park, CA. Reprinted by permission of Sage Publications, Inc.

Stressor event
An event that provokes a crisis for an individual in a family

stressor events. Pauline Boss (1988) has classified stressor events as shown in Table 15-1. As the table indicates, stressors vary in several ways; they may come from within or without the family, be predictable or unexpected, and so forth.

Stress in one area of life also tends to spill over into other areas of life. A person who is experiencing problems at work will probably bring those problems home to the family. This may cause increased stress because the family then becomes upset. Contrary to previous thinking, husbands are more likely than wives to bring their home stresses into the workplace. Husbands and wives bring work stress home equally, however (Bolger et al. 1989).

As noted earlier, severity of various stress situations varies according to how the family views the situation and the resources the family has to cope with the stress. Nevertheless, most families do find certain situations more stressful than others. McCubbin and Patterson (1983) have ranked various events by the relative severity of the stress produced. For example, most families find the death of a child more upsetting than the divorce of a child. Table 15-2 lists some of the most severe family stressors.

TABLE 15-2 RELATIVE SEVERITY OF SOME FAMILY STRESSORS (SCALE 1 to 100)	
Death of a child	99
Death of a spouse or parent	98
Separation or divorce of spouse or parent	79
Physical or sexual abuse between family members	75
Family member becomes physically disabled or chronically ill	73
Spouse or parent has an affair	68
Family member jailed or in juvenile detention	68
Family member dependent on drugs or alcohol	66
Pregnancy of an unmarried family member	65
Family member runs away from home	61

Source: McCubbin and Patterson 1983.

STRESS: HEALTHY AND UNHEALTHY

People tend to think of all stress as negative. You have probably read articles about the damage, both psychological and physical, stress can cause and have heard about the importance of reducing stress in your life. Yet everyone faces frustration, disappointment, and the resulting stress as life goals are pursued. A healthy person is not necessarily free of stress, but rather can cope with stress when it arises.

Tolerance to stress varies greatly between people. What may be stressful to you may not be stressful to someone else. The amount of stress tolerance you develop is unique to you as an individual. You can learn to understand your own personal reactions to stress and to cope with stress in healthful ways.

Furthermore, some stress in life can be healthful. For example, proper stress on muscles causes them to grow stronger. Weight lifting is healthful stressing of the body. Sometimes too little stress can be harmful. For example, individuals who experience a moderate amount of realistic fear before major surgery have milder emotional reactions after the surgery. After surgery their reaction is often, "Oh, it was not as bad as I feared it would be."

Research has also found that moderate stress, especially during childhood, may be related to later achievement. A study (Goertzel and Goertzel 1962) of over 400 famous twentieth-century men and women, including such individuals as the author Pearl Buck, the inventor Alexander Graham Bell, and the musician Louis Armstrong, found that:

1. Three-fourths of the individuals were troubled as children. Among the problems experienced were poverty, a broken home, rejecting or domineering parents, physical handicaps, and parental dissatisfaction over the child's failure at school or vocational choices.
2. One-fourth of the sample had experienced handicaps such as blindness, deafness, being crippled, having a speech defect, being homely, or being undersized or overweight.

Coping with Crises

TABLE 15-3
SIGNS OF STRESS

PHYSICAL SIGNS	PSYCHOLOGICAL SIGNS
Pounding of the heart; rapid heart rate.	Irritability, tension, or depression.
Rapid, shallow breathing.	Impulsive behavior and emotional instability; the overpowering urge to cry or to run and hide.
Dryness of the throat and mouth.	Lowered self-esteem; thoughts related to failure.
Raised body temperature.	Excessive worry; insecurity; concern about other people's opinions; self-deprecation in conversation.
Decreased sexual appetite or activity.	
Feelings of weakness, light-headedness, dizziness, or faintness.	Reduced ability to communicate with others.
Trembling; nervous tics; twitches, shaking hands and fingers.	Increased awkwardness in social situations.
Tendency to be easily startled (by small sounds and the like).	Excessive boredom; unexplained dissatisfaction with job or other normal conditions.
High-pitched, nervous laughter.	Increased procrastination.
Stuttering and other speech difficulties.	Feelings of isolation.
Insomnia—that is, difficulty in getting to sleep or a tendency to wake up during the night.	Avoidance of specific situations or activities.
Grinding of the teeth during sleep.	Irrational fears (phobias) about specific things.
Restlessness, an inability to keep still.	Irrational thoughts; forgetting things more often than usual; mental "blocks"; missing of planned events.
Sweating (not necessarily noticeably); clammy hands; cold hands and feet; cold chills.	Guilt about neglecting family or friends; inner confusion about duties and roles.
Blushing; hot face.	Excessive work; omission of play.
The need to urinate frequently.	Unresponsiveness and preoccupation.
Diarrhea; indigestion; upset stomach, nausea.	Inability to organize oneself; tendency to get distraught over minor matters.
Migraine or other headaches, frequent unexplained earaches or toothaches.	Inability to reach decisions; eratic, unpredictable judgment making.
Premenstrual tension or missed menstrual periods.	Decreased ability to perform different tasks.
More body aches and pains than usual, such as pain in the neck or lower back; or any localized muscle tension.	Inability to concentrate.
Loss of appetite; unintended weight loss, excessive appetite; sudden weight gain.	General ("floating") anxiety; feelings of unreality.
Sudden change in appearance.	A tendency to become fatigued; loss of energy; loss of spontaneous joy.
Increased use of substances (tobacco, legally prescribed drugs such as tranquilizers or amphetamines, alcohol, other drugs).	Nightmares.
Accident proneness.	Feelings of powerlessness; mistrust of others.
Frequent illnesses.	Neurotic behavior; psychosis.

In the ideal environment, stress will occur within a healthful range. But this range varies according to a person's adaptability and stress tolerance. Stress is harmful only when it becomes so strong that it causes an individual to behave in an unhealthful manner. Regardless of the source of stress, its physical and psychological symptoms are similar (see Table 15-3).

Moreover, individuals exhibit a pattern of response to stress called the *general-adaptation syndrome*. This response occurs in three phases: (1) alarm, (2) resistance, and (3) recovery or exhaustion.

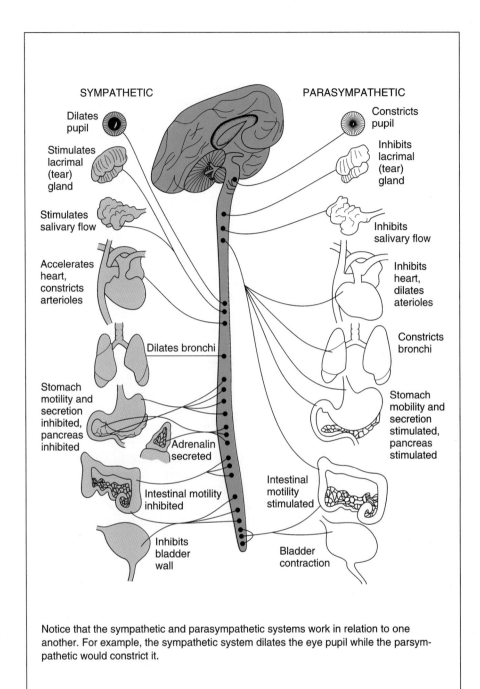

FIGURE 15-1
Autonomic nervous system

SYMPATHETIC

Dilates pupil

Stimulates lacrimal (tear) gland

Stimulates salivary flow

Accelerates heart, constricts arterioles

Dilates bronchi

Stomach motility and secretion inhibited, pancreas inhibited

Adrenalin secreted

Intestinal motility inhibited

Inhibits bladder wall

PARASYMPATHETIC

Constricts pupil

Inhibits lacrimal (tear) gland

Inhibits salivary flow

Inhibits heart, dilates aterioles

Constricts bronchi

Stomach mobility and secretion stimulated, pancreas stimulated

Intestinal motility stimulated

Bladder contraction

Notice that the sympathetic and parasympathetic systems work in relation to one another. For example, the sympathetic system dilates the eye pupil while the parasympathetic would constrict it.

In the first phase, the *alarm* reaction, a person experiences physical and psychological changes when confronted by a stressful situation (Table 15-3). These changes, which are largely automatic, are controlled by the sympathetic or parasympathetic nervous system (Figure 15-1). These two systems usually operate in opposition to one another; that is, if one system activates a response, the other counteracts the response.

Coping with Crises

If exposure to stress continues, the alarm reaction is followed by the second phase, *resistance*. During this stage, various physical responses appear to return to normal because the body has built up resistance to the stress.

The third phase, *exhaustion* or *recovery*, follows if stress continues. During this stage exhaustion occurs if many of the original symptoms return. In this case, the person often becomes physically ill. On the other hand, if the stress has been reduced to a tolerable level, the symptoms do not come back, and recovery ensues.

■ CRISIS MANAGEMENT ■

How you define and react to an event largely determines whether it is a crisis. Almost everyone would certainly define an event such as the death of a husband, wife, or child as a crisis. Being laid off from a job may be a crisis for one person, but not for another who may see it as an opportunity to return to school and change careers. Remember the word "crisis" has its roots in the Greek verb *krinein* meaning "to judge" and "to choose." Therefore a crisis is a moment when you must choose from among various alternatives and opportunities that present themselves.

The first step in crisis management is to describe the event in realistic terms and determine whether it is a crisis for you, your family, or your friend. It is important to face the facts squarely. Often the first reaction to crisis is disbelief and denial. "This isn't happening to me." "They aren't really going to lay me off from work." As long as you are in a state of denial, it is impossible to handle the crisis.

Sometimes defining the event can cause trouble within a family. Family members may describe and define an event differently. The mate of the person who is laid off may define the layoff as a crisis because he or she feels the family cannot survive financially. This definition of the situation will cause conflict if the partner wants to return to school and/or change careers regardless of the financial situation.

The second step in crisis management is to examine your emotions and reactions to the crisis situation. Uncontrolled emotions can disrupt the decision-making process. Emotions tend to blind us unless they are controlled and used in a positive manner.

Crisis situations are stressful, but stress can be helpful as well as disruptive. Stress can heighten your awareness and make you more efficient. Learning to control and use stress constructively in your life will be of great help in managing crises.

As a third step, seek support and help from friends and family who can help you to see alternatives. This step is especially important if you are extremely affected by your emotional reactions. Often your first reaction in a crisis is to feel trapped and think there is no way out, no answer. Friends and family can help you, however, to find answers that will bring you out of the crisis.

Fourth, consider all possibilities and take decisive action to resolve the crisis. Using outside resources may be necessary to resolve a crisis successfully. **Therapy** is a broad term used to describe actions taken to cure or solve any problem. Taking an aspirin is therapy for a headache. Counseling from a hospice after the death of a loved one is also therapy that will help you cope with the crisis caused by the death. Many groups and organizations help individuals cope with

Therapy
Any action taken to cure or solve a problem

crises in their lives. Outside individuals and groups have the advantage of being objective about problems. Although therapists and counselors can empathize with your feelings, they are not emotionally involved and thus may be able to see the problems more clearly.

In the past, families and friends were primarily responsible for helping in times of crisis. Although this is still true, the mobility of people means that family and friends may or may not be near enough to help at crucial times. Therefore the role of community agencies has become more important. Many agencies have resources for finding help. For example, the Catholic Charities and Jewish Family Services offer counseling services to families. Family Service of America, an organization found in many communities, also helps families. Teachers and school counselors can be of help directly and can also suggest other sources of assistance in the community. Often the public library can provide this information as well. Local churches and temples are another good source of help in times of trouble. Inset 15-1 describes some agencies and lists various hotlines that offer different kinds of help.

Crisis situations often tend to bring out the best in people. For example, during times of natural catastrophes—such as floods, earthquakes, and fires—not only family and friends but often strangers offer help and support.

> After the terrible hurricanes in Florida, Louisiana, and Hawaii in 1992 that destroyed thousands of homes and businesses, hundreds of people helped those who had lost their homes and belongings. Strangers gave food, money, housewares, and shelter to others. Stores offered goods at cost. Whole communities pitched in and offered help to those who needed it.

Your past experience with crises can be of great help when working through a new crisis. If you have successfully coped with past crises in your life, the crisis management skills you have learned will help you through future crises.

Remember that crisis management as the ability to solve problems constructively is one of the characteristics of a strong family. The better your family relations are and the stronger your family, the better you will be able to handle crises that arise in your life or that of your family.

■ DEFENDING AGAINST HARMFUL STRESS ■

We cannot always master every situation in which we find ourselves. Coping devices are ways of handling or dealing with stress, frustration, pain, fear, anxiety, and any other problems arising from stressful situations. Some coping devices are more helpful than others.

When you are confronting a stressful situation and are emotionally aroused, it helps to focus your energy. The emotional reactions caused by stress are often undirected. Under stress you may feel generally upset, angry, or fearful without directing your emotions toward anything in particular. *Anxiety* is a generalized fear without a specific object or source. For example, when you are afraid, you know what is causing your fear. In a state of anxiety, the source of the fear is unclear; yet the same emotional reactions are present. Anxiety often accompanies stress and frustration. If you focus your emotional reactions on the source of your stress, you can limit your anxiety. For example, "I am angry at the factory supervisor for firing me" rather than "I am angry at the world because I have been fired."

Coping with Crises

Tables 15-4 and 15-5 list telephone hotlines and various agencies that are available to help with crises.

TABLE 15-4
TELEPHONE HOTLINES TO HELP WITH VARIOUS CRISES

■ If you are thinking about running away or have run away: Call NATIONAL RUNAWAYS HOTLINE 800-231-6946 (in Texas 800-392-3352). They provide counseling on resolving home problems and referrals to local social service agencies and to safe shelters. They will send help to your home in an emergency abuse situation or refer you to OPERATION HOME FREE for free transportation home. Call NATIONAL HOTLINE FOR MISSING CHILDREN 800-843-5678. They provide counseling, referrals to local social service organizations, and recommendations of local shelters. Call NATIONAL RUNAWAY SWITCH-BOARD 800-621-4000. They provide help and guidance for such problems as drug abuse, child abuse, and sexual abuse, referral to local social service agencies and shelters, and transmittal of messages to parents without disclosing the runaway's location.

■ If you are the victim of or have observed child abuse: Call NATIONAL CHILD ABUSE HOTLINE 800-422-4453. They provide crisis intervention counseling and referrals to local services. All calls are confidential.

■ If you or someone you know has a drug problem: Call COCAINE HELPLINE 800-662-HELP (800-662-4357) or 800-COCAINE (800-262-2463). They provide counseling on drug problems, referrals to local support groups (such as Narcotics Anonymous and Cocaine Anonymous), to outpatient counseling programs, and to residential treatment centers.

■ If you have a drinking problem: Call AA (Alcoholics Anonymous). See your local telephone directory. They provide referral to their local support groups.

■ If you have a parent, friend, or relative with a drinking problem: Call ALATEEN. See your local telephone directory under Al-Anon. They provide referral to local support groups of teenagers who have relatives or friends with drinking problems.

■ If you feel depressed or suicidal: Call a local suicide prevention hotline. Most telephone directories list these and other crisis numbers in the community services section at the front of the White Pages.

■ If you discover cancer in yourself or family: Call for cancer information 1-800-638-6694.

■ If someone close to you becomes handicapped: Call for information on programs for the handicapped 1-800-424-8567.

■ If you are having problems as a parent: Call Parents Anonymous 1-800-421-0353.

■ If you discover that you or someone you know has the AIDS virus: Call for AIDS information 1-800-342-AIDS.

It is important yet difficult to relax in the midst of stress. By relaxing, you reduce emotional arousal and can then make better, more clearheaded choices and decisions about ways to reduce the stress that is causing your problems. The following steps may help you relax:

1. Assume a comfortable position, ideally in a quiet environment, and close you eyes.
2. Breath deeply.
3. Deliberately start to relax each muscle in your body starting with your feet and working up to your neck and face. This is called *progressive relaxation*.

TABLE 15-5
AGENCIES THAT CAN HELP WITH VARIOUS CRISES

RESOURCE	CLIENTELE	SERVICES
Aid to Families with Dependent Children	Families with children in need of assistance.	A government program that provides cash payments to families with needy children deprived of parental support because of the death, absence, or incapacity of one or both parents.
Alcoholics Anonymous	Victims of alcoholism.	Free local, self-help groups that follow rules of strict anonymity in overcoming alcoholism.
Al-Anon and Alateen	Families of victims of alcoholism.	Local support groups for parents, children, and friends of alcoholic victims.
American Red Cross	Provides services to families in the community.	Provides food, shelter, and other essentials for recovery to disaster victims and families in emergencies. Promotes health and safety awareness.
Battered Women's Center	Provides help for victims of family violence.	Offers shelter, counseling, public education, and advocacy for victims. Centers provide shelter, food, and clothing for victims and their children.
Big Brothers and Big Sisters	Provides adult companionship for children from single-parent families.	One-to-one relationship between adult volunteers and children, ages 7 to 15, from one-parent families. Adult provides guidance, social contact, and academic enrichment through regular weekly contacts.
Children's Protective Services (Agency name may vary.)	Children who are in need of protection due to abuse, neglect, abandonment, or sexual exploitation.	This government agency assigns social workers to supervise families against whom there have been complaints of abuse and/or neglect. In severe cases, the agency will remove children from the home and provide substitute care, supervision, and related services for the children.
Family Counseling Center(s)	Individuals, families, and groups needing counseling.	Family, marital, parent-child, and individual counseling is provided. Efforts are made to improve interpersonal relationships and family living.
Visiting Nurse	The general public.	Provides general help with injury and illness.
Hospice	The general public.	Offers help in coping with terminal illness.
YMCA and YWCA	The general public.	Programs include child care, camping, health and fitness groups, informal education, older youth programs, parent-child programs, senior citizen programs, and other related services.

4. Maintain a quiet attitude, letting your thoughts come and go, and allow relaxation to proceed at its own pace.

5. Once relaxed, let yourself remain in this state for fifteen to twenty minutes.

Some people may call this process self-hypnosis, meditation, yoga, or a number of other names for self-induced relaxation.

DEFENSE MECHANISMS

Defense mechanisms are methods that an individual uses to deny, excuse, change, or disguise behaviors that cause anxiety. There are many kinds of

Coping with Crises

defense mechanisms. Understanding and recognizing these mechanisms will lead to better, more open and honest communication. The following are a few of the more commonly used defense mechanisms:

1. *Repression* at first glance appears similar to forgetting, but is actually more complex. Repression is an unconscious blocking of whatever is causing the individual stress and frustration. For example, Jamie's mother sends him to the store to buy a number of items including liver. Jamie has always disliked liver. When he returns home with the groceries, his mother discovers that there is no liver—Jamie has forgotten to buy it. He did not do this deliberately. Forgetting the liver is an example of repression through which Jamie avoided the stress and frustration of having to eat something he doesn't like.

2. *Displacement* is a straightforward substitution of a less threatening behavior for another. For example, Richard's boss criticizes him unfairly. Richard is mad, but he's afraid to speak up for fear of being fired. That evening he becomes angry with his girlfriend for no apparent reason. It is less stressful and safer for Richard to take his anger out on his girlfriend. He has displaced or wrongly shifted his anger from his boss to his girlfriend.

3. *Rationalization* is a common defense mechanism. It involves finding an excuse for a behavior that is causing trouble. For example, Jeffrey is rationalizing when he tells his professor "I missed the test because I ran out of gas." Jeffrey is fooling himself. His professor, who sees that Jeffrey is just making an excuse instead of taking responsibility for his behavior, asks "Why didn't you look at the gas gauge?" Rationalization appears to others as "making excuses."

Lou and Alcohol

Lou, age thirty, has a severe drinking problem. Although all of his friends and family recognize that he is an alcoholic, he tells them that he really is only a social drinker and can quit any time he wishes. Whenever he gets drunk and causes a problem, Lou finds some reason or excuse for his behavior (rationalization). It is never his fault. He claims it is the fault of others or bad luck. It just happened, and he has no idea why. He is sure that he is not responsible.

When Lou's friends confront him about his drunkenness, he usually denies any problem. He feels that they are exaggerating. Sometimes he even accuses his friends of drinking and trying to blame him to escape their own guilt feelings.

WHAT DO YOU THINK?

1. Assuming that Lou really is an alcoholic, why do you think he doesn't recognize it even though his friends and family do?
2. Why do you think Lou always has an excuse or reason for his behavior?
3. Have you ever had a friend or family member with an alcohol or similar problem? Did they also make excuses for their behavior and deny that there was a problem? How did you react to this?

4. *Projection* is a defense mechanism whereby one's own characteristics or impulses are imposed upon others. Projection can take two different forms. It can justify one's own desires: Nancy tells her mother, "But, mother, everyone else is going to the party, why can't I?" Projection can also serve to rid one of unacceptable characteristics or behaviors: Lou sometimes claimed that his friends were drunks, not him. Projection is the major psychological mechanism used in **scapegoating** whereby a person or group is blamed for the mistakes and crimes of another. Scapegoating may also be evident when a person or group is blamed for some misfortune that is due to another cause.

Scapegoating
Blaming a person or group for some misfortune or mistake of another

5. *Sublimation* involves converting a socially unacceptable impulse into a socially acceptable activity. John is very aggressive and often feels like fighting. He joins the football team and is praised for his aggressiveness on the field.

6. *Compensation* allows a person to make up for a shortcoming in one area by becoming successful in another area.

Art and the Debate Team

Art has been active in sports since he was a small boy. In high school, he was a star football player and hoped he would make the team when he went on to college. At the university, however, Art faced competition from young men who had been stars on high school football teams all over the country. Although he was among the better players trying out, Art simply wasn't large enough or talented enough to make the team. Although he was extremely upset and disappointed, he joined the debate team at the suggestion of his speech class professor. At first Art thought debate was "wimpy" compared to football, but as time passed, he found that mental conflict in the form of debate took strength and courage, too. Soon he was competing in national contests and becoming known for his tough-minded debates. Art has compensated for his feelings of failure in football by his achievements in another area. He used the defense mechanism compensation in a positive manner.

WHAT DO YOU THINK?

1. Do you have areas in your life in which you feel unsuccessful? If so, what are they?

2. In what areas do you think you could be or are already successful? Could you substitute one of these areas for one in which you feel unsuccessful?

Some researchers think that defense mechanisms are unproductive ways of fooling ourselves. According to this interpretation, until Lou stops making excuses for his drinking habit, he will have no reason to change. Lou's defense mechanism is denying responsibility for himself, thus locking him into his behavior. "It's not my fault so why should I change?" In other words, defensive behavior keeps Lou from seeing the reality of his situation or behavior. This

Coping with Crises

From their research Lauer and Lauer (1988; 1991, 507–9) have identified a number of tools people use to deal successfully with stress situations:

■ *Take responsibility*. Rather than using denial, avoidance, and various defense mechanisms that deny responsibility, successful individuals and families assume responsibility for solving the problems they confront. They do not hide behind victimization and blame others for their problems. They assume that something can be done about the problems and set about making problem-solving decisions, which, in turn, lead to stress reduction.

■ *Affirm your and your family's worth*. Crises assault people's self-esteem. This makes it more difficult to deal with the crisis. Believing in yourself and in your ability to deal with difficult situations is an important part of being effective in a crisis. You need to remind yourself that you and your family are people with strengths and the capacity to cope successfully. You and your family are not victims with no control over your lives. Exercise control.

■ *Balance self-concern with other-concern*. A crisis tends to make people self-absorbed. We become so involved in the problem that we are unable to think about anything else or to listen to or care about others in our family. For example, the next section discusses the crisis of death in the family. Researchers studying families that had lost a child to cancer two to nine years earlier found that the families that handled the crisis best were those in which the individual family members were aware of the grieving of other family members and made efforts to empathize and support them (Davies et al. 1986).

■ *Learn the art of reframing*. Reframing, or redefining the meaning of something, is a way of changing your perspective on a situation. It isn't the situation that is changed, but the way you look at it. In essence, you learn to look at something that you had defined as troublesome and redefine it as adaptive and useful. Reframing is not denial. It is based on the fact that people can look at any situation in numerous ways. You can see a crisis as an intruder that has robbed you of your peace and happiness or as an obstacle that will ultimately lead to your growth as you overcome it.

makes adjustment to his drinking problem impossible. Nevertheless, defense mechanisms used in a moderate and recognizable manner can contribute to satisfactory adjustments. The following are potential positive uses of defense mechanisms:

1. Defense mechanisms can be used to gain time to adjust to a problem that might at first be overwhelming. For example, if you can find an excuse for your negative behavior, you feel more comfortable and perhaps are better able to work on the problem causing the behavior.

2. Defense mechanisms may lead to experimentation with new roles. For example, Francine has low self-esteem and feels worthless. She joins a prestigious club and brags about her membership in it to make herself feel better. However, joining the club does actually help her change for the better. Because the club members accept her, Francine's sense of self-worth improves.

3. Some behavior caused by defense mechanisms may be socially useful and even creative. A person may try to make up for shortcomings in one area of life by excelling in another. This is what Art did when he compensated for failing at football by becoming successful on the debate team.

Although they have positive uses, defense mechanisms also tend to block open and truthful communication. Emotional health is tied closely to the ability to communicate well. Stress and the resulting frustration tend to block communication. Thus, the better able you are to handle stress and the better you understand defense mechanisms, the better your ability to communicate will be.

DEATH IN THE FAMILY

■ NATURAL CAUSES ■

Almost everyone defines the death of a loved one as a crisis. In the following chapter, we will examine the crisis of marital failure—namely, divorce—which can cause many of the same feelings as death in family members. In both cases individuals may experience a sense of loss, grief, and loneliness.

Death is the other experience besides divorce that can end a family's existence. Loss of a husband or wife ends that particular family although the surviving spouse may start another family. Loss of a child does not end a family, but it creates a family crisis and an extreme sense of loss.

Death can result from many causes. Dying of natural causes, such as old age, may be gradual and expected. In this case the family can prepare for the death and coming changes in the family. But death by natural causes can also occur suddenly, such as from a severe heart attack. Death can also result from accidents, such as automobile accidents or fires. Any sudden death of a loved one creates an immediate and extremely traumatic shock and crisis for the family.

■ SUICIDE AND HOMICIDE ■

Death of a loved one through suicide or homicide is especially traumatic because the survivors are reacting to an intentional death. Suicides or homicides are generally unexpected. They usually cannot be reasonably explained. Family members, especially with a suicide, may feel partially responsible. "I should have known he or she felt this way. Perhaps I could have done something."

Unfortunately, suicide and homicide are not infrequent forms of death in our society (see Tables 15-6 and 15-7 and Figures 15-2 and 15-3 for statistics). The overall homicide rate in the United States was 9 per 100,000 in 1988. This rate continues to be three to eight times higher than rates in most other industrialized countries. Homicide was the leading cause of death among black males aged fifteen to thirty-four (U.S. Department of Health and Human Services March, 1991, 17).

The overall suicide rate in the United States has remained between 10 and 12 suicides per 100,000 population for the past fifty years. The overall homicide

TABLE 15-6
FREQUENCY OF HOMICIDE, LEGAL INTERVENTION, AND SUICIDE (DEATHS PER 100,000 POPULATION)

	HOMICIDE AND LEGAL INTERVENTION	SUICIDE
Caucasian male	7.7	19.8
Black male	58.2	11.8
Caucasian female	2.8	5.1
Black female	12.7	2.4

TABLE 15-7
DEATH RATES FOR SELECTED CAUSES FOR PERSONS 15–24 YEARS OF AGE (DEATHS PER 100,000 POPULATION)

	HISPANIC	ASIAN AMERICAN	AFRICAN AMERICAN	CAUCASIAN	NATIVE AMERICAN
Accidents	49	29	37	52	89
Homicide and legal intervention	28	7	59	8	22
Suicide	10	6	8	14	26
All other causes	25	15	41	21	24

Source: U.S. Department of Health and Human Services March 1991, DHHS pub. no. (PHS) 91-1232, 41.

FIGURE 15-2
Death rates for selected causes for persons fifteen to twenty-four years of age, according to race/ethnicity, 1988
Note: Data on Hispanic origin are from 26 states and the District of Columbia.
Source: National Center for Health Statistics, National Vital Statistics System, and U.S. Bureau of the Census, Current Population Surveys.

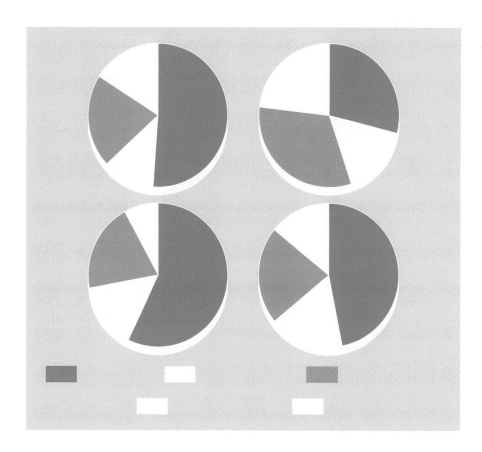

FIGURE 15-3
Weapons used in homicides among victims fifteen to thirty-four years of age, according to type of weapon and race of victim, 1986–1988
Note: Numbers of victims are in parenthesis.
Source: Federal Bureau of Investigation, Supplemental Homicide Reporting System.

rate in the United States has remained between 8 and 11 homicides per 100,000 population for the past twenty years. Homicides have increased in absolute numbers, however, because the population has grown.

The rate of suicide among white males aged fifteen to nineteen has increased during the past ten years. Suicide among young persons is particularly stressful to a family. "Young people have so much to live for." "Their whole life is ahead of them." "It's such a waste." The use of drugs is to blame for many youthful suicides. Nevertheless, society tends to view the family as somehow to blame for the suicide of a young person. "They must have been bad parents." "They should have known their son or daughter was using drugs." "Couldn't they see how depressed he or she was?"

Eleanor Whitney and Francis Sizer list some of the questions that are commonly asked about suicide:

1. *Why do young people want to die?* Experts say that, except for a tiny percentage, those who attempt suicide actually want to live. Thus, suicide may be the nation's number one preventable cause of death among young people.

2. *If suicidal persons want to live, why do they try to kill themselves?* Suicidal persons usually believe that they are not loved or accepted. They want desperately to know that someone cares. A suicide attempt is really a cry for help; it says, "Look at me, help me, save me!" In fact, some victims are found dead while holding the telephone, others call the police to say they plan an overdose of drugs. The majority of people attempt suicide in such a way that someone is sure to save them.

Death in the Family

3. *If a person's mind is set on suicide, can anyone or anything change it?* The overwhelming majority of people who survive a suicide attempt are glad they are alive. Only a few repeat the attempt and succeed. The wish to die generally lasts only a few hours or days, not a lifetime. If victims can be helped through the crisis period, chances are good that their life will go on normally afterward.

4. *Is it hard to face life after attempting suicide?* Of course, adjustment can be hard after an attempted suicide. With counseling and support from family and friends, however, life can be resumed.

5. *Do people who talk about killing themselves just want attention? Is it best to ignore their threats?* No. A person who often talks about suicide can lull friends and family into indifference. Meanwhile, the person is actually displaying suicidal intentions. By ignoring the suicide talk, friends and family members may even give the victim added reasons to follow through—to prove the seriousness of the intent.

6. *Are people who try to kill themselves emotionally ill?* Most people who commit suicide suffer from deep despair, loneliness, and hopelessness, but they usually don't have mental disorders. Some people contemplating suicide may be depressed, but others may be happier than they have been in a long while. They have decided on suicide as a way to solve their problems once and for all.

7. *What causes people to attempt suicide?*
- They may be trying to get attention.
- They may have an unrealistic, romantic view of death.
- They may be under too much pressure to succeed.
- They may not be able to express their anger or pain.
- They may feel rootless and lack the anchor of a strong parent-child relationship.
- They may not have firm values on which to base life decisions.
- They may have suffered a loss that has caused unbearable grief.
- They may have a parent or friend who committed suicide, making the act seem permissible.
- They may be under the influence of drugs and not realize exactly what they are doing.

8. *How can you tell if someone is about to commit suicide?* Be on the lookout for warning signs. Take seriously signs of severe depression. Watch for standoffish withdrawn behavior. Watch for the signs of drug use. Take suicide threats seriously.

9. *What can you do to help if you suspect an oncoming suicide attempt?* Take the person seriously and get involved. Don't wait to see what develops because tomorrow may be too late. Ask outright if the person is planning suicide. Do not be afraid to mention it. Chances are your friend already has the idea in mind, and talking about it with a clearheaded person can help. Be careful not to deny the seriousness of the intent. If you imply that your friend doesn't mean it, you may unknowingly be daring the person to do it. At the same time, show concern. Try to convey that you know the crisis is major, but offer reassurance that it is temporary. Try to help the person get professional help and counseling. If the person seems on the verge of making a suicide attempt:
- Phone a suicide or crisis intervention hotline immediately. If no hotline is available, call 911.
- Stay with the person until help arrives.

10. *What if you fail to prevent a suicide?* Accepting the suicide of someone close can be one of the hardest things in life to face. Still, you cannot change what has happened. You are not responsible for another person's suicide. Emotional support is available to survivors. Learning about the process of grief will also help.

11. *What if you sometimes feel like ending your own life?* Almost everyone feels that way sometimes. Things can seem very bad, but they can also get better, given time. You can talk to someone during bad times. Ask someone to listen to you. Most towns have suicide hotlines available twenty-four hours a day where you can talk with a counselor about your feelings. You can usually get the number from information. Enter group counseling with others who have similar feelings. Share your feelings with your family and friends who care about you.

■ GRIEF AND BEREAVEMENT ■

Death of a loved one almost always causes a crisis situation in a family. No matter how well you anticipate the death of a parent, the loss will be disturbing and adjustment will take time. Loss of a child or young adult is even more distressing. Everyone understands that death comes to us all. Hopefully, when parents pass away, you can look back on their lives and say, "I miss them, but they lived a good life." The death of a child or young adult is much more difficult to accept because you feel cheated: "My son's or daughter's life was all ahead of them. They didn't have a chance to enjoy life."

If death comes slowly to a loved one as with cancer or AIDS, you may go through the same basic emotional reactions to death that the dying person usually passes through:

1. *Denial and isolation.* A typical first reaction to impending death is an attempt to deny its reality. You try to ignore any information that points to impending death. You refuse to believe that your loved one is really going to die. "The lab reports are wrong." "Somebody mixed up the X rays." You may even refuse to discuss the subject of death.

2. *Anger.* "Why my wife or my child?" "I hate the world or God for taking this person from me." You may find that your anger spills over onto those still living. "Why is my husband being taken rather than another person?" You may find yourself angry and envious of the health of others.

3. *Bargaining.* You may find yourself bargaining for the life of your family member or friend just as those who are dying often bargain. "Just let my wife live a little longer, I'll treat her better than I have in the past."

4. *Depression.* Finally, as death draws near, you begin to recognize that it can't be prevented, there is nothing you can do about it. Usually, such recognition of the inevitability of death causes a profound sadness and temporary depression.

5. *Acceptance.* At last comes acceptance of the inevitable, followed by the actual death of your loved one and the process of bereavement.

Many, but not necessarily all, people pass through the stages in this list when death slowly approaches. It is also interesting to note that many of the same

Death in the Family

TABLE 15-8
LEADING CAUSES OF DEATH BY SELECTED AGE GROUPS
IN ORDER OF DECREASING DEATH

RANK	0–1 YEARS	1–14 YEARS	15–24 YEARS	35–44 YEARS	55–64 YEARS
1	Birth defects	Accident	Accident	Cancer	Heart disease
2	Sudden infant death syndrome	Cancer	Homicide	Heart disease	Cancer
3	Respiratory	Birth defects	Suicide	Accident	Stroke
4	Premature birth	Homicide	Cancer	Suicide	Accident
5	Complications from pregnancy	Pneumonia and influenza	Heart disease	Homicide	Liver disease

reactions accompany any major loss such as a divorce, loss of a job, and so forth.

After a friend or relative has died, whether the death is sudden or prolonged, grief usually follows. This reaction is natural and normal and is necessary for adjustment to the loss. At first there is a period of *numbness* and *shock.* You or the person grieving may seem to be adjusting well to the loss because during this period you may feel little emotion. This phase is followed fairly quickly by tears and the release of the bottled-up emotions.

The initial shock is followed by sharp *pangs of grief.* These are episodes of painful yearning for the dead person. During this period, agitated distress alternates with silent despair, and suffering is acute.

These sharp feelings of loss gradually give way to a prolonged period of dejection and periodic depression. Life seems to have lost meaning. There is a large gap in life that can't seem to be filled. Although the mourner is usually able to resume work and normal life ("life must go on"), listlessness, lack of energy, and difficulty concentrating continue. Gradually over time, maybe several years, life does return to normal for the mourning person. This does not mean that you never again mourn your loss. We all think often of lost loved ones and feel sad at the thought. But the mourning no longer dominates one's life (Coon 1992).

ACCIDENTS, INJURIES,
AND CATASTROPHIC ILLNESS

Accidents, injuries, and catastrophic illness are other kinds of major crises that can happen in any family. As Table 15-8 indicates, accidents are the most common cause of death and injury for young people aged one to twenty-four.

The accidents most likely to cause death for this age group involve motor vehicles, drowning, firearms, poison, and fires and burns.

A family with a child or parent who is severely injured because of an accident can be thrust into a crisis situation without warning. Many times a severe illness such as cancer develops gradually so that the family can plan ways to cope with the crisis. An accident, however, happens without warning so there is no time to prepare.

When an adjustment to the crisis of death has been made, the family can usually resume their everyday activities, even though the sadness and feelings of loss may persist for a long time as we noted. But the consequences of an accident or illness may cause a prolonged family crisis. Everyday activities may require adjustments that may continue for the rest of the family's life.

The Weinsteins

The Weinsteins are a middle-class family with two teenage children, Walt and Kara. They have some savings in the bank. The entire family is covered by Mr. Weinstein's health insurance at work. Walt is interested in cross-country mountain cycling. He has worked at a part-time job and bought a good mountain bike with his own money.

One day, riding in the hills with a group of friends, Walt loses control of his bicycle and goes over the side of the trail, dropping some fifty feet into a ravine. The search and rescue team finally gets him out, but he has a broken neck and is paralyzed.

Although the family's health insurance pays for the immediate expenses, it does not pay for prolonged physical therapy nor for at-home nursing care. Walt recuperates from the immediate injuries but will be confined to a wheelchair the rest of his life. He needs constant care in order to function.

WHAT DO YOU THINK?

1. Since the family's insurance doesn't cover at-home nursing care, how do you think the family will handle Walt's need for constant care?
2. What do you see as the family's most important adjustment to Walt's accident?
3. Do you know a family where a child or a parent has a serious long-term illness or injuries? How do they cope with the ongoing crisis?

Often we consider accidents as just that—accidents, or unfortunate events that occur unexpectedly or by chance. We become philosophical and say something about "being in the wrong place at the wrong time." In truth, accidents are not always chance or random events: they can be caused by ignorance or carelessness. Thus, many accidents are preventable. Statistics show that accidents do follow patterns (Reed and Long 1987); for example:

■ Males have more of every kind of accident than do females for every age after one year.
■ People under forty have more accidents than those over forty.
■ Most accident victims live in urban areas.
■ Most accidental deaths involve motor vehicles.
■ Most accidental injuries occur in the home.
■ Accident rates peak on certain days such as holidays.

By recognizing such patterns, preventive steps can be taken. For example, to help reduce the number of automobile accidents due to alcohol, police may stop cars at various checkpoints on holidays to check for drunken drivers.

Several factors increase the chances of becoming an accident victim. Physical conditions, such as fatigue, can lower a person's awareness and good judgment. Emotions, such as anger, grief, depression, or joy, can preoccupy people and thus increase the chances of an accident. Certain personality traits—including overconfidence in one's abilities, exaggerated self-importance, and impulsiveness—can lead people to make faulty decisions that lead to accidents (Reed and Long 1987).

Catastrophic illnesses, such as stroke, heart attack, AIDS, and cancer, are life threatening. They may disable a person for a long period of time—perhaps for the rest of the person's life. In this case, the family will have to find some way to care for the person long term as the Weinstein family had to do. Placing the person in some type of long-term care facility is often financially impossible for the average family. In that case, home care may be necessary. *Home care* means that family routines will probably have to change. This increases family stress. When accidents and injuries cause a crisis in a family, family members experience many emotions and are upset and worried about the person who has been hurt. Might the victim be crippled or die? Will he or she recover and, if so, how long will it take?

If a parent is injured and unable to work, the family may suffer economically. Usually, there is some short-term protection against this. An employee will have a number of sick days that can be taken (with pay) to recover. Workers injured on the job usually may draw worker's compensation payments for a set period of time. Some families will have disability insurance that pays them in the event of injury or accident.

The family may face large medical bills. Hospitalization can cost up to $1000 a day depending on the treatment. This may not even include doctor's bills. Many families have health coverage through their employer or from private insurance (see Figure 15-4). For families that do not have insurance, medical expenses can spell financial ruin.

Accidents and severe illness are unexpected. No one knows when or if an accident is going to happen or a severe illness contracted. When these crises occur, decision-making skills become very important because the family will have to make decisions quickly. These first decisions may be followed by a long period of adjustment or perhaps continual adjustment for the entire family.

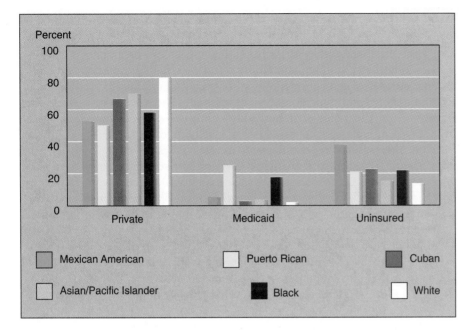

Percent

FIGURE 15-4
Health insurance coverage among persons under sixty-five years of age, according to race/ethnicity
Note: Percentages are age-adjusted annual averages.
Source: National Center for Health Statistics, *Health United States: 1990* March 1991.

FAMILY VIOLENCE

Violence within a family almost always leads to a crisis. Violence may occur within a family for many reasons. Family members who cannot talk to one another, don't listen to one another, and simply lack sufficient communication skills to make themselves understood are more likely to resort to violence. Children are often physically violent because they haven't learned how to communicate. In a way, adults who cannot communicate remain like children and often express themselves physically rather than verbally.

The family can be an important source of love, caring, and emotional support. Yet the possibility for violence and abuse within a poorly functioning family also exists. The family is an emotional hothouse. While the finest of emotions can be fully expressed in the strong family, the emotions of hate and anger can lead to violence in a poorly functioning family.

Family violence is difficult to measure and document because most of it occurs in the privacy of the home away from public view. However, family violence is coming increasingly into public view as newspapers, magazines, and television devote more attention to battered mates or abused children. Violence is reported between husbands and wives, between courting couples (see Chapter 4), and between parents and children. Definitions of abuse and violence vary. Abuse does not always refer to major physical and sexual abuse. Abuse means different things to different people. Some people consider spanking a form of parent-child abuse. Others regard shoving as spouse abuse. A single exposure to an exhibitionist may be considered child sex abuse. Hence the statistics on the amount of family abuse must be interpreted cautiously.

Family Violence

The most life-threatening situation a police officer can encounter is a family dispute. Emotions run high, and family members usually regard their problems as a private matter and consider the police officer an unwanted intruder. Homicide rates between husbands and wives are high. The number of wives killing husbands and the number of husbands killing wives are about equal. Most other physical violence between spouses usually involves the husband hurting his wife, although the reverse happens in a few cases.

In general, physical violence flares between spouses who do not have good communications skills. As a result of their inability to communicate, frustration and hostility build. Finally, something, such as an open conflict or alcohol or drug use, triggers an emotional outburst that culminates in violent behavior.

Most major cities now have battered women's shelters where a woman can go temporarily to escape an abusive relationship. The shelters usually have programs available to intervene in violent family situations. The criminal courts try to help by issuing restraining orders or jailing the violent partner for short periods. Unfortunately, some battered women return to the abusive relationship, even after seeking justice from the courts or staying in a shelter.

Violence also occurs between dating couples and cohabiting partners. One study compared violence among singles, cohabitants, and married couples and found that most violence occurred among cohabitants (Stets and Straus 1989). Numerous studies have reported violence among students who are dating, with females experiencing more violence than males (Burke, Stets, and Pirog-Good 1988; Lloyd 1991).

Family violence tends to follow a domino pattern; that is, those who experience courtship violence also tend to experience spousal violence. Those experiencing spousal violence tend to abuse their children. Abused children tend to abuse one another and become abusive adults. Do not take this to mean that every person who has ever been abused in turn abuses others. Indeed, most people who are abused do not necessarily abuse others.

■ CHILD ABUSE ■

Mistreatment of children by parents hardly seems compatible with mom, apple pie, and Sunday family outings. Yet many parents do emotionally and physically abuse their children. Increasing interest in child abuse has also revealed more sexual abuse and incest than previously had been thought to exist. Although numbers are hard to verify, studies report that anywhere from 9 to 28 percent of female children are sexually molested. Smaller percentages of male children are sexually abused. Some of the increase in child abuse can be attributed to the growing number of blended families (families with stepparents). In such families the incest taboo between the stepparent and stepchild is weaker than it is between the natural parent and child (see Chapter 17).

With the growing recognition of the prevalence of child abuse, new laws have been passed to protect children. In particular, states have made it mandatory for persons in contact with children to report cases of suspected abuse. Such provisions have helped greatly in uncovering cases that remained hidden in the past. These laws also account for the greatly increased numbers of reported child abuse incidents. In fact, child abuse may not actually have increased in recent years, but have simply been detected more frequently because of such laws.

The flood of publicity about child abuse has had negative as well as positive effects, however. One undesirable effect is that parents and school workers are becoming fearful of any kind of physical contact with children. Yet physical contact with adults in the form of affection and hugs is important to the development of young children. If in their efforts to protect children from abuse parents and child-care workers become afraid of any and all physical contact with children, more good may be lost than is gained.

Unfortunately, the flood of reports brought on by the changes in the laws and increased publicity has also greatly increased the number of unfounded reports. In 1975 about 35 percent of all reported cases of child abuse were closed because no evidence of abuse was found. By 1984 that number had increased to 65 percent (Johnson 1985).

At the same time, laws and publicity about abuse seem to have combined to reduce both spousal and child abuse. Using a large nationally representative sample, Straus and Gelles (1986) found that child abuse and wife abuse rates have decreased significantly. For an overview of research conducted through the 1980s on domestic violence and sexual abuse of children, see the work of Richard Gelles and Jon Conte (1991).

Three elements must usually be present in a family for child abuse to occur. First, the parent must be a person to whom physical punishment is acceptable. Often such an abusive parent was abused as a child. In addition, the abusive parent often has unrealistic expectations for the child and expects achievements that are impossible for the child's level of development. Second, the parent perceives the child as difficult and trying. Perhaps the child is sick much of the time or is very energetic and active. Third, usually a crisis of some kind has occurred in the family. The parent may have lost a job, be experiencing marital troubles, or have a lowered tolerance level due to something unrelated to the child, such as alcohol or drug use.

Some cities have created telephone hotlines that a parent can use to receive immediate help if he or she feels unable to cope with a child or children (see Inset 15-3).

■ SIBLING ABUSE ■

Violence between siblings is the most common form of family violence. Physical abuse is especially likely to occur between young children who have not yet learned other ways to express themselves. Young children have less self-control and often express their frustrations by physical means. The rate of violence declines as children become older and learn other ways to handle their frustrations. In general, boys are more violent than girls. Children in homes where adults are violent tend to copy the violence with one another. Almost 5 percent of families who were surveyed reported that a sibling had used a knife or gun at some time.

If brother-sister incest occurs, the effects on the children depend on a number of factors. Sex play among very young children, such as playing doctor—"I'll show you mine if you show me yours"—does not seem to be harmful as long as both children consent. However, sex play involving actual intercourse or continuous sexual episodes, occurring between children of widely different

In 1970, Claire W. Miles living in Santa Barbara, California, became so concerned about child abuse that she installed an extra phone in her home. She then placed an ad in the personal column of the local newspaper asking anyone who knew of an abused child to call the number. Within the next month, she received twenty-eight calls, many from parents who abused their own children. From this simple beginning, the Child Abuse Listening Mediation (CALM) program grew. In the first year, CALM was involved in 213 cases. Since that time the program has grown to include educational presentations throughout the country and visits to parents by volunteers, in addition to the immediate help offered by telephone. The following is an account of a case in which CALM volunteers became involved.

The mother had a son three years old. About two years ago, she had a nervous breakdown and was confined for some time in the psychiatric ward of a hospital. Her baby was cared for by his grandparents during her confinement. When she was able to take her baby back, she remarked how fat and healthy he was. The improvement in his physical condition seemed to accentuate her feelings of inadequacy as a mother and gave her a feeling of even greater insecurity in her relationship with her son. Her child was hyperactive, and her energy was often not a match for his. She had been trying to toilet train him without much success. When she tried to feed him, he threw food all over and refused to eat. Later he cried and was cross because he was hungry. Generally, she felt that he did nothing right and everything wrong. She was fearful that he was abnormal in some way.

She wanted to take him to a nursery school one or two days a week, so she could just be alone and rest, but she couldn't afford the private nurseries, which were the only ones that would take a child under three or one in diapers. She said, "I don't know what to do. I can't stand it much longer. Can you help me?"

She was told about the volunteer program, and she agreed to have someone come over the next day. A volunteer was selected who lived near her and had seven children of her own, ranging in age from ten to one, including a set of three-year-old twins.

The volunteer found that the woman has no friends in California since she had recently come from the East. She was lonely and over-anxious and tense from being a mother twenty-four hours a day, every day. On the initial visit, she didn't want the volunteer to leave, so the volunteer stayed as long as possible, then took the client and child home with her. For two or three weeks, the volunteer invited her over three mornings a week. She encouraged the girl to use her sewing machine to make kitchen curtains. The client gained assurance that there was nothing abnormal about her child, and through association with the volunteer's twins of the same age, the boy began to eat normally without throwing his food around. The mother observed many traits in the volunteer's children similar to those she had worried about in her son, and in a relatively short time, she expressed a relieved sense of relaxation in her relationship with her son. She is being more realistic in her expectations of him and is gaining self-confidence in her ability to care for him adequately.

ages, or taking place without mutual consent may have negative future consequences. In the future the child may feel ashamed and guilty and may have problems relating to sexuality as an adult.

PARENTAL ABUSE BY CHILDREN

Although abuse against parents sounds improbable, there are cases where children physically attack and even kill their parents. Although physical abuse of parents by their children is generally rare, verbal and psychological abuse is common. Children and adolescents tend to react verbally when they are frustrated. Consequently, verbal abuse heaped on parents by children is relatively common during adolescence.

Abuse of elderly relatives is another form of child-parent abuse. Estimates suggest that as many as 600,000 to 4 million elderly people are abused, neglected, or exploited. Such abuse often stems from the frustration felt by an adult child who must care for an elderly relative. Increasing life expectancy means that more and more children will have to cope with elderly parent care, however, so the problems faced by both the parent and the child are unlikely to diminish in the near future.

FACTORS ASSOCIATED WITH FAMILY VIOLENCE

Researchers have identified five factors that are frequently associated with family violence.

1. *The cycle of violence:* One of the consistent conclusions of domestic violence research is that individuals who have experienced violent and abusive childhoods are more likely to grow into violent adults. In other words, violence begets violence.

2. *Socioeconomic status:* Parental income and parental violence are inversely related: those with incomes below the poverty line have the highest rates of violence. Those struggling the hardest to support a family are more likely to be frustrated and unhappy.

3. *Stress:* Another consistent finding is that family violence rates are directly related to economic and social stress in families. Unemployment, financial problems, unwanted pregnancy, difficulties with single parenthood, and alcohol abuse are all related to higher incidence of violence in the family.

4. *Social isolation:* Social isolation increases the risk that severe violence will be directed at children or between spouses. Families who have religious affiliations, have a large circle of intimate friends, or participate in community and social activities report less familial violence.

5. *Traditional male role orientation:* Participants in violent relationships tend to hold a traditional view of the social roles of men and women. Abusive males have been described as very dominant, controlling, and "macho" in their outlook on women. They feel superior to women.

POVERTY AND UNEMPLOYMENT

Family well-being is intimately tied to economic well-being. A family that has economic problems also experiences frustration and stress. The family members must constantly worry that tomorrow may bring an emergency.

In the United States, poverty is usually defined in a relative way, and what we mean by poor differs greatly from what that status means in many other countries.

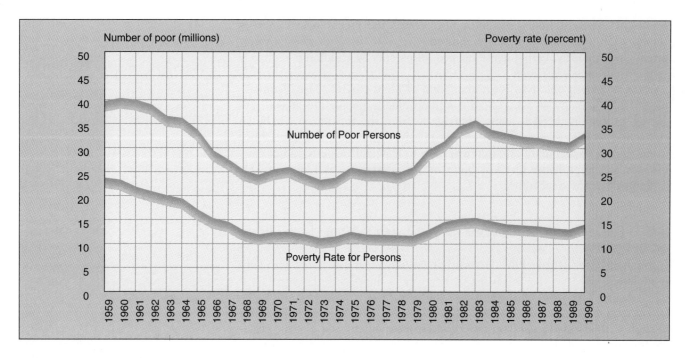

FIGURE 15-5
Number of poor and poverty rate,
1959–1990
Note: The data points represent the
midpoints of the respective years.
Source: U.S. Bureau of the Census
August 1991, 3.

TABLE 15-9 PERCENTAGE OF PERSONS BELOW THE POVERTY LEVEL BY RACE OR ETHNIC GROUP, 1990	
	PERCENT
Total	13.5%
Caucasian	10.7
Black	31.9
Hispanic	28.1
Asian American	12.2

Source: U.S. Bureau of the Census August,
1991, 4.

For example, the poverty threshold in the United States for a person living alone was $6,652 in 1990. The per capita income in Africa ranged from a low of $80 in Mozambique to a high of $2,520 in South Africa with the average for the whole of Africa being $630 (Population Reference Bureau 1992). The poverty threshold in the United States for a family of four was $13,359 in 1990.

As these statistics indicate, what Americans regard as poor hardly qualifies for the term in much of the rest of the world. Yet even though being poor in the United States does not mean that you will starve to death, being poor does cause great hardship to the poor individual or family.

As Figure 15-5 shows, the poverty rate (the percentage of people living below the poverty threshold) has varied since 1959 from a low of approximately 12 percent in 1973 and 1978 to a high of 22 percent in 1959. Figure 15-6 indicates that poverty rates for children are the highest for all age groups. This high percentage occurs because so many children live in single-parent female-headed households.

Poverty rates for single-parent female-headed families range from a high of 42.6 percent of such families in 1959 to a low of 30.4 in 1979. In 1990 the rate was 33.4 percent (U.S. Bureau of the Census August, 1991, 7).

Table 15-9 details the differences in poverty rates for various subgroups of Americans.

Most poor families move in and out of poverty depending on family composition and work patterns. The increased unemployment that occurs during economic downturns causes many families to drop into poverty. Once the economy recovers, many of these families move out of poverty again.

During the period of unemployment, however, the stress and strain on a family are great. Joblessness of a family member seriously affects the well-being

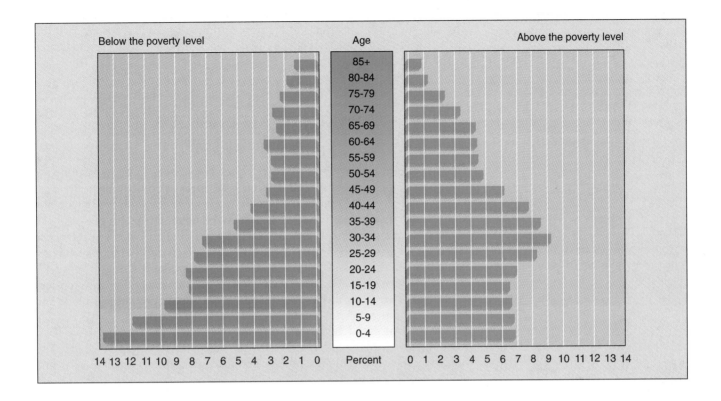

Below the poverty level	Age	Above the poverty level

Age (top to bottom): 85+, 80-84, 75-79, 70-74, 65-69, 60-64, 55-59, 50-54, 45-49, 40-44, 35-39, 30-34, 25-29, 20-24, 15-19, 10-14, 5-9, 0-4

Below the poverty level axis: 14 13 12 11 10 9 8 7 6 5 4 3 2 1 0

Percent

Above the poverty level axis: 0 1 2 3 4 5 6 7 8 9 10 11 12 13 14

of everyone in the family. The constant worry and strain, the loss of self-esteem and self-respect on the part of the unemployed family member, and the declining psychological and perhaps physical health of family members are all by-products of unemployment.

Changes in family composition also triggers movement in and out of poverty. For example, divorce throws many women and their children into poverty for a period of time. A young adult moving from home and setting up his or her independent household may find himself or herself beneath the poverty threshold, at least temporarily. A single woman giving birth may drop into poverty as a single parent.

Many people associate poverty only with unemployment, but in fact many working people live beneath the poverty threshold. They cannot earn enough to move out of the poverty status. These people are termed the **working poor.** They are usually members of families with children. More than half of the people who are poor live in families with at least one worker (Chilman 1991).

A number of public programs attempt to help people and families in poverty. Unemployment payments help families survive the period of joblessness until work is found. Retraining programs help workers improve their skills so that a wider variety of jobs will be open to them.

Since a large proportion of families in poverty are single-parent female-headed families, various laws have been passed to increase the level of child support by absent fathers. Child-care assistance, public subsidies for housing, food stamps, health-care assistance, and various tax credits that reduce taxes for poor people or families are all societal attempts to help the poor. Although efforts are being made to offer poor people economic help, many Americans feel that much more can be done. The creation of more and better-paying jobs

FIGURE 15-6
Distribution of the population above and below the poverty level by age, 1990
Source: U.S. Bureau of the Census August 1991, 3.

Working poor
People who are employed but cannot earn enough to move out of poverty status

Poverty and Unemployment

and the improvement of educational opportunities and standards are two important goals that American society much reach if poverty is to be eradicated in the United States.

DRUG AND ALCOHOL ABUSE

Good nutrition means eating the foods your body needs to be healthy. However, people ingest other substances that have little to do with nutrition, such as drugs and alcohol. Many of these substances can be harmful, both physically and psychologically, even though some may be taken for health reasons.

Defining the term *drug* is difficult. One definition of a **drug** is any substance taken for medical purposes or for pleasure that affects bodily functions. Thus, penicillin is a drug taken to fight disease, and morphine is a drug taken medically to relieve pain. Alcohol is a drug taken for pleasure and to ease tension, while marijuana is an illegal drug taken for the same purposes. Vitamins and minerals are drugs taken to promote and maintain health.

We are concerned here with the abuse of drugs and alcohol that leads to family crises. Many family problems are related to the misuse of both alcohol and drugs. For example, many, perhaps most, instances of spousal and child abuse occur when the abusing mate and/or parent is drinking or using drugs.

Drug
Any substance taken for medical purposes or for pleasure that affects bodily functions

DRUGS AND DRUG ABUSE

Many Americans express great concern about illegal drugs, such as cocaine, LSD, speed, and marijuana. Yet, in many ways Americans may be more threatened by legal drugs. For example, a person may go to sleep at night with the help of a sleeping pill, drink coffee as a stimulant to wake up the next morning, smoke a cigarette after lunch to ease tension, take a diet pill to reduce appetite for dinner, and drink several glasses of wine to be more relaxed and sociable at an evening party. Are these examples of abusing drugs?

As these examples illustrate, it is difficult to define *drug abuse*. This book will use the following definition: drug abuse is the persistent and excessive use of any drug that results in psychological or physical dependence or that the society labels as dangerous or illegal. Drug abuse can occur with legal drugs. If the person just described *must* follow that routine or any part of it to function normally, he or she is abusing drugs.

Susan and Crack

Susan was an honor student at the university. She worked evenings and on Saturdays to help pay her tuition. One Saturday when she was especially tired, one of her co-workers offered her a little crack cocaine, saying that it would make her feel better. Although a bit frightened, Susan was also curious. Shortly after smoking the crack, her fatigue left and she said, "I feel energetic and able to do anything."

Gradually, Susan started using crack before going to work. She found that the effects did not last long, and soon she was smoking more on her work break. As she needed more and more crack to maintain the high it gave her, the cost went beyond what she earned. Her co-worker who was supplying the crack offered to give her some free if she would go out with him. She soon found that he was not offering her free crack at all, but was trading crack for sex.

It wasn't long until she lost her job and stopped going to classes because consuming crack now occupied all of her time. Some months later she was arrested for shoplifting. Shortly after her release from custody, she was picked up again, this time for prostitution. She is now in a rehabilitation program and hopes to return to the university.

WHAT DO YOU THINK?

1. Have you any friends who have become consumed by a drug habit? How did they start using drugs?
2. If they are still using drugs, what do you think are their chances of kicking the habit? Why?
3. Why do you think some people are able to try a drug once or twice and not get hooked, while people like Susan seem to become addicted immediately? Which kind of person are you?

What is cocaine? Did Susan understand the long-term effects it would have on her body and her behavior? The major drug groups may be classified along a continuum from stimulating to depressing as shown in Figure 15-7. As the figure shows, drugs are capable of altering attention, memory, judgment, time sense, self-control, emotion, and perception.

When a person *must* use a drug to maintain bodily comfort, a *physical addiction* or *dependence* exists. The body often adapts to a drug and increases its *drug tolerance*, which means that an ever-increasing amount of the drug is necessary to maintain comfort. Once a physical addiction exists, any attempt to discontinue the drug usually causes both physical and mental *withdrawal symptoms*. Withdrawal from some drugs such as alcohol and heroin can be extremely unpleasant. Quitting heroin, for example, causes violent flu-like symptoms of nausea, vomiting, diarrhea, chills, sweating, and cramps.

Many people believe drugs that cause only psychological addiction are easier to give up than those causing physical addiction. Yet psychological addiction can be extremely difficult to overcome. For example, the eating disorder, anorexia nervosa, does not involve a physical addiction, yet the psychological addiction to the idea of being slim causes severe eating problems that lead to physical deterioration. Many therapists working with anorexic or bulimic young people find that the psychological addiction to faulty eating habits is extremely difficult to correct.

Drug and Alcohol Abuse

FIGURE 15-7

Continuum of drug action. Many drugs can be rated on a simulation-depression scale according to their effects on the central nervous system. Although LSD, mescaline, and marijuana are listed here, the stimulation-depression scale is less relevant to these drugs. The principal characteristic of hallucinogens is their mind-altering quality.

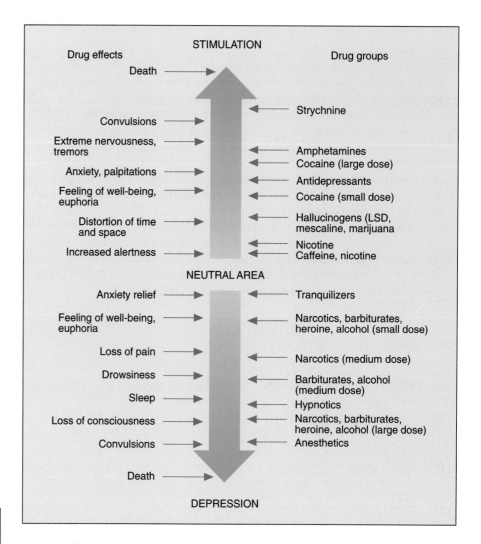

One of the dangers of doing drugs is mixing drugs. When different drugs are taken together, the effects of the drugs increase and confuse one's bodily reactions. The results can sometimes be fatal. Table 15-10 lists a number of celebrities who have died from taking a drug or mixture of drugs.

ALCOHOL

Alcohol is by far America's biggest drug problem. An estimated 14 to 18 million Americans have a serious drinking problem. Unfortunately, alcohol abuse seems to be increasing dramatically among adolescents and young adults. A 1990 study found that among adolescents aged twelve to seventeen, 27 percent of males and 24 percent of females reported alcohol use in the past month.

Contrary to popular belief, alcohol is not a stimulant. Actually, it slows or depresses bodily functions, such as reaction time. Small amounts of alcohol reduce mental control and produce feelings of relaxation. Alcohol also harms

TABLE 15-11	
THE DEVELOPMENT OF A DRINKING PROBLEM	
EARLY WARNINGS	SIGNALS NOT TO BE IGNORED
You are beginning to feel guilty about your drinking.	There are times when you need a drink.
You drink more than you used to and tend to gulp your drinks.	You drink in the morning to overcome a hangover.
You try to have a few extra drinks before or after drinking with others.	You promise to drink less and are lying about your drinking.
You have begun to drink at certain times or to get through certain situations.	You often regret what you have said or done while drinking.
You drink to relieve feelings of boredom, depression, anxiety, or inadequacy.	You have begun to drink alone.
You are sensitive when others mention your drinking.	You have weekend drinking bouts and Monday hangovers.
You have had memory blackouts or have passed out while drinking.	You have lost time at work or school because of drinking.
	You are noticeably drunk on important occasions.
	Your relationship to family and friends has changed because of your drinking.

sexual performance, especially for males. As William Shakespeare observed long ago, drink "provokes the desire, but takes away the performance."

Because alcohol abuse is such a common problem, it is important to recognize the danger signals of alcoholism. Table 15-11 points out some of the symptoms of a drinking problem.

Deaths in alcohol-related motor vehicle accidents are one of the most tragic side effects of drinking alcohol. Groups such as *Students Against Driving Drunk (SADD)* work to educate other students about the dangers of drinking and driving. Fortunately, such groups and the increasingly severe laws against driving and drinking have helped. Deaths from alcohol-related motor vehicle accidents have dropped from 57 percent of all traffic fatalities in 1982 to 49 percent in 1990.

Bruce and the Boys

Bruce is in his freshman year in college. He is elated to have made the football team as a wide receiver. He now spends most of his time with other members of the team.

His family has never used alcohol although they occasionally serve wine to friends who come to dinner. Bruce tasted both beer and wine

some time ago. He found them too bitter and sour for his taste and didn't like the aftertaste.

He has attended several parties with other members of the football team at which a great deal of beer was consumed. Because he did not like the taste of beer, he did not join in the drinking. His friends teased him calling his a "wimp" and a "nerd." Finally to shut them up, he joined them in their beer drinking at a party. He found the experience unpleasant and has now decided that he will just avoid those parties where beer is served.

WHAT DO YOU THINK?

1. If Bruce really didn't like beer, why do you think he finally joined his friends in drinking it?
2. How would you suggest Bruce handle his friends' pressure to drink at parties?
3. Do you agree with his decision to stop attending parties where beer is served? Why or why not?

Peer pressure played a large part in Bruce's drinking beer at the party. If you ask people who smoke, or drink, or do drugs how and why they started, many will blame it partially on their friends. "My boyfriend was doing drugs and wanted me to try it." "Everybody in my group smoked so it seemed like the thing to do." "On Saturday nights my friends competed to see who could drink the most beer, and I felt out of it if I did not participate."

Substance abuse can begin early in life. Part of maturity is making independent decisions for oneself. Young children must have decisions made for them. Adults who allow others to make important decisions about lifestyle and/or healthful living for them are acting as children. When Bruce drank the beer because of his friends, he was avoiding responsibility for his own behavior. To smoke, drink, or do drugs just because others are doing so is giving someone else the power to make important life decisions for you.

Saying "no" to alcohol, cigarettes, or drugs when friends offer them can be difficult. Inset 15-4 suggests a number of ways to say "no" to alcohol. With a few changes, these suggestions could apply equally well to saying "no" to drugs or cigarettes.

SUMMARY

1. *Stress occurs often in everyone's life.* Mild stress per se is neither good nor bad. It is how one handles stress that is important.
2. *People usually go through three phases in reacting to stress.* The first phase is alarm, the second phase is resistance, and the third phase is recovery or exhaustion.

■ Not now . . .
I'm in training for the _____
team.
I'm the driver.
I'm testing my will power.

■ I'd love one, but . . .
I'm counting my calories.
It gives me a headache.
I really don't like the taste.

■ Sorry, but . . .
I never drink on Saturdays.
It makes me sleepy.
I promised myself I wouldn't.
I just don't want to drink.

■ No, thank you . . .
I don't really care for any.
I feel great now, and I don't
want to spoil the feeling.

My date couldn't stand me if I
were more wound up.

■ What I would really like is . . .
A soft drink
Just a glass of water.
A nonalcoholic drink.

3. Successful crisis management involves five major steps:
■ Look realistically at the situation and determine if it really is a crisis situation.
■ Examine your emotions and reactions to the situation to be sure you are thinking clearly.
■ Seek support from family and friends who can help you to see the alternatives and make good choices.
■ Consider all of the possibilities and take decisive action to resolve the crisis.
■ Learn to recognize various defense mechanisms so that they can work for you rather than against you.

4. *Death of loved ones is a crisis that all people must face at times in their lives.* Natural death from old age is far easier to accept than death from homicide, suicide, or accident, especially if such a death occurs to a youthful loved one.

5. *Mourning and grief are natural reactions to a death.* Usually, the survivors first experience numbness and shock, followed by tears and emotional release after a few days or weeks. The initial shock is followed by pangs of grief and episodes of painful yearning for the dead person. Gradually, the survivors move into a prolonged period of dejection and periodic depression. Finally, life returns to normal although one may periodically feel the loss in the future.

6. *Injuries and prolonged illness can cause lasting changes in family life.* Unlike death, family members may have to live with the results for years.

7. *Family violence can come in many forms: spousal abuse, child abuse, sibling abuse, and parental abuse by children.* Five general factors have been associated with family abuse:
■ Violence begets violence. In other words, those who come from a violent environment tend to be violent themselves.
■ Family violence tends to be greater among families below the poverty line because they tend to experience greater stress and frustration.
■ High levels of stress contribute to family violence.
■ Social isolation tends to increase the risk of family violence.
■ An orientation to the traditional male role tends to increase the risk of family violence.

8. *Poverty and unemployment greatly increase the strains on the family.*

9. *Drug and alcohol abuse are contributing factors to many family problems.*

Summary

585

The following table will help you better understand the many legal and illegal drugs that can be abused.

TABLE 15-12
MAJOR DRUGS: THEIR USES AND EFFECTS

DRUG-TYPE	MOST COMMON TRADE NAME	LEGAL STATUS[a]	MEDICAL USE	STREET NAMES
Narcotics	Codeine	II	Analgesic, cough suppressant	Schoolboy
	Demerol	II		Demies
	Dilaudid	II		Little D
	Heroin	I	Analgesic	Smack, junk, downtown
	Methadone	II		Meth, dollies
	Morphine	II		M, Miss Emma, morph
	Opium	II	Paregoric	Blue velvet, black stuff
	Percodan	II	Analgesic	Perkies
Related analgesics	Darvon	IV	Reputed painkiller	None
	Talwin	IV		Ts
Barbiturates and related sedatives	Amytal	II		Blues, downers
	Nembutal	II		Yellow jackets, yellows
	Phenobarbital	IV		Phennies, purple hearts
	Seconal	II		Reds, F-40s
	Tuinal	II		Rainbows
	Doriden	III	Sedation, relief from tension, anesthetic	D
	Noludar	III		Downers
	Placidyl	IV		Dyls
	Quaalude, Sopor, Parest,	II		Ludes, 714s, Qs, sopors
	Optimil, Somnafac	II		
Minor tranquilizers	Dalmane	IV	Relief of anxiety, muscle tension, and the symptoms of alcohol withdrawal	Tranks, downs
	Equanil/Miltown	IV		
	Librium	IV		
	Serax	IV		
	Valium	IV		

586

TABLE 15-12
CONTINUED

SHORT-TERM EFFECTS OF AVERAGE DOSE	SHORT-TERM EFFECTS OF LARGE AMOUNTS	LONG-TERM EFFECTS OF CHRONIC USE OR ABUSE AND WITHDRAWAL SYMPTOMS, IF ANY
Masks pain by creating mental clouding, drowsiness, and, in some patients, mild to extreme euphoria. In contrast, some users experience nausea, vomiting, an itching sensation. Methadone is similar to other opiates but lasts 24–36 hours (compared with 2–4).	Effects of lower dosage are exaggerated: greater insensitivity to pain, increased sedation, nodding (a dreamlike state of relaxation, with total awareness and the appearance of sleep) or, paradoxically, a drive state of clarity and energy. Toxic overdose produces unconsciousness, slow and shallow breathing, cold and clammy skin, weak and rapid pulse. When mixed with any other depressant, may cause death.	Physical addiction (users take drug to avoid the discomfort of withdrawal sickness), lethargy, weight loss, inhibition of ejaculation and erection, loss of sexual interest. Withdrawal symptoms: restlessness, irritability, tremors, loss of appetite, panic, chills, sweating, cramps, watery eyes, runny nose, nausea, vomiting, muscle spasms
Talwin produces anxiety and hallucinations.	Darvon has relativity low lethal dose.	Similar to narcotics, including withdrawal.
Relaxation, sleep; used recreationally, the drugs are "like alcohol without the calories," producing mild intoxication, loss of inhibition (sexiness or aggressiveness), decreased alertness and muscle coordination.	All effects of lower dosage will be exaggerated, plus slurred speech, shallow and slow respiration, cold and clammy skin, weak and rapid heartbeat, hangover. Unconsciousness may move beyond sleep to coma and death.	Excessive sleepiness, confusion, irritability, severe withdrawal sickness. Warning: While tolerance to sedative effect increases, tolerance to lethal dose does not increase. A user may increase dosage to fatal level while attempting to regain previous high. Withdrawal symptoms: anxiety, insomnia, tremors, delirium, convulsions, and, infrequently, death
Similar to barbiturates, except users claim to feel euphoria without drowsiness; Reputed aphrodisiac	Longer acting than most barbiturates; consequently, the effect of an overdose is difficult to reverse; often fatal.	Similar to barbiturates
	Similar to barbiturates, except users may exhibit restlessness and excitement—rather than sedation—prior to convulsions.	Similar to barbiturates; however, while people who use barbs may substitute Ludes for the "down," Lude freaks seldom use barbs.
Mild sedative effect produces sense of well-being, ability to cope. May cause headaches and, in rare cases, an increase in anxiety and hostile behavior	Similar to barbiturates but considered less toxic; drowsiness, blurred vision, dizziness, slurred speech, stupor	Impairment of sexual function. Withdrawal symptoms indistinguishable from barbiturates. May appear one or two weeks after use stops (due to slow elimination of drug from body)

TABLE 15-12
MAJOR DRUGS: THEIR USES AND EFFECTS

DRUG-TYPE	MOST COMMON TRADE NAME	LEGAL STATUS[a]	MEDICAL USE	STREET NAMES
Alcohol	Beer, wine, spirits	None	Nighttime sedation, to improve appetite and digestion: painkiller, to relieve anxiety	Various trade names
Major tranquilizers	Mellaril Thorazine	None None	Control psychotic episodes, reduce hallucinations	None
Inhalants	Amyl nitrite Butyl nitrite Nitrous oxide	None None None	Smooth-muscle relaxant, controls heart spasms by lowering blood pressure Anesthetic	Poppers Locker room, Rush Laughing gas
Amphetamines and related stimulants	Benzedrine Biphetamine Desoxyn Dexedrine Methedrine Preludin Ritalin	II II II II II II II	Weight control (no longer recommended), to combat fatigue, depression, narcolepsy and hyperactivity in children	Bennies Black beauties Copilots Dex. speed Meth. crank Uppers
Cocaine	Cocaine hydrochloride	II	Local anesthetic for eye surgery; used with narcotics to treat intractable pain	Coke, snow, uptown
Caffeine	Caffeine	None	In combination with analgesics, decongestants, and antihistamines	Coffee, tea, cola, chocolate, No-Doz

TABLE 15-12
CONTINUED

SHORT-TERM EFFECTS OF AVERAGE DOSE	SHORT-TERM EFFECTS OF LARGE AMOUNTS	LONG-TERM EFFECTS OF CHRONIC USE OR ABUSE AND WITHDRAWAL SYMPTOMS, IF ANY
Relaxation, euphoria, loss of inhibition, increase in confidence, talkativeness, mood swings, decreased alertness and motor coordination	Effects of lower dosage are exaggerated; nausea, double vision, vertigo, staggering and unpredictable emotional changes (some people get hostile, some friendly), stupor, unconsciousness, severe hangover; rarely terminal	Light to moderate drinking does not have a serious effect on longevity. Chronic heavy use may cause malnutrition, impotence, ulcers, brain and liver damage, delirium. Withdrawal symptoms are similar to barbiturate withdrawal.
Heavy sedation, relief from anxiety, disorientation, an unpleasant trancelike stupor	Anxiety, rigidity of muscles, confusion, convulsions, possibly respiratory arrest and heart failure	Slowing of movement, rigidity, and painful muscle contractions. May cause dyskinesia (permanent disability of motor coordination)
Relaxation, euphoria, rapid heartbeat, dizziness, headache. Users claim that it heightens orgasm	Severe headaches, nausea, fainting, stupor	Permanent liver damage, no withdrawal
Giddiness, intoxication, drowsiness	Unconsciousness from oxygen deprivation, hallucination	Possible damage to bone marrow, several anemia, hearing loss, nerve damage
Decrease in appetite. Dramatic increase in alertness and confidence, mood elevation, improved physical performance and concentration, lessened sense of fatigue. Feeling of anxiousness, or "being wired"	Profound overstimulation, acute paranoia, agitation, insomnia, fear, irritability, sharp rise in blood pressure, fever, chest pain, headache, chills, stomach distress death from overdose is rare.	Tolerance develops rapidly. Psychological dependence and preoccupation with drug are usual. User may suffer from paranoia, auditory, visual, and tactile hallucinations (the feeling of bugs crawling under skin). Withdrawal symptoms include fatigue, hunger, crashing (long periods of sleep), disorientation, severe depression.
Similar to amphetamines but subjective reports claim the drug is smoother, more intensely felt. This may be due to route of administration, more rapid onset of drug, and shorter duration of effects.	Similar to amphetamine reaction; however, initial rapid pulse may become slow and weak, rapid breathing becomes shallow and slow. Possible convulsions, acute stomach pain, circulatory failure, and respiratory collapse; death from overdose is possible.	Economic disaster. Extensive long-term snorting may damage nasal tissue. Prolonged use has been reported to cause effects similar to amphetamine abuse— particularly paranoia and hallucination, high blood pressure, weight loss, muscle twitching.
Wakefulness, enhanced mental capacity, increase in heartbeat, reaction time and ability to work.	Stomach disorders, restlessness, insomnia, irritability, heart palpitations.	Stomach disorders, increased chance of heart attack. Withdrawal may produce mild anxiety, drowsiness, headache.

TABLE 15-12
MAJOR DRUGS: THEIR USES AND EFFECTS

DRUG-TYPE	MOST COMMON TRADE NAME	LEGAL STATUS[a]	MEDICAL USE	STREET NAMES
Nicotine	Nicotine	None	No medical use	Various trade names
Cannabis	Hashish	I	Under study for treatment of	Kif, herb
	Hash oil	I	glaucoma, asthma, side effects of	Honey
	Marijuana	I	cancer medication	Grass, ganja, weed
Hallucinogens	LSD	I		Acid
	MDA	I		The love drug
	Mescaline	I	No current use	Cactus
	Peyote	I		Buttons
	Psilocybin	I		Magic mushrooms
Related	Ketamine hydrochloride	None	Anesthetic	Green
	PCP phencyclidine	II	None for humans	Angel dust, krystal, DOA (dead on arrival)

[a]Federal penalties for trafficking: Classes I and II (fifteen years/$25,000), Class III (five years/$15,000), and Class IV (three years/$10,000).

TABLE 15-12
CONTINUED

SHORT-TERM EFFECTS OF AVERAGE DOSE	SHORT-TERM EFFECTS OF LARGE AMOUNTS	LONG-TERM EFFECTS OF CHRONIC USE OR ABUSE AND WITHDRAWAL SYMPTOMS, IF ANY
Relaxation, mild stimulation, increase in heartbeat	Headache, loss of appetite, nausea. Effects vary, depending on tolerance.	Has been linked to cancer, lung damage, heart and respiratory disease. Withdrawal: nervousness, increase in appetite, sleep disturbances, anxiety
Relaxation, euphoria, altered perception, fascination with visual and auditory phenomena, laughter	Confusion of time sense, inability to carry out mental tasks, sense of strangeness and unreality about self and surroundings, fear of dying, anxiety, panic, unwelcome introspection, hallucinations	Long-term use of heavy doses reported to cause impairment of concentration, memory, alertness, and the ability to perform complex tasks. Contradictory studies abound. THC remains in body fat for up to a month.
Users compare altered state of perception to religious, mystical experience. Rapid, drastic mood changes possible. With the exception of MDA, the hallucinogens usually produce visual and sensory distortion.	May exaggerate effects of low doses, increasing duration and intensity of trip. Possible panic, nausea, tremors, vomiting	Slight withdrawal; irritability, restlessness, insomnia. There is no medical consensus that the hallucinogens have any long-term effect. Many users report lower energy level day after use.
Varies from pleasant dreamlike state to confusion, paranoia, sense of drying, losing touch with your body, psychotic states, assaultive behavior	Exaggeration of the effects of smaller doses, plus sweating, flushing, drooling, visual distortions, muscle rigidity, and rarely seizures, coma, and death in combination with other drugs	Some evidence of memory loss, inability to concentrate, insomnia, chronic or recurrent psychosis. Withdrawal may produce short- to long-term depression.

CHAPTER

16

THE DISSOLUTION OF MARRIAGE

CONTENTS

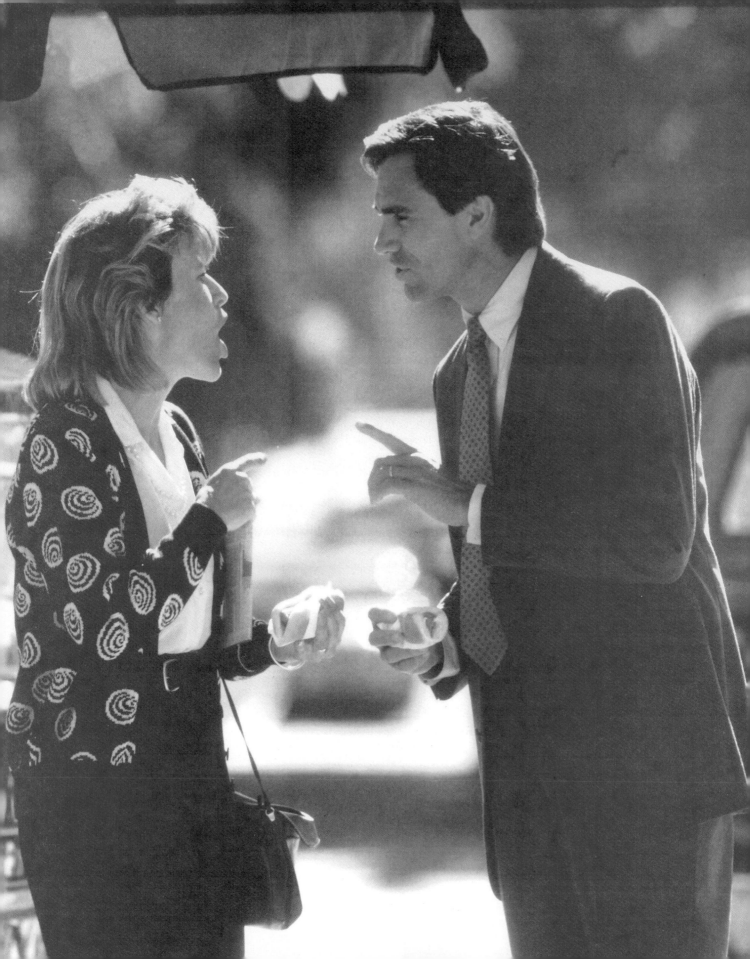

"In sickness and in health, till death do us part." This traditional part of the marriage ceremony might well be changed to the following in modern America: "In happiness and in good health, till divorce do us part."

A hundred years ago in this century, thirty out of every thousand marriages were ended each year by the death of one of the spouses. Only three marriages in a thousand were ended by divorce. Today divorce, separation, and desertion rather than death finish many marriages.

LET NO ONE PUT ASUNDER

It seems obvious that the "love match" marriage based on romance, self-gratification, and happiness—in other words, on the fulfillment of all one's needs—must suffer from a high rate of failure. In the past, a good marriage was measured by how well each spouse fulfilled the socially prescribed roles of husband and wife. Today Americans ask a great deal more of marriage, and the higher the stakes, the higher the chances of failure.

In addition, the greatly increased life span (since 1900, an additional twenty-four years for men and twenty-eight years for women, see p. 523) means that marriages are now expected to endure much longer than ever before. How realistic is it to ask a marriage to last for fifty or sixty years?

The rate of divorce in this country has been rising throughout the century. In 1900 there was about one divorce for every twelve marriages in a given year. By 1922 there was one divorce for every eight marriages, and in the late 1940s, there was approximately one divorce for every three and a half marriages. This peak was probably due to the dislocations arising from World War II. Between 1950 and 1964, the ratio of divorce to marriage leveled off at approximately one divorce for every four marriages. But the divorce rate started to rise again in 1967, and by 1984 approximately one divorce was occurring for every two marriages. The median duration of marriage today is approximately seven years.

The **crude divorce rate**—the ratio of divorces to each thousand persons within the population—is really a better, though less dramatic, measure of marital stability than the ratio of divorces to marriages in a given year (Table 16-1). Note that the crude divorce rate has remained quite stable since 1975, fluctuating between 4.7 and 5.3 (National Center for Health Statistics April 1992). If one considers all marriages, only about 2–3 percent of marriages end in divorce in a given year.

However, the overall divorce statistics do not yield a complete picture of the incidence of broken marriage. For example, there are differences among various groups (see Table 16-2).

Legal separation claims another 3 percent of all marriages. Desertion, another manner of breaking a marriage, is especially prevalent among the poor, although statistics on desertion are difficult to obtain because they rarely appear in the records. Usually, it is the husband who leaves, although more wives are now deserting than in the past.

Crude divorce rate
Ratio of divorces to each thousand persons

Let No One Put Asunder

| | | TABLE 16-1 | |
| | | NUMBER OF DIVORCES AND DIVORCE RATES | |
YEAR	NUMBER OF DIVORCES	PERCENTAGE CHANGE FROM PREVIOUS YEAR	RATE PER 1000 TOTAL POPULATION
1992	1,210,000	+ .01	4.7
1991	1,187,000	+ .01	4.7
1990	1,175,000	− .01	4.7
1989	1,186,000	.00	4.8
1988	1,183,000	+ .02	4.8
1987	1,157,000	− .03	4.8
1986	1,192,000	+ .01	5.0
1985	1,172,000	+ .01	4.9
1984	1,156,000	− .005	4.9
1983	1,158,000	− .01	4.9
1982	1,170,000	− .03	5.0
1981	1,213,000	+ .03	5.3
1980	1,182,000	.00	5.2
1979	1,181,000	+ .04	5.3
1978	1,130,000	+ .03	5.1
1977	1,090,000	+ .006	5.0
1976	1,083,000	+ 4.5	5.0
1975	1,036,000	+ 6.0	4.9
1974	977,000	+ 6.8	4.6
1973	915,000	+ 8.3	4.4
1972	845,000	+ 9.3	4.1
1971	773,000	+ 9.2	3.7
1965	479,000	+ 6.4	2.5
1960	393,000	− .5	2.2
1955	377,000	− .5	2.3
1950	385,000	− 3.0	2.6
1946	610,000	+ 25.8	4.3
1941	293,000	+ 11.0	2.2

Source: Wilson, B. National Center for Health Statistics. December 17, 1992.

Serial marriage
Marrying, divorcing, and marrying again; a series of legal marriages

In any case dissolution of American marriages seems to be relatively commonplace. In fact, America's divorce rate is the highest in the world. Some family experts call American marriages "throwaway marriages." A better name is **serial marriages;** that is Americans tend to marry, divorce, and remarry. In about one-half of all American couples marrying in a given year, one or both partners have previously been divorced. A high divorce rate apparently does not mean that Americans are disenchanted with marriage because the divorced remarry in great numbers and relatively quickly, depending on their age at the time of the divorce (see Chapter 17).

It is important to remember that statistics on divorce and separation must be interpreted cautiously. For example, the crude divorce rate is greatly influenced by the birthrate. A decrease in birthrate will produce a higher percentage of divorce, presuming the total number of divorces remains stable. Thus, the fact that the birthrate is at an all-time low in the United States accounts for some of the increase in the crude divorce rate.

To conclude that the institution of marriage and the family is in a state of decay and breakdown based on divorce statistics is not valid. Many marriages

TABLE 16-2

DIVORCED PERSONS PER THOUSAND MARRIED PERSONS WITH A SPOUSE PRESENT

Caucasian males	112		Caucasian females	153
Black males	208		Black females	358
Hispanic males	103		Hispanic females	155

Source: U.S. Bureau of the Census May 1991, 3–5.

still last a lifetime. Marriage is still high on most Americans' list of values. Marriage rates are higher among divorced persons than among single persons. What the high divorce tells us is that Americans in general are more accepting of divorce and that when they become disenchanted with their marital partner, they will leave that partner. Whether this is good or bad is another question.

REASONS FOR AMERICA'S HIGH DIVORCE RATE

The reasons for America's high divorce rate are many and varied. Many divorcing couples cite personal reasons, such as a breakdown in communication, sexual failure, or overuse of alcohol. More important, though, are the overriding influences that affect all marriages. These general social problems with their deep roots in American society and philosophy affect all relationships.

Americans ask a great deal of modern marriage, perhaps too much. High expectations often lead to disappointment and failure. If you ask nothing and receive nothing, "nothing" is not disappointing. If you ask a great deal and receive only a little, unhappiness often follows. Divorce in this context may mean not that the institution of marriage has failed, but that an attempt is being made to improve one's marriage and to improve the institution in general.

Tied closely to Americans' high expectations of marriage is the relative freedom of individuals to make marital choices. The first basic assumption of this book—that a free and creative society will offer many structural forms by which family functions can be fulfilled—is a second reason for America's high divorce rate. Many choices breed a certain amount of dissatisfaction. Is the grass greener on the other side of the fence? Might some alternative be better than what I have? Being surrounded by married friends who see marriage as you do and who are committed to it adds strength and durability to one's own marriage. Being surrounded by those who don't support your concept of marriage, who suggest or live alternate lifestyles, and who deride the kind of marriage you have is disruptive of your own marital patterns. Although such disruptions may lead to a better present marriage, they are just as apt to lead to marital complications.

Changing sex roles are part of the American interest in the general concept of change and its benefits. All those who question traditional sex roles place pressure on the institution of marriage. For example, a woman who decides that the role of mother is not for her, seeks a career, and leaves the care of their children to her husband is bound to face some disapproval from her family and friends. Certainly, the same holds true for the husband who decides at forty to quit his job as an accountant, cease supporting his family, and begin writing adventure stores. Although sex role changes may ultimately be liberating to individuals, the transitory results will be marital disruption for some people. Nevertheless, citing the changing roles of women and men as a major cause of divorce does not mean that such changes will not be good for the family in the long run. Certainly, many of those advocating change believe the family will benefit. Only time will tell.

Greater economic independence of women also encourages separation and divorce. When a wife had no economic alternatives, she was forced to put up with an unsatisfactory marriage in return for economic security for herself and her children. Now there are economic alternatives to an unsatisfactory marriage that allow women to fight back or leave such a marriage.

Another reason for the high divorce rate is America's heterogeneity. With so many kinds of people and so many beliefs, attitudes, and value systems, family and marriage will naturally mean many different things to various Americans. Even though people tend to marry people with similar backgrounds, there will still be differences in beliefs and attitudes. For example, consider the situation of a female college graduate interested in pursuing both a family life and a career; she marries an engineer from a traditional family background who believes the wife's place is in the home. Conflict seems inevitable.

America's heterogeneity also leads to a higher incidence of mixed marriages. People of differing marital and family values and philosophies are more apt to marry in America simply because they are here and freedom of marital choice is encouraged. When such persons marry, their differences make it more difficult to build a successful and enduring marriage.

The general mobility of Americans may also contribute to increased marital breakup. Families that move often may not create support networks. Other married friends, relatives, and membership in institutions such as churches all tend to support a marital relationship. A high degree of mobility tends to weaken such supports.

A list of the general reasons for marital failure would be incomplete if it failed to include social upheaval, economic problems, and the general health of the society. Certainly, job insecurity brought on by increased unemployment and scarcity of jobs during recession strains the family institution.

Continuing economic worries have also brought failure to many American marriages. Marital failure is highest among the poor and becomes progressively lower as economic status rises. As noted earlier, desertion tends to be high among the poor since it does not entail the costs of a divorce.

Acceptance of divorce by Americans is another important factor in the rising divorce rates. The stigma of divorce has largely vanished over the past thirty years. In fact, less stigma is probably attached to a forty-year-old divorced individual than to a person of the same age who has never been married. General social acceptance is also noticeable in the trend toward more lenient divorce laws and the increase in economic alternatives to marital dependency provided through various forms of government assistance.

Last on our list of reasons for increasing marital failure are the personal inadequacies, failures, and problems that contribute to each individual divorce. Regardless of the magnitude of the social problems and pressures that disrupt

TABLE 16-3
PERCEIVED CAUSES OF MARRIAGE BREAKDOWN

CAUSES[a]	PERCENTAGE OF ALL RESPONDENTS (n = 335)	PERCENTAGE OF MEN (n = 102)	PERCENTAGE OF WOMEN (n = 233)
Sexual incompatibility	45%	56%	40%
Lack of communication[b]	40	41	40
Husband's lack of time at home	40	28	46
Financial	32	24	36
Husband's associates with another woman[c]	31	17	37
Husband's drinking[d]	30	17	36
Husband's cruelty[e]	26	37	4
Wife's lack of interest[f]	26	25	26
Friction with relatives	23	29	21
Disagreements over children	20	22	19
Wife's association with another man[c]	19	35	12
Husband's lack of interest[f]	13	15	12
Wife's ill health	13	13	13
Inadequate housing	9	4	13
Religious differences	5	5	5
Husband's gambling	5	3	7

Source: Burns 1984, 551.

Note: Percentages do not add up to 100. Multiple complaints are included.

[a]Causes mentioned by less than 5 percent are not included.

[b]Includes lack of common interests.

[c]No homosexual relationships were mentioned.

[d]Includes husband's alcoholism.

[e]Includes wife's perception of husband as having sadistic, cruel, or brutal personality.

[f]Includes statement of resentment about the lack of stimulation.

marriage, the ultimate decision to end a relationship is made by one or both spouses. The specific reasons given for divorce by individuals are listed in Table 16-3. It must be remembered that the reasons listed by divorcing couples often bear little resemblance to the real reasons they are divorcing. For example, nowhere on the list do you find "falling in love" with another person.

EMOTIONAL DIVORCE AND THE EMOTIONS OF DIVORCE

Divorce is not a spontaneous, spur-of-the-moment act as marriage can be. In most cases dissolution occurs slowly, and divorce is the culmination of a prolonged period of gradual alienation. In many cases several years elapse between a couple's first serious thought of divorce and the decree. Willard Waller (1967) delineates the following steps in the alienation process:

1. Early in the process there is a *disturbance in the sex life and affectional response*. Rapport is lost, with an attempt to compensate for its lack in some cases. Emotional divorce begins here.

2. *The possibility of divorce is first mentioned*. This tends to clarify the relationship somewhat, with the initiator taking the lead and the partner remaining passive through the divorce cycle.

3. *The appearance of solidarity is broken before the public*. The fiction of solidarity is important as a face-saver. Once it is broken, the marriage cannot be the same again.

4. *The decision to divorce is made*, usually after long discussion, although at times it is made without forethought.

5. *A severe crisis of separation follows*. Severing a meaningful relationship is a traumatic experience at best, even if it is thought to be the only alternative.

6. *Final severance comes with the actual divorce*. This may come after a long period of delay and separation. Although the actual legal procedure is usually thought of as closing the case, another stage is necessary before the final adaptation can begin.

7. *A period of mental conflict and reconstruction closes the case*. The former partners enter new social worlds, and full estrangement takes place.

Waller's stages, though helpful to understanding the divorce process, are far simpler than the real process.

Long before legal divorce, a couple may find themselves beginning the process of emotional divorce. Often the beginnings of the process are not noticeable. Usually, they involve such things as a subtle withdrawal of one partner from the other, the erection of barriers that shield each from hurt by the other, a gradual shift of concern from "us" to "me," the tendency to meet more and more psychological needs outside the marriage, and finally the erosion of the couple's sex life. The actual facts or events that lead up to divorce are as varied as the individuals who marry, but one thing always happens: each partner begins to concentrate on the other partner's weaknesses, shortcomings, and failures rather than on that person's strengths. The "20 percent I hate you" becomes the focus of attention rather than the "80 percent I love you" (see Chapter 5, p. 161–162). The inability to accept the partner the way he or she is or to accept unwanted change in the partner is at the root of most emotional divorces.

Almost always there is an initiator who unilaterally begins the uncoupling process, consciously or unconsciously. This partner has the power in the breakup process because he or she knows earlier than the other partner that the relationship is in trouble and may have to be changed. Thus, the initiator often begins the process of withdrawing from the relationship, building a new and separate life, and preparing a new world for him- or herself long before the partner suspects that the relationship is in real trouble. When the initiator drops hints of dissatisfaction, the unknowing partner simply takes them to mean that there are problems to be worked out. "Every marriage has its ups and downs." Because the relationship is not in any "serious" trouble for the partner, he or she may remain blind to the growing discontent and the strength of the initiator's dissatisfaction. Many partners report shock and dismay and ignorance when the initiator finally makes it clear that she or he wants to end the relationship. "I was totally surprised when my wife indicated that she had seen a lawyer and was suing me for divorce. I had no idea that she was so unhappy and that our relationship was about to come to an end." In contrast, the initiator may say, "I have worked for years to make this relationship successful and it is not. I've known for a long time that our marriage was a mistake."

> The obvious contradiction between these statements of initiators and partners forces us to consider the possibility of some enormous failure in communication. How fascinating, yet how ironic, that when we begin relationships we develop sensitivity that allows us to pick up on the smallest cue. We are intent on discovering and knowing the other person. So much is understood on a non-verbal basis: a look across a room, a slight smile, a downcast glance, a frown. We are so tuned to each other, constantly exploring, checking, and testing the nature of our bond. Given this early attentiveness, what causes the failure in communication, especially when what is at issue is so central to the life and identity of both partners? (Vaughan 1987, 87).

Diane Vaughan asks an interesting question. How can a couple who have been in love, intimately close, perhaps for years, not communicate well enough to recognize that their relationship has severe problems? The fact is that the intensity of falling in love and courtship simply cannot be maintained in a long-term relationship. The emotional cost is too high. As relationships age, much of the daily interaction becomes routine. Systems are set up to simplify and make life comfortable, efficient, and convenient, thus conserving energy and time. Once a good relationship has been established the partners tend to assume that all is going well unless there are very strong indications to the contrary. Since the initiator does not arrive quickly and suddenly at the conclusion that the relationship must end, there are usually no obvious clues to draw the partner's attention. Since every relationship does have problems at times, the initiator's complaints are usually dismissed as trivial and certainly not indicative of serious relational problems. Even when the initiator does get the partner's attention, the partner usually assumes that changes can be made and the relationship saved. Unfortunately for the relationship, by the time the partner is aware of the seriousness of the situation, it is often too late to make the changes that might save the relationship. The initiator has already partially withdrawn and may have substituted other sources of need gratification so that the relationship is no longer as important to him or her as it is to the un-knowing partner. Generally, the initiator has the better chance of coming out of the divorce a winner although in Wallerstein and Blakeslee's study (1989, 40), in only 10 percent of the divorced couples were *both* husband and wife able to reconstruct happier, fuller lives by the ten-year mark after the divorce.

Although many breakups occur during the first few years of marriage, with the peak occurring about three years after marriage, nearly 40 percent of all broken marriages have lasted ten or more years. The median duration of a marriage at the time of divorce in the United States is approximately seven years. A couple usually decide on a legal divorce only after years of worsening relations.

Emotional Divorce and
the Emotions of Divorce

601

How can I be missing her after all the fighting and yelling we've been doing the past year or two? It's so nice to be in my own place and have peace and quiet. Damn, it sure is lonely. It's great to be a bachelor again, but after fifteen years of married life, who wants to chase women and play all those games? Wonder why the kids don't call? Keeping house is sure a drag. I wonder what she's doing. Do you suppose she is nicer to her dates than she was to me?

What really went wrong? Two nice kids, a good job, nice home, and I certainly loved her when we married. But she has been so unaffectionate and cold over the years. She never seemed to have time for me. Or was it that I never had time for her? When we dated, she was so flexible. She'd do anything with me, but after our first child, she seemed to become so conservative. She wouldn't do anything daring. I had so little leisure time what with working so hard to give the family a good life. Why couldn't she do what I wanted when I was free? It's really all her fault. Of course, I could have included her more in my work world. Maybe if I had shared more of my business problems with her, she'd have been more understanding. It's true I am awfully short-tempered when the pressure is on. Certainly, I didn't listen to her much any more. It seemed as if she only complained. I get enough of that at the office. You don't suppose there was some-

one else? Maybe it was all my fault. A failure at marriage, that's me. Never thought it could happen to me. When did it start? Who first thought of divorce? Maybe the idea came because all our friends seemed to be divorcing.

On and on the thoughts of this newly divorced man go. Anger, guilt, frustration, conflict, insecurity, and emotional upheaval are the bedmates of divorce. "Our culture says that marriage is forever and yet I failed to make a go of it. Why?" The whys keep churning up thoughts, and endless questioning follows marital breakdown. There are so many questions, doubts, and fears.

For first marriages, the duration is eight years, but for remarriages it is only six years. About 4 percent of divorcing couples have been married less than one year (National Center for Health Statistics May 21, 1991).

Once legal divorce proceedings are initiated, many emotions will be experienced including a sense of loss, the grief felt at the death of a loved one, and the loss of feelings of psychological well-being (see Inset 16-1). A lucky few—perhaps those divorcing quickly after marriage—will not experience grief and mourning. A very few may even feel happiness and joy over regaining their freedom. But most will go through a period of denial—this really isn't happening—followed by grief, mourning, and a mixture of the following:

- *Self-pity:* Why did this happen to me?
- *Vengeance:* I'm going to get even!
- *Despair:* I feel like going to sleep and never waking up again.
- *Wounded pride:* I'm not as great as I thought I was.
- *Anguish:* I don't know how I can hurt so much.
- *Guilt:* I'm really to blame for everything.
- *Loneliness:* Why don't our friends ever call me?

- *Fear:* No one else will want to marry me. I'll never be able to support myself.
- *Distrust:* He (or she) is probably conniving with attorneys to take all the property.
- *Withdrawal:* I don't feel like seeing anyone.
- *Relief:* Well, at least it's over, a decision has finally been made.
- *Loss of feelings of psychological well-being:* I feel awful, depressed, nervous, suicidal.

Unfortunately, our society offers no ritual or prescribed behaviors for the survivor of divorce. The community does not feel it necessary to help as it does in bereavement. Indeed, the fact that the spouse still lives often prevents the divorced person and the children of divorce from coming to a final acceptance of the breakup because there is always a chance, no matter how small, of recovering the spouse, the lost parent. Some rejected spouses exaggerate this remote chance and make it the sustaining theme of their lives for a long time after the legal divorce. Children and monetary involvement are often reasons for continued association. Even in cases where the marital breakup is hostile and bitter, the loneliness following the breakup may spur a mate to wish the spouse were home, even if only to have someone to fight with and ease the loneliness.

No matter how much one thinks about and prepares for a separation, there is still a shock when the actual physical separation occurs. Many persons, especially those who have been left, suddenly panic and feel abandoned.

> It's the same feeling you had as a child when you got separated from your mother in the supermarket. Although separation panic comes in many forms, most people experience it as apprehensiveness or anxiety. They feel physically and psychologically shaky, and have great difficulty concentrating on any complex task. As a thirty-five-year-old insurance agent described it, "I felt an alertness and constant vigilance. I had to be busy all the time but I couldn't concentrate on anything. I'd start to make a sandwich, only to forget it halfway as I began pacing through the house. I felt that something awful would happen, that I'd get sick or get too nervous to work." (McKay et al. 1984, 11).

Such feelings recede with time for many, but a divorced spouse may later feel a resurgence of hurt, hostility, and rejection on learning of the former spouse's new relationships. To hear that one's former mate is remarrying is often upsetting and may arouse past hostilities and regrets even though considerable time has passed. Much to the surprise of those who believe that time always heals, Wallerstein and Blakeslee's longitudinal long-term study (1989) of divorced families found that for many divorced persons, especially the children of divorce, the hurt, hostility, and anger don't disappear even after ten to fifteen years.

It is probably important for anger to be a part of divorce, because anger may be the means of finally breaking the emotional bonds that remain between the former spouses. Not until these bonds are broken will each be free. "Free" really is not the proper word. Few divorced persons are ever completely free of the earlier relationship as we shall see later in the chapter. Fortunately, many divorcing couples come to a turning point when their energies can finally be channeled from destruction to construction once again.

Emotional Divorce and
the Emotions of Divorce

DIVORCE BUT NOT THE
END OF THE RELATIONSHIP

Divorce is the death of a relationship, but strangely enough it is not the end of the relationship in most cases. Divorce can also be the rebirth of an individual. And rebirth is just as difficult as death. Once the mourning, grief, and anger begin to subside, the newly divorced individual faces important choices about life directions. What does one do when newly alone? Seek the immediate security of a new marriage? Prepare to live alone the rest of one's life? Make all new friends or keep old friends? Maintain ties to the past relationship? Escape into the work world? Seek counseling? Experiment with sexual involvements? More and more professionals as well as divorced persons themselves are saying, "Use the pain and suffering of divorce to learn about yourself. Seek the rebirth of a new, more insightful, more capable person out of the wreckage of failure." This is a wonderful goal, and some even talk about "creative divorce" and try to paint divorce as a positive experience that will bring growth and improvement to one's life if properly approached. Unquestionably, divorce does eventually lead to an improved and happier life for some persons.

Yet the attitude that divorce is simply a growth experience is a far cry from the way most people feel at the breakup of their marriages. Nevertheless, using divorce as a learning opportunity rather than seeing it only as a failure from which nothing good can be derived makes a great deal of sense. If divorced persons do not use the divorce to gain insight into themselves and their past relationships, they are doomed to make the same relational mistakes again; unfortunately, this is often exactly what they do.

The myth of romantic divorce has appeared, perhaps as a defense against guilt on the part of the growing numbers of divorced people in American society. In essence, this myth stresses only those aspects of divorce that can be perceived as positive. It tries to make divorce an exciting romantic adventure in the ongoing stream of life. However, this myth, with its emphasis on the joys of freedom and the delights of self-discovery, hardly prepares the divorcing couple for the traumas and problems they will experience in reaching these goals. Nor does it prepare people to reevaluate their broken marriages and themselves so that they can make more successful future marriages.

> The hooker in divorce is that in order to get over a marriage, you have to go back to it. To go forward to a new life, you have to go backward to the past. That's the agony of breaking up a marriage. It's not over yet, even after divorce.
> . . .
>   From what you see on television and in the movies, you'd think that getting a divorce was some yellow brick road to personal growth and happiness; all those stories of personal freedom, the joys of being single, the good sex out there; the jokes about falling off the marriage merry-go-round and having fun. The Great New Life.
>   But ask someone who's been through it. There is nothing funny or easy about divorce. It is a savage emotional journey. Where it ends, you don't know for a long time. (Trafford 1984, 1, 19).

Many people who contemplate divorce think it will end their misery by ending forever a relationship that has become intolerable. Yet this is not always true; it is certainly almost never true if children are involved. Divorced people often remain bound to one another by children, love, hate, revenge, friendship, business matters, dependence, moral obligations, the need to dominate or rescue, or habit. Increasingly, we are recognizing that divorce does not necessarily dissolve a family unit but simply changes its structure. This is especially true for children.

Every state has provisions for modifying judgments made by the court at the time of divorce. Requests for change of custody, support, or alimony can be made by either spouse at any time. If you believe marital problems end with divorce, you should attend "father day" in court. Many larger cities set aside specific days when motions are heard relative to an errant father's failure to pay child support or a mother's refusal to permit her former husband to visit their children. Sometimes these hearings are emotionally packed scenes, replete with name calling, charges, and countercharges years after the divorce has been granted.

On the positive side, some former spouses become good friends after the pain of divorce fades. Some divorced couples remain business partners. Even after one or both remarry, there may be friendly interaction between the couples and their new spouses.

Some professionals discourage relationships with former spouses. They contend that these continuing attachments drain energies that could be more productively spent in forming new relationships. They argue that the best policy for childless couples is to sever all ties.

It must be remembered that one's former spouse still has all the characteristics that attracted one to him or her in the first place. Therefore it seems unrealistic to expect that one will totally dislike the divorced spouse forever, though many divorced persons claim that they will. The best divorce adjustment is probably attained through an "amicable divorce," where there is a minimum of conflict and the marital relationship gradually is transformed into a friendship relationship.

PROBLEMS OF THE NEWLY DIVORCED

The newly divorced face several major dangers:

- They may make a prolonged retreat from social contact.
- They may jump quickly into a new marriage.
- They may base their life on the hope that the spouse will return.
- They may organize their life around hostility and getting even with the former mate.

Certainly, the first reaction after any loss may be a momentary retreat, as the individual turns inward to contemplation and avoids all situations reminding him or her of the hurt, disappointment, guilt, and shame of failure. Unfortunately, though, some divorced people make this reaction their lifestyle. In essence, such people die psychologically and end their lives in every way but physically.

1. What do you think is the single most important thing that a newly divorced person should avoid doing if he or she is to find the road to recovery? Why?
2. What are some things the newly divorced person should avoid doing if she or he wants to speed recovery?
3. If you were advising a newly divorced person, what would you tell him or her? Why?

A larger group of divorced people seek a new relationship as quickly as possible. Discounting those people who had a satisfying relationship with someone else before their divorce and are now fulfilling it as soon as possible, many people simply can't stand the thought of failure or being alone. They rush into the first available relationship. These people usually have not had time to reassess themselves or their motives. The idea of facing themselves and the challenges of becoming an independent person is simply too frightening. Often these people have never really been alone. They married early, and in a sense they may never have grown up psychologically. Even though their first marriage may have been unsatisfying, they still prefer marriage to assuming responsibility for themselves. Rushing into a new marriage, they will likely make the same mistakes again.

We have already looked at some of the problems of attempting to hold onto a past relationship. Living on the basis of false hope creates a prolonged situation in which hope and disappointment alternate. A life based on continuing anger and harassment of a former spouse may be the most destructive of all, however, because both the former spouse and the mate seeking revenge are harmed. The horror stories about this reaction to divorce are enough to keep people from ever marrying. In the usual scenario, one divorced spouse takes the other back to court repeatedly in an effort to punish him or her. Fortunately, few divorced persons react in this fashion for long.

Community divorce refers to the problems and changes in one's lifestyle and in one's community of friends that occur on divorce. Divorce affects not just the divorcing couple and their children but also their friends, their extended families, and their workplace. When an individual marries, single friends are gradually replaced by married-couple friends. When a couple divorce, another change of friends usually occurs. Unfortunately, changes of friendship after divorce tend to be more complicated both for the newly divorced and for the couple's friends. Some friends may side with one or the other member of a divorcing couple. Remaining friends with a newly divorced person is difficult for at least two reasons. First, the divorce causes the couple's married friends to reexamine their own marriages. Often a divorcing couple will inadvertently cause trouble in their friends' marriages. In fact, sometimes a domino effect occurs in that when one couple among a group of friends separates, other couples who are unhappy gain psychological support to separate also. Secondly, the married friends may experience conflict about which partner will remain a friend. In addition, still-married friends may view the newly single person as a threat or at least as a "fifth wheel." Generally, the newly divorced person will find that old friendships tend to fade and be replaced by new ones; often the new friends will have some of the same problems as the newly divorced.

Most divorced people start to date within the first year after their separation. The new dating partners bring with them a new circle of friends. Thus, most divorced people will experience a gradual change in their larger community of friends and contacts.

ECONOMIC CONSEQUENCES

The bottom line is that divorce brings about severe financial changes for the divorcing couple. In most divorcing couples with children, the man becomes single but the woman becomes a single parent, and poverty often begins with single parenthood.

> More than half the poor families in the United States are headed by single mothers. Children under eighteen constitute 40 percent of the poor (U.S. Bureau of the Census August 1991, 1–2).

Lenore Weitzman (1985, 323) found that divorced men experience a rise in their standard of living in the first year after divorce, while divorced women (and their children) experience a decline. Two factors tend to account for this disparity: men earn more than women, and they often don't pay what the court has directed them to pay. Men have always earned more than women (Chapter 9). This fact does not affect married women since they traditionally share in the man's resources. Once a woman is divorced, however, she no longer shares the man's higher earning power and must rely on court-ordered child or spousal support to make up the difference between her earning power and her former husband's.

The courts usually order child support to be paid, but if both divorced and separated mothers are considered, only about 60 to 70 percent of mothers are actually awarded child support (Buehler 1989, 79). Only about half of the mothers due court-ordered support from their children's father actually receive the full amount. Child support is awarded based on the child's or children's needs and the supporting parent's ability to pay.

Spousal support or alimony requires a showing of financial need and ability to pay, but the duration of the support may be reduced by expectations of the dependent spouse's economic rehabilitation. The trend toward "no-fault" divorce and away from fault-finding has tended to reduce alimony awards since they are no longer used to punish a guilty spouse.

If women have equal rights to men, theoretically they should be able to support themselves, and the courts now tend to use this rationale as the basis for awarding spousal support after divorce. This would be fine if women were indeed able to earn as much as men, but that is not yet the case, particularly for women who must care for children and have been long-term housewives (Chapter 9). Several states including South Carolina, Florida, Minnesota, New York, and California have amended their laws and changed procedures so that permanent or at least long-term alimony can again be awarded in some cases of special need (Quinn 1989, B-8). As with child support, only 50 to 75 percent of women awarded alimony actually receive payment from their ex-husbands.

These trends have led to a large increase in child poverty in the United States paralleling the increased number of divorces. At the current rate of divorce, about 60 percent of children born today will likely spend some of their childhood in a single-parent family, which increases their chances of living in poverty for at least that period of their lives.

In light of the poor child and spousal support payment records of noncustodial spouses, both state and local governments as well as the federal government have tried to enforce such payments through legislation. Congress unanimously approved legislation to strengthen child support collection through mandatory income withholding and the interception of federal and state income tax refund checks to cover past due support. A federal Parent Locator Service allows custodial parents access to various federal records, such as Internal Revenue Service information, to find an errant spouse. Finding the spouse is, of course, the first step in enforcing support payments. Other legislation allows states to provide information to consumer credit agencies on past due child support when the arrears are more than $1000. Late payments penalties may also be applied. Payments may be made through a state agency if requested by either parent, and mandatory wage assignments are required in most states as soon as child support is ordered by the court. All these enforcement tools have helped increase support payments. In those few jurisdictions that impose jail sentences on errant noncustodial parents, there seems to be quick compliance with the court-ordered payments.

The single-parent family created either by divorce or by having a child out of wedlock experiences not only economic problems but also severe time problems (Sanick and Mauldin 1986). To work and rear children successfully without an additional adult requires an almost superhuman effort. The complex logistics of working and providing child care at the same time, especially when money is in short supply, make it difficult for the single-parent family to function.

Many volunteer groups have sprung up to help newly divorced and single-parent families. "We Care" and "Parents Without Partners" are two such organizations. The latter is a nationwide organization whose goal is to help alleviate some of the isolation that makes it difficult for single parents to provide a reasonably normal family life for themselves and their children.

Fortunately, the single-parent family tends to be temporary. As we shall see in Chapter 17, the majority of divorced people remarry. Although having children might seem to make it harder to remarry, studies show that this is not true.

■ CHILDREN AND DIVORCE ■

The first problem for parents contemplating divorce is telling the children. There is no easy way to do this. Wallerstein and her colleagues (1980; 1984; 1989) report that 80 percent of the children studied were completely unprepared for their parents' separations. In a disturbingly high number of cases, a parent would simply disappear while a child was sleeping or away from home. Sharing an impending separation with one's children is an unpleasant task, but it is important to the child's well-being that it be done (see Inset 16-2).

It has generally been thought that divorce always has negative effects on the children involved. This belief has caused many couples to remain together "for the sake of the children" or to postpone divorce until the children were grown. Yet the effects of divorce on children are not at all clear. Certainly, the immediate effects are unsettling, but the long-term effects are probably mixed. Some children may suffer long-term damage. Others may be much better off after a divorce than they were when the conflicting parents were together. An unhappy marriage is an unhappy home for children; if divorce promotes parental happiness, the children should also benefit. Although this folk wisdom sounds reasonable, long-term study of divorced families only partially supports it.

Judith Wallerstein and her colleagues (1980; 1984; 1989) are doing a long-term study of sixty families who have gone through divorce. They interviewed them close to the time of divorce and at eighteen months, five years, ten years, and fifteen years after the divorce.

INSET 16-2
GUIDELINES FOR TELLING THE CHILDREN

Matthew McKay and his colleagues (1984, 142–44) suggest the following guidelines for telling children about an impending separation:

1. Tell children as clearly as you can what divorce means, and be prepared to repeat this information several times for younger children.

2. Describe some of your attempts to protect and improve your marriage.

3. Emphasize that both parents will continue to love and care for the children.

4. Do not assess blame. You can share your unhappiness and anger, but when you assess blame, you are asking the children to take sides.

5. Try to describe any changes the children may expect in their day-to-day experiences.

6. It is important to emphasize that the children in no way caused the divorce and are not responsible for problems between the parents. You are divorcing one another, not the children.

7. Assure the children that they will always be free to love both parents.

8. Encourage your children to ask questions throughout the process of divorce and adjustment.

Wallerstein and Blakeslee (1989) add the following:

9. Both parents should tell the children together. By representing unity, they convey the sense that a rational, mature decision has been made (285).

10. Tell the children all at once rather than separately so they can genuinely help one another (285).

11. Parents should indicate that the decision has been made rationally and reached sadly. The expression of sadness is important because it gives children permission to cry and mourn without having to hide their feelings of loss from adults and themselves (286).

Our overall conclusion is that divorce produces not a single pattern in people's lives, but at least three patterns, with many variations. Among both adults and children five years afterward, we found about a quarter to be resilient (those for whom the divorce was successful), half muddling through, coping when and as they could, and a final quarter to be bruised: failing to recover from the divorce or looking back to the predivorce family with intense longing. Some in each group had been that way before and continued unchanged; for the rest, we found roughly equal numbers for whom the divorce seemed connected to improvement and to decline. (1984, 67)

What factors appear to be associated with the 25 percent who adapted well to the divorce? Not surprisingly, children with strong, well-integrated personalities who were well adjusted before the divorce were making the best adjustments. Children also did significantly better when both parents continued to be a part of their lives on a regular basis. This was true only when the parents themselves were able to work out a satisfactory and nondestructive postdivorce relationship. Aside from these two factors, it was difficult to predict which children would do well and which would not (see Inset 16-3).

Although we have been discussing the general effects of divorce on children, it is important to realize that both the age and the sex of the child must be considered in understanding divorce effects. Younger children seem to have more severe immediate reactions to the divorce of their parents than adoles-

Problems of the Newly Divorced

INSET 16-3
WHAT RESEARCH TELLS US ABOUT THE CHILDREN OF DIVORCE

In general, past research has examined only the immediate consequences of divorce on children. Examining a national sample of 17,110 children under age eighteen, Dawson (1991) found that children living with single mothers or with mothers and stepfathers were more likely than those living with both biological parents to have experienced the following:

■ Repeated a grade in school.
■ Been expelled from school.
■ Been treated for emotional or behavioral problems.
■ Have elevated scores for behavioral and health problems.

Judith Wallerstein and her colleagues report the following from their long-term study of divorced families (1989):

■ Three out of five youngsters feel rejected by at least one parent.

■ Half grow up in settings in which the parents are continually at war with one another long after the actual divorce. Indeed, one-half of the mothers and one-third of the fathers were still intensely angry at their former partners despite the passage of ten years (29, 135).

■ Two-thirds of the girls, many of whom seemed to sail through the initial crises of family breakup, suddenly become deeply anxious in adolescence and as young adults appear unable to make lasting commitments and are fearful of betrayal in intimate relationships. Wallerstein terms this the "sleeper effect" (63).

■ Many boys, who were more overtly troubled in the postdivorce years, failed to develop a sense of independence, confidence, or purpose. About 40 percent were drift-

ing in and out of school and from job to job (18).

■ Only one in ten children experienced relief when their parents divorced (11).

■ The severity of the child's reaction at the time of the divorce does not predict how the child will fare five, ten, and fifteen years later (15).

■ Almost one-half of the children from families reporting abusive relationships formed abusive relationships themselves as young adults (117).

Essentially what Wallerstein is finding is that there is simply a reduction of parenting when a divorce takes place.

When marriage breaks down, most men and women experience a diminished capacity to parent. They give less time,

cent children. Yet ten years after the divorce, these same children seem better adjusted than their older siblings. In general, the younger siblings in divorced families are buffered as the older children bear the brunt of their parents' distress (Wallerstein and Blakeslee 1989, 175–76). Preschoolers (two to six years old) react to divorce with fright, confusion, and self-blame. Children seven to eight years old seem to blame themselves less but express feelings of sadness and insecurity. They have a problem expressing anger and a strong desire for parental reconciliation. Nine- to ten-year-old children can express their anger better, but they feel a conflict of loyalty, are lonely, and are ashamed of their parents' behavior. Adolescents express their anger, sadness, and shame most openly and seem better able to dissociate themselves from the parental difficulties (Lowery and Settle 1985).

Boys typically show more maladjustment and more prolonged problems than girls. Increased aggression, dependency, disobedience, and regressive behaviors are observed among more boys than girls (Lowery and Settle 1985).

Although not much studied, the role of former grandparents can also be important to children. Divorce removes the children not only from one parent

provide less discipline, and are less sensitive to their children, being caught up themselves in the personal maelstrom of divorce and its aftermath. (301)

This reduction in parenting suggests that increasing divorce will lead to an increasing number of unattached children (see Scenes from Marriage, Chapter 13). How much parenting a divorced parent will give is not easily predictable. Wallerstein was surprised to find that the quality of parenting before divorce did not predict the kind of parenting that would be offered after divorce. In some cases, a parent who was very loving and responsible toward his or her children ceased being so after the divorce while others continued to parent as they had before.

One thing is clear: Divorced parents who fight by means of their children will probably cause their children harm. One parent may try to turn the children against the former spouse. The visiting parent may use visitation rights to try to lure the child away from the custodial parent. The "Disneyland Dad" syndrome, in which the visiting parent indulges the child, may cause conflict with the custodial parent, who thinks that the "ex" is spoiling the children. Parents need to speak openly about the divorce but without speaking negatively about the former mate. Again Wallerstein was surprised by her finding that contrary to popular belief, the passage of time does not automatically diminish the feelings or memories of hurt, jealousy, and anger that the parents or the children of divorcing parents have

(30). Unless divorced parents can work out some mutually acceptable relationship that holds conflict to a minimum, adjustment will remain difficult for the children. In extreme cases recurring court battles may be fought over the children (approximately 10 to 12 percent of divorcing couples [196]). Or **child snatching** may occur, which is frightening, confusing, and possibly dangerous to the child; an estimated 163,000 abductions of children by a parent occurred in 1988 (Finkelhor, Hataling, and Sedlak 1991, 805).

but also from at least one set of grandparents. Moreover grandparents who have close and ongoing relationships with their grandchildren and then, because of divorce, are denied access to them are also victims of divorce (although generally unnoticed). Grandparents are one step removed from the conflicts of a divorce and therefore may be able to offer their grandchildren relative security and affection during the trying times. Recognition of the grandparent-grandchild relationship has led most states to protect grandparent visitation rights (Press 1983).

At this time we do not fully understand the effects of divorce on children. The immediate effects, usually negative, vary from child to child. Some children will be affected even as adults (Wallerstein and Blakeslee 1989). It is also clear that the divorced family is usually less adaptive economically, socially, and psychologically to the raising of children than the two-parent family. The one-parent family lacks the support and buffering effect of another adult (Wallerstein and Kelly 1980; Wallerstein 1984; Wallerstein and Blakeslee 1989).

Despite the general acceptance of divorce in our society, it remains an unpleasant and traumatic experience for most parents and a trying and difficult

Child snatching
The taking of children from the custodial parent by the noncustodial parent after a divorce

Problems of the Newly Divorced

611

time for most children. Fortunately, most divorced people remarry, thereby reconstituting the two-parent family. Of course, in this case children must establish a new successful relationship with the stepparent, which is another problem (Chapter 17).

TYPES OF CHILD CUSTODY

Courts have four choices when awarding custody of children in a divorce proceeding:

1. The most common is *sole custody* (65 to 70 percent). In this case the children are assigned to one parent, generally the mother (90 percent), who has sole responsibility for physically raising the children.

2. In *joint custody* the children divide their time between the parents, who share the various decisions about their children. Most states encourage joint custody with its appealing promise that the children of divorce can "keep both parents." This does not mean that the children spend equal amounts of time with each parent. It simply means that the parents share responsibility for major decisions regarding the children's health care, education, and the like. The trend toward joint custody has moderated somewhat as the courts have realized that custody conditions need to be tailored to each family rather than trying to use one type of custody in all situations (Chamberlin 1989). The question of whether states should mandate joint custody is currently provoking considerable debate (Ferreiro 1990). The perceived advantages of joint custody include the following:

■ Both parents continue parenting roles.
■ The arrangement avoids sudden termination of a child's relationship with one parent.
■ Joint custody lessens the constant child-care burden experienced by most single parents.
■ It has reduced the number of litigated custody cases.

Joint custody is a compromise that enables parents to save face by avoiding total loss of custody (Friedman 1992). However, joint custody also forces the parents to maintain a relationship; if they cannot do this successfully, there will be negative effects on the children. Joint custody can also give the child a sense of homelessness. A child who lives one week with mother and one week with dad may never be able to establish where his or her home and loyalties lie.

3. A third choice is termed *split custody*. In this case the children are divided between the parents. In most cases the father takes the boys and the mother the girls. This method has the major drawback of separating the children from one another. It does, however, reduce the burden on the parent who might otherwise have sole custody of all the children.

4. The court may award custody to someone other than a parent or parents. This is seldom done unless both parents are incompetent or offer such a poor environment for the children that the court decides parental custody would be harmful. In most such cases, grandparents or other near relatives gain custody of the children.

Custody and visitation plans often cause conflict between the divorcing couple. Yet in practice most children are still placed in the physical custody of their mother. Noncustodial fathers tend to gradually drop out of their children's lives. According to estimates, 10 percent to 40 percent of noncustodial fathers see their children once a year or less (Arditti 1990, 461–62; Haskins 1988; Furstenberg 1988; Seltzer 1991). The following are some of the factors that play a role in noncustodial fathers' failure to visit their children:

- Living some distance away from children.
- Conflict with the ex-spouse and/or a stepparent.
- New interests, family, or stepchildren.
- Guilt over nonpayment of support or failure to fulfill some other obligation to the former spouse and/or the children.
- Teenage children so busy with their own lives that little time was available for the noncustodial parent (Dudley 1991).

Little is known about the small percentage of noncustodial mothers. Generally, the courts do not demand as much monetary support from a noncustodial mother as they do from a noncustodial father (Christensen et al. 1990).

In the past couples with children tended to avoid or at least postpone divorce until the children were grown. This is no longer true, and with America's high divorce rate, increasing numbers of children will go through the divorce experience.

> In the 1950s, only 6 out of every 1000 children experienced parental divorce in a given year, but in the 1980s, the rate varied between 17 and 19 per 1000 (Bianchi 1990, 9).

DIVORCE: THE LEGALITIES

Historically, the American attitude toward divorce has been negative, stemming mainly from the majority Christian heritage. The stigma of divorce has a long history. As soon as the Christian church was established divorce was formally forbidden and made legally impossible. (There was no civil marriage or civil divorce until recent centuries.) To this day civil divorces of Catholics, even in non-Catholic countries, are not recognized by the Catholic church, and Catholics who obtain such a divorce and remarry are considered to be in a state of sin and therefore ineligible for communion, although they are no longer excommunicated. Ireland remains one of the few countries without legal divorce, having voted down a divorce statute in 1986.

The attitudes of many Americans, however, have changed; divorce is now a legitimate option. It is even considered a right and proper way to end an unsuccessful marriage.

Matrimonial law is one of the most dynamic fields of law in this country today. It is ever-changing and differs from most legal fields in that it is based less on historical precedents than on doing the "right thing" to achieve equity between the parties (Samuelson 1988). The credo of the American Academy of Matrimonial Lawyers is to preserve the best interests of the family and society.

WHAT DO YOU THINK?

1. Of the various types of child custody, which do you think would have been best for you if your parents had divorced when you were six years old?
2. Should parents stay together for the sake of the children?
3. If a noncustodial parent does not pay court-ordered child support, what do you think should be done?
4. If a parent denies visitation rights to his or her ex-spouse, what do you think should be done?
5. If visitation rights are denied and the noncustodial parent snatches his or her child away without permission, what do you think should be done?

No area of law requires greater emotional strength from the parties, the attorneys, and the judiciary than matrimonial law. There is no area where emotions run higher, where personal feelings obscure the facts more often, and where so many conflicting needs (father, mother, children) must be considered. Divorce is a situation where an all-out effort to win will only lead to losses for all involved.

Divorce laws vary from extreme restriction, as in Ireland where no divorce is allowed, to extreme permissiveness, as in Japan where divorce is granted simply on mutual consent. Even in the United States, there is great variety because divorce, like marriage, is regulated by individual states. The reason for such variety in divorce laws is the old philosophical battle between those who believe that stringent divorce laws will curtail marriage failure and those who believe that marriages fail regardless of the strictness of divorce legislation. The latter also believe that unrealistic laws do more harm than good.

In the past states laid down certain grounds for divorce—rules that if broken by one spouse allowed the other to divorce. Because one spouse had to be proved a wrongdoer, punishments were often established. For example, the American colonies commonly prohibited the guilty spouse from remarrying after a divorce. In the more recent past, payment by one spouse to the other (alimony) was sometimes used to punish the guilty spouse rather than simply to help a spouse become reestablished.

The necessity of proving one spouse guilty of marital misconduct was the only approach to divorce in America until the 1960s when several states passed **"no-fault"** divorce laws. Thus, the idea that a marriage might be terminated simply because it had broken down, without placing blame on one party or the other, found its way into both the law on the books (how the laws are written) and the law of action (how laws are actually applied).

Today the idea of limiting grounds for divorce to misconduct has lost favor, and most states have some form of no-fault divorce. All states have residency requirements for divorce (ninety days to a year or more). Each state recognizes a divorce granted in any other state providing the other state's residency requirements have been met. In actuality, even this requirement is not checked in the usual uncontested divorce (only 10 to 15 percent of divorces are ultimately contested). Theoretically, states do not recognize foreign divorces unless one party actually lives or has lived in the foreign country. But here again the formal law differs from the informal application, and states take no action about a foreign divorce, even if neither party lives abroad, unless a complaint is received. If a complaint is received and the divorce is contested, however, a state may invalidate a divorce where residency requirements have not been met. In such cases, spouses who have remarried have sometimes been prosecuted for bigamy when the divorce to the former spouse has been invalidated.

Today no-fault divorce laws usually ask only if there are irreconcilable differences between the parties or incompatibility although most states still recognize other grounds for divorce. A few states allow divorce by mutual consent, and a small number grant a divorce if the partners have lived apart for a time period ranging between one and five years. Since divorce laws are governed by the state and are continually being modified, it is important to check the laws of the state in which you reside if divorce is contemplated.

As the states passed no-fault divorce laws, they also modified their property division systems on the theory that marriage is a partnership and mere title to

No-fault divorce
Divorce proceedings that do not place blame for the divorce on one spouse or the other

the property should not necessarily control its ownership after divorce. As a result, nine states (as of 1992) have community property distribution systems, and the remaining states have equitable division systems. Community property systems essentially provide for an equal division of property while equitable division systems call for distribution based on a variety of factors such as the respective contributions of the spouses, the need for property for support purposes or to maintain a home for children, and the potential for economic viability in the future.

When a person applies for a no-fault divorce, the court simply asks if his or her marriage has broken down because of irreconcilable differences. The court does not inquire into the nature of the differences, though the court can order a delay or continuance if in its opinion there is a reasonable possibility of reconciliation. No-fault laws often have a unique section that bars evidence of misconduct on the part of either spouse:

> In any pleadings or proceedings for legal separation or dissolution of marriage under this part, ... evidence of specific acts of misconduct shall be improper and inadmissible, except where child custody is in issue and such evidence is relevant. (*West's Annotated California Codes* 1983, Section 4509)

To date the last point has been largely ignored by the courts.

Because misconduct of one partner or the other is no longer considered, property settlements, support, and alimony awards are no longer used as punishment. As long as the parties to the divorce agree and have divided their community property approximately evenly, the courts do not involve themselves in property settlements. The courts do set up support requirements for minor children, deeming such children the responsibility of both parents until they are of age. In practice, this generally means that the children live with the mother and the father pays support.

Although fault is no longer determined, the judge still has the right to award alimony or maintenance, though not as punishment for wrongdoing.

> In any judgment decreeing the dissolution of a marriage or a legal separation of the parties, the court may order a party to pay for the support of the other party any amount, and for such a period of time, as the court may deem just and reasonable having regard for the circumstances of the respective parties, including duration of marriage, and the ability of the supported spouse to engage in gainful employment without interfering with the interests of the children. (*West's Annotated California Codes* 1983, Section 4801)

In most cases the wife will receive "rehabilitative" alimony until she is able to get on her feet financially. Often a wife who has devoted herself exclusively to her family for years has lost what marketable skills she may once have had. If she is older, finding a job is even more difficult. Accordingly, judges are tending to award limited-term or reviewable alimony on the basis of need. **Reviewable alimony** can be extended at the end of the limited term if the need still exists. The amount is generally modified by the court if a material change occurs in either spouse's financial circumstances. In one case the court awarded a wife funds for a college education on the grounds that she had worked to put her husband through school when they first married, and now it would be fair for him to do the same for her. A number of courts are using

Reviewable alimony
An award of alimony that is reviewed periodically and changed if necessary

615

INSET 16-4
DIVORCE AND DAD

Wallerstein and Blakeslee (1989) make it clear that the usual loss of the father (immediate or gradual) in divorcing families has serious negative ramifications for the children, both male and female. The following stories point out some of the complications of continuing to parent as the noncustodial parent.

PAY BUT DON'T INTERFERE

I left home because it seemed easier for Elaine and the kids. After all, I was only one person, they were three. The children could remain in their schools with their friends and have the security of living in the home they had grown up in. I figured I'd come to visit often. I hoped that our separation and divorce would have minimal impact on the children and felt that the family remaining in our home was the way to achieve this.

It certainly hasn't worked out as I first imagined. Visiting the children often is no simple matter. Elaine has a new husband, the children have their friends and activities. And I seem to be busier than ever.

At first, I'd just drop by to see the children when time permitted, but this usually upset everyone concerned. Elaine felt I was hanging around too much and even accused me of spying on her. Actually, there may have been a little truth to this accusation, especially when she started dating. The children usually didn't have time for me because they had plans of their own. I felt rejected by them.

Next, Elaine and I tried to work out a permanent visitation schedule. I was to take the children one evening a week and one weekend a month. Then she accused me of re-

jecting the children because I wouldn't commit more time to them. But my work schedule only had a few times when I was sure I would be free and thus able to take the children.

At first, the set visiting times worked out well. I'd have something great planned for the children. Soon, however, Elaine told me that I was spoiling them. She said that they were always upset and out of their routine when I brought them home. Would I mind not doing this and that with them? Gradually, the list of prohibitions lengthened. She had the house, the children, and my money to support the kids, yet I seemed to have fewer and fewer rights and privileges with them.

Be sure child support payments arrive promptly but please leave the children alone—more and more

the following rough guidelines in awarding alimony. If the marriage has lasted less than twelve years, the period of support will not exceed half the duration of the marriage. In marriages of twenty years or more, awards of support may be permanent, that is, until death or remarriage. Generally, under no-fault proceedings, the amount and duration of alimony have been drastically reduced on the theory that once the marital partnership has ended and the property is divided, the parties should be able to care for themselves.

The simplified no-fault laws have encouraged a new "do-it-yourself" trend in divorce. In the past retaining an attorney to obtain a divorce was mandatory, if for no other reason than to help interpret the complicated divorce laws.

Divorced people often express negative sentiments about attorneys and the adversarial legal system. Sometimes the lawyer may simply have become a scapegoat for emotional clients with uncertain goals. On the other hand, the legal profession may need clearer guidelines for handling divorce as well as some training in counseling and interpersonal relations. In 1991 the American Academy of Matrimonial Lawyers published *The Bounds of Advocacy* proposing practice standards for lawyers and clients in matrimonial cases (Friedman

this was Elaine's message.

Since she remarried, my only parental role seems to be financial. I really have no say on what the children do. I feel as though I'm being taken every time I write a child support check.

THE MISSING DAD

When Bill and I divorced, I wanted him to see our two children as often as possible and told the judge that he could have unlimited visitation rights. Bill seemed happy and said he looked forward to seeing the children often, both at my place and in his new home. A year has now gone by, and Bill almost never visits the children. Each time I ask him about it, he has another excuse. At first, he told me that he was too busy moving into his place. Then he was working a lot of overtime and was just too pooped to

visit. Later, he said his new girlfriend was not comfortable with his visiting here. When I suggested that he take the children to his place, he told me that the complex did not allow children, something he hadn't realized when he moved in, he said.

I think that the children really need their dad. It is important to them, and they miss him. They ask where he is and why he doesn't come more often. I'm embarrassed when they ask since I don't know what to tell them. I really think he just doesn't care.

Even though the court ordered him to pay $200 a month for child support, he is very irregular about the payment, and often I have to remind him that it is due. This makes me very uncomfortable, too. Between asking him to visit the children more often and reminding

him to send the child support payment, all I seem to do is nag him. In fact, he accuses me of being a worse nag than when we were married, but what can I do?

WHAT DO YOU THINK?

1. How hard do you think it is for a father to have a relationship with his children after divorce?
2. How do you think the father in the first story should handle the situation?
3. What should the former wife do to get Bill to visit more often and make payments on time?
4. In your experience which of the two cases seems to occur more often? Why?

1992). Regardless of whether attorneys are involved, a couple who can work out their differences in an amicable manner before going to court are in a much better position to obtain a fair and equitable divorce. Without such an agreement, a couple put themselves in the hands of a judge who knows little or nothing of their personal situation. Certainly, a judge's decision will be more arbitrary than a mutual decision by the divorcing couple.

It is important that attorneys who handle divorce cases (1) realize that the termination of marital contracts involves psychological as well as legal considerations and (2) attend to these issues as they process the cases. Failure to recognize the psychological aspects of this area of law can lead to a multiplicity of problems and further complicate an already difficult situation. This is not meant to suggest that lawyers should become marriage counselors but to point out that nonlegal issues directly affect a divorce action. The lawyer's job is to shift the focus from emotions to facts without appearing unsympathetic or becoming too sympathetic. It is a difficult balance to maintain.

Many people are going directly to the courts, following simplified procedures from guidebooks written by sympathetic lawyers or knowledgeable citizens, and

Divorce: The Legalities

obtaining their own divorces for the cost of filing ($100 to $400). However, a do-it-yourself approach to divorce is not recommended unless the partners are relatively friendly; agree on all matters, including child custody and child support; and do not have a large income, assets, or liabilities. In any case, it is advisable to have a lawyer at least review the settlement to make sure something important hasn't been omitted. The court cannot be relied upon to do this.

STRICT VERSUS LIBERAL DIVORCE LAWS

Those favoring strict divorce laws claim that such laws act to strengthen marriage by forcing couples to work out their problems and assume responsibility for making their marriage work. Such persons consider divorce a sign of individual failure in marriage. In reality, however, divorce is not the problem; the problem is marital breakdown. Laws may preclude divorce, but they cannot prevent marriage breakdown; laws may prohibit remarriage after divorce, but they cannot prevent a man and woman from living together. Those favoring more liberal divorce laws say strict laws create undue animosity and hardship, lead to perjury and the falsification of evidence, and are simply unenforceable.

Rather than trying to maintain marriage through strict divorce laws, a better approach might be to make marriages harder to enter. The waiting period between the issuance of a marriage license and the actual marriage could be longer. Premarital counseling could be required. Trial marriages could be sanctioned. More couples seem to be forsaking formal marriage and simply living together, at least for a while, in what appears to be a trial union for some couples. This trend may lead to lower divorce rates, although research to date does not support this supposition (Chapter 4).

The real issue is whether laws can make marriage successful. Their ability to do so seems doubtful. Yet this does not mean the state should not be involved in marriage. Certainly, assigning responsibility for children, assuring some order in property division and inheritance, and guarding against fraud and misrepresentation are legitimate state concerns. But beyond those concerns, states' efforts to legislate successful marriage have not worked. Laws that support good human relations might be more helpful. For example, if a couple finds insurmountable obstacles to success in their marriage, the laws should support their mutual efforts to dissolve the marriage in the most amicable and beneficial manner to both partners.

Finding the perfect legislative formula for dissolving a marriage is difficult because the two parties to a marriage generally do not agree on when the marriage is over or what to do about their problems. The state must provide a framework for resolving differences in spousal perceptions of right and wrong in a fair and impartial manner. Whether the many reforms of divorce laws and procedures over the past twenty-five years have actually made the process fairer, simpler, and less acrimonious is a matter of serious debate. The fault lies not so much with the legislature, the lawyers, or the legal system as with the extraordinary emotional content of the subject matter. An angry spouse who is unwilling to accept the reality of his or her divorce will find something to fight over no matter how streamlined the system. The lawyer who tries to be fair will be accused of "selling his or her client down the river." Perhaps all that we can reasonably expect from divorce laws is a framework that will allow spouses to ventilate their anger and frustration while receiving fair protection under the law (Friedman 1992).

■ SOME CAUTIONS ABOUT NO-FAULT DIVORCE ■

There is little question that the implementation of no-fault divorce procedures has eased the immediate trauma of divorce by focusing on the demise of the marriage rather than on the guilt of one of the spouses. The fear that easier divorce laws would lead to skyrocketing divorce rates has proved unfounded. As noted earlier, the crude divorce rate has remained relatively stable since 1975.

Lenore Weitzman (1985) makes a strong case that the no-fault divorce laws have in practice caused severe economic hardship for a large proportion of divorced women and their children. For example, "equal" divisions of marital property have caused a dramatic increase in the sale of the family home. Because the home is most couples' major asset, the property cannot be divided equally unless the home is turned into cash via a sale. Court orders to sell the family home were issued in about one in ten divorces in 1968 before no-fault divorce laws. By 1977 such orders were issued in one out of three divorce cases (Weitzman 1985, 31). Sale of the family home adds additional stress and disorganization to the divorcing family because all parties must now find new housing. Selling the family home and splitting the proceeds usually leaves neither the wife nor the husband with enough money to buy a new home. In addition, if the family must move to a new neighborhood, the children's schooling and friendships will be disrupted when they most need continuity and stability. In most states the divorce judge can award temporary use of the home to the custodial party when children are involved, but judges don't always take this step.

Property settlements reached by divorcing couples under no-fault rules have been found to be incomplete and at times grossly unfair to one of the pair. An amicable agreement reached by a divorcing couple based on present circumstances may be totally inappropriate at some time in the future.

Another major factor working against custodial parents and their children is the reduction of the age of majority (legal adult status) from twenty-one to eighteen. As a consequence, college students who are over eighteen are no longer considered children in need of support. Thus, when expenses are apt to be greatest for the custodial parent, the noncustodial parent (the father in most cases) is under no legal obligation to help financially. As a result, many children of divorce have difficulty obtaining a higher education. In one study of families a decade after the divorce of the parents, 60 percent of the children over eighteen were getting less education than their fathers, and 45 percent were getting less than their mothers (Wallerstein and Blakeslee 1989, 157).

Ironically, many of the sex-based assumptions ridiculed by radical feminists a decade ago—assumptions about women's economic dependence, their greater investment in children, their need for financial support from their ex-husbands—have turned out not to have been so ridiculous after all. Rather they reflected the reality of married women's lives, and they softened the economic devastations of divorce for women and their children. In the early days

INSET 16-5
HUMANIZING DIVORCE PROCEDURES

Because the courts have for so long considered divorce an adversary procedure, the legal profession has had difficulty thinking in no-fault terms. Most of the legal terminology of divorce is derived from criminal law; thus the language used by attorneys and the courts comes from that same background (see Table 16-4).

A lawyer is trained to take the side of his or her client and to do the best possible for them. It is difficult for many lawyers to let go of that training (in fact, unethical to do so) and concern themselves with the entire family unit. Perhaps not every lawyer should handle divorces. Family law specialization is already a reality in many states. Such a specialization should encourage the lawyer to think in terms of protecting all members of the family. The family law attorney must think beyond the divorce, especially if children are involved, inasmuch as "parents are forever." All divorce really does is rearrange family relationships, not end them.

The family law attorney should encourage self-determination on the part of the divorcing couple. They each have strengths and weaknesses and are often better judges of how to change their relationship than attorneys and courts. The tradi-

TABLE 16-4
LEGAL TERMINOLOGY OF DIVORCE DERIVED FROM CRIMINAL LAW

TERM	CRIMINAL MEANING	DIVORCE MEANING
Custody	Holding of a criminal in jail	Giving of a child to a parent by the courts
Custodian	Prison guard	Parent having legal custody of the child after a divorce
Visitation	Friends and relatives visiting the person jailed	The noncustody parent visiting his or her child
Defendant	Person against whom legal action is taken	Person being sued for divorce
Plaintiff	Person or state taking legal action against defendant	Person suing for divorce
Suit	Legal action to secure justice	Legal action to secure divorce

tional attorney is trained to do everything for the client rather than encourage the client to take control of the process as much as possible. The family law attorney must learn to become a facilitator to the couple, complementing their strengths and weaknesses.

Emotions are not permissible facts in a court of law. Yet emotions are facts in most divorce proceedings. They must be considered because the close intimacy of marriage usually cannot be dissolved without them.

In recent years the law has recognized the need for family support during the crises of divorce. No-fault divorce, conciliation courts, joint child custody, and family law specialization for attorneys are all steps in the direction of humanizing divorce. The changes in the law are not enough; we must also work to bring the ideas of no fault and family well-being into the consciousness of those working in the legal system.

Source: Adapted from "Drawing Individual and Family Strengths from the Divorce Process," a talk given by Meyer Elkin, California conciliation court pioneer, at the California Council on Family Relations Annual Conference held in Santa Barbara, California, September 26–28, 1980.

of the women's movement, there was a rush to embrace equality in all its forms. Some feminists regarded alimony as a sexist concept that had no place in a society in which men and women were to be treated as equals. Alimony was an insult, a symbolic reflection of the law's assumption that all women were nonproductive dependents. But it soon became clear that alimony was a critical mechanism for achieving the goal of fairness in divorce. To a woman who had devoted twenty-five years of her life to nurturing a family and at age fifty had no job, career, pension, or health insurance, alimony was not an insult but a lifeline (Weitzman 1985, 359–60).

Such cautions about no-fault divorce are not meant to negate the advantages that no-fault divorce laws have brought to the procedure. They are simply meant to warn the reader that divorce under any circumstances is difficult. Even if divorce is not a legal trial, it is certainly an emotional one. Remember too that the no-fault divorce system does not relate to a particular support or property division system. Fault can still be found, and damage claims against spouses for such actions as causing injury or the willful infliction of emotional distress are still awarded.

DIVORCE COUNSELING AND MEDIATION

Going to court means giving up control of your relationship to a third party, namely, the judge. Generally, a good court settlement is one that leaves both parties feeling shortchanged. In other words, the parties accept a settlement with which neither fully agrees. In contrast, divorce mediation tries to provide a setting in which the divorcing couple can meet, communicate, and negotiate with professional help to reach their own settlement, which can then be presented to the court. In most cases, the court will accept such settlements.

Divorce mediation offers several advantages. If mediation is successful, the financial costs are far less than in a contested divorce. The emotional costs are also reduced since mediated divorce focuses on compromise rather than confrontation and seeks the best for all members of the family. By laying the groundwork for mutual cooperation in working out the postdivorce relationship (custody, visitation, support, and the like), divorce mediation reduces the chances of postdivorce conflict (McKay et al. 1984). Perhaps most important, the decisions are made by family members rather than imposed upon them by the court.

Some states have conciliation courts that attempt to ameliorate the negative effects of marital failure. The first goal of these courts is to save the marriage, but failing that they try to ensure an equitable divorce, "to protect the rights of children and to promote the public welfare by preserving, promoting, and protecting family life and the institution of matrimony, and to provide means for the reconciliation of spouses and the amicable settlement of domestic and family controversies" (West's Annotated California Codes 1983, 72).

Divorce mediation involves one or two professional mediators (a lawyer and/or a mental health worker) who meet with both the husband and wife to help them resolve conflicts, reach decisions, and negotiate agreements about the dissolution of their marriage. Usually, the first phase is predivorce counseling, which centers on the decision to divorce. At this point there is still a possibility of saving the marriage. The counselor acts as an objective third party (mediator) to help the couple contemplating divorce come to a good decision. The mediator acts as a neutral adviser, an expert source of information who suggests options from which the couple are free to choose. The spouses do not abdicate the decision-making responsibility but are helped to decide for themselves.

Actual divorce mediation begins when the decision is made and lawyers and/or legal proceedings enter the picture. It is important that both partners be willing to consent to full disclosure if mediation is to work.

Divorce counseling occurs after the divorce is final and is aimed at helping the individuals get life started again. In a few states, some divorce counseling is available through the courts, and occasionally courts require such counseling.

Persons using mediation should not expect to find support for their side or simple advice that will resolve their problems. They should also not expect to experience immediate improvement in themselves and their relationship with the former spouse. Rather they will find clarification and help in assessing their strengths and weaknesses so they can move toward better understanding and clearer communication. The better the couple's communication and understanding, the less traumatic the divorce will be, both for themselves and for any children they may have.

REDUCING DIVORCE RATES

A number of steps might be taken to help reduce the divorce rate:

■ More effective marriage and family training should be given at home and in the schools. Such courses are gaining popularity, and it is hoped that this interest by young persons will lead to sounder partner choices and improved marriages.

■ Perhaps more scientific methods of mate selection than the current haphazard system based largely on emotion can be developed.

■ Periodic marital checkups through visits to trained marriage counselors should be encouraged. As pointed out earlier, by the time most couples in difficulty seek help, their marriage is beyond help. Facing problems before they are insolvable and building problem-solving techniques into marriage are needed elements in American marriage.

■ Changing marriage laws to encourage couples to take their entry into marriage more seriously would also help reduce the necessity of divorce. California took a step in the direction of stricter marriage laws with Assembly Bill 402 (West's Annotated California Codes 1983), which became effective in 1970. This law, the first of its kind, empowers the court to require premarital counseling for any couple applying for a marriage license if either party is under eighteen years of age and the court deems such counseling necessary.

■ Child-care centers would help working couples with young children have more time for one another and more time to work positively on their marriage. Many couples simply do not have time for their marriage in the early child-rearing, work-oriented years. When the children are finally capable of independence and economic stability has been achieved, there is often not enough left of the marriage to be salvaged, much less improved.

■ Certainly, we need to give at least as much attention to the good aspects of marriage as we do to the negative aspects. Publicizing ways in which marriage can be improved, highlighting the strengths found in successfully married couples (see Chapter 1), and concentrating on relationship improvement will be of more value than exaggerating the problems inherent in marriage.

SUMMARY

1. Almost every society has some means of dissolving marriage. Divorce is America's mode of ending unsatisfactory marriages. *The divorce rate has increased drastically during this century, probably reflecting Americans' changing expectations for marriage and increasing tolerance of change.* Since 1975, however, the divorce rate has stabilized.

2. *There are many reasons for the high divorce rate in the United States.* Americans ask a great deal of marriage, and the more we ask of an institution, the more apt it is to fail. Changing sex roles, emphasis on the individual, heterogeneity of the population, mobility, and poverty all affect marriage and increase the chances for divorce.

3. *The decision to divorce is usually reached slowly and involves emotions similar to the feelings that one goes through after the death of a loved one.* Indeed, long before legal divorce and perhaps long after it as well, a couple will go through the suffering of an emotional divorce. Divorce is complicated by the presence of children and/or considerable property.

4. *Divorced people must cope with numerous problems.* They must make changes in their economic situation, their living situation, and their relations with family, friends, children, and co-workers. Most divorced persons eventually remarry. In order for the remarriage to be successful, divorcing people must learn from their past mistakes. Thus, the divorce must act as a catalyst to further self-insight.

5. *In the past few years, all states have instituted some form of no-fault divorce.* In these proceedings, neither party has to be proved guilty of misconduct providing grounds (a legal reason) for divorce. The only thing that must be proved is that the marriage has suffered an irremediable breakdown. No-fault divorce is not perfect. Laws cannot control emotions or eliminate the pain, disruption, and economic hardship that occur when a family breaks up.

In many cases divorce as a cure to a problematic marriage is worse than the disease. Although most family therapists see their job as helping people in troubled marriages, they usually remain neutral when the question of divorce is raised. "Whether you stay together or split up is your decision" is the standard answer of a marriage counselor to queries about divorce.

However, more and more family counselors are discovering that the problems surrounding divorce are often far worse than the problems within the marriage. Instead of remaining neutral, some marriage specialists now suggest that counselors should make strong efforts to save troubled marriages headed toward divorce (Smolowe 1991; Medved 1989; Weiner-Davis 1992).

People seeking a divorce are focused on what they see as unresolvable conflicts within their marriage. Often they believe the problem resides in their mate. Things are so bad in their relationship that leaving the relationship seems the only way to escape the situation. They believe that divorce means the end of their marital problems. Seldom does the person contemplating divorce anticipate the pain and upheaval divorce leaves in its wake. Seldom do they consider that divorce is usually not the end of the relationship and its problems. This is especially true if children are involved. Wallerstein and Blakeslee (1989) report that the painful effects of divorce often are felt for years by both the divorced mates and their children.

Michele Weiner-Davis (1992, 14–15) suggests that:

Battles over parenting issues don't end with divorce, they get played out with children as innocent bystanders or even pawns. Uncomfortable gatherings at future family weddings, bar mitzvahs, graduations, births and funerals provide never-ending reminders that divorce is forever.

I've met children of all ages who, even after both parents remarry, secretly hope their own parents will, someday, reunite. Many well-adjusted adults whose parents separated or divorced when they were children admit an emptiness that never goes away. Most parents recognize the fact that divorce will impact on their children, they just don't anticipate the lasting effects. I've heard too many divorced parents say "I wish I knew then what I know now." Gradually I have come to the conclusion that divorce is not the answer. It doesn't necessarily solve the problems it purports to solve. Most marriages are worth saving.

When you consider that most Americans marry for love, it seems plausible to believe that American marriages start out on a positive basis. The couple are attracted to one another, like one another, and find enough in common to marry. There will be problems but most problems are solvable. As Weiner-Davis (14) suggests, "I don't believe in saving marriages. I believe in divorcing the old marriage and beginning a new one—with the same partner." She strongly believes that working to solve marital problems is far less traumatic than the problems surrounding divorce. She asks, "If getting rid of one's problematic spouse is the solution to marital problems, why would 60 percent of second marriages fail?" In fact, as you saw in reading this chapter, divorce entails a myriad of new problems—financial difficulties, disputes over child custody and visitation rights, loneliness, how to meet potential new mates, how to handle old friends and extended family members, and so forth.

Too often mates dwell on what is

wrong with the relationship, the "20 percent I hate you," rather than on what is right, the "80 percent I love you." When this occurs, a negative vicious circle commences: I expect the worst, I see the worst, I invite the worst; it becomes a self-fulfilling prophecy. Weiner-Davis suggests that by examining what is positive in the relationship, a troubled couple can slowly, step by step, start a positive self-fulfilling prophecy. Her point is that since most marriages begin on a happy positive note, it makes sense to build on the strengths that brought the couple together in the first place rather than to concentrate on dissecting weaknesses when a couple comes for counseling.

Most couples go through a "honeymoon is over" period, a transitional period when the rose-colored glasses come off and expectations are slowly readjusted to reflect reality. This is not an easy process, but the end result, a workable marriage, is worth the effort. The couples who can't or won't make this transition are the couples whose relationship begins to worsen and who often travel the road to divorce.

Because troubled couples tend to become locked into circular action-reaction patterns, some kind of change—new behavior—is needed to break this cycle. Weiner-Davis finds that even a small change in behavior on the part of one mate necessitates change in the relationship. Too often both mates spend time diagnosing the problem rather than making behavioral changes. Of course, whether the diagnosis is right or wrong is immaterial to solving the couple's problems unless concrete behavior

changes occur in the relationship. Thus, she suggests starting with changes in behavior even if the changes are unilateral rather than being preoccupied with the possible reasons why the relationship is not working.

It is extremely important to set clear but small and simple goals. For example, a couple, after months of fighting, finally agree to "be more affectionate." But they don't define what this means in behavioral terms. Several weeks later they come back to the counselor accusing each other of not trying. Interestingly, each spouse believed that he or she had been trying but that the other had not tried. How did this happen? Because "being affectionate" had never been clearly defined, they were unaware that they had very different expectations. The wife defined "affectionate" as spending time together as a couple, doing thoughtful things like calling each other to say hello during the day, and giving and getting hugs. The husband defined "affectionate" as sexual foreplay or making love. When he approached her sexually, he felt he was trying, but she recoiled because he hadn't yet shown affection according to her definition. When she called him at work to let him know she was thinking about him, he seemed oblivious to her affection. They missed each other's attempts to improve their marriage because they could only spot signs of affection based on their own definitions, which they had failed to share with one another (Weiner-Davis 1992, 108). Table 16-5 illustrates how goals can be described in behavioral terms.

TABLE 16-5
DESCRIBING GOALS IN BEHAVIORAL TERMS

VAGUE GOALS	ACTION GOALS
Be respectful.	You will ask me about my day.
	I will compliment you about your work.
Be more loving.	You will tell me you love me at least once a week.
	I will volunteer to watch the kids so you can go out.
Be more sexual.	I will initiate sex once a week.
	I will suggest we try something different.
	You will be more verbal when we make love.
Be less selfish.	You will ask what I want to do on weekends.
	I will check with you before making plans.
	I will clean up if you make dinner.

Source: Weiner-Davis 1992, 111.

Another suggestion is that couples should focus on exceptions to their criticisms of their mates. Many couples coming for counseling make blanket black-and-white statements about each other: "He is *never* affectionate." "The *only* thing she ever does is nag." Yet in most cases, such statements simply are not true. He is affectionate at times. She does not nag all the time. By asking couples to think of exceptions to their blanket criticisms, the counselor can start moving the couple toward a more positive focus. Weiner-Davis (1992, 124–25) suggests that by recognizing exceptions:

■ The problems shrink because the black-and-white thinking is acknowledged.
■ Exceptions demonstrate that people *are* changeable. If a mate could behave in a desired way once, he or she can behave that way again. Individuals really can change.
■ Exceptions can supply solutions. The exception to the disliked behavior gives the mate an exact description, not of what is wrong, but of what can be done to improve the relationship.
■ Exceptions empower people. They realize for the first time in months (or years) that, despite the problems, they have been doing some things right. This realization often comes as a complete shock because most people feel they've tried everything and nothing works. Now they know that something does work.

Those persons suggesting that divorce is not the answer do not deny that marriages have problems. Of course, even the best relationships suffer at times. Rather their point is that energy spent on improving a relationship and trying to save a marriage may in the long run be more fruitful to the couple than a divorce. A divorce does not end a person's problems. Instead, most divorces introduce additional problems and complicate a person's life.

CHAPTER
17

REMARRIAGE: A GROWING WAY OF AMERICAN LIFE

CONTENTS

"It seems to me that John and Helen were just divorced, and here's an invitation to Helen's wedding."

"Not only that, but I met John and his new girlfriend at lunch yesterday and from the way they were acting, I'll bet we'll soon get an invitation to their wedding."

"It's hard to understand. They were so eager to escape their marriage and now it seems they can hardly wait to get back into another marriage."

Nothing restores adult self-esteem and happiness after divorce as quickly and as thoroughly as a love affair or a successful second marriage. No matter how badly the men and women in our study were burned by their first marriages, not one turned his or her back on the possibility of a new relationship. (Wallerstein and Blakeslee 1989, 225–226).

Divorced people as a group are not against marriage. For every age group remarriage rates are higher than first marriage rates, although like first marriage rates, they have been dropping. Remarriage rates for men are higher than for women, and remarriage rates for the divorced are higher than for the widowed. Statistically single divorced people are a minority in America's population.

Since divorced people, in general, are not against marriage and the United States has a high divorce rate, it is clear that many (approximately 46 percent) American marriages will be remarriages for one or both of the partners. Overall about 30 percent of American families are **blended or reconstituted families** (National Center for Health Statistics August 26, 1991, 4; London and Wilson 1988).

> Four out of five divorced men remarry and three out of four divorced women remarry although these proportions appear to be dropping (Furstenberg and Spanier 1987; Glick 1989). On the average, he remarries at age thirty-eight to a woman aged thirty-three. She remarries at age thirty-four to a man aged thirty-seven. Remarriage rates drop rapidly as age increases. Remarriage rates have also dropped overall, perhaps due to the increase in cohabitation during the 1980s. Not only do divorced persons remarry in large numbers but they also tend to remarry quickly. The median interval before remarriage for previously divorced women is 2.5 years; for previously divorced men, the median is 2.3 years (National Center for Health Statistics August 26, 1991, 5).

Although the high rate of remarriage is often presented as a major change in American family structure, this rate is actually about what it has always been historically. The difference is that remarriages in past centuries occurred because of widowhood, not divorce. Originally, the term *step* in *stepfather, stepmother* and *stepfamily* meant "orphan." The stepchild of yesteryear had almost always lost a biological parent to death. Most of today's stepchildren have both biological parents as well as one and perhaps two new stepparents.

Age differences between remarried spouses tend to be greater than between first-married couples. For first-married couples, the age difference has consistently been two years. In marriages between never-married women and divorced men, however, the age difference averages seven years. For remarriages of both spouses, the age difference is four years. The only category in which brides are generally older than their grooms (approximately one year) are mar-

Blended or reconstituted family
Husband and wife, at least one of whom has been married before, and one or more children from previous marriages

riages of previously married women to never-married men (National Center for Health Statistics 1986, 3; August, 1991).

May-December marriages—marriages between older men or women and much younger women or men—are more common among divorced people than among people entering their first marriage. Although we have little empirical data on the success of such marriages, many such couples express high levels of marital satisfaction. The younger partners appreciate the security and stability that the older partners often can offer. The older partners express pleasure with the generally high energy level and flexibility of their younger partners.

From the remarriage statistics, we can conclude that divorce serves not so much as an escape hatch from married life as a recycling mechanism that gives individuals a chance to improve their marital situation (Furstenberg and Spanier 1987). Considering the rise in divorce rates, the lengthening life span, and the younger ages at which Americans divorce, the incidence of remarriage appears likely to remain high in the future.

> About 29 percent of divorcing husbands and 37 percent of the wives are in their twenties at the time of divorce (National Center for Health Statistics May, 1991, 11).

Serial monogamy
Having several spouses over a lifetime but only one at a time

What Americans experience is not monogamy, but **serial monogamy**—that is, several spouses over a lifetime but only one at a time.

Although we have concentrated on the remarriage of divorced persons, the widowed also remarry. They stay single longer than the divorced, though, and their remarriage rates are lower because choice is more limited for older people.

RETURNING TO SINGLE LIFE

Many people married for some time, burdened with the responsibilities of a growing family and missing the flush of romance that brought them together with their mate, feel pangs of envy when their friends divorce and reenter the singles world. Remembering their dating and courting days, they relive nostalgic memories of the excitement of the "new date" and the boundless energies they expended when they were young pursuing and being pursued. Except for a few individuals, such dreams of married people are just that—dreams.

The return to the singles world can be frightening for both men and women, especially for those married for some years. "Can I be successful as a single person?" is a question that cannot be answered at first. Most people have experienced a severe blow to their self-esteem with the divorce and are reluctant to face the potential rejections involved with meeting new people. Those who have been left against their will are more likely to find single life intimidating than those who have voluntarily left their marriage. Those who divorce because they have found someone else while married may avoid a return to single life altogether.

The point at which divorced persons are ready to return to the single social life varies greatly. Most take about a year after the divorce to get themselves emotionally back together. Those who had an ongoing extramarital relationship are in a different position and often remarry as soon as legally possible.

Learning, or rather relearning, to date and relate to the opposite sex as a single person is especially difficult for anyone who has been married for a long time because his or her self-image has for so long been that of one member of a couple. Once the divorced (or widowed) persons reenter the social world, though, they are often surprised at how many people share their newly single status. Except for the very young divorced, most reenter a world of single but formerly married people rather than one of never-married people. This eases the transition inasmuch as the people they meet have also experienced marital collapse. In about 19 percent of remarriages, both spouses have been divorced (National Center for Health Statistics August, 1991, 4). Divorced persons respond to problems with a certain empathy, which helps the newly divorced person feel more acceptable. In fact, the discovery that they can meet and interact with people of the opposite sex in their new single role can be exciting and heartening. "Maybe I'm not such a failure after all," is a common response.

A newly divorced person, especially a person who was rejected by the spouse and did not want a divorce, may initially engage in sexual experimentation. To be desired sexually is a boost to shattered self-esteem. To be close to another person physically—to be held, touched, and sexually pleasured—makes the rejected person feel loved and cared for and also verifies his or her sexual desirability. For these reasons newly divorced persons must guard against sexual exploitation and not make the error of equating sex with love.

Dating has already been discussed in Chapter 4, but it is important to realize that the dating practices of divorced or widowed persons tend to be different from the dating practices of young, unmarried individuals. For example, the divorced and widowed have more problems meeting new people than young, never-married people. Sometimes friends, relatives, and business associates supply new acquaintances. Organizations such as *Parents Without Partners* and *We Care* can be meeting places. Often the lofty educational and helping goals of these groups are secondary to their social functions. The stated goals may make it easier for people to join activities without appearing to be "mate hunting." Although young, never-married persons may use any of the methods discussed here, they tend to be used more by older, divorced persons.

Many singles clubs make introductions their major purpose. Such clubs sometimes frighten and intimidate those just recuperating from marital failure. Many people are uncomfortable attending singles parties that have a "meat market" atmosphere.

Although long used in Europe, the personal newspaper advertisement is relatively new in the United States. Discounting the ads for sexual partners in underground newspapers, legitimate classified advertising is increasingly being used, especially by divorced persons, to seek desirable companions and potential mates. Those using such ads should take precautions to make sure that the person one decides to meet is sincere. Using a post office box or telephone number rather than one's home address and arranging for the first meeting to be in a public place are sensible safeguards.

Technology has found a place in the formerly marrieds' new single life in the form of computer and video dating. For a fee, a computer dating service will search its large bank of personal information on many single clients to find an appropriate date. The new client is asked about background, interests, feelings about sexual relations, and the qualities sought in prospective dates. The computer then makes a match based on stated interests, hobbies, habits, education, age, and so on. Computer dating is based on the theoretical notion

ATTRACTIVE refined widow seeks real gentleman, 60s. Home loving, likes music, trips, books, gardening; financially secure; wants to enjoy lasting companionship.

EXPERIENCED sailboat skipper, fifties, single, yacht club member, wants to meet compatible outdoor gal who would like to go sailing.

MAN seeking intelligent, independent, intuitive female companion (21–35) for social events. Send photo.

MALE 39, desires pleasant, attractive easy-going female. Enjoys good home life, occasional outdoor activities, flying, fishing, ghost towning. Photo & phone.

RETIRED lady loves nature, fine music. Sincere, kind, honest, sense of humor; wants same kind of person as bus travel companion or share your trans. No smoking.

cathy®

by Cathy Guisewite

of "homogamy," that those of similar interests, backgrounds, and the like will be attracted to one another.

Often the client then has the opportunity to look at videotapes of people who share his or her interests. Videotapes have the advantage of giving an overall impression of the person before any meeting. Clients of videodating services report that they put a great deal of thought into composing their biographical statement and selecting pictures. They say that the chance to prescreen dates is the most attractive feature of videodating (Woll and Young 1989, 483). Some agencies estimate that about 25 percent of their clients eventually marry someone they met through the computer's selection process although few statistics are available on success rates of such dating methods (Woll and Cozby 1987; Woll and Young 1989). Computer and video dating can also involve considerable expense. Membership charges can run as high as $1000.

With the increasing availability of home computers, potential dating partners can contact one another via modems. Some large computer services such as Compuserve Information Services have set up special channels that can be used for a small fee for meeting other computer owners. The users talk to one another by typing out messages on their computers.

There are many other ways to meet new people. The most important step the newly divorced can take is to participate actively in the singles' world. Unless an individual is out in society, meeting new people is difficult. The newly divorced person in a small town probably stands the poorest chance of meeting someone new.

When divorced and widowed persons date, children are often part of the dating equation. The romantic rendezvous for two more and more frequently includes three or four. With the high divorce rate and increased numbers of single-parent families, many singles now find that dating someone new means getting acquainted with the date's children. "I recently started dating Jean. When I went to pick her up for our first date, I rang the bell and put on my best smile. But it wasn't Jean who opened the door, it was a ten-year-old kid. He seemed to be checking me out the way date's fathers used to when I was a teenager."

About 53 percent of divorcing couples have children under eighteen. Of divorcing couples, 26 percent have one child, and 27 percent have two or more children (National Center for Health Statistics May, 1991a, 2).

The presence of children after divorce complicates dating and courting and movement toward remarriage. The custodial parent in particular must consider the effect dating will have on the children. Dating and serious courtship will drastically affect the children's hopes and dreams of reconciliation between their divorced parents. Children may even directly resist dating on the part of their divorced parents. Thus, a divorced parent has many concerns that do not trouble a single individual: What will children think of the new date? Would the new date make a good stepparent? How do I handle sexual relations while I am dating? What will the children think if a date stays overnight? What will the children tell my "ex" about my dates?

Dating and courtship also affect the ex-spouse. Some who hold onto thoughts of reconciliation will regard dating by their former partner as threatening. Others who themselves are dating may be relieved that the ex-spouse is also starting to date. Dating by the former spouse can relieve guilt feelings and give the other ex-spouse more autonomy. It can also remove pressure on the former spouse since the dating spouse now channels some energy toward a new person. In addition, dating can serve as a final break to the old relationship. Dating by a former spouse may also give the other an excuse to change the divorce settlement. For example, a noncustodial parent may seek a change of custody or a change in financial support claiming that the dating custodial parent is shirking parental duties or using money for the dating partner instead of the children. As these examples illustrate, dating and courtship after divorce differ considerably from premarriage dating and courtship.

Despite the complications of dating after divorce, the high remarriage rates indicate that most people who divorce do meet new prospective mates. And the new mate is often in the same situation; divorced people tend to marry divorced people.

Dates often come from the person's present or past group of acquaintances. Although few statistics have been compiled on the number of divorced and/or widowed persons seeking out past friends to date, there are many stories about couples who knew one another in high school or at some other time making contact and marrying. Recently, your author's father-in-law married a

| WHAT DO YOU THINK? |

1. What do you think the major dating problems would be for the newly divorced man?
2. For the newly divorced woman?
3. If you were newly divorced, how would you go about meeting potential dates?
4. Would you use a dating service? Why or why not?
5. Would you place a personal ad in the newspaper seeking friends? Why or why not?

Returning to Single Life

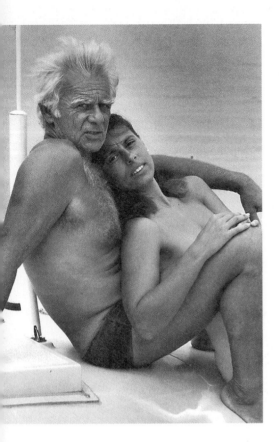

woman that he had known years earlier when both couples had lived in the same town and been friends. Both had recently lost their spouses.

In general, divorced men tend to remarry more quickly and at a higher rate than divorced women. It is interesting that males over the age of thirty tend to have courtships that end in remarriage about half as long as those of younger males. The length of courtship before remarriage does not seem to vary according to age for females. In general, less educated, lower-income women marry more quickly the second time around while the reverse is true for divorced men (O'Flaherty and Eells 1988, 505).

COHABITATION AS A COURTSHIP STEP TO REMARRIAGE

Research on cohabitation among never-married young persons found that its relationship to later marital success was negative or at best neutral (Chapter 4). Contrary to this finding, divorced persons who cohabitate seem to increase their chances of success in a remarriage. Lawrence Ganong and Marilyn Coleman (1989) found that the primary way that people prepare for remarriage is by living together. Fully 59 percent of their sample cohabited before remarriage. Cohabitation had more positive effects on a subsequent remarriage for men than for women. Men reported less conflict and more affection for their wives than noncohabiting men while women reported fewer disagreements. The positive effects of cohabitation appear to be limited to the marital relationship; stepparent-child relationships, parent-child relationships, and extended-family affect did not change. Perhaps cohabitation helps those planning to remarry because they have so many additional problems to sort out, especially if children are present. Having failed once at marriage, the person or couple are simply more cautious about entering a new union. By living together before remarriage, they can resolve many of the problems. If the problems are not resolved, the couple can leave the relationship and thereby avoid another unsuccessful marriage.

REMARRIAGE: WILL I MAKE THE SAME MISTAKES AGAIN?

As noted earlier, high remarriage rates among divorced people indicate that the divorced are still interested in marriage and the role of "being married." In fact, most activities in the American culture, for better or worse, revolve around the married pair, the couple. High remarriage rates seem to suggest that it is important to have someone with whom to share, to be intimate, to feel closeness, and to experience a part of something larger than oneself.

To love and be loved are important to most Americans. As unhappy as a marriage may have been, most people can recall a time when they experienced love and closeness. Indeed, loss of this intimacy may have been a major reason for leaving the marriage. Finding intimacy is certainly a factor in most remarriages just as it was in the first marriage.

The route to marriage for young unmarried Americans is fairly clear. You date, you fall in love, you become engaged, you marry. In remarriages, though, the simplicity of ignorance has been replaced by the knowledge and, for some, the anxiety of past experience.

The divorced react to the idea of remarriage in many different ways. Some remarry quickly because they already have another relationship in place at the time of the divorce. Others remarry quickly on the rebound, out of loneliness, out of insecurity, or simply because they know no other way of life but to be married. Such persons often married young, going straight from their parents' homes into marriage, and thus have had no practice at being a single adult. Often they remarry the *transition person*. This is an individual who out of friendship and sympathy helps another person through a difficult period such as divorce.

A minority of divorced persons (approximately 20–25 percent of divorced men and 25–30 percent of divorced women) do not remarry. These percentages appear to be increasing, but since a remarriage can take place at any age, it is too early to tell if this is really a trend toward increasing lifetime singleness or simply a postponement of remarriage as first marriage is now being postponed. These statistics are misleading because remarriage is closely related to age at divorce. Remarriage rates are very high for people under the age of forty but decrease dramatically for those over forty.

The reasons for not remarrying are many. Some people may simply enjoy the autonomy and independence of single life. Others may want to remarry but fail to find an acceptable mate. Still others may have been so hurt in their first marriage that they avoid relationships that might lead to remarriage. A few who choose not to remarry may be psychologically unable to give up their lost spouse. This is especially true of the widowed, who sometimes feel disloyal to the deceased spouse if they form a new relationship. Sometimes the children of a widowed spouse discourage remarriage of their remaining parent for fear that the stepparent may take what they feel is rightfully theirs.

The most common reaction, however, tends to be a careful, cautious relationship-testing period leading to remarriage. For persons approaching re-marriage slowly, the risk of a second mistake is their main concern. Most divorced persons believe that they were deluded in their first marriage and therefore approach a second marriage with extra care, no longer naïve about the difficulty of achieving a successful marriage. They realize that they must work out the problems of their first marriage and establish a new independent and strong self-image. In this way they hope that their new relationship will be one of equality and maturity in contrast to their first immature relationship. They also realize that without such care and work remarriage will be a triumph of hope over experience and very apt to fail.

The partners in a remarriage must deal with all the problems any newly married pair faces. In addition, they must deal with attitudes and sensitivities within themselves that were fostered by their first marriage. They may enter remarriage with many prejudices for and against the marital relationship. They need to divest themselves of these attitudes if they are to face the new partner freely and build a new relationship that is appropriate to both. In a remarriage the mate is new and must be responded to as the individual she or he is, not in light of what the past spouse was. An additional task in every remarriage, then, is the effort partners must make to free themselves from inappropriate

attitudes and behaviors stemming from the first marriage. In essence, second marriages are built on top of first marriages. Prior spouses remain to haunt remarriages.

Bob had been married for twelve years to Alice, had two children by the marriage, and was established economically when the marriage ended in divorce. Two years later, he married Carol, eight years his junior, who had one child by her previous husband, Ted.

Bob and Carol both approached their marriage carefully, giving much thought to their relationship. Both agree that their new marriage is a big improvement over their past marriages. They find that their biggest problem is making sure they react to one another as individuals rather than on the basis of their past relationships. This is not always easy.

Bob's past wife, Alice, is emotionally volatile, which both attracted and repulsed him. He liked Alice's displays of happiness and enthusiasm but hated her fits of temper and general unhappiness.

Carol is placid and even-tempered. In fact, these personality traits were part of what drew him to her. When they do things together, however, he keeps asking her if she is having fun, is she enjoying herself? He asks so often that Carol becomes upset at what she regards as harassment. One day she blew up at him over this. Bob reacted strongly to her negative emotional display. Once everything was calm again, they both discovered that the problem grew out of his past marriage. Bob simply expected Carol to show her enjoyment in the same way Alice had. He was not relating to Carol as an individual but was reacting in light of his past experiences with Alice. When Carol blew up at him, his reaction was much stronger than necessary. Her emotional blast activated all of his past dislike of Alice's fits of temper.

Inasmuch as most divorced persons marry other divorced persons, another couple is involved in remarriages, namely, the former spouses as in the story about Bob and Carol. This phantom couple often dictates to the newly remarried pair, if not directly through the courts and divorce settlements, then indirectly via years of previous interaction.

A remarriage between divorced persons is more difficult than a first marriage for a number of reasons besides the influence, often negative, of past spouses:

1. Each mate may have problems of *low self-esteem* stemming from the divorce.
2. The divorced are *less apt to tolerate a poor second marriage*. They have been through divorce and know that they have survived. Life after divorce is not an unknown any longer and is therefore less threatening than before. Divorced persons tend to end an unhappy remarriage more quickly than they ended their first marriage; approximately 60 percent of remarriages also end in divorce. Remarriages for blacks tend to be more stable than their first marriages,

which is not true for whites (Furstenberg and Spanier 1984, 183; 1987; Ihinger-Tallman and Pasley 1987, 73; Coleman and Ganong 1990, 926).

3. *The past relationship is never really over.* Even if a couple successfully overcomes the kind of dynamics illustrated by Bob, Carol, Ted, and Alice, the past marriage can still directly affect the new marriage. For example, payments to a former spouse may be resented by the new spouse, especially if the current marriage seems shortchanged monetarily. First marriages also indirectly affect remarriage. Although remarried couples go to considerable lengths to differentiate marital styles between their first and second relationships, this very effort to change relationship styles suggests that the second relationship is influenced by reactions to their first marriage.

4. *A remarriage that involves children will experience a great many more complications.* Family law is also inadequate in dealing with the blended family. For example, there are no provisions for balancing husbands' financial obligations to spouses and children from current and previous marriages. What are the support rights of stepchildren in stepfamilies or in stepfamilies that end in divorce? The courts have traditionally held that first families take priority over second families (Rotenberg 1987, 6; Fine 1989; 1992).

5. *The society around the remarrying person tends to expect another failure.* "He (she) couldn't make it the first time, so he'll (she'll) probably fail this time, too." "After all, most divorced people don't learn; they usually remarry the same kind of person as their earlier spouse." "Once a failure, always a failure." This lack of support can create a climate of distrust in the minds of the remarried couple themselves and lead to a self-fulfilling prophecy.

Many studies find that remarrieds list money and children (particularly discipline of children) as their two major problems (Ihinger-Tallman and Pasley 1987, 66); these are also the top two reasons listed for remarriage failure (Berman 1987, 27).

Remarried families are often strapped financially because money must go to support the man's prior family. In some cases the former wife uses the new wife's earnings as grounds for requesting an increase in support payments.

Jill and Michael have been married for six years and have two children. Michael was married previously and also has two children by his former wife. Although Jill works, support payments to Michael's first family make it difficult to survive financially. As Michael's first children have grown, his ex-wife has returned to court twice seeking higher support payments because older children cost more. The court did not order an increase the first time since Michael's income had not changed. Jill was expecting their first child and was not working. However, the second time, an increase was granted. Jill was working full-time, and the court considered Michael and Jill's combined incomes, her income becoming a mere extension of her husband's. Even though the higher support payments drastically cut into Michael's ability to provide for his second family, the court considered only the needs of his first family.

Remarriage: Will I Make
the Same Mistakes Again?

Mark Fine (1989; 1992) reviewed family law relating to remarriage and stepfamilies. His overall finding was that family law does not currently provide clear and comprehensive rules to define the responsibility of parties to the stepparent-stepchild relationship (1989, 53), but legislatures and courts are becoming more sensitive to this relationship (1992, 334). Presently the only way that stepparents can assure themselves of the same rights as biological parents is through adoption.

CHILD SUPPORT OBLIGATIONS

Only fourteen states have statutes that obligate stepparents to support stepchildren and these are usually limited in scope, applying only when the stepchildren are living with the stepparents. Although the legal support for such statutes varies, essentially they are based on the common law doctrine of "in loco parentis." Under this doctrine a person who intentionally assumes parental obligations (actively participates in childrearing, school, social and recreational functions, and so forth) can be treated as the parent in some cases. Unlike biological parents, however, stepparents may terminate this relationship and its responsibilities at any time. While

support obligations for biological parents remain after divorce, courts and legislatures have generally not extended such support after the end of a remarriage. Nothing in present family law speaks to the problem of supporting stepchildren when the stepparent has the higher obligation of supporting biological children. The law assumes that the biological parents of stepchildren will supply the support. Statistics about child support payments refute this assumption. Also, nothing in the law protects children conceived in the remarriage from partial loss of economic support that goes to previous biological children.

CUSTODY AND VISITATION OF STEPCHILDREN FOLLOWING DISSOLUTION OF A REMARRIAGE

Since stepchildren are not considered "children of the marriage," stepparents usually do not have any custody or visitation rights upon divorce. In a few cases where the biological parent in the remarriage has died, custody has remained with the stepparent in the best interests of the children. In these cases, the noncustodial biological parent has normally had little interaction with the children for an extended period of time.

States are becoming more liberal in granting "fit" nonbiological parents custody. According to Victor et al. (1991), 25 states have passed legislation that allows third parties to file for custody of minor children whether or not they are already in their care. In specific cases, a broad range of factors has been considered in custody determinations, including character and resources of parents and third parties, the nature of the relationship between adults and the involved children, the advantages and disadvantages that may accrue to the child from various custody options, and the length of time the adult has lived with the child (1992, 336).

Although a stepparent has no innate visitation rights, those stepparents who argue that they acted "in loco parentis" are increasingly being granted visitation rights. All fifty states now grant some third party visitation, although the rights of the child's grandparents have been recognized to a greater extent than have those of stepparents (Victor et al. 1991). Alaska, California, Pennsylvania, Kentucky, Utah and Oklahoma are a few of the states now granting stepparent rights of visitation if they would be in the best interest of the children.

The number of remarried families in America must lead to an increased recognition and acceptance of second families. Since the average child is six at the time of the parents' divorce, the chances are high that his or her divorced parents will become parents or at least stepparents in their next marriage. In a sense the courts penalize the children of remarriages for not being born in the first marriage (Bilbrey 1987, 8). Of course, if earnings are low, it may be impossible for a parent to support both the former and current families.

Despite the increased problems faced in remarriage, those remarrying seem to take few active steps to increase the chances of success. Only about 25 percent of men and 38 percent of women receive counseling. Only 2 percent of men and 8 percent of women attend a support group of any kind. However, 34 percent of men and 47 percent of women do report reading self-help materials and books (Ganong and Coleman, 1989).

That some Americans divorce remarry, and then redivorce indicates the necessity for remarriage education (Kaplan and Hennon 1992, 127). It is important for people considering remarriage to understand how remarriages differ from first marriages. An understanding of the additional problems faced in remarriage, especially if children are involved, is also a necessity if remarriage is to be successful.

What are the statistics on success and failure of second marriages? Unfortunately, the statistics do not present a clear picture. Most studies comparing the divorce rates of first marriages with those of second marriages do report that a remarriage is more likely to break up than a first marriage (Ihinger-Tallman 1987). The differences are small; most studies indicate about 60 percent of remarriages will end in divorce. Paul Glick (1984) estimates that 49 percent of men and women will divorce but 54 percent of women and 61 percent of men who remarry will divorce a second time. But these studies do not take into account the small group of divorce-prone people who marry and divorce often and in the course of these repeated divorces tend to overinfluence the remarriage-divorce figures.

Marital satisfaction studies also show mixed results with the differences being small. People in first marriages indicate slightly greater marital satisfaction than those in remarriages. Men tend to be more satisfied than women with their remarriages. Stepfathers and stepmothers indicate about the same level of remarriage satisfaction (Vemer et al. 1989).

Perhaps more important than comparisons of divorce rates are the subjective evaluations made by those remarrying. Most remarried couples report a moderate to high degree of marital happiness. Remarriages of divorced persons that do not end quickly in divorce are on the whole almost as successful as intact first marriages.

Remarriages seem to be judged by different criteria than first marriages, perhaps because they are based on different factors. None of the variables that have often served as good predictors of marital satisfaction in first marriages (presence of children, age at marriage, social class, and similarity of religion) seem to be strongly related to remarriage satisfaction. Perhaps the romantic illusion is gone for those remarrying. Overall, though, divorce and remarriage seem to have been effective mechanisms for replacing poor marriages with good ones and for keeping the level of marital happiness fairly high for at least some people.

Furstenberg and Spanier (1987) find that couples in successful remarriages repeatedly state that their marriage is different from their first marriage. Most importantly they feel they have married the right person, that is, "someone who allows you to be yourself." In other words, they have chosen a better mate for themselves. Because of this better choice, they feel that their remarriage is better than their first marriage. They feel this is true because they have learned to communicate differently and now handle conflicts more maturely. Better communication also leads to better decision making. Because both partners feel they are more equal, the division of labor in remarriage tends to be more equitable.

Furstenberg and Spanier (1987, 65) also point out that hostility toward the remarried couple's former spouses tends to be a part of the successful remarriage:

> Most interviews yielded liberal expressions of hostility displayed toward former partners. . . . Repudiating the former spouse heightens solidarity in the new relationship. Expressions of hostility serve to demonstrate loyalty to the new spouse, thus reducing the potential for jealousy. The couple could unite in outrage over past injustices inflicted by a former spouse. In the in-depth interviews, a partner would sometimes tell stories that had become a part of the lore of their marriage. In recounting such incidents, the current spouse can provide reassurance that things really are different now. The husband or wife hearing his or her biography replayed can affirm just how much change has occurred and usually responds by declaring that he or she is married to the right person this time. Through this dramatic interplay, assurance is provided that the second marriage is essentially different from the first.

Although such hostility may be helpful in cementing the remarried couple's relationship, it can make coparenting of a divorced couple's children much more difficult. Divorced couples who can resolve their differences and work together amicably can make remarriage for either or both much more pleasant and conflict-free. Those who feel only anger and hostility forever toward their former mate forget that they chose their mate and were at one time in love with that person. All of the qualities that drew them to the person in the first place probably still exist. Thus, to have only negative feelings toward a former mate is somewhat unrealistic.

Even though the statistics are mixed on the success of remarriages, it is clear that a great many are successful despite the extra problems involved. As divorce becomes more prevalent and acceptable, the problems facing those wishing to remarry may diminish. Perhaps social support for remarriage will be greater in the future as more and more people marry more than once during their lifetime.

HIS, HERS AND OURS: THE STEPFAMILY

For many years children in the home precluded the parents' divorcing. Everyone "knew" the dire consequences to children if divorce occurred. Many couples stayed together for years after their marriage had failed in order to spare the children the trauma of divorce.

Having children no longer seems to impede divorce, however. More than one million children under the age of eighteen have been involved in divorce in the United States every year since 1972 (National Center for Health Statistics May, 1991). Some people are reasoning that strain and conflict are as harmful to children as divorce. People in discordant marriages who divorce and remarry often believe they are taking positive steps to improve their home situation and provide a healthier environment for children than was possible within the original family.

Many people believe that the divorced person who has custody of the children stands much less chance of remarriage. In actuality, if age is held constant, having children does not seem to have a significant influence on one's chances of remarriage. In fact, remarriages may well involve at least three different sets of children. Both spouses may bring their own children into the new marriage, and they may also have children together. Hence his, hers, and ours is often a correct description of the children in a reconstituted family. Generally, remarried families with children are stepfather families since mothers receive custody in approximately 90 percent of divorces. There are five residential stepfathers for every residential stepmother (Giles-Sims and Crosbie-Burnett 1989a).

Literature is replete with many examples of the poor treatment accorded stepchildren. The ogre **stepparent** is a popular stereotype in fairy tales like *Cinderella*. Yet, in reality, there is little evidence to support this stereotype. Certainly, the transition to a new parent is not always easy. Children generally remain with their biological mother, and the stepparent is a new father. Because ties are usually closest to the mother, this is probably an advantage for most children. Also, some preparation and training for parents in stepfamilies improve the parent-stepparent-children relationship (Nelson and Levant 1991).

One might get the impression from the mass media that more children are now being placed in the custody of their father after a divorce. In absolute

Stepparent
The husband or wife of one's parent by a later marriage

His, Hers and Ours:
The Stepfamily

641

numbers this is true. But the number of children living with a divorced mother has increased at the same rate.

> Over the years a fairly constant 10 to 11 percent of all children living with a divorced parent live with the father. Children living with their father only for all reasons (widowed, separated, divorced) has increased from 9 percent in 1980 to 13 percent in 1990 (U.S. Bureau of the Census May, 1991b).

Research findings on the effects of remarriage on children are mixed. For example, though there is some conflicting evidence, earlier research indicates that children in stepfamilies don't appear to differ significantly in self-image or personality characteristics from children in their original families (Ganong and Coleman 1984 [a review of approximately forty studies]). On the other hand, Wallerstein and Blakeslee (1989) report serious problems for a large percentage of the children of divorce ten and fifteen years after the divorce.

Counselors and therapists also report that stepchildren and stepparents do have a great deal of trouble in their relationships. Stepparents often feel confusion about their roles; children feel loyalty conflicts; and coparenting of children with former spouses may split parental authority (Ganong and Coleman 1986, 313; Wallerstein and Blakeslee 1989; Ihinger-Tallman and Pasley 1987). Perhaps the data on stepchildren are mixed because each situation is unique and one cannot generalize about the effects of divorce or a stepparent on children. It may well be that a well-adjusted child with a healthy personality will cope successfully with the family breakup and become a more mature, independent child. If the child is unstable, however, divorce may cause even greater maladjustment.

To learn what effect divorce and remarriage have on a child, we need to know the answers to the following questions:

■ What were the preconditions to the divorce (much fighting; calm, quick decision; long, slow decision; emotional; rational, and so on)?
■ How well adjusted was the child?
■ What age was the child?
■ With which parent did the child go?
■ Did the child want to go with that parent?
■ What kind of person is the stepparent?
■ How long was the child given to adjust to the stepparent?
■ How many siblings went with the child into the remarriage?
■ Were other children present from the stepparent?
■ What sort of family atmosphere was created?
■ Did the natural parent support or disrupt the child's adjustment?

With so many questions to answer, it is not surprising that the research findings are mixed. The only valid conclusion is that some children suffer more than others from divorce and remarriage.

Probably the single most important thing divorcing parents can do to reduce the negative consequences of divorce and remarriage on their children is to maintain a reasonable relationship with the divorced mate. Fighting over children or using them against a former spouse will lead to negative consequences for the child.

Stepparents face additional problems beyond those of natural parents. To begin with, they must follow a preceding parent. If the child and the natural parent had a positive relationship, the child is apt to feel resentful and hostile toward the stepparent. The child may also feel disloyal to the departed parent if a good relationship is established with the stepparent. This sense of disloyalty may provoke negative behavior toward the stepparent in an effort to counteract growing feelings of affection.

It is important to give the stepchild permission to like the stepparent. "It is all right to like your new stepparent. It doesn't mean that you don't like mom (or dad) anymore. A person can like many people at the same time." Children need to be reassured that having a warm relationship with a stepparent will not endanger the relationship with the biological parent.

Often a child feels rejected and unloved by the parent who leaves the household. In this case the child may cling more tightly to the remaining parent as a source of security and continuity. The remaining parent's subsequent remarriage can be threatening to such a child. "This stepparent is going to take my last parent away from me." In this case, the stepparent may be met with anger and hostility.

In fact, children can break up a remarriage (the divorce rate is higher in remarriages with stepchildren). This is especially true of adolescents who can assume a great deal of power in a blended family (Giles-Sims and Crosbie-Burnett 1989b; Chapman 1991). Children can create divisiveness between spouses and siblings by acting in ways that accentuate differences between them. Children have the power to set parent against stepparent, siblings against parents, and stepsiblings against siblings (Ihinger-Tallman and Pasley 1987, 93–95).

Joyce had two teenage children when she remarried Bill. Her fourteen-year-old daughter was deadset against the marriage. She claimed to hate Bill and showed it in every way she could. She would not eat at the same table with him. She swore at him and called him names both privately and publicly. Finally, in frustration Bill made her come to the dinner table one evening and sit with the family. Without telling anyone, she called the police and reported that her stepfather was molesting and beating her. The police appeared at the door shortly after dinner and took Bill down to headquarters and charged him with child abuse. Although the charges were completely untrue and quickly dropped, the episode caused such trauma to the family that Bill decided he could take no more and left the home. After a long period of counseling, the daughter came to terms with her mother's divorce and remarriage. But the damage to the couple's relationship may never be repaired.

When the child's relationship with the departed parent was not good, hostility remaining from this prior relationship can be displaced onto the step-

The natural family presents hazards enough to peaceful coexistence. Add one or two stepparents, and perhaps a set of ready-made brothers and sisters, and a return to the law of the jungle is virtually ensured. Some guidelines for survival include the following advice for stepparents:

1. *Provide neutral territory.* Stepchildren have a strong sense of ownership. The questions: "Whose house is it? Whose spirit presides here?" are central issues. Even the very young child recognizes that the prior occupation of a territory confers a certain power. When two sets of children are brought together one regards itself as the "main family" and the other as a subfamily, and the determining factor is whose house gets to be the family home. One school of thought suggests that when a couple remarries, they should move to a new house, even if it means selling the family heirlooms (Kuyper 1987, 109). If it is impossible to finance a move to neutral territory, it is important to provide a special, inviolate place

that belongs to each child individually.

2. *Don't try to fit a preconceived role.* When dealing with children, the best course is to be straight right from the start. Each parent is an individual with all his or her faults, peculiarities, and emotions, and the children are just going to have to get used to this parent. Certainly, a stepparent should make every effort to be kind, intelligent, and a good sport, but that does not mean being saccharine sweet. Children have excellent radar for detecting phoniness, and are quick to lose respect for any adult who lets them walk all over him or her.

3. *Set limits and enforce them.* One of the most difficult areas for a natural parent and stepparent living together to decide on is disciplinary measures. The natural parent has a tendency to feel that the stepparent is being unreasonable in demanding that the children behave in a certain way. If the parents fight between themselves about discipline, the children will quickly force a wedge between them. It is important that the parents themselves

work out the rules in advance and support one another when the rules need to be enforced.

4. *Allow an outlet for feelings by the children for natural parents.* It is often difficult for the stepparent to accept that his or her stepchildren will maintain a natural affection for their natural parent who is no longer living in the household. The stepparent may take this as a personal rejection. Children need to be allowed to express feelings about the parent who is absent. Their feelings should be supported in a neutral way so that the children do not feel disloyal.

5. *Expect ambivalence.* Stepparents are often alarmed when children appear to show both strong love and strong hate toward them. Ambivalence is normal in all human relationships, but nowhere is it more accentuated than in the feelings of the stepchild toward the stepparent.

6. *Avoid mealtime misery.* For many stepfamilies meals are an excruciating experience. This, after all, is the time when the dreams of blissful family life confront reality.

parent. The stepparent simply represents the natural parent in the eyes of the child.

Because children constantly make comparisons between biological parents and stepparents, many stepparents make the mistake of trying too hard, especially at first. Usually, it is better for the stepparent to move slowly, because the child needs time to adjust to the new situation and to reevaluate the past parental relationship (see Inset 17-2). It is also important to the child to figure out just what the remaining parent's feelings are toward the new mate. Making this adjustment is even more difficult when the stepparent tries to replace the

Most individuals cling to a belief in the power of food to make people happy. Since it is the mother who is most often charged with serving the emotionally laden daily bread, she often leaves the table feeling thoroughly rejected. If the status quo becomes totally unbearable, it is forgivable to decide that peace is more important and turn a blind eye, at least temporarily, to nutrition. Some suggested strategies include daily vitamins, ridding the house of all "junk" foods and letting the children fix their own meals, eating out a lot, and/or letting father do some of the cooking so he can share in the rejection. Stepfathers tend to be less concerned about food refusal but more concerned about table manners.

7. *Don't expect instant love.* One of the problems facing a new stepparent is the expectation of feeling love for the child and expecting that love to be returned. It takes time for emotional bonds to be forged, and sometimes this never occurs. All stepparents must acknowledge that eventuality.

Alternately, nonacceptance by the children is often a major prob-

lem. Some children make it very clear that "You are not my mother or father!" This can be very painful or anger provoking, especially if the stepparent is doing the cooking and laundry and giving allowances. Most children under three have little problem adapting with relative ease. Children over five have more difficulty.

8. *Don't take all the responsibility. The child has some too.* Ultimately, how well the stepparent gets along with the stepchild depends in part upon the kind of child he or she is. Like adults, children come in all types and sizes. Some are simply more lovable than others. If the new stepmother has envisioned herself as the mother of a cuddly little tot and finds herself with a sullen, vindictive twelve-year-old who regards her with suspicion, she is likely to experience considerable disappointment. Like it or not, the stepparent has to take what he or she gets. But that doesn't mean taking all the guilt for a less than perfect relationship.

9. *Be patient.* The words to remember here are "things take time." The first few months and

often years have many difficult periods. The support and encouragement of other parents who have had similar experiences can be an invaluable aid.

10. *Maintain the primacy of the marital relationship.* Most stepparenting relationships have resulted from divorce by one or both members of the couple. A certain amount of guilt about the breakup of the previous relationship may spill over into the present relationship and create difficulties when there are arguments. The couple needs to remember that their relationship is primary in the family. The children need to be shown that the parents get along together, can settle disputes, and most of all will not be divided by the children. While parenting may be a central element in the couple's relationship, both partners need to commit time and energy to the development of a strong couple relationship; this bond includes, but is greater than, their parental responsibilities.

Source: Turnbull and Turnbull 1983.

natural parent, especially if the child is still seeing that parent. Probably, the best course for the stepparent is to assume a supplemental role, meeting the needs of the child not met by the noncustodial parent. In this way the stepparent avoids direct competition with the natural parent.

Approximately half of the women who remarry give birth in their second marriage, most within twenty-four months of the remarriage; this pattern holds true for both blacks and whites (Wineberg 1990, 31). When a remarried family has children of its own, additional problems may arise with stepchildren. The stepchild may feel even more displaced and alienated. The remaining parent

His, Hers and Ours:
The Stepfamily

1. What would you find most difficult about becoming a stepparent?
2. Do you think it would be easier for a stepmother or a stepfather to be successful? Why?
3. What do you think is most difficult for a young child becoming a stepchild?
4. What do you think is most difficult for an adolescent becoming a stepchild?
5. Why do you think so many noncustodial parents slowly lose contact with their children?
6. If contact is lost with the noncustodial parent, should children try to reestablish contact when they are older?

may seem to have been taken away, first by the new stepparent and now by their new child. On the other hand, having brothers or sisters takes the focus off the stepchild, allowing a more natural adjustment for both parent and child. A new child can be a source of integration in a stepfamily because everyone finally has someone to whom all are related (Papernow 1984).

The role of parent is often difficult. The role of stepparent can even be more difficult, yet an empathic, caring stepparent can give a great deal to a child. The stepparent can be an additional source of love, support, and friendship and, by making the family a two-parent family again, can solve some of the childrearing problems of the single parent. If a stepparent enters a child's life when the child is young, the child often comes to look on the stepparent as his or her real parent, which alleviates the child's feelings of loss. The stepparent can bring new ideas into a family that help family members to grow and expand their horizons.

Russ was an avid outdoorsman and sports lover. His wife Jennifer had two adolescent sons from a former marriage who were both very bright and excellent students. Their natural father was an intellectual who was uninterested in sports and outdoor activities. Through Russ's influence, both boys grew to love the outdoors. Both became active in school sports and earned varsity letters in track and field.

DEALING WITH SEXUALITY IN THE STEPFAMILY

One of the most difficult issues for stepfamily members to deal with is sexuality (Chapman 1991). Stepfamilies experience a loosening of sexual boundaries, which is related to the nonbiological structure of the stepfamily. A stepfamily has not had a long developmental period in which to form intimate parent-child ties and develop strong aversions to incest. The more affectionate, sexual atmosphere in the home during the time when the new couple are more romantically involved may also contribute to heightened sexual intensities. It is not unusual for stepfamily members to experience sexual fantasies, increased anxiety, distancing behavior, or even anger in responding to and trying to cope with these sexual issues. In more extreme circumstances, a sexual relationship can develop between a stepparent and stepchild or between stepsiblings (Covi and Robinson 1985, 123). Research indicates that opposite-sex adolescent stepsiblings tend to be sexually involved with each other much more frequently than opposite-sex biological siblings (Baptiste 1987, 91). Stepsiblings often fight against sexual feeling for one another through open conflict and statements of dislike for each other.

Thus far, we have concentrated on the problems of the stepfamily with custody of the stepchildren. Periodic visitations of noncustodial children may be another facet of remarriage.

At a recent stepfamily meeting, Carla, a stepmother, talked of the coming and going of children on weekends, and how uncomfortable they made her. During the week, Carla and her husband Tim live with Carla's two sons, ten-year-old Ron and eight-year-old Peter, and with Tim's oldest daughter Shelley, age twelve. Ron and Peter spend every weekend with their father, and three weekends a month Shelley is away with her mother. Tim's other two daughters, Franny and Paula, ages nine and seven, come every other weekend.

Such complex arrangements are not unusual in stepfamilies. In Carla and Tim's family, there are sometimes five children at home, sometimes two rarely none. Working out a month in advance who will be home for a particular weekend is an intellectual challenge. Carla told the group, "I don't know who is in my family and who is not." In nuclear families this complaint would never arise, because children don't shuttle like boxcars between stations. . . .

Weekends are difficult for the visiting child as well as the entire family. The visiting child may resent having to follow a schedule instead of being free like other kids on weekends. It can also be upsetting to see Dad living in another home with another set of kids and a new wife. It can feel unfair sleeping on a sofa-bed or an army cot in a strange room, when her kids have beds and rooms of their own.

If the stepfather hears complaints, he is apt to feel unjustly accused. He is doing his best, yet he is unappreciated. One stepfather said: "I live with Laura's kids all the time. I feel that when my children come over, Laura's kids shouldn't gripe about having to double up."

There is no magic remedy for the dislocations and hurt feelings that visiting causes. These feelings are manageable, however, when people are open about their emotions, respectful of each other, and committed to making their stepfamily work. . . .

HELPFUL HINTS FOR WEEKEND VISITS

Give the visiting child a permanent place such as a drawer, shelf, or closet to keep his or her things. Also make sure things are left behind: a toothbrush, comb, or books.

Establish consistent routines to follow or chores to do during visits. Assign the child a place at the dinner table, so it won't be musical chairs when he or she comes for the weekend.

Don't overdo special activities. Let a natural, relaxing environment evolve for the entire family.

Spend time alone with each child in the family.

Encourage the child to bring a friend for the weekend.

Use family meetings to get children involved in the workings of the households.

Reprinted by permission of publisher, from *Making Remarriage Work* by J. Belovitch (Lexington, Mass.: Lexington Books, D.C. Heath and Co. Copyright 1987, G and R Publications Inc.

Jane brought her fourteen-year-old daughter into a remarriage with Rich who had two children, one a sixteen-year-old son. All three children lived in the new home with the stepparents. For the first year or so, the two older children fought like cats and dogs driving the parents to distraction. The parents insisted that the two get along and become friends. The two finally ceased hostilities much to the relief of the parents and became inseparable. The parents returned home unexpectedly from a weekend trip and discovered the two in bed together. Predictably, they were shocked and outraged. Upon being confronted, the daughter commented, "Well, you wanted us to become friends. How much closer can we get?"

Although all states have laws governing sexual relations between blood relatives, most states do not regulate sexual relations between members of reconstituted families.

The following measures can reduce the likelihood of a sexual relationship developing in a stepfamily:

■ Be prepared to discuss sexual feelings that might arise in the stepfamily situation.
■ Discuss the facts of life with pubescent children.
■ Encourage the children to verbalize their sexual fantasies.
■ Resist the temptation to push opposite-sex stepsiblings to become closer friends than they want or can tolerate at the time.
■ Accept as all right the usual intersibling hostilities (Baptiste 1987).

THE NEW EXTENDED FAMILY

Although we have spoken only of stepparents, it is important to realize that the blended family will bring another set of kin into the relationships. By and large, new kin do not replace old kin but add to those from the first marriage. For example, there will now be stepgrandparents and probably the new spouse of the noncustodial parent as well. A blended family's immediate family tree can be unimaginably complex. As an extreme, imagine the many relationships of the following blended family:

Former husband (with two children in the custody of their natural mother) marries new wife with two children in her custody. They have two children. Former wife also remarries man with two children, one in his custody and one in the custody of his former wife, who has also remarried and had a child with her second husband who also has custody

of one child from his previous marriage. The former husband's parents are also divorced and both have remarried. Thus, when he remarries, his children have two complete sets of grandparents on his side, plus one set on the mother's side, plus perhaps two sets on the stepfather's side.

The example could go to any level of complexity; indeed, trying to sort out all of the relationships in some blended families is an impossible task. When one considers the complexities of the blended family, it is surprising that as many remarriages are as successful as they seem to be.

The immediate effect of divorce on relative interaction is that it intensifies contacts between blood relatives and curtails relations with former in-laws. Unless the relatives (mainly grandparents) of the noncustodial parent make real efforts to remain on close terms with the children, contact is slowly lost just as it is with the noncustodial parent (Furstenberg and Spanier 1987). With remarriage, however, the children's circle of relatives suddenly expands greatly, especially if they have been able to maintain contact with relatives of the noncustodial parent. Whether such expansion occurs or not depends in part on the proximity of the relatives. If a remarried family lives at a great distance from one set of relatives, that set tends to have less contact with the family than relatives who live close by.

Furstenberg and Spanier (1984, 160–61; 1987) found that:

What remarriage does is not to subtract but to add relatives. Contrary to our expectation, contacts with biological and with stepgrandparents were not inversely related. Contact with stepgrandparents did not diminish the child's interaction with the family of his or her noncustodial biological parent. . . . Individuals have the option but never the obligation to define people as relatives when they are not closely related by blood. Kinship is often achieved rather than ascribed. Remarriage illustrates this principle by creating an enlarged pool of potential kin. To a large extent, it is up to the various parties involved to determine the extent to which potential kin will be treated as actual relatives.

In the past remarriage was brought about far more often by death than by divorce. Remarriage after death, of course, meant the replacement of a parent rather than the addition of a parent as remarriage after divorce means. Today remarriage most often means the addition of a parent plus all of the stepparent's relatives. In a way remarriage has brought the idea of extended family (granted, not blood relatives) back into American society. Potentially, children in a remarried family can have many, many sets of grandparents as we saw in the example. They may have two sets of biological grandparents and four sets of stepgrandparents if both their biological parents remarry. If all these grandparents live close by and maintain relationships with the blended family, holidays such as Christmas can become logistical feats (Sanders and Trygstad 1989). At the same time, a wide circle of relatives can also offer much support and love to children in the blended family.

BUILDING STEPFAMILY STRENGTHS

A review of popular literature about stepfamilies found the following potential strengths were discussed:

■ Stepchildren learn problem-solving, negotiation, and coping skills and also become more flexible and adaptable.
■ The presence of more adults adds support and exposes children to a wider variety of people and experiences.
■ Stepfamilies are better for children than single-parent families.
■ More role models are available to children.
■ Stepparents try harder to be good parents; thus children may gain an additional parent from whom they can learn and love and be loved.
■ Blended families tend to experience less trauma and crisis (Ihinger-Tallman and Pasley 1987).
■ Hopefully, both adults and children can learn what it is like to be in a happy, successful relationship.

Although there is little empirical evidence to support these supposed advantages for stepchildren and their families, it is worthwhile to examine potential strengths that can be built up in blended families. Naturally, all of the family strengths enumerated in Chapter 1 will be equally or even more important to the blended family because the blended family tends to be more complicated organizationally than a first-marriage family. It also lacks the societal support usually afforded intact nuclear families.

One step that would help build blended family strength is for society to recognize the blended family as a legitimate alternative to the nuclear family. This would help do away with the "wicked stepparent" myth that can cause harm to the stepfamily. Such recognition would also facilitate the creation of model roles and rules for the functioning of the stepfamily.

THE PRENUPTIAL AGREEMENT

Although we discussed the prenuptial agreement earlier, it is more important in a remarriage than in a first marriage. The couples entering remarriage may bring with them an extended history, household furnishings, financial investments such as a home, obligations to prior families, and so forth. All of this tends to make the remarriage much more complicated and thus more prone to conflict. By establishing many of the rules ahead of time, remarrying couples can head off many potential problems. Naturally, any such agreements cannot nullify state laws concerning marriage. Generally, prenuptial agreements cover what happens to the children and the couple's property if either dies, the division of property in case of divorce, spousal maintenance, and more specific daily living plans.

Since finances and children are the two major sources of conflict in a remarriage, both need to be discussed in detail. Perhaps the most important financial decision is whether to combine money into a single pot or to keep the partners' money separate. Since people remarrying often bring considerable resources into the remarriage, many couples opt to keep money separate, with both partners donating to a household fund used for daily living. Perhaps the couple is living in a home owned by one party. The home may remain separate property, with the incoming spouse picking up the monthly costs. One spouse may be receiving child support payments and will keep them separate to be used only for that purpose. Keeping money separate usually means that a tighter bond will be maintained with the first family and may reduce cohesion in the stepfamily. At the same time, however, separate finances will normally reduce conflicts, especially if the parties entering the remarriage both have considerable resources and prior obligations.

Questions are likely to arise about who will pay for insurance, health benefits, children's illnesses, luxuries, credit cards, prior debts, and so on. If the courts give some freedom in child custody arrangements, what will the arrangements be? What role will religion play in the family? What changes need to be made in wills? The questions are endless, but the more that are answered ahead of time, the less conflict there will be later and the stronger the remarried family will become.

MEDIATION TO SETTLE CONFLICTS

Remarrying couples who have divorce in their background have probably gone through a great deal of conflict at the time of their divorce. If they enter a new marriage and encounter new conflicts, the relationship will start off negatively. As we have seen, conflict is even more inevitable in a remarriage than in a first marriage. Couples who managed to divorce in an amicable manner will enter a remarriage with an advantage. Unfortunately, many couples enter a remarriage at a disadvantage having engaged in vigorous conflict with their ex-spouse.

Mediation with an objective third party whose goal is to help the couple solve their problems and reach their own goals greatly reduces potential conflict. Although few divorcing or remarrying couples consult mediators or counselors before they marry, such an experience is demonstrably worthwhile. To spend some money heading off problems seems infinitely more intelligent than to lose money trying to escape a conflict. Obtaining counseling and mediating problems and conflicts ahead of time usually strengthen the remarriage and stepfamily.

Because remarriages are more complicated and difficult than first marriages, perhaps cultivating a sense of humor is one of the best ways to build a healthy stepfamily. There will be times when your stepfamily would make a good situation comedy. If you can step back and put yourself into the role of an audience at these times and laugh at the comedy and at yourself and share your laughter with the rest of the family, stress and strain will decrease.

> After all you are pioneering a new lifestyle. You are proving that you don't have to be a biological parent to be loving, and you certainly don't have to be a biological parent to put your foot down. Being proud of your new family and appreciating your spouse's efforts can give you a sense of a new identity as a person, as a couple, and as a family. (Keshet 1987, 98)

In many ways the remarried family has the chance of being even stronger than a first-marriage family. Each new spouse brings a wealth of information and experience to a remarriage. By utilizing that experience and knowledge to the full, they can create a strong and healthy new family.

SUMMARY

1. *High remarriage rates indicate that the high divorce rates do not necessarily mean that Americans are disenchanted with marriage as an institution.* The divorce rates may simply indicate that Americans have high expectations for marriage as well as the freedom to end marriage when their expectations are not fulfilled.

2. *The majority of divorced persons remarry, most of them within a few years of divorce.* A few remarry as soon as possible, but the rest usually remain single for at least a short period of time. The adjustment to single life is often difficult, especially for those who have been married a long time. Learning to date and interrelate with the opposite sex as a single person after many years of marriage is especially difficult because the newly single person's self-image has for so long been that of a married person, part of a couple. The newly single person may also be insecure and may suffer from feelings of failure and guilt. These feelings make it hard to relate to new people.

3. *Remarriage is sought by most divorced people.* Yet making the actual decision to remarry is often difficult because the idea of marriage evokes negative

attitudes based on their negative experiences with marriage. *People marrying for a second time carry with them attitudes and expectations from their first marital experience.* In many cases they also must still cope with their first family. Visiting children, child support, and alimony payments may add to the adjustment problems in the second marriage.

4. *Children from prior marriages often add to the responsibilities of second marriage.* Becoming a stepparent to the new spouse's children is not easy. A second family may have children from several sources. Each spouse may have children from his or her previous marriage, and in time they may have children together. Children from previous marriages often mean continued interaction between the formerly married couple when the former mate visits with or takes the children periodically. Many remarriages, especially when children from the previous marriages are present, actually involve relationships among four adults. The remarried pair naturally have their own relationship, but in addition each will have some level of relationship with the divorced spouse.

5. *About 20 to 30 percent of those divorcing never remarry.* For these persons, single life becomes permanent. As divorce rates rise, however, the likelihood of remarriage also increases because there are more potential partners. At present about 30 percent of American marriages involve at least one person who was formerly married. Remarriage, then, has definitely become a way of life for a significant number of Americans.

THE ROLE OF MYTHS IN MARRIAGE AND FAMILY LIFE

A *myth* has been defined as "an unfounded or false notion; a traditional story of ostensibly historical events that serves to unfold part of the world view of a people or explain a practice, belief or natural phenomenon; a popular belief or tradition that has grown up around someone or something" (*Webster's Ninth New Collegiate Dictionary* 1991). Myths are oversimplified, but firmly held, beliefs that guide perceptions and expectations. Myths usually incorporate an element of truth because if a cultural myth contained no truth, it would quickly lose its power. That myths are generally unfounded does not reduce their power to influence both attitudes and behavior. Problems develop when myths serve as blinders to actual experience and lead people into painful situations that could have been prevented.

REMARRIAGE MYTHS

1. *Things must work out.* For some couples the goal of remarriage is to "get it right" this time. Everything will work out because this time it is *really* love. Those who had a simple first wedding ceremony may opt this time for multiple bridesmaids, a long, white gown, and other trappings of a traditional wedding. Those who had a traditional ceremony the first time may choose something simpler or just different in an attempt to change their luck and get it "right." This approach merely incorporates the original marriage myth, with a note of added intensity or desperation.

2. *Always consider everybody first.* The remarriage version of the second myth may take several forms. Variations may include "always consider yourself first," "always consider the other person first," "always consider your marriage first," "always consider yourself and *your* children first" (as compared to your spouse and his or her children), and finally, "always consider everybody first." These mutually exclusive myths may all be operating at one time.

People who had few financial resources as single parents may have felt deprived. If they developed an assertive style of obtaining resources for themselves and their children during this period, they may continue to use that style on behalf of their children after remarriage; at the same time, however, they may feel guilty for not trusting their spouses and putting them first. Attorneys contribute to this problem by encouraging people to consider themselves and their children first legally and financially and by advising them to arrange prenuptial agreements, marriage contracts, and trusts.

Stepfamilies often consist of a man living with a woman and her children. The stepfather is faced with the task of joining a single-parent family system that may have been functioning for some time. The woman, who is trying to put her children first, may feel protective and interfere when the stepfather disciplines them. She may then feel guilty because she has failed to consider her husband first (the original marriage myth). The children may resent having to share their mother's attention with the stepfather, and she may feel guilty about giving them less attention. Thus, trying to juggle everyone's needs is not only stressful, it is impossible.

An alternative myth often fostered by counselors "always consider the marital relationship first" is related to the first remarriage myth: If the relationship does not come first, then the marriage may fail, and it *must* succeed. Empirical evidence, however, supports the idea that satisfaction with stepparent-stepchildren relationships is more important to family happiness than is satisfaction with the marital relationship (Crosbie-Burnett 1984).

3. *Keep criticism to oneself and focus on the positive.* Some remarried partners believe that if they had adhered to this myth in their first marriage, they might still be married. Consequently, they return to this myth with a vengeance in remarriage. It may be even more difficult to adhere to in remarriage, however, because there often are more people and things to criticize (i.e., stepchildren former spouses, former in-laws, new in-laws). This myth also incorporates the pseudomutuality that arises because of the intense fear of failure. *Pseudomutuality* among remarried people and stepfamilies is the tendency to deny history, ambivalence, and conflict (Sager et al 1983). As a result, the marriage remains frozen and static because poking and prodding might uncover a fatal flaw. Children also may support this myth by becoming overtly upset if their parents and stepparents argue or by being unnaturally "good" around stepparents.

Few would fault a couple who show strong determination to make their remarriage work. The problems occur when an intense fear of failure interferes with direct, open communication between the partners (Jacobson 1979). Intimate relationships normally involve disagreements and conflict. Totally avoiding conflict would be impossible, yet for the person overly concerned with becoming a two-time loser, conflict may create extreme anxiety. The result is often pseudomutuality.

4. *If things are not going well, focus on what went wrong in the past and make sure it does not happen again.* This myth also pushes for pseudomutuality and denial rather than honest communication. It is reworking of the old relationship to "get it right" instead of an attempt to build a new and unique relationship. A corollary myth is to "criticize the past and focus on the future." Couples who convince themselves that everything was negative in their previous marriages (proof of which is that the marriage failed) and that everything is going to be perfect in their new marriage are building a relationship based on denial. The first sign of any pattern resembling that of the previous marriage may cause panic.

5. *See oneself as part of the couple first, as an individual second; see oneself as an individual first, as part of a couple second.* This myth is actually a combination of two myths. The first version is identical to the marriage myth and is held by remarried persons who are attracted to the sense of security they perceive as a benefit of being married. These individuals may have rushed quickly into remarriage following divorce (or even following death of a spouse).

The second version is identical to the divorce myth and is held by remarried persons who consider themselves sadder but wiser after their first marriages—the major lesson they learned is that one must look out for oneself.

6. *What is mine is mine, what is yours is yours.* This myth tends to move developmentally through family stages from marriage ("what is mine is yours"), to divorce ("what is yours

is mine"), to single parenthood ("what is mine is mine"), to remarriage ("what is mine is mine, what is yours is yours"). A problem with this myth is the lack of an "ours" orientation. There may be good reason to maintain some individual control of financial assets, but establishing intimacy in an atmosphere of a business corporation may be difficult, if not impossible.

Stepfamilies tend to organize their finances in one of two ways: *common pot* or *two pot*. Fishman and Hamel (1983) found the two-pot agreement to be satisfactory when both partners were contributing approximately equal resources to the household. They found it to be much less satisfactory when contributions were blatantly unequal and one set of children was "richer" or "poorer" than the other. They also found that a couple's economic stability was a matter of perspective; sometimes one spouse perceives the family's economic stability as solid and the other views it as shaky. They believed that a shared perspective of the family financial situation was an important factor in stepfamily unity and that neither the common-pot nor the two-pot approach would guarantee a remarriage free of conflict over financial resources.

7. *Marriage makes people significantly happier.* This myth is dramatically reinstated at the time of remarriage. It is not only imperative that people be happy in their remarriages, but even happier than they were in their first marriages. A related remarriage myth is that if two people are happy and love each other enough, then everyone will be happy, including children, grandparents, and former spouses.

The myth of "instant love," or "if you love me you will love my children," often operates at the time of remarriage and can cause a great deal of grief and misunderstanding. The couple, caught up in the bliss of a new romantic love relationship, may at first be oblivious to the fact that other family members (e.g., children) are less enthralled. It takes extraordinary efforts to love a step child who blatantly ignores your existence or who is cleverly rude.

The wise couple may decide they cannot ensure the happiness of their children in the stepfamily. Rather than concentrating on making the children "happy," they should concentrate on providing structure and reasonable rules and limits so that the children are at least aware that they will not be allowed to dominate the family with their unhappiness.

Remarriage may make the remarried couple significantly happier, but they may find their circle of marital bliss surrounded by unexpected ripples of discontent and unhappiness on the part of others. If the remarriage does not result in happiness quickly enough or great enough, believers in this myth may seek someone to blame (stepchildren are good candidates for scapegoats) or may begin to plan or anticipate the dissolution of the marriage.

8. *What is best for us must be harmful for the children.* The final remarriage myth is a watered-down version of the divorce myth. Although the effects of parental remarriage on children are typically not perceived as negative as are the effects of parental divorce on children, there is clearly a widespread belief in our society that all stepchildren have a difficult time. The empirical research on stepchildren, however, does not support the view that parental remarriage always has harmful effects on children.

Paradoxically, many remarrying parents entertain both this myth and myths that seem to be diametric opposites. "Having a 'real' family again is best for everyone" and "what is best for us is best for the children" are remarriage myths that essentially are denials of the notion that children will have to make adjustments and experience stress when parents remarry. Adherents to these myths may really believe that their children have been harmed by their changing family structure but react by convincing themselves that a two-parent family is a panacea.

Finally, it should be noted that the list of remarriage myths discussed here is not exhaustive. There are probably hundreds of fallacies related to remarriage and hundreds more related to broader stepfamily issues.

Source: Adapted from Coleman and Ganong 1985.

CHAPTER
18

ACTIVELY SEEKING MARITAL GROWTH AND FULFILLMENT

CONTENTS

Marriage is a process or set of processes. From this point of view, marriage cannot be understood as an institution or structure. The man and woman commit themselves to the sharing of certain processes, sharing economic responsibility for one another, sharing sexual intimacy, sharing procreation. The mutual commitment of wife and husband involves them freely in a growing changing way of life rather than in a static "state of life." (Rogers 1972).

This final chapter stresses the idea that every person has the ability to improve his or her marriage. Marriages tend to get into trouble because we often believe that we can't do much about our marriages and simply don't take the time to nourish them and make our relationships healthier. We also tend to get into trouble because security and comfort may lull us into avoiding risks, and we must remain willing to take risks if we expect to grow and maintain positive movement in our lives and relationships. This does not mean that we must work on our relationships every minute of every day. That would be stifling and take away some of the fun that should exist in every relationship. But some time must be devoted to nurturing our relationships and our marriages.

Marriages grow and change. This is the essence not only of the marital relationship but of all relationships. Relationships are not stagnant. They do not remain forever as they were when you initiated them. Since relationships are processes, they must be attended to and worked on, or the process will pass you by. People who accuse their spouse of changing—"He (or she) is not the person I married"—have not attended to the relationship. Of course, the person you marry will change, but active participation in the relational changes is what leads to growth. Good marriages grow as the couples themselves change and grow. Poor marriages stagnate or grow without direction or participation and guidance from both partners.

We began our journey of marriage and family study by examining the characteristics of strong, successful families. You'll remember those characteristics:

- Commitment to one another and the relationship.
- Appreciation of all family members.
- Good communication.
- Spending time together.
- Building a value system.
- Dealing with problems constructively.

These six ideal characteristics give us a goal, a direction for the changes to take in our relationships.

Can we commit ourselves to relationships in which we appreciate our mates and develop good communication patterns so that the time we spend together is fulfilling and growth producing? Can we develop a value system and problem-solving skills that will allow us to deal positively with crises and stress? If we can do these things, we stand a good chance of creating a strong family for ourselves and loved ones. To accomplish this, we must be actively involved in our relationships. We cannot just assume that our relationships will take care of themselves because we love our partners. It is true that the relationship will evolve and change, but will the change be in positive directions that lead to strength and stability, happiness, and fulfillment?

What can we do to make our intimate relationships more fully functioning? Although everything we have discussed thus far bears on this question, this concluding chapter will specifically attend to the goal of seeking marital growth and fulfillment.

"AND THEY LIVED HAPPILY EVER AFTER"

The American scenario of marriage concludes with "and they lived happily ever after." In other words, once you find the right person, fall in love, and marry, all your problems will be over. Of course, this is a fairy tale. We know that all married couples will face problems. Yet this myth persists, even if only at the unconscious level, and hampers many Americans' efforts to realize the fullest possible potential in their marriages. To find out if you are influenced by the myth, examine your reaction to the following statement: "All married couples should periodically seek to improve their marriage through direct participation in therapy, counseling, or marriage enrichment programs."

What do you think? Some typical reactions are:

■ "It might be a good idea if the couple are unhappy or having problems."
■ "I know couples who need some help, but Jane and I are already getting along pretty well. It wouldn't help us."

- "We already know what our problems are. All we need to do is. . . ."
- "I'd be embarrassed to seek outside help for my marriage. It would mean I was a personal failure."
- "We're so busy now, what with work, the children, and social engagements, we wouldn't have time for any of those things."
- "John is a good husband [Mary is a good wife]. I really couldn't ask him [her] to participate in anything like that. He [she] would feel I wasn't happy with him [her] or our marriage."
- "I could be happier, but overall our marriage is fine."

It is true that not all married couples need to seek help from a third party, but it is also true that to be successful, a marriage needs more than just to be maintained.

Although drawing an analogy between marriage and an automobile is superficial and a gross oversimplification, it may clarify this point. An unmaintained car quickly malfunctions and wears out; a well-maintained car gives less trouble and lasts longer. Over and beyond maintenance, however, a car can be improved (by buying better tires or changing the carburetion, exhaust, compression, gearing, and so on) and modified to run better (faster, smoother, and more economically). Most Americans spend most of their adult lives married. Yet they spend little time and energy improving their marriages. If the marriage becomes too bad, they leave it to seek a new marriage that will be better. The new marriage may be better for a while, but without maintenance and improvement, it too will soon malfunction.

Some Americans expend a fair amount of energy seeking a new mode of marriage. Perhaps communes are the answer. Maybe just living together (cohabiting) and avoiding legal marriage is the answer. Yet the "improved" alternatives to marriage quickly lead to disenchantment. The new commune member who had problems communicating with his or her spouse finds that communicating intimately with seven other people is even more difficult. The cohabiting couple who thought that limited commitment was the way to avoid the humdrum in their life together may find that a prolonged lack of commitment leads to increased insecurity and discomfort. Perhaps the energy spent seeking some ideal alternative to marriage might be better spent working on the marriage itself.

After all most of us marry the people we do because we love them, want to be with them, and want to do things for them. We marry by our own decision in most cases. We start out supposedly with the best of all things—love—going for us. Where does love go? Why isn't love able to solve all of our problems? Might it be that the fairy tale—"and they lived happily ever after"—keeps us from working to build a better marriage? Do we think that love will automatically take care of everything?

In reality, a number of factors combine to keep most Americans from working more actively to improve their marriages. The fairy tale we have been discussing has been called the **myth of naturalism.** This is the idea that marriage is "natural" and will take care of itself if we just select the right partner. Many people believe that outside forces may support or hinder their marriage but that married couples need do little to have a well functioning marriage, especially when the outside forces are good (full employment, little societal stress, and so on).

Myth of naturalism
The idea that marriage is "natural" and will take of itself if we select the right partner.

Privatism
The belief that marriage and family are private matters that are not to be shared publicly.

Another factor is the general **privatism** that pervades American culture. "It's nobody else's business" is a common attitude about problems in general and marriage in particular. It's bad taste to reveal our intimate and personal lives publicly. Seeking outside help to improve marriage means sharing personal information, which is often viewed as an invasion of privacy.

A third factor is the *cynicism* that treats marriage as a joke and thus heads off attempts to improve it. "You should have known better than to get married. Don't complain to me about your problems." This attitude contradicts the romantic concept of marriage but operates just as strongly to keep people from deliberately seeking to improve their marriages. "Why would anyone want to improve this dumb institution?" Even though American society is marriage oriented, marriage still evokes a great deal of ridicule and stories about "the ball and chain." Facing up to and countering the antifamily themes in American society is an important step toward revitalizing marriage and the family (Etzioni 1983). Much of the presidential debate during the 1992 elections centered on *family values* or the lack thereof.

Despite these factors, people in growing numbers are actively seeking to improve their marriages. For example, more than two million couples have participated in the Roman Catholic Marriage Encounter program since it started in 1967. Although created for Catholics, this program is open to all couples who wish to participate. Such programs indicate that the idea of marriage improvement is finding a place in society. The April 1992 issue of *Family Relations* devoted much of its content to prevention programs for families and children (Holman 1992). A sampling of the article titles demonstrates the high degree of interest to be found today in improving relationships and heading off problems before they occur:

■ "The Prevention and Relationship Enhancement Program (PREP): An Empirically Based Preventive Intervention Program for Couples."
■ "Premarital Relationship Enhancement: Its Effects on Needs to Relate to Others."
■ "Description and Evaluation of the Orientation for Divorcing Parents: Implications for Postdivorce Prevention Programs."
■ "Designing a Primary Intervention to Help Dual-Earner Couples Share Housework and Child Care."
■ "Return and Reunion: A Psychoeducational Program Aboard U.S. Navy Ships."

In order to improve a marriage, it is first necessary to believe that relationships can be improved. In other words, the myth of naturalism must be overcome. A marriage will not just naturally take care of itself. In addition, the privatism and cynicism that surround marriage must be reduced if effective steps are to be taken to enrich a marriage.

To improve their marriage, a couple must work on three things: (1) themselves as individuals, (2) their relationship, and (3) the economic environment within which the marriage exists. We have already looked at these elements. For example, in Chapter 5 we discussed the self-actualized person in the fully functioning family; in Chapter 6 we looked at ways to improve communication within a relationship; in Chapters 8 and 9 we examined marriage as an economic institution and found that the economics of one's marriage will drastically affect the marital relationship.

Although this chapter deals specifically with activities designed to improve marital relationships, it is important that a couple work to improve the other two influences on marriage: themselves as individuals and their economic situation. Neglect of any of these influences or emphasis on only one can lead to marital failure. In fact, a couple can be extremely successful in one of the three areas and still fail miserably at marriage, as the following cases demonstrate.

Bill and Susan both worked to buy the many things they wanted: a house, fine furnishings, nice clothes, a fancy car, and so on. Bill even held two jobs for a while. Certainly, no one could fault their industriousness and hard work. In time their marital affluence became the envy of all who knew them. After seven years of marriage, they divorced. Their friends were surprised: "They had everything, why should they divorce?" Unfortunately, Bill and Susan didn't have much of a relationship except to say hello and goodby as they passed on the way to and from work. In addition, they both worked so hard that they had no time for self-improvement. No self-improvement means no growth or change; this eventually leads to boredom with the relationship, and boredom often portends failure.

Bill and Susan were successful with their marital economic environment but did not pay enough attention to improving themselves as individuals or to improving their relationship.

Jack and Mary believed that the key to a successful marriage was self-improvement. Both took extension classes in areas of their own interest. They attended sensitivity training groups and personal expansion workshops. Unfortunately, they could seldom attend these functions together because of their conflicting work schedules. Soon they were so busy improving themselves that they had little time for one another. The house was a shambles, the yard grew up in weeds, and their relationship disappeared under a maze of "do-your-own-thing" self-improvement projects. After seven years, they divorced. Their friends were surprised: "After all, they're so dynamic and interesting, why should they divorce?" Jack and Mary had become so self-oriented that their relationship had disappeared and their living environment had become unimportant.

"And They Lived Happily Ever After"

Jack and Mary worked so hard to improve themselves individually that they had no time for each other or for their home.

Both of these scenarios happen every day. The second is becoming more prevalent with the growing interest in the human potential movement. The very concepts used in this book—self-actualization, self-fulfillment, and human growth orientation—can all be taken to such an individual extreme that marriage is disrupted. If the human potential movement ignores the relational aspect of people by making self-fulfillment the central goal, it can work to the disadvantage of an intimate relationship such as marriage, which requires a great deal of unselfishness.

More and more family researchers as well as general observers of American society see excessive hedonism as America's greatest enemy. Stressing individuality at the expense of mutuality overlooks the importance of successful human relationships, which many see as a basic human need, even for successful individual functioning. Amitai Etzioni (1983) suggests that mutuality, the basic need for interpersonal bonds, is not something each person creates on his or her own and then brings to the relationship. Rather it is constructed by individuals working with one another. This working together is the essence of the healthy family.

To make marriage as rewarding and fulfilling as possible, a couple must be committed first to the idea that effective family relationships do not just happen, but are the result of deliberate efforts by members of the family unit. Then they must be prepared to work on all three facets of marriage: to improve themselves as individuals, to improve their interactional relationship, and to improve their economic environment. These three areas encompass developing oneself in the physical, social, emotional, intellectual, and spiritual realms.

Such a commitment helps a couple anticipate problems before they arise rather than simply reacting to them. When both partners are committed to the active management and creative guidance of a marriage, the marriage can become richly fulfilling and growth enhancing, both for the family as a social unit and for the individuals within the family.

MARRIAGE IMPROVEMENT PROGRAMS

Many techniques are now available to help families who seek assistance. Some techniques aim at solving existing problems, others aim at general family improvement. We will briefly examine some of these techniques in the hope of accomplishing two goals:

1. To help families seek experiences that benefit them.
2. To alert families to some of the possible dangers involved in unselective, nondiscriminative participation in some of the popular techniques.

Help for family problems in the past usually came from relatives, friends, ministers, and family doctors. The idea of enriching family life and improving already adequate marriages simply did not occur to most married people. Marriage traditionally was an institution for childrearing, economic support, and

proper fulfillment of marital duties defined in terms of masculine and feminine roles. If there were problems in these areas, help might be sought. If not, the marriage was fine.

Marriage in modern America, however, has been given more and more responsibility for individual happiness and emotional fulfillment. The criteria used to judge a marriage have gradually shifted from how well each member fulfills roles and performs marital functions to whether both partners have achieved personal contentment, fulfillment, and happiness.

Marital complaints now concern sex roles dissatisfaction, loss of individuality, unequal opportunities for growth and personal fulfillment, personal unhappiness and emotional dissatisfaction, and feelings that the marriage is short-changing the individual partners. In other words, more and more marriage problems revolve around personal dissatisfactions than around traditional marital functioning. The "me" in today's marriage often seems more important than the "us."

A successful family is able to find a balance between personal freedom and happiness on the one hand and family support and togetherness on the other. The "me" and the "us" come into an acceptable balance. The precise balance will vary from family to family. At one end of the continuum are joint conjugal relationships where the balance favors the "us." These couples are close emotionally and share most areas of their lives. Their leisure activities almost always involve one another, and their outside friendships are almost always couple friendships. At the other end of the continuum are separated conjugal relationships where the balance favors the individual. Such couples usually have separate leisure activities and friends. It is interesting to note that in the past the two ends of this "togetherness" continuum related loosely to economic levels. Those at higher economic levels tended to emphasize togetherness while those at lower economic levels tended to emphasize individuality. Today with the entry of so many wives into the work force, the women's liberation movement, and the general social support for individual growth and fulfillment, the

Mr. and Mrs. Smith have been married for fifteen years. They have two children, Colin, thirteen, and Beth, ten. Their church recently started a series of family retreat weekends at a nearby mountain camp. After some discussion, the family members agree that it would be fun and rewarding to go on one of the weekends.

At noon the twenty families gather in the cafeteria/meeting hall for lunch. Everyone is given a name tag and the leaders are introduced. After lunch the families introduce themselves. Much to the children's delight, many other children are present. The leaders assign each family to one of five family subgroups. After lunch the family groups meet, and the four families become better acquainted. The group leader then introduces the first work session, entitled "Becoming More Aware." There are exercises in identification of feelings, and attention is given to feelings the participants would like to experience more often and those they would like to experience less.

After a break the group leader discusses methods the families might use to reduce unwanted feelings and increase desired feelings. Each family then practices some of these methods while the others ob-

serve. After each family finishes, group members offer a general critique.

The families are free after the work session until dinner. After dinner short movies on various developmental problems are shown to the children. At the same time the parents attend a sexuality workshop where they learn message techniques designed to relax and give physical pleasure. They are then asked to practice the techniques in their individual cabins. They are assured of privacy because the children will be occupied for at least another hour. The children meanwhile form small groups and discuss how the children shown in the films can be helped with the developmental problems portrayed.

Next morning, the first work session is devoted to the theme "Being Free." This involves learning openness in experiencing each other. The children of the four families talk to one another about things they like and don't like while the parents sit and listen. Then the roles are reversed. Afterward, the families exchange children and are given a hypothetical problem to solve. Each newly constituted family has a half hour to work on the problem while the other families observe.

At noon each family group eats together and then uses the hour recreational period to do something together, such as hiking, boating, or fishing.

The afternoon work session again separates the parents and children. In each case the assignment is the same. The children are asked to form family groups where some children play the parents' roles. They are given problems to work out as a family unit. The parents also form family groups with some parents taking children's roles.

In the final dinner meeting, all of the families come together. Both the families and the leaders try to summarize the experiences of the weekend and their significance. Then the leaders outline several homework assignments, and each family has to choose one and promise to work on it at home.

WHAT DO YOU THINK?

1. What do you see as the major benefits such an experience could provide a family?
2. Would you be willing to participate with your family in such an experience? Why or why not?
3. Do you have any friends who have participated in any kind of marriage enrichment experience? How did they respond to it?

---

differentiation between economic classes has lessened. The lifestyles of most American families have moved slowly toward separated conjugal relationships.

Emphasis on emotional fulfillment as the most important aspect of marriage makes an enduring marital union much more difficult to attain. According to one authority, "Emotional fulfillment has always occurred in the family; probably more so in the past than is usual today. But it was never before seen as the primary function of the family. It was a lucky 'by-product' " (Putney 1972). For example, when Australia was first colonized by male convicts, a brisk trade in mail-order wives took place because there were no available women in the country. Most of these marriages seem to have been successful for the simple reason

> that the prospective husband and wife expected things of each other that the other could provide. The man needed assistance and companionship of a woman in the arduous task of making a farm, and he wanted sons to help him. He expected certain skills in his wife, but all girls raised in rural England were likely to have them. Her expectations were similarly pragmatic. She expected him to know farming, to work hard, and to protect her. Neither thought of the other as a happiness machine. If they found happiness together more often than American couples do, it may have been they were not looking so hard for it. They fulfilled each other because they shared a life; they did not share a life in the hope of being fulfilled. (Putney 1972)

The search for emotional fulfillment has led to the development of many new techniques to gain this end. Sensitivity training, encounter groups, family enrichment weekends, sex therapy, sexuality workshops, communication improvement groups, massage and bodily awareness training, psychodrama, women's and men's liberation groups, and many other experiential activities have sprung up in recent years to help Americans enrich their lives.

Although this chapter's overview cannot hope to do justice to the many marriage improvement techniques that are emerging, let's take a brief look at some typical ones before we examine marriage enrichment in more detail.

1. *Courses on marriage and the family:* These courses, which are offered by most colleges, aim to help people better understand the institution of marriage. Many schools offer even more specialized courses, often in the evening, on marital communication, economics of marriage, childrearing, and so on.

2. *Encounter groups:* These consist of group interactions, usually with strangers, where the masks and games used by marital partners to manipulate one another and conceal real feelings are stripped away. The group actively confronts the person, forcing him or her to examine some problems and the faulty methods that may have been used to solve or deny the problems. Participants in such groups release a great deal of emotion. Couples contemplating attending an encounter group should carefully consider the guidelines on page 668.

3. *Family enrichment weekends:* Here the entire family goes off to a retreat setting where they work together to improve their family life. The family may concentrate on learning new activities to share. They may listen to lectures, see films, and participate in other learning experiences together. They may interact with other families and learn through the experiences of others. Family members may participate in exercises designed to improve family communication or general family functioning (see Inset 18-1).

4. *Women's and men's consciousness raising groups:* These groups center their discussions and exercises on helping people escape from stereotypical sex roles and liberate the parts of their personalities that have been submerged in the sex role. For example, women who believe that the typical feminine role has been too passive may work to become more assertive. Men who feel the typical masculine role has repressed their ability to communicate feelings may work to become more expressive.

5. *Married couples' communication workshops:* These workshops may be ongoing groups or weekend workshops in which communication is the center of attention. Role playing, learning how to fight fairly, understanding communication processes, and actively practicing in front of the group all help the couple toward better communication. An important aspect of a workshop is the group critique; a couple discusses something that causes a problem for them and then hears a critique of their communication skills from other group members.

6. *Massage and bodily awareness training:* This training is often included in sexuality workshops. It is aimed at developing the couple's awareness of their own bodies and teaching them the techniques involved in physically pleasuring each other through massage. The art of physical relaxation is part of bodily awareness training.

7. *Psychodrama:* This is a form of psychotherapy developed by J. L. Moreno. Couples dramatize problems by acting them out with other group members as the players. In the case of marriage enrichment, psychodrama is used to help individuals in the family better understand the roles of other family members. This understanding is accomplished mainly by having the individuals participating in the drama make timely role changes under the direction of the group leader. Shifting roles also helps each player understand how the other persons in the drama see the situation and feel about it.

8. *Sensitivity training:* This training consists of exercises in touching, concentrating, heightening awareness, and empathizing with one's mate. The exercises increase each partner's self-awareness and sensitivity toward the other.

9. *Sex therapy and sexuality workshops:* These workshops focus on a couple's sexual relationship and use sex therapy to overcome sexual problems. The workshops are designed more to help couples improve this aspect of their relationship than to cure severe problems. Such a workshop assumes that the couple has no major sexual problems. The goal is to heighten sexual awareness so that the couple's sexual relations may be enriched. Films, discussion, mutual exploration, sensitivity, and massage and bodily awareness techniques are all used to reduce inhibitions and expand the couple's sexual awareness.

10. *Marriage counseling and family service organizations:* These services are aimed more at couples with real marital and family difficulties. For example, *Parents Without Partners (PWP)* is an active volunteer organization to help and support single parents. *Planned Parenthood* helps families with reproductive problems such as finding the best contraceptive. The *American Association of Marriage and Family Counselors* will help a couple find a reputable marriage counselor. The *Stepfamily Association of America* is aimed directly at couples who remarry and form stepfamilies.

GUIDELINES FOR CHOOSING MARRIAGE IMPROVEMENT PROGRAMS

Unfortunately, the large demand for marriage improvement programs has brought some untrained and unscrupulous people into the fields of marriage counseling and marriage enrichment. For example, it is relatively simple as well as monetarily rewarding to run a weekend encounter group of some kind.

All you need is a place where the people can meet. Some participants have found that not all such experiences are beneficial or even accomplish what they claim. In a minority of cases, unexpected repercussions, such as divorce, job change, and even hospitalization for mental disturbance, have occurred after some supposedly beneficial group experience. Consider what happened to the following couple because one partner could not tolerate the intensity of the group experience.

David and Melissa have been married for eleven years and have two children. David has always been shy and uncomfortable among people, but has nevertheless worked out a stable, satisfying relationship with Melissa. She is more socially oriented than David and began to attend a series of group encounter sessions out of curiosity. As her interest increased, she decided that David would benefit from a group experience. She asked him to attend a weekend marathon. Unfortunately, the group turned its attention too strongly toward David's shyness, causing him acute discomfort that finally resulted in his fleeing from the group. He remained away from his home and work for ten days. On returning, he demanded a divorce because he felt that he was an inadequate husband. Fortunately, psychotherapeutic help was available, and David was able to work out the problems raised by the group encounter.

Evaluation studies of the Marriage Encounter program (a popular church-sponsored enrichment program) indicate that only about 10 percent of the participants experience potentially harmful effects (Doherty and Lester 1982, 9). But since there are possible negative effects, it is worthwhile to list what they might be:

1. The perceived benefits may be illusory or at best temporary.
2. The stress on the relationship may tend to deny individual differences.
3. There may be divisive influences on the couple's relationship with other family members.
4. The communicative techniques taught may rigidify the couple's communication patterns, and failure to practice the techniques may lead to guilt or resentment.

Because marriage enrichment experiences can be so beneficial to couples, it is important to reduce the potential negative aspects to a minimum. Couples seeking marital enrichment or help for marital problems are advised to check out the people offering such services. They should also discuss the kind of experiences they want and make sure that those are the experiences offered. For example, if a couple decide that they would like to improve their sexual relations and wish to do so by seeking some general sensitivity training (learning to feel more comfortable with their bodies, be more aware, and give and accept bodily pleasure), they might be rudely shocked if the group leader conducts a nude encounter group with the goal of examining each person's emotional hang-ups about sex.

Couples who have a reasonably satisfactory marriage can use the following guidelines in choosing a marriage enrichment activity:

1. Choose the activity together and participate together if possible.
2. If only one mate can participate, do so with the consent of the other and bring the other into the activity as much as possible by sharing your experiences.
3. In general, avoid the one-time weekend group; it is often too intense and no follow-up is available if needed.
4. Never jump into a group experience on impulse. Give it a lot of thought, understanding that experiences leading to growth may be painful.
5. Do not participate in groups where the people are friends and associates if the group's goal is total openness and emotional expression. What occurs in a group session should be privileged information.
6. Don't remain with a group that seems to have an ax to grind, insists that everybody be a certain type of person, or insists that all must participate in every activity.
7. Participate in groups that have a formal connection with a local professional on whom you can check. The local profession is also a source of follow-up help if necessary.
8. A group of six to sixteen members is optimum size. Too small a group may result in scapegoating; too large a group cannot operate effectively.

Such cautions are not meant to dissuade couples from trying to improve their marriages. They are simply meant to help couples select experiences that are beneficial and supportive rather than threatening and disruptive. Legitimate marriage counselors throughout the United States are working to upgrade their profession and tighten the rules guiding counseling practices. Many states now have licensing provisions for marriage and family counseling.

AN OUNCE OF PREVENTION IS WORTH A POUND OF CURE: MARRIAGE ENRICHMENT

Only recently have those working in the field of marriage and family counseling turned their attention away from marital problems and focused instead on marriage enrichment. In the past marital services tended to be remedial in nature. When a couple had a marital problem, they could seek help from numerous sources. Marriage enrichment places the emphasis on the preventive side with the objective of facilitating positive growth. In other words, the goal is to help couples with "good" marriages further improve their relationship and head off potential problems. Marriage enrichment is proactive rather than only reactive. Guerney and Maxson (1990, 1127) offer the following formal definition: *Marital and family enrichment comprises psychoeducational programs designed to strengthen couples or families so as to promote a high level of present and future family harmony and strength, and hence long-term psychological, emotional, and social well-being of family members.*

Whenever seeking help, regardless of recommendations, always check credentials. The foremost organization in the nation for accrediting and certifying marriage counselors is the American Association of Marriage and Family Therapists, 1717 K Street N.W. #407, Washington, D.C. 20006. At no charge it will supply a list of three or more accredited marriage counselors in your area.

Psychologists are also active in marital counseling and enrichment training. Membership in the American Psychological Association (APA) indicates that the person has met minimum training requirements and has agreed to abide by a strict set of ethics in client relationships. Your local phone book usually lists members of the national and/or state psychological associations in the yellow pages.

The American Association of Sex Educators and Counselors has established certification standards for sex therapists. You can receive a copy of these standards and a list of certified sex therapists by writing to Sex Therapy Certification Committee, American Association of Sex Educators, Counselors and Therapists, 11 Dupont Circle, Suite 220, Washington, D.C. 20036.

In addition more than 350 marriage-and-family-oriented non-profit social service organizations throughout the nation are affiliated with the Family Service Association of America, 11700 Westlake Park Drive, Milwaukee, WI 53224, and the National Association of Social Workers, 1425 H Street N.W., Suite 600, Washington, D.C. 20005.

Many churches also offer family counseling and enrichment programs. In fact, some churches have been pioneers in the marriage enrichment movement. You can also contact Worldwide Marriage Encounter, 1908 Highland Avenue, San Bernardino, CA 92404. Such programs are run all over the United States. Another source of information is the Association for Couples in Marriage Enrichment, P.O. Box 10596, Winston-Salem, NC 26108.

The Stepfamily Association of America offers help to remarried couples. There are many local branches. The national headquarters may be contacted at 602 East Joppa Road, Baltimore, MD 21204.

Marriage enrichment programs are for couples who perceive their marriage as functioning fairly well and wish to make it even more mutually satisfying. Because the emphasis is on education and prevention rather than on therapy, these programs are not for couples with serious problems in their marriage. Enrichment programs are generally concerned with enhancing the couple's communication, emotional life, or sexual relationship; fostering marriage strengths; and developing marriage potential while maintaining a consistent and primary focus on the couple's relationship.

The purpose of marriage enrichment is to teach couples attitudes, communication behaviors, and knowledge about family and marital relationships. This education is designed to help them develop relationships that meet personal needs and enhance individual development. This is education in the best sense of the term, experiencing new ideas and new approaches to relating, not just learning about them. It is education that enables spouses to change the way they think, what they feel, and how they care for each other. (Garland 1983, 217)

Some people in the field make a distinction between marriage enrichment and family life enrichment programs. The latter involve not only the primary couple but the entire family in the program. Again, they are designed for families without severe problems.

Marriage Improvement Programs

If couples are to direct and improve their marriage, they must increase their awareness. You can't improve anything unless you recognize what is taking place. It is helpful to organize awareness into four subcategories (Hill 1961): topical; self, partner, and relationship. Marriage enrichment programs usually spend a great deal of time helping couples or families to become more aware in each of these categories.

For example, in the category of *self-awareness*, enrichment programs offer sensitivity training exercises to help you focus on your internal sensory, thinking, and emotional processes. Goals include achieving a realistic self-picture, openness to your feelings, and minimal defensiveness as well as eliminating some emotional hang-ups.

Partner awareness involves knowing accurately what your partner is experiencing in terms of his or her own self-awareness. How does this behavior affect my partner? Is my partner happy, sad, or indifferent? How can I best communicate with my partner? What does my partner think or feel about this? Answering such questions accurately is the goal of partner awareness training.

Relationship awareness shifts the focus from the behavior of one individual to the interactional patterns of the couple or the entire family. For example, who starts an argument, who continues it, and who ends the interaction? Does each individual contribute self-disclosures, feeling inputs, and negative and positive communications? Do the family members play unproductive games? If so, who initiates the game? What are the rules by which the family interacts?

Every interrelationship has boundaries or constraints that either encourage or discourage certain types of awareness and various types of behavior. These rules are usually outside our direct awareness, but they create and maintain meaning and order. We like to conceptualize rules in terms of who can do what, where, when, how, and for what length of time. These rules can be applied to any issue in a relationship. For example, does a family allow personal criticism? Who is allowed to criticize? When? And to what degree? What is a family's mode of handling conflicts? Some families talk directly about issues and make active efforts to solve them. Other families pretend that conflicts don't exist and ignore them in the hope they will go away. Others deal with the issue in some stereotypical manner that usually fails to solve the conflict but allows family members to ventilate hostility.

Topical awareness is less important than the three categories we have just discussed. Topical awareness encompasses references to events, objects, ideas, places, and people—topics that constitute most of everyday conversation. By increasing topical awareness, the couple can focus on their interests and find where they differ and where they coincide. In this way they can find areas in which they can work and play together. They can also recognize and tolerate areas of their spouse's interests that they don't share.

Another purpose of marriage enrichment programs is to help couples and families develop a game plan for handling disputes and conflicts. What are the rules, how can they be clarified, and what procedure can change them? If you don't have a set of rules for handling conflict, your relationship is likely to degenerate into a series of arguments and squabbles. Thus most marriage enrichment programs spend a great deal of time on the development of communication skills, including the kinds of skills discussed in Chapter 6. For example, identifying problem ownership, self-assertion, empathic listening, negotiation, and problem solving are all emphasized.

Marriage Encounter is one of the earliest programs designed to help people improve both their marriage and family life. Started by a Spanish Catholic priest (Fr. Gariel Calvo) in the 1960s for Catholic families, the movement has broadened to other denominations. Although church related, the program has a long history of success in helping people regardless of religious affiliation build stronger, more successful relationships.

Father Calvo lists ten major points as basic to the process of marriage encounter:

1. *Discovering oneself:* Before we can move toward the "you," we have to find the "I." We have already examined this idea when we discussed love in Chapter 3. If you are not at peace and accepting of yourself, it is difficult to give love and establish an intimate relationship.

2. *Talking to the other:* Father Calvo is speaking of more than simply conveying information between people. He is speaking of a mutuality between persons in which each person really listens to the other and really tries to understand her or his partner at the deepest

level. He suggests that a husband and wife who truly listen to one another will launch a revolution in their own lives and relationship. By applying the principles discussed in Chapter 6, couples can improve their communication.

3. *Mutual trust:* Without mutual trust a close intimate relationship would be impossible to achieve. Such trust is not the work of a single day, but grows out of the little personal confidences between husband and wife that occur all of the time in a growing relationship.

4. *Growth in knowledge of each other:* Mutual trust leads to greater knowledge of one another. Couples that fall prey to the illusion that if there is a strong attraction between them, all will be well in their marriage often fail to increase their knowledge of one another. They are married but are, in fact, strangers to one another.

5. *Understanding each other:* Knowledge of one another leads to a true understanding of each other, and with this understanding can come acceptance.

6. *Acceptance of each other:* So often we are unable to accept some characteristics and behaviors in our partners. However, a true acceptance of the other person can give

that person the confidence in the relationship that can also enable him or her to change. True acceptance yields confidence.

7. *Helping one another:* Mutual help is a sign of true friendship. One of the advantages of marriage is that it is a partnership—two people are working together to solve the problems of life. Being able to rely on another is a great help and comfort.

8. *Growth in love and union:* All of the previous steps lead to a growing relationship and foster a sense of mutual gratitude and profound joy in one another. As the love between the couple strengthens, it broadens to include greater love for the family, kin, and community.

9. *Opening up to others:* The establishment of a loving union gives the couple the security to turn love outward to others and to the broader community.

10. *Love transcendent:* For Father Calvo, all of this will lead in the end to a love of God. Regardless of one's religious orientation or acceptance of this final step, the first nine qualities he describes are important elements in any successful intimate relationship.

Esteem building is another area of concern in enrichment programs. We sometimes forget this area when lauding the improvement of communication skills, but better communication can equip a person to be destructive as well as constructive. Emphasizing esteem building, communicating with a positive intent or spirit, and valuing both the self and the partner make communication constructive and growth enhancing. Esteem building is particularly difficult for

Marriage Improvement Programs

a partner who feels devalued and inferior. Thus enrichment programs stress the importance of building a relationship that negates such feelings and supports positive feelings of value and high esteem in family members.

The fact that a family is interested in and open to the idea of marriage enrichment is an extremely important strength. Certainly, the kinds of goals sought by the marriage enrichment movement are worthwhile. These goals, however, are not as important as the family's general attitude toward marriage. The family that takes an active role in guiding, improving, and working toward better family relations is the family that stands the greatest chance of leading a long, happy, and meaningful life.

How successful are family and/or marriage enrichment programs? In general, participation in such programs leads to positive changes in a couple's or family's relationships. Real changes and improvement in interaction behavior are noted. Particular programs vary in their effectiveness, but all of the programs investigated indicate positive changes (Giblin, Sprenkle, and Sheehan 1985; Guerney and Maxson 1990; LeCroy et al. 1989; Mattson 1990).

MARRIAGE WITH PURPOSE: EFFECTIVE MANAGEMENT

Popular lore has it that the love marriage simply happens (the myth of naturalism that we discussed earlier). If we are in love, then the other factors necessary to a successful relationship and marriage will fall into place automatically as if by magic. There is no reason to worry about problems ahead of time. Of course, difficulties will arise, but they can be worked out successfully by any couple truly in love.

It is almost a sacrilege to suggest that people entering a love relationship should make a conscious effort to guide and build that relationship. In fact, many argue that attempts to guide and control a relationship will ruin it. Their advice is to "relax and let it happen." This attitude implies a great tolerance on the part of each individual, because what happens may not be something the other wants. How tolerant are we? Does love mean that we must never judge our mate? Are we to accept any behavior from our mate in an effort to "let it happen"?

Most people are tolerant only up to a given point, after which certain behavior becomes unacceptable. Most of us are tolerant in some areas of our life and intolerant in other areas. Of course, everyone can learn to be more tolerant, but total tolerance of all things is probably impossible. People have many and varying standards. As a result, when we let a relationship "just happen," it usually isn't long before we discover some of our intolerances. Then we try to change our relationship or our mate. Conflict usually follows because our mate may not want to change or have the relationship change in the direction we desire. Without mutually acceptable ways of handling conflict, unconscious games and strategies may take over, and soon communication will be lost.

Marriage and family require management skills. Work, leisure, economics, emotions, interests, sex, children, eating, and maintaining the household all require effective management in the fully functioning family. We have discussed most of these matters elsewhere in the book, but tying them all together under the concept of effective management seems a proper way to end.

"Surely you can't be serious? Effective management belongs in business, not in my marriage." Yet every married couple, especially if they have children, are running a business. For example, just planning what the family will eat for the next week, buying the food, preparing it, and cleaning up afterward require considerable management and organizational skills, especially if money is in short supply. Furthermore, recurrent personal and family crises are likely to throw off schedules and plans.

In addition to day-to-day management, a family needs to plan to achieve long-range goals. For some families, life seems to be a constant struggle from one catastrophe to the next. Other families seem to move smoothly through life despite the crises that arise periodically. What is the difference? Often the difference is simply a matter of efficient planing and management versus lack of planning and management. Compare attitudes toward money of the following two couples:

Jim and Marge went to college with Bill and Sally. They remained close friends after college, as both Jim and Bill got jobs with the same company. Each couple has two children. Marge works periodically, and the money she earns is always saved or used for some specific goal such as a trip or an addition to the house. Sally works most of the time also, but she and Bill don't care much about things like budgeting. As long as there is enough money to pay the bills, nothing else matters.

"You and Jim are always so lucky. Bill and I have wanted to add a master bedroom for ourselves so we could have a retreat away from the children, but we'll never be able to afford it," complains Sally.

"Luck has nothing to do with it. Jim and I have planned to add the bedroom for a number of years. We always budget carefully so our monthly expenses are covered by Jim's salary. That way all of the money I earn less child-care costs goes into savings. The new bedroom represents my last three years of work. I'd hardly call it luck," replies Marge.

Naturally, Sally isn't interested in hearing Marge's response. "Luck" is an easier way to explain her friend's new bedroom. Besides, what Marge is telling her is, "Be a better money manager, and you, too, can add a new bedroom." This advice will only make Sally feel guilty and inadequate. "It isn't worth all the trouble to budget money and be tightwads to get a new bedroom," Sally will probably think to herself.

Creative management in all areas helps the family run smoothly and achieve its desired goals. Effective management reduces frustrations and conflicts because it gives family members a feeling of success. Careful planning also helps a family maintain the flexibility necessary to cope with unforeseen emergencies. Such flexibility gives family members a feeling of freedom because they can make choices rather than having choices forced upon them by events beyond their control.

One reason many married persons feel trapped is that they do not take the initiative to plan and guide their lives but simply react to circumstances. Of course, there are times and situations when one can do nothing but react. The poor in particular often have so little control over their lives that they give up planning altogether and live by luck and fate.

Family control and rational planning become more difficult as social institutions multiply and infringe on family responsibilities. Some of these external stresses on the family have emerged out of necessity. When a society begins to develop beyond a primitive level, its members soon find that many tasks are better performed by agencies other than the family. The clergy take over the job of interceding with the supernatural; police forces, armies, and fire brigades take over the job of protecting the family from physical harm; and schools undertake to educate children. In the complex modern world, the family often has little say over what kind of work its members will perform or where or for how long. These matters may be decided by the impersonal forces of the marketplace or by distant corporations, unions, or government bureaus.

In such a situation, it becomes even more important for planning, foresight, and management to be an integral part of family life so that the family can cope successfully with outside pressures. The family that actively takes control of its destiny is most often the family that grows and prospers, thereby helping every member toward self-fulfillment.

THE FAMILY WILL REMAIN AND DIVERSIFY

Many people have tried to predict the future of the American family. These predictions vary from an early death to the emergence of new and improved families that will be havens of fulfillment for their members. It is unlikely, however, that families will disappear or that there is any single ideal family structure. All families face both external environmental pressures and internal stresses and strains. Older generations will probably always think they are seeing the deterioration of the family because their children choose different lifestyles from their own. Yet differences in lifestyle and family structure do not necessarily mean deterioration. Perhaps with increased affluence and education, each individual will be able to choose from a wider variety of acceptable lifestyles, thereby increasing the chances that the family will be satisfying and fulfilling to its members.

The family has always been with us and always will be. And it will also always change. Indeed, the flexibility of the family allows it to survive. The family is flexible because humans are flexible and create institutions that meet their purposes at a given time. When we forget the basic flexibility of humans, we feel threatened by changes in institutions, even though the changes may in fact be helping people meet their needs.

The concept of family has always been controversial, but it has also always been one of the central concepts whenever people have congregated into a society. For example, in Japan there is even a rent-a-family service where children can hire actors to visit their elderly parents. The actors come complete with hugs, kisses, and maybe even a baby grandchild (Rivenbark 1992). Such a stand-in family certainly says something negative about the elderly couple's children who hire professional visitors rather than taking the time to visit themselves. On the other hand, the story also says something about the importance of family.

Change is an integral part of the concept of family. As Elise Boulding (1983, 259) has suggested: "The family has met fire, flood, famine, earthquake, war, economic and political collapse over the centuries by changing its form, its size, its behavior, its location, its environment, its reality. It is the most resilient social form available to humans."

The presidential election of 1992 found both Republicans and Democrats, conservatives and liberals united in their concern over family values and the importance and centrality of the family in society. The debate was not over whether the family is an important building block of society, but rather how best to strengthen the family and improve its functioning.

The following suggestions might help the family to better meet the challenges of the 1990s:

1. The workplace must be made "family friendly" (Bayme 1990, 256). Chapters 7 and 9 offer numerous suggestions for accomplishing this end. If employers join in partnership with families, both the families and the employers will benefit.

2. Family life education must begin early and train young people in the art of healthy marital communication and family relationships. A pro-marriage, pro-family bias needs to be encouraged. For example, divorce need not be stigmatized, yet it should be presented as a course of last resort to be used only after all efforts to save a relationship have failed.

3. The image of marriage and family conveyed in the popular culture and media needs to be improved. For example, people need to advocate television programming that portrays realistic role models and suggests that conflicts can be resolved if family members are committed to working together to iron out difficulties.

Stable families both provide opportunities for personal growth and hold the key to society's future through the socialization of children. For these reasons, we should be willing to assert our cultural preferences for traditional norms such as marriage and the two-parent home while at the same time accommodating and reaching out to those who have chosen to lead their lives within alternative settings. We need have no nostalgia for the mythical nuclear family of the 1950s. At the same time, we have no need to redefine the family so as to regard all possible living arrangements as being equally preferable. Rather, we need to advocate programs that encourage responsible preparation for marriage and parenthood and that communicate that if society acknowledges family cohesion as a desirable personal and communal goal, it is the responsibility of society to support families (Bayme 1990, 258).

SUMMARY

1. The American dream "and they lived happily ever after" remains only an unfulfilled dream unless *the newly married couple commit themselves to the idea of working not only to maintain but also to improve their relationship.*

2. *Unfortunately, a number of factors work against such commitment to improve a relationship.* One factor is the myth of naturalism that claims love will take care of any problems that arise if you marry the "right" mate. Another is the general "privatism" that pervades American culture and precludes sharing the very intimate problems that arise in marriage. The third factor is the cynicism that often surrounds the idea of marriage.

3. *To improve an intimate relationship, a couple must work on three things: (1) themselves as individuals, (2) their relationship, and (3) the economic environment within which their relationship exists.* Ignoring any of these increases the chances that the relationship will experience problems.

4. *There are now many marriage improvement programs from which couples may choose.* However, couples need to use caution in choosing such programs. Although most programs are beneficial, there is always the potential for damage to the relationship if the couple is unprepared for the experience or if the particular program is poorly presented.

5. *Marriage and family enrichment programs are aimed at families that do not have serious problems.* Enrichment programs are for families that are getting along pretty well but want to improve their relationships and the quality of their lives.

6. *As unromantic as it may sound, a fulfilling marriage and family life is largely based on good management.* The family that remains in control of its day-today life as well as its future is most apt to be successful. Good planning and follow-through are essential to maintaining such control.

7. Although the family today faces many problems just as it has in the past, *the flexible nature of the family allows it to survive as the major institution for intimate interaction.* Just what form the family will take in the future remains to be seen, but it will survive as it always has.

A

SEXUAL ANATOMY

When describing human anatomy, we think in terms of two descriptions, male and female. Yet the development of male and female anatomical structures rests on a common tissue foundation. As described in Chapter 7, hormonal action triggered by chromosomal makeup differentiates the tissues into male and female organs. Figures 1 and 2 show this differentiation, as well as the homologues (similar in origin and structure but not necessarily in function) of external and internal male and female genitals. The contrast between the sexes begins around the fifth or sixth week after conception.

Human sex organs always seem to have been of more interest to people than other organs. Many past societies have glorified the genitals in their arts. But the advent of Christianity brought a more negative attitude toward sexuality as the church generally attempted to limit it to reproduction. The interest in sexuality as pleasure went underground, so to speak, and graphic display of sexual activities became known as pornography. (See Debate the Issues on pp. 366–367).

The **genitals** have long been studied medically in modern America, but only recently have they been studied as organs of sexuality. Masters and Johnson in their classic study, *Human Sexual Response* (1966), pioneered the study of the genitals as pleasure organs. Today every aspect of human sexuality—whether physical, psychological, or social—is a legitimate area of study. For example, the following papers were presented at a recent regional meeting of the Society for the Scientific Study of Sex: "Feminine Sexual Hygiene," "Penile Sensitivity, Aging and Degree of Sexual Activity," "Clitoral Adhesions: Myth or Reality," and "The Vaginal Clasp."

Genitals
The external reproductive organs

FIGURE 1

External male and female genitals:
development from undifferentiated
to differentiated stage

Undifferentiated

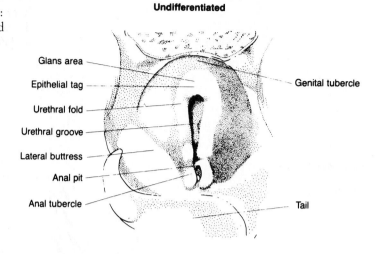

Glans area

Epithelial tag

Urethral fold

Urethral groove

Lateral buttress

Anal pit

Anal tubercle

Genital tubercle

Tail

Male   **Embryo**   **Female**

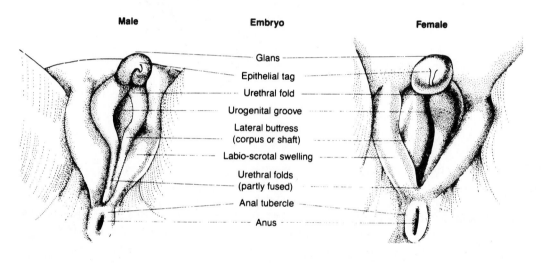

Glans

Epithelial tag

Urethral fold

Urogenital groove

Lateral buttress
(corpus or shaft)

Labio-scrotal swelling

Urethral folds
(partly fused)

Anal tubercle

Anus

Fully Developed

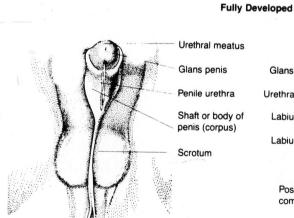
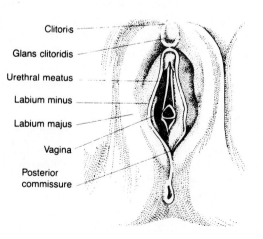

Urethral meatus

Glans penis

Penile urethra

Shaft or body of
penis (corpus)

Scrotum

Clitoris

Glans clitoridis

Urethral meatus

Labium minus

Labium majus

Vagina

Posterior
commissure

FIGURE 2

Internal male and female genitals: development from undifferentiated to differentiated stage

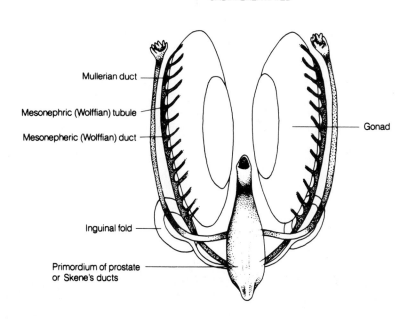

UNDIFFERENTIATED

Mullerian duct

Mesonephric (Wolffian) tubule

Mesonepheric (Wolffian) duct

Gonad

Inguinal fold

Primordium of prostate
or Skene's ducts

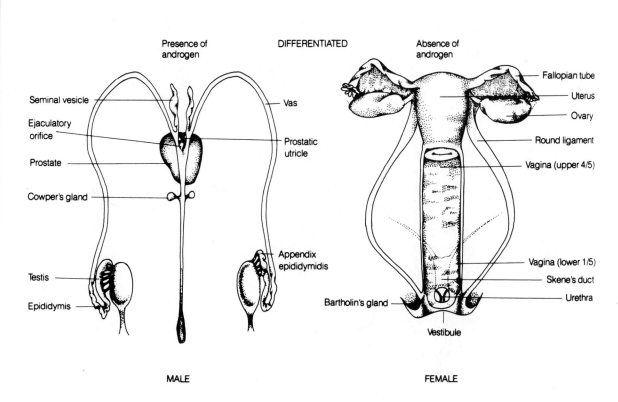

DIFFERENTIATED

Presence of androgen

Absence of androgen

Seminal vesicle

Ejaculatory orifice

Prostate

Cowper's gland

Vas

Prostatic utricle

Testis

Epididymis

Appendix epididymidis

Fallopian tube

Uterus

Ovary

Round ligament

Vagina (upper 4/5)

Vagina (lower 1/5)

Skene's duct

Urethra

Bartholin's gland

Vestibule

MALE

FEMALE

Testosterone
An important component of the male sex hormone androgen; responsible for inducing and maintaining the male secondary sexual characteristics

FIGURE 3
The male reproductive system

Although most people's interest focuses on the male external organs because of their obvious sexual connotations, the internal ones are regarded as the primary organs of procreation (see Figures 3 and 4).

The testes in the male produce *spermatozoa* (*sperm* for short). If the coiled tubules within the testes that produce and store the sperm were straightened out, they would be several hundred feet long. Other special cells within the testes produce the important hormone **testosterone.** This hormone directs the developing tissue toward maleness and, at adolescence, causes the maturing of the sexual organs and the appearance of secondary sexual characteristics, such as deepening voice and facial and body hair. Figure 5 shows the course taken by the sperm in ejaculation. Sperm are matured and stored in the *epididymis*. With ejaculation they travel up the *vas deferens* where it joins the duct of the

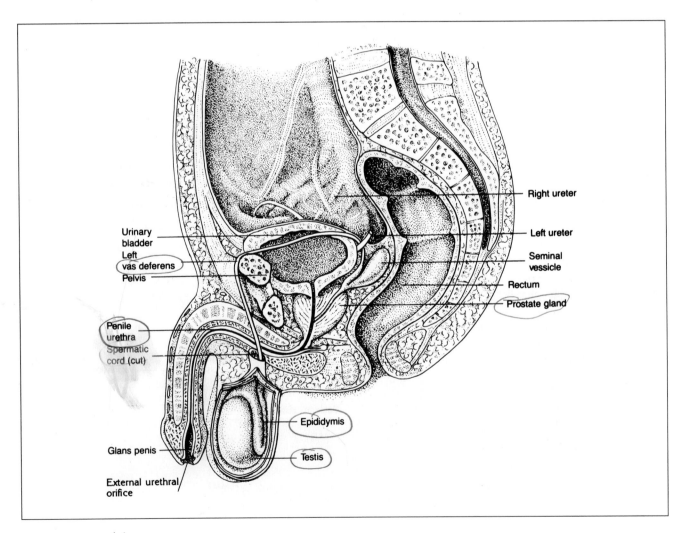

Urinary bladder
Left vas deferens
Pelvis
Penile urethra
Spermatic cord (cut)
Glans penis
External urethral orifice
Right ureter
Left ureter
Seminal vessicle
Rectum
Prostate gland
Epididymis
Testis

FIGURE 4
A longitudinal section of the penis

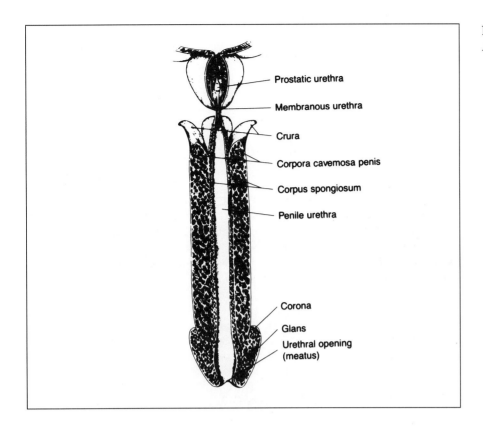

- Prostatic urethra
- Membranous urethra
- Crura
- Corpora cavemosa penis
- Corpus spongiosum
- Penile urethra
- Corona
- Glans
- Urethral opening (meatus)

seminal vesicle in the lower abdomen. The two seminal vesicles produce the secretion **semen** to increase the volume of the ejaculatory fluid, which empties into the ejaculatory ducts. These ducts empty into the *urethra,* which is the canal extending through the penis. (The urethra is also the canal through which urine is discharged, but urine and semen can never pass through at the same time. Sexual arousal and ejaculation inhibit the ability to urinate.) The *prostate gland* surrounds the first part of the urethra as it leaves the bladder. This gland secretes a thin fluid that helps alkalize the seminal fluid. In addition, the muscle part of the prostate helps propel the ejaculatory fluid out of the penis. The last contribution to the seminal fluid comes from the *Cowper's glands,* two pea-sized structures flanking the urethra. During sexual arousal they secrete an alkaline fluid that further neutralizes the acidic environment of the urethra and provides penile lubrication to facilitate intercourse.

The process of **ejaculation** begins with contractions of the ducts leading from the seminiferous tubules in the testes and simply continues on through the system. The actual amount of ejaculate varies according to the male's physical condition and age and the time elapsed between ejaculations. Usually, about a teaspoon of fluid is ejaculated; it contains about 300 million sperm. To be considered of normal fertility, the ejaculate must contain a minimum of 60 to 100 million sperm per cubic centimeter of semen. The ejaculatory amount is reestablished in the healthy male within twenty-four hours.

The strength of the ejaculatory response also varies: The semen may simply ooze out of the urethra or may be discharged as far as several feet beyond the penis. Figure 6 diagrams the route taken by the sperm for fertilization to take place.

Semen
The secretion of the male reproductive organs that is ejaculated from the penis during orgasm and contains the sperm cells

Ejaculation
The expulsion of semen by the male during orgasm

Male Sex Organs

FIGURE 5
The passage of sperm

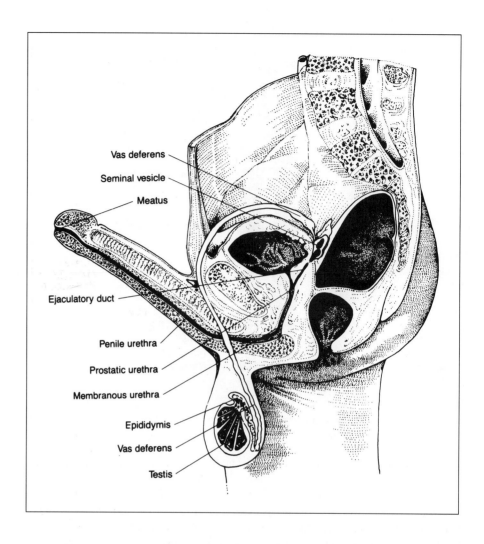

Vas deferens

Seminal vesicle

Meatus

Ejaculatory duct

Penile urethra

Prostatic urethra

Membranous urethra

Epididymis

Vas deferens

Testis

Ejaculation is accompanied by a highly pleasurable sensation known as *orgasm*. This was discussed more fully in Chapter 10.

The testes are particularly sensitive to temperature and must remain slightly cooler than the body to produce viable sperm. Hence when the temperature is hot, the sac containing them hangs down farther. When the temperature is cold, the testicles are pulled up close to the body. Since high temperatures in the testes reduce sperm count, it is unwise for a man to spend long periods of time in a hot tub or sauna if his mate is trying to get pregnant. Occasionally, the testicles don't descend into the scrotum properly, which causes sterility. Surgery and hormone treatment can usually correct this. Sometimes only one testicle descends, but one is usually enough to ensure fertility.

In order to have intercourse, it is necessary for the male to have an erection. Both erection and ejaculation can occur without physical stimulation, such as with a nocturnal emission that usually is accompanied by an erotic dream (wet dream).

Figure 4 shows the three cylindrical bodies of spongy erectile tissue that run the length of the penis. Sexual arousal causes the dilation of blood vessels within the penis, and small valvelike structures (polsters) emit blood into the

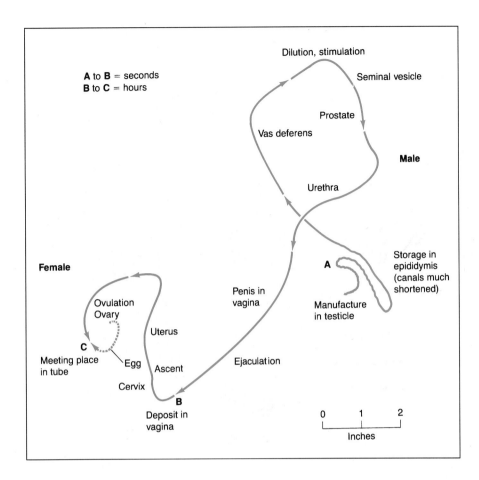

vascular spaces of the erectile tissue. Because the rate of blood inflow is greater than the rate of outflow, the volume of blood in the penis increases. As the erectile tissue becomes engorged with blood, the penis stiffens into an erection. The average penis is three to four inches long in a flaccid state and six to seven inches long when erect. Size variations are less in the erect state than they are in the flaccid state and are not related to virility. Men do not have voluntary control of erection and cannot always be sure that they will be capable of intercourse. This fact sometimes leads to sexual insecurity in males. Failure to achieve and hold an erection long enough for sexual intercourse is called **impotence.**

Modern technology has succeeded in duplicating the erection's mechanism, and the device has been successfully implanted to aid men who cannot become erect. See Figure 7 for an illustration and description of the device.

Impotence
Usually temporary inability of a man to experience erection; may be caused by either physical or psychological factors

FEMALE SEX ORGANS

To focus our discussion of the female reproductive system (see Figure 8), let us trace the course of development and ultimate fertilization of the female egg

FIGURE 7

The inflatable penile prosthesis. The operation of the inflatable penile prosthesis mimics the natural action of the erection process. A miniature hydraulic system transfers fluid to implanted cylinders, which causes the cylinders to fill and expand, creating an erection. When an erection is no longer desired, the man activates a deflation mechanism to return the penis to a normal flaccid state.

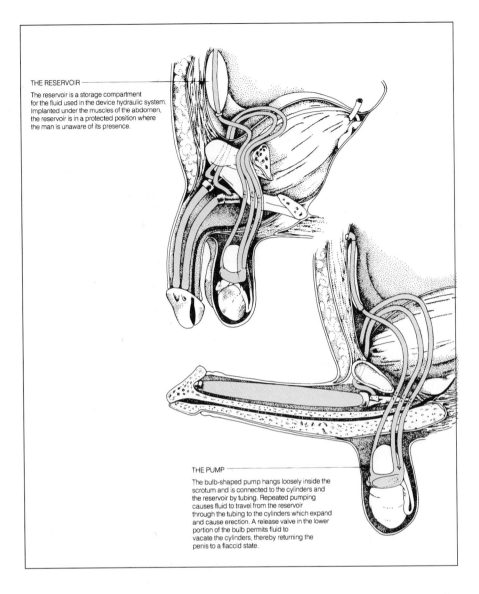

THE RESERVOIR

The reservoir is a storage compartment for the fluid used in the device hydraulic system. Implanted under the muscles of the abdomen, the reservoir is in a protected position where the man is unaware of its presence.

THE PUMP

The bulb-shaped pump hangs loosely inside the scrotum and is connected to the cylinders and the reservoir by tubing. Repeated pumping causes fluid to travel from the reservoir through the tubing to the cylinders which expand and cause erection. A release valve in the lower portion of the bulb permits fluid to vacate the cylinders, thereby returning the penis to a flaccid state.

Ovum
The female reproductive cell (egg) that when fertilized develops into a new member of the same species

Ovaries
The female sex glands in which the ova (eggs) are formed

Fallopian tubes
The two tubes in the female reproductive system that link the ovaries to the uterus; passageway for eggs

Ovulation
The regular monthly process in the fertile woman whereby an ovarian follicle ruptures and releases a mature ovum (egg)

(ovum). Eggs are released from the female gonads or **ovaries.** Each ovary contains an estimated 50,000 to 200,000 tiny sacs or *follicles,* but only 250 to 400 will become active during a woman's lifetime and produce eggs (see Figure 9). Each woman is born with a lifetime supply of eggs and does not actually produce them as the male produces sperm. After puberty, normally once every twenty-eight days, one egg ripens, bursts from a follicle, and enters the **Fallopian tube,** where fertilization may occur.

Each month the ripe egg travels through the Fallopian tubes to the uterus where, if fertilized, it implants in the blood-rich uterine lining that has built up during the month to receive it. This cycle is known as the menstrual cycle, and release of the ripe egg from the follicle is called **ovulation.** If the egg is not fertilized, it will be shed, along with the thickened uterine lining, as menstrual flow. The easiest way to describe this process is to label the first day of menstrual flow as day 1 because it is easy to observe. On the average the cycle

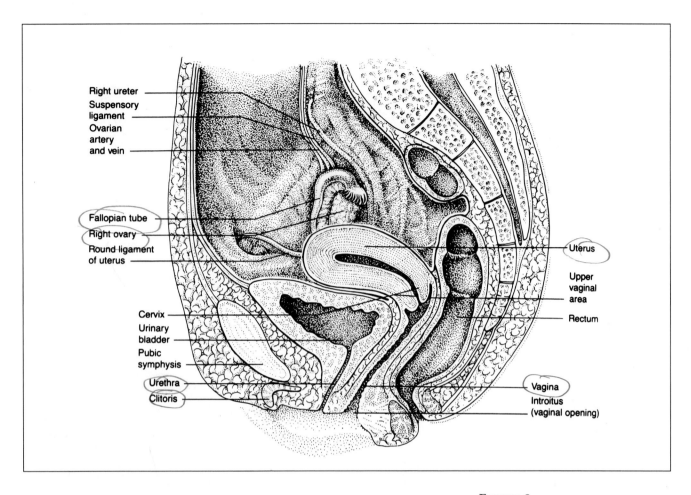

Right ureter
Suspensory ligament
Ovarian artery and vein

Fallopian tube
Right ovary
Round ligament of uterus

Cervix
Urinary bladder
Pubic symphysis

Urethra
Clitoris

Uterus

Upper vaginal area

Rectum

Vagina
Introitus (vaginal opening)

FIGURE 8
The female reproductive system

lasts twenty-eight days, with menstruation lasting five days. Individuals may vary considerably from these averages.

Follicle-stimulating hormone (FSH) is released from the anterior lobe of the pituitary gland, which is a pealike gland suspended from the base of the brain. The follicle-stimulating hormone activates the ovarian follicles, and two to thirty-two eggs begin to ripen. The follicles mature at different rates of speed. By the tenth day, the most mature follicles look like rounded, fluid-filled sacs. The maturing follicles begin to produce **estrogen,** which prepares the uterus for implantation of the fertilized egg. At this time one of the follicles speeds its growth. The others, developed to various extents, regress, and die. Occasionally, a woman may produce more than one ripe egg per cycle and thus be prone to multiple births. Many women taking certain chemicals designed to increase their fertility have had multiple births, indicating that the chemicals stimulate numerous follicles to continue ripening.

By about day 13, the egg is ready to be released. This is accomplished by the *luteinizing hormone (LH),* also produced by the pituitary gland. The luteinizing hormone causes the follicle to rupture, which is ovulation.

The egg survives for about twenty-four hours. Sperm, on the other hand, can normally survive from one to three days after being deposited in the vagina. If ovulation occurs between the twelfth and sixteenth days of the cycle,

Estrogen
Often called the "female hormone"; directs the differentiation of embryonic tissue into female genitals and of prenatal brain tissue that governs female physiological functions; responsible for the development of female secondary sexual characteristics

Female Sex Organs

A9

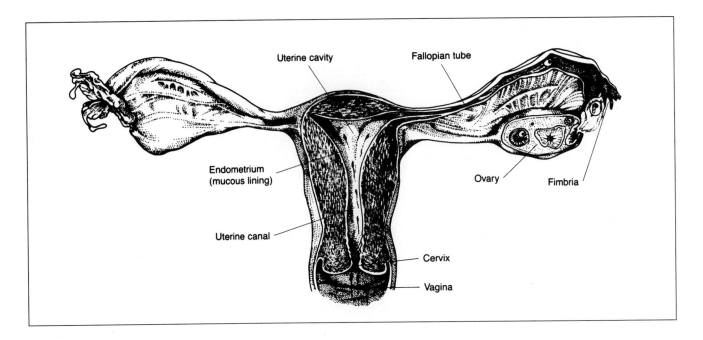

FIGURE 9
A schematic illustration of the development of a fertilized egg. An ovum is shown leaving the ovary. Later it is fertilized in the upper Fallopian tube. The fertilized ovum, or zygote, will divide continuously as it travels through the Fallopian tube to the uterus. It floats in the uterus for several days and then is implanted in the uterus wall.

FIGURE 10
Timing of the menstrual cycle

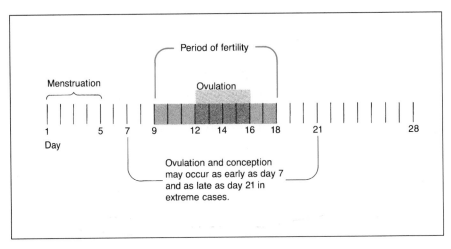

Menstruation
The discharge of blood from the uterus through the vagina; normally occurs every twenty-eight days in women from puberty to menopause

intercourse any time between the ninth and the eighteenth days may cause pregnancy (see Figure 10).

As the egg has been developing, estrogen has also worked to enrich and thicken the uterine lining, or *endometrium* (see Figure 11). Blood engorges the tissue to provide a nourishing environment for the fertilized egg. If fertilization does occur, the fertilized egg will be implanted in the thickened uterine wall, and the menstrual cycle will be suspended for the duration of the pregnancy (see Chapter 12). Usually, however, fertilization does not take place, and the menstrual cycle is completed. Without fertilization the estrogen level falls and the thickened uterine lining, as well as the remnants of the unfertilized egg, are shed as **menstruation** through the cervix and vagina. About two ounces of blood are lost in an average menstrual period. There may be some cramps in the pelvic region as well as general discomfort at this time. Many women also report some fatigue, irritability, depression, and psychic distress just before

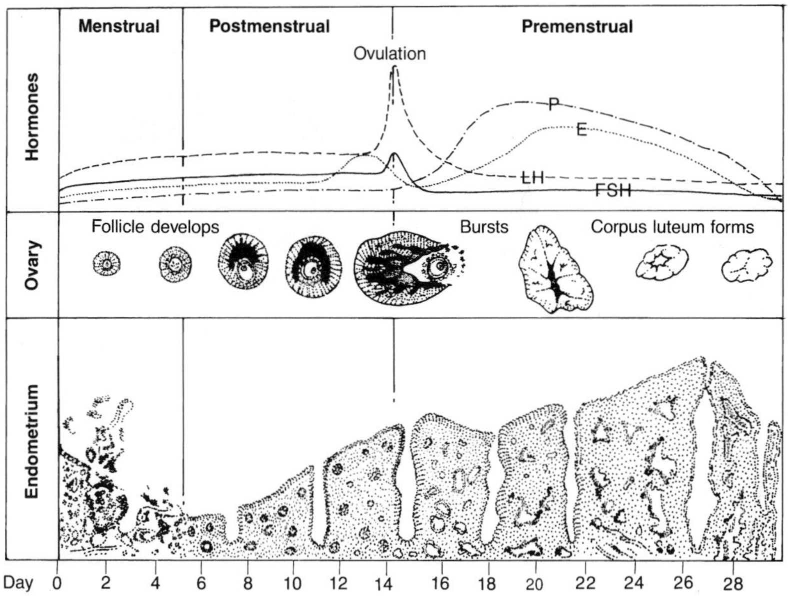

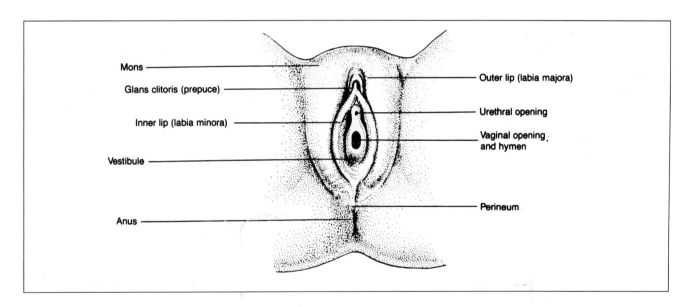

FIGURE 11
Uterine lining buildup

FIGURE 12
External female genitals

menstruation. This premenstrual tension is probably the result of the shifts in hormonal levels. (See pp. 356–357.)

The remaining organs of the female reproductive system, the *vagina*, *clitoris*, and other external genitals (Figure 12) are important to sexual behavior. The vagina is about three and a half inches long when it is relaxed and can stretch considerably during intercourse and childbirth (see Chapter 12). The clitoris is important to female sexuality, being highly erogenous. It is located just under the upper part of the labia minora.

Female Sex Organs

GLOSSARY

Abortion   Induced or spontaneous termination of a pregnancy before the fetus is capable of surviving on its own.

Abstinence   One of several premarital sexual values, based on the belief that sexual intercourse between unmarried men and women is wrong.

Adolescence   The general social as well as biological changes a child experiences in becoming an adult.

Adultery   Voluntary sexual relations between a married person and someone other than their spouse.

Agapé   Greek term for spiritual love.

AIDS   Acquired Immune Deficiency Syndrome.

Alienation   A feeling of not being a part of a society.

Alternative birth center   A special birth center that creates a homelike atmosphere for birth.

Ambivalence   Simultaneous liking and disliking of an object or person.

Amniocentesis   An important prenatal diagnostic tool. A long hollow needle is inserted through the mother's abdomen and into the amniotic sac, where a sample of the amniotic fluid is drawn off. This fluid contains sloughed-off cells from the fetus that may be examined microscopically for signs of disease or birth defects, enabling early treatment to be instituted. This technique may also determine the baby's gender.

Amniotic fluid   The fluid that surrounds and insulates the fetus in the mother's womb.

Anaphrodisiac   A drug or medicine that reduces sexual desire.

Androgen   The dominant male hormone, which is thought to have an effect on aggression.

Androgynous   The quality of having both masculine and feminine personality characteristics.

Aprodisiac   A chemical or other substance used to induce erotic arousal or to relieve impotence or infertility.

Areola   The pigmented area surrounding the nipples of the breasts, a significant erogenous zone for about half of the male and female population.

Artificial insemination   Induction of semen into the vagina or uterus by artificial means.

Bankruptcy   Being financially insolvent, unable to pay one's bills.

Bigamy   Being married to two people at the same time.

Binuclear family   A family that includes children from two nuclear families; occurs when one or both of the divorced parents remarry.

Birth control   Deliberate limitation of the number of children born.

Bisexuality   Having sexual relationships with partners of the same and opposite sex.

Brainstorming   A group problem-solving technique that invalues spontaneous contribution of ideas from all members of the group.

Budget   A plan for balancing expenses with estimated income.

Cesarean section   The delivery of a baby by means of a surgical incision through the mother's abdominal and uterine walls. Cesareans are generally performed when the physical condition of the mother or the fetus is such that one or both might not survive the stress of vaginal delivery.

Child snatching   The taking of children from the custodial spouse by the noncustodial spouse after a divorce.

Clique   A narrow exclusive circle or group of persons and/or friends.

Clitoris   The small organ situated just under the upper portion of the labia minora of the female genitalia. It is the homologue of the male penis, consists of a shaft and a glans, and becomes erect with sexual arousal. It is also the chief organ for erotic arousal in most women.

Cluster family   An artificially contrived family group that meets for companionship, recreation, and other meaningful experiences without the members actually living together.

Cohabitation   A man and woman living together in an intimate relationship without being legally married.

Common-law marriage   A marriage that becomes legally recognized after the woman and man have lived together for some time as though they were wife and husband.

Commune   A group of people who live together by choice rather than because of blood or legal ties. Also referred to as an intentional community.

Conception   Fertilization of the egg by the sperm to start a new human life.

Condom Also known as a "rubber" or "prophylactic," the condom is a thin sheath, usually made of latex, which is rolled over and down the shaft of the erect penis prior to intercourse. While used primarily as a method of contraception, it also protects against venereal disease.

Congenital defect A condition existing at birth or before, caused by the intrauterine environment; as distinguished from a genetic defect.

Consumer Price Index (CPI) A sample of costs of goods and services collected by the Bureau of Labor Statistics, which are then compared with some arbitrarily set base period.

Contraception A deliberate action to prevent fertilization of the ovum as a result of copulation.

Contraceptive Any agent used to prevent conception.

Credit buying Purchasing goods by making payments for them over a period of time.

Cunnilingus Oral contact with female genitalia.

D&C (dilatation and curettage) A procedure usually used to induce an abortion during the first twelve weeks of pregnancy. It involves dilating (stretching) the cervix and scraping away the contents of the uterus with a sharp instrument (curette). The operation requires no incision, recovery is usually rapid, and most patients are in the hospital only overnight. (Used as a diagnostic procedure, a D&C is performed to determine the cause of abnormal menstrual bleeding or to determine the cause of bleeding after the menopause.)

Dating Social interaction and activity with a person of the opposite sex.

DES Abbreviation for diethylstilbestrol, known as the morning after pill. It contains high doses of estrogen and terminates a pregnancy if taken within twenty-four hours of intercourse.

Diaphragm A contraceptive device consisting of a circular piece of thin rubber that is fitted by a physician so that it spans the back of the vagina and covers the cervix. Spermicidal jelly often is used in conjunction with the diaphragm.

Discount interest Interest paid on the full amount initially borrowed even though some of the loan is repaid each month.

Double standard Different standards of appropriate sexual behavior for men than for women; the acceptability for men but not for women of all types of sexual behavior.

Douche Flushing the vagina with water or with a spermicidal agent after intercourse. A relatively unreliable method of contraception.

Dual-career family A marriage in which both spouses pursue their own careers.

Ectopic pregnancy Implantation of the fertilized egg elsewhere than in the uterus.

Ejaculation The expulsion of semen by the male during orgasm.

Embryo The developing organism from the second to the eighth week of pregnancy, characterized by differentiation of organs and tissues into their human form.

Empty-nest stage Period in a marriage that begins when the last child leaves home and continues until either spouse retires or dies.

Enculturation The process of learning the mores, rules, ways, and manners of a given culture.

Endogamy The inclination or the necessity to marry within a particular group.

Engagement The final courtship stage before marriage; characterized by public knowledge of the coming marriage.

Episiotomy A surgical incision made in the mother's perineum during childbirth in order to prevent tearing of the vaginal tissues.

Eros The physical, sexual side of love; termed "Cupid" by the Romans.

Estrogen Often called the "female hormone," it is active in many important ways, such as directing the differentiation of embryonic tissue into female genitalia, directing the differentiation of prenatal brain tissue that governs various female physiological functions, and directing the development of female secondary sexual characteristics at puberty. It is produced chiefly in the ovaries and adrenal cortex of the female and, to a lesser extent, in the testicles and adrenal cortex of the male.

Estrus A regularly occurring period of time when the female of most mammals can become pregnant.

Exogamy The inclination or the necessity to marry outside a particular group.

Extended family A nuclear or polygamous family and the parental generation. The typical extended family includes the husband, wife, their children, and the parents (or aunts/uncles) of the spouses.

Fallopian tubes The two tubes in the female reproductive system which link the ovaries to the uterus. Eggs released from the ovaries move down these tubes to the uterus.

Family A group of two or more persons who are related by blood, marriage, or adoption (U.S. Census definition). The term usually implies the presence of children, a common residence, and economic cooperation.

Family enrichment programs Groups of three to five families who meet together for mutual care and support and for the development of family potential.

Family life cycle A model designed to explain the behavior patterns of married couples. It divides marriage into various stages according to the number, age, and health of a married couple's children.

Family of orientation The family into which an individual is born or adopted.

Family of procreation The family which one begins by marrying and having one's own children.

Family planning Controlling the number and spacing of children through systematic use of contraceptive methods.

Feedback (in communication) Telling the speaker what you think he or she said.

Fellatio Oral contact with male genitalia.

Fetal monitoring Using various instruments to measure the vital signs of the fetus during the birth process.

Fetoscopy   Examining the fetus through a small viewing tube inserted into the mother's uterus.

Fetus   The name given to the developing human organism from eight weeks after conception until birth.

Franchise   The right granted to an individual or group to market a company's goods or services in a particular territory.

Gender   Attitudes and behavior associated with each of the two sexes.

Genes   The subcellular structures within the chromosomes in the cell nucleus that contain the DNA molecules and determine the traits of the differentiating cells of the organism.

Genetic defect   An abnormality in the development of the fetus that is inherited through the genes, as distinguished from a congenital defect.

Genitalia   The external reproductive organs.

Genotype   The underlying genetic trait that, in contrast to the *phenotype*, is not readily observable.

Gonorrhea   A venereal disease caused by gonococci. Unlike syphilis, which typically involves the entire body, gonorrhea usually remains localized in the genitalia and is self-limiting, although it may persist and cause serious and permanent damage, including sterility. Symptoms are common in men, but the disease is often asymptomatic in women and difficult to detect.

Gross National Product (G.N.P.)   Total value of a nation's annual output of goods and services.

Halo effect   The tendency for a first impression to influence subsequent judgments about something.

Hermaphrodite   A person who has both male and female organs, or organs that are indeterminant (such as a clitoris that resembles a penis).

Heterogamy   The mutual attraction and compatibility of persons with opposite and complementary personality traits—for example, dominance-submission, nurturance-dependence, achievement-vicarious.

Home birth   Giving birth at one's home rather than in a hospital.

Homogamy   The strongly practical attraction of persons who share similar objective characteristics, such as race, religion, ethnic group, intelligence, education, social class, age, and interests and skills.

Hysterectomy   A surgical procedure which removes a woman's uterus. While hysterectomies result in sterility for the woman, they are usually conducted because of a malignancy.

Impotence   The inability of a man to experience erection. It may be caused by either physical or psychological factors and is usually temporary.

Incest   Copulation between closely blood-tied relatives. The degree of closeness that is considered incestuous depends on social attitudes, but all societies proscribe sexual relations between parents and children and between siblings.

Infanticide   The deliberate killing of infants as a measure to control population or for some other socially accepted purpose.

Infertility   Inability to produce children.

Inflation   A sustained rise in the average of all prices.

Inflationary recession   A falling off of business activity at the same time that prices are rising.

Intimacy   Experiencing the essence of oneself in intense intellectual, physical, and/or emotional relationships with others.

Intrauterine device   Known as the IUD, it is a small object that a physician inserts into a woman's uterus to prevent conception from occurring.

Investment   Use of money to earn more money, such as putting it in a business or in stocks.

Jealousy   The state of being resentfully suspicious of a loved one's behavior toward a suspected rival.

Labor   Changes in a woman's body as it prepares to deliver a child, consisting mainly of muscle contractions and dilation of the cervix.

Latchkey child   A young child of working parents or parent who must spend part of the day at home unsupervised.

Laparoscopy   A sterilization procedure for females involving the use of a telescope instrument (laparoscope) to locate the Fallopian tubes, which are then cauterized.

Legal separation   A legal decree that forbids cohabitation by husband and wife and provides for separate maintenance and support of the wife and children by the husband. A legally separated couple is still bound by the marital contract and may not remarry.

Macrosociology   Study of social structures and organizations.

Marriage contract   A written agreement between married partners outlining the responsibilities and obligations of each partner.

Masturbation   Any voluntary erotic activity that involves self-stimulation.

Menopause   The cessation of ovulation, menstruation, and fertility in the woman. It usually occurs between ages forty-five and fifty.

Menstruation   The discharge of blood and the unfertilized ovum from the uterus through the vagina; normally occurs every twenty-eight days in women from puberty to menopause.

Mental health   A mode of being in which a person is free of mental problems and/or disease.

Microsociology   Study of the interaction between individuals.

Middlescence   The second adolescence experienced in middle age, usually involving reevaluation of one's life.

Midlife crisis   The questioning of one's worth and values, usually beginning sometime in one's forties or early fifties.

Midwife   A person, usually a woman, trained to assist in childbirth or, in some countries, to perform delivery.

Miscarriage   A spontaneous abortion.

Miscegenation   Marriage or interbreeding between members of different races.

Modeling   Learning vicariously by observing others' behavior.

Monogamy   The state of being married to one person at a time.

Natural childbirth   Birth wherein the parents have learned about the birthing process and participate via exercises such as breathing techniques so as to minimize pain.

Naturalism, myth of   The belief that two people will naturally get along in marriage if they love each other.

No-fault divorce   Divorce proceedings that do not place blame for the divorce on one spouse or the other.

Norm   Accepted social rules for behavior.

Nuclear family   A group of persons, consisting of a married couple and their children, who live by themselves. The children may be natural or adopted by the couple.

Open marriage   A relationship that emphasizes role equality and the freedom for each partner to maximize his or her own potential; may or may not involve extramarital sex.

Oral contraceptive   Hormonal materials (in pill form) that suspend ovulation and therefore prevent conception.

Orgasm   The climax of excitement in sexual activity.

Osteoporosis   A condition characterized by a decrease in bone mass producing bone fragility.

Ovaries   The female sex glands in which the ova (eggs) are formed.

Ovulation   The regular monthly process in the fertile woman whereby an ovarian follicle ruptures and releases a mature ovum (egg).

Ovum   The female reproductive cell (egg) that when fertilized develops into a new member of the same species.

Paracervical anesthesia   Injection of a pain killer, such as Novocain, into the cervix to reduce pain during childbirth.

Phenomenology   The study of how people subjectively experience their environment.

Philos   Greek term for the love found in deep, enduring friendships; a general love of mankind.

Placenta   The organ that connects the fetus to the uterus by means of the umbilical cord.

Polyandry   A form of marriage in which one woman has more than one husband.

Polygamy   Marriage with multiple spouses (as opposed to *monogamy*, with one spouse).

Polygyny   A form of marriage in which one man has more than one wife.

Postpartum depression   Also known as the blues, it is a feeling of depression, after giving birth, characterized by irritability, crying, loss of appetite, and difficulty in sleeping. Such feelings are thought to be a result of numerous physiological and psychological changes that occur as a result of pregnancy, labor, and delivery.

Premature ejaculation   The inability to delay ejaculation as long as the male or his partner wishes.

Prenatal   Existing or occurring before birth.

Prenuptial agreement   An agreement as to duties and obligations made before marriage.

Promiscuous   Having numerous sexual partners.

Propinquity   Nearness in time or place.

Puberty   Biological changes a child goes through to become an adult capable of reproduction.

Recession   A temporary falling off of business activity.

Reconstituted family   A husband and wife, at least one of whom has been married before, and one or more children from previous marriage(s).

Rh factor   An element found in the blood of most people that can adversely affect fetal development if the parents differ on the element (Rh negative versus Rh positive).

Rhythm method   A birth-control method involving avoidance of sexual intercourse when the egg is in the Fallopian tubes. The "calendar method" and the "temperature method" are used to predict this time. The rhythm method is a relatively unreliable contraceptive technique.

Role   Particular type of behavior one is expected to exhibit when occupying a certain place in a group

Role equity   Freedom to establish roles within a relationship that allow each person to fulfill his or her own capabilities to the greatest possible degree with acceptance by the partner.

Romantic love   Love at first sight, based on the ideas that there is only one true love and that love is the most important criterion for marriage.

Rooming-in   The practice of placing the newborn in the mother's room after delivery so that the mother (and father) can care for it.

Saline abortion   An abortion-inducing procedure in which a salt solution is injected into the amniotic sac to kill the fetus, which is then expelled via uterine contractions.

Self-actualization   The process of developing one's cognitive, emotional, social, and physical potential.

Semen   The secretion of the male reproductive organs that is ejaculated from the penis during orgasm and contains the sperm cells.

Sensitivity training   Training in learning to understand and be more aware of one's body, its feelings and functioning.

Serial marriage   The process of having a series of marriages, one after the other.

Sex therapy   Therapy of any kind designed to help persons overcome sexual problems.

Sexually transmitted disease (STD)   Any contagious disease communicated mainly by sexual interaction.

Simple interest   Interest paid only on the unpaid balance of a loan.

Socialization   The process of a person's learning—from parents, peers, social institutions, and other sources—the skills, knowledge, and roles necessary for competent and socially acceptable behavior in the society.

Spermaticides   The chemical substances that destroy or immobilize sperm and are used as contraceptives.

Stepparent   The husband or wife of one's parent by a later marriage.

Sterility   The permanent inability to reproduce.

Sterilization   Any procedure (usually surgical) by which an individual is made incapable of reproduction.

Surrogate mother A woman who becomes pregnant and gives birth to a child for another woman who is incapable of giving birth.

Swinging Agreement by married couples to swap mates sexually.

Syphilis A venereal disease caused by a microorganism called a *spirochete*. Syphilis goes through four stages, each with separate and distinct characteristics, and can involve every part of the body. It is transmitted by contact of mucous membrane or broken skin with an infectious syphilitic lesion.

Testosterone An important component of the male sex hormone androgen. It is responsible for inducing and maintaining the male secondary sexual characteristics.

Transsexualism A compulsion or obsession to become a member of the opposite sex through surgical changes.

Transvestism A sexual deviation characterized by a compulsive desire to wear garments of the opposite sex.

Trial marriage Cohabitation between two people who intend to marry.

Tubal ligation A sterilization procedure for females in which the Fallopian tubes are cut or tied.

Ultrasound Sound waves directed at the fetus that yield a visual picture of the fetus; used to detect potential problems in fetal development.

Umbilical cord A flexible cordlike structure connecting the fetus to the placenta and through which the fetus is fed and waste products are discharged.

Uterus The hollow, pear-shaped organ in females within which the fetus develops; the womb.

Vacuum aspiration An abortion-inducing procedure in which the contents of the uterus are removed by suction.

Vasectomy A sterilization procedure for males involving the surgical cutting of the vas deferens.

Virginity Not having experienced sexual intercourse.

Withdrawal Removing the penis from the vagina before ejaculation. A relatively unreliable method of contraception.

REFERENCES

Abbott, D. A.; Berry, M.; and Meredith, W. H. 1990. "Religious Belief and Practice: A Potential Asset in Helping Families." *Family Relations* (October): 443–448.

Abel, E. 1984. "Opiates and Sex." *Journal of Psychoactive Drugs* 16: 205–216.

Abrahamse, A. F.; Morrison, P. A.; and Waite, L. S. 1988. *Beyond Stereotypes: Who Becomes a Single Teenage Mother?* Santa Monica, Calif: Rand Corporation, January.

Adams, B. 1986. *The Family: A Sociological Interpretation.* New York: Harcourt, Brace and Jovanovich.

Addiego, F., et al. 1980. "Female Ejaculation?" *Medical Aspects of Human Sexuality* (August): 99–103.

Adler, T. 1989. "Sex-based Differences Declining, Study Shows." *APA Monitor.* Washington, D.C.: American Psychological Association, March 6.

Aldous, J., and Dumon, W. 1990. "Family Policy in the 1980s: Controversy and Consensus." *Journal of Marriage and the Family* (November): 1136–1151.

Aldous, J.; Ganey, R.; Scott, T.; and Marsh, L. 1991. "Families and Inflation: Who Was Hurt in the Last High-inflation Period?" *Journal of Marriage and the Family* (February): 123–134.

American Psychologist. 1989. "Special Issue: Children and Their Development: Knowledge Base, Research Agenda, and Social Policy Application." Washington, D.C.: American Psychological Association, February.

Amick, R. E., and Calhoun, K. S. 1987. "Resistence to Sexual Aggression: Personality, Attitudinal and Situational Factors." *Archives of Sexual Behavior* 16: 153–163.

Anderson, B. M. (C.L.U.) 1988. Personal correspondence. 2290 Eastex Freeway, Beaumont, Texas.

Anderson, D., and Collins, P. 1989. "The Impact on Children's Education: Influence on Cognitive Development." In "Watching T.V., Children Do Learn," edited by S. Landers. *APA Monitor.* Washington, D.C.: American Psychological Association, March 25.

Anson, D. 1989. "Marital Status and Women's Health Revisited: The Importance of a Proximate Adult." *Journal of Marriage and the Family* (February): 185–194.

Archer, J. 1984. "Gender Roles as Developmental Pathways." *British Journal of Social Psychology* 23: 245–256.

Archer, J., and Lloyd, B. 1985. *Sex and Gender.* Cambridge, England: Cambridge University Press.

Arditti, J. 1990. "Noncustodial Fathers: An Overview of Policy and Resources." *Family Relations* (October): 460–465.

Associated Press. 1980. "No Differences Seen in Childbirth Methods." *Santa Barbara News Press* (April 15): A–5.
———. 1992. "Ownership Rate of Homes Stabilizes." *Santa Barbara News Press* (July 7): A–4.
———. 1992. "Study: Fertility Drugs Contribute to Rise in Costly Multiple Births." *Santa Barbara News Press* (July 15).

Avery, C. S. 1989. "How Do You Build Intimacy in an Age of Divorce?" *Psychology Today* (May): 27–31.

Bachrach, C. A. 1986. "Adoption Plans, Adopted Children, and Adoptive Mothers." *Journal of Marriage and the Family* (May): 243–253.

Bachrack, C.; London, K.; and Maza, P. 1991. "On the Path to Adoption: Adoption Seeking in the United States: 1988." *Journal of Marriage and the Family* (August): 705–718.

Bader, E. 1981. *Do Marriage Preparation Programs Really Help?* Paper presented at the National Council on Family Relations Annual Conference at Milwaukee, Wisconsin.

Baker, L. 1983. "In My Opinion: The Sexual Revolution in Perspective." *Family Relations* (April): 297–300.

Baker, R. 1982. *Growing Up.* New York: New American Library.

Bandura, A. 1969. *Principles of Behavior Modification.* New York: Holt.

Baptiste, D. A. 1987. "How Parents Intensify Sexual Feelings between Stepsiblings." In *Making Remarriage Work,* edited by J. Belovitch, 91–94. Lexington, Mass.: D. C. Heath.

Barkley, S. C. 1989. "Drug Use during Pregnancy Exacts an Unconscionable Toll from Unborn." *Santa Barbara News Press* (April 30): A–17.

Barnett, R., and Baruch, G. 1983. "Women Still Do the Majority of Childcare and Housework." Report on their study by Susan Cunningham (staff writer) as found in *APA Monitor.* Washington, D.C.: American Psychological Association (November): 16.

Barnhill, L. 1979. "Healthy Family Systems." *Family Coordinator* (January): 94–100.

Barrett, C., and Noble, H. 1973. "Mother's Anxieties versus the Effects of Long-distance Move on Children." *Journal of Marriage and the Family* (May): 181–188.

Barrett-Connor, E. 1986. "Postmenopausal Estrogens—Current Prescribing Patterns of San Diego Gynecologists." *Western Journal of Medicine* 6: 620–621.

Bayme, S. 1990. "Conclusion: Family Values and Policies in the 1990s (part 2)." In *Rebuilding the Nest,* edited by D. Blankenhorn,

S. Bayme, and J. Elshtain. Milwaukee, Wis: Family Service America.

Beck, S. H., and Beck, R. W. 1984. "The Formation of Extended Households during Middle Age." *Journal of Marriage and the Family* (May): 277–287.

Bell, R. 1981. *Worlds of Friendship*. Beverly Hills, Calif.: Sage Publications, 131–150.

Bellah, R., et al. 1985. *Habits of the Heart: Individualism and Commitment in American Life*. Berkeley, Calif.: University of California Press.

Belovitch, J. 1987. *Making Remarriage Work*. Lexington, Mass.: Lexington Books, D. C. Heath, G & R. Publications.

Belsky, J., and Pensky, E. 1988 "Marital Change across the Transition to Parenthood." *Marriage and Family Review* 12: 133–156.

Belsky, J.; Lang, M. E.; and Rovine, M. 1985. "Stability and Change in Marriage across the Transition to Parenthood: A Second Study." *Journal of Marriage and the Family* (November): 855–865.

Belsky, J.; Learner, J.; and Spanier, G. B. 1984. *The Children in the Family*. Reading, Mass.: Addison-Wesley.

Belsky, J.; Spanier, G. B.; and Rovine, M. 1983. "Stability and Change in Marriage across the Transition to Parenthood." *Journal of Marriage and the Family* (August): 567–577.

Bengtson, V. L. 1985. "Diversity and Symbolism in Grandparental Roles." In *Grandparenting*, edited by Y. L. Bengtson and J. F. Robertson, 11–15. Beverly Hills, Calif.: Sage Publications.

Benin, M., and Agostinelli, J. 1988. "Husbands' and Wives' Satisfaction with the Division of Labor." *Journal of Marriage and the Family* (May): 349–361.

Bennett, N.; Blanc, A.; and Bloom, D. 1988. "Commitment and the Modern Union: Assessing the Link between Premarital Cohabitation and Subsequent Marital Stability." *American Sociological Review* 53: 997–1008.

Berardo, D. H.; Shehan, C. L.; and Leslie, G. R. 1987. "A Residue of Transition: Jobs, Careers, and Spouses' Time in Housework." *Journal of Marriage and the Family* (May): 381–390.

Berelson, B. 1972. *The Population Council Annual Report*. New York: Population Council.

Berger, K. S. 1986. *The Developing Person through Childhood and Adolescence*. New York: Worth.

Berk-Fenstermaker, S. 1985. *The Gender Factory: The Apportionment of Work in American Households*. New York: Plenum Press.

Berman, C. 1987. "The Cold Facts about Remarriage: Money, Prenuptial Agreements and Wills." In *Making Remarriage Work*, edited by J. Belovitch, 15–17. Lexington, Mass.: D.C. Heath.

Beutler, I. F.; Burr, W. R.; Barr, K.; and Herrin, D. A. 1989. "The Family Realm: Theoretical Contributions for Understanding Its Uniqueness." *Journal of Marriage and the Family* (August): 805–816.

Bianchi, S. 1990. "America's Children: Mixed Prospects." *Population Bulletin*. Washington, D.C.: Population Reference Bureau, June.

Biddle, B. J. 1976. *Role Theory: Expectations, Identities and Behaviors*. Chicago: Dryden.

Bilbrey, D. 1987. "Second Families Go Unprotected by the Law." In *Making Remarriage Work*, edited by J. Belovitch, 79–81. Lexington, Mass.: D.C. Heath.

Blankenhorn, D. 1990. "American Family Dilemmas." In *Rebuilding the Nest*, edited by D. Blankenhorn, et al. Milwaukee, Wis.: Family Service America.

Blankenhorn D., et al. 1990. *Rebuilding the Nest: A New Commitment to the American Family*. Milwaukee, Wis.: Family Service America.

Blieszner, R., and Alley, J. 1990. "Family Caregiving for the Elderly: An Overview of Resources." *Family Relations* (January): 97–102.

Blizard, D. A. 1983. "Sex Differences in Running-Wheel Behavior in the Rat: The Inductive and Activational Effects of Gonadal Hormones." *Animal Behavior* 31: 378–384.

Blumstein, P., and Schwartz, P. 1983. *American Couples*. New York: Pocket Books.

Bohannan, P. 1984. *All the Happy Families*, chap. 7. New York: McGraw-Hill.

Bolger, N.; DeLongis, A.; Kessler, R.; and Wethington, E. 1989. "The Contagion of Stress across Multiple Roles." *Journal of Marriage and the Family* (February): 175–183.

Bond, M., and Stillblower, L. 1988. Reported in the *Santa Barbara News Press* (February 14): G–13.

Boss, P. 1988. *Family Stress Management*. Newbury Park, Calif.: Sage Publications.

Boston Women's Health Book Collective. 1992. *The New Our Body, Ourselves*. New York: Simon & Schuster, originally published 1973, 1976, 1984.

Boulding, E. 1983. "Familia Faber: The Family as Maker of the Future." *Journal of Marriage and the Family* (May): 257–266.

Bouvier, L. F., and Gardner, R. W. 1986. "Immigration to the U.S.: The Unfinished Story." *Population Bulletin* 41, Washington, D.C.: Population Reference Bureau (November): 17.

Bowe, C. 1986. "What Are Men Like Today?" *Cosmopolitan* (May).

Brecher, E. M., and the editors of Consumer Reports Books. 1984. *Love, Sex and Aging: A Consumer Union Report*. Boston: Little Brown.

Bretschneider, S. G., and McCoy, N. L. 1988. "Sexual Interest and Behavior in Healthy 80- to 101-year-olds." *Archives of Sexual Behavior* 17 (2): 109–129.

Brinkerhoff, D. B., and White, L. K. 1988. *Sociology*. St. Paul, Minn.: West.

Brinley, M. 1984. "Should You Have a Baby?" *McCall's* (January): 28.

Broman, C. 1988. "Household Work and Family Life Satisfaction among Blacks." *Journal of Marriage and the Family* (August): 743–748.

———. 1991. "Gender, Work, Family Roles and Psychological Well-Being of Blacks." *Journal of Marriage and the Family* (May): 509–520.

Browder, S. 1988. "Is Living Together a Good Idea?" *New Woman* (June): 120, 122, 124.

Brubaker, T. 1990. "Family in Later Life: A Burgeoning Research Area." *Journal of Marriage and the Family* (November): 959–981.

Brubaker, T. H. 1985. *Later Life Families*. Beverly Hills, Calif.: Sage Publications.

Buehler, C. 1989. "Influential Factors and Equity Issues in Divorce Settlements." *Family Relations* (January): 76–82.

Bumpass, L. 1989. "Marriage Researchers Question Cohabitation." *Santa Barbara News Press* (June 9): A–10.

Bumpass, L., and Sweet, J. 1988. *National Survey of Households*. Madison, Wis.: University of Wisconsin.

Bumpass, L. L.; Sweet, J. A.; James, A.; and Cherlin, A. 1991. "The Role of Cohabitation in Declining Rates of Marriage." *Journal of Marriage and the Family* 53 (November): 913–927.

Burke, P.; Stets, J.; and Pirog-Good, M. 1988. "Gender Identity, Self Esteem, and Physical and Sexual Abuse in Dating Relationships." *Social Psychology Quarterly* 51: 272–285.

Burkett, L. 1989. *Debt-Free Living: How to Get Out of Debt (And Stay Out)*. Chicago: Moody Press.

Burns, A. 1984. "Perceived Causes of Marital Breakdown and Conditions of Life." *Journal of Marriage and the Family* (May): 279–287.

Burr. W. 1990. "Beyond I-Statements in Family Communication." *Family Relations* (July): 266–275.

Business Week. 1985. "Women at Work." (January 28): 80–85.

Buunk, B., and Bringle, R. G. 1987. "Jealousy in Love Relationships." In *Intimate Relationships: Development, Dynamics and Deterioration*, edited by D. Perlman and S. Duck, 123–147. Newbury Park, Calif.: Sage Publications.

Calderone, M. S. 1972. "Love, Sex, Intimacy, and Aging as a Life Style." In *Sex, Love, and Intimacy–Whose Life Styles?*, edited by M. Calderone. New York: SIECUS.

Calderone, M. S., and Johnson, E. W. 1989. *The Family Book about Sexuality.* New York: Harper & Row.

Campbell, A. 1981. *A Sense of Well-being in America.* New York: McGraw-Hill.

Canfield, E. 1979. "On The Sex Education Frontiers." Talk given at the California Council on Family Relations Annual Conference, October 18–20, at Anaheim, California.

Caplan, P. J., et al. 1985. "Do Sex-related Differences in Spatial Abilities Exist?" *American Psychologist* (July): 879–888.

Carlson v. Olson. 1977. 256 N.W.2d 249.

Carlson, B. E. 1987. "Dating Violence: A Research Review and Comparison with Spouse Abuse." *Social Casework* 68, no. 1 (January): 16–23.

Carlson, M. 1990. "It's Our Turn." *Time* (Fall): 16.

Carnes, P. 1986. "Sex Can Be an Addiction." *SIECUS Report* (July): 14.

Cash, T. F.; Winstead, B.; and Janda, L. H. 1986. "The Great American Shape-up." *Psychology Today* (April): 30–37.

Casler, L. 1969. "This Thing Called Love." *Psychology Today.* December.

Catton, T. 1991, "Child-care Problems: An Obstacle to Work." *Monthly Labor Review.* Washington, D.C.: U.S. Department of Labor (October): 3–9.

CBS News/New York Times Poll. 1989. "Attitudes towards Marriage." February 13.

CBS Reports. 1986. "Vanishing Families: Crises in Black America." January 25.

Chafetz, J. 1974. *Masculine/Feminine or Human?* Itasca, Ill.: Peacock.

Chamberlin, C. R. 1989. "Joint Custody Can Work, But Not in Every Situation." *Los Angeles Daily Journal* (February 7).

Chance, P. 1987. "The Chinese and the Eskimos." *Psychology Today* (July): 44–47.

———. 1988. "The Trouble With Love." *Psychology Today* (February): 22–23.

Chapman, S. F. 1991. "Attachment and Adolescent Adjustment to Parental Remarriage." *Family Relations* (April): 232–237.

Chasnoff, I. J., et al. 1985. "Cocaine Use in Pregnancy." *New England Journal of Medicine* (September 12): 666–669.

Cherlin, A., and Furstenberg, F. F. 1985. "Styles and Strategies of Grandparenting." In *Grandparenthood*, edited by V. L. Bengtson and J. F. Robertson, 97–116. Beverly Hills, Calif.: Sage Publications.

Chilman, C. S. 1991. "Working Poor Families: Trends, Causes, Effects and Suggested Policies." *Family Relations* (April): 191–198.

China Daily. 1986. "IUD Widely Used." March 15.

Chira, S. 1984. "Town Experiment Cuts TV." *New York Times* (February 11).

Christensen, D.; Dahl, C.; and Rettig, K. 1990. "Noncustodial Mothers and Child Support: Examining the Larger Content." *Family Relations* (October): 388–394.

Clabes, J. 1989. "Caught in the Middle: Sandwich Generation." *Santa Barbara News Press* (May 1): B–10.

Clark, H. H. 1980. *Cases and Problems on Domestic Relations.* 3d ed. St. Paul, Minn.: West.

Clark, J. R. 1961. *The Importance of Being Perfect.* New York: McKay.

Clarke-Steward, K. 1989. "Infant Day Care." *American Psychologist* (February): 266–273.

Clayton, R., and Bakemeier, J. L. 1980. "Premarital Sex in the Seventies." *Journal of Marriage and the Family* (November): 759–775.

Client's Monthly Alert. 1990. "The High Cost of Raising Junior." A bulletin sent out by many tax accountants and consultants to their clients. October.

Cline, F. 1978. *Understanding and Treating the Severely Disturbed Child.* Evergreen, Colo.: Evergreen Consultants in Human Behavior.

Close, H. 1968. "To the Child: On Parenting." *Voices* (Spring).

Cochran, M. M., and Gunnarsson, L. 1985. "A Follow-up Study of Group Day Care and Family-based Childrearing Patterns." *Journal of Marriage and the Family* (May): 297–309.

Coleman, M., and Ganong, L. 1985. "Remarriage Myths: Implications for the Helping Professions." *Journal of Counseling and Development* (October): 116–120.

———. 1990. "Remarriage and Stepfamily Research in the 1980s: Increased Interest in an Old Family Form." *Journal of Marriage and the Family* (November): 925–940.

Collins, B. 1990. "Pornography and Social Policy: Three Feminist Approaches." *Journal of Women and Social Work* 5, (4): 8–26.

Collins, J. G., and Thornberry, O. T. 1989. "Health Characteristics of Workers by Occupation and Sex: United States, 1983–1985." Advance Data from Vital and Health Statistics, no. 168. DHHS pub. no. (PHS) 89–1250. National Center for Health Statistics. Hyattsville, Md.: U.S. Department of Health and Human Services, April 25.

Condron, M. K. 1988. "A Preliminary Examination of the Pornographic Experience of Sex Offenders, Paraphiliacs, Sexual Dysfunction Patients and Controls based on Meese Commission Recommendations." *Journal of Sex and Marital Therapy* 14 (4): 285–298.

Consumer Reports. 1989. "Can You Rely on Condoms?" (March): 135–141.

———. 1992. "Has Our Living Standard Stalled?" (June): 392–393.

Cooke, B. 1991. "Thinking and Knowledge Underlying Expertise in Parenting: Comparisons between expert and Novice Mothers." *Family Relations* (January): 3–13.

Coombs, R. A. 1991. "A Healthy Marriage." *American Demographics* (November): 40–43.

Coon, D. 1992. *Introduction to Psychology.* St. Paul, Minn.: West.

Corder, J., and Stephan, C. 1984. "Females' Combination of Work and Family Roles: Adolescent's Aspirations." *Journal of Marriage and the Family* (May): 391–402.

Costa, P. T., and McCrae, R. R. 1985. "Hypochondriasis, Neuroticism and Aging." *American Psychologist* (January): 19–28.

Covi, R. B., and Robinson, B. E. 1985. "Stepfamilies: A Review of the Literature with Suggestions for Practitioners." *Journal of Counseling and Development* (October): 121–125.

Covington, T. R., and McClendon, J. F. 1987. *Sex Care*. New York: Pocket Books.

Coward, R.; Mullens, R.; and Christopherson, V. 1990. "Family Care-givers." *Family Relations* (January): 14–67.

Cox, F. 1988. *Premarital Sex and Religion*. Unpublished study. Santa Barbara, Calif.: Santa Barbara City College.

———. 1993. *The AIDS Booklet*. Dubuque, Iowa: William C. Brown.

Crawford, L. E. 1988. "Comparable Worth: Precedent or Appeasement." *The Humanist* (March/April).

Crooks, R., and Baur, K. 1987. *Our Sexuality*. 3d ed. Menlo Park, Calif.: Benjamin/Cummings.

Crosbie-Burnett, M. 1984. "The Centrality of the Step Relationship: A Challenge to Family Theory and Practice." *Family Relations* 33: 459–464.

Crosby, J. F. 1980. "A Critique of Divorce Statistics and Their Interpretation." *Family Relations* (January): 51–58.

———. 1985. *Reply to Myth: Perspectives on Intimacy*. New York: Wiley.

———. 1991. *Illusion and Disillusion: The Self in Love and Marriage*. Belmont, Calif.: Wadsworth.

Cross, R. J. 1989. "What Doctors and Others Need to Know: Six Rules on Human Sexuality and Aging." *SIECUS Report* 17 (January/February): 14–16.

Cunniff, J. 1991. "Forecast on Prices Shocker." *Santa Barbara News Press* (December 30): B–1.

Curran, D. 1983. *Traits of a Healthy Family*. New York: Ballintine.

Danziger, S., and Gottschalk, P. 1986. "Poverty and the Underclass." Testimony before the House Select Committee on Hunger, August 5.

Darling, C. A.; Kallen, D. S.; and VanDusen, J. E. 1984. "Sex in Transition, 1900–1980." *Journal of Youth and Adolescence* 13, no. 5.

Davis, K. E. 1985. "Near and Dear: Friendship and Love Compared." *Psychology Today* (February): 22–28, 30.

Dawson, D. 1991. "Family Structure and Children's Health and Well-being: Data from the 1988 National Health Interview Survey of Child Health." *Journal of Marriage and the Family* (August): 573–584.

DeMaris, A. 1984. "A Comparison of Remarriages with First Marriages on Satisfaction in Marriage and Its Relationship to Prior Cohabitation." *Family Relations* 33 (July): 443–449.

DeMaris, A., and Leslie, G. R. 1984. "Cohabitation with the Future Spouse: Its Influence upon Marital Satisfaction and Communication." *Journal of Marriage and the Family* 46 (February): 77–84.

Demming, Bill. 1992. Personal telephone conversation. Washington, D.C.: Bureau of Labor Statistics, April 30.

Denhan, T., and Smith, C. 1989. "The Influence of Grandparents on Grandchildren: A Review of the Literature and Resources." *Family Relations* (July): 345–350.

Dick-Read, G. 1972. *Childbirth without Fear*. 4th ed. New York: Harper & Row.

Dietsch, R. 1989. "Some Small Businesses Spawn More Millionaires." *Santa Barbara News Press* (March 12): F-4.

Dix, C. 1985. *The New Mother Syndrome: Coping with Postpartum Depression*. New York: Doubleday.

Doherty, W. J., and Lester, M. E. 1981. "Casualties of Marriage Encounter Weekends." *Family Therapy News* 13: 4, 9.

Dolgin, J. L. 1990. "Surrogacy Agreements: Valid Contracts or a Vi-

olation of Women's Dignity?" *Daily Journal Report* no. 90–12 (December 28): 2–18.

Donnelly, B., and Voydanoff, P. 1991. "Factors Associated with Releasing for Adoption among Adolescent Mothers." *Family Relations* (October): 404–410.

Dreskin, W., and Dreskin, W. 1983. *The Daycare Decision: What's Best for Your Child*. New York: M. Evans.

Duberman, L. 1974, 1977. *Marriage and Its Alternatives*. New York: Praeger.

Dudley, J. R. 1991. "Increasing Our Understanding of Divorced Fathers Who Have Infrequent Contact with Their Children." *Family Relations* (July): 279–285.

Durden-Smith, J., and DeSimone, D. 1982. "Is There a Superior Sex?" *Playboy* (May).

Earle, R. H. 1990. "Sexual Addiction: Understanding and Treating the Phenomenon." *Contemporary Family Therapy* 12 (2): 89–104.

Ehrenreich, B. 1983. *The Hearts of Men*. New York: Doubleday.

———. 1990. *Time* (Fall): 15.

Ehrhardt, S. 1989. "Wonder of Birth Reborn among Swirl of Controversy." *Santa Barbara News Press* (April 30): D–8.

———. 1990a. "Waterbirth: Hospital vs. Home Central to Debate." *Santa Barbara News Press* (February 18): D–1.

———. 1990b. "Waterbirth: Option Making Steady Progress." *Santa Barbara News Press* (February 18): D–1.

Ekman, P. 1985. *Telling Lies: Clues to Deceit in the Marketplace, Politics and Marriage*. New York: Norton.

Elkin, M. 1980. "Drawing Individual and Family Strengths from the Divorce Process." A talk given to the California Council on Family Relations Annual Conference, September 26–28, at Santa Barbara, California.

English, D. V. 1981. "The War against Choice: Inside the Abortion Movement." *Mother Jones* (February/March).

Erikson, E. H. 1963. *Childhood and Society*. 2d ed. New York: Norton.

Ettinger, B., et al. 1985. "Long-term Estrogen Replacement Prevents Bone Loss and Fractures." *Annals of Internal Medicine* 102: 319–29.

Etzioni, A. 1983. *An Immodest Agenda: Rebuilding America before the 21st Century*. New York: McGraw-Hill.

Fabes, R.; Wilson, P.; and Christopher, F. 1989. "A Time to Reexamine the Role of Television in Family Life." *Family Relations* (July): 337–341.

Faludi, S. 1991. *BackLash: The Undeclared War against Women*. New York: Crown Publishers.

Family Relations. 1989. "Child Care and the Family. Participation of Fathers. Single Parents." Minneapolis, Minn.: National Council on Family Relations, October.

Farel, A. 1980. "Effects of Preferred Maternal Roles, Maternal Employment, and Sociodemographic Status on School Adjustment and Competence." *Child Development* 51: 1179–1186.

Federal Bureau of Investigation. 1991. Supplemental Homicide Reporting System as found in *Health: United States 1990*. DHHS pub. no. (PHS) 91–1232. Hyattsville, Md.: National Center for Health Statistics (March): 17.

Fehr, B. 1988. "Prototype Analysis of the Concepts of Love and Commitment." *Journal of Personality and Social Psychology* 55(4): 557–579.

Ferreiro, B. 1990. "Presumption of Joint Custody: A Family Policy Dilemma." *Family Relations* (October): 420–426.

Final Report of the Attorney General's Commission on Pornography. 1986. Nashville, Tenn.: Rutledge Hill.

Fine, M. A. 1989. "A Social Science Perspective on Stepfamily Law: Suggestions for Legal Reform." *Family Relations* (January): 53–58.

Fine, M. A., and Fine, D. R. 1992. "Recent Changes in Laws Affecting Stepfamilies: Suggestions for Legal Reform." *Family Relations* (July): 334–340.

Finkelhor, D.; Hataling, G.; and Sedlak, A. 1991. "Children Abducted by Family Members: A National Household Survey of Incidence and Episode Characteristics." *Journal of Marriage and the Family* (August): 805–817.

Finley, N. 1989. "Theories of Family Labor as Applied to Gender Differences in Caregiving for Elderly Patients." *Journal of Marriage and the Family* (February): 79–86.

Fortune. 1988. "The Invincible Grays." (March 28): 155–156.

Fowles, J. 1992. *Why Viewers Watch: A Reappraisal of Television's Effects.* Newbury Park, Calif.: Sage Publications.

Francoeur, R. T. 1991. *Becoming a Sexual Person.* New York: Macmillan.

Freiberg, P. 1991. "Killing by Kids Epidemic Forecast." *APA Monitor* (April): 1, 31.

Friedan, B. 1963. *The Feminine Mystique.* New York: Dell.

———. 1981. *The Second State.* New York: Summit Books.

Friedman, J. T. 1992. Personal correspondence. Member of the Law Offices of Davis, Friedman, Zavett, Kane and MacRae. Chicago, Illinois: May 27.

Frieze, I., et al. 1978. *Women and Sex Roles.* New York: W. W. Norton.

Fromm, E. 1956. *The Art of Loving.* New York: Harper and Row. Reprinted by Bantam Books, 1970.

Furstenburg, F., Jr. 1988. "Marital Disruptions, Child Custody and Visitation." In *Child Support: From Debt Collection to Social Policy,* edited by S. Kamerman and A. Kahn, 277–305. Beverly Hills, Calif.: Sage Publications.

———. 1991. "As the Pendulum Swings: Teenage Childbearing and Social Concern." *Family Relations* (April): 127–138.

———. 1992. "Teenage Childbearing and Cultural Rationality: A Thesis in Search of Evidence." *Family Relations* (April): 239–243.

Furstenberg, F., Jr., and Spanier, G. 1984, 1987. *Recycling the Family: Remarriage after Divorce.* Beverly Hills, Calif.: Sage Publications.

Galbraith, J. K. 1958. *The Affluent Society.* Boston: Houghton Mifflin.

Gallagher, W. 1988. "Sex and Hormones." *Atlantic Monthly* (March): 77–82.

Galvin, K. M., and Brommel, B. J. 1986. *Family Communication: Cohesion and Change.* 2d ed. Glenview, Ill.: Scott, Foresman. 1st ed. 1982.

Ganong, L. H., and Coleman, M. A. 1984. "The Effects of Remarriage on Children: A Review of the Empirical Research." *Family Relations* (July): 389–406.

———. 1989. "Preparing for Remarriage: Anticipating the Issues, Seeking Solutions." *Family Relations* (January): 28–39.

Gardner, J. W. 1981. *Self-Renewal: The Individual and the Innovative Society.* Rev. ed. New York: Norton.

Gardner, R. W.; Roley, B.; and Smith, P. C. 1985. *Asian Americans: Growth, Change and Diversity* 40, no. 4. Washington, D.C.: Population Reference Bureau, October.

Garland, D. R. 1983. *Working with Couples for Marriage Enrichment.* San Francisco: Jossey-Bass.

Gellis, R., and Conte, J. 1991. "Domestic Violence and Sexual Abuse of Children: A Review of Research in the Eighties." In *Contemporary Families: Looking Forward, Looking Back,* edited by A. Booth. Minneapolis, Minn.: National Council on Family Relations.

General Mills. 1977. "Raising Children in a Changing Society." In *The General Mills American Family Report, 1976–1977.* Minneapolis, Minn.: General Mills.

Geronimus, A. T. 1991. "Teenage Childbearing and Social and Reproductive Disadvantage: The Evolution of Complex Questions and the Demise of Simple Answers." *Family Relations* (October): 463–471.

———. 1992. "Teenage Childbearing and Social Disadvantage: Unprotected Discourse." *Family Relations* (April): 244–248.

Gibbs, N. 1989. "The Baby Chase." *Time* (October 9): 86–95.

Giblin, P.; Sprenkle, D.; and Sheehan, R. 1985. "Enrichment Outcome Research: A Meta Analysis of Premarital, Marital, and Family Interventions." *Journal of Marital and Family Therapy* 11: 257–271.

Giles-Sims, J., and Crosbie-Burnett, M. 1989. "Adolescent Power in Stepfather Families: A Test of Normative-Resource Theory." *Journal of Marriage and the Family* (November): 1065–1078.

———. 1989. "Stepfamily Research: Implications for Policy, Clinical Interventions, and Further Research." *Family Relations* (January): 19–23.

Glenn, N. 1990. "Quantitative Research on Marital Quality in the 1980s: A Critical Review." *Journal of Marriage and the Family* (November): 818–831.

Glenn, N. D. 1991. "Quantitative Research on Marital Quality in the 1980s: A Critical Review." In *Contemporary Families: Looking Forward, Looking Back,* edited by A. Booth. Minneapolis, Minn.: National Council on Family Relations.

Glick, P. 1955. "The Life Cycle of the Family." *Marriage and Family Living.* 17: 3–9.

———. 1984. "Prospective Changes in Marriage, Divorce, and Living Arrangements." *Journal of Family Issues* 1.

———. 1989. "The Family Life Cycle and Social Change." *Family Relations* (April): 123–129.

———. 1989. "Remarried Families, Stepfamilies and Stepchildren." *Family Relations* (January): 24–27.

Glick, P., and Spanier, G. 1980. "Married and Unmarried Cohabitation in the United States." *Journal of Marriage and the Family* 43 (February): 19–30.

Glick, P., and Lin, S. L. 1986. "More Young Adults Are Living with Their Parents: Who Are They?" *Journal of Marriage and the Family* (February): 107–112.

Godwin, D. D. 1990. "Literature and Resource Review Essay." *Family Relations* (April): 221–228.

Goertzel, V., and Goertzel, M. 1962. *Cradles of Imminence.* Boston: Little, Brown.

Goldstine, D., et al. 1977. *The Dance-Away Lover and Other Roles We Play in Love, Sex, and Marriage.* New York: Morrow.

Goleman, D. 1978. "Special Abilities of the Sexes: Do They Begin In the Brain?" *Psychology Today* (November).

Goodman, E. 1991. "Defining the Limits of Surrogate Mothers." *Santa Barbara News Press* (August 9): A–15.

Gordon, M., and Miller, R. L. 1984. "Going Steady in the 1980s: Exclusive Relationships in Six Connecticut High Schools." *Sociology and Social Research* 68.

Gordon, T. 1970. *Parental Effectiveness Training.* New York: Peter Wyden.

Gorman, C. 1992. "Sizing Up The Sexes." *Time* (January 20): 42–51.

Gotwald, W. H., and Golden, G. 1981. *Sexuality: The Human Experience*. New York: Macmillan.

Gove, W.; Style, C.; and Hughes, M. 1990. "The Effect of Marriage on the Well-being of Adults." *Journal of Family Issues* (March): 4–35.

Goy, R. W., and McEwan, B. S. 1980. *Sexual Differentiation in the Brain*. Cambridge, Mass.: MIT Press.

Graham, S. 1992. "What Does a Man Want?" *American Psychologist* (July): 837–841.

Greer, G. 1984. *Sex and Destiny*. New York: Harper & Row.

Grosskopf, D. 1983. *Sex and the Married Woman*. New York. Simon & Schuster.

Guelzow, M.; Bird, G.; and Koball, E. 1991. "An Explanatory Path Analysis of the Stress Process for Dual-Career Men and Women." *Journal of Marriage and the Family* (February): 151–164.

Guerney, B., and Maxson, P. 1990. "Marital and Family Research: A Decade Review and Look Ahead." *Journal of Marriage and the Family* (November): 1127–1135.

Gwartney-Gibbs, P. A.; Stockard, J.; and Bohmer, S. 1987. "Learning Courtship Aggression: The Influence of Parents, Peers and Personal Experiences." *Family Relations* (July): 276–282.

Hagan, R., and D'Agostino, S. 1982. "Smoking May Be a Hazard to Male Sexual Response." *Brain-Mind Bulletin* 7 no. 3.

Halpern, H. 1986. "Midlife Crises: Frontline Dispatches." *Los Angeles Times* (May 12): V–2.

Hanna, S. L., and Knaub, P. K. 1981. "Cohabitation before Marriage: Its Relationship to Family Strengths." *Alternative Lifestyles* 4: 507–522.

Hansen, G. L. 1982. "Reactions to Hypothetical Jealousy Producing Events." *Family Relations* (October): 513–518.

———. 1991. "Balancing Work and Family: A Literature and Resource Review." *Family Relations* (July): 348–353.

Hanson, J. E., and Schuldt, W. J. 1984. "Marital Self-disclosure and Marital Satisfaction." *Journal of Marriage and the Family*: 923–926.

Hanson, S. L., and Ooms, T. 1991. "The Economic Costs and Rewards of Two-Earner, Two-Parent Families." *Journal of Marriage and the Family* (August): 622–634.

Hanson, S. M., and Bozett, F. W. 1987. "Fatherhood: A Review and Resources." *Family Relations* (July): 333–340.

Hansson, R., et al. 1990. "Adult Children with Frail Elderly Parents: When to Intervene?" *Family Relations* (April): 153–158.

Haskins, R. 1988. "Child Support: A Father's View." In *Child Support: From Debt Collection to Social Policy*, edited by S. Kamerman and A. Kahn, 306–327. Beverly Hills, Calif.: Sage Publications.

Hatcher, R. A., et al. 1990. *Contraceptive Technology 1990–1992*. Falls Village, Conn.: The Brambel Co.

Hatfield, E., and Sprecher, S. 1986. "Mirror, Mirror." In *The Importance of Looks in Everyday Life*. New York: SUNY Press.

Hatfield, E., and Walster, G. W. 1978. *A New Look at Love*. Reading, Mass.: Addison-Wesley.

Hawrylyshyn, P. A., et al. 1981. "Risk Factors Associated with Infection Following Cesarean." *American Journal of Obstetrics and Gynecology* (February): 294.

Hayghe, H. V. 1988. "Employees and Child Care: What Roles Do They Play?" *Monthly Labor Review* (September): 38–44.

———. 1991. "Volunteers in the United States: Who Donates the Time?" *Monthly Labor Review* Washington, D.C.: U.S. Department of Labor (February): 17–23.

Heath, Julia. 1988. "Labor and Love Lost." *Psychology Today* (April): 16.

Hechinger, F. 1986. "Children in the United States: Victims of a Self-Serving Population." *Santa Barbara News Press* (May 9): A–11.

Hendrick, S., and Hendrick, C. 1992. *Liking, Loving and Relations*. 2d ed. Pacific Grove, Calif.: Brooks/Cole.

Hewitt Associates. 1990. "What Employers Provide." *Los Angeles Times* (October 14): D–4.

Hewitt v. Hewitt. 1986. *Family Law Quarterly* 19: 433.

Hewlett, S. A. 1987. *Lesser Life: The Myth of Women's Liberation in America*. New York: Warner Books. 1st ed., 1986.

———. 1990. "Good News: The Private Sector and Win-Win Scenarios." In *Rebuilding the Nest*, edited by D. Blankenhorn, S. Bayme, and J. Elshtain. Milwaukee, Wis.: Family Service America.

Hicks, M., and Platt, M. 1970. "Marital Happiness and Stability: A Review of Research in the Sixties." *Journal of Marriage and the Family* (November): 553–574.

Hill, E. A., and Dorfman, L. T. 1982. "Reaction of Housewives to the Retirement of Their Husbands." *Family Relations* (April): 195–200.

Hill, W. F. 1961. *Hill Interaction Matrix Scoring Manual*. Los Angeles: University of Southern California, Youth Studies Center.

Hines, M. Reported in T. Adler, "Early Sex Hormone Exposure Studies." *APA Monitor*. Washington, D.C.: American Psychological Association (March): 6.

Hochschild, A., with Machung, A. 1989. *The Second Shift*. New York: Viking.

Hofferth, S., and Cain, V. 1987. Reported in S. Chollar, "Latchkey Kids: Who Are They?" *Psychology Today* (December): 12.

Hogan, M. J., and Bauer, J. W. 1988. "Problems in Family Financial Management." In *Employment and Economic Problems: Families in Trouble Series*, edited by C. S. Chilman, F. M. Cox, and E. W. Nunnally. New York: Sage Publications.

Holman, T. B. 1992. "Prevention Programs for Families and Children." *Family Relations* (April): 141–192.

Hopson, J., and Rosenfeld, A. 1984. "PMS: Puzzling Monthly Symptoms." *Psychology Today* (August): 30–35.

Houlgate, L. D. 1988. *Family and State: The Philosophy of Family Law*. Washington, D.C.: Family Research Council of America.

Houston, P. 1986. "Five Million Women Earning More Than Husbands Do." *Los Angeles Times* (May 7): I–23.

Hull, J. B. 1985. "Women Find Parents Need Them Just When Careers Are Resuming." *Wall Street Journal* (September 9).

Hunt, M. 1959. *The Natural History of Love*. New York: Knopf.

———. 1974. *Sexual Behavior in the 1970s*. Chicago: Playboy Press.

Hunt, R., and Rydman, E. 1976. *Creative Marriage*. Boston: Holbrook.

Hupka, R. B. 1977. "Societal and Individual Roles in the Expression of Jealousy." In *Sexual Jealousy*, chaired by H. Sigall. Symposium presented at the meeting of the American Psychological Association, August, at San Francisco.

Huston, T., and Levinger, G. 1978. "Interpersonal Attraction and Relationships." *Annual Review of Psychology*. Palo Alto, Calif.: Annual Reviews.

Ihinger-Tallman, M., and Pasley, K. 1987. *Remarriage*. Beverly Hills, Calif.: Sage Publications.

Information-Please Almanac. 1991. Prodigy Service, U.S. Bureau of the Census.

Jackson, J. 1991. *Life In Black America*. Newbury Park, Calif.: Sage Publications.

Jacobs, E.; Shipp, S.; and Brown, G. 1989. "Families of Working Wives Spending More on Services and Nondurables." *Monthly Labor Review*. Washington, D.C.: U.S. Department of Labor, February.

Jacobson, D. 1979. "Stepfamilies: Myths and Realities." *Social Work* 24: 202–207.

Jacoby, S. 1987. "The Private Life of the American Family." *Family Circle* (October 20): 2, 14, 83–85.

Jacques, J., and Chason, K. 1979. "Cohabitation: Its Impact on Marital Success." *The Family Coordinator* (January): 35–39.

Jampolski, G. 1989. *Love Is Letting Go of Fear*. Putnam Valley, N.Y.: Cogent Publishing.

Johnson, A. G. 1989. *Human Arrangements: An Introduction to Sociology*. New York: Harcourt, Brace and Jovanovich.

Johnson, J., et al. 1992. "Abortion, the Future Is Already Here." *Time* (May 4): 27–33.

Johnson, R. 1983. *We: Understanding the Psychology of Romantic Love*. New York: Harper & Row.

Johnson, S. 1985. "Many Child Abuse Reports Unfounded, Expert Claims." *Santa Barbara News Press* (December 18): B–11.

Johnson, W. R., and Skinner, J. 1986, *American Economic Review* 76, no. 3. As reported in "Working Women and Divorce: Cause or Effect." *Psychology Today* (October 1986): 12–13.

Joint Center for Housing Studies at Harvard University. 1989. Reported in P. Reeves, "Renting Cheaper in Some Areas." Scripps Howard News Service. *Santa Barbara News Press* (August 6): F–8.

Jones, E. E., and Jones. H. C. 1977. *Sensual Drugs*. New York: Cambridge University Press.

Jorgenson, S. R. 1986. *Marriage and the Family*. New York: Macmillan.

Jorgenson, S. R., and Gaudy, J. C. 1980. "Self-disclosure and Satisfaction in Marriage: The Relationship Examined." *Family Relations* (July): 281–287.

Jourard, S. M. 1963. *Personal Adjustment*. New York: Macmillan.

Journal of Family Issues. 1992. "Special Edition: Intergenerational Relationships." December.

Kahn, H., and Weiner, A. 1973. "The Future Meanings of Work: Some 'Surprise-Free' Observations." In *The Future of Work*, edited by F. Best. Englewood Cliffs, N.J.: Prentice-Hall (Spectrum).

Kain, E. 1990. *The Myth of Family Decline*. New York: Lexington Books.

Kalmuss, D.; Davidson, A.; and Cushman, L. 1992. "Parenting Expectations, Experiences, and Adjustments to Parenthood: A Test of the Violated Expectations Framework." *Journal of Marriage and the Family* (August): 527–536.

Kaplan, L., and Hennon, C. B. 1992. "Remarriage Education: The Personal Reflections Program." *Family Relations* (April): 127–134.

Kasl, C. D. 1989. *Women, Sex, and Addition*. New York: Technor and Fields.

Kaye, K. 1988. "Turning Two Identities into One." *Psychology Today* (November): 46–50.

Kealing, J. 1990. "Sexual Fantasies of Heterosexual and Homosexual Men." *Archives of Sexual Behaviors* 19 (5): 461–475.

Kelly, C.; Huston, T. L.; and Cate, R. M. 1988. "Premarital Rela-

tionship Correlates of the Erosion of Satisfaction in Marriage." *Journal of Sociology and Personal Relationships* 2: 167–178.

Kerkhoff, A., and Davis, K. E. 1962. "Value Consensus and Need Complimentarity in Mate Selection." *American Social Review* 27: 295–303.

Keshet, J. K. 1987. "Strengthening Your New Family." In *Making Remarriage Work*, edited by J. Belovitch, 95–98. Lexington, Mass.: D. C. Heath.

Kieffer, C. 1977. "New Depths in Intimacy." In *Marriage and Alternatives: Exploring Intimate Relationships*, edited by R. Libby and R. Whitehurst, 267–293. Glenview, Ill.: Scott, Foresman.

Kimura, D. 1985. "Male Brain, Female Brain: The Hidden Difference." *Psychology Today* (November): 50–58.

Kinsey, A., et al. 1948. *Sexual Behavior in the Human Male*. Philadelphia: Saunders.

———. 1953. *Sexual Behavior of the Human Female*. Philadelphia: Saunders.

Klassen, A. D., and Wilsnack, S. C. 1986. "Sexual Experience and Drinking among Women in a U.S. National Survey." *Archives of Sexual Behavior* 15 (5): 363–389.

Knouse, S.; Rosenfeld, P.; and Culbertson, A. 1992. *Hispanics in the Workplace*. Newbury Park, Calif.: Sage Publications.

Knox, D. 1983. *The Love Attitude Inventory*. Saluda, S.C.: Family Life Publications.

———. 1984. *Human Sexuality*. St. Paul, Minn.: West.

———. 1985. *Choices in Relationships*. St. Paul, Minn. West.

Knox, D., and Wilson, K. 1983. "Dating Behavior of University Students." *Family Relations* (April): 225–258.

———. 1983. "Dating Problems of University Students." *College Student Journal* 17: 225–228.

Kochanek, K. D. 1989. "Induced Terminations of Pregnancy: Reporting States, 1985 and 1986." *NCHS Monthly Vital Statistics Reports* 37, no. 12, Supp.-DHHS. pub. no. (PHS) 89–1120. Public Health Service. Hyattsville, Md.: National Center for Health Statistics, April 28.

Kolodny, R. 1981. "Effects of Marijuana on Sexual Behavior and Function." Paper presented at the Midwestern Conference of Drug Use, February 16, at St. Louis, Missouri.

———. 1985. "The Clinical Management of Sexual Problems in Substance Abusers." In *Current Management of Alcoholism and Substance Abuse*, edited by T. E. Bratter and G. Forest. New York: Free Press.

Koss, M. P. 1988. "Hidden Rape: Sexual Aggression and Victimization in a National Sample of Students in Higher Education." In *Rape and Sexual Assault II*, edited by A. Burgess, 3–25. New York: Garland Press.

Koss, M. P.; Dinero, T. E.; Seibel, C. A.; and Cox, S. L. 1988. "Stranger and Acquaintance Rape: Are There Differences in the Victim's Experience?" *Psychology of Women Quarterly* 12: 1–24.

Krauthammer, C. 1989. "Crime and Responsibility." *Time* (May 8).

Lacayo, R. 1989. "Between Two Worlds." *Time* (March 31).

Lacayo, R.; Johnson, J.; Painton, P.; and Taylor, E. 1992. "Abortion: The Future Is Already Here." *Time* (May 4): 27–32.

Lamb, M. E., et al, eds. 1992. *Childcare in Context*. Hillsdale, N.J.: Laurence Erlbaum.

Landers, A. 1989a. "Readers Report: Thrill Leaves after Marriage." *Santa Barbara News Press* (January 22): D–8.

———. 1989b. "Survey Results: American Comments." *Santa Barbara News Press* (January 23).

Landers, S. 1989a. "Koop Will Not Release Abortion Effects Report." *APA Monitor*. Washington, D.C.: American Psychological Association (March): 1, 24.

————. 1989b. "Severe Stress after Abortions Is Rare." *APA Monitor*. Washington, D.C.: American Psychological Association (May): 32.

Lane, K. E., and Gwartney-Gibbs, P. A. 1985. "Violence in the Context of Dating and Sex." *Journal of Family Issues* 6: 45–49.

Lang, A. R. 1985. "The Social Psychology of Drinking and Human Sexuality." *Journal of Drug Issues* 15 (2): 273–289.

Langley, P. 1991. "The Coming of Age of Family Policy." *Families in Society: The Journal of Contemporary Human Services* 72 (2): 116–120.

LaRossa, R., and LaRossa, M. M. 1981. *Transition to Parenthood.* Beverly Hills, Calif.: Sage Publications.

Larson, J. 1988. "The Marriage Quiz: College Students' Beliefs in Selected Myths about Marriage." *Family Relations* (January): 3–11.

Lasswell, M. E. 1973. "Looking Ahead in Aging: Love after Fifty." In *Love, Marriage, Family,* edited by M. Lasswell and T. Lasswell. Glenview, Ill.: Scott, Foresman.

Lasswell, M. E., and Lobsenz, N. 1980. *Styles of Loving.* Garden City, N.Y.: Doubleday.

Latham v. Latham. 1976. 274 Ore. 421, 541 P.2d 144.

Lauer, J., and Lauer, R. 1985. "Marriages Made to Last." *Psychology Today* (June): 22–26.

Lauer, R., and Lauer, J. 1988. *Watersheds: Mastering Life's Unpredictable Crises.* New York: Little Brown.

————. 1991. *The Quest for Intimacy.* Dubuque, Iowa: William C. Brown.

Lawson, A. 1988. *Adultery: An Analysis of Love and Betrayal.* New York: Basic Books.

Leboyer, F. 1975. *Birth without Violence.* New York: Knopf.

LeCroy, C.; Carrol, P.; Mewlso-Becker, H.; and Sturlaugson, P. 1989. "An Experimental Evaluation of the Caring Days Techniques for Marital Enrichment." *Family Relations*, 15–18.

Lederer, W. J., and Jackson, D. D. 1968. *The Mirage of Marriage.* New York: Norton.

Lee, G., and Shehan, C. 1989. "Retirement and Marital Satisfaction." *Journal of Gerontology* 44: S226–S230.

Lee, K., and Rittenhouse, A. 1991. "Prevalence of Premenstrual Symptoms in Employed Women." *Women & Health* 17 (3): 17–32.

Leo, J. 1984. "The Revolution Is Over." *Time* (April 9): 74–84.

LeShan, E. J. 1973. *The Wonderful Crisis of Middle Age.* New York: David McKay.

Leslie, G. 1979. "Personal Values, Professional Idealogies and Family Specialists: A New Look." *The Family Coordinator* (April): 157–162.

Leslie, L.; Huston, T.; and Johnson, M. 1986. "Parental Reactions to Dating Relationships: Do They Make a Difference?" *Journal of Marriage and the Family* (February): 578–66.

Levine, M., and Troiden, R. 1989. "The Myth of Sexual Addiction." In *Taking Sides,* edited by R. Franscolur. Guildford, Conn.: Dushkin.

Lewis, S., and Cooper, G. 1988. "Stress in Dual-Earner Families." In *Women and Work,* vol. 3, edited by B. Gutek, et al., 139–168. Beverly Hills, Calif.: Sage Publications.

Lewis, S.; Izraeli, D.; and Hootsmans, H., eds. 1992. *Dual-Earner Families.* Newbury Park, Calif.: Sage Publications.

Libby, R. W., and Whitehurst, R. N. 1977. *Marriage and Alternatives: Exploring Intimate Relationships.* Glenview, Ill.: Scott, Foresman.

Liese, L.; Snowden, L.; and Ford, L. 1989. "Partner Status, Social Support and Psychological Adjustment during Pregnancy." *Family Relations* (July): 311–316.

Life. 1986. "Having Babies." (March): 33.

Lindemann, B. 1976. "The Sex Role Revolution." In *American Marriage: A Changing Scene?* edited by F. Cox, 175–188. Dubuque, Iowa: William C. Brown.

Lindemann, B. 1986. Professor of Women's Studies, Santa Barbara City College, Santa Barbara, California. Personal discussion. March.

Linton, R. 1936. *The Study of Man.* New York: Appleton.

Lloyd, S. A. 1991. "The Dark Side of Courtship: Violence and Sexual Exploitation." *Family Relations* 40 (January): 14–20.

London, K.; Mosher, W.; Pratt, W.; and Williams, L. 1989. "Preliminary Findings from NSFG, Cycle IV." Paper presented at the annual meeting of the Population Association of America at Baltimore, Maryland.

Lopata, H. Z. 1979. *Women as Widows.* New York: Elsevier.

Los Angeles Times. 1985. "Nonwhite Children Adjust Well When Adopted by White Families, Study Reports." (December 26): Part 1, 11.

Los Angeles Times. 1989. (March 19): 26.

Lowenthal, M. F.; Thurnher, M.; and Chiriboga, D. 1975. *Four Stages of Life: A Comparative Study of Women and Men Facing Transitions.* San Francisco: Jossey-Bass.

Lowery, C. R., and Settle, S. A. 1985. "Effects of Divorce on Children: Differential Impact of Custody and Visitation Patterns." *Family Relations* (October): 455–463.

Ludtke, M. 1990. "To Grandmother's House We Go." *Time* (November 5): 86,90.

Lyness, J. L.; Lepetz, M.; and Davis, K. 1972. "Living Together: An Alternative to Marriage." *Journal of Marriage and the Family* 34 (May): 305–311.

MacAdam, M. N., and Meadows, F. L. 1985. "Company-supported Child Care." *Business to Business* (April): 69–73.

Maccoby, E., and Jacklin, C. 1974. *The Psychology of Sex Differences.* Palo Alto, Calif.: Stanford University Press.

McCubbin, H. I., et al. 1988. *Family Types and Strengths: A Life Cycle and Ecological Approach.* Edina, Minn.: Bellwether; Bellwether, Burgess, 1986.

McCubbin, H. I., and McCubbin, M. 1988. "Typologies of Resilient Families: Emerging Roles of Social Class and Ethnicity." *Family Relations* (July): 247–259.

McCubbin, H., and Patterson, J. 1983. "Stress: The Family Inventory of Life Events and Changes." In *Marriage and Family Assessment: A Sourcebook for Family Therapy,* edited by E. Filsinger, 285–286. Beverly Hills, Calif.: Sage Publications.

MacDermid, S.; Huston, T.; and McHale, S. 1990. "Changes in Marriage Associated with the Transition to Parenthood: Individual Differences as a Function of Sex-role Attitudes and Changes in the Division of Household Labor." *Journal of Marriage and the Family* (May): 475–486.

MacDonald, S. 1992. Wedding consultant. Personal communication.

Mace. D. 1980. "Strictly Personal." *Marriage and Family Living* (September).

Mace, D., ed. 1983. *Prevention in Family Services: Approaches to Family Wellness.* Beverly Hills, Calif.: Sage Publications.

Mace, D., and Mace, V. 1977. "Counter-Epilogue." In *Marriage and*

Its Alternatives: Exploring Intimate Relationships, edited by R. Libby and R. Whitehurst, 390–406. Glenview, Ill.: Scott, Foresman.

———. 1985. "Family Wellness: Wave of the Future." In *Family Strengths*, vol. 6, edited by R. Williams, et al. Lincoln, Nebr.: University of Nebraska Press.

McGinnis, A. 1979. *The Friendship Factor*. Minneapolis, Minn.: Augsberg.

McGuiness, D., and Pribram, K. 1979. "The Origins of Sensory Bias in the Development of Gender Differences in Perception and Cognition." In *Cognitive Growth and Development*, edited by M. Bortner. New York: Brunner-Mazel.

McHale, S., and Huston, T. 1985. "A Longitudinal Study of the Transition to Parenthood and Its Effects on the Marriage Relationship." *Journal of Family Issues* 6: 409–433.

McHenry v. Smith. 1986. *Family Law Quarterly* 19: 432.

McKay, M., et al. 1984. *The Divorce Book*. Oakland, Calif.: New Harbinger Publications.

Macklin, E. 1983. "Nonmarital Heterosexual Cohabitation: An Overview." In *Contemporary Families and Alternative Lifestyles*, edited by E. Macklin and R. Rubin. Beverly Hills: Calif.: Sage Publications.

McLanahan, S., and Booth, K. 1989. "Mother-Only Families: Problems, Prospects and Politics." *Journal of Marriage and the Family* (August): 557–588.

McLanahan, S., and Garfinkel, I. 1989. "Single Mothers, the Underclass and Social Policy." *Annals of the American Academy of Political and Social Science* 501: 92–104.

Madden, J. F. 1985. "The Persistence of Pay Differentials: The Economics of Sex Discrimination." In *Women and Work: An Annual Review*, edited by L. Larwood, et al. Beverly Hills, Calif.: Sage Publications.

Magid, K., and McKelvey, C. A. 1987. *High Risk: Children without Conscience*. New York: Bantam Books.

Malamuth, N., and Donnerstein, E., eds. 1984. *Pornography and Sexual Aggression*. New York: Academic Press.

Malatesta, V. J. 1982. "Acute Alcohol Ingestions and Female Orgasm." Researcher referred to by R. C. Kolodny at a Masters and Johnson Institute Seminar on Human Sexuality, December 6–7, at Los Angeles.

Mall, J. 1986. "Men Send Mixed Signals on Attitudes." *Los Angeles Times* (April 27): VI, 1–20.

Maloney, E. R. 1982. *Human Sexuality*, 128–129. New York: McGraw-Hill.

Mancini, J. 1989. *Aging Parents and Adult Children*. Lexington, Mass.: Lexington Books.

Marino, V. 1989. "Lure of Plastic Money Miring More in Debt." *Santa Barbara News Press* (January): 22.

Marvin v. Marvin. 1976. 18 Cal.3d 660, 134 Cal.Rep. 815, 557 P.2d 106.

Marvin v. Marvin. 1979. *Family Law Reporter* 5: 3109.

Marvin v. Marvin. 1981. *Family Law Reporter* 7: 2661.

Maslow, A. H. 1968. *Toward a Psychology of Being*. 2d ed. Princeton, N.J.: Van Nostrand.

———. 1971. *The Farther Reaches of Human Nature*. New York: Viking.

Masters, W. H., and Johnson, V. 1966. *Human Sexual Response*. Boston: Little, Brown.

———. 1981. "Sex and the Aging Process." *Journal of American Geriatrics Society* (September): 385–390.

Masters, W. H.; Johnson, V. E.; and Kolodney, R. C. 1988. *Human Sexuality*. Glenview, Ill.: Scott, Foresman.

Mattox, W. R. 1990. "The Family Time Famine." *Family Policy*. Washington, D.C.: Family Research Council, 3 (1): 2.

Mattson, D. 1990. "The Effectiveness of a Specific Marital Enrichment Program: Time." *Individual Psychology* 46 (January): 89–92.

May, R. 1970. *Love and Will*. New York: Norton.

Mead, M. 1948, 1968. "Jealousy: Primative and Civilized." In *Woman's Coming of Age*, edited by S. D. Schmalhausen and V. E. Calverton. New York: Morrow.

Medved, D. 1989. *The Case against Divorce*. Santa Monica, Calif.: Donald I. Fine.

Mehren, E. 1986. "Working Wives; Negative Effect on Husbands." *Los Angeles Times* (March 31): Part V, 1, 4.

Mellman and Lazarus, Inc. 1989. *Mass Mutual American Family Value Study*. Washington, D.C.: Mellman and Lazarus, Inc.

Mellman, M., et al. 1990. "Family Time, Family Values." In *Rebuilding the Nest*, edited by D. Blankenhorn, S. Bayme, and J. Elshtain, 73–79. Milwaukee, Wis.: Family Service America.

Merewood, Anne. 1991. "Sperm under siege." *Health* (April): 53–57, 76–77.

Miller, B. C., and Sollie, D. L. 1980. "Normal Stresses during the Transition to Parenthood." *Family Relations* (October): 459–465.

Miller, B. C., and Heaton, T. B. 1991. "Age at First Sexual Intercourse and the Timing of Marriage and Child Birth." *Journal of Marriage and the Family* 53 (August): 719–732.

Miller, B. C., and Moore, K. A. 1990. "Adolescent Sexual Behavior, Pregnancy and Parenting: Research through the 1980s." *Journal of Marriage and the Family* 52 (November): 1025–1044.

Miller, R. L. 1984. *Economic Issues for Consumers*. St. Paul, Minn.: West.

Mimenauer, J., and Carroll, D. 1982. *Singles: The New Americans*. New York: Simon & Schuster.

Mishell, D. R. 1989. "Contraception." *New England Journal of Medicine* (March): 777–787.

Money, J., and Ehrhardt, A. A. 1972. *Man and Woman, Boy and Girl: The Differentiation and Dimorphism of Gender Identity from Conception to Maturity*. Baltimore: Johns Hopkins University Press.

Money Magazine. 1989. "Financial Planning." (March): 56–57.

Monroe, P., and Garand, J. C. 1991. "Parental Leave Legislation in the U.S. Senate: Toward a Model of Roll-call Voting." *Family Relations* (April): 208–218.

Montagu, M. F. A. 1972. *Touching: The Human Significance of Skin*. New York: Harper & Row.

———. 1989. *Growing Young*. Granby, Mass.: Bergin and Garvey.

Monthly Labor Review. 1988. Washington, D.C.: U.S. Department of Labor (February): 75.

———. 1992. "Selected Labor Force Indicators by Sex, Age, Race, and Hispanic Origin." Washington, D.C.: U.S. Department of Labor (January): 56.

Mooney, D. 1986. "Blush," "blur," "backlash," and "balance" were terms for family life stages described in N. Hellmich, "Marriage: Don't Call It Unpredictable." *USA Today* (May 9): 7D.

Moore, K. A.; Nord, C.; and Petersen, J. 1989. "Nonvoluntary Sexual Activity among Adolescents." *Family Planning Perspectives* 21: 110–114.

Morgan, E. A. 1987. *Pioneer Research on Strong, Healthy Families*. Washington, D.C.: Family Research Council of America.

Morris, D. 1971. *Intimate Behavior*. New York: Random House.

Morris, J. 1974. *Conundrum*. New York: Harcourt Brace Jovanovich.

Moses, S. 1991. "Gender Gap on Tests Examined at Meeting." *APA Monitor*. Washington, D.C.: American Psychological Association (December): 38.

Mosher, W. D., and Pratt, W. F. 1987. "Fecundity, Infertility, and Reproductive Health in the United States, 1982." *Vital and Health Statistics*, ser. 23, no. 14, DHHS pub. no. (PHS) 87–1990. National Center for Health Statistics. Washington, D.C.: U.S. Department of Health, May.

Moss, M. 1987. "One in Eight Female Students Is a Victim of Date Rape or a Rape Attempt." *Behavior Today Newsletter* 18, no. 7 (February).

Moynihan, D. P. 1965. "Counting Our Blessings: Reflections on the Future of America." *America*.

———. 1986. *Family and Nation*. New York: Harcourt Brace Jovanovich.

Mulligan, T. 1991. "Sexuality and Aging in Male Veterans: A Cross-Sectional Study of Interest, Ability and Activity." *Archives of Sexual Behavior* 20 (1): 17–25.

Murdock, G. 1950. "Sexual Behavior: What Is Acceptable." *Journal of Social Hygiene* 36: 1–31.

Murren, S.; Perot, A.; and Byrne, D. 1989. "Coping with Unwanted Sexual Activity: Normative Responses, Situational Determinants and Individual Differences." *Journal of Sex Research* 26: 85–106.

Murstein, B. I. 1974. *Love, Sex, and Marriage through the Ages*. New York: Springer.

———. 1980. "Mate Selection in the 1970s." *Journal of Marriage and the Family* (November): 777–792.

———. 1986. *Paths to Marriage*. Beverly Hills, Calif.: Sage Publications.

Myers, L. 1992. "Women Pay Price for Career Gaps." *San Diego Union* (January 11): D–1.

Myricks, N. 1980. "Palimony: The Impact of Marvin vs. Marvin." *The Family Coordinator* (April): 210–215.

———. 1983. "The Law and Alternative Lifestyles." In *Contemporary Families and Alternative Lifestyles*, edited by E. D. Macklin and R. H. Rubin. Beverly Hills, Calif.: Sage Publications.

Nass, G. D., and Libby, R. W. 1984. *Sexual Choices*. 2d ed. Monterey, Calif.: Wadsworth Health Sciences Division. 1st ed., 1981.

National Center for Health Statistics. May 2, 1986. "Advance Report of Final Marriage Statistics: 1983." *Monthly Vital Statistics Report*. Hyattsville, Md.: U.S. Department of Health and Human Services.

———. September 26, 1990. "Wanted and Unwanted Childbearing in the United States: (1973–1988)." *Advance Data* no. 189. Washington, D.C.: U.S. Department of Health and Human Services.

———. March 1991. *Health United States: 1990*. DHHS pub. no. (PHS) 91–1232. Hyattsville, Md.: U.S. Department of Health and Human Services.

———. May 21, 1991. "Advance Report on Final Divorce Statistics, 1988." *Monthly Vital Statistics Report*. Hyattsville, Md.: U.S. Department of Health and Human Services.

———. August 26, 1991. "Advance Report on Final Marriage Statistics, 1988." *Monthly Vital Statistics Report*. 40 no. 4. Hyattsville, Md.: U.S. Department of Health and Human Services.

———. March 12, 1992. "Births, Marriages, Divorces and Deaths for November 1991." *Monthly Vital Statistics Report*. 40 no. 11. Hyattsville, Md.: U.S. Department of Health and Human Services.

———. April 8, 1992. "Births, Marriages, Divorces, and Deaths for 1990." *Monthly Vital Statistics Report*. Washington, D.C.: U.S. Department of Health and Human Services.

———. April 15, 1992b. "Advance Report of New Data from 1989 Birth Certificates." *Monthly Vital Statistics Report*. Hyattsville, Md.: U.S. Department of Health and Human Services.

———. April 15, 1992. "Birth, Marriages, Divorces and Deaths for 1991." *Monthly Vital Statistics Report*. 40 no. 12. Hyattsville, Md.: U.S. Department of Health and Human Services.

———. June 26, 1992. "Births, Marriages, Divorces and Deaths for February 1992." *Monthly Vital Statistics Report*. Hyattsville, Md.: U.S. Department of Health and Human Services.

———. September 1992. "Annual Summary of Births, Marriages, Divorces, and Deaths: United States, 1991." Hyattsville, Md.: U.S. Department of Health and Human Services.

———. November 2, 1992. "Births, Marriages, Divorces, and Deaths for June 1992." *Monthly Vital Statistics Report*. Hyattsville, Md.: U.S. Department of Health and Human Services.

Nelson, W., and Levant, R. 1991. "An Evaluation of a Skills Training Program for Parents in Stepfamilies." *Family Relations* (July): 291–296.

Neugarten, B. L., and Neugarten, D. A. 1987. "The Changing Meaning of Age." *Psychology Today* (May): 29–33.

Nevid, J. S. 1984. "Sex Differences in Factors in Romantic Attraction." *Sex Roles* 11: 401–411.

———. 1985. "Choose Me." *Psychology Today* (August): 66–67.

New Jersey Supreme Court. *In the Matter of Baby M*. A–39–87. Argued September 14, 1987. Decided February 3, 1988.

Noller, P. 1985. "Negative Communication in Marriage." *Journal of Social and Personal Relationships*, 289–301.

Norton, A. J., and Glick, P. C. 1986. "One Parent Families: A Social and Economic Profile." *Family Relations* (January): 9–17.

O'Connell, J. C. 1987. "Children of Working Mothers: What the Research Tells Us." In *The Psychology of Women: Ongoing Debates*, edited by M. Walsh, 367–377. New Haven, Conn.: Yale University Press.

O'Flaherty, K. M., and Eeels, L. W. 1988. "Courtship Behavior of the Remarried." *Journal of Marriage and the Family* (May): 499–506.

O'Hara, K. 1989. "43.6% of Kids Have T.V. in Bedroom." Report of the Superintendent of Schools, Santa Barbara County. *Santa Barbara News Press* (April 30): B–1.

O'Hare, W.; Pollard, K.; Mann, T.; and Kent, M. 1991. "African Americans in the 1990s." *Population Bulletin* 46 no. 1. Washington, D.C.: Population Reference Bureau.

Olds, S.; London, M.; and Ladewig, P. 1988. *Maternal Newborn Nursing*. 2d ed. Reading, Mass.: Addison-Wesley.

Olson, D. 1986. *Prepare*. St. Paul, Minn.: University of Minnesota Press.

———. 1986. "What Makes Families Work?" In *Family Strengths 7: Vital Connections*, edited by S. Van Zandt, et al., 1–12. Lincoln, Nebr.: University of Nebraska Press.

Olson, D. H., et al. 1983. *Families: What Makes Them Work?* Beverly Hills, Calif.: Sage Publications.

Orlinsky, D. E. 1972. "Love Relationships in the Life Cycles: A Developmental Interpersonal Perspective." In *Love Today: A New Exploration*, edited by H. A. Otto, 135–150. New York: Dell.

Packard, V. 1958. *The Hidden Persuaders*. New York: Pocket Books.

Papalia, D., and Olds, S. 1986. *Human Development*. New York: McGraw-Hill.

Papernow, P. 1984. "A Baby in the House." *Stepfamily Bulletin* (Winter).

Parrot, W. G., and Smith, R. H. 1987. *Differentiating the Experiences of Envy and Jealousy*. Paper presented at the annual meeting of the American Psychological Association, August, at New York.

Pearle, D. 1984. "Violence and Aggression." *Society* (September): 17–22.

Pearson, J. C. 1989. *Communication in the Family*. New York: Harper & Row.

Pecher, V. 1988. "The New Aphrodisiacs." *Men's Health* (Spring): 43–44.

Perry, J. D., and Whipple, B. 1981. "Pelvic Muscle Strength of Female Ejaculation: Evidence in Support of a New Theory of Orgasm." *Journal of Sex Research* 17: 22–39.

Pillemer, V., and Suitor, J. 1991. "Will I Ever Escape my Children's Problems? Effects of Adult Children's Problems on Elderly Parents." *Journal of Marriage and the Family* (August): 585–594.

Pincus, J., and Wolhandler, J. 1992. "If You Think You Are Pregnant: Finding Out and Deciding What to Do." In *The New Our Bodies, Ourselves*. New York: Simon & Schuster. 1st ed., 1984.

Pines, A. 1985. As reported in C. Turkington, "Finding What's Good in Marriage." *APA Monitor*. Washington, D.C.: American Psychological Association.

Pleck, J. H., and Rustad, M. 1980. "Husbands' and Wives' Time in Family Work and Paid Work in the 1975–1976 Study of Time Use." Working paper. Wellesley, Mass.: Wellesley College Center for Research on Women.

Pleck, J. H.; Sonenstein, F.; and Leighton, C. 1991. "Adolescent Males' Condom Use: Relationships between Perceived Cost-Benefits and Consistency." *Journal of Marriage and the Family* (August): 733–745.

Popenoe, D. 1991. "Breakup of the Family: Can We Reverse the Trend?" *USA Today Magazine*. Society for the Advancement of Education (May): 50–53.

Popular Mechanics. 1991. "Prenatal Heart Monitor." (December): 16.

Population Reference Bureau. 1991. *1991 World Population Data Sheet*. Washington, D.C.: Population Reference Bureau, April.

———. 1992. *1992 World Population Data Sheet*. Washington, D.C.: Population Reference Bureau, April.

Postman, N. 1982. *The Disappearance of Childhood*. New York: Delecorte.

Pratt, W. F. 1990. *Premarital Sexual Behavior, Multiple Partners and Marital Experience*. Paper presented at the annual meeting of the Population Association of America, at Toronto, Canada.

Press, A. 1983. "Divorce American Style." *Newsweek* (January 10): 42–43.

Presser, H. 1989. "Can We Make Time for Children?" *Population Today*. Washington, D.C.: Population Research Bureau, May 2.

Putney, S. 1972. *The Conquest of Society*. Belmont, Calif.: Wadsworth.

Queen, S. A., and Habenstein, R. W. 1985. *The Family in Various Cultures*. Philadelphia: Lippincott.

Quinn, J. 1989. "Permanent Alimony Is Making a Comeback." *Santa Barbara News Press* (February 8): B–8.

Rappaport, R., and Rappaport, R. 1975. "Men, Women and Equity." *The Family Coordinator* (October): 421–432.

react. 1984. "Viewing Goes Up." *Action for Children's Television Magazine* 13: 4.

Redbook. 1987. "Special Survey Results." September.

Reed, R., and Long, T. 1987. *Health Behaviors*. St. Paul, Minn.: West.

Reiss, I. L. 1960. "Toward a Sociology of the Heterosexual Love Relationship." *Marriage and Family Living* (May).

———. 1988. *Family Systems in America*. 5th ed. New York: Holt.

Repetti, R.; Matthews, K.; and Waldron, I. 1989. "Employment and Women's Health." *American Psychologist* (November): 1394–1401.

Richardson, L. 1985. *The New Other Woman*. New York: Free Press.

———. 1986. "Another World." *Psychology Today* (February): 22–27.

Ricks, S. S. 1985. "Father-Infant Interactions: A Review of Empirical Research." *Family Relations* (October): 505–511.

Ridley, C.; Peterman, D.; and Avery, A. 1978. "Cohabitation: Does It Make for a Better Marriage?" *The Family Coordinator* (April): 135–136.

Risman, B. J., et al. 1981. "Living Together in College: Implications for Courtship." *Journal of Marriage and the Family* 43: 77–83.

Rivenbark, C. 1992. "Families for Rent, Not Cheap." *Santa Barbara News Press* (July 26): D–1.

Robinson, I., et al. 1991. "Twenty Years of Sexual Revolution: 1965–1985: An Update." *Journal of Marriage and the Family* 53. (February): 216–220.

Robinson, J. 1988. Reported by R. Schmid, "Women Still Dominate Domestic Engineering." *Santa Barbara News Press* (December 1).

Robinson, J. P. 1977. *How Americans Use Time: A Social Psychological Analysis of Everyday Behavior*. New York: Praeger.

Rodman, H. 1991. "Should Parental Involvement Be Required for Minor's Abortions?" *Family Relations* (April): 155–160.

Rogers, C. 1951. "Communication: Its Blocking and Facilitation." Paper read at Centennial Conference on Communications, October 11, at Northwestern University.

———. 1972. *Becoming Partners: Marriage and its Alternatives*. New York: Delacorte.

Rokachi, A. 1990. "Content Analysis of Sexual Fantasies of Males and Females." *Journal of Psychology: Interdisciplinary and Applied* (January): 427–436.

Roleder, G. 1986. *Starting Your Marriage*. Special Products Manager. 426 So. 5th St., Minneapolis, Minn.: Augsburg Fortress.

Roncek, D.; Bell, R.; and Chaldin, H. 1980. "Female-headed Families: An Ecological Model of Residential Concentration in a Small City." *Journal of Marriage and the Family* (February): 157–169.

Rosenthal, D. 1986. "You Can Still Make a Million Dollars." *Parade* (January 26): 4.

Rosenthal, R., and Jacobson, L. 1968. *Pygmalian in the Classroom*. New York: Holt.

Rossi, A. 1977. "A Biosocial Perspective on Parenting." *Daedalus* (Spring): 1–31.

———. 1978. "The Biosocial Side of Parenthood." *Human Nature* (June): 72–79.

Rotenberg, E. 1987. "Reflections of a Family Court Judge." In *Making Remarriage Work*, edited by J. Belovitch. Lexington, Mass.: D. C. Heath.

Rouse, L. P.; Breen, R.; and Howell, M. 1988. "Abuse in Intimate Relationships: A Comparison of Married and Dating College Students." *Journal of Interpersonal Violence* 3: 414–429.

Rubin, Z. 1973. *Liking and Loving*. New York: Holt.

———. 1983. "Are Working Wives Hazardous to Their Husband's Health?" *Psychology Today* (May).

Rubin, Z., et al. 1980. "Self-Disclosure in Dating Couples: Sex Roles and the Ethics of Openness." *Journal of Marriage and the Family* (May): 305–317.

Rubinstein, E. A. 1983. "Research Conclusion of the 1982 NIMH

Report and Their Policy Implications." *American Psychologist* (July): 820–825.

Rubinstein, C. 1982."Wellness Is All." *Psychology Today* (October): 27–37.

Ruble, D.; Fleming, A.; Hackel, L.; and Stangor, R. 1988. "Changes in the Marital Relationship during the Transition to First Time Parenthood: Effects of Violated Expectations Concerning Division of Household Labor." *Journal of Personality and Social Psychology* 55: 78–87.

Russell, B. 1936, 1957. "Our Sexual Ethics." In *Why I Am Not a Christian*, 171–172. New York: Simon & Schuster.

Sager, C., et al. 1983. *Treating the Married Family*. New York: Brunner/Mazel.

Salovey, B. 1985. "The Heart of Jealousy." *Psychology Today* 19: 22–25, 28–29.

Salovey, B., and Rodin, J. 1989. "Envy and Jealousy in Close Relationships." In *Close Relationships*, edited by C. Hendrick, 221–246. Newbury Park, Calif.: Sage Publications.

Samuelson, E. D. 1988. *The Divorce Law Handbook*. New York: Human Sciences Press.

Sanders, G., and Trygstad, D. 1989. "Stepgrandparents and Grandparents: The View from Young Adults." *Family Relations* (January): 71–75.

Sanders, G. F., et al. 1985. *Family Strengths of Older Couples and Their Adult Children*, edited by R. Williams, et al., 85–98. Lincoln, Nebr.: University of Nebraska Press.

Sanick, M., and Mauldin, T. 1986. "Single versus Two Parent Families: A Comparison of Mother's Time." *Family Relations* (January): 53–56.

Santa Barbara News Press. 1985. "Dutch Mothers Opt for Home Delivery." (August 22): D–7.

———. 1989. "Senate Backs Democrats' Plan on Child Care." June 23.

———. 1991. "Woman Gives Birth to Own Grandchildren." October 13.

Sargent, A. G. 1977. *Beyond Sex Roles*. St. Paul, Minn.: West.

Scarr, S.; Phillips, D.; and McCartney, K. 1989. "Working Mothers and Their Families." *American Psychologist* (November): 1402–1409.

Schmind, R. 1988. "Median Age in Nation Heads toward Record High." *Santa Barbara News Press* (November 17): A–14.

Schnittger, M., and Bird, G. 1990. "Coping among Dual-Career Men and Women across the Family Life Cycle." *Family Relations* (April): 199–205.

Schumm, W. R., et al. 1986. "Self-Disclosure and Marital Satisfaction Revisited." *Family Relations* 34: 241–247.

Schwartz, F. 1992. *Breaking with Tradition*. New York: Warner Books.

Scoresby, A. L. 1977. *The Marriage Dialogue*. Reading, Mass.: Addison-Wesley.

Seligmann, J. 1992. "A Condom for Women." *Newsweek* (February 10): 45.

Seltzer, J. 1991. "Relationships between Fathers and Children Who Live Apart: The Father's Role after Separation." *Journal of Marriage and the Family* (February): 79–102.

Shapiro, H. 1988. *The New Birth Control Book*. New York: Prentice-Hall.

Shapiro, J. L. 1987. "The Expectant Father." *Psychology Today* (January): 36–39.

Shaver, P., et al. 1988. "Love as Attachment: The Integration of Three Behavioral Systems." In *The Psychology of Love*, edited by R. Sternberg and Mr. Barner. New Haven, Conn.: Yale University Press.

Shotland, R. L. 1989. "A Model of the Causes of Date Rape in Developing and Class Relationships." In *Close Relations*, edited by C. Hendrick, 246–270. Newbury Park, Calif.: Sage Publications.

Siegel, R. K. 1982. "Cocaine and Sexual Dysfunction." *Journal of Psychoactive Drugs* 14: 71–74.

Sillers, A. L., et al. 1987. "Content Themes in Marital Conversations." *Human Communication Research* 13: 495–528.

Singer, D. 1983. "A Time to Reexamine the Role of Television in Our Lives." *American Psychologist*. Washington, D.C.: American Psychological Association (July): 815–816.

Singer, J., and Sherrod, L. R. 1979. "Prosocial Programs in the Context of Children's Total Pattern of TV Viewing." Paper presented at the biennial meeting of the Society for Research in Child Development, March, at San Francisco.

Singer, J., and Singer, D. 1981. *Television, Imagination and Aggression: A Study of Preschoolers*. Hillsdale, N.J.: Erlbaum.

Skelton, G. 1989. "Many in Survey Who Had Abortion Cite Guilt Feelings." *Los Angeles Times* (March 19): 28.

———. 1989. "The Times Poll. Most Americans Think Abortion Is Immoral." *Los Angeles Times* (March 19): 26.

Skidmore, D. 1992. "Bankruptcies Reach Record High." *Santa Barbara News Press* (March 3): C–4.

Skolnick, A. 1978, 1983. *The Intimate Environment: Exploring Marriage and the Family*. 2d and 3d eds. Boston: Little, Brown.

———. 1991. *Embattled Paradise: The American Family in an Age of Uncertainty*. New York: Basic Books.

Skolnick, A., and Skolnick, J. 1981. *Family in Transition*. Boston: Little, Brown.

Small, M. 1991. "Sperm Wars." *Discover* (July): 48–53.

Smith, D. S. 1985. "Wife Employment and Marital Adjustment: A Cumulation of Results." *Family Relations* 34 (October): 483–490.

Smith, J. P., and Welch, F. R. 1986. *Closing the Gap: Forty Years of Economic Progress for Blacks*. Santa Monica, Calif.: Rand Corporation, February.

Smith, M. J. 1980. "The Social Consequences of Single Parenthood: A Longitudinal Perspective." *The Family Coordinator* (January): 75–81.

Smolowe, J. 1991. "Can't We Talk This Over?" *Time* (January 7): 77.

Sonenstein, F. L.; Pleck, J. H.; and Ku, and L. C. 1989. "Sexual Activity, Condom Use and AIDS Awareness among Adolescent Males." *Family Planning Perspectives* 21: 152–158.

Spanier, G. B. 1986. "Cohabitation in the 1980s: Recent Changes in the United States." In *Contemporary Marriage: Comparative Perspectives on a Changing Situation*, edited by K. Davis and A. Grossband-Sliechtman. New York: Russell Sage.

Spitze, G., and Logan, J. 1990. "Sons, Daughters, and Intergenerational Social Support." *Journal of Marriage and the Family* (May): 420–430.

Spock, B. 1980. "What about Our Children?" In *Family Strengths: Positive Models for Family Life*, edited by N. Stinnett, et al. Lincoln, Nebr.: University of Nebraska Press.

Sponaugle, G. C. 1989. "Attitudes toward Extramarital Relations." In *Human Sexuality: The Social and Interpersonal Context*, edited by K. McKinney and S. Sprecher. Norwood, N.J.: Ablex Publishing.

Sprecher, S. 1987. "The Effects of Self-Disclosure Given and Received on Affection for an Intimate Partner and Stability of Relationship." *Journal of Social and Personal Relationships* 4: 115–127.

Sprenkle, D. H. 1987. "Treating a Sex Addict through Marital Sex Therapy." *Family Relations* (January): 11–14.

Staines, G.; Patrick, K.; and Fudge, M. 1986. "Wives' Employment and Husbands' Attitude toward Work and Life." *Journal of Applied Psychology* (February).

Stein, H. 1984. "The Case for Staying Home." *Esquire* (June): 142–149.

Steinem, G. 1982. "Steinem: Reproductive Freedom Basic Right." *Planned Parenthood Review* 2 (Winter): 5–6.

Steiner, C. M. 1986. *When a Man Loves a Woman: Sexual and Emotional Literacy for the Modern Man.* New York: Grove Press.

Stephan, C., and Corder, J. 1985. "The Effects of Dual-Career Families on Adolescents' Sex-Role Attitudes, Work and Family Plans, and Choices of Important Others." *Journal of Marriage and the Family* 47 (November): 921–930.

Stets, J. E. 1991. "Cohabiting and Marital Aggression: The Role of Social Isolation." *Journal of Marriage and the Family* 53. (August): 669–680.

Stets, J. E., and Straus, M. A. 1989. "The Marriage License as a Hitting License: A Comparison of Assaults in Dating, Cohabiting and Married Couples." In *Violence in Dating Relationships: Emerging Social Issues,* edited by M. Perog-Good, and J. Stets, 33–52. New York: Praeger.

Stinnett, N. 1979. "In Search of Strong Families." In *Building Family Strengths,* edited by N. Stinnett, B. Chesser, and J. Defrain, 22–30. Lincoln, Nebr.: University of Nebraska Press.

———. 1986. "Strengthening Families: An International Priority." Talk given at the International Conference on Family Strengths sponsored by Pepperdine College, April 20–22, at Los Angeles International Airport Hilton.

Stinnett, N., and DeFrain, J. 1985. *Secrets of Strong Families.* Boston: Little, Brown.

Stokols, D. 1992. "Establishing and Maintaining Healthy Environments." *American Psychologist* (January): 6–22.

Stout, A., et al. 1986. "Premenstrual Symptoms in Black and White Community Samples." *American Journal of Psychiatry* (143): 1436–1439.

Straus, M. and Gelles, R. 1986. "Societal Change and Change in Family Violence from 1975 to 1985 as Revealed by Two National Surveys." *Journal of Marriage and the Family* (August): 465–479.

Strong, J. R. 1983. *Creating Closeness.* Ames, Iowa: Human Communication Institute.

Sugimoto, E. 1935. *A Daughter of the Samuri.* Garden City, N.Y.: Doubleday.

Suitor, J. J. 1991. "Marital Quality and Satisfaction with Division of Household Labor across the Family Life Cycle." *Journal of Marriage and the Family* (February): 221–230.

Surra, C. A. 1990. "Research Theory on Mate Selection and Premarital Relationships in the 1980s." *Journal of Marriage and the Family* 52 (November): 844–865.

———. 1991. "Research and Theory on Mate Selection and Premarital Relationships in the 1980s." In *Contemporary Families: Looking Forward, Looking Back,* edited by A. Booth. Minneapolis, Minn.: National Council on Family Relations.

Tanfer, K. 1987. "Patterns of Premarital Cohabitation among Never-Married Women in the U.S." *Journal of Marriage and the Family* (August): 483–498.

Tannen, D. 1990. *You Just Don't Understand: Women and Men in Conversation.* New York: Ballentine Books.

Tavris, C. 1984. *The Longest War: Understanding Sex Differences.* 2d ed. New York: Harcourt Brace Jovanovich.

Tavris, C., and Sadd, S. 1977. *The Redbook Report on Female Sexuality.* New York: Redbook.

Thomas, V. 1990. "Determinants of Global Life Happiness and Marital Happiness in Dual-Career Black Couples." *Family Relations* (April): 174–178.

Thompson, A. P. 1983. "Extramarital Sex: A Review of the Literature." *Journal of Sex Research* 19: 1–22.

Thompson, E., and Collela, V. 1992. "Cohabitation and Marital Stability: Quality or Commitment." *Journal of Marriage and the Family* (May): 259–268.

Thompson, R., et al. 1989. "Grandparents' Visitation Rights." *American Psychologist* (September): 1217–1222.

Tillich, P. 1957. *Dynamics of Faith.* New York: Harper & Row.

Tilly, C. 1991. "Reasons for Continuing Growth of Part-time Employment." *Monthly Labor Review.* Washington, D.C.: U.S. Department of Labor, March.

Time. 1981. "Not So Merry Widowers." (August 10): 45.

———. 1985. "More and More, She's the Boss." (December 2): 64–65.

———. 1986. "Cocaine Babies." (January 20): 50.

———. 1987. "The Cost of Kissing and Not Telling." (June 8): 78.

———. 1988. "Older, But Coming on Strong." (February 22): 76–78.

———. 1988. "The Battle of Baby K." (May 2): 60.

———. 1988. "Children." (August 8): 32–54.

———. 1988. "A New Alternative." (August 15): 65.

———. 1988. "Crack Comes the Nursery." (September 19): 85

———. 1989. "Trying to Fool the Infertile." (March 13): 53.

———. 1989a. "The Rat Race: How America Is Running Itself Ragged." (April 29): 58–67.

———. 1989b. "Ma Bell's Family Way." (June 12): 51.

———. 1989c. "Death by Gun." July 17.

———. 1990. "It's All in the (Parental) Genes." (November 15): 77.

———. 1991. "Making Babies." (September): 56–63.

———. 1992. "Abortion, The Future is Already Here." (May 4): 76–78.

———. 1992. "Unsettling Report on an Epidemic of Rape." (May 4): 15.

Touliatos, J. 1991. *Inventory of Marriage and Family Literature, 1990–91.* St. Paul, Minn.: National Council of Family Relations.

Trafford, A. 1984. *Crazy Time: Surviving Divorce.* New York: Bantam Books.

Troll, L. E. 1983. "Grandparents: The Family Watchdogs." In *Family Relationships in Later Life,* edited by T. Brubaker, 63–74. Beverly Hills, Calif.: Sage Publications.

Trzcinski, E., and Finn-Stevenson, M. 1991. "A Response to Arguments against Mandated Parental Leave: Findings from the Connecticut Survey of Parental Leave Policies." *Journal of Marriage and the Family* 53 (May): 445–460.

Turkington, C. 1983. "Lifetime of Fear May Be the Legacy of Latchkey Children." *APA Monitor.* Washington, D.C.: American Psychological Association, November.

Turnbull, S. K., and Turnbull, J. M. 1983. "To Dream the Impossible Dream: An Agenda for Discussion with Stepparents." *Family Relations* (April): 227–230.

Udry, J., 1974. *The Social Context of Marriage*. 3d ed. Philadelphia: Lippincott.

Uhlenberg, P. 1980. "Death & the Family." *Journal of Marriage and Family History* 5 (Fall): 313–320.

Ullian, D. Z. 1976. "The Development of Conceptions of Masculinity and Femininity." In *Exploring Sex Differences*, edited by B. Lloyd and J. Archer. London: Academic Press.

U.S. Bureau of the Census. July 1985. "Persons 65 Years Old and Over—Characteristics by Sex: 1960–1983." *Current Population Reports*. Series P–20, no. 389; Series P–23, nos. 57, 59, 917, & 949; Series P–60, nos. 142 & 144. In *Statistical Abstract of the United States*, 30. 105th ed. Washington, D.C.: U.S. Government Printing Office.

———. June 1988. "Money Income of Households, Families and Persons in the United States: 1986." *Current Population Reports*. Series P–60, no. 159. Washington, D.C.: U.S. Government Printing Office.

———. August 1988. "Money, Income and Poverty in the United States: 1987." *Current Population Reports*. Series P–60, no. 161. Washington, D.C.: U.S. Government Printing Office.

———. January 1989. "Marital Status and Living Arrangements: March 1988." *Current Population Reports*. Series P–20, no. 433. Washington, D.C.: U.S. Government Printing Office.

———. March 1989. "The Hispanic Population in the United States." *Current Population Reports*. Series P–20, no. 444. Washington, D.C.: U.S. Government Printing Office.

———. April 1989. "Population Profile of the United States, 1989." *Current Population Reports*. Series P–23, no. 159. Washington, D.C.: U.S. Government Printing Office.

———. June 1989. "Studies in Marriage and the Family." *Current Population Reports*. Series P–23, no. 162. Washington, D.C.: U.S. Government Printing Office.

———. August 1989. "Changes in American Family Life." *Current Population Reports*. Series P–23, no. 163. Washington, D.C.: U.S. Government Printing Office.

———. October 1989. "Money, Income and Poverty Status in the United States: 1988." *Current Population Reports*. Series P–60, no. 166. Washington, D.C.: U.S. Government Printing Office.

———. December 1990. "Household and Family Characteristics: March 1990 and 1989." *Current Population Reports*. Series P–20, no. 447. Washington, D.C.: U.S. Government Printing Office.

———. May 1991. "Marital Status and Living Arrangements: March 1990." *Current Population Reports*. Series P–20, no. 450. Washington, D.C.: U.S. Government Printing Office.

———. August 1991. "Poverty in the United States: 1990." *Current Population Reports*. Series P–60, no. 175. Washington, D.C.: U.S. Government Printing Office.

———. August 1991. "Money Income of Households, Families and Persons in the United States: 1990." *Current Population Reports*. Series P–60, no. 174. Washington, D.C.: U.S. Government Printing Office.

———. October 1991. "Fertility of American Women: June 1990." *Current Population Reports*. Series P–20, no. 454. Washington, D.C.: U.S. Government Printing Office.

———. October 1991. "Studies in American Fertility." *Current Population Reports*. Series P–23, no. 176. Washington, D.C.: U.S. Government Printing Office.

———. February 1992. "Household and Family Characteristics: March 1991." *Current Population Reports*. Series P–2, no. 458. Washington, D.C.: U.S. Government Printing Office.

———. April 1992. "Marital Status and Living Arrangements: March 1991." *Current Population Reports*. Series P–20, no. 461. Washington, D.C.: U.S. Government Printing Office.

———. January 1993. Personal communication with Shirley Smith, Income Statistics Branch, Room 307–1, Iverson Mall, Washington, D.C.

U.S. Department of Education. 1991. *1991 Edition, Educational Statistics*. Washington, D.C.: U.S. Department of Education.

U.S. Department of Labor. December 1985. *Monthly Labor Review*. Washington, D.C.: Bureau of Labor Statistics.

———. March 1989. *Monthly Labor Review*. Washington, D.C.: Bureau of Labor Statistics.

———. March 1991. *Monthly Labor Statistics*. Washington, D.C.: Bureau of Labor Statistics.

———. March 1992. "Employment Status of the Population by Sex, Age, Race and Hispanic Origin: Monthly Data Seasonally Adjusted." *Monthly Labor Review* 115, no. 3. Washington, D.C.: U.S. Government Printing Office.

———. October 1992. Personal conversation with Bureau of Labor Statistics personnel.

Vaughan, D. 1988. *Uncoupling*. New York: Vintage Books.

Verbrugge, L. M. 1983. "Multiple Roles and Physical Health of Women and Men." *Journal of Health and Social Behavior* 24: 16–30.

Verbrugge, L. M., and Madans, J. 1985. "Social Roles and Health Trends of American Women." *Milbank Memorial Fund Quarterly/Health and Society* 63 (Fall).

Verbrugge, L. M., and Madans, J. H. 1986. "National Health Interview." *American Demographics* (March).

Vemer, E.; Coleman, M.; Ganong, L. H.; and Copper, H. 1989. "Marital Satisfaction in Remarriage: A Meta-analysis." *Journal of Marriage and the Family* (August): 713–725.

Verney, T., and Kelly, J. 1981. *The Secret Life of the Unborn Child*. New York: Simon & Schuster.

Veum, J. R., and Gleason, P. M. 1991. "Childcare Arrangements and Costs." *Monthly Labor Review*. Washington, D.C.: U.S. Department of Labor (October): 11.

Victor, R. S.; Robbins, M. A.; and Bassett, S. 1991. "Statutory Review of Third-Party Rights Regarding Custody, Visitation, and Support." *Family Law Quarterly* 25: 19–57.

Vinovekis, M. 1987. "Historical Perspective on the Family and Parent-Child Interactions." In *Parenting across the Life Span: Biosocial Dimensions*, edited by Lancaster et al. New York: Alpine.

Voydanoff, P. 1987. *Work and Family Life*. Beverly Hills, Calif.: Sage Publications.

Walker, A.; Pratt, C.; and Oppy, N. 1992. "Perceived Reciprocity in Family Caregiving." *Family Relations* (January): 82–85.

Wall Street Journal. May 10, 1985, 22.

Wallenberg, B. J. 1984. "The Good News Is the Bad News Is Wrong." *Esquire* (November).

Waller, W. 1967. *The Old Love and the New: Divorce and Readjustment*. Carbondale, Ill.: Southern Illinois University Press.

Wallerstein, J. 1984. "Children of Divorce—Preliminary Report of a Ten-Year Follow-up of Young Children." *American Journal of Orthopsychiatry* 54: 444.

———. 1988. In G. Kalata, "Child Splitting." *Psychology Today* (November): 34–36.

Wallerstein, J., and Blakeslee, S. 1989. *Second Chances*. New York: Ticknor & Field.

Wallerstein, J., and Kelly, J. 1980. "California's Children of Divorce." *Psychology Today* (January): 67–76.

Wallis, C. 1985. "Children Having Children." *Time*. (December 9): 76.

Walsh, M. R., ed. 1987. *The Psychology of Women: Ongoing Debates.* New Haven, Conn.: Yale University Press.

Ward, R.; Logan, J.; and Spitze, G. 1992. "The Influence of Parent and Child Needs on Coresidence in Middle and Later Years." *Journal of Marriage and the Family* (February): 209–221.

Washington Post. 1987. "Nation Spent $17.9 Billion on Teen-Age Mothers Last Year." May 28.

Watson, M. A. 1981. "Sexually Open Marriages." *Alternate Lifestyles* 4 (February).

Watson, R. E. 1983. "Premarital Cohabitation vs. Traditional Courtship: Their Effects on Subsequent Marital Adjustment." *Family Relations* (January).

Watson, R. E., and DeMeo, P. W. 1987. "Premarital Cohabitation vs. Traditional Courtship and Subsequent Marital Adjustment: A Replication and Follow-up." *Family Relations* (April): 193–197.

Webster's Ninth New Collegiate Dictionary. 1991. Springfield, Mass.: Merriam-Webster.

Weiner-Davis, M. 1992. *Divorce Busting.* New York: Summit Books.

Weinstein, S., and Gottheil, L. 1986. "Cocaine Abuse: What the Family Needs to Know." *Medical Aspects of Human Sexuality* 2: 87–89.

Weis, D., and Felton, J. 1987. "Marital Exclusivity and the Potential for Future Marital Conflict." *Social Work* 32: 45–49.

Weiss, D. 1988. "100 Percent American." *Good Housekeeping*, 120.

Weitzman, L. 1975. "Sex-role Socialization." In *Women: A Feminist Perspective*, edited by J. Freeman, 105–144. Palo Alto, Calif.: Mayfield.

———. 1981: *The Marriage Contract.* New York: Free Press.

———. 1985. *The Divorce Revolution: The Unexpected Social and Economic Consequence for Women and Children in America.* New York: Free Press.

———. 1988. In G. Kolata, "Child Splitting." *Psychology Today* (November): 34–36.

West's Annotated California Codes. 1989. Vol. 12A, Cumulative Pocket Part. St. Paul, Minn.: West.

West's Annotated California Codes: Civil Code. 1986. Sections 4000–5099. St. Paul, Minn.: West.

White, B. 1984. *The First Three Years of Life: A Guide to Physical, Emotional and Intellectual Growth of Your Baby.* 2d ed. New York: Avon.

White, G. L. 1980. "Inducing Jealousy: A Power Perspective." *Personality and Social Psychology Bulletin* 6: 222–227.

Whitney, E., and Sizer, F. 1988. *Life Choices: Health Concepts and Strategies.* St. Paul, Minn.: West.

Wienberg, H. 1990. "Childbearing after Remarriage." *Journal of Marriage and the Family* (February): 31–38.

Willie, C. V. 1988. *A New Look at Black Families.* New York: General Hall.

Wilson, B. 1992. Personal communication with personnel at the National Center for Health Statistics, Hyattsville, Maryland. December 17.

Wilson, B. F. 1987. Reported in B. Gavzer, "Why More Older Women Are Marrying Younger Men." *Parade Magazine* (May 24): 12–13.

Wilstein, S. 1987. "Electronic Pioneer Hewlett Reflects on Career." *Santa Barbara News Press* (February 15): G-3.

Wisensale, S. K. 1990. "Approaches to Family Policy in State Government: A Report on Five States." *Family Relations* (April): 136–140.

Wisensale, S. K., and Allison, M. D. 1989. "Family Leave Legislation: State and Federal Initiatives." *Family Relations* (April): 182–189.

Woll, S. B., and Young, P. 1989. "Looking for Mr. or Ms. Right: Self-presentation in Videodating." *Journal of Marriage and the Family* (May): 609–618.

Woll, S. B., and Cozby, P. C. 1987. "Videodating and Other Alternatives to Traditional Methods of Relationship Initiation." In *Advances in Personal Relationships* vol. 1, edited by T. W. Jones and D. Perlman, 69–198. Greenwich, Conn.: JAI Press.

Working Woman. 1992. "Best-Paid Corporate Women." (January): 52.

Zimmerman, S. L. 1991. "The Welfare State and Family Breakup: The Mythical Connection." *Family Relations* (April): 139–147.

AUTHOR INDEX

SUBJECT INDEX

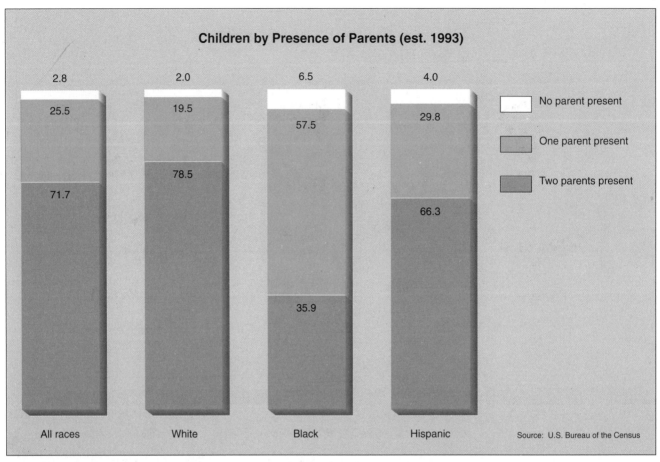

Children by Presence of Parents (est. 1993)

	No parent present
	One parent present
	Two parents present

All races: 2.8 / 25.5 / 71.7

White: 2.0 / 19.5 / 78.5

Black: 6.5 / 57.5 / 35.9

Hispanic: 4.0 / 29.8 / 66.3

Source: U.S. Bureau of the Census

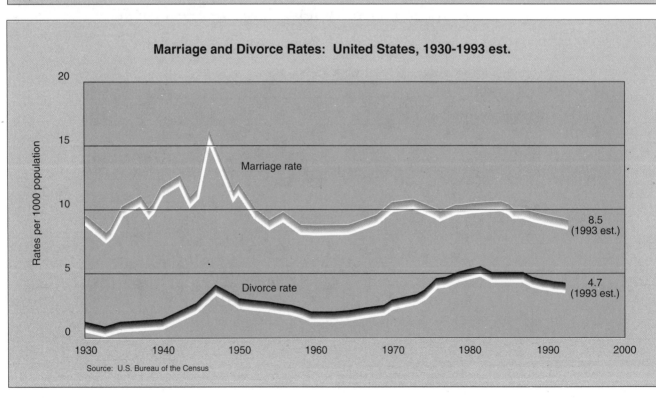

Marriage and Divorce Rates: United States, 1930-1993 est.

Rates per 1000 population

Marriage rate — 8.5 (1993 est.)

Divorce rate — 4.7 (1993 est.)

Source: U.S. Bureau of the Census